ideas, interests, and issues

READINGS IN INTRODUCTORY POLITICS

George A. MacLean | UNIVERSITY OF MANITOBA

Brenda O'Neill | UNIVERSITY OF MANITOBA

PEARSON

Prentice
Hall

Toronto

Library and Archives Canada Cataloguing in Publication

MacLean, George A. (George Andrew), 1967–
    Ideas, interests and issues : readings in introductory politics / George A. MacLean,
    Brenda O'Neill.

Includes bibliographical references.
ISBN 0-13-127191-1

    1. Political science. I. O'Neill, Brenda, 1964– II. Title.

JA66.M248 2005   320   C2005-901271-4

ISBN 0-13-127191-1

Vice-President, Editorial Director: Michael J. Young
Executive Acquisitions Editor: Christine Cozens
Signing Representative: Duncan Mackinnon
Marketing Manager: Cynthia Smith
Developmental Editor: Matthew Christian
Production Editor: Charlotte Morrison-Reed
Copy Editor: Jonathan Dore
Proofreader: Gillian Scobie
Production Coordinator: Janis Raisen
Manufacturing Coordinator: Susan Johnson
Page Layout: B.J. Weckerle
Art Director: Mary Opper
Cover Design: Michelle Bellemare
Cover Image: Photonica

1 2 3 4 5   10 09 08 07 06

Printed and bound in the United States of America.

TABLE OF CONTENTS

MODULE 3   ISSUES

Preface

It is commonplace to hear the word "politics" used in everyday exchange to identify the worst form of decision-making or, pejoratively, to disparage an outcome or process. The perceptions underlying these practices matter and tell us much about the state of democracy. Our hope is, however, that the study of politics reveals its complexity and, through this, that one develops an understanding of the difficult challenges faced by those who devote themselves to public life. And it is precisely this complexity that we believe makes the study of politics so engaging and which presents a challenge to the ultimate objective of the discipline—to develop a set of decision-making structures within society to maintain peace and order. It is our hope that these readings can convey, in an accessible manner, the complexity of politics as well as the important distinction between the study and the practice of politics.

We have chosen a set of articles that provide a balanced perspective on the ideas, interests and issues that dominate contemporary politics at both the domestic and international levels. Some readings have a particular perspective but as a whole, the combination of readings provide a balanced view of the discipline. We both firmly believe that the passion of politics should appear in the material offered to students who study it; to do otherwise is to sanitize what is inherently messy and often emotional. Respectful debate and dialogue are the keys to developing our understanding of politics; we hope this reader provides a tool that helps this to occur.

Thanks are due to the many people we have worked with at Pearson Education Canada, but especially Matthew Christian, our developmental editor, who most ably kept two busy academics fairly close to the publication schedule, and Christine Cozens and Duncan MacKinnon, who originally approached us with the idea of putting together a reader for introductory courses in political science.

We also would like to note the comments and criticisms made by our external reviewers, including Peter G. Boswell, Paul Howe, Nigmendra Narain, Lydia Miljan, Hamish Telford, Greg McElligott, Harold Jansen, and Gerard Boychuk. We are indebted to you for your time and your suggestions, which have contributed to this final work.

Thanks are also due to the various authors who so graciously allowed their work to be reproduced in this volume. It goes without saying that we all benefit from their efforts and from their willingness to share their work.

And without question the greatest debt of thanks goes to our respective spouses and children, for providing the refuge of love and laughter when it is needed most.

POLISCI SUPERSITE

The PoliSci supersite (www.pearsoned.ca/polisci) is Pearson Education Canada's online resource for students of political science. This website includes information about the study of politics, material on the various areas of study in politics, useful links to textbooks and other sources, supplementary information for course work and study, and a glossary of key terms from the text.

In addition, the PoliSci supersite contains several pages of content relating specifically to Ideas, Interests, and Issues. Organized by the sections of this reader, the supersite includes lists of relevant websites, as well as suggestions for further reading. Visit these pages if you are beginning to research an essay or if you want additional ammunition for a debate.

LIST OF CONTRIBUTORS

Louise Arbour, former Supreme Court of Canada Justice (1999–2004) is the United Nations High Commissioner for Human Rights.

Jennifer Baumgardner, a self-described "professional feminist," is a former editor at *Ms.* and writes for *The Nation*, *Jane*, *Nerve*, and *Out*.

André Blais is Professor of Political Science at Université de Montréal.

Gerard W. Boychuk is Associate Professor of Political Science at the University of Waterloo.

J. Patrick Boyer, Progressive Conservative Member of Parliament for Etobicoke (1984–1993), is Adjunct Professor at the University of Guelph.

Sir Bernard Crick is Emeritus Professor of Birkbeck College, University of London, and Honorary Fellow in Politics at the University of Edinburgh.

Claude Couture is Professor of History at the Centre d'Études Canadiennes de la Faculté Saint-Jean, University of Alberta.

Elisabeth Gidengil is Professor of Political Science, McGill University, Montréal.

Carol Gould is Professor of Humanities and Social Sciences at the Imperatore School of Sciences and Arts, Stevens Institute of Technology, Hoboken, New Jersey.

John Hannigan is Professor of Sociology at the University of Toronto.

David Held is Graham Wallas Professor of Political Science at the London School of Economics and Political Science.

Janet L. Hiebert is Associate Professor of Political Studies at Queen's University, Kingston.

Andrew F. Johnson is Professor of Political Science at Bishop's University, Lennoxville, Quebec.

Terry Lynn Karl is Professor of Political Science, Stanford University, California.

Nathalie Kermoal is Instructor at the School of Native Studies, Faculté Saint-Jean, University of Alberta.

Russell Kirk (1918–1994) was a Guggenheim Fellow, a senior fellow of the American Council of Learned Societies, a Constitutional Fellow of the National Endowment for the Humanities, and a Fulbright Lecturer in Scotland.

George A. MacLean is Associate Professor of Political Studies at the University of Manitoba, Winnipeg.

Elizabeth May is Executive Director of the Sierra Club of Canada.

Beverley McLachlin is Chief Justice of the Supreme Court of Canada.

Kenneth Minogue is Emeritus Professor of Political Science at the London School of Economics and Political Science.

Richard Nadeau is Professor of Political Science at Université de Montréal.

Neil Nevitte is Professor of Political Science, University of Toronto.

Kim Richard Nossal is Professor and Head of Political Studies at Queen's University, Kingston.

Rory O'Brien is Professor of Political Science at Cabrillo College in Aptos, California.

Darren J. O'Byrne is Senior Lecturer and Programme Convener (Human Rights), University of Surrey, Roehampton.

Brenda O'Neill is Associate Professor of Political Studies at the University of Manitoba, Winnipeg.

Amy Richards is a contributing editor at *Ms.* and co-founder of the Third Wave Foundation, an activist group for young feminists.

Kent Roach is Professor of Law and Criminology at the University of Toronto.

Philippe C. Schmitter is Professor of Political and Social Sciences at the European University Institute of Florence, Italy.

Daniel Schwanen is Senior Economist at the Institute for Research on Public Policy, Montreal.

Denis Stairs is McCulloch Professor in Political Science at Dalhousie University, Halifax.

Maurice Strong is Senior Advisor to United Nations Secretary General Kofi Annan, former Secretary-General of the United Nations Conference on the Human Environment, and Executive Director of the United Nations Environment Programme.

Ramesh Thakur is Senior Vice-Rector, Peace and Governance Programme, United Nations University, Tokyo, Japan.

Stella Z. Theodoulou is Dean of the College of Social and Behavioral Sciences, California State University, Northridge.

Reg Whitaker is Distinguished Research Professor Emeritus at York University, Toronto, and Adjunct Professor of Political Science, University of Victoria.

Jonathan B. Wight is Associate Professor of Economics and International Studies at the University of Richmond, Virginia.

Oliver H. Woshinsky is Emeritus Professor of Political Science at the University of Southern Maine.

THEMATIC DIRECTORY

Canadian politics: Boyer; Hiebert; Whitaker; CRIC; Citizen's Assembly; Nossal; May; Schwanen; McLachlin; Boychuk; Couture and Kermoal; Roach

Civil Society: Held; Minogue 1 and 2; Woshinsky; Boyer; Hiebert; Whitaker; Hannigan; Schmitter and Karl; Johnson; CRIC; Gidengil et al.; Citizen's Assembly; Couture and Kermoal

Comparative politics: Held; Woshinsky; Schmitter and Karl

Democracy: Held; Gould; Boyer; Whitaker; Schmitter and Karl; Johnson; CRIC; Gidegil et al.

Electoral systems: Held; Minogue 2; Boyer; Whitaker; Schmitter and Karl; Johnson; CRIC; Citizen's Assembly

Environment: May; Strong

Globalization: Held; Woshinsky; Gould; Hannigan; Johnson; Stairs; May; McLachlin; Roach

Identity: Held; Woshinsky; Minogue 2; Schmitter and Karl; Johnson; Gidengil et al.; Citizen's Assembly; McLachlin; Couture and Kermoal; O'Byrne

Ideology: Held; Woshinsky; Kirk; Wight; Baumgartner and Richards; Gould; Hannigan; Schmitter and Karl; Stairs; Couture and Kermoal

Institutions: Boyer; Hiebert; Whitaker; Boychuk

Interest groups: Held; Minogue 1; Baumgartner and Richards; Hiebert

International relations: Gould; Hannigan; Nossal; Thakur; Stairs; Arbour; May; Schwanen; Strong; Roach

Justice: Baumgartner and Richards; Boyer; Hiebert; Arbour; O'Byrne

Rights: Minogue 1 and 2; Baumgartner and Richards; Hiebert; Arbour; McLachlin; Couture and Kermoal; O'Byrne

Political analysis: Minogue 1; Woshinsky; Theodoulou and O'Brien; Minogue 2; Kirk; Wight

Political economy: Gould; Hannigan; Schwanen

Political systems: Held; Crick; Boyer; Whitaker; Schmitter and Karl; Johnson; CRIC; Citizen's Assembly; Stairs

Political theory: Crick; Theodoulou and O'Brien; Minogue 2; Kirk; Wight; Baumgartner and Richards; Gould; Schmitter and Karl

Public administration: Crick; Boyer; Whitaker; CRIC; Boychuk

Protest: Minogue 1; Baumgartner and Richards; Hannigan; May; O'Byrne

Terrorism: Thakur; Stairs; Roach

CREDITS

Page 8: From Archibugi, Daniele, David Held, and Martin Kohler, eds. "Re-imagining Political Community: Studies in Cosmopolitan Democracy." Copyright © 1998 Polity Press.

Page 21: Bernard Crick, "In Praise of Politics," in *In Defence of Politics*, 5th ed., (London: Contiuum, 2000). Reprinted by permission of the Continuum International Publishing Group.

Page 34: Kenneth Minogue, "The Experience of Politics: How to be an Activist," in *Politics: A Very Short Introduction*, (New York: Oxford, 2000). Reprinted by permission of the publisher.

Page 40: Oliver H. Woshinsky, "The Impact of Culture on Politics." Reprinted by permission of Oliver H. Woshinsky, Professor Emeritus of Political Science, University of Southern Maine, Portland, Maine, USA.

Page 59: Kenneth Minogue, "The Classical Greeks: How to Be a Citizen," in *Politics: A Very Short Introduction*, (New York: Oxford, 2000). Reprinted by permission of the publisher.

Page 64: pp. 1-12. "Where We Stand Today: The State of Modern Political Science" in Theodoulou, Stella Z.; O'Brien, Rory, *Methods for Modern Political Enquiry: The Discipline, Philosophy and Analysis of Politics*, 1st Edition, © 1999. Reprinted by permission of Pearson Education, Inc., Upper Saddle River, NJ.

Page 77: Russell Kirk, "Ten Conservative Principles." This reading Copyright Annette Y. Kirk.

Page 83: Excerpts from Wight, Jonathan B., "Saving Adam Smith: A Tale of Wealth, Transformation, and Virtue," 1st Edition, © 2002. Reprinted by Permission of Pearson Education , Inc., Upper Saddle River, NJ.

Page 89: "Prologue: A Day Without Feminism" and "Epilogue: A Day With Feminism" from *Manifest: Young Women, Feminism and the Future* by Jennifer Baumgardner and Amy Richards. Copyright © 2000 by Jennifer Baumgerdner and Amy Richards. Reprinted by permission of Farrar, Straus and Giroux, LLC.

Page 100: Carol Gould, "Socialism and Democracy," *Praxis International*, 1 (1981): 5–58. Reprinted by permission of Blackwell Publishing and the author.

Page 110: J. Patrick Boyer, "Responsible Government Won and Lost" in J. Patrick Boyer, *Just Trust Us: The Erosion of Accountability in Canada*, (Toronto: Breakout Educational Network, 2003). Reprinted by permission of the Breakout Educational Network. For more information, visit the Underground Royal Commission Website at www.theurc.com.

Page 121: Janet L. Hiebert, "From Equality Rights to Same-Sex Marriage – Parliament and the Courts in the Age of the Charter," in *Policy Options*, *24* (October 2003). Reprinted by permission of the Institute for Research on Public Policy

Page 130: Reg Whitaker, "Virtual Political Parties and the Decline of Democracy," *Policy Options* June 2001: 16–22. Reprinted by permission of the Institute for Research on Public Policy

Page 138: "The Global Entertainment Economy" was first published in David R. Cameron and Janice Gross Stein, eds., *Street Protests and Fantasy Parks: Globalization, Culture and the State* (Vancouver: University of British Columbia Press, 2002) and is reproduced by permission of the publisher. All rights reserved.

Page 166: Schmitter, Phippe C. and Terry Lynn Karl. "What Democracy is. . . And is Not." *Journal of Democracy 2*:3 (1991), 75–87. © National Endowment for Democracy and the Johns Hopkins University Press. Reprinted with Permission of the Johns Hopkins University Press.

Page 177: Andrew F. Johnson, "Democracy, Prosperity, Citizens and the State," in *Canadian Foreign Policy*, *10* (Fall 2002). Reprinted with permission.

Page 195: "Voter Participation in Canada: Is Canadian Democracy in Crisis?" *The CRIC Papers*, (Oct. 2001), abridged from the original available online at www.cric.ca/pdf/cahiers/cricpapers_nov2001.pdf.

Page 224: Elisabeth Gidengil, Andre Blais, Neil Nevitte and Richard Nadeau, "Turned Off or Tuned Out? Youth Participation in Politics" in *Electoral Insight 5*:2 (2003), 9–14 (also available at www.elections.ca). Reprinted with permission of Elections Canada.

Page 231: Issued by the Citizens' Assembly on Electoral Reform at Morris J. Wosk Centre for Dialogue, March 21, 2004. *A Preliminary Statement to the People of British Columbia*. Reprinted by permission of the British Columbia's Citizen's Assembly on Electoral Reform.

Page 241: Kim Richard Nossal, "Canada: Fading Power or Future Power?" *Behind the Headlines*, *59* (Spring 2002). This article was first published by the Canadian Institute of International Affairs in *Behind the Headlines*, Vol. 59 No. 3.

Page 247: Ramesh Thakur, "Security in the New Millenium," *Canadian Foreign Policy*, *10* (Fall 2002). Reprinted with permission.

Page 262: Denis Stairs, "9/11 'Terrorism,' 'Root Causes' and all that: Political Implications of the Socio Cultural Argument," in *Policy Options*, *23* (September 2002). Reprinted by permission of the Institute for Research on Public Policy

Page 268: Louise Arbour, "The Responsibility to Protect and the Duty to Punish," *Behind the Headlines*, *59* (Autumn 2001). This article was first published by the Canadian Institute of International Affairs in *Behind the Headlines*, Vol. 59 No.1.

Page 275: Elizabeth May, "From Montreal to Kyoto: How We Got From Here to There – Or Not," in *Policy Options*, *24* (December 2002-January 2003). Reprinted by permission of the Institute for Research on Public Policy.

Page 281: Daniel Schwanen, "Canada and Free Trade – 15 Years On, in *Policy Options*, *25* (February 2004). Reprinted by permission of the Institute for Research on Public Policy.

Page 306: Gerard W. Boychuk, "The Illusion of Financial Unsustainability of Canadian Health Care," in *Policy Options*, *23* (November 2002). Reprinted by permission of the Institute for Research on Public Policy.

Introduction:
The Reader and its Goals

There are many ways to introduce the subject of politics. Your first course in politics is the product of your instructor's ideas, the content of your textbook, and events taking place in daily life. Every year, thousands of students are presented with the study of politics in courses such as the one you are taking. And many of those courses are vastly different from yours. Your instructor will shape the material for your course in his or her own way, and the textbooks you read will influence the course as well. However, whether the course is entitled "Political Science," "Political Studies," or simply "Politics," there are topics and themes that tend to appear regularly.

There is no single "customary" way to teach or to learn politics, but there are constants in most introductory courses in the subject. Politics is about ideas that communities have about governing themselves. Politics is an extension of the way that we deal with each other. Politics is about the many diverse interests that exist in our societies. Politics is about power, influence, control, and making our world a better place. Politics is often considered negative or pessimistic, but it is really a positive and optimistic discipline. Studying politics helps us to decide how to make our societies better and improve our world. In practice, of course, we often fail to achieve these goals.

Your first course in political science should be stimulating, timely, provocative, and thought-provoking. This reader hopes to provide a vehicle for bringing the "stuff" of politics alive for the first-time politics student, in a manner unlike introductory textbooks. Textbooks can be stimulating, to be sure, but often their objectives can make it difficult to maintain a consistent level of stimulating reading. Textbooks must span the breadth of the discipline, reviewing the key concepts, approaches, and methods employed in its study. A reader, on the other hand, does not need to provide a comprehensive review of the discipline, and so has the flexibility of offering a more limited set of issues and questions upon which to focus. This freedom makes it easier to develop a package of readings that we hope will push you to challenge your ideas, to investigate new ways of thinking, and to develop an awareness of the challenges and rewards that come with the study of politics. We encourage you to engage with the material that we have collected in this volume, both on your own and with your peers and instructors.

THE STRUCTURE OF THE BOOK

The title of this book is instructive. We believe that politics is about many things, but it is best understood and explained if we look at the *ideas* that underpin our societies, the *interests* that exist in our political systems, and the changing *issues* that affect all walks of political life. These are constants in politics, and thus are constants in the study of politics as well.

The book is divided into three modules, reflecting the themes of ideas, interests, and issues in modern political life. The first module deals with some of the many ideas that people have had about the relationship that exists between citizens and government. Ideas are not just abstract theoretical notions. In fact, all political systems are based on ideas, which often change with the wishes of governments or their citizens.

This first module of the book presents some essays on the study of politics, and some theoretical frameworks that have been used in political life for centuries. To begin Section 1, David Held's "Democracy and Globalization" examines the relatively new concept of "globalization," which appears to be an idea that can be used by anyone for almost any purpose. He argues that globalization is more than just a political phenomenon. Its various forms have real meaning for politics, he claims, and it is crucial for us to examine the dynamics of globalization so as to ground ourselves in the reality of modern national and international affairs. Held looks at the development of democracy worldwide, and suggests that "cosmopolitan democracy," which takes into account both regional and global factors that affect the democratic process, is a better conceptual tool for our understanding.

Bernard Crick's classic essay "In Praise of Politics" follows. First published in 1962, and reprinted many times since, this piece suggests that politics is society's only alternative to government by coercion. He reminds us that politics is all about debate and compromise in an effort to create the most effective society. In "The Experience of Politics: How to be an Activist," Kenneth Minogue reasons that we cannot be complacent when we engage in politics. Activism, he suggests, is crucial to the kind of debate and compromise that Crick speaks of in his essay. "The Impact of Culture on Politics," by Oliver Woshinsky, considers the impact that culture has on politics today. Culture, Woshinsky proposes, is the basis of community identity, and affects politics in a most direct way. The result is that political systems are as diverse as the cultures in which they have been created.

In Section 2, Kenneth Minogue discusses the emergence of "citizenship" under the ancient Greeks in "The Classical Greeks: How to Be a Citizen." Minogue's choice of time period is fitting, since so much of modern political analysis stems from the era of the Greek city states. Stella Theodoulou and Rory O'Brien provide some historical background for political studies in "Where We Stand Today: The State of Modern Political Science." They maintain that politics is the result of a long process, and is a puzzle made up of many pieces that may not make much sense when examined on their own. Putting them together, however, provides a clearer view of the discipline.

In Section 3, the theories of nationalism, conservatism, and liberalism are scrutinized. Russell Kirk succinctly recounts the elements of conservative ideology in "Ten Conservative Principles." Jonathan Wight offers an imagined account of the great liberal thinker Adam Smith, alive again and infuriated at the way modern society has used liberalism. Carol Gould puts a contemporary twist on socialism, offering up a realistic explanation of how it affects our lives today. Feminist writers Jennifer Baumgardner and Amy Richards build on a long-standing tradition of political ideas, and pose two scenarios: a world without the advances of feminism and one with feminism.

The second module of the book deals with how different interests are represented in political systems. No system is made up of one point of view, or one ambition. As Module 1 demonstrates, there are many different ideas and ideologies that push our communities to move in different directions, and they are often opposed to one another. Canada is a good example of a political system that is truly "pluralistic," which means that many different views exist, often competing with one another, but cooperating as well. Multiculturalism, religious diversity, economic disparity, and regional distinctions are just a few of the many forces that lead to an assortment of interests in any political system.

People who study politics recognize the meaning of "interests." The courts, legislatures, political parties, protest movements, election campaigns, even the very nature of democracy itself, are the product of numerous interests in society. J. Patrick Boyer raises concerns about accountability among elected officials in Section 4. He argues in "Responsible Government Won and Lost" that our assumptions about the responsibility of politicians do not match reality. Boyer exposes what he calls the "myths" of responsible government (government in which the executive branch is accountable to the legislative branch). Janet Hiebert applies the role of the Courts to a topical issue in politics today: same-sex marriage. In "From Equality Rights to Same-Sex Marriage: Parliament and the Courts in the Age of the Charter," Hiebert contends that an issue such as same-sex marriage could not have been anticipated by the framers of the Charter of Rights and Freedoms more than two decades ago, so that the Charter may now be used as an excuse by governments that are unwilling to delve into particularly controversial issues.

Reg Whitaker maintains that political parties are no longer the bastions of diverse ideologies, but now are more akin to the branding and packaging of a product for mass consumption. Whitaker's essay, "Virtual Political Parties and the Decline of Democracy," contends that the very nature of our democracy is threatened by this packaging of politics. John Hannigan, meanwhile, feels that major changes in the way people see themselves as "citizens," and the forces of globalization, in part explain the new protest movements. In "The Global Entertainment Economy," Hannigan argues that the growth of global entertainment, marketing, corporations, and information has real implications for who we think we are, and what we think we stand for.

Philippe Schmitter and Terry Lynn Karl provide a much-needed breakdown of the concept of democracy in "What Democracy Is . . . And Is Not" in Section 5. Schmitter and Karl dissect the concept, which they suggest is used today to describe all manner of political systems. Their reading sets the tone for the following essays, which further scrutinize democracy in contemporary politics.

Changing priorities in modern societies have led to a clash between democratic principles and the forces of the market. Andrew Johnson states in "Democracy, Prosperity, Citizens and the State" that the separateness of governments and markets has eroded, leading to a blurred image of the two. Political discontent is the result, he suggests, reflecting some conclusions that link with those made in Section 4 by both Boyer and Whitaker.

Issues relating to elections and voting behaviour are discussed in the following three essays: the Centre for Research and Information on Canada's "Voter Participation in Canada: Is Canadian Democracy in Crisis?," Gidengil, Blais, Nevitte, and Nadeau's "Turned Off or Tuned Out? Youth Participation in Politics," and the Citizen's Assembly on Electoral Reform report entitled "A Preliminary Statement to the People of British Columbia." Controversies abound with every election in Canada, and as these readings point out, there are serious implications for representation, participation, and democracy itself in Canada.

Global politics are examined in Section 6 in the third module, called "Issues." Kim Richard Nossal argues that Canada's influence in global politics, and in its relationship with the United States, has been damaged due to recent foreign policies. In "Canada: Fading Power or Future Power?" Nossal examines ways that Canada might return to its former position of relevance. Tackling one of the most important issues in politics today, Ramesh Thakur describes the changing nature of international security in "Security in the New Millennium." And in a closely related essay, Denis Stairs considers the topic of global terrorism in "9/11 'Terrorism,' 'Root Causes' and All That: Political Implications of the Socio-Cultural Argument."

Louise Arbour, Canada's Supreme Court Justice and former Chief Prosecutor of the International War Crimes Tribunals for the former Yugoslavia and Rwanda, discusses international rights, and the possibility that national principles such as Canada's Charter of Rights and Freedoms could be extended to the international arena. In "The Responsibility to Protect and the Duty to Punish: Politics and Justice in a Safer World," Arbour considers the future of state rights, and the need to ensure basic rights for citizens in every nation.

Climate change has emerged as one of the most debated topics in global politics. In her essay "From Montreal to Kyoto: How We Got From Here to There—Or Not," Elizabeth May warns that political inaction endangers the global environment. And on the economic front, Daniel Schwanen looks as the pros and cons of free trade, and its effects on the Canadian economy.

The final section of the book considers topics that are not exclusively national or international. Rather, they straddle both levels. Beverley McLachlin, Chief Justice of the Supreme Court of Canada, confronts the issue of identity and politics in "The Civilization of Difference." Perhaps the most fundamental of political issues, identity politics has the power to drive communities apart, and often leads to the worst forms of violence. However, as McLachlin argues, our similarities, rather than our differences, may be the basis for overriding our violent tendencies. Dispelling the conventional impression that Canadian health care is in trouble, Gerard Boychuk argues in "The Illusion of Financial Unsustainability of Canadian Health Care" that health care is not endangered by economic reasons, but rather by political disputes that exist between federal and provincial governments. Maurice Strong poses a futuristic picture of a world suffering the ill effects of environmental degradation. Claude Couture and Nathalie Kermoal delve into the roots of identity in Quebec politics. Kent Roach considers the implications of the 9/11 attacks for Canadians, and—wrapping up this section—Darren O'Byrne discusses one of the most studied but perhaps least understood topics in politics, human rights.

At first, politics might seem fairly straightforward, since we all have our own opinions about the world around us. However, studying politics can be challenging for the first-time student because of the many contested concepts and multiple approaches, and the lack of established "standard" theories. Politics is not like biology or astronomy; we don't have a series of accepted concepts and theories that have been verified with scientific rigour. This is because politics is about human interaction, which is far more than a simply physical or biological one. Subjecting human interaction to definitive statements about behaviour is impossible, since our impulses are so variable and complex. Politics students come to see this, to say nothing of the further challenge of discovering where one's own beliefs lie.

One important distinction to understand, however, is the distinction between the normative and positivist streams of political research. Normative research seeks to understand how the political system *ought* to be structured. Answering this question necessitates the establishment of a set of assumptions (e.g. What is the essential nature of men and women? Are they fundamentally nasty and brutish or good-hearted?) and of a set of values (e.g. What priorities should be kept in mind in thinking about the structures and processes of a political system? Liberty? Equality? Protection of minority interests?). Such questions form one key branch in the study of politics.

The second key branch, the positivist stream, asks how the political system and its processes *are* structured. Like the normative stream, however, understanding how the political system operates also requires the establishment of a set of assumptions regarding the key actors and processes at play (e.g. Is the key to understanding politics found in an investigation of institutions? Or is a true understanding to be found through the lens of public choice, with its emphasis on rational actors?). The distinction is an important one; while the positivist stream seeks to describe and explain, the normative stream is more focused on developing prescriptions for action. Developing an understanding of the degree to which our assumptions shape our conclusions is often difficult for students of political science; developing an understanding of which set of assumptions we subscribe to can be even more difficult.

We hope that this reader helps your knowledge and appreciation of politics. We have assembled a set of readings that we think will support what you learn in lectures and textbook readings. But this reader should do more than just help you in your politics course. You should think of the reader as a tool for developing a number of the skills that you'll need as a post-secondary student.

The first is simply the ability to digest and understand material. To help you with this, each section of the reader provides a short summary of the key points of the set of readings, and a set of questions that stimulate you to think more deeply about the material covered from the perspective of a political scientist. You should realize that you will probably need to read an article twice in order to develop a solid understanding of it. The first reading should be devoted simply to understanding. The second should include note-taking and/or highlighting in an effort to ensure that the material stays with you. This is a strategy you can use in other courses as well.

A second skill you'll develop is the ability to apply the conceptual tools learned in a discipline-specific course to a particular reading. So, the textbook you use contains definitions and explanations of key concepts. This book does as well; but it also gives you some insights into what these terms really mean for everyday use. The practical application of your education is always important. Third, you will see how these readings use very different writing styles and approaches; this shows the importance of diverse thinking. Fourth, these readings come from many sources: academic journals, web pages, periodicals, speeches, and books. What this indicates is that there is no single place to get your information. As these readings show, you should keep your mind open to the places where you might find useful information for your course work.

Simply put, these readings are meant to get you to think. Politics is all around us, and it is unavoidable in our daily lives. Politics affects us all, and it is crucial that we think about politics in an open and critical manner. We all have our own ideas, interests, and issues in political life. The readings in this book will confirm or challenge yours.

Section 1

Politics in a Complex Age

SECTION SUMMARY

What makes your lectures in politics, your textbook, or this book of readings different from simply reading the daily newspaper or watching news about politics on television? Why not simply read stories and commentary posted on the internet and come to your own conclusions about politics that way? It might seem appealing to become informed about politics without having to attend class; for most people, that is sufficient.

Studying politics is not the same as watching the news or reading the newspaper. It's not even the same as engaging in political debate with friends and colleagues, as useful and constructive as that may be. If we watch the news or read the paper, we might be able to explain events taking place around us. But studying politics enables us to move further: to understand these events. The formal study of politics permits us to peek behind the façade of daily political events to the deeper questions about why things happen, and what causes change.

It goes without saying that we are living in an era of change. Of course, every era is one of change; can you imagine a period in time when people thought that nothing new was happening, or that nothing was changing? It's true that politics is about change. However, it's also about continuity. As the saying goes, "plus ça change, plus c'est la même chose": the more things change, the more they stay the same. It's amusing to think that people who believe the world is changing too fast are often the same people who feel that things will never change!

Our world is changing. What's more, some of these changes are simply unprecedented. No previous generation has had access to information as easily as yours has. On his 1992 album *Human Touch*, Bruce Springsteen sang that there were "57 Channels (And Nothin' On)." Not much more than a decade later, one might wonder if he could afford something more than basic cable. These days we have more information at our fingertips than ever before. The problem is that so much of this information is being marketed to us by major multinational firms. Is our information unfiltered? Are there biases in what we hear or read? The irony may be that while we have more information at our disposal, we are less informed.

In 1989 the world witnessed a revolutionary end to the Cold War. That had been a period marked by a global split between capitalist and communist countries; the Cold War influenced all political, economic, and social life, and our greatest fear was nuclear war between the Soviet Union and the United States. That worry is largely gone, but it is safe to say that others have taken its place. Global terrorism, pandemic diseases, economic inequality, and a general political malaise are all part of the "new" world.

This section offers some ideas about the current state of our political world. "Globalization," a term that was usually met with derision during the Cold War, is now given respect. Some even suggest it is the best way to describe our world today. Nevertheless, globalization is a complex idea, and encompasses much more than just the political world. In this section, David Held gives us some insight into what may be the most important political concept in our contemporary world.

What does this mean for politics? Pollsters tell us that voter turnout in democratic elections continues to slump, fewer people than ever subscribe to daily newspapers, and talk of current events usually takes the place of real political discussions today. Election campaigns are sorely lacking in real, substantive debate, and citizens' decisions about candidates (when they do vote) is often based on superficial reasons, such as character or likeability. Is there a need for politics today? In their brief essays, Bernard Crick and Kenneth Minogue sound a call to arms for the study of politics. Nothing is more important in society than an interested electorate, and the only way that we can effect change is to become involved.

Globalization also brings up questions of cultural difference. Today we travel more than we ever did in the past, at lower cost and with greater ease. Being more aware of events nationally and internationally means that we are also more aware of cultures other than our own. But being more aware does not necessarily make us more accepting. Indeed, the very act of creating a political community means that some groups are excluded. Oliver Woshinsky speaks of this in his contribution to this section.

Politics is more alive today than it ever has been. Our ideas, our interests, and the issues that surround us are charged with politics. In an age of globalization, understanding as well as explaining politics in all its facets makes us better citizens of our country, and of our world.

Democracy and Globalization

DAVID HELD*

*David Held is Graham Wallas Professor of Political Science at the London School of Economics and Political Science.

There is a striking paradox to note about the contemporary era: from Africa to Eastern Europe, Asia to Latin America, more and more nations and groups are championing the idea of democracy; but they are doing so at just that moment when the very efficacy of democracy as a national form of political organization appears open to question. As substantial areas of human activity are progressively organized on a regional or global level, the fate of democracy, and of the independent democratic nation-state in particular, is fraught with difficulty.

Throughout the world's major regions there has been a consolidation of democratic processes and procedures. In the mid-1970s, over two-thirds of all states could reasonably be called authoritarian. This percentage has fallen dramatically; less than a third of all states are now authoritarian, and the number of democracies is growing rapidly.[1] Democracy has become the fundamental standard of political legitimacy in the current era. Events such as the release of Nelson Mandela from prison and the tearing down of the Berlin Wall are symbolic of changes indicating that, in more and more countries, citizen-voters are in principle able to hold public decision-makers to account. Yet at the same time the democratic political community is increasingly challenged by regional and global pressures and problems. How can problems such as the spread of AIDS, the debt burden of many countries in the 'developing world', the flow of financial resources which escape national jurisdiction, the drugs trade and international crime be satisfactorily brought within the sphere of democracy? What kind of accountability and control can citizens of a single nation-state have over international actors, such as multinational corporations, and over international organizations, such as the World Bank? In the context of trends towards regionalization, European integration, fundamental transformations in the global economy, mass communications and information technology, how can democracy be sustained? Are new democratic institutions necessary to regulate and control the new international forces and processes? How can citizens participate as citizens in a new and more complex internationally organized world? In a world organized increasingly on regional and global lines, can democracy as we know it survive?

Of course, there is nothing new about the emergence of global problems. Although their importance has grown considerably, many have existed for decades, some for centuries. But now that the old confrontation between East and West has ended, many regional and global

I should like to thank Daniele Archibugi, Martin Köbler, Joel Krieger and Craig Murphy for comments on this chapter. A version was previously published in *Global Governance*, 3.3 (1997), pp. 251–67.

[1] See D. Potter, D. Goldblatt, M. Kiloh and P. Lewis (eds), *Democratization* (Cambridge: Polity Press, 1997).

issues have come to assume an urgent place on the international political agenda. Nonetheless, profound ambiguity still reigns as to where, how and according to what criteria decisions about these matters can be taken.

Democratic theory's exploration of emerging regional and global problems is still in its infancy. While students of democracy have examined and debated at length the challenges to democracy that emerge from within the boundaries of the nation-state, they have not seriously questioned whether the nation-state itself can remain at the centre of democratic thought; the questions posed by the rapid growth of complex interconnections and interrelations between states and societies, and by the evident intersection of national and international forces and processes, remain largely unexplored.[2] By contrast, this chapter seeks to address these questions by, first, examining the nature of globalization and, second, laying out a novel conception of democratic options in the face of the new global circumstances.[3]

GLOBALIZATION

Globalization is a much contested word. On the one hand, there are those who claim that we live in an integrated global order. According to this view, social and economic processes operate predominantly at a global level and national political communities are inevitably 'decision takers'.[4] This development represents a fundamental break in the organization of human affairs - a shift in the organizational principle of social life. On the other hand, there are those people who are very sceptical about the extent of globalization and who still think the national state is as integrated and robust as it ever was. They point out, for instance, that contemporary forms of international economic interaction are not without precedent and that nation-states continue to be immensely powerful, with an impressive range of political options.[5]

Both these views are misleading in significant respects. We live in a world which is changing due to processes of globalization. The interconnectedness of different peoples today is more extensive and intensive than it has ever been. But globalization is not a new phenomenon; societies have always been connected with one another to some degree. Conceptions of globalization need to be sensitive to the historical variation in forms of globalization, as well as to their variable impact on politics. It is easy to exaggerate the extent to which globalization signals 'the end of the nation-state'. Global processes should not be assumed to represent either a total eclipse of the states system or the simple emergence

---

[2]   For an elaboration of this theme, see my *Democracy and the Global Order: From the Modern State to Cosmopolitan Governance* (Cambridge: Polity Press, 1995).

[3]   In focusing on processes of globalization I would like to acknowledge my debt to David Goldblatt, Anthony McGrew and Jonathan Perraton, with whom I have collaborated over the last four years on a research project investigating the changing enmeshment of states in global flows and transformations. The conception of globalization along with many of the examples in the following section are drawn from our joint work. See D. Goldblatt, D. Held, A. McGrew and J. Perraton, *Global Transformations: Concepts, Evidence and Arguments* (Cambridge: Polity Press, 1998).

[4]   See for example, K. Ohmae, *The Borderless World* (London: Collins, 1990); and R. Reich, *The Work of Nations* (New York: Simon and Schuster, 1991).

[5]   See P. Hirst and G. Thompson, *Globalization in Question* (Cambridge: Polity Press, 1996).

of a global society. Accordingly, before proceeding further, the concept of globalization needs clarification.

Globalization is best understood as a spatial phenomenon, lying on a continuum with 'the local' at one end and 'the global' at the other. It denotes a shift in the spatial form of human organization and activity to transcontinental or interregional patterns of activity, interaction and the exercise of power. It involves a stretching and deepening of social relations and institutions across space and time such that, on the one hand, day-to-day activities are increasingly influenced by events happening on the other side of the globe and, on the other, the practices and decisions of local groups or communities can have significant global reverberations.[6]

Globalization today implies at least two distinct phenomena. First, it suggests that many chains of political, economic and social activity are becoming interregional or intercontinental in scope and, secondly, it suggests that there has been an intensification of levels of interaction and interconnectedness within and between states and societies.[7] What is noteworthy about the modern global system is the stretching of social relations in and through new dimensions of activity and the chronic intensification of patterns of interconnectedness mediated by such phenomena as modern communication networks and new information technology. It is possible to distinguish different historical forms of globalization in terms of (1) the extensiveness of networks of relations and connections; (2) the intensity of flows and levels of enmeshment within the networks; and (3) the impact of these phenomena on particular communities.

Globalization is neither a singular condition nor a linear process. Rather, it is best thought of as a multidimensional phenomenon involving diverse domains of activity and interaction, including the economic, political, technological, military, legal, cultural and environmental. Each of these spheres involves different patterns of relations and activity. A general account of globalization cannot simply predict from one domain what will occur in another. It is important, therefore, to build a theory of globalization from an understanding of what is happening in each one of these areas.

The significance of globalization, of course, differs for individuals, groups and countries. The impact of various global flows on, for instance, policy-making in the economic domain will alter considerably depending on whether the country in question is the United States, Peru or Spain. For individuals and groups as well, variable enmeshment in global flows is the norm. The elites in the world of politics, law, business and science are often quite at home in the global capitals, the leading hotels, and in the major cultural centres. Their access and use of these different facilities is clearly in marked contrast to those peoples, for example villagers in sub-Saharan Africa, who live at the margins of some of the central power structures and hierarchies of the global order. But such peoples are by no means unaffected by changing processes and forms of globalization. On the contrary, they are often in the position of being profoundly influenced by these processes and forms, even if they cannot control them. What often differentiates their position from what some have called the new 'cosmopolitan elite' is differential, unequal and uneven access to the dominant organizations, institutions and processes of the new emerging global order.

---

6   See A. Giddens, *The Consequences of Modernity* (Cambridge: Polity Press,1990).

7   See A.G. McGrew, 'Conceptualizing Global Politics', in A.G. McGrew and P.G. Lewis (eds), *Global Politics: Globalization and the Nation-State* (Cambridge: Polity Press, 1992).

At the heart of this 'differential access' is power, where power has to be conceptualized as the capacity to transform material circumstances—whether social, political or economic—and to achieve goals based on the mobilization of resources, the creation of rule systems, and the control of infrastructures and institutions. The particular form of power that is of concern to a theory of globalization is characterized by hierarchy and unevenness. Hierarchy connotes the asymmetrical access to global networks and infrastructures, while unevenness refers to the asymmetrical effects of such networks on the life chances and the well-being of peoples, classes, ethnic groupings and the sexes.[8]

In order to elaborate a theory of globalization, it is necessary to turn from a general concern with its conceptualization to an examination of the distinctive domains of activity and interaction in and through which global processes evolve. This task cannot be pursued here at any length. But some significant changes can be highlighted. An obvious starting point is the world economy and, in particular, trade, financial flows and the spread of multinational corporations.

TRADE

There are those who are sceptical about the extent of the globalization of trade in the contemporary period and they sometimes point out that trade levels in the late twentieth century have only recently reached the same levels as in 1914. This sceptical view is open to doubt. First, using constant price data, it can be shown that the proportion of trade to gross domestic product (trade–GDP ratios) surpassed that of the gold standard era (that is, the period 1875–1914) by the early 1970s, and was considerably higher by the late 1970s and 1980s. In other words, trade has continued to expand as a proportion of GDP. Export–and import–GDP ratios were around 12–13 per cent for advanced industrial countries during the gold standard era but rose to 15–20 per cent—or even higher for some developed countries—from the late 1970s onwards.

In addition, if one removes government expenditure from the enquiry, and focuses on trade in relation to the size of national economic activity, it can be demonstrated that the proportion of trade to such activity has grown markedly, by as much as a third. Technological developments have made many classes of goods, particularly those in the service sector, tradeable where previously they were not.

The evidence also shows that there has not been a simple increase in intraregional trade around the world. Measures of the intensity of trade reveal sustained growth between regions as well (albeit concentrated among Europe, North America and Pacific Asia). Growth in trade within regions and growth among regions are not contradictory developments; rather, they appear to be mutually complementary.

What these points suggest is that trade has grown rapidly, especially in the postwar period, reaching unprecedented levels today. More countries are involved in trading arrangements, such as India and China, and more people and nations are affected by such trade. In the context of the lowering of tariff barriers across the world one can reasonably expect these trends to continue. Any argument that suggests that the world's three key trading blocks—the EU, NAFTA and Pacific Asia—are becoming more inward-looking and

---

[8]   See R. Falk, *On Humane Governance: Toward a New Global Politics* (Cambridge: Polity Press, 1995).

protectionist is not supported by the evidence. Although contemporary trading arrangements stop far short of a perfectly open global market, national economies are enmeshed in a pattern of increasingly dense, competitive international trade. When linked to changes in finance and the organization of production and banking, this has significant political implications.

FINANCE

The expansion of global financial flows around the world has been staggering in the last ten to fifteen years. Foreign exchange turnover is now over a trillion dollars a day. The volume of turnover of bonds, securities and other assets on a daily basis is also without precedent. A number of things can be said about these flows:

1. The relationship of foreign exchange turnover to trade has mushroomed from 11 dollars to 1 to over 55 dollars to 1 in the last thirteen to fourteen years; that is, for every 55 dollars turned over in the foreign exchange markets, 1 dollar is turned over in real trade.

2. A great deal of this financial activity is speculative—it generates fluctuations in values in excess of those which can be accounted for by changes in the underlying fundamentals of asset values.

3. While the net movement of capital relative to GDP is smaller for some countries today than in earlier periods, this has nothing to do with diminishing levels of globalization, that is, lower levels of integration of capital markets. The liberalization of capital markets in the 1980s and early 1990s has created a more integrated financial system than has ever been known.

4. The effects of global financial flows on economic policy are profound. Among the most important are:
   a) the increased possibility of rapid and dramatic shifts in the effective valuation of economies, as illustrated, for instance, in Mexico in January 1995;
   b) the increasing difficulty for countries of pursuing independent monetary policies and independent exchange rate strategies in the face of the current volume of international turnover in currencies and bonds;
   c) the erosion of the option to pursue Keynesian reflationary strategies in a single country—the costs and benefits of these strategies have shifted against the pursuit of such options in many places;
   d) and, finally, as can be seen in the growing macroeconomic policy convergence across political parties in the present period, a deepening acknowledgement of the decline in the economic manoeuvrability of individual governments. Recent examples of this can be found in the reshaping of economic policy among the social democratic parties of Europe. The transformation of the economic policy of the Labour Party in Britain—from policy emphasizing demand management to policy prioritizing supply-side measures (above all, in education and training) to help meet the challenges of increased competition and the greater mobility of capital—is a particular case in point.

Many of these changes might not be of concern if financial market operators had a monopoly of economic expertise, but they clearly do not. Their actions can precipitate crises and can contribute to making sound policies unworkable. In addition, they can erode the democratic quality of government. This does not necessarily lead to political impotence—although it has done so in some countries in some respects—but it creates new political questions.

MULTINATIONAL CORPORATIONS

The globalization of production and the globalization of financial transactions are organized in part, familiarly enough, by fast-growing multinational companies (MNCs). Two central points need to be made about them. First, MNCs account for a quarter to a third of world output, 70 per cent of world trade and 80 per cent of direct international investment. They are essential to the diffusion of technology. And they are key players in international money markets.

Secondly, although evidence indicates that many of the largest MNCs still generate most of their sales and profits from domestic business, this is largely due to the influence of US companies, which have, of course, a particularly large home market.[9] The proportion of sales and profits generated domestically are much lower for non-US companies and, significantly, for higher-technology companies. Moreover, although a company like Ford or General Motors may well have the majority of its assets in one particular country—in these cases, the US—it would be wrong to suggest that their performance is not substantially affected by their overseas activities. Even if a minority of assets are held overseas—say 20 to 30 per cent—this still represents a significant interlocking of a company's assets with overseas market conditions and processes. Companies are highly vulnerable to changes in economic conditions wherever they are. Marginal decreases in demand can profoundly affect the operations of a company.

Multinational corporations in general have profound effects on macroeconomic policy; they can respond to variations in interest rates by raising finance in whichever capital market is most favourable. They can shift their demand for employment to countries with much lower employment costs. And in the area of industrial policy they can move their activities to where the maximum benefits accrue. Irrespective of how often MNCs actually take advantage of these opportunities, it is the fact that they could do so in principle which influences government policy and shapes economic strategies. But the impact of MNCs should not just be measured by these indicators alone. They have a significant influence on an economy even when their levels of capitalization are not particularly high. For example, in Zimbabwe, the Coca-Cola bottling plant is not a big factory by global standards, yet it has a major influence on local management practices and on aspects of economic policy more broadly.

Economic globalization has significant and discernible characteristics which alter the balance of resources, economic and political, within and across borders. Among the most important of these is the tangible growth in the enmeshment of national economies in global economic transactions (thus a growing proportion of nearly all national economies involves international economic exchanges with an increasing number of countries). This

---

9   For a fuller account of these points see J. Perraton, D. Goldblatt, D. Held and A. McGrew, 'The Globalization of Economic Activity', *New Political Economy*, 2.2 (July 1997). I am particularly grateful for Jonathan Perraton's guidance on these matters.

increase in the extent and intensity of economic interconnectedness has altered the relation between economic and political power. One shift has been particularly significant: 'the historic expansion of exit options for capital in financial markets relative to national capital controls, national banking regulations and national investment strategies, and the sheer volume of privately held capital relative to national reserves. Exit options for corporations making direct investments have also expanded... the balance of power has shifted in favour of capital vis-à-vis both national governments and national labour movements.'[10] As a result, the autonomy of democratically elected governments has been, and is increasingly, constrained by sources of unelected and unrepresentative economic power. These have the effect of making adjustment to the international economy (and, above all, to global financial markets) a fixed point of orientation in economic policy and of encouraging an acceptance of the 'decision signals' of its leading agents and forces as a, if not the, standard of rational decision-making. The options for political communities, and the costs and benefits of those options, ineluctably alter.

CULTURAL AND COMMUNICATION TRENDS

Interlinked changes in trade, finance and the structure of multinational corporations are somewhat easier to document and analyse—even if their implications remain controversial—than the impact of globalization in the sphere of the media and culture. Evidence of globalization in this domain is complex and somewhat uncertain. A great deal of research remains to be carried out. Nonetheless, a number of remarkable developments can be pointed to. For instance:

1. English has spread as the dominant language of elite cultures—it is the dominant language in business, computing, law, science and politics.

2. The internationalization and globalization of telecommunications has been extraordinarily rapid, as manifested in the growth of, for instance, international telephone traffic, transnational cable links, satellite links and the Internet.

3. Substantial multinational media conglomerates have developed, such as the Murdoch empire, but there are many other notable examples as well, including Viacom, Disney and Time Warner.

4. There has been a huge increase in tourism. For example, in 1960 there were 70 million international tourists, while in 1995 there were nearly 500 million.

5. And the transnationalization of television programmes and films is also striking: 60 to 90 per cent of box office receipts in Europe, for instance, come from foreign movies (although this is largely the story of American dominance).

None of these examples, or the accumulated impact of parallel instances, should be taken to imply the development of a single global, media-led culture—far from it. But taken together, these developments do indicate that many new forms of communication and media range in and across borders, linking nations and peoples in new ways.

---

[10]   D. Goldblatt, D. Held, A. McGrew and J. Perraton, 'Economic Globalization and the Nation-State: Shifting Balances of Power', *Alternatives*, 22.3 (1997), p. 281.

Accordingly, national political communities by no means simply determine the structure and processes of cultural life in and through which their citizens are formed. Citizens' values and judgements are now influenced by a complex web of national, international and global cultural exchange. The capacity of national political leaders to sustain a national culture has become more difficult. For example, China sought to restrict access and use of the Internet, but found it extremely difficult to do.

THE ENVIRONMENT

Contemporary environmental problems are perhaps the clearest and starkest examples of the global shift in human organization and activity, creating some of the most fundamental pressures on the efficacy of the nation-state and state-centric politics. There are three types of problems at issue. First, there are shared problems involving the global commons, that is, fundamental elements of our ecosystem. The clearest examples of the environmental commons are the atmosphere, the climate system and the oceans and seas. And among the most fundamental challenges here are global warming and ozone depletion. A second category of global environmental problems involves the interlinked challenges of demographic expansion and resource consumption. An example of the profoundest importance under this category is desertification. Other examples include questions of biodiversity and challenges to the very existence of certain species. A third category of problems is transboundary pollution of various kinds, such as acid rain or river pollutants. More dramatic examples arise from the siting and operation of nuclear power plants, for instance, Chernobyl.

In response to the progressive development of, and publicity surrounding, environmental problems, there has been an interlinked process of cultural and political globalization as illustrated by the emergence of new cultural, scientific and intellectual networks; new environmental movements with transnational organizations and transnational concerns; and new institutions and conventions like those agreed in 1992 at the Earth Summit in Brazil. Not all environmental problems are, of course, global. Such an implication would be quite false. But there has been a striking shift in the physical and environmental circumstances—that is, in the extent and intensity of environmental problems—affecting human affairs in general. These processes have moved politics dramatically away from an activity which crystallizes simply around state and interstate concerns. It is clearer than ever that the political fortunes of communities and peoples can no longer be understood in exclusively national or territorial terms.

POLITICS, LAW AND SECURITY

The sovereign state now lies at the intersection of a vast array of international regimes and organizations that have been established to manage whole areas of transnational activity (trade, the oceans, space and so on) and collective policy problems. The growth in the number of these new forms of political organization reflects the rapid expansion of transnational links, the growing interpenetration of foreign and domestic policy, and the corresponding desire by most states for some form of international governance and regulation to deal with collective policy problems. These developments can be illustrated by the following.

1. New forms of multilateral and multinational politics have been established and with them distinctive styles of collective decision-making involving governments, international governmental organizations (IGOs) and a wide variety of transnational pressure groups and international non-governmental organizations (INGOs). In 1909 there were 37 IGOs and 176 INGOs, while in 1989 there were nearly 300 IGOs and 4,624 INGOs. In the middle of the nineteenth century there were two or three conferences or congresses per annum sponsored by IGOs; today the number adds up to close to 4,000 annually. Against this background, the range and diversity of the participants at the Earth Summit in Rio de Janeiro in 1992 or the Conference on Women in Beijing in 1995 may not seem quite as remarkable as the occasions initially suggested.

2. All this has helped engender a shift away from a purely state centred international system of 'high politics' to new and novel forms of geogovernance. Perhaps one of the most interesting examples of this can be drawn from the very heart of the idea of a sovereign state—national security and defence policy.

3. There is a documentable increase in emphasis on collective defence and cooperative security. The enormous costs, technological requirements and domestic burdens of defence are contributing to the strengthening of multilateral and collective defence arrangements as well as international military cooperation and coordination. The rising density of technological connections between states now challenges the very idea of national security and national arms procurement. Some of the most advanced weapons systems in the world today, such as fighter aircraft, depend on components which come from many countries. There has been a globalization of military technology linked to a transnationalization of defence production.

4. Moreover, the proliferation of weapons of mass destruction makes all states insecure and prolematizes the very notion of 'friends' and 'enemies'.

Even in the sphere of defence and arms production and manufacture, the notion of a singular, discrete and delimited political community appears problematic. As a result, the proper home and form of politics and of democracy becomes a puzzling matter.

RETHINKING DEMOCRACY

The developments documented above have contributed to the transformation of the nature and prospects of democratic political community in a number of distinctive ways. First, the locus of effective political power can no longer be assumed to be national governments—effective power is shared and bartered by diverse forces and agencies at national, regional and international levels. Second, the idea of a political community of fate—of a self-determining collectivity which forms its own agenda and life conditions—can no longer meaningfully be located within the boundaries of a single nation-state alone. Some of the most fundamental forces and processes which determine the nature of life chances within and across political communities are now beyond the reach of individual nation-states. The system of national political communities persists of course; but it is articulated and re-articulated today with complex economic, organizational, administrative, legal and cultural processes and structures which limit and check its efficacy. If these processes and structures are not acknowledged and brought into the political process themselves, they may bypass or circumvent the democratic state system.

Third, it is not part of my argument that national sovereignty today, even in regions with intensive overlapping and divided political and authority structures, has been wholly subverted—not at all. But it is part of my argument that the operations of states in increasingly complex global and regional systems both affect their autonomy (by changing the balance between the costs and benefits of policies) and their sovereignty (by altering the balance between national, regional and international legal frameworks and administrative practices). While massive concentrations of power remain a feature of many states, these are frequently embedded in, and articulated with, fractured domains of political authority. Against this background, it is not fanciful to imagine, as Bull once observed, the development of an international system which is a modern and secular counterpart of the kind of political organization found in Christian Europe in the Middle Ages, the essential characteristic of which was a system of overlapping authority and divided loyalties.[11]

Fourth, the late twentieth century is marked by a significant series of new types of 'boundary problem'. If it is accepted that we live in a world of overlapping communities of fate, where, in other words, the developmental trajectories of each and every country are more tightly entwined than ever before, then new types of boundary problem follow. In the past, of course, nation-states principally resolved their differences over boundary matters by pursuing reasons of state, backed, ultimately, by coercive means. But this power logic is singularly inadequate and inappropriate to resolve the many complex issues, from economic regulation to resource depletion and environmental degradation, which engender an intermeshing of 'national fortunes'. In a world where transnational actors and forces cut across the boundaries of national communities in diverse ways, and where powerful states make decisions not just for their peoples but for others as well, the questions of who should be accountable to whom, and on what basis, do not easily resolve themselves. Overlapping spheres of influence, interference and interest create dilemmas at the centre of democratic thought.

In the liberal democracies, consent to government and legitimacy for governmental action are dependent on electoral politics and the ballot box. Yet the notion that consent legitimates government, and that the ballot box is the appropriate mechanism whereby the citizen body as a whole periodically confers authority on government to enact the law and regulate economic and social life, becomes problematic as soon as the nature of a 'relevant community' is contested. What is the proper constituency, and proper realm of jurisdiction, for developing and implementing policy with respect to health issues such as AIDS or BSE (Bovine Spongiform Encephalopathy), the use of nuclear energy, the harvesting of rain forests, the use of non-renewable resources, the instability of global financial markets, and the reduction of the risks of nuclear warfare? National boundaries have traditionally demarcated the basis on which individuals are included and excluded from participation in decisions affecting their lives; but if many socioeconomic processes, and the outcomes of decisions about them, stretch beyond national frontiers, then the implications of this are serious, not only for the categories of consent and legitimacy but for all the key ideas of democracy. At issue is the nature of a constituency, the role of representation, and the proper form and scope of political participation. As fundamental processes of governance escape the categories of the nation-state, the traditional national resolutions of the key questions of democratic theory and practice are open to doubt.

---

[11] H. Bull, *The Anarchical Society* (London: Macmillan, 1977), pp. 254–55.

Against this background, the nature and prospects of the democratic polity need re-examination. The idea of a democratic order can no longer be simply defended as an idea suitable to a particular closed political community or nation-state. We are compelled to recognize that we live in a complex interconnected world where the extensity, intensity and impact of issues (economic, political or environmental) raise questions about where those issues are most appropriately addressed. Deliberative and decision-making centres beyond national territories are appropriately situated when those significantly affected by a public matter constitute a cross-border or transnational grouping, when 'lower' levels of decision-making cannot manage and discharge satisfactorily transnational or international policy questions, and when the principle of democratic legitimacy can only be properly redeemed in a transnational context. If the most powerful geopolitical interests are not to settle many pressing matters simply in terms of their objectives and by virtue of their power, then new institutions and mechanisms of accountability need to be established.

It would be easy to be pessimistic about the future of democracy. There are plenty of reasons for pessimism; they include the fact that the essential political units of the world are still based on nation-states while some of the most powerful sociopolitical forces of the world escape the boundaries of these units. In part in reaction to this, new forms of fundamentalism have arisen along with new forms of tribalism—all asserting the a priori superiority of a particular religious or cultural or political identity over all others, and all asserting their sectional aims and interests. But there are other forces at work which create the basis for a more optimistic reading of democratic prospects. A historical comparison might help to provide a context for this consideration.

In the sixteenth and seventeenth centuries, Europe was marked by civil conflict, religious strife and fragmented authority; the idea of a secular state, separate from ruler and ruled, and separate from the church, seemed an unlikely prospect. Parts of Europe were tearing themselves to pieces, and yet, within 150–200 years, a new concept of politics became entrenched, based around a new concept of the state. Today, we live at another fundamental point of transition, but now to a more transnational, global world. There are forces and pressures which are engendering a reshaping of political cultures, institutions and structures. First, one must obviously note the emergence, however hesitatingly, of regional and global institutions in the twentieth century. The UN is, of course, weak in many respects, but it is a relatively recent creation and it is an innovative structure which can be built upon. It is a normative resource which provides—for all its difficulties—an enduring example of how nations might (and sometimes do) cooperate better to resolve, and resolve fairly, common problems.

In addition, the development of a powerful regional body such as the European Union is a remarkable state of affairs. Just over fifty years ago Europe was at the point of self-destruction. Since that moment Europe has created new mechanisms of collaboration and of human rights enforcement, and new political institutions in order not only to hold member states to account across a broad range of issues, but to pool aspects of their sovereignty. Furthermore, there are, of course, new regional and global transnational actors contesting the terms of globalization—not just corporations but new social movements such as the environmental movement, the women's movement and so on. These are the 'new' voices of an emergent 'transnational civil society', heard, for instance, at the Rio Conference on the Environment, the Cairo Conference on Population Control and the Beijing Conference on Women. In short, there are tendencies at work seeking to create new forms of public life and new ways of debating regional and global issues. These are, of course, all in early stages of development, and there are no guarantees that the balance of political contest will allow them to develop. But they point in the direction of establishing new ways of holding transnational power systems to account—that is, they help open up the possibility of a cosmopolitan democracy.

Cosmopolitan democracy involves the development of administrative capacity and independent political resources at regional and global levels as a necessary complement to those in local and national polities. At issue would be strengthening the administrative capacity and accountability of regional institutions like the EU, along with developing the administrative capacity and forms of accountability of the UN system itself. A cosmopolitan democracy would not call for a diminution per se of state power and capacity across the globe. Rather, it would seek to entrench and develop democratic institutions at regional and global levels as a necessary complement to those at the level of the nation-state. This conception of democracy is based on the recognition of the continuing significance of nation-states, while arguing for a layer of governance to constitute a limitation on national sovereignty.

The case for cosmopolitan democracy is the case for the creation of new political institutions which would coexist with the system of states but which would override states in clearly defined spheres of activity where those activities have demonstrable transnational and international consequences, require regional or global initiatives in the interests of effectiveness and depend on such initiatives for democratic legitimacy. At issue, in addition, would not merely be the formal construction of new democratic mechanisms and procedures, but also the construction, in principle, of 'broad access' avenues of civic participation at national and regional levels. Table 1.1 provides an outline of some of the constitutive features of cosmopolitan democracy.[12]

IN SUM

The theory of cosmopolitan democracy is one of the few political theories which examines systematically the democratic implications of the fact that nation-states are enmeshed today in complex interconnected relations. Our world is a world of overlapping communities of fate, where the fate of one country and that of another are more entwined than ever before. In this world, there are many issues which stretch beyond the borders of countries and challenge the relevance of those borders in key respects. Many of these issues have already been referred to—pollutants, resource use questions, the regulation of global networks of trade, finance, etc. Can these be brought within the sphere of democracy? The theory of cosmopolitan democracy suggests this is not only a necessity, but also a real possibility.

---

[12] For further discussion and elaboration of these and related features, see Daniele Archibugi and David Held (eds), *Cosmopolitan Democracy: An Agenda for a New World Order* (Cambridge: Polity Press, 1995) and Held, *Democracy and the Global Order* (Cambridge: Polity Press, 1995).

TABLE 1.1	Cosmopolitan democracy

Principle of justification

In a world of intensifying regional and global relations, with marked overlapping 'communities of fate', democracy requires entrenchment in regional and global networks as well as in national and local politics. Without such a development, many of the most powerful regional and global forces will escape the democratic mechanisms of accountability, legitimacy and considered public intervention.

Illustrative institutional features

Short-term	Long-term

Polity/governance

1	Reform of leading UN governing institutions such as the Security Council (to give developing countries a significant voice and effective decision-making capacity)	1	New Charter of Rights and Obligations locked into different domains of political, social and economic power.
2	Creation of a UN second chamber (following an international constitutional convention).	2	Global parliament (with limited revenue-raising capacity) connected to regions, nations and localities.
3	Enhanced political regionalization (EU and beyond) and the use of transnational referenda	3	Separation of political and economic interests; public funding of deliberative assemblies and electoral processes.
4	Creation of a new, international Human Rights Court. Compulsory submission to ICJ jurisdiction.	4	Interconnected global legal system, embracing elements of criminal and civil law.
5	Establishment of an effective, accountable, international military force.	5	Permanent shift of a growing proportion of a nation-state's coercive capability to regional and global institutions.

Economy/civil society

1	Enhancement of non-state, non-market solutions in the organization of civil society.	1	Creation of a diversity of self regulating associations and groups in civil society.
2	Systematic experimentation with different democratic organizational forms in the economy.	2	Multisectoral economy and pluralization of patterns of ownership and possession.
3	Provision of resources to those in the most vulnerable social positions to defend and articulate their interests.	3	Social framework investment priorities set through public deliberation and government decision, but extensive market regulation of goods and labour remain.

General conditions

1) Continuing development of regional, international and global flows of resources and networks of interaction.

2) Recognition by growing numbers of peoples of increasing interconnectedness of political communities in diverse domains including the social, cultural, economic and environmental.

3) Development of an understanding of overlapping 'collective fortunes' which require collective democratic solutions—locally, nationally, regionally and globally.

4) Enhanced entrenchment of democratic rights and obligations in the making and enforcement of national, regional and international law.

5) Transfer of increasing proportion of a nation's military coercive capability to transnational agencies and institutions with the ultimate aim of demilitarization and the transcendence of the states' war system as a means of resolving conflicts of national interest.

In Praise of Politics

BERNARD CRICK*

***Sir Bernard Crick** is Emeritus Professor of Birkbeck College, University of London, and Honorary Fellow in Politics at the University of Edinburgh.*

And every man that striveth for the
mastery is temperate in all things.
St Paul
In the prison of his days
Teach the free man how to praise.
From W. H. Auden, 'In Memory of W. B. Yeats'

Politics deserves much praise. Politics is a preoccupation of free men, and its existence is a test of freedom. The praise of free men is worth having, for it is the only praise which is free from either servility or condescension. Politics deserves praising as—in Aristotle's words—'the master-science', not excusing as a necessary evil; for it is the only 'science' or social activity which aims at the good of all other 'sciences' or activities, destroying none, cultivating all, so far as they themselves allow. Politics, then, is civilizing. It rescues mankind from the morbid dilemmas in which the state is always seen as a ship threatened by a hostile environment of cruel seas, and enables us, instead, to see the state as a city settled on the firm and fertile ground of mother earth. It can offer us no guarantees against storms encroaching from the sea, but it can offer us something worth defending in times of emergency and amid threats of disaster.

Politics is conservative—it preserves the minimum benefits of established order; politics is liberal—it is compounded of particular liberties and it requires tolerance; politics is socialist—it provides conditions for deliberate social change by which groups can come to feel that they have an equitable stake in the prosperity and survival of the community. The stress will vary with time, place, circumstance, and even with the moods of men; but all of these elements must be present in some part. Out of their dialogue, progress is possible. Politics does not just hold the fort; it creates a thriving and polyglot community outside the castle walls.

Politics, then, is a way of ruling in divided societies without undue violence. This is both to assert, historically, that there are some societies at least which contain a variety of different interests and differing moral viewpoints; and to assert, ethically, that conciliation is at least to be preferred to coercion among normal people. But let us claim more than these minimum grounds: that most technologically advanced societies are divided societies, are pluralistic and not monolithic; and that peaceful rule is intrinsically better than violent rule, that political ethics are not some inferior type of ethical activity, but are a level of ethical life fully self-contained and fully justifiable. Politics is not just a necessary evil; it is a realistic good.

Political activity is a type of moral activity; it is free activity, and it is inventive, flexible, enjoyable, and human; it can create some sense of community and yet it is not, for instance, a slave to nationalism; it does not claim to settle every problem or to make every sad heart glad, but it can help some way in nearly everything and, where it is strong, it can prevent the vast cruelties and deceits of ideological rule. If its actual methods are often rough and imperfect, the result is always preferable to autocratic or to totalitarian rule—granted one thing alone, that sufficient order is created or preserved by politics for the state to survive at all. Praise, in politics as in love, beyond the early days of idealization, can only hearten if it paints a picture plausible enough to be lived with. It must be asked, when is politics possible at all? It is possible when there are advanced or complicated societies, societies with some diversity of technical skills and which are not dependent for their prosperity or survival on a single skill, a single crop, or a single resource. Not all societies (or people) are in this position. Some primitive societies may be so near the margin of survival, so dependent on constant toil and on the precarious success of harvests or trade in a single commodity, that they never amass any capital, hence no leisure, no margin for tolerance, and hence no possibility of political culture. Diversity of interests, which creates a speculative recognition of alternatives, may simply not exist, or if so, be a luxury endangering sheer physical survival. Advanced states in times of war or emergency revert to this condition; if everything depends on the military, then everything is subordinated to military considerations. But, of course, a people who have known politics will be more reluctant to accept this condition on trust; they will take some chances with survival in order to preserve liberty.

Diversity of resources and interests is itself an education. Men living in such societies must appreciate, to some degree, alternative courses of action—even if just as speculative possibilities. There is then not just a technique of doing some one thing, but an abstract knowledge of how other things are done. Some division of labour exists and this, of itself, creates attempts at seeing their relationships: abstract knowledge. The Greek *polis* was perhaps the first circumstance in which a division of labour went together with a division of interests (or speculative alternatives) to a sufficient degree to make politics a plausible response to the problem of ruling such a society. Politics is, as it were, an interaction between the mutual dependence of the whole and some sense of independence of the parts. Obviously the small size of these cities helped to make politics possible. The idea and the habit of politics stood little chance of administrative survival in an Empire as large as Rome, when so many parts of the Empire were entirely dependent on their immediate crops and on the military power of the centre. In an Empire politics must expand from the Mother City, or perish under the burden of the struggle for sheer survival and the habits of autocratic rule which it is forced to create in the true citizens. Part of the price of the Commonwealth's remaining a British Empire would almost certainly have been autocracy in Britain itself—as France came at least so near in the attempt to keep Algeria. And the Romans did not even have the fortunate necessity of having to negotiate politically with other independent powers—the quasi-politics of international relations.

Thus diversity of resources and interests is itself the education which is necessary for politics. There is no a *priori* level of education—even literacy or any such test—which can be laid down as necessary for politics. The level of education will be relative to the level of technological development. The unique modern problem arises when advanced, Western industrial technology is suddenly introduced into a hitherto colonial or underdeveloped area. Then there will almost inevitably be a time lag, at least, between a country's ability to handle these particular skills itself and its ability to develop or recognize a speculative sense, even, of the alternative uses to which these skills and this capital can be put. The simultaneous introduction of Western ideas, including that of free politics itself, may help; this is also a resource and a skill. But politics has to strive against an initial sense that the introduction of scientific and industrial technology is one unified and overwhelming good. Industrialism becomes at first a comprehensive slogan. The fact of new machines is confused with the doctrine of 'technology': that technology solves everything and that all problems are technological. Perhaps only time can show that not merely are real choices of policy called for at every stage of industrialization, but that new and real differences of interests are created.

Here is, of course, the great hope of many that freedom will grow even in the Soviet Union, even in China. The complexity of industrial society, it is argued, will force genuine negotiation first between the party and the managers, and then with the scientists and perhaps even the skilled workers. At least the managers and the scientists, it is argued, because of their function cannot be prevented from meeting together, from developing corporate interests divergent from those of the party and the party ideology. This is a reasonable hope, but it is only a hope. Certain conditions of the modern age work against it. There is the power of bureaucracy. One of the great conditions for, and achievements of, the process of state consolidation and centralization in the whole modern period has been the growth of centralized, skilled bureaucracies. The idea of a rational bureaucracy, of skill, merit, and consistency, is essential to all modern states. Like democracy, as we have seen, bureaucracy is a force that strengthens any state—political, autocratic, and totalitarian alike. The bureaucracy, like the priesthood of medieval Christendom, can become more than an intermediary between the scientists, the managers, the workers, and the seat of power; it can become a conservative power on its own acting in the name of whoever controls the state at the time when these great changes begin. This ambivalent factor of bureaucracy, necessary to all states, strengthening free and unfree alike, has then to be seen in the context of a second obstacle to the hope that industrialization by itself creates freedom.

There is also, as part of industrialization, as we have been at sad pains to insist, a genuine revulsion from, hatred of, and theoretical attack upon, politics. Politics itself is attacked for dividing communities, for being inefficient, for being inconclusive and—with a completely false but powerful idea of science—for being anti-scientific. Political thinking is replaced by ideological thinking. The force of abstract ideas is not to be ignored—though it is the academic fashion of today to do so. So if we ask when is political rule possible, we must also add—far from formally—that it is possible only when at least some powerful forces in a society want it and value it. And it follows that politics is not possible when most people do not want it. The element of will is not independent of circumstances, but it may often and has often weighed the scales one way or the other. Certainly, there is little doubt at the moment which of the two great fruits of Western civilization—politics and technology—is in greater demand in the non-Western world. If Western history demonstrates that they did emerge together, this is no guarantee that in their migration they will always be received together.

Skilled manpower is itself a crucial factor for the possibility of politics in underdeveloped areas. The demand on educational resources, on the very small skilled talent available at all, for scientists, doctors, and engineers, may make the vocation of politics seem either an unjustifiable luxury, or else seem a refuge for not merely the second-rate, who anyway are the bulk of steady representative figures in free societies, but for the utterly third-rate. In this dilemma it is worth noticing that the lawyer often holds a key position. In Nigeria, for instance, and in most of the present and former British colonial dependencies, the profession of law is highly esteemed and sought after. It was almost the only avenue of social advance for the educated, and the most likely springboard for politics. The supply of lawyers is already greater than the demand, at the moment, for strictly legal work. This can mean that political values are kept alive—when politics becomes the arena of the talented underemployed. But, of course, it can also mean that if political opposition has been silenced out of principles or alleged necessity, the supply of skill for a despotic bureaucracy is ensured. Hope and fear spring, once again, from precisely the same factors.[1] The decision depends, once again—in large part at least—on a conscious affection for politics or disaffection from it.

Closely related to this decision is what some writers mean by praising 'political ethics' or 'constitutional ethics' as a condition of free societies: simply that people must agree to, or accept, the solution of social problems by political and legal means. Problems can always be attacked by autocratic means. There was a time, as we have seen, when liberals had a profound distrust of party and faction. James Madison argued in the great Tenth Paper of *The Federalist* (one of the masterpieces of political literature) that factions were, indeed, selfish and divisive. But he argued that they were inevitable (he said 'natural') and could be eliminated (which they could be) only at the cost of eliminating liberty; they could and should be restrained, but not destroyed. Indeed, as the state has grown larger and more complex, we go beyond this and say that such organized factions—better still, parties as things which are capable of forming responsible governments—are essential to free politics in the modern state. They should pursue their 'selfish' ends, for they are devices, whatever their doctrines or lack of doctrine, by which an electorate may hold a government responsible for its actions; and they are gauges by which a government may learn what it can safely and properly do. But they must be forced to pursue their aims in a way which does not endanger public order and their aims should be limited, if they are to be worthy of support by free men, to things which can be done without destroying politics. However convinced men are of the rightness of their party, they must compromise its claims to the needs of some electoral and legal framework, at least so far that the only way of removing it from power does not have to become revolution. Political compromises are the price that has to be paid for liberty. Let us not delude ourselves that we are not paying a price; but let us summon reasons to think that it is normally worth paying.

Political power is power in the subjunctive mood. Policy must be like a hypothesis in science. Its advocates will commit themselves to its truth, but only in a manner in which they can conceive of and accept its possible refutation. Politics, like science, must be praised for being open-minded, both inventive and sceptical. One is not acting politically if one pursues as part of a policy devices intended to ensure for certain that it can never be overthrown. This condition embraces both the well-meaning but futile attempts of constitution makers to put something permanently above politics (though it may be part of politics to make the gesture), and the autocratic attempt to forbid or destroy opposition. The true activity of scientists, not the myth of 'scientism', should give some comfort—if only by analogy—to politicians. When anything is deemed to be fixedly true by virtue of the

---

[1] Perhaps it is not merely pride which has made several 'national leaders' recently cancel the scholarships of students studying abroad, who are reported, amid the heady freedom of London or New York, to have expressed even slight doubt that their leader has all the virtues of, shall we say, Mohammed and Lenin combined. Such men depend on the skills and the support of such youths. One knows the cost and the risk, but such youths may be in a stronger position than they think—if they are in earnest with their scepticism.

authority who pronounces it, this thing can be neither politics nor science. Everything has to be put to the test of experience—though some men are better at framing hypotheses or policies than others. If all boats are burnt, if assertions are made categorically, as in a totalitarian party, then the pace of the advance can only be intensified and made desperate. Politics is to be praised, like science, for always retaining a line of retreat.

For independent positions in society to survive there must be some institutional framework. And this framework can be thought of as guaranteeing these independencies. There is a long tradition of Western political thought which sees the essence of freedom as the cultivation of constitutional guarantees. The laws or customs which define the framework of government and representation must be put on some different footing to ordinary customs or acts of legislation. There must be, it is said, some fundamental law, something entrenched against the momentary caprice of government or electorate—something at least made more difficult to change than ordinary laws. Some writers, then, properly aware of the difficulties and dangers of calling free regimes 'democratic', call them 'constitutional democracies' and speak of 'constitutionalism' as the key to free politics. This view deserves praise—but a qualified praise.

Let us simply realize that this is desirable but impossible to ensure. Some political societies survive without such a strengthening of their foundations. Constitutionalism is itself a doctrine of politics. Like any doctrine of politics it says that something is the case and that something *should* be. It says that political government is limited government: that governments cannot do everything we or they may want. This is true. But it also says that we should guarantee that they should not try—and this is impossible. There are no guarantees in politics. Guarantees may have to be offered as part of politics. But while guarantees stop short of giving independence to a former sub-group or dependency, they remain themselves things subject to change, negotiation, and, even in the most rigid-seeming written Constitution, interpretation. Constitutionalism is vitally important to politics. It is one of the great themes of Western thought and a fruitful concept in that it leads us always to see abstract ideas as needing institutional expression, and to see existing institutions as existing for some purpose. But the praise of politics as constitutionalism needs to be realistic; it needs to be seen that it is the belief itself in fundamental or constitutional law which gives this law force. No law can survive the withering of the belief. No law can survive the growth of new needs and demands; if the fundamental law is not in fact flexible, it can hinder more than help free politics. Constitutions are themselves political devices. They may be viewed as self-sufficient truths in the short run; but in the long run it is political activity itself which gives—and changes—the meaning of any constitution. When we praise a constitution we are doing no more than praise a particular abridgement of a particular politics at a particular time. If the abridgement was a skilful one and circumstances are kind, it may last into a long middle period and help to give stability to a state. But, in the long run, though the words are the same and formal amendments to it may be few, the meaning of it will be different. Even the old Anglo-American Whigs, the arch-constitution-makers, used to say that no constitution was better than the character of the men who work it.

Certainly, at any given time a settled legal order is necessary for freedom and politics. Law is necessary in any society at all complex and people should be able to find out what it is fairly precisely and to use it fairly cheaply. (Litigation, not politics, is the necessary evil of free states.) The autocrat was, indeed, an arbitrary ruler—making laws without any process of consultation or litigation. And the totalitarian leader thinks of law as policy: people are judged not for specific breaches of the law, but for not living up to the general ideals of the régime. Certainly politics should be praised in procedures. Since the business of politics is the conciliation of differing interests, justice must not merely be done, but be seen to be done. This is what many mean by the phrase 'the rule of law'. The framework for conciliation will be a complexity of procedures, frustrating to both parties, but ensuring that decisions are not made until all significant objections and grievances have been heard. Procedure is not an end in itself. It enables something to be done, but only after the strength behind the objections has been assessed. Procedures help to stop both governments and litigants from making claims which they cannot enforce. Procedures, legal or Parliamentary, if given some temporary independent power themselves, tiresome, obstructive, and pettifogging though they may be, at least force great acts of innovation to explain themselves publicly, at least leave doors open for their amendment if the government has misjudged the power of the forces opposed to it. More praise, then, for politics as procedure than for politics as constitutional law, since, while there is no doubt that procedures are necessary for politics, there is also no doubt that every particular procedure is limited to time and place. Justice Frankfurter once asked the interesting question whether one would rather have American substantive law and Russian procedures or Russian substantive law and American procedures. Every essay should be pardoned one enigma.

Some common views about constitutions are more helpful if restated in political terms. Some claims for necessary legal elements in political order need seeing, by just a shift of perspective, as themselves parts of political order, or as possible but not exclusive types of political order. Consider the view that free government depends upon legally instituted checks and balances and the division of powers. People at times have felt extremely certain about this.

Alexander Hamilton wrote in the Ninth Paper of *The Federalist:*

> *The science of politics, however, like most other sciences, has received great improvement. The efficacy of various principles is now well understood, which were either not known at all, or imperfectly known to the ancients. The regular distribution of power into distinct departments; the introduction of legislative balances and checks; the institution of courts composed of judges holding their offices during good behaviour; the representation of the people in the legislature by deputies of their own election: these are wholly new discoveries, or have made their principal progress towards perfection in modern times.*

But these are not 'principles' at all. They are already the summary of an existing political practice in which power was divided, indeed to an extraordinary degree; and in which legislative checks and balances already existed in most of the separate Colonial or Provincial Assemblies as the procedural products of a long struggle between the Royal Governors and the Assemblies, indeed between factions in the Assemblies themselves. The American Federal Constitution was an invention intended to summarize and synthesize an existing division of powers into a Federal Union which had itself only the minimum power necessary to ensure common survival. (Federalism has been a practical response to divided power more than a way of dividing it as a matter of principle.) And in America these divisions had been astonishingly political in nature. They were predominantly the separate interests of thirteen existing fully political units. Only through these political units could 'national' and sectional economic and social differences express themselves.

This is not to say, however, else our praise would be but faint and local, that Hamilton's 'principles' (even if not strict principles) had relevance only to American Colonial conditions. As we have argued, there already exist in certain advanced societies divisions of power, group interests with independent strength from the state itself—independent at least in the sense that the central state is not willing to risk destroying them, but is conscious that it must conciliate them. It is these divisions which make the Constitution necessary; they are not created by it. The constitutional principle of the division of powers only affirms the reasons for which politics arises at all, and attempts to make them secure amid the need for strong government to maintain both internal and external safety. The constitutional principle of checks and balances only affirms the need for organized participants in politics to remember that their will is not the only will. Even when this will does seem to be in fact the only will, typically in the first generation of some colonial Liberation, it affirms the need for this unified majority to set obstacles against itself developing illusions of infallibility and permanence. In the constitutions of many of the American states there was, indeed, the praiseworthy spectacle of a unified majority willing to bind itself against itself. The binding can never be permanent, but it can set up sufficient obstacles for second thoughts to follow any initial impetus for great innovations.

So the relativity to time and place of all constitution-making does not mean that we are driven back merely to the maintenance of order as the only clear criterion of good government. Mere order is not enough to satisfy men as they are. Politics will fail if it cannot maintain order, as at the end of the French Fourth Republic; but it is a counsel of despair to think that all that can be hoped for is public order and 'merciful and just rulers'. We live in a democratic age whether we like it or not. And if none of the devices for limiting power and for subjecting governments to control, even when they extend their control of the economy vastly, are permanent or sure, yet we have learned more about such devices, even about constitution-making, than the tired or despairing conservative will usually allow. Politics, again we insist, is a lively, inventive thing as well as being conservative. We can use it for good and deliberate ends.

Political rule should be praised for doing what it can do, but also praised for not attempting what it cannot do. Politics can provide the conditions under which many non-political activities may flourish, but it cannot guarantee that they will then flourish. 'One cannot make men good,' said Walter Bagehot, 'by Act of Parliament.' No state has the capacity to ensure that men are happy; but all states have the capacity to ensure that men are unhappy. The attempt to politicize everything is the destruction of politics. When everything is seen as relevant to politics, then politics has in fact become totalitarian. The totalitarian may try to turn all art to propaganda, but he cannot then guarantee that there will be art as distinct from propaganda—indeed by his concern to destroy or enslave the abstract speculation of the philosopher or the creativity of the artist, activities apparently quite irrelevant to mere political power, he demonstrates that these irrelevancies are necessary to free life and free society. The totalitarian, like the autocrat, may try to make use of religion until he is powerful enough to destroy it, but he is driven to degrade men in order to try to prove that there is no soul which need not fear the body's harm.

To ensure that there be politics at all, there must be some things at least which are irrelevant to politics. One of the great irrelevancies to the total-politician is simply human love:

How can I, that girl standing there,

My attention fix

On Roman or on Russian

Or on Spanish politics?

—the poet rightly asks. The girl, of course, may happen to be involved in politics—Yeats had his Maud Gonne and Zhivago his Larissa—but the value of the involvement between the poet and the girl is not political. Yeats called this poem 'Politics' and headed it with a remark of Thomas Mann's: 'In our time the destiny of man presents itself in political terms.' Would Mann, one wonders, have disagreed with this splendidly contemptuous criticism, or would Yeats have made it, were either sure that the other was using politics in the narrow sense which we have striven to show is its best sense, and not as standing for all forms of power and authority? If man has a destiny, politics is obviously incompetent to legislate about it; but it can keep him alive and free to seek it. If artistic activity is an end in itself, then it is the denial of politics to start laying down laws about art. No wonder poets and writers have constantly explored the theme of the clash between political values and art and love. The independence of art and love, it is some comfort to think, are not merely the sure signs of a free society, but have a deep influence in making men think freedom worth while amid the temptations there are to surrender ourselves to the sense of certainty offered by an ideology. Politics does not need to defend itself against the anarchy and irresponsibility of the artist and the lover; it does not need even to claim that it is necessary for everyone to be involved in and to support politics. (It can withstand a lot of apathy; indeed when the normally apathetic person suddenly becomes greatly interested in political questions, it is often a sign of danger.) But if the politician, too, has a little proper pride in his vocation, he can at least ask such critics whether they are not sometimes confusing state power in general with political rule in particular, or, more subtly, are not accusing political regimes of being purely democratic—democracy, again, as the belief that because men are equal in some things, they are equal in all. It is this belief against which the very existence of the philosopher, the artist, and the lover is a unique testimony.

Even in true politics, however, there is no guarantee that there will not, in some unhappy circumstances, be a clash between the public interest and private conscience. Indeed the paradigm-case of political philosophy, the point at which this new thing began, was Plato's picture of the trial of Socrates as just such an event. Plato, of course, leaves us in no doubt that love of wisdom—*philosophia*—should be put before love of country; and he was condemning a particular democratic régime. But—the mark of the great artist—he could not help but give us enough of the other side of the case to show that Socrates really could be thought a danger to the state, by corrupting the most able youth of the city with a technique of self-doubt at a time when the city was struggling in war for very survival, and needed every ounce of military ability and civic patriotism available. Certainly Plato's Socrates himself saw no way out of the dilemma but death. He could not promise, as an inspired philosopher, to hold his tongue for the duration of the hostilities. Nothing can guarantee us against genuine tragedy—that moral virtues can lead to disaster in certain circumstances—except belief in an ideology which abolishes tragedy by making every sacrifice a pragmatic calculation towards gaining future benefits for the collective cause.

One of the great disappointments of modern liberalism, made possible by democracy, was the need and the ability to introduce military conscription, first in time of war, and then even in times of the mere threat of war. Conscription taught liberals a sad lesson in the primacy of survival over personal liberties. But how great and praiseworthy was the fact that even in the Second World War, even in genuinely total war, Great Britain, and to a lesser extent the United States, solemnly made provision for conscientious objection to military service. Let one be as critical as one likes of the bizarre concept of 'conscience' which arose in the tribunals. Let one be as Machiavellian as one can and call it a mere gesture, something which would never have been tolerated if the numbers involved, or the example, had proved in the least bit a hindrance to the war effort. But the gesture was a gesture towards the kind of life which a political régime thought it was trying to preserve. If someone's sense of self-identity was so deeply bound up with feeling it impossible to kill a fellow human being, then that sense of self-identity had to be respected. Perhaps pacifism as a social force did not matter very much. And a pacifist was just as useful—as some of them sadly realized—replacing an agricultural labourer for service in the infantry as he would have been serving himself—probably more so. But it is the mark of political regimes that they do not, as ideological regimes do, condemn even ineffective opposition out of sheer arrogant principle. It is the mark of freedom that, even if ideas may have to be prevented from achieving institutional and powerful form, the ideas themselves are not forbidden and hunted down. We cannot always get what we want, but if we lose the ability to think of wanting other things beside what we are given, then the game is lost for ever.

Political activity is important not because there are no absolute ideals or things worth doing for themselves, but because, in ordinary human judgement, there are many of these things. Political morality does not contradict any belief in ideal conduct; it merely sets a stage on which people can, if they wish, argue such truths without degrading these truths into instruments of governmental coercion. If the truth 'will set you free' and if the service of some ideal is held to be 'perfect freedom', let this be so, so long as the advocates are prevented from involving others in the fraudulent freedom of coerced obedience. The view that the belief in absolute ideals (or what Professor K. R. Popper has called 'essentialism') is dangerous to political freedom is itself intolerant, not a humanistic view of society but a gelded view, something so over-civilized and logically dogmatic as to deprive many of any feeling that anything, let alone free institutions, is worth while. Freedom and liberty are not ends in themselves, neither as methods nor as substitute moralities; they are part of politics and politics is simply not concerned, as politics, with absolute ends. It need neither affirm nor deny. And when sceptics or true believers are in fact acting politically, it should teach us to take with a grain of salt the 'purely practical' or 'the purely ideal' construction which they put on their own involvement. Political morality is simply that level of moral life (if there are other levels) which pursues a logic of consequences in the world as it is. To act morally in politics is to consider the results of one's actions.

Lincoln once set out to define the position of the new Republican Party on the slavery question. He said (in a speech of 15 October 1858):

> *The real issue in this controversy—the one pressing upon every mind—is the sentiment on the part of one class that looks upon the institution of slavery as a wrong, and of another class that does not look upon it as a wrong. . . . The Republican Party . . . look upon it as being a moral, social, and political wrong, and while they contemplate it as such, they nevertheless have due regard for its actual existence among us, and the difficulties of getting rid of it in any satisfactory way, and to all the constitutional obligations thrown about it. . . . I repeat it here, that if there be a man amongst us who does not think that the institution of slavery is wrong in any one of the aspects of which I have spoken, he is misplaced, and ought not to be with us. And if there be a man amongst us who is so impatient of it as a wrong as to disregard its actual presence among us and the difficulty of getting rid of it suddenly in a satisfactory way, and to disregard the constitutional obligations*

thrown about it, that man is misplaced if he is on our platform. We disclaim sympathy
with him in practical action.

This is true political morality—indeed political greatness. If anyone is not willing to walk this kind of path he might be happier to realize that he has in fact abandoned politics. He may abandon them for the lead of the benevolent autocrat who will promise the end of slavery tomorrow, or he may simply do nothing because he is not willing to muddy his conscience with such 'terrible compromises' or equivocation. As regards the greatness of a man who can sharpen the issue so clearly, I admit that there is always an alternative interpretation of such words—hypocrisy. Someone may just be offering excuses for not doing something which he does not believe in anyway. This is a matter of judgement—and perhaps the motive does not matter if the right public actions follow, except to the man's own soul and to his biographer. 'Hypocrisy,' said Swift, 'is the tribute that vice pays to virtue.' What matters in politics is what men actually do—'sincerity' is no excuse for acting unpolitically, and insincerity may be channelled by politics into good results. Even hypocrisy, to a very, very small degree, keeps alive something of the idea of virtue. Certainly on an issue such as slavery, some people must keep a pure moral vision alive, but such visions, perhaps held only by 'saints', fanatics, reformers, intellectuals, will be partially fulfilled only when there is an attempt to realize them in terms of public policy. There is little doubt in Lincoln's case that he did truly believe that slavery was a 'moral, social, and political wrong'. But it is rare good fortune for the leader of a state himself to combine absolute ethics and the ethics of responsibility. And these are things only to be reconciled through time.

The politician must always ask for time. The hypocrite and the enemy of reform uses time as an excuse for inaction—literally the 'time-server' or the slave to time, he whose vision is entirely limited to the immediate. But 'eternity', said the poet Blake, 'is in love with the products of time'. 'Eternal values' cannot be treated as immediate values; but time in itself is nothing but a tedious incident on the way to death unless in it and through it we strive to achieve—what the Greeks looked for in the public life—'immortal actions', ever memorable reforms, monuments to the belief that civilization can advance. In 1955 the United States Supreme Court declared that racial segregation in all American schools supported by public funds was unconstitutional. It enjoined the responsible authorities to integrate, not immediately—which would have been impossible, without the use of force incredible to imagine in a free society—but with 'deliberate speed'. This was an act not merely of great moral (and presumably legal) significance, but of political wisdom. *The law* is now known. That is as far as a Court or a moralist can go. But it will be an act of political cowardice if the Federal executive cannot now constantly nudge the unreconstructed time-servers to implement the law. Time by itself solves nothing; but time is needed to attempt anything politically.

Now let us continue to praise Lincoln as a great politician on even harder grounds, which may scare away still more fair-weather friends of politics—or men who would do good if it did not mean walking, like Bunyan's Pilgrim, through both Vanity Fair and the Valley of the Shadow of Death. In the middle of the hardest time of the American Civil War, Horace Greeley, a militant abolitionist, challenged Lincoln to commit himself to immediate emancipation as a matter of principle. Lincoln replied:

My paramount object in this struggle is to save the Union, and is not either to
save or destroy slavery. If I could save the Union without freeing any slave, I
would do it; and if I could do it by freeing all the slaves, I would do it; and if I

could do it by freeing some and leaving others alone, I would also do that. What I do about slavery and the coloured race, I do because I believe it helps to save the Union, and what I forbear, I forbear because I do not believe it would help to save the Union . . . . I have here stated my purpose according to my view of official duty, and I intend no modification of my oft expressed personal wish that all men, everywhere, could be free.

Lincoln put preservation of the Union, the political order itself, above everything else, not because he did not care for Negro suffering and exclusion—he did; but because only if there was a Union again, a common political order again between North and South, could any of these problems be tackled. Suppose I will risk the case of politics on even more unhappy grounds than Lincoln actually had to face—that a man in his position could have felt confident of winning the war and preserving the Union only by promising *not* to use his emergency powers as Commander-in-Chief to emancipate the slaves. Would this have been justified? I think the hard answer is obviously—yes. The first responsibility of a leader is to preserve the state for the benefit of those to follow. Suppose such a leader had privately believed that after his making such a promise the legislature would, immediately after the war, overrule him. This is no deceit; he could not have been held responsible for their actions—or if so, it would have been an agony for the private conscience faced with the primacy of public responsibility. Suppose even the darkest situation of all, that he had privately believed that once his promise was made and once his war-time powers were gone, the legislature would not emancipate the slaves. The personal agony of such a position as this cannot be evaded, and it would be hard to blame a man who would abandon politics in such a situation in the sense of resigning from office. But even then such a man as Lincoln would probably not have abandoned power, for the true political statesman knows that while there is *political* power at all, while there is a representative assembly, nothing is really certain, no single aspect of policy is not negotiable somehow, realizable in however small a part in the flexibility and management of a free assembly.

The example of Lincoln is not too bad a one on which to rest this case for politics—however much pietistic myths have obscured the grosser human tale of political action. He offended beyond reason many responsible men of his day by rarely being willing to talk seriously in private, by his infuriating retreats into badinage and the telling of old jokes. His dignity was a very variable quality. He seems to have been an indifferent administrator, disorderly, inconsistent, and even slothful; his relations with Congress were often inept and usually bad. But, for all that, he is as great an example of a mere politician as can be found. If this claim actually sounds more odd to American than to English ears, it is because American English, or rather American liberalism, has debased the word 'politician'. True, he preserved the State as a statesman; but he sought to do it, even at the height of the emergency, politically. (It is not helpful to inflate, as is done in American vernacular, every small but honest politician into a 'statesman'.) Lincoln, before his death, made it quite clear that he would oppose Congress if they sought to treat the South as a conquered territory without constitutional rights. The task, he said, was that of 'doing the acts necessary to restoring the proper practical relations between these States and the Union'; he scorned 'deciding, or even considering' whether these States had ever been out of the Union; he ironically suggested, almost parodying his own best style, that 'each for ever after, innocently indulge his own opinion whether, in doing the acts, he brought the States from without, into the Union, or only gave them proper assistance, they never having been out of it'. Politics, as we have seen, is indeed a matter of 'practical relations', not of deduction from higher principles.

Lincoln had little dignity, but he had enough authority and he did not have pride. Pride is an easy vice for any whose business must be in the public eye. But a true politician cannot afford it. The politician lives in a world of publicity, calumny, distortion, and insult. He is often looked down upon by polite society as being a mere 'fixer' and an 'opportunist' (though it is puzzling why this last word always has a bad meaning); and he is mocked by intellectuals for rarely having ideas of his own:

a politician is an arse upon

which everyone has sat except a man

—which is the whole of an easy poem by e. e. cummings. And, indeed, the politician, beneath his necessary flexibility, will rarely be a man of less than normal pliability and ambitions. He will provoke such cheap mockery from spectators. But he will not take these things to heart. The successful politician will learn how to swallow insults. The successful politician keeps in mind the English nursery proverb:

Sticks and stones may break my bones

But names will never hurt me.

He does not store up memories of insults and nor does he, when in power, take opposition personally, making a matter of principle or of *lèse majesté* of every ungenerous suspicion hurled upon him. A politician, like any of us, may not be above such pettiness; but he has no need for it, so he must not show it. The temptation is great, however. It is now [1962] an offence in Ghana's criminal code, punishable by up to three years in prison, to defame or insult President Nkrumah. This law is a sad monument to a man who showed such zest and ability for politics when in opposition himself. It is sad to think that this tender soul may not even have enjoyed such politics. Lincoln once remarked, with pragmatic humility: 'A man has not the time to spend half his life in quarrels. If any man ceases to attack me, I never remember the past against him.' He told one of his generals: 'I wish you to do nothing merely for revenge, but that what you may do shall be solely done with reference to the security of the future.' The politician has no more use for pride than Falstaff had for honour. And if when suddenly dismissed from favour, he then invokes pride and asks for employment and honour, he is just kicking against the terms of his trade which he, like any of us, had ample opportunity to study. Politics as a vocation is a most precarious thing, so we should not grudge the politician any of the incidental rewards he can pick up. But we must always beware that he does not grow bored or frustrated with 'mere politics'—that all this need for compromise stops him from doing what is obviously best for the nation. The price of politics is eternal involvement in politics ourselves.

The political leader, as we have seen, may have to take risks with liberty to preserve the nation. He may have to invoke 'sovereignty' and, at this point, the leader who cannot lead is not worth having. But he will lead so that politics can survive. Lincoln wrote to General Hooker: 'I have heard, in such a way as to believe it, of your recently saying that both the army and the government needed a dictator. Of course it was not for this, but in spite of it, that I have given you command. Only those generals who gain successes can set up dictators. What I now ask of you is military success, and I will risk the dictatorship.' Free politics is a risky business, though not so risky as dictatorship. And 'free politics', as I have sought to show, is really a pleonasm—either word will do. If a politician has pride, it must be, as Aristotle distinguished, a 'proper pride'—in his skill at his conciliatory vocation, not *hubris,* the attempt to be more than a man, which commonly makes a man less than a man.

Conciliation is better than violence—but it is not always possible; diversity is better than unity—but it does not always exist. But both are always desirable. Perhaps it all comes down to the fact that there are two great enemies of politics: indifference to human suffering and the passionate quest for certainty in matters which are essentially political. Indifference to human suffering discredits free regimes which are unable, or which fear, to extend the habits and possibility of freedom from the few to the many. The quest for certainty scorns the political virtues—of prudence, of conciliation, of compromise, of variety, of adaptability, of liveliness—in favour of some pseudo-science of government, some absolute-sounding ethic, or some ideology, some world-picture in terms of either race or economics. Perhaps it is curious, or simply unnatural, that men who can live with dignity and honour in the face of such endemic uncertainties as death, always so close in the normal possibilities of accident and disease; as love, its precariousness and its fading, its dependence on the will and whims of others, yet can go mad for certainty in government— a certainty which is the death of politics and freedom. A free government is one which makes decisions politically, not ideologically.

There is no end to the praises that can be sung of politics. In politics, not in economics, is found the creative dialectic of opposites: for politics is a bold prudence, a diverse unity, an armed conciliation, a natural artifice, a creative compromise, and a serious game on which free civilization depends; it is a reforming conserver, a sceptical believer, and a pluralistic moralist; it has a lively sobriety, a complex simplicity, an untidy elegance, a rough civility, and an everlasting immediacy; it is conflict become discussion; and it sets us a humane task on a human scale. And there is no end to the dangers that it faces: there are so many reasons that sound so plausible for rejecting the responsibility and uncertainty of freedom. All that we have tried to do is to show why political activity is best seen as only one form of power relationship and political rule as only one form of government; and then to advance some arguments to show why the political solution to the problem of government is normally to be preferred to others. The only end to such an incomplete essay of defence and praise is to repeat drily what it is we have been describing.

Aristotle repeated his definition in almost the same words as we quoted at the beginning:

> *The object which Socrates assumes as his premise is... 'that the greatest possible unity of the whole* polis *is the supreme good'. Yet it is obvious that a* polis *which goes on and on, and becomes more and more of a unit, will eventually cease to be a* polis *at all. A* polis *by its nature is some sort of aggregation. If it becomes more of a unit, it will first become a household instead of a* polis, *and then an individual instead of a household. . . . It follows that, even if we could, we ought not to achieve this object: it would be the destruction of the* polis.

The Experience of Politics:
I. How to Be an Activist

KENNETH MINOGUE*

***Kenneth Minogue** is Emeritus Professor of Political Science at the London School of Economics and Political Science.

Those who study politics are called political scientists, and we must presently consider politics as a science. First, however, we must look to what it is that scientists have to study: namely, the actual experience of engaging in politics.

This experience is sometimes compared to theatre. Politicians and actors certainly belong to related tribes. Much of the architecture of public life recalls the Classical inspiration of the Roman forum, especially that of Washington. In London, the Houses of Parliament, rebuilt in the middle of the nineteenth century, have been appropriately described as 'a basically classical structure with neo-Gothic detail'. The architecture of the Kremlin and its communist embellishments reflect the remoteness and grandiosity of despotism. French public architecture is imperial in its grandeur. That the British prime minister lives in a more or less ordinary house in a more or less ordinary street reveals something of the studied casualness of British public life.

These are the national theatres of politics, but most political drama, even in a televisual age, takes place in local and regional offices, in dusty halls and on windy street corners where electors can be harangued. Politics has its own logistics: it requires agents, premises, contacts with printers, a pool of supporters, money, and generally, as the condition of all these things, an established political party. The rich and famous are sometimes inclined to start a party from scratch, but it is a difficult option. The typical route taken by the ambitious politician is from the periphery to the centre, and each step of the way resembles a game of snakes and ladders.

The politician needs, for a start, the same kind of knowledge as the concerned citizen; just more of it. What American politician could move a step without a close knowledge of the Constitution, the Bill of Rights, and many of the decisions of the Supreme Court? Knowledge of history is indispensable, supplying a range of memories, references, and metaphors without which political talk is unintelligible. From the War of Independence, through the Civil War, to the very songs and slogans of the American past, the politician must be able to pick up the references, many of them highly local, which constitute the culture of those whom he seeks to represent. He must know how the Senate and Congress work in detail, not to mention the way in which the states relate to them. Much of this is low-level, slightly tedious, descriptive material, but without it the politician's understanding hardly rises above gossip.

Traditions of politics vary greatly. In beginning by contrasting politics with despotism, we have already suggested that there is an immense gulf dividing the possible ways of ordering a society. The very idea of what a human being is, and what is due to men, and especially to women, will in many countries be remote from what is believed by the average reader of this book. A tradition is something 'handed down' from one generation to another, and (perhaps re-described as 'political culture') must be the central object of under-standing in any political system. It is composed of many strands, and what people say about the state may give very little sense of the reality of politics. A population long accustomed to being exploited by tax collectors, for example, has an attitude to the census, to governmen-tal forms, and the rhetoric of leaders quite different from that which used to be found in European liberal democracies. In some traditions, people are sanguine about what can be changed, in others cynical and fatalistic. The very language in which the thoughts and senti-ments pass down over the generations reveals a conceptual structure which affects political possibility. All languages have some analogue for 'justice', for example, but there are many variations on this broad theme—such as the idea of fairness—which can only be imported from other languages. Even European languages which are culturally similar to English do not yield a genuine translation of the subtitle—*Justice as Fairness*—of John Rawls's *A Theory of Justice*. Again, the Chinese character for 'freedom' connotes slipperiness and ego-ism rather than the courage and independence with which Europeans associate the term.

Most political knowledge generalizes experience. The politician cannot help but learn a great deal from the past, and especially from exemplary heroes and villains. Machiavelli recommended a close attention to the great deeds of ancient Rome, but modern history is not a whit less fertile in suggestive examples, and certainly much more revealing about our own political traditions. A British politician, for example, must know something of Magna Carta, Roundhead and Cavalier, Whig and Tory, the Reform Bills of the nineteenth centu-ry, the contrasting political styles of prime ministers such as Melbourne, Peel, Disraeli, Gladstone, Churchill, Attlee, and Wilson, not to mention the events of the twentieth cen-tury. Much of this will be legend, and what is heroic to some will be deplorable to others. A Labour politician might regard Ramsay MacDonald's formation of the National Government in 1931 as an act of treason to the party; a Conservative would treat the event quite differently, and would certainly see it as less important. Politicians train for the real world by endless talk about past landmarks and present possibilities, and they do so in a special language of their own. Thus 'appeasement' is no longer in politics the name of a type of response to someone's discontent, but refers to a dispute about foreign policy in the 1930s. For several decades after the Second World War it denoted an episode of shame and cowardice. Then came revision, an attack on the reputation of Churchill, the great critic of appeasement, and the argument that Britain's lone stand against Hitler in 1940 had mere-ly delivered her into the hands of the rising empires of the USA and the USSR. It is very seldom that events stand still for long, and the paradox is that the past is nearly as opaque as the future.

For the aspiring politician in a country such as France, the past hangs more heavily than it commonly has in Anglo-Saxon countries. The French Revolution split France pro-foundly, largely along religious and secular lines, and the Nazi occupation left memories which determined political allegiances for the rest of the century. Irish politics has been similarly haunted by memory. The United States has, in general, been more fortunate, though the legacy of the Civil War has been bitter.

Since politics is talk, political skill requires wit, and politicians are remembered for their phrases. Winston Churchill is remembered both for the speeches which articulated 'the lion's roar' during the Second World War and for a string of witticisms, some of them malicious, like his description of Clement Attlee as 'a sheep in sheep's clothing'. Lincoln's political success came from his wisdom, but it is hard to imagine his political skill with-out his dazzling capacity for oratory. These men all belong, of course, to a vanished time when citizens attended like connoisseurs to long and complicated political speeches. Gladstone once took four hours to introduce his budget to the House of Commons—fortified, it is said, with raw eggs and sherry. That culture has been destroyed by the trivializing effect of radio and television, which provide such abundant distraction for the mind that politics must be fitted into a much smaller space: the 'sound-bite'. The sound-bite belongs to the simplified world of the slogan and the banner, but this does not diminish the need of the politician for the phrasemaker.

In modern democracies, a politician is a spokesman for some broadly based opinion, and what he or she hopes to become is the holder of an office. *Spokesmanship* and *office* are the polarities within which the men and women who go in for politics must live, and each reveals much about politics.

Spokesmanship is representation, and modern government must be conducted by representatives rather than by the citizens themselves because legislative enactments, often some hundreds of pages long, are too complicated to be mastered without unusual skill and attention. But the representative function of the politician begins long before policies emerge. It is the skill of constructing a position which will appeal to many people because it can harmonize conflicting desires. The superficial critic of politicians can see the vagueness and indeterminacy which are certainly often necessary for this, but generally fails to appreciate the trick of finding some essence of an issue that can unite different opinions. A skilful politician resembles a magician in his capacity to set an object before the mind of one audience, while keeping it invisible to others, sometimes in the same hall. Simple-minded rationalists sometimes stigmatize this characteristic of politicians as nothing but support-seeking duplicity, and journalists have taken to 'decoding' their speeches and disclosing the supposed 'message' behind the words. Better understood, this technique is the tact which allows people with very different judgments and preferences to live together in one society; where it fails—as, for example, in the difficulty Canadian politicians have had in projecting a 'Canada' that would accommodate Francophone and Anglophone opinion—then society moves to the brink of dissolution. American politicians finessed the division over slavery for as long as they could, for they suspected that the real alternative was civil war, and they were right.

Constrained by his representative function, the politician is further circumscribed by the responsibilities of his *office*. The raw brutalities of power are largely converted into the suavities of authority, and it is important to distinguish these two phenomena. The outsider is often impressed by the power of those who hold important positions in the state, but power, while attractive as a kind of melodrama, is mostly exaggerated. The office of a prime minister or president is constitutionally limited, and idealists quickly find that their capacity to improve the world requires whole streams of concessions they would prefer not to make, As Harry S. Truman remarked: 'About the biggest power the President has is the power to persuade people to do what they ought to do without having to be persuaded.' The power of an office is merely the skill by which a ruler can use his authority to get the right things done. Otherwise, when people talk of 'power' they merely mean the pleasure an office-holder may get from a purely personal exercise of will, which is basically a trivial thing. Most trivial of all is the pleasure in being the constant focus of attention in public places, and the capacity to please—but also to frustrate—the ambitious people by whom the politician is surrounded. It can no doubt be exploited for illicit purposes. President Kennedy notoriously used his prestige as president to induce large numbers of women to sleep with him, though since he was also handsome and rich, he hardly needed presidential prestige for that. It may be that, like the kinds of political groupie the Hungarian writer Arthur Koestler talked about, some of them 'wanted to sleep with history'. Such power is not a thing possessed by the power-holder, but a moral relationship between the power-holder and the person over whom the power is supposedly exercised. Where it is a form of corruption, it involves the corruption of both parties.

The fact that persuasion lies at the heart of politics has one central implication: the reasons a politician decides upon a policy are categorically distinct from the reasons by which he publicly defends it. The two sets of reasons may overlap, or they may not, but in neither case need we conclude that politics is a cynical business. The reason lies in what we may call the *dimensions* of a political act. One such dimension concerns the practicality of the act in question. Will it have the desirable effects expected of it? What are its costs, and possible longer-term consequences? For the government to guarantee everyone an old age pension, for example, will certainly alleviate hardship, but it will also have economic consequences because the incentives to thrift and saving will diminish, and that will affect the economy. The real test is the long term. As the nineteenth century journalist Walter Bagehot observed, one cannot judge the consequences of any reform until the generation in which it was passed has left the scene.

A second dimension: what is the consequence of pursuing this particular *type* of policy? It will infallibly become a precedent used in arguing for further policies of the same type. If it fails, there may be demands that the policy be pursued even further, rather than abandoned. When central direction of some economic activity produces anomalies, for example, the typical demand is that further central direction should be invoked to deal with the anomalies. Another dimension: what effect will this policy have on the short- and long-term prospects of its promoter? The promoter here is both the individual and the party legislating the policy. The Welfare State, for example, created in Britain after 1945, diffused benefits widely over the electorate, and its short-term effects might therefore have been to increase support for the Labour Party which carried it out. In the event, this did not happen—Labour lost the 1951 election. More seriously still, some welfare measures of the period have been thought to have 'gentrified' the working class and detached them from the Labour Party. As politicians sometimes say, nothing fails like success.

A typical form of cynicism revolves around concepts such as the 'public interest' or the 'common good'. It is easy to discredit such terms by pointing out that nearly every act of government will have both good and bad consequences for different sets of people. But it is to mistake the meaning of public interest to think it can be judged in terms of individual costs and benefits. Ideas of this kind are formal terms of political argument whose specific meaning can only emerge from the public debate itself. They are the necessary formal conditions of any political advocacy. It would be absurd for a politician to say: 'I want to do this because it is good for *me*.' Such a line would provide no reason why anyone else should do it. No doubt there is a vague sense in which everything any politician advocates is the best thing for him in the circumstances, but this does not at all mean that he is a hypocrite out for nothing else but personal benefit. There is plenty of self-serving conduct in politics, though it is reasonable to think that politicians are generally more rather than less public-spirited than the rest of us. That may not be much, of course, but it is something.

None of this is to deny the lowness of much of politics. A certain craftiness is essential. To know, for example, the rule whereby when votes are equal in a committee, the motion is lost, tells the crafty politician whether to frame a precarious motion in negative or in positive terms. For if, opposing the policy, he frames it in positive terms, and the vote is tied, then the motion is lost and he gets what he wants. In the 1994 Euro-elections in Britain, one candidate got thousands of votes from an unsophisticated electorate by calling himself the 'literal' (rather than liberal) democratic candidate. To have a name beginning with the early letters of the alphabet gives a candidate a slight but measurable advantage from the dimness of some citizens who simply fill in the ballot-paper from the top down. And no one called 'Kennedy' can fail to pick up extra votes in many American states. The main delinquencies of politicians, however, arise from highly prevalent human vices: cowardice in failing to challenge the fashionable opinion which the politician senses is wrong, fear of being thought stupid, desire to take up a virtuous-seeming posture, a preference for the comfortable option when the politician knows that the chickens will come home to roost some time after he has left the scene, and so on.

Politicians form a kind of club, sharing a culture in liberal democracies which cuts across party divisions. Friendships, for example, are often warmer *across* parties than within them. Certain ideas are always dominant in this culture, and some of these ideas may run counter to the opinions (known here as prejudices) of the people at large. In recent times, capital punishment, multiculturalism, and international idealism are examples of this class of idea, and politicians sometimes confuse them with the quite different thing called principle. The significance of this fact is that in certain respects politicians as a class constitute an oligarchy whose tendency is at odds with that of the population it rules. This oligarchic tendency is even more pronounced in countries whose electoral system requires voters to support party lists. When the gap between what politicians admire and what the people want widens, the general stock of politicians goes down, and they are recognized less as representing than as trying to hoodwink the people. The familiar ambiguities of politics become explicit sophistry. This is, of course, a dangerous situation in which opportunities for demagogues multiply.

The politician facing the question: how may my policy be commended to my audience? will think more of his audience than of his own introspections. Sometimes that audience will be colleagues, sometimes his own party, and sometimes the electorate as a whole. We may assume that he is persuaded of its wisdom, but the reasons which seem decisive to him may well not be decisive to others. The problem of persuasion is to find the reasons that will be decisive to the audience. In doing that, the politician must take off from whatever common ground he shares with them. The first act in persuasion is for the persuader to convince his audience of his fellow-feeling with their broad aims, and only then can he commend his own policy as something fitting in with those aims.

What this account of persuasion suggests is that the politician must be a special type of person, one capable of keeping his deepest convictions to himself. The rest of us can shoot off our mouths to our hearts' content, indulging in that massive new pleasure the modern world has invented, being opinionated about matters on which we are ignorant. The politician must generally consider the effect of his opinions on his likely future, and requires a special kind of personality structure. But it should not be concluded from this that a politician is simply a hypocrite. Such a person is engaged in a high-risk occupation in which he must always be looking to future developments. Opportunism is certainly part of the talent, but unless the politician has genuine convictions—both moral convictions, and convictions about how things are likely to move—he will lack the clear profile which is usually necessary for the greatest success. Statesmen—the highest grade of politician—are those who can balance inner conviction with the talent of turning every opportunity to advantage. Charles de Gaulle called for resistance to Germany from London in 1940, and withdrew from French politics in 1946, taking risks in both cases which could have doomed him to obloquy and insignificance. Churchill's stand against appeasement in the 1930s might have been a mere swansong to a moderately successful career. Barry Goldwater, who took disastrous risks in bidding for the presidency in 1964, turned out to be preparing the soil for the Reagan victory of 1980. The secret of politics is to care about success, but not too much.

The Impact of Culture on Politics

OLIVER H. WOSHINSKY*

***Oliver H. Woshinsky** is Emeritus Professor of Political Science at the University of Southern Maine.

People behave, from one place to another, in remarkably dissimilar ways. Brazilians bear hug when they meet friends. The French shake hands formally, and the Japanese bow. Transferring the behavior of one culture to another can produce dramatic misunderstandings. Bear hugging a Japanese businessman would hardly improve your chances for a contract. Fail to shake hands with a Frenchwoman each time you meet, and she will see you as a boor and a cad.[1]

Ian Robertson has written amusingly about the variety of human behavior.

> *Americans eat oysters but not snails. The French each snails but not locusts. The Zulus eat locusts but not fish. The Jews eat fish but not pork. The Hindus eat pork but not beef. The Russians eat beef but not snakes. The Chinese eat snakes but not people. The Jalé of New Guinea find people delicious.*[2]

Anecdotal accounts of human diversity can be fascinating, and they can also make a serious point. It pays to understand the variety of human mores, because every social pattern impinges in some way on politics. Candidates for office in Japan or France don't throw their arms around constituents while campaigning; in Brazil they do. Try it in Japan, or fail to do it in Brazil, and you will get nowhere in your bid for office.

In the same manner, what you eat (far-fetched though it may seem) will influence your political fortune. Imagine a politician in Israel known to dine on roast pig. Or an American politician who admits to loathing hot dogs and apple pie. George Bush [Sr.] had to claim that he loved pork rinds in order to win the trust of Texas voters, and Bill Clinton is known to enjoy that quintessential American food, the Big Mac. Had these men ever admitted, early in the political careers, that they preferred locusts and snakes to good old American food, they would never have had political careers, and none of us today would have heard of them.

P. J. O'Rourke, the flamboyant American journalist, once described some harrowing (though hilarious) adventures in Lebanon for his best-seller *Holidays in Hell*. One day he and his guide roamed the countryside looking for a farmer he was supposed to interview.

> *It's hard to know what your driver is doing when he talks to the natives. He'll pull up somewhere and make a preliminary oration, which draws five or six people to*

---

[1]   For an engaging account of the social significance of body language in different cultures, see Roger E. Axtell, *Gestures: The Do's and Taboos of Body Language around the World* (New York: John Wiley & Sons, Inc. 1991).

[2]   Ian Robertson, *Sociology* (New York: Worth Publishers, 1981) p. 63.

the car window. Then each of them speaks in turn. There will be a period of ges-turing, some laughter, much arm clasping and handshaking, and a long speech by the eldest or most prominent bystander. Then your driver will deliver an impas-sioned soliloquy. This will be answered at length by each member of the audience and anybody else who happens by. Another flurry of arm grabbing, shoulder slap-ping and handshakes follows, then a series of protracted and emotional good-byes. 'What did you ask them?' you'll say to your driver. 'Do they know your friend.' 'What did they tell you?' 'No.'[3]

Cultures vary. People differ radically from each other, depending on where they live and how they have been raised. People are emphatically *not* "just the same the world over," as the old cliché would have it. And as human behavior varies from one culture to anoth-er, so too does political behavior. The direct, straightforward American manner of asking questions would get nowhere in a Lebanese village. Just as obviously, a "straight-talking" American politician would fail miserably in a bid for office there. On the other hand, the bombastic, circuitous, and loquacious style of Lebanese interaction would produce career disaster for any American politician dim enough to adopt it in the United States.

POLITICS AND CULTURE

Politics everywhere reflects the culture of a time and place. This argument underpins the perspective of modern political science. To understand politics anywhere, you must first understand the culture within which political acts are embedded.

An intriguing item once appeared in my local newspaper: "In the Tonga Islands it is a compliment for a young man to say to your woman, 'Oh, fat liver full of oil, let us go and watch the moonrise.'"

Can you imagine using that line at a Saturday night fraternity party? It would prove a dismal failure in U.S. culture. The current American's ideal of beauty is often expressed in that famous cliché, "You can never be too rich or too thin." Studies show that the vast majority of American women consider themselves "too fat," when in fact most of them are not, by any reasonable standard, overweight.[4] But in a culture that glorifies slenderness, those who deviate even slightly from the reigning ideal of beauty see themselves (and indeed, are seen by others) as disadvantaged.

As it turns out, most cultures have fairly rigid notions of attractiveness, and those notions vary widely. Many societies prefer heftier body types than those admired in the West. A thin woman, attractive by American standards, once told me that growing up in West Africa in a missionary family, she was shunned by the young men of her village. Her plump sister, however, was considered stunning, and men came from miles around to offer her father many cows for the privilege of making her their bride.

---

[3]   P. J. O'Rourke, *Holidays in Hell* (London: Pan Books, Ltd., 1989), p. 36.

[4]   According to a recent survey, "three-quarters of American adults are not overweight." See "Losing Weight: What Works, What Doesn't," *Consumer Reports* 58 (June 1993): 347–52. See also Morton G. Harmatz. "The Misperception of Overweight in Normal and Underweight Women," *Journal of Obesity and Weight Regulation* 6 (1987): 38–54; and Marika Tiggemann and Esther D. Rothblum, "Gender Differences and Social Consequences of Perceived Overweight in the United States and Australia," *Sex Roles* 18 (1988): 75–86.

As this example suggests, attractiveness, however defined by a particular culture, is an asset. Study after study has shown that benefits accrue to "attractive" people—that is, to people deemed attractive by the standards of their specific culture. Compared to others, attractive people are better liked, believed to be more intelligent, and prove more likely to get and hold any given job.[5] They not only receive "undeserved" benefits from life, they avoid its worst punishments. For instance, these same studies show that attractive people are less likely than others to be arrested; if they are arrested, they are less likely than others to be convicted; and if they are convicted, they are less likely than others to serve time in jail. To cap this process of injustice, even when attractive people do go to jail, they spend less time there than other convicts.[6]

Continuing this examination of attractiveness, we know that Americans prefer tall to short and white to black. As we would expect, therefore, when a white or black person, equally qualified, apply for any given job, the white person is likely to be chosen.[7] Similarly, a tall person is more likely than a short person to be given a job, even when both hold the same credentials.[8] Indeed, this pattern is so powerful that in the entire history of American presidential elections, a candidate clearly shorter than the other has won office only four times.[9]

Deviation from a culture's norm of beauty is hardly fatal to our life chances. Still, it represents a modest hurdle. It subtly detracts from one's career potential. On an individual basis, it must be dealt with, compensated for. Consider famous people (the short Napoleon, the plain Eleanor Roosevelt, the handicapped Toulouse-Lautrec or Stephen Hawking) who have achieved brilliant success despite falling seriously short of their society's attractiveness norms. We can also think of individual examples, from among people we know, who are successful but not especially attractive, or—on the contrary—attractive but not particularly successful. "History" (and by implication, social science) "knows probabilities but not certainties," writes Stephen White,[10] reminding us that there are few rules of human behavior that don't allow for a number of exceptions.

Still, social science prefers generalization to exception, rule to deviant case; that is, attractiveness is an advantage. On the whole, those who come closest to their culture's ideal

---

[5] For a recent summary of these findings, see Robert B. Cialdini, *Influence: Science and Practice*, 3rd ed. (New York: Harper Collins College Publishers, 1993), pp. 140–42; see also David G. Myers, *Social Psychology*, 4th ed. (New York: McGraw-Hill, Inc., 1993), pp. 473–76.

[6] See the evidence cited in Myers, op. cit., pp. 354–55.

[7] See, for example, Richard Jenkins, *Racism and Recruitment: Managers, Organizations, and Equal Opportunity in the Labour Market* (Cambridge: Cambridge University Press, 1986), pp. 116–88. See also Andrew Hacker, *Two Nations: Black and White, Separate, Hostile, Unequal* (New York: Ballantine Books, 1992), especially his discussion of black–white differentials in income and employment in the U.S., pp. 93–133.

[8] For a summary and critique of the literature, see Wayne E. Hensley and Robin Cooper, "Height and Occupational Success: A Review and Critique," *Psychological Reports* 60 (1987): 843–49.

[9] The Clinton victory over Bush in 1992 may provide a fifth case. On paper, both candidates were listed as six feet, two inches tall, but most observers gave Bush a half-inch advantage over his challenger. This marginal difference does little to undermine the generalization that Americans like their leaders to be tall, since both men stood well above the height of the average middle-aged American male (around five feet, nine inches). Now if [Ross] Perot (five feet, four inches) had won the election, *that* would have represented a serious deviation from the pattern!

[10] Stephen White, *Political Culture and Soviet Politics* (London: Macmillan, 1979), p. *x*.

of beauty will, other things being equal, be better rewarded than others (with whatever that culture's idea of reward might happen to be—money, cows, penthouses, or poems written in their honor).

Those who doubt this point might ask themselves why one rarely sees an unattractive popular singer—especially in these days of MTV. Did nature really contrive to distribute musical potential only to those with pretty faces? From among the many talented singers available, generally we elevate to musical stardom only those people who also happen to meet our standards of beauty. The same point applies to a host of other social positions. Why are news anchors uniformly pleasant to look at? Is there really some correlation between looks and the ability to read from a teleprompter? Clearly, we can find thousands of excellent reporters in any country. Hundreds of these would be more than able to read aloud the day's news for us. From among this group, however, only the best-looking are chosen for this straightforward task.

You may be wondering: What on earth does this have to do with politics? The answer is simple. Politics is not some arcane ritual divorced from the life of society. It is intertwined in the most integral way with all other social activity. *Political activity cannot be considered apart from society as a whole*, any more than blood can be considered apart from the body in which it circulates.

Political behavior reflects the culture in which it occurs. If a given society adulates strength, it will reward strong individuals. All social leaders of that culture, including political decisionmakers, will be aggressive. (Even those who aren't will strive to appear so, if they wish to achieve social status.) If a society prefers friendliness, it will choose amiable, cooperative types for all leadership posts, from president on down to head of the local animal shelter. Pugnacious types in that culture will work at toning down their rough edges—or risk being ostracized.

Ruth Benedict found this precise pattern when she examined various North American indigenous peoples in the 1920s. The Pueblos, a peaceful and cooperative bunch, chose relatively weak, nonauthoritarian individuals to head their group. The Kwakiutl, on the other hand, an aggressive lot, chose their toughest and most assertive members for leadership positions.[11]

The simple *politics-reflects-culture* axiom explains a good deal about politics everywhere. In a highly religious society, for example, political leaders will be emissaries of God on earth. Witness the doctrine of the divine rights of kings in the Middle Ages. Witness the political power of the Ayatollah Khomeini in the ardently religious Iran of the 1980s. By way of contrast, in a nonreligious (or antireligious) society (say, Russia under Marxist rule), political leaders too will be nonreligious or antireligious. In reverse, deeply religious people in a nonreligious society will rarely gain political power. They will most often be scorned and treated as outcasts, even persecuted as subversives.

In a moderately religious society like the United States, political leaders must be moderately religious—or at least believed to be. They must be seen going to church, invoking

---

[11] See Ruth Benedict, *Patterns of Culture* (New York: The New American Library, 1934), esp. pp. 62–120 and 156–95. On the relation between cultural values and societal leadership patterns, see also Ruth Benedict, *Tales of the Indians* (Washington, D.C.: U.S. Government Printing Office, 1931), Margaret Mead, *Sex and Temperament in Three Primitive Societies* (New York: W. Morrow & Co., 1935), and David Riesman, *The Lonely Crowd: A Study of the Changing American Character* (Garden City, NY: Doubleday & Company, Inc., 1953), pp. 191–217.

God's will, praying publicly. Imagine the doleful fate awaiting the first presidential candidate bold enough (or foolish enough) to admit: I don't see much evidence of God's existence. In my humble opinion, prayer and churchgoing are a colossal waste of time, and I won't insult the intelligence of the American people by pretending otherwise. No such political leader exists in the United States today, nor should we expect one in the foreseeable future. On the other hand, excessive piety also works against someone seeking to rise in mainstream American politics. Many Americans feel uncomfortable around people who give voice regularly to intense religious fervor. Truly devout people rarely gain political power in the United States, thus joining atheists at the fringes of American politics.

Political activity, then, reflects cultural expectations. The proposition, used as a starting point, yields any number of useful predictions. We can confidently assert, for instance, that Americans will not soon elect any nonreligious person to the presidency. We also feel confident that they won't elect any clearly unattractive person to the Oval Office.

We must qualify and expand this last point. Remember the Tonga Islander's appreciation of fat? We can well imagine that the Tonga political leader is a large, burly fellow. (Indeed, I once came across a photograph of him and his wife, both towering over Great Britain's Queen Elizabeth, who was touring the island during a royal visit.) What one culture considers attractive, another may find distasteful. What, then, will an elected American president look like?

To begin, he will be a man—for reasons to be explained shortly. He will be tall—for reasons already explained. He will not be bald—Americans like men with a good head of hair. Indeed, in the history of this country (or at least since wigs went out of fashion), only two balding men have ever attained the presidential office. One was a national hero—General Dwight David Eisenhower. The other was something of a fluke: Gerald Ford. Through an odd chain of improbable events, Ford became president without ever facing the American electorate.[12] When he did try to win the voters' approval, in 1976, he lost a close race against Jimmy Carter, a man with a stylish head of hair. These two exceptions out of thirty-five presidents in the post-wig era do nothing but reinforce our conclusion: Men lacking in hirsute qualities will rarely make it to the top of the American political ladder.[13]

On another point of personal appearance, the president of the United States must be relatively thin. He certainly must not be overweight. Americans are so fanatical on this point that we can lay down the simple law: Anyone over ten percent heavier than average for his height and build will not be elected president. Think of all the significant presidential candidates we have seen in recent years: Jesse Jackson, Al Gore, Jerry Brown, Bob

---

[12]   Ford was the beneficiary—the only one so far—of the 25th Amendment to the U.S. Constitution, ratified only in 1967. This amendment set up a way to fill any vacancy that might occur in the vice-presidency. The amendment was put to use in 1973, when Spiro Agnew resigned from that office after corruption charges against him surfaced. President Richard Nixon then nominated Ford, minority leader in the House of Representatives, to replace Agnew, and Congress approved the appointment, making Ford vice-president. When Nixon himself resigned from the presidency a year later to avoid facing impeachment charges over the Watergate scandal, Ford acceded to the White House—having never faced the American electorate. Only residents of Michigan's Fifth Congressional District had ever voted for Ford before he gained the presidency.

[13]   Every ambitious politico is well aware of the phenomenon. More than one has addressed himself to the "misfortune" of hair loss. Within the last two decades, at least two senators who harbored hopes for the presidency undertook hair transplant treatment: William Proxmire and Joseph Biden.

Dole, Jack Kemp, Pat Robertson, Ross Perot. To a man, none is overweight. (When Ted Kennedy decided to run for president in 1980, he went on a diet and lost fifty pounds.) Among presidents themselves, none has been clearly obese since the days of William Howard Taft (1909–1913), who, at 300 pounds, stands out as an exceptional case. Exceptions can always occur, but we don't want to bet on them. Given the facts of American culture and the pattern of recent history, we can only conclude that it is advantageous to be thin if you harbor presidential ambitions.

Another matter of external appearance is crucial if you wish to become president. You must possess a friendly smile, one which gives you the appearance (at least) of being amiable and possessing a good sense of humor. Americans value these traits. Not all presidents have them, but most presidential contenders work at *appearing* to possess them—especially in recent years with the need to enhance one's television image uppermost in politicians' minds.[14]

Once into the spirit of this discussion, we can generate dozens of additional qualifications for candidates to the U.S. presidency. Among other requirements, for example, they must be (or at least seem to be) happily married and must have produced at least one healthy offspring. Nearly all our presidents fit this description. Only [James] Buchanan [1857–1861] was a bachelor. All other presidents were married, and most fathered several children.

American presidents, then, will be tall and well proportioned, possess a good head of hair, and show good teeth in a friendly smile, which they will display on all occasions. They will also have a supportive wife and at least one adoring child. To summarize: How many small, bald, overweight, scowling, single, childless men do you know with a serious chance at reaching the Oval Office?

What happens in politics, as these example illustrate, cannot be divorced from what happens in the rest of society. *A culture's deepest held values will be expressed in all its social institutions*. If society glorifies attractiveness, and if attractiveness is defined by height, hair, and smile, then those who are tall with nice hair and a cheerful grin will be advantaged in the struggle for political power.

WOMEN AND POLITICAL POWER

I have tried to use some amusing examples to get your attention. They may seem frivolous, but the principle they illustrate is profoundly important. Let us now apply it to a serious phenomenon. Our discussion of the attractiveness of U.S. presidential candidates focused entirely on men. The reason is obvious: We cannot generalize about the ideal features of a successful female presidential candidate. Not only have we never seen a successful woman candidate for president, but through the 1992 election we have not even seen a serious *potential* woman candidate for president!

---

[14] No one would quarrel with the assertion that television has stiffened the attractiveness requirement in all realms of American life, especially for those who must meet the public in their job—and that's one of the prime requirements for politicians. In short, the need for presidents to meet some kind of societal photogenic ideal has grown markedly in recent years, although I contend that it has never been absent from our history. The shrewd George Washington, for example, knew well the benefits of presenting an attractive image. He purposely made sure that he was always seen riding on a large white horse—to enhance his overall stature. (You will find no paintings of him on a steed of grey or brown.)

Some might argue this last point. Here's how I justify it. Let's define "a serious potential candidate" as anyone whom knowledgeable political observers would, one year before
the next presidential election, place among the twenty people most likely to attain the
Presidency. Under this admittedly loose definition, it is difficult to name *any* woman who
might have *ever* qualified. Perhaps Pat Schroeder or Elizabeth Dole in 1987 would have
made someone's list at number nineteen or twenty. Perhaps (though less likely) Shirley
Chisholm might have made someone's list in 1971. But that's about it. The rule is clear. To
be a serious candidate for president of the United States, even in this current era of feminism, you must be a man. (As I write these words in mid-1994, not one woman is being
seriously suggested by anyone as a likely challenger to Bill Clinton in 1996.)

This absence of women at the very top of the political ladder is hardly a fluke. We don't
find many women at the next rungs down either. No vice-president has ever been a woman.
Only one vice-presidential *nominee* (out of roughly a hundred major party nominations)
has ever been a woman—Geraldine Ferraro in 1984. We have never had more than four
women in the Cabinet (out of ten to fourteen members, depending on the year), but the
average number over the last twenty years has been two. (Before that, during the preceding 180 years, it was roughly zero.)

This pattern continues. No women can be found among the 101 justices named to the
U.S. Supreme Court during its first 191 years. The first woman (Sandra Day O'Connor)
reached the Court in 1981, and the second (Ruth Bader Ginsburg) twelve years later in
1993. (That makes two women currently on the nine-member Court—two out of the 108
Justices who have served since 1789.) The U.S. Senate has, over the past forty years, aver-
aged two women members out of a hundred, although it had by mid-1993 reached its highest number ever: seven. The U.S. House of Representatives saw twenty to twenty-five
female members (out of 435) from most of 1970 to 1990. (Before the 1994 elections, that
number was approaching fifty—roughly, eleven percent of the total.) As late as 1994, the
country had never had more than four women Governors in office at any given time (out
of the fifty states). The total number of women in all state legislatures never attained the
twenty percent level until 1993. The story continues in this vein; few women are in power,
right down to school boards and town councils throughout the land.

Because women comprise the majority of the electorate, their drastic underrepresenta-
tion in nearly every political and governmental body is one of the most striking facts of
American political life. To see this point more clearly, go back thirty years—or fifty. In
those days, women were practically invisible in American politics.

They were, we must note in fairness, invisible in the political system of all other countries as well. Except for the occasional oddity of a powerful queen, women were missing
from positions of power everywhere in the world until well into the twentieth century.

This absence of women from the structures of power is a vital political fact. After all,
a number of studies suggest that when women do reach decision-making positions, they
make different choices from those made by men.[15] For one thing, their energy is devoted
to different issues. They work for day care funding, health services, and improvements to

---

[15]   For a good summary of this literature, see Rita Mae Kelly, Michelle A. Saint Germain, and Jody D.
Horn, "Female Public Officials: A Different Voice?" *Annals of The American Academy of Political
and Social Science* 515 (1991): 77–87. See also Debra Dodson and Susan Carroll, *Reshaping the
Legislative Agenda: Women in State Legislatures* (New Brunswick, NJ: Center for the American

education rather than on tax policy, roadbuilding, and defense. They also vote differently from men. They show more support for social welfare programs and less for defense expenditures and business subsidies.

Whether you prefer these positions or not, the task of political analysis is to understand how politics works, and the point here is simple: *This dramatic absence of powerful women produces clear effects.* We as citizens get more conservative public policies than we would get if women were represented at something like their number in the population.

This phenomenon—the paucity of political women—is a central issue that touches us all. As students of politics, we must devote some time to understanding why it occurs. That means we must return to the concept of culture. It would be utterly impossible to explain the lack of women in power without reference to American norms, values, and social expectations. In other words, we must consider the broader culture within which U.S. politics take place.

Notice that if we try to understand this issue by examining narrower frameworks—the world of professional politics, for instance, or the realm of law—we get nowhere. Women aren't legally forbidden to run for political office. The political parties don't have rules preventing women from competing for nomination to public office. Voters don't even punish women who run for office by voting for their male competitors. When a man and a woman run against each other for any given office, studies show that (other things being equal) the man has no particular advantage.[16]

As far as law and politics go, then, women may freely compete for and win party nominations, go on to contest elections for office, and suffer no negative voter reaction when they do. Why, then, don't we find as many women *inside* politics as we do *outside* it, among the electorate?

Scholars have developed dozens of theories to explain this well-known phenomenon. We would need an entire book to account fully for it.[17] Yet one variable stands out as a central inhibitor of women's political activism. That is a simple but deepseated norm of American culture: Women, not men, have prime responsibility for the duties of homemaking and childrearing. Nowhere is this statement written down as law, but deeply implanted cultural beliefs have a stronger effect on human behavior than laws, which themselves are merely a reflection of those cultural beliefs. It will pay us to examine this norm and its many ramifications.

First, let's acknowledge it: Support for this norm is diminishing rapidly. We are all familiar with the changing relationship between men and women in our times, with the decline of traditional gender roles and norms. Still, the idea that women are homemakers and childrearers continues to maintain a significant hold on our society. But *even if it didn't*, I am going to argue, its near-universal acceptance in the recent past goes a long way toward explaining the small number of powerful women in the United States of the 1990s.

Woman and Politics, 1991); Susan Carroll, Debra Dodson, and Ruth Mandel, *The Impact of Women in Public Office* (New Brunswick, NJ: Center for the American Woman and Politics, 1991), esp. chap. 5; Sue Thomas, *How Women Legislate* (New York: Oxford University Press, 1994); and Joni Lovenduski and Pippa Norris, *Gender and Political Parties* (London: Sage, 1993).

[16] See, for example, the evidence cited in R. Darcy, Susan Welch, and Janet Clark, *Women, Elections and Representation* (New York: Longman, 1987), pp. 51–57 and 75–77.

[17] Many books already exist on the subject. Among the more useful, see Darcy Welch, and Clark, op. cit., and Vicky Randall, *Women and Politics* (New York: St. Martin's Press, 1982).

Why? Let us begin with a straightforward assertion: *power takes time to accumulate.* You have to work your way up the hierarchies of influence. Just as no one springs full-blown into the presidency of General Motors, so no one leaps from obscurity into the U.S. Senate.[18] Those who reach the upper levels of the American political system need first to attain education, status and wealth and then convert those assets into the skills that produce political clout.

Many skills are needed to become a political leader: speaking ability, self-confidence, and persuasiveness, to name a few. You also need a variety of resources. Wealth is perhaps the most obvious one. Having good connections is another.

But of all the resources needed to become influential in American politics, two are especially crucial for explaining the predominance of men over women at the upper levels of power. First, you need a good deal of *time* to develop those political skills, mentioned previously, that are crucial to political success. You also need time to convince a broad public segment that you actually have those skills and should be rewarded for having them.

In other words, you don't graduate from high school and get elected a senator. You have to study for and earn a college degree then work for and attain a graduate degree (typically the law), then win a seat on some local or regional body (city council, county board of commissioners), then spend some time in the state legislature, go on to win a statewide office (attorney general, lieutenant governor), then perhaps gain your state's governorship or a seat in the U.S. House of Representatives, and finally after several years in one of these latter posts, make your bid for a U.S. Senate seat.

Naturally, there are other ways up the ladder of power, but all of them have this in common: They take time, and they don't come easily.

The difficulty of attaining political success leads to the second key requirement for gaining that success: *motivation.* There are few accidental powerholders in this world. *Those who get power want it and want it badly.* Consider the enormous expenditure of effort it takes to follow the previous scenario for political success. To be willing to exert yourself doggedly onward for years in order to rise to some serious level of political influence you must be deeply motivated. That is to say, you must be career oriented, focused on making your way into the world, and willing to suffer those "slings and arrows of outrageous fortune," which are always associated with the bruising career path you have chosen. You must eat, sleep, and breathe politics—for years and years, from young adulthood to middle age—to have a reasonable chance of arriving at the upper-middle to upper levels of the political power hierarchy.[19]

Now who is likely to start out in young adulthood with that orientation? Consider the U.S. political hierarchy as it currently exists (the mid-1990s). Given the time it takes to

18   Well, almost no one. Exceptions do occur, on occasion. One of the most dramatic was the election of Joseph Biden to the U.S. Senate from Delaware in 1972. At the time he was twenty-nine years old, and his entire political experience prior to that date consisted of two years on the Wilmington (Del.) City Council! In fact, Biden was so young that he did not turn thirty until two weeks *after* his election to the Senate and had to keep reassuring people during the campaign that he would be old enough to take his seat if elected. (The U.S. Constitution forbids anyone under thirty from serving as a U.S. senator, although it doesn't prohibit voters from *electing* someone under thirty to the Senate.)

19   On the energy needed to move forward in politics, see James L. Payne and Oliver H. Woshinsky, "Incentives for Political Participation," *World Politics* 24 (1972): 518–46, esp. pp. 518–21.

reach a serious level of political power, we can see that few powerholders will be much under forty years of age.[20] Of course, there will be many exceptions, but let's focus on the norm. The median age of the average powerholder in the United States today is somewhere in the range of forty-five to sixty years.

We start, then, with this age factor. You are going to be middle-aged or older before reaching serious political power. And this power doesn't just come and tap you on the shoulder. You need to make an intense commitment of your energies and resources for years and years if you wish to gain power. You don't, in other words, spend twenty years as an accountant or an architect or an assembly-line worker and then suddenly decide to become governor or senator. Or to put it more accurately, if you do decide to make that kind of midlife career decisions, you have little hope of fulfilling it. If you haven't decided on a political career path by age thirty (or better still, by twenty or twenty-five), you aren't likely to rise far in politics.

I can think of one modest exception to this point. A person can occasionally trade power in some other line of work for political clout. A few people manage to make these lateral transfers from some other activity into political positions of real power; General Eisenhower, Ronald Reagan, and even Ross Perot are good examples. These people represent the world of the military, celebrityhood, and business. Going further back into the past, we can find similar examples: George Washington and Andrew Jackson from the military, for instance, celebrities like Horace Greeley or Will Rogers, and businessmen like William Randolph Hearst and Wendell Wilkie. All converted their fame from nonpolitical achievements into political influence of one kind or another *without* spending decades in the political process itself.

These seeming exceptions, on close examination, do little more than support the basic rule: You *still* must start early in life if you wish to attain political power. After all, these people who moved into politics from nonpolitical careers had first gained power for themselves in *another* key decision-making arena of society. All had clearly started early in life down the road toward power attainment. All had been obliged to struggle upward for years in their chosen profession. All needed decades of perseverance to reach a point at which they could trade the resource of power in their own career path for power in the world of politics.

These "exceptions" merely underline, then, the main proposition. *Political power is rarely attained without two or three decades of grueling effort,* beginning usually during the ages of twenty to thirty.

We must confront one additional fact before putting this argument together to explain why few women are currently found in positions of political power in the United States. A number of studies have shown that the average person's value system (his or her outlook on life) is shaped, roughly, during ages fifteen to twenty-five.[21] It will, of course, vary considerably from person to person. Furthermore, beliefs, once developed, aren't permanent;

---

[20] By "powerholder" in the United States, I am referring essentially to the president, vice-president, Cabinet and sub-Cabinet officers, House members, senators, Supreme Court justices, federal judges, governors, state legislative leaders, big-city mayors, top lobbyists, top political aides, and top media people.

[21] See, for example, Angus Campbell, Philip E. Converse, Warren E. Miller, and Donald Stokes, *The American Voter* (Chicago: University of Chicago Press, 1960), chap. 7; and M. Kent Jennings and Richard G. Niemi, *Generations and Politics: A Panel Study of Young Adults and Their Parents* (Princeton: Princeton University Press, 1981), chap. 4.

most people undergo modest changes in their thinking during the course of life. Still, the bulk of evidence suggests that after age thirty, at the latest, most of us will not deviate seriously from the central perspectives on life that we developed by that age.

By thirty, that means, most of us are pretty well set in our views on politics, religion, and society. We are liberal or conservative, feminist or traditionalist, religious or agnostic, rigid toward minorities or tolerant. For most of us, those perspectives developed early and often unconsciously, came to be understood and expressed between ages fifteen and twenty, then matured and hardened in the following decade. By thirty, we have a full-fledged world outlook and cling to it for the rest of life. With these facts in mind we conclude by simple mathematics that Americans aged about fifty today began to absorb their essential view of gender roles some time in the late 1950s.

Let us now put all of these points together. Average powerholders in the United States today are forty-five to sixty years old. These people must have *decided* to start seeking power in their twenties. There basic outlook on life started being shaped ten years before that—in their teens. The vast majority of people who currently hold power today, then, came of age between 1950 and 1970. Imprinted on their brain cells are the ideas that dominated that era. And what were those ideas? Whatever else we associate with that time, it was characterized by traditional norms about the division of labor between men and women. It was the era of suburbia and the baby boom. Men were to have careers, whereas women were to raise children and keep house. Public activities (like politics) were for men, whereas private activities (the home) was the proper sphere for women.

"The past is a foreign country," said L. P. Hartley. "They do things differently there."[22] It is always hard to enter the mind-set of another era, but we must try. Although it may seem incredible, women were *forbidden* to enter most law schools as late as the early 1970s. Women were legally *forced* to take their husband's name upon marriage. They could not get credit in their own names. Single women could not obtain mortgages to buy houses. These examples could continue for pages. The National Organization for Women (NOW), a crucial pressure group for women's rights in our time, was not even founded until 1966. No one noticed the event. NOW hardly entered national consciousness until the 1970s. *Ms. Magazine* published its first issue in 1972. The first woman elected governor in her own right (not as the spouse of some famous politician) was Ella Grasso of Connecticut in 1974.

People coming of age in the 1940s, 1950s, and 1960s—that is, those people most likely to be at the height of their political careers in the *1990s*—would have developed their political and social beliefs at a time when current feminist ideals stressing women's equality with men were hardly imagined by the average American citizen, male *or* female. Indeed, the precept that men have careers and women raise children was perhaps *at its height* when Americans who are currently middle-aged first came of political and social consciousness.

This cultural outlook, deeply ingrained in the children of the 1950s, gave a tremendous power advantage to the young men of that time over young women. A female baby boomer, by ages fifteen to twenty, would have accepted the norm that her social duty was to get married and start raising children. She might someday expect to "get a job," primarily to

---

L.P. Hartley, *The Go-Between* (London: H. Hamilton, 1953), Prologue, p. 9.

"help out" with family expenses, but she was rarely expected to *have a career*, especially not in any walk of life involving competition for power.

In only a few work areas was the 1950s woman actually allowed a career. We know those specialties are the "caring" or "nurturing" professions (teaching, nursing, secretarial help). They symbolized an extension of the "primary" female role and, as such, presented no threat to men. These jobs derived from activities centered on the home, from the women's role there as nurturer, caregiver, and helper. Most men didn't want these jobs, so women moved into them. Indeed, men encouraged them to do so.

Teenage males, by way of contrast, had been raised in the expectation of spending their entire lives building careers. At the least, they knew that they had to prepare for a life of continuous work outside the home, work in the paid labor force, in order to support a family (that is, wife and children).

Society taught these norms to most young people in the 1940s, 1950s, and 1960s. True, not everyone conformed. Some women raised in the 1950s sought careers and attained power. Some men of that era stayed home and raised children. They were the exceptions, however. The vast majority of people raised in that time behaved as the norms of that day dictated. Men finished school and went right to work. Many pursued careers associated with power—in the world of business, the military, law, or politics. Women raised children and shunned careers—except in a few traditional areas that never lead to societal power. (Quick! Name a famous librarian. Name a renowned nurse. Name a celebrated fourth-grade teacher. Get the point?)

These norms and work patterns devastated women's chances of ever reaching political power. First, they made women feel that the world of politics was for men only; hence, they simply stayed out of it. Furthermore, the skills that women developed from the activities they did engage in (childrearing) were not, in any obvious way, directly transferable to the world of politics. Knowing how to potty train a two-year-old does not help you learn to give a rousing political speech. Knowing how to teach a six-year-old to read doesn't help you become an expert on defense policy. Knowing how to cook macaroni-and-cheese doesn't help you learn the subtle art of winning party nominations.

Finally, the time and effort that women had to put into the years of childbearing, childrearing, and homemaking insured that they would be unable to devote much attention to the world of power gathering until it was essentially "too late." That is, if a woman in her early twenties started having children and had three or four (as was the norm for 1950s families), she would probably find herself in her early forties before her last child had entered the teen years and become reasonably independent. If she *then* decided to embark on a career that might lead to a power position, notice how greatly disadvantaged she became, in comparison to her male contemporaries (also in their early forties) who had been doggedly pursuing that very career path for the last twenty years.

Of course, the knowledge gained by women in those intervening years counts for something. Maturity and experience are assets that can be converted into skills that are useful in the struggle for power. But even with the best efforts and the best will in the world from well-wishers in society, any person, male or female, just starting out to achieve something at forty-two is at a severe disadvantage compared with another person of forty-two who has been pursuing that same objective since age sixteen (or twenty-three or twenty-eight).

This chain of reasoning suggests that by the time some woman, who doesn't decide until her forties to get into politics, starts to amass a serious amount of influence, she will be reaching, roughly, age sixty or older, a time when most people are more likely to be thinking of retirement than of continuing the difficult struggle for political power. Furthermore, voters and party activists (especially in youth-obsessed America) may start looking for a younger candidate to fill whatever job the sixty-year-old woman has her eye on.

In short, even if a middle-aged woman successfully gets past her early socialization into traditional gender roles, completes her decades of childrearing with some reasonable level of energy left to embark on her own career, and even if she does quite well at developing that career, she is *still* likely to arrive too late at the threshold of power to be able to make the leap over that threshold and into real power itself before deciding, or having the matter decided for her by a fickle electorate, that she is "too old" to be promoted any further up the rungs of the political ladder.

As if these facts weren't harsh enough, we must add yet another array of grim data. The older any population gets, the more likely it is that its members will fall by the wayside, succumbing to a variety of illnesses that either kill them or force them out of serious competition for power. These are statistical generalizations, but overall they hurt women badly in the struggle for upward political mobility. Let's say it takes twenty-five years on average to go from the day you receive your law degree to the U.S. Senate. If you get your degree at age twenty-seven, you will become senator at fifty-two. Few healthy Americans of age twenty-seven die before age fifty-two. Most don't even get seriously ill in that time frame.

But if you don't decide to start law school until age forty-two (when your children are grown), then you don't get your law degree until age forty-five, and you don't get to the Senate until you are seventy! Now many more Americans die, or become seriously ill, between forty-two and seventy than between twenty-two and fifty. Simply on the basis of these cruel facts of illness and mortality, we would expect that many fewer women than men would get to high levels of power, *if* women start their careers twenty years later. And we have already shown that they are likely to do exactly that, if they were born in the United States some time between 1945 and 1970.

Notice how far we have come. We have gained some serious insights into a key political pattern, by following a simple line of reasoning.

> *Cultures affect politics. Specifically, cultures affect politics by implanting deep-seated norms into people's heads, norms that affect how people behave in the social world. One deep-seated norm in American society of the 1940s and 1950s held that men and women were to play different roles in life, men seeking careers aimed at giving them wealth, power, fame, and status, and women staying at home to raise families. This gender-division norm from the 1950s explains why men dominated American politics in the 1980s and 1990s.*

This example illustrates the power of a social analysis that begins by focusing on culture.

WOMEN AND POLITICS: A NEW ERA

Incidentally, we can use this same approach to explain a dramatic new trend on the American political scene. The era of few women in American politics is coming to an end. Indeed, we are now witnessing the definite emergence of women onto the political scene and their rise to the upper level of American institutions. The 1990s appears to be the decade when women finally gained a serious share of political power.

Why have women gained their recent clout in politics? To answer that question, we must return to the same reasoning we used to explain why women were rarely found in politics in earlier years. If the norms young people absorb in their teenage years traditionally helped men and hurt women in the long-term struggle for political power, then changing those norms could make the playing field level. And changing norms is exactly what happened.

Even before the mid-1960s, some Americans had started questioning traditional gender roles.[23] Traditional attitudes began seriously eroding by 1970, and by the mid-1970s the modern feminist movement was in full swing. Indeed, by the 1980s it was taken for granted by the majority of Americans that women should have legal equality with men, that they had the right to pursue careers of their own, and that governments should work to obliterate the most egregious forms of gender discrimination.[24]

Given this development, we fully expect to find, as time goes by, an increasing number of women at the upper levels of all prestigious, power-wielding institutions of American life. Specifically, we can even predict that by the time women who were around fifteen in 1975 reach fifty, the number of women in serious positions of political power will look a great deal more like equality than it does now. That means keep a sharp eye out for the year 2010!

Just to be cautious, I'll predict numerical gender equality at all levels of American politics by the year 2020. I will also predict an increasing number of women in political power as each year passes between now and then.

We don't have to wait long to check on this prediction. Just in case it doesn't pan out, however, I have an explanation at the ready. Change is a law of life, but no trend is irreversible. The drive toward a redefinition of woman's traditional homemaker's role could peter out or reverse itself, depending on future social, economic, and cultural developments, which no one can foresee. Perhaps the Dan Quayle-Pat Robertson perspective on these matters will gather steam and overwhelm the forces of the Hillary Clintons and Donna Shalalas. I doubt it, but stranger developments have occurred in history. Who would have predicted the rise of fundamental Islam in the Middle East, setting back for decades the cause of women's rights in that region? I am personally betting on the advance of gender equality in the United States (and everywhere else, for that matter), but ultimately only time will tell.[25]

It is important to note that there exist few universal generalizations about human behavior. A given pattern today may or may not exist tomorrow. That depends on what

---

[23] The most famous and influential example of this questioning came in 1963 from Betty Friedan in her groundbreaking and eloquent plea for feminism, *The Feminine Mystique* (New York: Dell Publishing Company, 1963). For a survey of efforts on behalf of women's rights in this era, see Susan M. Hartmann, *From Margin to Mainstream: American Women and Politics since 1960* (New York: Alfred A. Knopf, 1989), esp. pp. 48–71.

[24] On recent American attitudes toward gender equality, see the data reported by Virginia Sapiro, "Feminism: A Generation Later," in *Annals of the American Academy of Political and Social Science* 515 (1991): 10–22.

[25] For a chilling vision of a different future from the one I imagine, a future in which American women lose all rights and become oppressed slaves, read Margaret Atwood's grim novel, *The Handmaid's Tale* (Boston: Houghton Mifflin, 1986).

caused the pattern and on whether or not those causes change. Change the cause of some human behavior, and you will change the behavior as well.[26]

These propositions apply specifically to the issue under discussion: gender equality. The cause of male political domination lies in the gender norms of our culture, which have been undergoing change. We should hardly be surprised to see these new norms produce a different set of effects. Our societal values once favored men; now they stress equality. They insured male domination of politics in the past. Now and into the foreseeable future they encourage a trend toward male-female sharing of political power.

Whether one hates or supports this development, it exists and it produces important political outcomes. Our job is to describe and explain. Powerful women were scarce in the past because of traditional cultural norms. Powerful women are more numerous now and will be much more numerous in the future because of modern cultural norms. If you wish to understand American politics—past, present, and future—you have to know these facts.

Now if you want to reverse or quicken the trend, that's another matter altogether. You must then get involved in politics and work to achieve your goals. The analyst's job is not to teach what your goals should be, but to help you understand the world as it is. What you wish the world to be is your own business. When you start trying to change the world to match your own desires, you become a political participant, an activist, and part of the very world that analysts like me work to explain. If you take that route, I wish you the very best of luck as you set off to realize your aims. In the meantime, I shall get back to the task at hand: explaining the world of politics as it currently works.

SUMMARY

Norms—deepseated beliefs about how people should behave—produce a powerful effect on society. When most people in any culture share a norm, they will act in a manner congruent with that norm. Norms, to put it simply, influence social behavior. It follows that any norm in any culture will influence political behavior, since all behavior is intertwined. We cannot separate social from economic from political activity.

This [text] has provided several examples of the way cultural norms affect politics. These examples merely scratch the surface. We could multiply them indefinitely. To understand the wellsprings of political action, we must learn the norms that underpin human thought. When we see any given pattern of political behavior, we must ask what cultural outlook has produced that particular way of dealing with political issues. This perspective, one that owes much to the insights of *cultural anthropology*,[27] will guide our thinking as we move forward to learn about the many, varied forms of political behavior.

---

[26] Of course, change may be a long time in coming, especially if the original cause has existed for decades and has had time to create deeply imbedded attitudes and behavior patterns.

[27] For the classic expression of this perspective, see Benedict, *Patterns of Culture*, op. cit. For a recent summary of the approach, see Michael C. Howard, *Contemporary Cultural Anthropology*, 2nd ed. (Boston: Little, Brown and Company, 1986).

SECTION 1 TERMINOLOGY

Activist

Authoritarian

Autocratic

Conservative

Constitutionalism

Culture

Decision-Making

Democracy

Despotism

Developing World

Electorate

EU (European Union)

Federalism

GDP (Gross Domestic Product)

Globalization

Gold Standard

Hierarchy

ICJ (International Court of Justice)

IGO (International Governmental Organizations)

INGO (International Non-Governmental Organizations)

Keynesian System

Liberal

Liberal Democracy

Liberty

Macroeconomic Policy

Multinational Corporation

NAFTA (North American Free Trade Agreement)

Nation-State

Norms

Polis

Political Culture

Politics

Public Interest

Regionalization

Security Council

Socialist

Sovereignty

Totalitarian

Welfare State

World Bank

SECTION 1 DISCUSSION QUESTIONS

1. Is it possible to truly understand politics without taking culture into account? How does culture affect governance?

2. Why is there such cynicism about politics? Would we be better off without politics, or, as Crick might suggest, does politics provide for a better life? Why do we ignore politics at our peril?

3. Can we be "political" and apathetic at the same time? What is it about politics that makes it so "activist"?

4. Does democracy "travel"? Is it a Western ideal, or universal in nature? Is there a sound "alternative"?

5. Is politics a "science"?

6. How is politics about "choice"? Why is decision-making so important for politics?

POLISCI SUPERSITE

Pearson Education Canada's PoliSci Supersite (**www.pearsoned.ca/polisci**) contains a set of text-specific pages for *Ideas, Interests, and Issues*. Visit the Supersite to access a list of relevant weblinks and interesting additional readings tailored to the content of each section.

Section 2

Approaching Politics

SECTION SUMMARY

Few would dispute that politics is very much the core focus of the discipline of political science. And most would accept that power is one of the key concepts studied within the discipline. Moving beyond these very basic statements, however, one is much less likely to encounter agreement within the political science community. This diversity of approaches can be extremely confusing for students, and can mistakenly be interpreted as evidence of the discipline's failings. This set of readings hopes to identify the various approaches employed within the study of politics and, more importantly, to establish the significance of this diversity. Whatever the approach taken, the study of politics strives to develop a fuller understanding of politics and political systems, in the hopes of predicting, to the limited degree possible when dealing with human nature, political outcomes. This knowledge and predictability are fundamental to the development of "better" political systems.

You may well have heard people suggest that democracy is the "best" political system or that a presidential system is "better" than a parliamentary system. The study of politics is very much about laying out the methods or approaches that can be employed to study these very questions. It asks both "what is and why?" and "what ought to be?" The former is referred to as a positivist approach, and the latter as a normative approach; the first relates primarily, but not exclusively, to facts, and the latter primarily to values. What makes political science a *discipline* is that such questions are studied in a particular way: knowledge is developed in an organized manner, arguments are structured logically, and evidence is systematically collected and analyzed. It is more, then, than casual attention to politics and government, and more than punditry.

As a beginning student of political science, you should develop an understanding of the various approaches that are employed in the discipline, since the approach directly determines the questions that researchers ask, the focus of their gaze, and thus, to a certain extent, the answers and conclusions that are reached. Minogue's reading provides insight into the earliest civilization to inform much of modern democratic politics and political science—Ancient Greece. Fundamental democratic tenets—the equality of citizens, the rationality of humans, and freedom of expression—grounded politics in this early civilization. Plato, Aristotle, and others were the first to attempt to describe existing political systems properly, but also the first to argue for the "ideal" regime, based on a particular set of evaluative criteria. Their arguments remain part of the core curriculum in political philosophy.

Theodoulou and O'Brien's article summarizes key periods in the study of politics, including its more modern branches. As the authors make clear, the focus and central concerns of each period often originate in the perceived weaknesses of the approach adopted in the preceding period. Moreover, they make an important argument for ensuring that the study of politics remains relevant—that is, that the practice of government and politics are sufficiently important to warrant the attention of those who study them.

The Classical Greeks:
How to be a Citizen

KENNETH MINOGUE*

*__Kenneth Minogue__ is Emeritus Professor of Political Science at the London School of Economics and Political Science.

Politics among the ancient Greeks was a new way of thinking, feeling, and above all being related to one's fellows. Citizens varied in wealth, beauty, and intelligence, but as citizens they were equal. This was because citizens were rational, and the only appropriate relation between rational beings is that of persuasion. Persuasion differs from command in assuming equality between speaker and listener. Plato provides a noble vision of this form of political life in his dialogue the *Crito*. The philosopher Socrates, having been sentenced to death for corrupting the youth, refused the offer of help to escape Athens, arguing that to flee would be rationally inconsistent with the commitment to the city expressed in the way he had lived his whole life. Even the mode of his execution reflected this basic belief that violence was not an appropriate relation between citizens: he was given a cup of hemlock to drink. The Greek freely obeyed the law of his *polis* and was proud to do so. His very identity was bound up with his city. The worst of fates was exile, a form of civic death sometimes imposed by the convention of ostracism on Athenian statesmen whose power was thought to threaten the constitution.

Among the Greeks we find most of the conditions of freedom: a life lived among equals, subject only to law, and ruling and being ruled in turn. The Greeks were the first historical people to create societies having this form; certainly they were the first to create a literature exploring it as an experience. Politics was the activity specific to this new thing called a 'citizen'. It might take many forms, even the debased forms of tyranny and usurpation, but on one thing the later classical Greeks were adamant: oriental despotism was not politics.

Such is the formal position, and these were the forms which left so deep an imprint on our civilization. The reality was no doubt a great deal more complex. Democratic and oligarchic factions fought bitter battles within cities. Farmers lived on the edge of destitution, and bad harvests might impel them towards debt slavery. Equality within cities was not matched by equal relations *between* cities, and war was endemic. The Greeks were a talkative, passionate people, and their politics was often violent and sometimes corrupt. None of this qualifies, however, the fact that they were capable of brilliant exploits, such as their victory in repelling (and ultimately conquering) their Persian neighbours. In reading much of the literature of their time, we find it easy to think of them as our contemporaries: being rationalists, they speak across the millenniums to us, their cultural descendants, with a deceptive fluency. For all the common ground, however, they were immensely different from us, in their religion, their customs, and their conception of human life. It is this difference which makes studying their civilization so exhilarating.

The Greeks were humanists, but of a kind strikingly different from the humanism (transformed by Christianity) found in the modern world. Their basic proposition was that man is a rational animal, and that the meaning of human life is found in the exercise of rationality. When men succumbed to the passions, they were shamefully descending to a lower form of being. When pride, or hubris, led them to think they were gods, they lost sight of their human limitations and suffered nemesis, the destructive resentment of the gods. The secret of life was human self-knowledge, and a balanced expression of one's human capacities. In deliberating about law and public policy, man found his highest and purest form of self-expression. It could only be enjoyed in the political life of a city.

Humanists often look to the Greeks as ancestors, but their view of the world has one remarkable (and in modern terms, disturbing) implication. Since some are less rational than others, so also are they less human. Slaves in particular are defective in rationality when compared to masters. Those who explored this view, above all the philosopher Aristotle, were perfectly aware that some slaves are clever and some masters stupid; they were merely expounding what they took to be the rational foundation of the institution itself. Again, women were taken to be less rational than men, though Aristotle considered the barbarians to be quite wrong in thinking that they were indistinguishable from slaves. Citizenship was thus confined to free adult males, and in some cities not even to all of those. The activity of politics and that of waging war merged with each other, and it thus seemed natural that women should live domestic lives: they could hardly stand their ground in a phalanx. It might seem that, in taking this view, the Greeks were the prisoners of the prejudices of their time. Being immensely imaginative in their exploration of the world, however, they had no difficulty imagining women doing any number of things: becoming warriors in the form of Amazons; going on a sexual strike to enforce peace in the *Lysistrata* of Aristophanes: taking the role of philosopher-rulers in the Guardians of Plato's *Republic*; but these images were not the reality of everyday life.

The laws and policies of a Greek city emerged, then, not from the palace of a despot, but from discussion among notionally equal citizens in the *agora*, the market-place which also generally served as the arena of politics. Citizens enjoyed equality before the law (*isonomia*, a term sometimes used as a synonym for democracy) and an equal opportunity to speak in the assembly. In a large city such as Athens, thousands of people might turn up to such meetings, so that the speakers were predominantly aristocrats who had studied the art of speaking, or notable leaders who had managed to acquire a band of supporters. In democracies, many offices were filled by lot, but the main officers were elected and were commonly from powerful families. In Thucydides' history of the Peloponnesian War we can see the democratic process at work—for example in the Athenian debate, reported in Book Ill, as to how the people of Mitylene, who had rebelled against Athenian hegemony, should be punished. In this debate, the popular leader Cleon put the case for confirming the decision already taken to kill the men and sell the women and children into slavery. Cleon appealed to realism: if you want to have an empire, he argued, then you must be prepared to do the ruthless things necessary to keep it together. His opponent, Diodotus, argued for clemency on the ground that ruthlessness would merely turn every occasion of revolt among the clients of Athens into a life and death struggle. It was Diodotus who triumphed in this vivid intellectual contest.

The citizens who participated in the debates belonged in their private lives to households (*oikia*) which were the basic productive units of this ancient world. The *oikos* (from which our term 'economics' derives) was a system of orderly subordination described by Aristotle: subordination of female to male, of children to parents, and of slaves to masters. The household was the sphere in which the Greeks enjoyed family life and largely supplied their material needs: for food, warmth, shelter, procreation, and so on. Here was the world of nature in which everything had its season. In many civilizations, the distinction between artifice and nature is not developed, but it was the basis of the Greek understanding of the world. The idea that wisdom consisted in following the dictates of nature led to divergent philosophies, according to the way in which the concept of 'nature' developed. Greek political philosophy began in meditation upon the tension between recognizing that the *polis* was in one sense natural and in another sense a thing of artifice.

On becoming an adult, the young Greek male could step out of the household into the *agora,* where he found the freedom to transcend natural necessity and take responsibility, uttering words worth remembering and doing deeds that might give him a kind of immortality. The Greeks of the classical period were self-conscious enough to see themselves as a distinct culture, and it is in creating a historical understanding of themselves and their world that they were opening up quite new possibilities of human experience. Politics and history were thus born together, for they share the same conception of what a human being is, and what is worth remembering.

History was the memory of words and deeds, and words were the vehicles of memory. in political activity, men addressed each other in speech, which is a skill to be learned. It requires the marshalling of ideas, the construction of arguments, the capacity to understand an audience, a recognition of the dominant passions of human nature, and much else. For the first time in history, public decisions were made in the clear light of day and subject to open criticism. The skill of rhetoric was codified by teachers called 'sophists' for the benefit of ambitious young aristocrats whose power depended on swaying a popular audience. A speech was a performance to be remembered down the ages. Thucydides tells the story of the Peloponnesian War largely in terms of the arguments adduced in the speeches of the participants; taken together, these speeches amount to a comprehensive manual on political wisdom and political folly.

This approach to political thought and action was the product of one striking false belief, which remains influential to this day: the idea that everything in the world was the result of deliberate design. The Greeks believed their own cities to have been founded by semi-divine figures, such as Lycurgus in the case of Sparta, and Thekus in the case of Athens. Wise men were sometimes called on to restore some such design if it had fallen into disrepair. In politics, the most famous case of this was that of Solon at Athens in the early part of the sixth century BC. Two features of Solon's reforms illustrate essential features of Greek politics.

The first is that he was careful to base politics on territorial units which mixed up clan or tribal loyalties. The modern constituency, which lumps together all the heterogeneous people living in a given area, has the same effect of breaking down natural loyalties and encouraging people to act politically in terms of broad interests shared widely throughout a community.

The second is that, after establishing his reforms, Solon was careful to leave Athens for ten years so that the new constitution could be operated by others—an early version of the principle of the separation of powers. For the key to politics in the strict sense is that it is a nexus of abstract offices to which duties are attached, and in principle the work may be done by any competent office-holder. Whereas despotism depends on the personality (and often the caprice) of the individual despot, political rulers act in terms of the duties attaching to their offices.

The set of offices by which a *polis* was governed, and the laws specifying their relation, are the constitution. Government without a constitution would lack the specific kind of moral limitation which distinguishes politics. Constitutions function in two essential ways: they circumscribe the power of the office-holders, and as a result they create a predictable (though not rigid and fixed) world in which the citizens may conduct their lives. It is constitutions which give form to politics, and the study of them led to the emergence of political science.

A science of politics (as opposed to despotism) is possible because politics itself follows regular patterns, even though it is ultimately at the mercy of the human nature from which it arises. All that one can confidently say about despotism is that able rulers will sooner or later be followed by mad or feeble heirs. A despotism is thus subject to a fixed rhythm of rise and fall, like the seasons, and this confirmed the Greeks in their belief that despotisms, as associations of slaves, were unfree and belonged to the non-rational sphere of nature. But constitutions, because they belong to the sphere of rationality, can be studied in a more scientific way than despotisms, despite their ultimate fallibility.

For one thing, they can be classified according to certain characteristics which reveal dominant tendencies. In all constitutions, the ruler is either a monarch, or a small group of powerful leaders, or a popular assembly. There are no other possibilities than that rule must be by one, or a few, or by the many. During the classical period of Greek politics, the main division was between oligarchic states, which were thought to favour the rich and powerful, and democracies, which responded to the interests of the poor, and which were commonly thought violent and unstable.

Greek political science studied constitutions and generalized the relation between human nature and political associations. Perhaps its most powerful instrument was the theory of recurrent cycles. Monarchies tend to degenerate into tyranny, tyrannies are overthrown by aristocracies, which degenerate into oligarchies exploiting the population, which are overthrown by democracies, which in turn degenerate into the intolerable instability of mob rule, whereupon some powerful leader establishes himself as a monarch and the cycle begins all over again. This is the version of political science we find influentially expounded by a later Greek called Polybius whose main concern was to explain the character of Roman politics to his fellow Greeks; other versions of a political cycle are to be found in Plato and Aristotle.

Knowledge, as [Sir Francis] Bacon remarked, is power, and the knowledge of this cyclical rhythm in politics provoked the thought that institutions might be arranged in such a way as to break the cycle, allowing states to achieve, if not immortality, at least some long-term stability. The secret of breaking the cycle of decline lay in two propositions. The first was that government consists of a number of functions which may be parcelled out among different offices and assemblies. Executive decision requires a leader, deliberation about policy requires a small group of experienced citizens, while the acceptability of laws and the responsiveness of government depend upon effective ways of consulting the people. This is an argument for constructing a constitution in which power is distributed between the one, the few, and the many. The second proposition is that the very same distribution may also balance the interests of rich and poor, to prevent either from using political power for the purpose of economic exploitation. Such balance in politics was the equivalent of health in the body, and might keep corruption at bay for a very long time. Such is the theory of the balanced constitution which has played a central part in the politics of the West. It represents as a theory what practical politicians often evolve for themselves. The English constitution, for example, evolved into a balance between monarch, Commons, and Lords and is often cited as an example of this theory. Lawyers and statesmen were, indeed, aware of the theory, and sometimes it helped to guide them, but the actual institutions of British politics responded basically to the specific conditions of life in Britain.

It was Aristotle's view that some element of democracy was essential to the best kind of balanced constitution, which he called a 'polity'. He studied many constitutions, and was particularly interested in the mechanics of political change: revolutions, he thought, always arose out of some demand for equality. Concerning himself with both politics and ethics, he posed one question which has been found especially fascinating: can a good citizen be a good man? Rulers in some states may demand of their subjects actions which are wrong. Greek politics (like everything else in the Greek world) was powerfully theorized, to such an extent that it has often been thought that we rattle around within the limited set of possibilities revealed to us by Greek experience. Political judgement, to put the matter another way, is a choice between finite possibilities. This view assumes that human nature is fixed, and has been challenged, especially in modern times, by the view that human beings are always the creatures of their society. Very few possibilities that we discuss were not recognized in one form or another by the Greeks, who also left behind—indeed, it was their speciality—visions of the ideal: in philosophy, Plato's *Republic*, and in politics, the account of Athens put into the mouth of Pericles by Thucydides in his history of the Peloponnesian War.

Where We Stand Today: The State of Modern Political Science

STELLA Z. THEODOULOU AND RORY O'BRIEN*

Stella Z. Theodoulou is Dean of the College of Social and Behavioral Sciences, California State University, Northridge. *Rory O'Brien* is Professor of Political Science at Cabrillo College in Aptos, California.

In this chapter, we will look at how political science developed as a discipline. Most people use the word *politics* without fully defining what it is they are interested in. However, it is easy to know when you are involved in a political discussion. In this sense, there seems to be a shared definition we all seem to work with in society to understand one another when we are talking about politics. The study of political phenomenon by applying scientific techniques involves multiple steps, including theory development, hypothesis building and testing, the drawing of conclusions that are based on the strengths or weaknesses of those hypotheses, and, ultimately, the proving of the theories themselves. In this way, political science operates in a circle, with empirical research being fueled by theory development, and theory, in turn, being the outcome of research findings.

We begin with an assessment of where our discipline is today and where it has come from. Political science, especially in terms of research methodology, has come into its own during the latter half of the twentieth century. As we step into the next millennium, we need to create a map for practitioners of our trade to follow. Before we can do that, we must first establish the groundwork in which the discipline finds its genesis.

TRACING THE DEVELOPMENT OF THE DISCIPLINE

Since the beginning of time, people have observed, thought about, evaluated, and analyzed politics. Thus, the study of politics is not a new phenomenon, and the broad questions and interests of political scientists remain in many ways the same over time. However, what has changed is the way in which political scientists have tried to find the answers to the questions. There is a growing body of literature that identifies and discusses the evolution of the discipline.[1] Within such a discussion, it is clear to see that political scientists over time have taken different paths in their study of politics. Authors might disagree on whether to label these paths eras, approaches, orientations, models, or methods, but at least there is

---

[1] See Gabriel Almond, *A Discipline Divided, Schools and Sects in Political Science* (Newbury Park: Sage Publishing, 1990); David Easton, *Political Science in the United States: Past and Present* (London & New York: Routledge, 1991); David Easton, John G. Gunnell, and Luigi Graziano (eds), *The Development of Political Science: A Comparative Study* (London & New York: Routledge, 1991); James Parr and Raymond Seidelman, *Discipline & History: Political Science in the United States* (Ann Arbor: University of Michigan Press, 1993).

general consensus that at different times different directions have been taken and are still being taken by political scientists in their quest for political knowledge.

In the following discussion, we will identify four general paths that political scientists have taken over the years. Some may be surprised at the omission of what they consider to be other paths, such as feminism, discourse analysis, rational choice theory, and Marxism. However, it is our opinion that all of these are approaches that fall within our four general paths rather than being distinctive paths themselves.

Many would argue that we can trace the development of the discipline directly to the social disorder of the Athenian city-state and the response to it by Socrates, Plato, and Aristotle. These first political philosophers and those that follow them take a theoretical path in their study of politics.

THE THEORETICAL PATH (FROM 600 B.C.)

Perhaps the most audacious statement we can make from an epistemological point of view is embodied in our fundamental assumption that it is even possible for us to possess knowledge about human social interaction. Observation might easily lead us to conclude that human behavior is too erratic to ever be understood fully, and, if understood, is difficult to predict. And yet, these are the foundational aspects of how we go about studying society. Since the early nineteenth century, our study of society has been based on the positivism of [Auguste] Compte [1798–1857]. This French *philosophe* advanced the theory that the social order could be studied in a logical fashion. In contrast to the metaphysical reasoning of the Age of Enlightenment preceding him, and in a continued reaction to the earlier Christian era in Europe, Compte sought to ground a view of society in the sober logic of empirical investigation and analysis.

Thus, in the modern age, many have fallen victim to merely focusing on the empirical, and in the process an important aspect of what gives motivation to the research process itself has been missed. Research gives expression to theories, or ideas. Without those ideas, the research project would be meaningless. If we think of political ideas as a series of questions that are posed to humankind across a tradition, and political phenomena as the tangible (and testable) manifestations of possible answers to those questions, we see the relationship between theory and scientific research more clearly. Throughout our history each age has presented us with both questions and answers, What we think of as *political theory* is a coherent body of work that has, in some sense, transcended time to provide us with enduring questions that continue to help us to evaluate current circumstances, as well as create solutions as we look towards the future.

Theory provides the context for the study of political science through the development of models and through the development of normative conclusions or prescriptions. Whereas empirical research yields empirical conclusions, normative pursuits involve questions about "what ought to be" or what "should be." Normative prescriptions are, thus, suggestions or recommendations concerning how society might best be configured.

Normative theory leads to empirical research in two ways. First, normative questions can drive empirical projects. In order to conduct research of any kind one must begin with a question, the answer to which may be elusive. The research questions that lead to fruitful hypotheses are grounded in a theoretical foundation. Moving in this way from theory to practice, scientific research gives practical application to the solely theoretical.

Second, theory can, and regularly does, arise from the practice of normal scientific enquiry. As social scientists realize how and in what ways their theoretical foundations differ from reality they are able to adjust their theories so as to better describe and predict the political world. Very few political theorists think like Plato did that the abstract forms of physical things are distinct from those things themselves. Instead, political theorists are involved in a journey of discovery that allows them to constantly update and refine theoretical perspectives so as to more effectively represent testable circumstances. Ultimately these adjustments to theory lead to further scientific investigation, beginning the process anew.

Finally, political theory creates models that political scientists can utilize to gain a broader understanding of their concepts and hypotheses. Models are artificial structures constructed by political scientists. They are human artifacts, made with the express purpose of developing ways in which students of society can more easily view the political order. Models are merely ways for us to get our minds around a concept as big as society itself. In essence, models provide the testing ground for hypotheses. But in a deeper context, the logical tests performed by our own intellects provide the most fertile ground for the creation of new political ideas and insights.

What Are We Looking For?

For the purpose of better understanding society in general and the political order in particular, political theorists have traditionally looked at various fundamental aspects of both social ideas and social organizations. Among these are our notions of what human nature is, what constitutes the "good life," and what terms such as *justice* and *equality* really mean to us. Additionally, the way we conceptualize freedom, democracy, power, and social cohesion all say something about our views of politics. Human society is dynamic and rarely, if ever, static. As the social and political order of societies change it is crucial to have some enduring ideas about how to assess that change. This is precisely what political theory provides in the form of a conceptual framework. Political philosophy is about developing ways and means for not only thinking about such things, but for using our ideas constructively to better understand society.

Human Nature

We'll begin by considering our motivations and activities in society based on who we are. This is what philosophers refer to as *human nature*. We often take for granted the composition of psychological elements that we refer to as our nature. Generally, we do not have to think about such things. But at the heart of any political theory is a conception of human nature. This is because society, which is made up of many individuals, is but a reflection of our nature, or our essential characteristics, on a large scale. When we view society as the reflection of many individuals, we can ask questions such as "Why are certain policies popular, or unpopular?" and "Why do some forms of government work better than others?"

Some political theorists take a dim view of human nature, pronouncing us to be wild beasts if not constrained by the forces of a strong and powerful government.[2] Other theorists

---

[2]   See David Easton, John G. Gunnell, and Luigi Graziano (eds.) *The Development of Political Science: A Comparative Study* (London & New York: Routledge, 1991).

speak to the human spirit, and seek ways to aid in its liberation and fulfillment.[3] Some thinkers find us to be hard-working and generous, while others see us as lazy and mean-spirited. But in every case, political theorists utilize their view of human nature to help them in the construction of their model of the social order.

The Good and the Just

In everyday language we talk about what is right and wrong, just or unjust, without taking the time to really formulate a position on these matters. In posing questions about what is *good* and what is *just*, the theorist develops ideas that help us to consider social successes (as well as failures) in order to further our general knowledge about the social world. At the same time we create categories through which we interpret our world.

When we talk about *the good* we are referring to our highest ideals. The best, finest, mostly highly valued are all captured by our notion of the good. When political theorists refer to the good they do not mean merely what we as individuals think is good. This *good* is not simply the opposite of *bad*. Humans often find that which is expedient to be the good. In other words, we may casually think of what we like as being good, or what is easiest as being the best. In many instances, modern society emphasizes that which is expedient over that which we know is truly good. Through the process of focusing on what is expedient we lose sight of any deeper value that the good may represent.

The notion of "the good life" makes reference to how each member of society might live so as to work toward developing his or her individual potential, and help to create a stronger community The good life leads to happiness, in that excellence is its own reward.[4] When philosophers talk about happiness, they mean something that goes beyond material possessions.

By the same measure, *justice,* as well as our notions of the just, have at their roots the way we conceive of community. Every aspect of how a society is oriented tells us about that society's notions of justice. From distribution of wealth to welfare policy, from tax codes to educational requirements, all of these things refer us back to a concept of justice. And, if the members of society believe that in order to live together there must be a commonly agreed upon set of ideas about what is right and wrong (as every society does), the rules that are created on the basis of that contract will dictate the outlines of a theory of justice.[5]

Everything Put Together, Sooner or Later, Falls Apart

Politics is sometimes defined simply as power, and the ways in which power is distributed in society. All of the important structures and benefits of a society are arranged on the basis of the distribution of power. In most cases, the extent to which justice is dispersed in

---

[3]   See St. Augustine; for instance, *City of God* (New York: Doubleday & Company, Inc.,1958); or Thomas Hobbes, *Leviathan* (New York: Penguin Books, 1968). See Karl Marx and Friedrich Engels, *The Communist Manifesto* (New York: Bantam Books, 1992).

[4]   We refer here to the way Aristotle in the *Nicomachean Ethics* (Indianapolis: Bobbs-Merrill Educational Publishing, 1962), characterizes the good life.

[5]   See chapter one of John Rawls, *A Theory of Justice* (Cambridge, Massachusetts: The Belknap Press, 1971).

society also has to do with the distribution of power. And the actual foundations of justice are often created as a form of compromise between competing interests. In fact, virtually all aspects of the political realm are influenced by how we construe power. But regardless of the ways in which power has been configured in various societies, across many cultures and throughout time (what we refer to as *transculturally* and *transhistorically*) power alone has never held a social group together. This leads us to ask, "Why do humans stay together in social groups?" And, it further begs the question, "Why do those groups sometimes disintegrate?" We'll take this up when we discuss *social contract* and *alienation*.

Social Contract

The *contractarian* view of society is based on the notion that in order to stay together, a group of people must have some common purposes.[6] Furthermore, the political order must be based on ideas that are agreeable to a sizable portion of the population. Contractarian perspective says that these political ideas form a *contract,* or agreement, between the people and the government. Here we are using the idea of a social contract to help us understand a larger concept, social cohesion. For instance, Aristotle thinks that part of what keeps human societies together is the fact that we are "social animals" in the sense that we only function well in the social milieu. Without others to live with in society, Aristotle notes, we would never be able to do our "civic duty," which, in part, involves our virtuously following common moral and ethical rules.

In his view, the pleasure derived from the experience of excellence as a social being far outstrips that enjoyed as a consequence of one of our generally hedonistic pursuits. Furthermore, according to Aristotle, we are in essence social animals. Much of Aristotle's view of the world is based on the notion that everything is made up of essential qualities that make particular things what they are.[7] Said differently, we can only reach our own individual potential if we exist in a social world.

Taking another political thinker, John Locke, we get a further elaboration of how a society is held together. In Locke's view, the power of government is controlled only through a formal procedural development like a constitution. In fact, we can view a constitution as the physical manifestation of a social contract. Although the contract itself goes far beyond the structure of any document, the reality is that the constitution (and the laws that are generated fromm it) are the embodiment of the broader contract. The point here is that citizens, in a sense, own the document itself. That they not only agree to its tenets, but, on a deeper level, are the source of the contents of the constitution. In this way, a temporal, material document has the ability to truly represent the wishes and finer aspirations of a social group.

People form together in social groups primarily because the alternative is relatively distasteful. In the main, human beings have found it far easier to agree to some set of rules, or compact, than they have found it to live together each with his or her own total license. Locke articulated this clearly, fully realizing that the better instincts in humankind would almost always prove to be subordinate to our baser motives. However, the point for those

---

6   This notion is fully discussed in the second of John Locke's *Two Treatises on Government* (New York: New American Library, 1963).

7   The best discussion of this idea is found in Section X of Aristotle, *Nicomachean Ethics.*

of us who are students of politics is that there appears to be a human striving for the safety and security of an organized social order. This observation alone may give us hope to move forward into the future armed with the sense that regardless of the countless examples of ruined societies, we may, in time, find ways to live with one another while reducing friction.

At the same time, Locke's entire project is held together on the basis of another tenet. According to Locke, the *legitimacy* of government rests in the consent of those who are governed. Said differently, the true power of government ought to lie in the fact that the people of a nation accept, or consent to that government, not merely in the government's ability to coerce the citizenry. A liberal government, founded on the consent of those governed, allows for the development of some of our most cherished political ideas. Equality, freedom, and democracy are nurtured in the Lockean-liberal schema, and representation in government is a natural outcome of legitimacy based on consent.

Alienation

Why don't societies stay together? A quick review of human history shows us that, in general, we seem to like changing social orders on a regular basis. There have been few governments throughout time that have been able to hold societies together for more than a few generations. Often governments are overthrown through revolutions. The revolutionary change of existing social orders has been a common thread around the world during the past three hundred years, and yet we have not learned much that helps us predict exactly where or when a revolution might next take place. Although we understand the larger social forces that *may* lead down the revolutionary road, when a revolution *will* take place is most often a function of how long the human spirit will endure before demanding liberating change.[8] In some societies (such as Europe during the Middle Ages), it has taken centuries to bring about change. In other situations (China during the twentieth century), change has come about quite rapidly.

We may be able to better understand more readily yet a different aspect of social cohesion, or the lack thereof. Social scientists use the term *alienation* to refer to a sense of being disconnected or separated from other people, things, experiences, and even ourselves. For instance, in the Marxist model of society, alienation is utilized to help explain why people feel a lack of connection with the work they are doing. In essence, when we are alienated from our work we are alienated from our own lives. If the level of this alienation is high enough, or if it goes on for too long a period of time, Marxist theory suggests that the social order may break down, leading to revolution.[9]

Although Marx's concern with alienation is focused in the economic sphere, this concept is also helpful in describing other ways in which people become disengaged from society. When a government is repressive, its citizens become alienated from the political order itself. The most effective way to overcome this disconnectedness between the people and the distribution of power in a society is through radical change. Whether one advocates

---

[8] See Barrington Moore, Jr., *Social Origins of Dictatorship and Democracy* (Boston: Beacon Press, 1967).

[9] See Isaac D. Balbus, *Marxism and Domination* (Princeton, New Jersey: Princeton University Press, 1982).

Lockean liberalism or Marxist economics makes little difference. The reality is that the lack of efficacy (or feeling of possessing political power), that groups of citizens, or entire populations often experience leads to a form of alienation which is remedied through the overthrow of an existent government.

In summary, political theory functions to provide a groundwork, or foundation for our continued research and observation of social phenomena. By probing some of our deeper questions about society and our own nature, theory gives us the ability to logically arrange our knowledge about the political order. By gaining a greater understanding of both those things that we can empirically measure and those that we only draw normative conclusions about, we learn about all aspects of the social world.

THE TRADITIONALIST PATH (FROM THE 1850s)

This is essentially a collection of different emphases brought together under the generic heading of *traditionalism.* However, within the tradition we can identify three dominant thrusts. The first is the *historical* thrust, which argues that the primary method of understanding politics is to draw lessons from history and apply them to politics. Much of the work undertaken in this area results in what we call *case studies.* Extensive use of generalizations are made in this type of research as the case study is used to test the assumptions of the researcher. The main problem with such research is that it is hard to apply findings beyond the case under study.

The second major thrust within traditionalism is the *legalistic* perspective, which views political science as mainly the study of laws, structures, institutions, and constitutions founded upon law. The last major thrust is the *institutional* view, which came about as a reaction to the historical and legalistic directions that the study of politics was undertaking. The emphasis is on the description of political institutions and structures. Thus, institutionalists would argue that political institutions should be researchers' primary focus, and that when we discuss them we should do so by looking at their powers, roles, and functions. The vast majority of introductory American government textbooks are written from this perspective. The weakness with the institutional emphasis is it goes little beyond description and thus there is little explanation as to the why or how of events or trends.

THE BEHAVIORALIST PATH (FROM THE 1950s)

Behavioralism came about as a protest to traditionalism, in particular to the institutionalist emphasis. The behavioralist path was advocated by a group of political scientists who claimed that traditionalism was not producing truly reliable political knowledge, and that rather than study structures and how they are supposed to function, we should be concerned with what is actually happening within the polity. The behavioralist path concentrates on the behavior of political actors and stresses the use of scientific method to study politics. Thus behavioralists argue that, although we cannot ignore institutions and their structural components, it is the activity within and the behavior around an institution that is of more concern. Yes, it is important to *know* the structure of the executive office, but it is more crucial to know why one president has more power than another, or why one bill gets passed by Congress and another does not. In their study of politics, behavioralists use scientific methodology and thus stress the empirical. They argue we should adopt natural science as a model for social inquiry. Thus, all political research should display scientific principles and characteristics [such] as determinism, observation, objectivity, verification, explanation, classification, and prediction. In their quest for scientific method and the need for rigorous and systematic research, behavioralists introduce statistical, mathematical, and other quantitative analyses of data to the discipline.

Behavioralism has by no means been universally accepted by political scientists. In fact, it has been criticized on many fronts. Critics are both political scientists who adhere to the traditionalist and theoretical paths as well as those who have attempted to push the boundaries of what we study and how we study politics into new applied settings. Such political scientists we will label as *neoeclectics*. They have most commonly been referred to as *postbehavioralists*.[10] The logic behind this is that they came just after behavioralism. However, this hides the diffuse and varied interests and activities of such political scientists. They have, in fact, formulated the latest path in studying politics. However, before we look at what they do we should consider two main criticisms of behavioralism, for that will explain neoeclecticism to a great degree.

The first criticism of behavioralism is that in their desire to follow the scientific method and their obsession with quantification, behavioralists have not always studied the most important political questions. A second criticism of behavioralists is that they have avoided normative issues and a discussion of values and thus there is no discussion of what should be. In short, the critique of behavioralism is that there is an obsession with methodology at the expense of what we study as political scientists.

THE NEOECLECTIC PATH (FROM THE 1970s)

The neoeclectic view has been taken by a group of political scientists who argue political science has to become relevant once again. They argue that attention should be focused beyond the empirical and that value judgements about government and politics must be considered. Neoeclectics are interested in describing both the goals of political activity as well as how to achieve those goals. Thus, there is an explicit place for normative considerations alongside empirical applications in the study of politics. Neoeclectics are not advocating an end to the scientific study of politics; rather, they argue such skills should be applied to the solution of crucial social and political problems. Neoeclectics use quantification to aid them in this quest and attempt to show the utility of quantification in the study of politics. Thus, we can term the neoeclectic path as the applied study of politics. Neoeclectics do not have a single method or focus; rather, they try to push the boundaries of how and what we study. They often consider problems that traditionalists and behavioralists would consider outside of the realm of political science. Many neoeclectics study public policy.

---

10   See David Easton, "Political Science in the United States: Past and Present," in *Discipline and History: Political Science in the U.S.: Part 4*. (ed.) James Farr and Raymond Seidelman (Ann Arbor: University of Michigan Press, 1993).

WHERE WE STAND TODAY AND WHAT WE HAVE BECOME

In recent years, it seems as if we have gotten lost in *how* we study politics, rather than in *what* we study about the world of politics. Said differently, we have allowed our attention to focus on our methods instead of our actual areas of concern. We have become adept at the manipulation of empirical data while leaving behind the very reasons that we seek knowledge about politics in the first place. Through our interest in quantifiable bits of information we have taken the *politics* out of political science. This obsession with quantification, we will argue, has come at the expense of our understanding of society and the polity.

We have left behind the larger questions about social and political life in our rush towards neutrality. For decades, political scientists have struggled to be perceived as "value free" when in reality we have needed the opposite, to return what value sensitivity we have lost and develop an even greater ability to infuse value into our discussion of politics in the future. Political scientists need to be intersubjective rather than value free; that is, to acknowledge our values and how they frame our inquiry. To a great degree, we have learned that neutrality extinguishes debate. It is precisely to the degree that political science is capable of bringing a deeper level of value into our discourse on the political order that we will be successful in appropriately responding to a diversity of ideas.

As a discipline, the challenge to political science is to move forward in meaningful ways. It is not enough to trace where we have come from or merely to establish where we stand today. As previously discussed, the empirical is crucial in terms of our understanding of political and social phenomena. But, the key element here is to reintroduce the normative into our current discussion of the political world. Ultimately, the symbiotic relationship between empirical and normative theory construction allows the discipline to come full circle where scientific research is fueled by more profound considerations.

The important questions regarding politics have always been the same. In many ways, it seems as if political scientists are constantly trying to come up with a new list. Often, in our rush to find quantifiable answers we leave the dynamic qualities out of our study. Academics routinely write and lecture about the political realm as if it is some sort of fossil or specimen frozen in time. Those of us who have a passion for politics must return the zest to our pursuit of knowledge about the political world so that we can move together towards answering the enduring questions. The question before us concerns the nature of the discipline itself. Are we history, law, or philosophy? Or, are we the behaviorists and postbehaviorists, and all those "post-posts" who have come since? Indeed, political science is all of these disparate things, having its roots in the study of philosophy and its future in sophisticated, computerized statistical analysis. But the true science of politics is an *ideal* that combines all of these areas.

In other words, it is possible to construe political science as a sort of ideal type that integrates a diversity of intellectual categories, each of which has something to offer the other. If we view our discipline in this manner, it is possible to imagine political scientists creating the context for our continued study and greater understanding of the political world.

The context of our discipline is similar to a large jigsaw puzzle, and each subdiscipline is another piece of the puzzle. While we can understand separately the different elements of political science, the whole thing lacks a clarity of perspective until all of the pieces are in place. Essentially, the pieces themselves are no more, or less, than separate paradigms, in the sense that each subdivision of the discipline tends to see the world through its own lens. These paradigmatic lenses, or mental templates, that drive our study of the political world each reflect a different interpretation of reality. Collectively, the mosaic of these sub-disciplines in political science gives a richness to the whole that is not at all diminished by their number.

As the various component elements of political science represent different viewpoints we must have some sense of the entire discipline as a project in order to understand it. We need to know where the discipline is at today and indeed where it is headed in the future. By thinking about political science as a *project* (rather than as *merely* an academic area of interest, for instance), we remind ourselves that our discipline is constantly changing and evolving. It is also necessary to gain a general understanding of what the discipline is all about before it is truly possible to analyze the conclusions of political science appropriately. It is only by assessing the tapestry made up of the many sub-fields that we bring sharply into focus the *teleology,* or final cause, in Aristotle's words, of political science.

Our second question is, "Why do we want to know what it is we want to know?" As we have become sure of the hows and whats of the research process, we need to recapture our sense of *why* we pursue knowledge about politics and political life. What does it take for dedicated political scientists to return this intellectual curiosity to our pursuit? Finally, in order to return politics to the intersubjective study of the dynamic between people and institutions in society we must allow ourselves to consider the normative as well as the empirical. The question is, how can researchers accomplish this, thus allowing empirical investigation to be informed by normative considerations?

SECTION 2 TERMINOLOGY

Agora	Epistemological	Polis
Alienation	Human Nature	Political Philosophy
Behaviouralism	Humanists	Political Theory
Citizen	Hypothesis	Positivism
Concepts	Institutionalism	Social Contract
Constitution	Legitimacy	Sophists
Democracy	Normative (research)	Tyranny
Despotism	Oligarchy/Oligarchic States	
Empirical (research)	Paradigm	

SECTION 2 DISCUSSION QUESTIONS

1. The modern practice of democracy rests on the premise that all citizens are capable of making rational decisions within the public realm, at least in the form of voting for political representatives. Can and should an argument be made for restricting the vote to a smaller, more qualified group of citizens?

2. Ancient Greece is often held up as an example of the purest form of democracy. What limitations can you identify in attempting to adopt this system of government in today's modern world?

3. What is your view of "human nature"? Can you think of ways in which your view informs your understanding of politics, policy and government?

4. How does your understanding of the study of politics fit with the paths described by Theodoulou and O'Brien?

 POLISCI SUPERSITE

Pearson Education Canada's PoliSci Supersite (**www.pearsoned.ca/polisci**) contains a set of text-specific pages for *Ideas, Interests, and Issues*. Visit the Supersite to access a list of relevant weblinks and interesting additional readings tailored to the content of each section.

Section 3

Political Theories and Perspectives

SECTION SUMMARY

The word "philosophy" is based on two ancient Greek words, "philos" (love) and "sophia" (wisdom), so the word means, loosely, "love of wisdom." All forms of philosophy involve the quest for understanding. Political philosophy, or political theory, is an inquiry into the nature of politics. These theories and perspectives about politics are more about the significance of political studies than they are about the mechanics of political structures or institutions. Ultimately, the objective of political theory is to pose new and better ways to deal with the problems of human society.

In addition to dealing with perennial questions such as "what is the good life?" and issues such as equality or the relationship between governments and citizens, political theory is more important in our daily lives than we might think. What distinguishes the Conservative Party from the Liberals or New Democrats in Canada, or the Democrats from the Republicans in the United States? What makes "socialists" think the way they do, and why do people call themselves "fiscal conservatives"? The answers to these questions are all about ideas and philosophies about how our society ought to be organized. Societies have seen the creation of many, many political philosophies. None of them can offer the "universal truth," but all aspire to bring change in political systems.

The readings in this section of the book take a contemporary view of major political ideologies. Perhaps you have your own philosophy of political life. Will it change after you have finished these readings? Russell Kirk points out that conservatism means many different things, but that there are some central tenets (his "conservative principles") that define modern conservatives. Jonathan Wight provides a twist on our understanding of liberalism. What would happen if Adam Smith, one of the founders of modern liberalism, were alive today? What would he think of our "liberal" world? Would he agree with it? Wight's contribution here is a fictionalized story of Adam Smith in the modern world, trying to "save" the ideology he believes has been misused and distorted over time.

Carol Gould brings socialism up to date by offering some non-polemical thoughts about the ideology. Much as Anthony Giddens has argued with his "Third Way,"

Gould suggests that we don't simply have to choose one perspective or another. She contends that modern democratic societies need socialist thought. Instead of just outlining the feminist movement, Jennifer Baumgardner and Amy Richards provide two contrasting scenarios: first, the reality of life for women in 1970 in the United States, and second, an imagined world in which feminism's goals have been achieved and the movement is no longer needed.

Any field of study has its own "philosophies." We study them because they tell us about our political lives, and they link our political ideas with real policies that get put into practice. They often lead to conflict, as anyone who has watched a political debate might agree, but this shows the relevance of philosophies. Rather than being in decline in modern life, political philosophies frame the way we see the world, and the changes we would like to implement.

Ten Conservative Principles

RUSSELL KIRK*

*__Russell Kirk__ (1918–1994) was a Guggenheim Fellow, a senior fellow of the American Council of Learned Societies, a Constitutional Fellow of the National Endowment for the Humanities, and a Fulbright Lecturer in Scotland. This extract is adapted from the author's The Politics of Prudence (ISI Books, 1993).

Being neither a religion nor an ideology, the body of opinion termed *conservatism* possesses no Holy Writ and no *Das Kapital* to provide dogmata. So far as it is possible to determine what conservatives believe, the first principles of the conservative persuasion are derived from what leading conservative writers and public men have professed during the past two centuries. After some introductory remarks on this general theme, I will proceed to list ten such conservative principles.

Perhaps it would be well, most of the time, to use this word "conservative" as an adjective chiefly. For there exists no Model Conservative, and conservatism is the negation of ideology: it is a state of mind, a type of character, a way of looking at the civil social order.

The attitude we call conservatism is sustained by a body of sentiments, rather than by a system of ideological dogmata. It is almost true that a conservative may be defined as a person who thinks himself such. The conservative movement or body of opinion can accommodate a considerable diversity of views on a good many subjects, there being no Test Act or Thirty-Nine Articles of the conservative creed.

In essence, the conservative person is simply one who finds the permanent things more pleasing than Chaos and Old Night. (Yet conservatives know, with Burke, that healthy "change is the means of our preservation.") A people's historic continuity of experience, says the conservative, offers a guide to policy far better than the abstract designs of coffee-house philosophers. But of course there is more to the conservative persuasion than this general attitude.

It is not possible to draw up a neat catalogue of conservatives' convictions; nevertheless, I offer you, summarily, ten general principles; it seems safe to say that most conservatives would subscribe to most of these maxims. In various editions of my book *The Conservative Mind* I have listed certain canons of conservative thought—the list differing somewhat from edition to edition; in my anthology *The Portable Conservative Reader* I offer variations upon this theme. Now I present to you a summary of conservative assumptions differing somewhat from my canons in those two books of mine. The diversity of ways in which conservative views may find expression is itself proof that conservatism is no fixed ideology. What particular principles conservatives emphasize during any given time will vary with the circumstances and necessities of that era. The following ten articles of belief reflect the emphases of conservatives in America nowadays.

1. AN ENDURING MORAL ORDER

First, the conservative believes that there exists an enduring moral order. That order is made for man, and man is made for it: human nature is a constant, and moral truths are permanent.

This word *order* signifies harmony. There are two aspects or types of order: the inner order of the soul, and the outer order of the commonwealth. Twenty-five centuries ago, Plato taught this doctrine, but even the educated nowadays find it difficult to understand. The problem of order has been a principal concern of conservatives ever since *conservative* became a term of politics.

Our twentieth-century world has experienced the hideous consequences of the collapse of belief in a moral order. Like the atrocities and disasters of Greece in the fifth century before Christ, the ruin of great nations in our century shows us the pit into which fall societies that mistake clever self-interest, or ingenious social controls, for pleasing alternatives to an oldfangled moral order.

It has been said by liberal intellectuals that the conservative believes all social questions, at heart, to be questions of private morality. Properly understood, this statement is quite true. A society in which men and women are governed by belief in an enduring moral order, by a strong sense of right and wrong, by personal convictions about justice and honor, will be a good society—whatever political machinery it may utilize; while a society in which men and women are morally adrift, ignorant of norms, and intent chiefly upon gratification of appetites, will be a bad society—no matter how many people vote and no matter how liberal its formal constitution may be.

2. CUSTOM, CONVENTION, AND CONTINUITY

Second, the conservative adheres to custom, convention, and continuity. It is old custom that enables people to live together peaceably; the destroyers of custom demolish more than they know or desire. It is through convention—a word much abused in our time—that we contrive to avoid perpetual disputes about rights and duties: law at base is a body of conventions. Continuity is the means of linking generation to generation; it matters as much for society as it does for the individual; without it, life is meaningless. When successful revolutionaries have effaced old customs, derided old conventions, and broken the continuity of social institutions—why, presently they discover the necessity of establishing fresh customs, conventions, and continuity; but that process is painful and slow; and the new social order that eventually emerges may be much inferior to the old order that radicals overthrew in their zeal for the Earthly Paradise.

Conservatives are champions of custom, convention, and continuity because they prefer the devil they know to the devil they don't know. Order and justice and freedom, they believe, are the artificial products of a long social experience, the result of centuries of trial and reflection and sacrifice. Thus the body social is a kind of spiritual corporation, comparable to the church; it may even be called a community of souls. Human society is no machine, to be treated mechanically. The continuity, the life-blood, of a society must not be interrupted. Burke's reminder of the necessity for prudent change is in the mind of the conservative. But necessary change, conservatives argue, ought to he gradual and discriminatory, never unfixing old interests at once.

3. STANDING ON THE SHOULDERS OF GIANTS

Third, conservatives believe in what may be called the principle of prescription. Conservatives sense that modern people are dwarfs on the shoulders of giants, able to see farther than their ancestors only because of the great stature of those who have preceded us in time. Therefore conservatives very often emphasize the importance of *prescription*— that is, of things established by immemorial usage, so that the mind of man runneth not to the contrary. There exist rights of which the chief sanction is their antiquity—including rights to property, often. Similarly, our morals are prescriptive in great part. Conservatives argue that we are unlikely, we moderns, to make any brave new discoveries in morals or politics or taste. It is perilous to weigh every passing issue on the basis of private judgment and private rationality. The individual is foolish, but the species is wise, Burke declared. In politics we do well to abide by precedent and precept and even prejudice, for the great mysterious incorporation of the human race has acquired a prescriptive wisdom far greater than any man's petty private rationality.

4. PRUDENCE IS CHIEF AMONG VIRTUES

Fourth, conservatives are guided by their principle of prudence. Burke agrees with Plato that in the statesman, prudence is chief among virtues. Any public measure ought to be judged by its probable long-run consequences, not merely by temporary advantage or popularity. Liberals and radicals, the conservative says, are imprudent: for they dash at their objectives without giving much heed to the risk of new abuses worse than the evils they hope to sweep away. As John Randolph of Roanoke put it, Providence moves slowly, but the devil always hurries. Human society being complex, remedies cannot be simple if they are to be efficacious. The conservative declares that he acts only after sufficient reflection, having weighed the consequences. Sudden and slashing reforms are as perilous as sudden and slashing surgery.

5. THE PRESERVATION OF DIFFERENCES

Fifth, conservatives pay attention to the principle of variety. They feel affection for the proliferating intricacy of long-established social institutions and modes of life, as distinguished from the narrowing uniformity and deadening egalitarianism of radical systems. For the preservation of a healthy diversity in any civilization, there must survive orders and classes, differences in material condition, and many sorts of inequality. The only true forms of equality are equality at the Last Judgment and equality before a just court of law; all other attempts at leveling must lead, at best, to social stagnation. Society requires honest and able leadership; and if natural and institutional differences are destroyed, presently some tyrant or host of squalid oligarchs will create new forms of inequality.

6. RESISTING THE UTOPIAN AND ANARCHIC IMPULSE

Human nature suffers irremediably from certain grave faults, the conservatives know. Man being imperfect, no perfect social order ever can be created. Because of human restlessness, mankind would grow rebellious under any utopian domination, and would break out once more in violent discontent—or else expire of boredom. To seek for utopia is to end in disaster, the conservative says: we are not made for perfect things. All that we reasonably can expect is a tolerably ordered, just, and free society, in which some evils, maladjustments, and suffering will continue to lurk. By proper attention to prudent reform, we may preserve and improve this tolerable order. But if the old institutional and moral safeguards of a nation are neglected, then the anarchic impulse in humankind breaks loose:

"the ceremony of innocence is drowned." The ideologues who promise the perfection of man and society have converted a great part of the twentieth-century world into a terrestrial hell.

7. FREEDOM AND PRIVATE PROPERTY ARE RELATED

Seventh, conservatives are persuaded that freedom and property are closely linked. Separate property from private possession, and Leviathan becomes master of all. Upon the foundation of private property, great civilizations are built. The more widespread is the possession of private property, the more stable and productive is a commonwealth. Economic leveling, conservatives maintain, is not economic progress. Getting and spending are not the chief aims of human existence; but a sound economic basis for the person, the family, and the commonwealth is much to be desired.

Sir Henry Maine, in his *Village Communities*, puts strongly the case for private property, as distinguished from communal property: "Nobody is at liberty to attack several property and to say at the same time that he values civilization. The history of the two cannot be disentangled." For the institution of several property—that is, private property—has been a powerful instrument for teaching men and women responsibility, for providing motives to integrity, for supporting general culture, for raising mankind above the level of mere drudgery, for affording leisure to think and freedom to act. To be able to retain the fruits of one's labor; to be able to see one's work made permanent; to be able to bequeath one's property to one's posterity; to be able to rise from the natural condition of grinding poverty to the security of enduring accomplishment; to have something that is really one's own—these are advantages difficult to deny. The conservative acknowledges that the possession of property fixes certain duties upon the possessor; he accepts those moral and legal obligations cheerfully.

8. VOLUNTARY COMMUNITY VS. INVOLUNTARY COLLECTIVISM

Eighth, conservatives uphold voluntary community, quite as they oppose involuntary collectivism. Although Americans have been attached strongly to privacy and private rights, they also have been a people conspicuous for a successful spirit of community. In a genuine community, the decisions most directly affecting the lives of citizens are made locally and voluntarily. Some of these functions are carried out by local political bodies, others by private associations: so long as they are kept local, and are marked by the general agreement of those affected, they constitute healthy community. But when these functions pass by default or usurpation to centralized authority, then community is in serious danger. Whatever is beneficent and prudent in modern democracy is made possible through cooperative volition. If, then, in the name of an abstract Democracy, the functions of community are transferred to distant political direction—why, real government by the consent of the governed gives way to a standardizing process hostile to freedom and human dignity.

For a nation is no stronger than the numerous little communities of which it is composed. A central administration, or a corps of select managers and civil servants, however well intentioned and well trained, cannot confer justice and prosperity and tranquility upon a mass of men and women deprived of their old responsibilities. That experiment has been made before; and it has been disastrous. It is the performance of our duties in community that teaches us prudence and efficiency and charity.

9. POWER AND PASSION REQUIRE RESTRAINT

Ninth, the conservative perceives the need for prudent restraints upon power and upon human passions. Politically speaking, power is the ability to do as one likes, regardless of the wills of one's fellows. A state in which an individual or a small group are able to dominate the wills of their fellows without check is a despotism, whether it is called monarchical or aristocratic or democratic. When every person claims to be a power unto himself, then society falls into anarchy. Anarchy never lasts long, being intolerable for everyone, and contrary to the ineluctable fact that some persons are more strong and more clever than their neighbors. To anarchy there succeeds tyranny or oligarchy, in which power is monopolized by a very few.

The conservative endeavors to so limit and balance political power that anarchy or tyranny may not arise. In every age, nevertheless, men and women are tempted to overthrow the limitations upon power, for the sake of some fancied temporary advantage. It is characteristic of the radical that he thinks of power as a force for good—so long as the power falls into his hands. In the name of liberty, the French and Russian revolutionaries abolished the old restraints upon power; but power cannot be abolished; it always finds its way into someone's hands. That power which the revolutionaries had thought oppressive in the hands of the old regime became many times as tyrannical in the hands of the radical new masters of the state.

Knowing human nature for a mixture of good and evil, the conservative does not put his trust in mere benevolence. Constitutional restrictions, political checks and balances, adequate enforcement of the laws, the old intricate web of restraints upon will and appetite— these the conservative approves as instruments of freedom and order. A just government maintains a healthy tension between the claims of authority and the claims of liberty.

10. PERMANENCE AND CHANGE MUST BE RECOGNIZED AND RECONCILED

Tenth, the thinking conservative understands that permanence and change must be recognized and reconciled in a vigorous society. The conservative is not opposed to social improvement, although he doubts whether there is any such force as a mystical Progress, with a Roman P, at work in the world. When a society is progressing in some respects, usually it is declining in other respects. The conservative knows that any healthy society is influenced by two forces, which Samuel Taylor Coleridge called its Permanence and its Progression. The Permanence of a society is formed by those enduring interests and convictions that gives us stability and continuity; without that Permanence, the fountains of the great deep are broken up, society slipping into anarchy. The Progression in a society is that spirit and that body of talents which urge us on to prudent reform and improvement; without that Progression, a people stagnate.

Therefore the intelligent conservative endeavors to reconcile the claims of Permanence and the claims of Progression. He thinks that the liberal and the radical, blind to the just claims of Permanence, would endanger the heritage bequeathed to us, in an endeavor to hurry us into some dubious Terrestrial Paradise. The conservative, in short, favors reasoned and temperate progress; he is opposed to the cult of Progress, whose votaries believe that everything new necessarily is superior to everything old.

Change is essential to the body social, the conservative reasons, just as it is essential to the human body. A body that has ceased to renew itself has begun to die. But if that body is to be vigorous, the change must occur in a regular manner, harmonizing with the form and nature of that body; otherwise change produces a monstrous growth, a cancer, which devours its host. The conservative takes care that nothing in a society should ever be wholly old, and that nothing should ever be wholly new. This is the means of the conservation of a nation, quite as it is the means of conservation of a living organism. Just how much change a society requires, and what sort of change, depend upon the circumstances of an age and a nation.

Such, then, are ten principles that have loomed large during the two centuries of modern conservative thought. Other principles of equal importance might have been discussed here: the conservative understanding of justice, for one, or the conservative view of education. But such subjects, time running on, I must leave to your private investigation.

The great line of demarcation in modern politics, Eric Voegelin used to point out, is not a division between liberals on one side and totalitarians on the other. No, on one side of that line are all those men and women who fancy that the temporal order is the only order, and that material needs are their only needs, and that they may do as they like with the human patrimony. On the other side of that line are all those people who recognize an enduring moral order in the universe, a constant human nature, and high duties toward the order spiritual and the order temporal.

Saving Adam Smith:
A Tale of Wealth,
Transformation, and Virtue

JONATHAN B. WIGHT*

*__Jonathan B. Wight__ is Associate Professor of Economics and International Studies at the University of Richmond, Virginia.

"So, Dr. Smith," I asked, "what is this urgent message for the world? You want people to know the secrets of wealth? The gains from trade?"

"Of course, of course. Quite essential"

. . . The sunlight coming through the half-drawn shades of Julia's living room cast his face in partial shadow.

"But perhaps that's rushing the cart," he continued. "Perhaps people worry about wealth, when they should ask whether wealth is the final goal? Eh?"

"We can assume that most people want wealth."

"Yes, we can assume that," he sighed, "but use logic. If something happens to be an important goal, does that make it the most important?"

"A heavy stone in the garden isn't necessarily the heaviest."

"So, we can stipulate that increasing wealth is highly desirable, even as something else could be more desirable, something even . . . intangible?"

"Intangibles can't be measured or counted," I said.

"Ah—you like to count. Then how do you measure a successful life? Bear with me, if you can. How would you determine that?"

I shrugged, "Happiness?"

"Yes. And happiness is the consequence of?" He waited expectantly.

"Dying with the most toys?" I joked.

He rapped his cheek with his knuckles. "No, no, no, think! Something basic."

I thought of my faded eight-year-old station wagon, its sticky transmission needing overhaul. If I had the money, I'd trade it in for a new Saab turbo. Wasn't that basic to my happiness? Then there's the vacation cottage on the Rappahannock River I coveted. The down payment was out of reach, but that cottage would bring real joy: kayaking the river by day and rocking on the porch at night with a cold beer. But getting real basic, winning the Samuelson Prize would provide the career boost I needed, to catapult me to a research university with untold consulting opportunities. I'd have to move, but that was a small price for recognition and status.

Smith threw up his hands. "It's *peace of mind*."

"Huh?" I woke from my reverie.

"Tranquility of being! That's the basis for happiness."

"It's hardly the driving desire for me or anyone else," I shot back.

"Ah, but it must be cultivated! Humans need to acquire skills in moral development as well as in material development."

I rolled my eyes. "We spout peace and love on Sundays. What does this have to do with economics?"

. . . Smith paced a patch of rug. After a minute he slowed and drew up in front of one of Julia's paintings: a bumblebee, drawn to huge scale, hovered over a field of clover. Smith raised a hand as if to stroke the tiger belly.

He turned suddenly. "Answer this, are you happy?"

"What's the relevance? Why drag economics over a philosophical abyss?"

. . . Smith's voice came out a whisper. "How can I justify, in a sentence, ideas I labored over for forty years? My masterwork explains all this."

I was startled. "*The Wealth of Nations*?" Smith's masterpiece was the cornerstone of my discipline. Although I'd never read it, we all knew this was Smith's epistle to laissez faire economics, to hands-off government. Economics without Smith's "invisible hand" of the market seemed unthinkable.

Smith shook his head. "No, no, no. My *Theory of Moral Sentiments*. It's the foundation."

I'd never heard of it.

He raised a finger, addressing an imaginary audience. "The danger to freedom is forgetting moral meaning. Before it's too late, I must awaken people to it in this day and age."

"Are you saying," I asked, "that you think your most important accomplishment was in moral development, not economic development?"

"Quite. Every man is rich or poor according to the degree to which he can afford the necessities, conveniences, and amusements of life. But that same richness, that same poverty, has no essential corollary with his happiness." He sat back relaxed, as if he thought I finally understood.

In my two years of front-line teaching, it had been a constant struggle to harden the romantic hearts of students to the real world, to the truth that businesses inexorably pursue profits to the last marginal dollar, that countries relentlessly boost Gross Domestic Product, even to the possible detriment of the environment and future generations. I thought about the Adam Smith I imagined who was the guide and cheerleader for this joyously avaricious, free market scramble for material wealth. It crystallized in my mind that my dissertation sat untended while I listened to the drivel of this untutored, quixotic fossil.

Irritated, I blurted: "You expect me to believe that Adam Smith cared more about morality than markets?"

Julia rose and stood with her arms crossed. "Rich . . . "

The Smith fellow opened his mouth but I'd worked myself into a warm flush. "Why for a minute should I believe you're the real Adam Smith!"

I picked up my tape recorder and headed for the door. Julia didn't stop me.

"You're supposed to be to be the academic," he yelled after me, his voice carrying through the open door. "Do your homework. Doesn't anybody read anymore?"

. . . Walking relaxed me, but not today. I resented the shifting of positions that made me the focus of inquiry. Of course I wasn't content with my life. I assumed that finishing my dissertation and later receiving tenure at a prominent university would bring that feeling, sometime in the future. Having those milestones would bring me money, prestige, even fame. After that, I could worry about other things.

. . . My encounter with this channeled Smith-voice still troubled me. I could hear his parting words: my supposing to be an academic! Well, it's true I didn't have a Ph.D. yet, making me touchy on the subject of my qualifications. . . . What did I know of Smith's writings? I rose wearily before my bookcase.

Where had I put it? There, used as a bookend for my research folders, was Adam Smith's *An Inquiry into the Nature and Causes of The Wealth of Nations*, published in 1776. I'd found it at a yard sale, and strange as it sounds, I never cracked it in school. Why should I have? History of economic thought was a dying field during my graduate school days, populated by those who couldn't stomach calculus and matrix algebra. Older historians of thought died off or retired, and their replacements were scholars in the modern fields of game theory, econometrics, and macroeconomic dynamics. With the proliferation of knowledge in the present, who had time to deal with antiques from the past? No, the pithy Adam Smith quoted in textbook blurbs was all the Smith anyone needed today.

I turned to the editor's introduction:

Before proceeding to the economics it may therefore be useful to review the main elements of the other branches of Smith's work, and to elucidate some of their interconnections. . . . Smith himself taught the elements of economics against a philosophical and historical background . . . concerned with much more than economics as that term is now commonly understood . . . .

What this meant was soon apparent: Smith's questions focused on, *"Wherein does virtue consist?"* and *"How is this character of mind recommended to us?"*

"Damn." I slammed the book shut. I wanted easy, quantifiable answers, not complicated intangible ones. An eighteenth century discourse on virtue sounded like a dreary waste of time. . . .

Crossing the central quadrangle I barely avoided colliding with a group of prospective students and their parents on a college tour. I mounted the steps to Lee Library, last remodeled in 1985. A large glass and steel addition now assaulted its Georgian façade. The new wing was hermetically sealed, offering stale re-circulated air, heavy with the fumes of carpets, drapes, and printer's ink. The metal chairs were spindly with ninety-degree angled backs. No architect or college administration would put up with this sterile, depressing place. Yet somehow they imagined students and faculty would.

Entering the marbled foyer of the older structure, I passed the security check area and stopped at a bank of computers. A few clicks of the keyboard and the answer to my search popped up on the screen. Descending circular stairs, I entered the underground collections. The second basement was a mere seven feet high, and books were perched on metal shelves floor-to-ceiling. It was as oppressively claustrophobic as a submarine. Fluorescent lights stuttered; the antiquated ventilation system droned, pinged, and hiccupped, adding to the dreamlike, underwater illusion.

I meandered through this murky confine, looking at call numbers. At the "BJ1000s" I turned right, down a narrow row. A few moments later my forefinger rested on a thick volume. This was it! *The Theory of Moral Sentiments*. Its brown leather cover was faded and cracked. I lifted it gently, wiping dust from its binding.

I moved to a library carrel and sat down. Cautiously I lifted the cover. The lending card showed it had been checked out only once. But the spine was stiff, the pages uncut. This book had never been read by anyone. I fished a penknife from my pocket and began freeing pages. The frontispiece instantly caught my eye. The subtitle was an eighteenth century teaser, "*An essay towards an analysis of the principles by which men naturally judge the conduct and character first of their neighbour, and afterwards of themselves.*"

I turned to the first chapter, and soon was reading, blinking, and murmuring. My expectation had been of a dull irrelevant treatise on moral philosophy. I was having trouble reconciling that view with the effervescent insights and sparkling writing that jumped from the pages. I was mesmerized. Unlike the colorless prose and methodological rigidity of my graduate training in economics, this was new and invigorating. After a half hour I set the book aside.

"Haaaa!" My discovery brought equal parts unease and chagrin. I re-read the passage that had so upset my equilibrium:

> *Happiness consists in tranquility. . . . What can be added to the happiness of the man who is in health, who is out of debt, and has a clear conscience? To one in this situation, all accessions of fortune may properly be said to be superfluous. . . . Do they imagine that their stomach is better, or their sleep sounder in a palace than in a cottage? The contrary has been so often observed, and, indeed, is so very obvious. . . .*

. . . Why had I never heard of this aspect of Smith's reasoning? Did it refute *The Wealth of Nations*? The laws of economics? More importantly, was any of it relevant for business and society today?

If I could be ignorant of this work, what of my colleagues? Did they know of Smith's *Moral Sentiments*?...

"Mr. Burns," the librarian smiled, "you just missed one of your admirers. Your ears must be burning!"

"Oh?"

"He said he was a former student... very nice. He asked all about you, what you were researching. I told him about your work on Russia."

I dislike idle gossip. "What did he look like?"

She pondered, lifting a hand to her mouth. " L... Like most students. You know, sunglasses, blue jeans, blonde hair. Looked a little older than most, though. Said he graduated five years ago."

"Mrs. Peabody, I wasn't teaching here five years ago. How could I possibly have had him as a student?"

She looked flustered. "I'm sorry, I haven't seen you all summer."

"I don't come in much," I replied. I wanted to add that libraries were becoming an anachronism, that on-line databases accessible from my home and office now gave me far more information than the printed tomes stuck in some inaccessible library basement. Aside from being a cruel thing to say, it wouldn't even be true, since I now clutched under my arm Smith's *Moral Sentiments*, two biographies of Smith, and three history of thought surveys. But my patience was almost to its limit.

. . . Instead, I said, "Thanks for thinking of me, Mrs. Peabody. I've found some jewels here."

THE POOR MAN'S SON

"There's a paradox," I said to Smith as we pulled back on the highway. "You're animated about expanding wealth, yet the first time we spoke, you bit my head off for saying wealth was the objective."

"I'm an empiricist." Smith said, rapping the dashboard. "I like to record observable facts. As such, it's my obligation to examine whether material things make people happy. The issue is complicated, I'll admit, but are economists today so narrow-minded the issue doesn't seem important?"

I felt rebuked. "A growing national output or GDP is almost always considered a sign of a 'healthy' economy," I replied. "Oh, there are people on the fringes who talk about *Small is Beautiful* and the *Genuine Progress Indicator* (GPI)—which subtracts from GDP the negative impacts of pollution, crime, rising inequality, and such things—but most economists don't take time to consider these issues. Virtually all our models assume that higher output is the goal without a second thought."

"Let me lay out the broad picture," Smith said, "saving specifics for later?" He was covering a lot of ground, and I wasn't sure I had the patience, or he the stamina, to finish. Nevertheless, I nodded.

"It's clear to me," he said, "that one's material station in life isn't the ultimate factor explaining happiness. This is corroborated by numerous observations, naturally anecdotal ones, but enough surely to cloud the *unexamined* notion you so easily accept. No," he paused to punctuate his words, "happiness is fairly immune to economic fortune."

"You think peace of mind determines happiness?"

"Ultimately," he said.

"Doesn't wealth affect your peace of mind, your security for the future?"

"To a point. Man's existence requires many things that are external to him. Abject starvation isn't conducive to peace of mind; the utility of wealth can't be questioned in that regard. Eliminating such scourges is critical because it eases real, physical burdens. Perhaps a third of the earth's people still need to feel those benefits." Smith stroked his chin. "But for those who are beyond abject destitution, there's little real difference between the potential happiness of a rich person and a poor person."

"But there's a difference, holding all else constant?" I asked.

"Some, but not that great. And can you really hold all else constant?"

Smith looked at me. "May I tell you a story from my *Theory of Moral Sentiments*? One of my favorites."

I nodded.

"It's the 'Parable of the Poor Man's Son.'" He closed his eyes, and began to recite:

A poor man's son, whom heaven in its anger visited with ambition, begins to look around himself and admire the condition of the rich. He finds the cottage of his father too small for his accommodation, and fancies he should be lodged more at his ease in a palace. He is displeased with being obliged to walk a-foot, but sees his superiors carried about in carriages, and imagines that in one of these he could travel with greater convenience. He judges that a numerous retinue of servants would save him from a great deal of trouble. He thinks if he had attained these conveniences he would sit contentedly in the tranquility of his situation. He is enchanted with the distant idea of this felicity.

Smith's voice became deeper and louder, and I found myself drawn in to this story as if it were my own unhappy fate.

To obtain these conveniences, he submits in the first year, nay in the first month of his application, to more fatigue of body and more uneasiness of mind than he could have suffered through the whole of his life from the want of them! He slaves to distinguish himself in some laborious profession which he hates, forces himself to be obsequious to people he despises, and, by so doing, finally acquires all the material riches he so long sought. But by now he's in the last dregs of life, his body wasted with toil and diseases, his mind galled and ruffled by the memory of a thousand injuries and disappointments, and he begins at last to realize that wealth and fame are mere trinkets of frivolous utility, no more adapted for procuring ease of body or tranquility of mind than the tweezer-cases of the lover of toys.

"What's a tweezer-case?" I asked

"A small box for tiny tools. Men of leisure carried them," Smith said. He waited for this to sink in. "Anyway, the poor man's son threw away the key to happiness which was with him all along. The stumbling block to happiness lay in his mind, not in his luxuries." Smith looked at me as if I should extract some particular meaning.

I didn't respond. It was a poignant parable, but I struggled to accept the claim that money couldn't buy peace of mind.

Socialism and Democracy

CAROL C. GOULD*

Carol Gould is Professor of Humanities and Social Sciences at the Imperatore School of Sciences and Arts, Stevens Institute of Technology, Hoboken, New Jersey.

I. INTRODUCTION

Perhaps the leading problem for both political practice and political theory today [1981] is the relation between democracy and socialism. The problem in practice is that both Western democratic societies and contemporary socialist societies fail in different ways to provide the conditions for full individual freedom and meaningful social cooperation. Thus contemporary socialist societies, both in Eastern Europe and in the Third World, are undemocratic in that they fail to protect individual civil liberties, such as freedom of expression and association, and political rights, such as the right to choose one's political representatives freely and the equal right to stand for office. Furthermore, while such societies attempt to introduce cooperation as a principle of economic and social life, yet they exhibit serious domination in the form of extensive bureaucracy, state control, the repression of individual differences, and personal and psychological domination. On the other hand, Western democratic societies, while they protect individual civil liberties and political rights to a significant degree, nonetheless are not flatly democratic in that they do not permit effective political participation by the poor, disadvantaged minorities, and even by the working people who comprise the large majority of the population. This results from the distortion of the political process by the power of wealth and lobbying by special interest groups. Such societies are also not fully democratic in that social and economic life outside the political sphere are characterized by economic exploitation, special privilege, and forms of personal domination. Furthermore, Western democratic societies fail to take seriously the principle of social cooperation as a condition for full human freedom.

Correlative to these defects in practice are defects in the respective political theories of socialism and liberal democracy. Socialist theory, in its development, places emphasis on the social whole and on the state as the articulator of the needs of the whole and disregards the importance of individuality and of individual rights. Furthermore, in its stress on economic production, socialist theory fails to take into account the significance of the social and political dimensions as spheres of human cooperation and self-development. By contrast, liberal democratic theory places emphasis on individual freedom and individual rights and disregards the importance of social cooperation and community as a condition for the full development of this individual freedom. Moreover, liberal theory takes democracy as pertaining to political life alone and not also as applying to social and economic life.

Thus socialism and liberal democracy, both in practice and in theory, are faulty and stress one of the principles of social and political reality—namely, either individuality or social cooperation—at the expense of the other. In light of these defects in contemporary political theory, I would like to propose a new theoretical framework which brings the values of individual freedom and social cooperation to bear on each other in a coherent way.

Such a theory would also suggest concrete forms in which these values could be realized in economic, social, and political life. In terms of this framework it will become clear that socialism and democracy, on a certain interpretation, are not only not incompatible with each other, but in fact entail each other.

Such an understanding that socialism and democracy are essentially related may be seen to gain support from an examination of the root meanings of the terms. In its original connotation, democracy meant self-rule by the people through a process of co- determination. Furthermore, at least in modern political theory, the concept of democracy was closely tied to that of individual freedom, in that political democracy was seen as the mode in which the equal individual liberty of the citizens could be preserved. Similarly, in its original connotation, socialism meant the control by the people over their own activities in economic, social and political life, through a process of social cooperation and co-determination. Here, too, the concept of socialism is closely connected to that of freedom, in the sense of freedom from domination and exploitation and in the sense that socialism is supposed to provide an equality of condition which would permit all individuals to develop themselves freely. Hence, both democracy and socialism in their root meanings involve the ideas of self-rule and co-determination as conditions for freedom. This connection between the concepts of democracy and socialism needs to be reclaimed. However, such a synthesis cannot remain at the abstract level of the original meanings of the terms. Rather, what is required is a new theoretical framework which would provide a philosophical foundation for the intimate relation between individuality and community or social cooperation, as well as the proposal of some concrete ways in which such a synthesis might occur. In this paper, I can only give a sketch of these philosophical ideas and a few concrete proposals as to how they could be realized.

II. PHILOSOPHICAL FOUNDATION FOR A RECONSTRUCTED DEMOCRATIC THEORY

If political theory is to satisfy the requirements which are set forth above, namely, to give an adequate account of individual freedom and social cooperation and of the relation between them, then the fundamental philosophical concepts and the normative grounds should be clarified at the outset. I would propose that the fundamental value which a system of social relations ought to serve is that of freedom, taken in the sense of the freedom of individuals to realize themselves. . . . This sense of freedom may be characterized as positive freedom or freedom *to* realize or develop oneself. Yet the realization of the purposes of an individual requires social interaction as its condition. That is, particular forms of social relations are necessary for the expression and development of human purposes and capacities. In addition, various material conditions also serve as necessary conditions for individual self-realization. Together, such social and material conditions may be characterized as the objective conditions for such self-development or human freedom. Thus, freedom requires access to these objective conditions. Such availability of conditions is part of what is connoted by the term "positive" in the idea of positive freedom. Thus on this view, freedom connotes more than free choice as a capacity; it involves the freedom to realize oneself through acting with others and by transforming the material means to suit one's purposes or ends. Yet this sense of freedom presupposes free choice as a universal feature of human activity. Such free choice is implicit in the structure of human activity as a process of fulfilling purposes. This feature of human activity constitutes the capacity for freedom as self-development. However, self-development or self-realization does not follow from this capacity alone, since it requires the availability of conditions in terms of which one's purposes can be fulfilled.

Since every human being equally possesses such a capacity for freedom inasmuch as they are human, no individual has more of a right to the exercise of this capacity than any other. That is to say, they have an equal right to self-development. But, as I have said, self-development requires access to objective conditions, both social and material. Therefore, the equal right to self-realization implies an equal right to access to such conditions.[1] Such an equal right to self-realization constitutes the value of equal positive freedom which is a cornerstone of the new democratic theory.

However, inasmuch as positive freedom presupposes that one exercise free choice, such positive freedom presupposes an absence of constraint on the free choice of agents. This means absence of constraint by other agents or by the state. Such absence of constraint, or "freedom from," has been characterized in classical liberal theory as negative freedom. Thus equal positive freedom has as its presupposition equal negative freedom. Such negative freedom includes the basic liberties, namely individual civil liberties and political rights. Thus on this theory too, each individual has a right to the full realization of these basic liberties compatible with a like right on the part of each of the others. Thus the liberal rights such as freedom of speech, press, association, etc., as well as the political rights of citizenship are seen to be crucial elements in the theory of positive freedom. It may be seen that such liberties and rights are among the social conditions for freedom as self-development. Beyond this, the theory of positive freedom implies that each individual has a right to the fullest self-realization compatible with a like right on the part of others. It therefore follows that no individual has a right to dominate or exploit any other. Each individual has the right to freedom from domination and exploitation. On this theory, therefore, the idea of negative freedom extends beyond the sphere of civil liberties and political rights and includes the right to absence of constraint in the domains of social and economic life.

. . . Since the concept of equal positive freedom entails that each individual has an equal right to such self-control, it follows from this concept that each individual has an equal right to participate in the co-determination of the social activities in which they are engaged. This may be called the *principle of democracy*, and it serves as a norm for the achievement of equal positive freedom. With respect to those social relations which are interpersonal and not institutional, the principle implies a mutual determination on the part of the individuals involved, so that none dominates or controls the activity of the others. In institutional social relations, e.g., in politics, the principle implies an equal right to democratically decide with others how such institutions are to be organized and how they are to function.

---

[1]   C. B. Macpherson presents a similar view concerning the equal right of access to what he calls "the means of labor," and also stresses the value of positive freedom and self-development. See his *Democratic Theory: Essays in Retrieval* (Oxford, 1973), especially Chapters 1, 3, 5 and 6. However, there are important differences between the theory presented here and his. Among these are differences concerning the interpretation of self-development, the meaning of property, the importance given to social relations, and the scope and nature of participatory democracy. For a further discussion of these and other differences, see my "Contemporary Legal Conceptions of Property and their Implications for Democracy" *(Journal of Philosophy,* Vol. LXXVII, No. 11, November, 1980) and my "Freedom, Reciprocity and Democracy" (unpublished manuscript).

An important consequence of this view is that democratic decision-making must be extended beyond the political sphere to which classical political theory has assigned it. From the principle presented here, it follows that individuals have a right to co-determine all social decisions that affect them, whether these are in the domain of politics, culture, or social or community life more generally.

A second principle follows from the concept of equal positive freedom. It concerns the objective conditions of action, both material and social. It will be recalled that positive freedom requires the availability of conditions for the actions of an individual or a group of individuals, in order that their purposes may be achieved. We have also seen that equal positive freedom implies an equal right to the social and material conditions of action and further that freedom defined as self-development involves control over the conditions required for realizing one's purposes in activity. But I would argue that control over the conditions or means of activity is the meaning of property and this includes both social and material conditions. Therefore, there is an equal right to such property. This gives rise to what we may call the *principle of property right*. Namely, individuals have an equal right to means of subsistence and personal means for their self-realization, which belong to them as their personal or private property; and they have an equal right to control the material and social conditions or means of their common activity, which take the form of social property. The first aspect of this property right, namely the right to personal property, connotes that each has a right to means of subsistence and to the conditions of their own self-expression compatible with a like right on the part of the others. The second aspect, namely the right to social property, connotes that all those who engage in a common productive activity or joint project have an equal right to control of conditions, that is, to co-determine their use and function. It therefore excludes the possibility that only some of those engaged in the activity would control it to the exclusion of others or that any external agents not engaged in the activity would be in control of it. Thus this second aspect of the principle of property rules out denomination and exploitation in productive life and in social activity, just as the first aspect rules out domination in personal relations. Thus the principle excludes private ownership of social means of production, and it also excludes control by others over the means or conditions which individuals need for their individual or social activity.

From the analysis of the philosophical foundations thus far, it is clear that the concepts of democracy and socialism, on a certain interpretation, entail each other. For the principle of democracy states that each individual has an equal right to participate in the co-determination of all social activities in which he or she is engaged. As we have seen, this includes not only the sphere of political decision-making, but also decisions in economic, social and cultural life as well. But such co-determination or common control over social activity in these spheres, if it is to be meaningful, requires also co-determination or common control over the conditions for this activity. For if control over the conditions of such activity belongs to others, then the democracy involved in control over the activity would remain severely limited. But the common control over the conditions by those engaged in the activity is precisely what I designated as social property, which is one of the fundamental aspects of socialism. Conversely, the principle of social property was seen to involve common control over the social and material conditions of social production by means of democratic participation in decision-making concerning the use of such means. But this is a mode of democratic decision-making concerning the means which is closely related to the principle of democracy.

The equal right to participate in social decisions concerning both the activity and the means, as I have discussed it earlier, also has implications for the form and nature of the democratic process. Specifically, it implies that where feasible, the form of democratic decision-making should be participatory. For where such participation is feasible and an individual is excluded from such participation, then others are making decisions for that individual and violating the equal right which he or she has to co-determine these decisions. Furthermore, a participatory rather than a representative process is the most direct and surest way of taking into account each individual's choices. In addition, participation serves to develop the range of choices which an individual has, as well as the individual's capacities to deal with diverse situations. In this sense, also, it is a means for the fuller development of an individual's freedom. The realization of equal rights in social decision-making thus requires the extension and development of participatory processes. However, such processes of direct participation clearly cannot be instituted in all contexts, as for example in large-scale and centralized policy-making in government, industry, and cultural affairs. Here, what is required is an adequate system of representation founded on participation at the lower levels. Such participation and representation would not only characterize the political sphere but would also apply to decisions in economic, social and cultural life as well. In these various spheres, each would have an equal right to be represented and to serve as a representative. Furthermore, the representatives or delegates would be held accountable to those whom they represent by regular elections and regular consultations with those whom they represent, as well as by being subject to recall.

III. THE NEW DEMOCRACY—SOME CONCRETE PROPOSALS

The theoretical model of democracy and the value of equal positive freedom on which it is based need to be interpreted in terms of concrete social and institutional forms which would serve to realize them. The general political, economic and social forms which I will propose here seem to me to be required by the principles which I have discussed, although particular details of these forms may vary. In the formulation of these concrete proposals, I am concerned not only with the realization of these principles and values, but also with the feasibility of the institutional forms. In particular, it is important that they be suitable for large, complex societies and not serve simply as suggestions for small social experiments.

The first set of concrete proposals concerns the economic sphere. The four points I will deal with here are workers' self-management, the market, planning and regulatory func-tions, and the distribution of income. One of the most decisive features of the proposed social structure is the democratic management of economic activity by the workers them-selves. This would be in the form of ownership, control and management of each firm by those who work there.[2] Such worker self-management means that the workers in a given

---

[2] Similar proposals for workers' self-management have been made by a number of other authors, among them M. Marković's "New Legal Relations for New Social Institutions," in *Proceedings of the IVR World Congress,* 1975, and "Philosophical Foundations of the Idea of Self-Management," in B. Horvat *et al.* ed., *Self-Managing Socialism* (New York, 1975), pp. 327–350; C. Pateman, *Participation and Democratic Theory* (Cambridge, 1970); R. Selucký, *Marxism, Socialism, Freedom*

firm jointly determine the planning and production for the firm, and the work process (including allocation of work, rates of production, hours of work and work discipline). They also decide on the distribution of the firm's income, including reinvestment in production, depreciation costs and the division of wages to be paid among themselves. In addition, the workers control the sale of their firm's products. The capital of the firm is the workers' joint or social property, which is to say that they have the legal rights to possess, use, manage or alienate this property.

Such workers' self-management does not entail that all the workers decide on every feature of the production and sale of their products. They may well decide to appoint directors or managers of various aspects of the firm's activities. However, such delegation of powers and functions rests entirely upon the democratic decision of the workers. This democratic decision-making should involve the direct and immediate participation by the workers up through as many levels of the firm's activities as is feasible.

It may be seen that these forms of democratic and participatory control by the workers of their own economic activity are required by the principle of equal positive freedom. For, as will be recalled, such equal positive freedom implies each individual's right to control the conditions of his or her activity, and thus it implies the right to co-determine those common activities in which an individual is engaged, as well as the conditions for such activity. Therefore, the workers' activity as well as the objective conditions of this activity, namely the means of production, must be under their own control. This requirement is realized in workers' self-management, as I have described it.

The second major feature of the proposed economic structure is the market. Firms are free to buy and sell to other firms, institutions, or to individual consumers. The market therefore determines prices and serves as an instrument for adjusting supply and demand. Thus, the market functions as the locus for the exchange of commodities. However, unlike the capitalist market, what is excluded here is the market between capital and labor. Rather,

---

(New York, 1979); D. Schweickart, "Should Rawls be a Socialist? A Comparison of his Ideal Capitalism with Worker-Controlled Socialism," in *Social Theory and Practice,* vol. 5, no. 1 (Fall, 1978), pp. 1–27; J. Vanek, *The General Theory of Labor-Managed Market Economies* (Ithaca: N.Y., 1977); P. Rosanvallon, *l'Age de l'autogestion?* (Paris, 1978).

Although my proposal is similar in many respects to these, yet it differs from each of them in important ways. Thus, for example, although my proposal shares with Marković's an emphasis on participatory democracy in all spheres of social life, it differs from his in keeping the political and economic spheres separate from each other. Again, my proposal has in common with Selucký's an emphasis on the role of the market, on political democracy, and on the importance of the protection of individual rights. Yet my view, while holding that the market is important, does not regard it as the most decisive factor, as his does. Moreover, unlike him, I stress the need for the further democratization of the political sphere in addition to the economic sphere. Although my proposals are similar to Schweickart's in basic features of worker control, market and democracy, my differences with him concern his insufficient emphasis on democratizing the political sphere, and what seems to me an overextended planning function of the state, inasmuch as on his view it controls virtually all new investment, and dispenses it through a general plan. Furthermore, as will be seen, my proposal differs from several of those above in that it regards the social means of production as the common property of the workers in each firm rather than as belonging to society as a whole. However, some large-scale social means of production, e.g., utilities and railroads, and some natural resources should be owned by society as a whole.

the workers' incomes are determined by their own division of the net revenue or profits of the firm among themselves.

In terms of the values and principles discussed earlier, the virtues of such a market scheme are three: First, it preserves the freedom of workers to determine what to produce and the freedom of consumers to determine what, and from whom, to buy. In the market, the firms relate to each other and to individual consumers as free and equal exchangers. Second, the market is an efficient means of reflecting the needs and wants of consumers and of adjusting supply to meet the effective demand. Third, the market fosters variety in what is produced because it expresses the multiplicity of wants and it leaves producers free to satisfy them. In all these respects, the market is superior to a centralized planning scheme in which decisions are made from the top down, as they are in many contemporary socialist countries. Such centralized planning removes the autonomy of the workers in determining production, is often inefficient, and fails to provide variety because the planning bureaucracies tend to be insensitive to differentiated demands and cumbersome in adjusting supply to demand.[3] However, in claiming that the market is well-suited to realize the principles, I do not mean to imply that it is the only system that could satisfy these principles. But the market form is already available and well-developed and requires no third party to intervene between producers and consumers, or to validate their choices.

The third feature of the proposed economic structure is that there should be planning and market-regulatory commissions. The planning commissions would affect the direction of production in the economy indirectly, by making funds available for new investment to existing or prospective worker-managed firms. The commissions would derive these funds from taxation of the social capital of firms. They would operate regionally where possible, though some national planning would be necessary.

All of these commissions would be political bodies in the sense that they would be made up of elected representatives of the people. They would not be chosen as representatives of the workers in the firms, but rather by the workers in general, in their capacity as citizens, who would presumably be in a better position to make decisions in the interests of society as a whole. The unit to be represented on the planning commissions will, therefore, be a political unit at the most local levels possible, rather than an economic unit (e.g., a firm or an industry).

The market-regulatory commissions will function to see to it that the market is free of abuses, such as price-fixing, monopolistic practices, violations of contract, or deceptive advertising or merchandising practices. Thus, these commissions are not intended to control the market, but to permit it to operate fairly and effectively. Like the planning commissions, the market-regulatory commissions will also be democratically elected entities representing the public.

Both the planning commissions and the market-regulatory commissions are necessary to correct malfunctions of the economy and to help it to meet social needs. Thus, although worker self-managed firms together with the market are seen as the principal moving force and adjustment mechanism, respectively, of the economy, nonetheless, these cannot be expected to meet all needs optimally, or may sometimes meet them in a haphazard or

---

[3]   On the importance or usefulness of the market, cf. Selucký, *op. cit.*, esp. Chapter 5; and Schweickart, *op. cit.*

distorted way. The commissions, in representing the general social interest, are thus balancing the corrective mechanisms, and can also foster innovation to meet important social and economic needs.

The fourth feature of the proposed scheme concerns the principles and mode of distribution of income. It combines elements of the two well-known principles of distribution according to work and distribution according to needs. The scheme excludes deriving income from investment or from exploitation of the work of others.

Most generally, income will be distributed by the workers in each firm, by a process of participatory democratic decision in which they determine the allocation of the net revenue of that firm among themselves. Since this is an autonomous democratic procedure, the principle that they use for distributing income is up to them. However, since the amount of net revenue to be distributed among the workers in a firm depends in part on their work, the principle of distribution of income is to this degree a principle of distribution according to work.

In terms of the principle of equal positive freedom, the justification of such democratic allocation of income follows from the requirement for common control over the activity of production. I take such activity to include not only the conception and process of production, but also its product. Therefore, each worker has an equal right to control the common product of his or her work, and therefore also an equal right to co-determine the distribution of the income from that work.

This principle is complemented by the principle of distribution according to need in important areas of social and economic life. Thus, every individual is assured of free access to education and health-care according to their needs. In the case of education, this should be taken to include the provision of higher education to all those who want it. A principle of need should also be in effect with regard to subsistence needs which should be available to all regardless of their work. With respect to those unable to work because of age or illness, or those who are unemployed, this would mean that they should be provided with incomes approximating the average of those who work. With respect to those (hopefully few) who refuse to work, this principle would mean the provision of minimal subsistence needs. The principle of distribution according to need may also require that the state guarantee a minimum income for those who work, which would provide not merely means of subsistence but also means of self-development.

It may be seen that this combination of principles of distribution according to work and need is required by the value of equal positive freedom as discussed above, at least under the conditions of scarcity. This value was seen to imply not only the equal right to control over the work activity, but also the right of each individual to the means of subsistence and the conditions for self-realization, compatible with a like right on the part of each of the others. This latter aspect of the principle excludes exploitation of some by others, or some profiting from the work of others, in two senses: it excludes the accumulation and control of capital by those who have not produced it; and it also excludes parasitism, in the sense of those unwilling to work benefiting from the labor of others. Yet, because of the supreme value of human life, the principle of equal positive freedom implies that everyone has a right to the means of subsistence. These interpretations of the second part of the principle of equal positive freedom, combined with the first part which asserts the equal right of everyone to control their activity, seem to me to yield the principles of distribution sketched above.

Just as democracy is necessary in the economic sphere, so too is it necessary in the organization and relations of social and cultural life. I therefore turn to the question of how the social and cultural institutions and activities of society may be democratized. These institutions and activities include educational institutions such as schools and universities; cultural institutions such as museums and various arts organizations and activities; health services, including hospitals, community health organizations, etc.; welfare organizations; scientific institutions; sports; the media, e.g., newspapers, radio, T.V.; religious organizations; and charitable organizations. There would also be a wide variety of voluntary associations of individuals organized to pursue their various social and cultural interests. One may also include under the general heading of social and cultural life, the family and other child-raising and living arrangements.

With respect to the funding of these institutions, one would expect that some would operate wholly within the market, some would be publicly funded, some funded by firms, some privately funded, and many, perhaps most, would derive their funds from a mixture of these sources. It seems to me that in social and cultural affairs, such a proliferation of funding sources is important. Thus, for example, it would be good if the arts were funded from a multiplicity of sources, in order to preserve diversity and to prevent any control by the state, as well as to prevent the subservience of the arts to market fashions or requirements.

Here, as in the economic sphere, the institutions should be self-managing, and for the same reason: namely, to provide the conditions for the individuals' self-development by participating in the control of their own social activity. Thus, each such institution will have a managing board made up of those who work there or those who are involved in the range of that institution's activities. More specifically, where the social or cultural institutions operate in the market and are therefore subject directly to considerations of what consumers want, it is sufficient to have the board made up of the workers in the institution, who together decide upon the policy and activities of that institution. Where the institutions are partly or wholly exempt from market function, and depend largely on public funds, it would seem appropriate to include on the board not only those who work in the institution but also representatives of those who benefit from or use the institution, as well as representatives from the public at large, or the state.[4] In addition, there are those institutions which have to take into account the needs of consumers in a way which is more direct than a market permits, even though such institutions may function in the market. In such cases, the managing boards should have representatives of the users, in addition to those who work in the institution. Examples of this latter type of institution would be privately funded universities or hospitals which would operate in addition to those publicly funded ones that provide free education and health benefits.

In social and cultural institutions as in economic ones, self-management should be understood to operate in a participatory way. That is to say, the workers in such institutions, as well as representatives of those who use them or take part in their activities, have a right to participate in formulating policy and procedures. This is not to say that everyone should participate in deciding on all aspects of the institution's operation. Rather, all have a right to decide general matters of policy, as well as to make decisions concerning those areas directly related to their functions. Furthermore, decisions which require special expertise in order to make competent judgments should be reserved to those who are certifiably

---

[4]   A similar point is made by Selucký, *op. cit.,* p. 182.

competent to make such judgments. An example of this requirement of expertise would obviously be medical or surgical judgments.

The democratization of social and cultural institutions has to be understood as founded upon greater mutuality in interpersonal relations. That is, changes in the institutions can be fully effective only if people at the same time generally relate to each other as equals and with respect for each other's individuality. The reason for this is that the very process of participatory democratic decision-making which is required for the functioning of these institutions, if the principle of equal positive freedom is to be realized, entails that each participant treat the others as fully equal, and that they respect the differences among themselves. Such participation at the institutional level would very likely be undermined by lack of reciprocity in interpersonal relations, and would not endure for very long without such reciprocity. Conversely, the achievement of full mutuality in personal relations requires some changes in institutions, as well as the introduction of new institutions. Among the important interpersonal relations are male–female relations. Greater equality and mutuality here seem to me to require not only the elimination of domination, but also greater freedom to introduce new forms of child-raising, as well as new forms of living arrangements. In addition, in order to achieve women's equality at work, which would be one of the foundations of their equality more generally, extensive day-care facilities would be necessary. These proposals for the democratization of social and cultural life, together with economic democracy, bear upon the democratization of the political sphere to which I now turn.

The political sphere has traditionally been the domain in which democracy has been thought to apply. Democracy in this sphere has connoted forms of political representation, popular elections, and the protection of civil and political rights of individuals, among other features. Such features are also important in my proposed structure. Thus, a crucial aspect of democracy is the constitutional protection of equal civil liberties or basic freedoms (such as freedom of speech, press, association, etc.) as well as equal political rights (such as the right to vote, to be elected, etc.).

The principle of the separation and balance of powers is also of great importance, both among the various functions of government, as well as among the levels of government. Thus, the division of powers among the legislative, executive and judicial functions of government, together with a system of checks and balances, helps to prevent any one of these branches of government from dominating the others. A similar check on the over-centralization of power is provided by the division of political decision-making into various levels, e.g., local, state, regional, national. In addition, the separation of the political sphere itself from the economic sphere is also important in preventing the excessive concentration of power in either of these spheres. Furthermore, the universal right to vote, periodic free elections and a system of representation are important features of the proposed political democracy. As is clear, these are already features of modern political states. Yet, even with such features, these states are not fully democratic. This is in part because their political democracy is undermined by the lack of democracy in the economic and social spheres. Thus, the power of concentrated wealth can be used to influence the political process in its own interests. Or again, economic and social alienation may lead to feelings of political powerlessness and to voter apathy, leaving the process of governing without genuine popular support. The democratization of economic and social life in the structure proposed here should contribute to the elimination of alienation and of the distortion of the political process by the power of money. The proposed structure would therefore permit the fuller realization of these forms of political democracy.

These proposals concerning the concrete structures and practices of economic, social and political life are intended as realizations of the values and principles discussed earlier, namely, the value of equal positive freedom and the principles of democracy and of property right. My attempt was to synthesize the best features of liberal democracy on the one hand, and of socialism on the other, both in the theoretical system which I presented and in the specific proposals which I have discussed. However, I do not see this as a combination of presently existing forms of democracy and socialism, or of presently available theories. Rather, it seems to me that a start has to be made which, though it draws on both these traditions, introduces a decisively new foundation for social theory, namely, one which takes fully seriously both the values of individual freedom and of social cooperation.

A Day Without Feminism

JENNIFER BAUMGARDNER AND AMY RICHARDS*

*__*Jennifer Baumgardner*__, *a self-described "professional feminist," is a former editor at* Ms. *and writes for* The Nation, Jane, Nerve, *and* Out. __*Amy Richards*__ *is a contributing editor at* Ms. *and co-founder of the Third Wave Foundation, an activist group for young feminists. This article is divided into two separate chapters, "Prologue: A Day Without Feminism" and "Epilogue: A Day With Feminism."*

PROLOGUE: A DAY WITHOUT FEMINISM

We were both born in 1970, the baptismal moment of a decade that would change dramatically the lives of American Women. The two of us grew up thousands of miles apart, in entirely different kinds of families, yet we both came of age with the awareness that certain rights had been won by the women's movement. We've never doubted how important feminism is to people's lives—men's and women's. Both of our mothers went to consciousness-raising-type groups. Amy's mother raised Amy on her own, and Jennifer's mother, questioning the politics of housework, staged laundry strikes.

With the dawn of not just a new century but a new millennium, people are looking back and taking stock of feminism. Do we need new strategies? Is feminism dead? Has society changed so much that the idea of a feminist movement is obsolete? For us, the only way to answer these questions is to imagine what our lives would have been if the women's movement had never happened and the conditions for women had remained as they were in the year of our births.

Imagine that for a day it's still 1970, and women have only the rights they had then. Sly and the Family Stone and Dionne Warwick are on the radio, the kitchen appliances are Harvest Gold, and the name of your Whirlpool gas stove is Mrs. America. What is it like to be female?

Babies born on this day are automatically given their father's name. If no father is listed, "illegitimate" is likely to be typed on the birth certificate. There are virtually no child-care centers, so all preschool children are in the hands of their mothers, a baby-sitter, or an expensive nursery school. In elementary school, girls can't play in Little League and almost all of the teachers are female. (The latter is still true.) In a few states, it may be against the law for a male to teach grades lower than the sixth, on the basis that it's unnatural, or that men can't be trusted with young children.

In junior high, girls probably take home ec; boys take shop or small-engine repair. Boys who want to learn how to cook or sew on a button are out of luck, as are girls who want to learn how to fix a car. *Seventeen* magazine doesn't run feminist-influenced current columns like "Sex + Body" and "Traumarama." Instead the magazine encourages girls not to have sex; pleasure isn't part of its vocabulary. Judy Blume's books are just beginning to be published, and *Free to Be . . . You and Me* does not exist. No one reads much about masturbation as a natural activity; nor do they learn that sex is for anything other than procreation. Girls do read mystery stories about Nancy Drew, for whom there is no sex, only her blue roadster and having "luncheon." (The real mystery is how Nancy gets along without a purse and manages to meet only white people.) Boys read about the Hardy Boys, for whom there are no girls.

In high school, the principal is a man. Girls have physical-education class and play half-court basketball, but not soccer, track, or cross country; nor do they have any varsity sports teams. The only prestigious physical activity for girls is cheerleading, or being a drum majorette. Most girls don't take calculus or physics; they plan the dances and decorate the gym. Even when girls get better grades than their male counterparts, they are half as likely to qualify for a National Merit Scholarship because many of the test questions favor boys. Standardized tests refer to males and male experiences much more than to females and their experiences. If a girl "gets herself pregnant," she loses her membership in the National Honor Society (which is still true today) and is expelled.

Girls and young women might have sex while they're unmarried, but they may be ruining their chances of landing a guy full-time, and they're probably getting a bad reputation. If a pregnancy happens, an enterprising gal can get a legal abortion only if she lives in New York or is rich enough to fly there, or to Cuba, London, or Scandinavia. There's also the Chicago-based Jane Collective, an underground abortion-referral service, which can hook you up with an illegal or legal termination. (Any of these options are going to cost you. Illegal abortions average $300 to $500, sometimes as much as $2,000.) To prevent pregnancy, a sexually active woman might go to a doctor to be fitted for a diaphragm, or take the high-dose birth-control pill, but her doctor isn't likely to inform her of the possibility of deadly blood clots. Those who do take the Pill also may have to endure this contraceptive's crappy side effects: migraine headaches, severe weight gain, irregular bleeding, and hair loss (or gain), plus the possibility of an increased risk of breast cancer in the long run. It is unlikely that women or their male partners know much about the clitoris and its role in orgasm unless someone happens to fumble upon it. Instead, the myth that vaginal orgasms from penile penetration are the only "mature" (according to Freud) climaxes prevails.

Lesbians are rarely "out," except in certain bars owned by organized crime (the only businessmen who recognize this untapped market), and if lesbians don't know about the bars, they're less likely to know whether there are any other women like them. Radclyffe Hall's depressing early-twentieth-century novel *The Well of Loneliness* pretty much indicates their fate.

The Miss America Pageant is the biggest source of scholarship money for women. Women can't be students at Dartmouth, Columbia, Harvard, West Point, Boston College, or the Citadel, among other all-male institutions. Women's colleges are referred to as "girls' schools." There are no Take Back the Night marches to protest women's lack of safety after dark, but that's okay because college girls aren't allowed out much after dark anyway. Curfew is likely to be midnight on Saturday and 9 or 10 p.m. the rest of the week. Guys get to stay out as late as they want. Women tend to major in teaching, home economics, English, or maybe a language—a good skill for translating someone else's words. The women's studies major does not exist, although you can take a women's studies course at six universities, including Cornell and San Diego State College. The absence of women's history, black history, Chicano studies, Asian-American history, queer studies, and Native American history from college curricula implies that they are not worth studying. A student is lucky if he or she learns that women were "given" the vote in 1920, just as Columbus "discovered" America in 1492. They might also learn that Sojourner Truth, Mary Church Terrell, and Fannie Lou Hamer were black abolitionists or civil-rights leaders, but not that they were feminists. There are practically no tenured female professors at any school, and campuses are not racially diverse. Women of color are either not there or they're lonely as hell. There is no nationally recognized Women's History Month or Black History Month. Only 14 percent of doctorates are awarded to women. Only 3.5 percent of MBAs are female.

Only 2 percent of everybody in the military is female, and these women are mostly nurses. There are no female generals in the U.S. Air Force, no female naval pilots, and no Marine brigadier generals. On the religious front, there are no female cantors or rabbis, Episcopal canons, or Catholic priests. (This is still true of Catholic priests.)

Only 44 percent of women are employed outside the home. And those women make, on average, fifty-two cents to the dollar earned by males. Want ads are segregated into "Help Wanted Male" and "Help Wanted Female." The female side is preponderantly for secretaries, domestic workers, and other low-wage service jobs, so if you're a female lawyer you must look under "Help Wanted Male." There are female doctors, but twenty states have only five female gynecologists or fewer. Women workers can be fired or demoted for being pregnant, especially if they are teachers, since the kids they teach aren't supposed to think that women have sex. If a boss demands sex, refers to his female employee exclusively as "Baby," or says he won't pay her unless she gives him a blow job, she either has to quit or succumb—no pun intended. Women can't be airline pilots. Flight attendants are "stewardesses"—waitresses in the sky—and necessarily female. Sex appeal is a job requirement, wearing makeup is a rule, and women are fired if they exceed the age or weight deemed sexy. Stewardesses can get married without getting canned, but this is a new development. (In 1968 the Equal Employment Opportunity Commission—EEOC—made it illegal to forcibly retire stewardesses for getting hitched.) Less than 2 percent of dentists are women; 100 percent of dental assistants are women. The "glass ceiling" that keeps women from moving naturally up the ranks, as well as the sticky floor that keeps them unnaturally down in low-wage work, has not been named, much less challenged.

When a woman gets married, she vows to love, honor, and obey her husband, though he gets off doing just the first two to uphold his end of the bargain. A married woman can't obtain credit without her husband's signature. She doesn't have her own credit rating, legal domicile, or even her own name unless she goes to court to get it back. If she gets a loan with her husband—and she has a job—she may have to sign a "baby letter" swearing that she won't have one and have to leave her job.

Women have been voting for up to fifty years, but their turnout rate is lower than that for men, and they tend to vote right along with their husbands, not with their own interests in mind. The divorce rate is about the same as it is in 2000, contrary to popular fiction's blaming the women's movement for divorce. However, divorce required that one person be at fault, therefore if you just want out of your marriage, you have to lie or blame your spouse. Property division and settlements, too, are based on fault. (And at a time when domestic violence isn't a term, much less a crime, women are legally encouraged to remain in abusive marriages.) If fathers ask for custody of the children, they get it in 60 to 80 percent of the cases. (This is still true.) If a husband or a lover hits his partner, she has no shelter to go to unless she happens to live near the one in northern California or the other in upper Michigan. If a woman is downsized from her role as a housewife (a.k.a. left by her husband), there is no word for being a displaced homemaker. As a divorcée, she may be regarded as a family disgrace or as easy sexual prey. After all, she had sex with one guy, so why not all guys?

If a woman is not a Mrs., she's a Miss. A woman without makeup and a hairdo is as suspect as a man with them. Without a male escort she may be refused service in a restaurant or a bar, and a woman alone is hard-pressed to find a landlord who will rent her an apartment. After all, she'll probably be leaving to get married soon, and, if she isn't, the landlord doesn't want to deal with a potential brothel.

Except among the very poor or in very rural areas, babies are born in hospitals. There are no certified midwives, and women are knocked out during birth. Most likely, they are also strapped down and lying down, made to have the baby against gravity for the doctor's convenience. If he has a schedule to keep, the likelihood of a cesarean is also very high. *Our Bodies, Ourselves* doesn't exist, nor does the women's health movement. Women aren't taught how to look at their cervixes, and their bodies are nothing to worry their pretty little heads about; however, they are supposed to worry about keeping their little heads pretty. If a woman goes under the knife to see if she has breast cancer, the surgeon won't wake her up to consult about her options before performing a Halsted mastectomy (a disfiguring radical procedure, in which the breast, the muscle wall, and the nodes under the arm, right down to the bone, are removed). She'll just wake up and find that the choice has been made for her.

Husbands are likely to die eight years earlier than their same-age wives due to the stress of having to support a family and repress an emotional life, and a lot earlier than that if women have followed the custom of marrying older, authoritative, paternal men. The stress of raising kids, managing a household, and being undervalued by society doesn't seem to kill off women at the same rate. Upon a man's death, his beloved gets a portion of his Social Security. Even if she has worked outside the home for her entire adult life, she is probably better off with that portion than with hers in its entirety, because she has earned less and is likely to have taken time out for such unproductive acts as having kids.

Has feminism changed our lives? Was it necessary? After thirty years of feminism, the world we inhabit barely resembles the world we were born into. And there's still a lot left to do.

EPILOGUE: A DAY WITH FEMINISM

Women and men are paid equal wages for work of comparable value, as is every race and ethnic group, co-parenting is a given, men lengthen their lives by crying and otherwise expressing emotion, and women say "I'm sorry" only when they truly should be. To the extent that we can imagine this even now, this is the equality feminists have been working for since that day in Seneca Falls in 1848. With each generation, the picture will get bigger and at the same time more finely detailed.

When Elizabeth Cady Stanton and her crew wrote the Declaration of Sentiments, they knew that this nation's Declaration of Independence would have no justice or power unless it included the female half of the country. For these women, equality was being full citizens who were able to own and inherit property, just as men were, to have the right to their own children, and the ability to vote. In 1923, Alice Paul had the vision to write the Equal Rights Amendment so that laws could not be made based on sex, any more than they could be made based on race, religion, or national origin. By the 1970s, Betty Friedan, Audre Lorde, Gloria Steinem, and Shirley Chisholm could imagine women's equality in the paid workforce, a new vision of family and sexuality, and legislative bodies that truly reflected the country. They could not have foreseen a twenty-three-year-old White House intern who owned her own libido and sexual prowess the way Monica Lewinsky did. (They certainly wouldn't have imagined that a woman with that much access to power would just want to blow it.)

Now, at the beginning of a new millennium, we have witnessed a woman running for President who has a chance of winning, a first lady who translates that unparalleled Washington experience into her own high-flying political ambitions, easily reversible male birth control, gay parenting, a women's soccer team that surpasses the popular appeal of men's, and parental leave for both parents. And we can imagine more: federally subsidized child-care centers for every child and legalized gay marriage in all fifty states. A number of leaps are still needed to bring us to a day of equality, but at least we can begin to picture what such a future might hold.

Whether children are born to a single mother, a single father, two mothers, two fathers, or a mother and a father, a family is defined by love, commitment, and support. A child who has two parents is just as likely to have a hyphenated last name, or choose a whole new name, as she or he is to have a father's or birth mother's name. Carrying on a lineage is an individual choice, not the province of the father or the state.

Men work in child-care centers and are paid at least as well as plumbers, sanitation workers, or firefighters. When kids sit down to their breakfast Wheaties, they are as likely to confront a tennis star like Venus Williams as a golf pro like Tiger Woods. On TV, the male and female newscasters are about the same age and, whether black or white, are as likely to report foreign policy as sports. In general, people on camera come in all shapes and sizes. If you are watching drama, women are just as likely to be the rescuers as the rescued, and men are just as likely to ask for help as to give it. Women are as valued for their sense of humor as men are for their sex appeal. On Monday-night television, women's soccer or basketball is just as popular as men's basketball or football. Barbie no longer has feet too tiny to stand on or finds math hard; nor do girls. G.I. Joe, now a member of a peacekeeping force, likes to shop at the mall. In grade school, boys and girls decorate their bedrooms with posters of female athletes.

By the time girls hit junior high, they have already had the opportunity to play sports, from soccer to Little League, hockey to wrestling, and they share gymnastics and ballet classes with boys. Boys think ballet and gymnastics are cool. Kids hit puberty fully aware of how their bodies work: erections, nocturnal emissions, periods, cramps, masturbation, body hair—the works. These topics still cause giggling, curiosity, and excitement, but paralyzing shame and utter ignorance are things of the past. In fact, sweet-sixteen birthdays have given way to coming-of-age rituals for both genders, and don't assume that the birthday kid has never been kissed. Around the time that girls and boys are learning how to drive, both have mastered manual stimulation for their own sexual pleasure.

In high school, many varsity teams have coed cheerleaders, athletes all, but mostly cheering is left to the fans. Differences in girls' and boys' academic performance are as indistinguishable as differences in their athletic performance though they are very different as unique individuals. Some girls ask other girls to the prom, some boys ask boys, and that is as okay as going in as a mixed couple. Some go alone or not at all, and that's okay, too. Athletic scholarships have no more prestige or funding than arts scholarships.

Students take field trips to local museums where women are the creators of the art as often as they are its subjects. In preparation for this trip, students study art history from Artemisia Gentileschi to Mark Rothko, from Ndebele wall paintings to Yayoi Kusama. The museums themselves were designed by architects who may have been among the 11 percent of architects who were female in the 1990s. Military school is open to everyone and teaches peacekeeping as much as defense. Women's colleges no longer exist, because women no longer need a compensatory environment, and women's history, African-American history, and all those remedial areas have become people's and world history.

Women achieved parity long ago, so the idea of bean counting is irrelevant. At Harvard, 75 percent of the tenured professors are women, and at nearby Boston College, 30 percent of the tenured faculty is female. History courses cover the relevance of a movement that ended sexual violence against women. Though there is still a throwback incident now and then, men are even more outraged by it than women are. Once a year, there is a party in the quad to commemorate what was once called Take Back the Night.

Women walking through a park at night can feel just as safe as they do during the day, when kids play while white male nannies watch over them, right along with women and men of every group. In fact, it's as common to see a white man taking care of a black or a brown baby as it is to see a woman of color taking care of a white baby.

Sex is separate from procreation. Because there is now a national system of health insurance, birth control and abortions are covered right along with births, and the Hyde Amendment's ban of federal funding for abortions is regarded as a shameful moment in history, much like the time of Jim Crow laws. A judicial decision known as *Doe* v. *Hyde* effectively affirmed a woman's right to bodily integrity, and went way past the right to privacy guaranteed by *Roe* v. *Wade*. Abortion isn't morally contested territory because citizens don't interfere with one another's life choices, and women have the right to determine when and whether to have no children, a single child, or five children.

Environmentally sound menstrual products are government subsidized and cost the same as a month's worth of shaving supplies. After all, women's childbearing capacity is a national asset, and young, sexually active men often opt for freezing their sperm or undergoing a simple vasectomy to control their paternity. Many men choose vasectomies, given that it's the least dangerous and most foolproof form of birth control—as well as the easiest to reverse. Men are screened for chlamydia, human papilloma virus, herpes, and other sexually transmitted diseases during their annual trip to the andrologist. Doctors learn how to detect and treat all of the above, in both men and women. Although the old number of three million or so new cases of STDs each year has dropped to half that amount, STDs are still as common (and about as shameful) as the common cold and are finally acknowledged as such.

The Equal Rights Amendment has put females in the U.S. Constitution. There are many women of all races in fields or institutions formerly considered to be the province of men, from the Virginia Military Institute and the Citadel to fire departments and airline cockpits. Women are not only free to be as exceptional as men but also as mediocre. Men are as critiqued or praised as women are. Women's salaries have jumped up 26 to 40 percent from pre-equality days to match men's. There are no economic divisions based on race, and the salary categories have been equalized. This categorization is the result of legislation that requires the private sector—even companies that employ fewer than 50 people—to report employees' wages. Many older women are averaging half a million dollars in back pay as a result of the years in which they were unjustly underpaid. Women and men in the NBA make an average of $100,000 per year. Haircuts, dry cleaning, and clothes for women cost the same as they do for men.

The media are accountable to their constituency. Magazines cover stories about congressional hearings on how to help transition men on welfare back into the workforce. Many of these men are single fathers—by choice. Welfare is viewed as a subsidy, just as corporate tax breaks used to be, and receiving government assistance to help rear one's own child is as destigmatized as it is to be paid to rear a foster child. Howard Stern, who gave up his declining radio show to become a stay-at-home granddad, has been replaced on radio by Janeane Garofalo, who no longer jokes primarily about her "back fat" and other perceived imperfections. (Primary caregiving has humanized Stern so that people no longer have to fear for his influence on his offspring.) Leading ladies and leading men are all around the same age. There is always fanfare around *Time* magazine's Person of the Year and *Sports Illustrated*'s coed swimsuit issue. *Rolling Stone* covers female pop stars and music groups in equal numbers with male stars, and women are often photographed for the cover with their shirts on. Classic-rock stations play Janis Joplin as often as they play Led Zeppelin.

Women who choose to have babies give birth in a birthing center with a midwife, a hospital with a doctor, or at home with a medicine woman. Paid child-care leave is for four months, and it is required of both parents (if there is more than one). Child rearing is subsidized by a trust not unlike Social Security, a concept pioneered by the welfare-rights activist Theresa Funiciello and based on Gloria Steinem's earlier mandate that every child have a minimum income. The attributed economic value of housework is figured into the gross national product (which increases the United States' GNP by almost 30 percent), and primary caregivers are paid. Whether you work in or out of the home, you are taxed only on your income; married couples and people in domestic partnerships are taxed as individuals, too. When women retire, they get as much Social Security as men do, and all people receive a base amount on which they can live.

The amount of philanthropic dollars going to programs that address or specifically include women and girls is now pushing 60 percent, to make up for all the time it was about 5 percent. More important, these female-centered programs no longer have to provide basic services, because the government does that. All school meals, vaccinations, public libraries, and museums are government-funded and thus available to everybody. Taxpayers have made their wishes clear because more than 90 percent of the electorate actually votes.

"Postmenopausal zest" is as well documented and as anticipated as puberty. Women in their fifties—free from pregnancy, menstruation, and birth control—are regarded as sexpots and envied for their wild and free libidos. "Wine and women," as the saying goes, "get better with age."

Every man and woman remembers exactly where they were the moment they heard that the Equal Rights Amendment passed. The President addressed the nation on the night of that victory and said, "Americans didn't know what we were missing before today . . . until we could truly say that all people are created equal." The first man stood at her side with a tear running down his face.

The social-justice movement, formerly known as feminism, is now just *life*.

SECTION 3 TERMINOLOGY

Anarchy	Feminism	Market Economy
Bureaucracy	Free Market	Morality
Checks and Balances	Game Theory	Norms
Civil Liberties	GDP (Gross Domestic	Prescription
Civil Servants	Product)	Prudence
Command Economy	Glass Ceiling	Rights
Conservatism	Ideology	Socialism
Democracy	Invisible Hand	Society
Democratization	*Laissez-faire*	Third World
Econometrics	Liberty	Utopia

SECTION 3 DISCUSSION QUESTIONS

1. Is it simplistic to think that political theories can contribute to a better life?
2. It is quite easy to get conservatism and liberalism confused, in spite of the fact that they are quite different. But they have both changed over time. In what way?
3. Some say that we need socialism for a fair society. Why?
4. Can ideology be constructive, or does it just cause conflict?
5. Is liberalism a progressive ideology? Is it fair to describe liberalism as the "ideology of business"?
6. Is feminism a theory of its own, or is it the product of other ideologies?

 POLISCI SUPERSITE

Pearson Education Canada's PoliSci Supersite (**www.pearsoned.ca/polisci**) contains a set of text-specific pages for *Ideas, Interests, and Issues*. Visit the Supersite to access a list of relevant weblinks and interesting additional readings tailored to the content of each section.

Structures and Processes

SECTION SUMMARY

It is often said that the act of governing has become far more complex given the increased pace with which decisions must be made, the tangle of domestic and international regulations that have to be navigated to protect legislation and policies from challenge, and the increasing number of actors claiming a legitimate place at the decision-making table. Developing an understanding of modern politics and governing necessarily requires an understanding of the many actors, institutions, and processes involved. The lack of transparency that often accompanies political decision-making can make this a difficult endeavour. Yet such an understanding is critical, for it brings with it an ability not only to identify the various forces and actors that shape and influence political decision-making, but also when and how these actors and forces come into play.

The next set of readings identifies several key issues facing governments within modern democracies. The first reading, by J. Patrick Boyer, provides a critical evaluation of the principle of responsible government as it is practised in Canada's parliamentary system. Boyer's key concern, the lack of government accountability, is especially important in modern systems that claim to respond to the "will of the people" and which are often rocked by scandals. His premise, that the myths and fictions shrouding modern government in Canada provide the executive branch with a level of power that goes largely unchecked, speaks to the root causes of much of the political dissatisfaction currently displayed among citizens.

The relationship between the government and the courts is the focus of Janet Hiebert's article on equality rights within the Charter of Rights and Freedoms. The key debate, the right of a democratically elected legislature to legislate the "will of the people" versus the Supreme Court's right and, some might argue, duty to uphold the rights and freedoms outlined in the Charter, represents a very real example of the difficulties of bringing the separation of powers into practice. Reg Whitaker, on the other hand, addresses the changes that have taken place in one of the core institutions in democratic systems—political parties. Likening party strategy to the marketing of a product, Whitaker sees a "democratic deficit" resulting from a hollowing out of parties' ideological cores, in turn caused by the single-minded pursuit of electoral victory focused on the party brand and leader. He argues that political parties are an essential link between civil society and the state—because they perform functions that interest groups and social movements cannot—and that reforming the current political system is unlikely to be successful if political parties are not included in the process.

In an argument that speaks to some of the same concerns as Whitaker's, John Hannigan highlights the policy-making process and the forces at play in that arena. Governments are under competing pressures, on the one hand, to encourage economic investment in their urban spaces, and on the other hand, to protect urban and national spaces from foreign investment challenges. The "global entertainment economy" provides an important example of the challenges facing modern governments—in a move to revitalize downtown cores, policy decisions can result in communities dominated by "foreign brands" with little or no connection to the local population. In this respect, "glocalization" refers to the attempt to mitigate the universalizing tendencies of global enterprises on local environments. Policy choices, particularly those that have a direct impact on community life, are of particular concern in modern politics.

The political system is just that—a *system*, made up of various parts that must work together to function efficiently. And like any system of parts, a malfunction in one area is felt throughout. Just as important, however, is the degree to which the various parts of that system work together to perform the task at hand, which in a political system is to make decisions regarding the allocation of both goods and values—that is, decisions regarding what we can access, and importantly, who has that access.

Responsible Government Won and Lost: Parliamentarians Play-Act Their Accountability Roles

J. PATRICK BOYER*

*J. Patrick Boyer, Progressive Conservative Member of Parliament for Etobicoke (1984–1993), is Adjunct Professor at the University of Guelph.

Getting to Parliament, newly elected MPs are often shocked to find that on a functional level we do not have responsible government. Before I was first elected in 1984 I'd spent years training and preparing to participate in an accountable parliamentary process as the representative of the 100,000 citizens in my district, but I discovered there simply were no effective means by which to do so. My experience was no aberration. For most MPs, getting to Parliament Hill is like going to play hockey in an arena but finding no ice to skate on. In recent decades many MPs on both sides of the House have given vent, often in acute frustration and occasionally with considerable eloquence, to this sense of futility. It's even a bit ominous because the historical conditions that first gave rise to responsible government in Canada seem so familiar in our present circumstances. You start to wonder if history doesn't repeat itself.

Consider, for example, that in the early 1800s government was run by a small group of the powerful and privileged, or what is called an oligarchy. As confident in their own plans as they were arrogant in their use of power, these colonial leaders paid little heed to elected representatives in the legislature, and didn't really need to. By about 1815 demands for reform began to build. By the 1830s our expanding Loyalist colonies of British North America, increasingly outgrowing the forms of overseas government laid down at the close of the American Revolution, were growing less content to be ruled from above by a local oligarchy. As grievances piled up, reform movements developed. More people began expressing an impatient desire to gain local control over local affairs.

The British government in London neglected this pressure. The oligarchy gave only token attention to petitions, resolutions, practical grievances and real problems. (Is the picture looking familiar?) For its part the government seemed focused instead on its international trade agenda. The economy was globalizing. Britain's rise as an industrial power meant the world wanted its manufactured products, not just access to its colonial markets controlled under the older mercantilist trading system. After the American Revolution the remnant British North American colonies were being marginalized, losing their relative importance in the new patterns of world trade. In matters of governance the creaking colonial system continued to operate almost as a matter of habit, and Britain was largely content to keep things as they were, which meant supporting an increasingly unpopular political system. (Does this not seem to be echoing across the years too?)

The parallels don't end there. Back then the colonial assemblies represented the people but did not fully control either law making or public finances, and reformers felt these important roles should be taken up more rigorously and responsibly; they even wrote about the absence of accountability in publications of the day. Some main sources of government revenue were not under the control of elected representatives. Their enacted laws were often revised by the Cabinet ministers, vetoed by the governor or set aside for consideration by the overseas imperial authorities. Government was not responsible—or accountable—to the elected assemblies, and the constituency representatives complained, then as today, about being as impotent as the people they represented.

Real power lay in the hands of the small governing executive, an oligarchy in each colonial province called, for example, the "Council of Twelve" in Nova Scotia, the "Chateau Clique" in Quebec and the "Family Compact" in Ontario. The situation was not dissimilar in other British North American colonies such as Newfoundland, Prince Edward Island, Vancouver Island and British Columbia. Each colony faced particular issues and unique grievances, but sooner or later all roads led back to the same central problem of the unaccountable exercise of power by those in positions of privilege. Elected members in the legislative assemblies, weak against the inertia of a solidly planted establishment, expressed frustration over being ineffectual and sought to expose the hollowness of these nominal institutions of representative democracy. As decades passed it grew clearer that little could be achieved to respond to people's needs until these self-reinforcing oligarchies had been dislodged, or at least made to govern in some accountable fashion. The battle to gain responsible government was under way.

In Nova Scotia, Quebec (Canada East) and Ontario (Canada West) moderate reform parties emerged under strong leaders such as Joseph Howe, Louis Lafontaine and Robert Baldwin pushing politically for responsible government. Others, such as Louis-Joseph Papineau and William Lyon Mackenzie, sought swifter changes to the shortcomings and abuses of the existing system, leading armed rebellions in 1837 to overthrow the oligarchy by force. After British soldiers suppressed this Canadian revolution-in-the-making, Lord Durham was quickly dispatched from the Home Office in London to figure out what the devil was wrong in the colonies.

Given that ministers in government were not paying much attention to the people's elected representatives in the legislature, Durham recommended making them live together under one roof. Then they'd be forced to talk together, listen, debate, answer, argue and explain. There were to be other benefits to Durham's forced marriage of Cabinet and legislature. Elected representatives could no longer just give fiery speeches atop a country stump or in a village hall, or to one another in the echoing legislative chamber, but would now have to address their sharp complaints directly to those wielding power. Ministers of the Crown, by the same token, could no longer make decisions or set policies without facing directly those who might criticize and even improve them. Moreover, by imposing a new rule that ministers themselves had to be chosen from among the members of the legislature, ministers and members would now share a common footing; they would moderate one another, a process that institutionalized accountability and ensured more focused responsibility in providing peace, order and good government.

By 1848, with Durham's proposal implemented in a new Constitution enacted by Britain's Parliament, responsible government was in full swing in Canada East, Canada West and Nova Scotia. Within the decade it had also been gained by Britain's other eastern colonies: Prince Edward Island, New Brunswick and Newfoundland. This plan for responsible government was carried forward into the new Canadian Constitution in 1867. Other provinces that subsequently joined Confederation operated on the same plan.

The theory of responsible government is one thing; the present-day operation of government in Canada, quite another. It would be overly dramatic to say that responsible government in Canada has collapsed, but there is very little remaining to actually support it. To come to grips with the absence of accountability in the way Parliament works, not in theory but in practice, it is instructive to begin with some of the myths, fictions and misconceptions pertaining to governing doctrines. Perhaps four of the greatest myths are the following:

Myth #1: Accountability is enhanced because power is divided between different levels of government.

Myth #2: The re-election of a government shows that people endorse it.

Myth #3: MPs go to Ottawa to run the country.

Myth #4: General elections give the winning party a mandate to govern.

Let's consider each in turn to see how our actual government system has become shrouded behind these misconceptions and myths.

Myth #1: Accountability is enhanced because power is divided between different levels of government.

Jurisdictional clarity, which is a precondition for accountability, and which is represented in our Constitution by the division of powers between the national and provincial governments, no longer exists in Canada today.

. . . In the case of the Canada Infrastructure Works Program—not to mention in the more challenging areas of health, transportation, security, environment, trade, labour and social services—when it comes to figuring out who is responsible for government spending, the buck stops nowhere; the result is that *accountability is impossible*. Over time, combining a parliamentary system with our federal system, which formally has two levels of government (national and provincial) and operationally has three (national, provincial and local), actually fragmented jurisdictional accountability, to the point where it has been lost completely. Seldom in all my years around government did I find anyone who said, "I did that, I'm the one responsible." Instead it was invariably, "I'll have to consult my advisors on this." When it comes to the way our government works today, no one really knows who is doing what, or who is responsible.

Myth #2: The re-election of a government shows that people endorse it.

The Canadian electoral system does not accurately measure voter support. Winning an election does not mean that a party is supported by a majority of the population; nor can the victory be cited as evidence that the public approves of the party's style of governing.

Our electoral system is dysfunctional in terms of its ability to translate levels of popular support for different parties across the country into a comparable ratio of seats in Parliament. Because the system was designed to determine elections fought between only two parties, it has been out of date since the 1920s when the country moved from a two-party to a multiparty system. Yet privilege and inertia have kept this defective system in place, which is just one more reason why many Canadians are increasingly disowning the electoral process and the distorted results it generates.

Our country does not speak with one voice, but is divided into some 300 constituencies. Within these constituencies, or ridings, those who are elected often assume office with only a plurality, not a majority, of the votes cast by people living there. A plurality just means getting more votes than any other candidate, which is all it takes to win. Typically, four, five or even six candidates run in each riding. The result is that many MPs go to Ottawa with only a minority of voters having cast ballots for them. For example, when I was elected to Parliament in 1984, it was with 44 percent of the popular vote; when I was re-elected in 1988, it was again with 44 percent of the popular vote; when I was defeated in 1993, it was still with a mid-40s mark of popular vote. Whether I won—or lost—depended not on the accuracy of a representative electoral system, but on the relative fates and fortunes of the numerous other candidates also in the field. Although the majority of voters in my riding of Etobicoke-Lakeshore did not vote for me, there I was in Parliament, voting for the GST, for borrowing bills, for free trade, for Meech Lake. When I looked around the Commons at the 294 other elected "representatives," I saw a number of MPs from all parties who won with considerably narrower victories and even lower pluralities than mine.

The second Chrétien Liberal government, with its "huge majority" of seats in the Commons, took office having won only 38 percent of the popular vote. In 2000 Jean Chrétien and the Liberals won their third majority in a row, with the support of a minority of the electorate—42 percent of the popular vote. Nevertheless, the Liberals secured 172 of the 301 seats in the Commons, or 57 percent of the seats. Holding a majority of seats gives the appearance of a majority government because of the distorting hall-of-mirrors effect of our antiquated (though much tinkered with) electoral system. The reality, however, is that the levels of representation in our national legislative assembly are not an accurate reflection of the levels of voter support, of citizens' considered electoral conclusions.

So once again we discover that we do not have "representative government" in Canada and that our political superstructure, along with the laws and institutions it brings into being, rests upon shaky supports.

Myth #3: MPs go to Ottawa to run the country.

It is *not* Parliament's role to run the country. That's what the government does.

In the overall structure of Canadian government, the primary role of Parliament is to provide accountability in the way government is being run. If people (including MPs) don't know what government is really doing, it is a measure of how greatly Parliament has failed to shed light on the proper object of its attention.

Unfortunately there is confusion here because many people *think* that Parliament is the government. Even many MPs think and act this way with embarrassing frequency. The bleak truth about the role of MPs in Canada is that—and I'm speaking as someone who once was one—their main task ends the very night they are elected. That's when their aggregated numbers determine which party, and which small group within that party, will form the government. Having then served their leadership-selection function, MPs are kept busy and generally out of trouble for several years with highly public make-work projects until it's time for the party's leaders to again work MPs up into a state of partisan fervour sufficient, the leaders hope, to win another election.

Perhaps the distinction between the government and Parliament can best be illustrated by comparing Cabinet ministers in Parliament to a hand in a glove. The fact that one fits inside the other, so that they move as one and even function together, does not mean they are the same thing. Because our MPs and government leaders (the prime minister and Cabinet ministers) are combined institutionally within the legislative assembly, the hand is in the glove. This reality, and the appearance of it, contributes to the confusion of roles. It is the government that runs the country, and it is the job of Parliament to hold that government to account. Today, however, Parliament is failing to perform its primary role. Parliament, in fact, is no longer an institution of representative democracy, but has instead become a *government institution*. The elected representatives of the people do not hold the government to account, but rather function as extensions of the government itself, and generally are satisfied and proud to do so. Canadian legislatures do perform important roles in recruitment and education, for it is through the legislative chamber that new people are constantly drawn into government service, and it is also from MPs that a stream of publications, speeches and public-service advertisements flows to the public. Yet neither of these functions has much to do with holding government accountable. They are, if anything, just the opposite: a measure of how far and in how many ways our national legislature has devolved into little more than an operating extension of government—its recruitment office and public relations bureau.

Some political scientists add that Parliament performs a legitimizing role. By this they mean that when the government has decided to do something, it may appear more acceptable to the country or to the international community if Parliament enacts a law or passes a resolution endorsing it. Legitimacy is extremely important for a government because if the people (and the governments of other countries) believe someone is legitimately in power, or is acting with the endorsement of the country's principal democratic institution, they will obey even if they don't agree. Again, however, according legitimacy to a government is in many important respects the very antithesis of holding it accountable.

Myth #4: General elections give the winning party a mandate to govern.

The "mandate theory," even in the best of circumstances, was never more than a convenient constitutional fiction.

Powerful governments have long promoted a doctrine of parliamentary democracy which holds that once elected by virtue of winning the most seats in a general election, regardless of the size of the party's popular vote, the government has a mandate to deal with any issue that comes up during the life of that Parliament. Most political scientists and media commentators also operate within this accepted view and have, along with many compliant politicians, reinforced its popularity by their teachings, commentaries and behaviour. This doctrine makes sense as a practical approach to the many details and issues that can never be aired and debated, let alone anticipated, in an election campaign. It nevertheless enshrines a very bold fiction in a country that operates with the theory of being a representative parliamentary democracy: it is one of the major reasons why Canadian governments have lost credibility and Canadian legislatures are generally viewed with disrespect, even by many who are members of them.

To assert that a government can go to war, amend the country's constitution or reverse a whole pattern of trade policies or immigration programs without ever talking about such courses of action in its election campaign is to stretch the mandate doctrine further than is reasonable in a parliamentary democracy. Yet each of these has happened in Canada. To brazenly reverse aspects of the mandate—clear promises made by the political party that won voters' endorsement during the campaign—such as freezing prices and wages (as Prime Minister Trudeau did, although he'd pledged he wouldn't) or cancelling the acquisition of nuclear-powered submarines (as Prime Minister Mulroney did, even though he'd said his government would buy them) or continuing the GST and the free trade treaty (as Prime Minister Chrétien has, despite ardently campaigning against both) stretches the doctrine to the point of meaninglessness, and, not surprisingly, the government loses its authority and legitimacy. If prime ministers shrug with indifference, so will citizens.

People reasonably understand that some issues not addressed in an election campaign may later emerge and influence the stated positions of the party in office. Most Canadians also accept that the government basically governs as it must, and even as it chooses, provided it can maintain majority support in the Commons. The mandate doctrine itself, however, is increasingly untenable. Many Canadians are now prepared to challenge it by declaring that a mandate does not empower a government to deal with any and all issues or crises that arise over its term in office, especially if those issues were never discussed in the previous election campaign. All political parties campaign on the basis of some program; the party that forms the government may even try to implement part of it! Yet many Canadians have grown increasingly skeptical about the election promises of parties right across the political spectrum, based on practice and performance. Part of the reason for this shift is that we understand an election is no longer principally an accountability session. Elements of renewal and accountability assuredly remain part of an election, but only a part.

To reveal the different ways a majority government mandate can cover vastly different practices and policies, just contrast the two Liberal majority governments, both headed by Pierre Trudeau, elected in 1974 and 1980. When the Liberals won a convincing majority in the 1974 general election, we saw how the parliamentary theories about an electoral mandate camouflaged the actual practices of the government that had received the public's "blank cheque" to govern. Prime Minister Trudeau, suggests Richard Gwyn in his biography of him, "interpreted a majority victory as a mandate to goof off." When the Conservatives, led by Joe Clark, defeated the Liberals in May 1979, Marc Lalonde, a principal minister in the Trudeau Cabinet, looked back bleakly and saw no significant achievement of his government in many portfolios, especially the economic ones. "It was quite clear in our minds that if we came back, it would have to mean something," Lalonde later explained in a 1982 interview.

Back in power following the 1980 election, the Liberals displayed a newfound conviction, according to authors Robert Sheppard and Michael Valpy, that Ottawa "must reassert itself in a number of key fields—energy, regional economic development, fiscal transfers and constitutional reform." The revived Trudeau government soon "embarked on a new age of confrontational politics—competitive rather than co-operative federalism." In the spring of 1980, the same writers said, Pierre Trudeau was "probably wielding more raw prime ministerial power than any of his predecessors. He had a majority government and was facing a dispirited opposition . . . his caucus and party were beholden to him for leading them out of the wilderness; and . . . his few promises in the winter campaign effectively gave him a free hand to pursue the national interest in his own fashion."

This gap between what leaders say during campaigns and then do in office is not a uniquely Liberal phenomenon. After the Progressive Conservatives won a huge majority government in 1984, Prime Minister Mulroney used his "licence to govern" to initiate a free trade treaty with the United States, thereby reversing the historic position of the Conservative Party and his own position during his successful PC leadership campaign, when he had made specific statements opposing "continentalism." His government soon began to get into real trouble on this issue, "not because they had promised more than they had delivered," observed pollster and author Michael Adams, "but because they had delivered more than they had promised, namely the free trade agreement with the United States." Free trade, which had not been mentioned during the 1984 election campaign and thus could not in any sense be considered part of the people's mandate given to the Mulroney Conservatives, consequently became the central issue of the 1988 election campaign.

These important policy reversals by Liberal and Progressive Conservative governments show how, at a theoretical and policy level, the ballot box is not necessarily an effective mechanism for ensuring accountability—at least not if one examines the correlation between election campaign promises and subsequent government actions. This flip-flop approach has become endemic in recent decades—on such matters as new military helicopters, repeal of the GST and renegotiation of the free trade treaty—a discrepancy between promise and performance that cannot be ignored as a factor contributing to the decline in the credibility of our political leaders and a growing embarrassment about our governmental processes.

These four political myths or constitutional fictions are no longer believable in the face of the reality of Parliament's structural operations and performance record. Parliament has lost credibility and relevance not only among most Canadians, but also with senior civil servants and many highly frustrated MPs. Parliament has turned into a scene of bittersweet theatre, sadly incapable of being accountable even unto itself. Does this have consequences for Canadians? Unfortunately, and sometimes tragically, the answer is yes. Nowhere is the increasing irrelevance of Parliament, as well as the government's tendency to ignore or overstep its mandate, more evident than in the realm of military and defence policy. The same accountability issues relevant to any area of government apply to the Canadian military too, except that the consequences of incompetence and unaccountability are more serious because "mistakes" may risk the lives of Canadians in uniform and the lives of others. Accordingly, in a system of responsible government decisions regarding the Canadian Armed Forces should call for the very highest standards of accountability.

When I was parliamentary secretary for the Department of National Defence in 1992, in Washington one morning driving with Defence Minister Marcel Masse to a meeting at the Pentagon, we learned that External Affairs Minister Barbara McDougall had announced Canada would send a further 1,200 soldiers overseas for the UN peacekeeping mission in the former Yugoslavia. We were reading faxed copies of a newspaper report. There had been no consultation, not even an inquiry to ascertain the availability of military personnel for this mission—at least none that either of us knew anything about. Certainly there had been no debate about it in Parliament, let alone a vote by Parliament to authorize and support the deployment. Similarly, during the summer of 1990 when the Iraqi forces of Saddam Hussein invaded Kuwait, Prime Minister Mulroney announced, not before the House of Commons but into a television camera, that Canadian ships, aircraft and military personnel were being dispatched to the Persian Gulf. Canadians learned the news of this major commitment as a fait accompli, a military mission overseas, undebated and unauthorized by Parliament.

The ascendancy of prime ministerial power at the expense of parliamentary accountability has transformed the country in profound ways, as these matters concerning the deployment of the Canadian Forces overseas demonstrate. Colonel (Ret) John English explained to researchers for the *underground royal commission*, "Over the years we got in this business of deploying peacekeeping forces by order-in-council or by Cabinet decision—that they will go over and there will be no parliamentary debate called. There will be no debate within the Canadian public at large." A succession of Canadian prime ministers—William Lyon Mackenzie King, John Diefenbaker, Lester Pearson, Pierre Trudeau, Brian Mulroney, Jean Chrétien—has sought to play a major role on the international stage; these leaders have appropriated for themselves through the Privy Council Office a significant role in relation to foreign policy and defence matters. "No minister likes to mess with the food on a prime minister's plate," observed John Dixon, who served as Kim Campbell's senior advisor when she was defence minister, "so he stands back to let the prime minister run foreign policy and defence. Meanwhile, the prime minister rightly thinks his minister is running the Defence Department. So there is a deep confusion that has been institutionalized in our structure of government."

This confusion has only been increased by the absence of Parliament from any decision-making or review process with respect to foreign policy and defence matters. While it is not Parliament's role to run the government, it is Parliament's job to air issues, debate different considerations, approve the annual budgets of the Defence and Foreign Affairs ministries, vote to ratify treaties and authorize military involvement overseas. So why doesn't it? The rise of "partyism" in Parliament means that our national legislature now functions more as an arena for team sport than as a centre for contending issues and serious debate on legitimate differences of policy. Party solidarity, considered a prime virtue in this setting at all times, is especially valued and enforced in times of crisis and international confrontation. The government's instinct to show solidarity with our allies in collective security arrangements when a global crisis hits is then refracted back into its control over Parliament. Why give hostility and dissent a chance to display itself on the floor of the House of Commons when we want to show unanimity and solidarity of purpose?

With respect to these fundamental military matters, Parliament no longer plays its historic and proper role, is no longer an instrument for accountability on the national political scene or touching the affairs of state. Our country's original policy was that no Canadian in uniform could ever be sent beyond our borders without parliamentary authorization. The prime minister and ministers of defence and foreign affairs would have to justify such life-and-death policies to the people's elected representatives. For some even that seemed inadequate. When debating Canadian participation in the Boer War in 1899, for example, Sir Wilfrid Laurier suggested holding a national referendum on the question. At a minimum Parliament was always fully involved in authorizing war activity. In August 1914 Prime Minister Robert Borden interrupted his Muskoka vacation to summon Parliament, which debated and voted to declare war on Germany. The Borden government had, moreover, also been on the brink of holding a national referendum on going to war, but pulled back at the last moment—a hesitation in taking the matter directly to the people that Arthur Meighen, attorney general of Canada at the time and later Conservative Party leader and prime minister, came to openly regret. In 1939 Parliament, now under the leadership of Prime Minister Mackenzie King, again voted, following debate, upon a resolution for a declaration of war. However, when Canadian forces sailed in 1950 for Korea, they did so without the approval of Parliament; the Cabinet of Prime Minister St. Laurent, dispensing with the required parliamentary debate, merely issued an order-in-council as authorization. The limp excuse that Korea was a so-called "police action" by the United Nations, not a war, was already enough to persuade some folks that Parliament didn't have to be involved. Although it was not a "war," 27,000 Canadians served overseas under arms and over 800 died in the "action." From Wilfrid Laurier to Louis St. Laurent, the country had turned 180 degrees and a new pattern was set. Our prime ministers in the modern era came to think that Canadians should just trust them to do the right thing.

Thus it was Cabinet, not Parliament, that approved the decision to intervene in Somalia in October 1992. The mission was presented in the Commons during Question Period and to the media in press briefings as traditional peacekeeping, but it was not in any fashion like other United Nations military missions with which Canadians were familiar. The nature and purpose of the military's role, having been neither clarified nor endorsed by Parliament, was ambiguous and uncertain to those in the field, a situation that recurred in late 2001 and 2002 when Canadian troops were sent to Afghanistan in an cloud of uncertainty about their overall mission, and even about such matters as taking prisoners.

Our soldiers' experiences in Bosnia in the early 1990s highlight the problems encountered when accountability is avoided for long periods. Ambush greeted the Canadian soldiers who thought they had been sent on a peacekeeping mission. Hatred between different ethnic groups created deep and mean responses, and Canadians found themselves right in the middle. Even the seasoning gained from Canada's decades' long role in keeping peace between Turks and Greeks in Cyprus was no preparation for what the soldiers faced in Bosnia. Furthermore, silence on the home front covered this operation with a mask of unreality. Canadian soldiers, on the ground in a hot war, discovered no one in Ottawa was seriously accountable for what was unfolding. This examination of Parliament's role (or lack thereof) in military matters shows that the consequences of inaction, or action based on inaccurate or incomplete information, can be extremely serious. While the stakes are higher and the results of decisions more dramatic, the lack of accountability evident in both Parliament's and the government's attitude toward the Canadian Armed Forces is indicative of the way in which contemporary Canadian government operates in general.

In theory government is subject to a number of constraints. It must be accountable to an official Opposition in the House of Commons. It must enact new laws through Parliament. It is constitutionally obligated to meet Parliament every year, submit a budget and all spending estimates to Parliament annually and call a general election at least every five years. The government's laws and actions can be challenged in court and scrutinized by an independent judiciary. Provincial governments can balance Ottawa's broad power. All the while a competitive and often critical news media continually examines the government's exercise of power. Yet in reality, for every minute of reckoning achieved by Parliament, there are hours of non-accountability. For every law passed openly in Parliament, a dozen more are enacted inconspicuously by orders-in-council. For every budget items scrutinized, a thousand others are deemed approved unexamined. For every election held when the government's back is to the wall or its constitutional time limit of five years has run out, three more are self-servingly called at the moment most propitious to those who already hold power. Parliament, once central to expressing peoples' views on issues facing Canadians, has become an anachronism ever since this role was scooped out by government-hired public opinion pollsters, leaving the House of Commons a hollow chamber rather than a connector between Canadians and our government's policies and programs. Parliament's role in controlling government spending has been eviscerated, procedurally and behaviourally, step by step over the past 30 years, to the point where MPs no longer control the public purse strings either.

As citizens we no doubt conclude, the more we watch television or read newspaper accounts about the increasing role of lobbyists and interest groups and the ineffectiveness of our elected representatives, that our own chance to individually influence public decisions grows slimmer and more remote with each passing day. We do not have representative government so much as a system of government where representations are made behind closed doors and away from any mechanisms of accountability. So it's hardly a surprise that, as reported by Leger Marketing in April 2002, 69 percent of Canadians think that the federal government is corrupt. Some citizens have expressed their growing dissatisfaction with the decision making of elected and appointed officials by suggesting that government should hold community forums and town hall meetings as a regular part of the ongoing governing process. People do not advance such alternatives unless they feel dissatisfied with the existing arrangements. Those who make these suggestions are trying to improve a system evidently in need of an overhaul. Others just boycott it altogether, staying away from polling stations on election day.

The power of Parliament to monitor the government's activities and provide accountability to the Canadian people once came about through the mechanism of approving the government's spending program, voting for taxes, approving of borrowing, questioning Cabinet ministers and enacting or amending the laws that the government introduced in Parliament. Along the way there was debate, sometimes humour, and invariably deep differences of opinion. Today these parliamentary powers are exercised formally but seldom substantively. However, in considering the ephemeral nature of governmental accountability in our Canadian context, it would he wrong to focus on Parliament alone; Parliament was once our most important national political institution, but not the only one. It functions within a matrix of institutions that connect and interact. One's role picks up where another's leaves off. If Parliament no longer exercises much effective power, it is not because power has evaporated, but because it has flowed and been taken elsewhere. Each governmental institution in our capital and across the country is part of a larger picture we need to see more clearly for accurate perception of our functioning realities.

Most Canadians believe, and are in fact encouraged to think, that the MP is our connector. We believe that MPs, individually and collectively, make the system work, especially in terms of accountability. Isn't that also what we teach our children? Don't we say the meaning of responsible government—the executive held to account—is all about answering to the people's elected representatives in Parliament? The truth is, the Parliament of Canada is no longer a seriously functioning part of the accountability equation. As an MP I was no connector. I was a pushed and battered shock absorber between the needs of the people I represented and the predetermined plans of a tightly controlled top-down government. In my case it was the Mulroney government because I was elected as a Tory; had I run and been elected as a Grit, I'd have experienced the same phenomenon under the Trudeau or Chrétien governments. This is not a partisan issue; it is a parliamentary issue. Until you've been there to experience this, you cannot hope to know with just how much excruciating humiliation parliamentarians are forced to absorb and internalize our governing system's deepest contradictions—while seeking to salvage a measure of human dignity with a broken smile toward constituents and into the cameras.

During its cross-country interviews the *underground royal commission* encountered many MPs and former MPs who had similar views about their experiences in Parliament. Reg Alcock, Liberal MP for Winnipeg-South, was both perceptive and clear:

> *The House actually has enormous authority, but at certain key points, who exercises that authority is controlled by one person—the prime minister. We need to*

*separate that to allow the House to function as a body to demand accountability
from the government. That's what it has to be.*

In a similar way George Baker, a Newfoundland Liberal MP for some 30 years before
being appointed to the Senate in 2002, pointed out that once MPs are elected to the House
they face "a situation where a member has to be in good standing with the party even to
get on Question Period. A member has to be in good standing with the party leader and the
whip in order to even speak in the House of Commons. Where does this leave members of
Parliament?" Former Conservative Cabinet minister John Crosbie was candid too. He said
an MP can be "a good representative of their area but as members of a party influencing
policy, what a government actually does, rather than settling up this man's unemployment
claim or this woman's rent problem, they basically don't have much influence. They are a
very frustrated group."

Having been in Parliament, I share the contradictory feelings of Canadians who are
disenchanted with the way our country's system of government works, but are also aware
of so much that is good and of permanent value in it. The problem? Our democratic theory is premised on citizens and citizens' elected representatives playing an active and
informed role in the political system, but theory is not matched by opportunity. Instead,
MPs and the people they represent are relegated to the periphery of political life by government officials who prefer to say, in effect, "Just trust us." In this atmosphere it's most
beneficial for members to portray themselves as ombudsmen for their constituents and
lean heavily toward service and problem solving and speaking up for local concerns, all
helpful for getting re-elected. That's how Canadians evidently perceive them too.

For instance, a 1999 Environics poll asked respondents to rank the most important
functions of MPs from a list provided. "Representing local concerns to Parliament" was
chosen by 42 percent; 24 percent said it was "solving constituents' problems"; 22 percent
picked "providing their constituents with information on government?" Only nine percent
said the fourth role, "supporting the objectives of their political party," should rank as most
important. Even more revealing is that none of the "most important" roles identified in the
question had anything to do with holding government accountable or scrutinizing spending. The pollsters, being realists, didn't even bother to ask. They, too, know that what we
teach the children about responsible government is not the way it really works. On good
days the most that happens is that MPs play-act at accountability.

With this evaluation of the institutional and behavioural problems facing those who
represent the people of Canada in mind, it makes sense to now step back a little further, or
rise above the parliamentary fray a little higher, and see the nature of just who we are, the
Canadian citizens that our MPs endeavour to represent.

From Equality Rights to Same-Sex Marriage: Parliament and the Courts in the Age of the Charter

JANET L. HIEBERT*

*__Janet L. Hiebert__ is an Associate Professor in the Department of Political Studies at Queen's University.

Should the definition of marriage change to include same-sex unions? This issue has prompted more controversy than any other area of social policy affected by Canada's decision in 1982 to adopt the Canadian Charter of Rights and Freedoms. Lesbians and gay men argue that no principled reason exists to deny them the opportunity to marry, and they are confident that the Supreme Court of Canada will soon rule that a legal prohibition on same-sex marriage is unconstitutional. Yet a sizeable and increasingly vocal segment of the Canadian population remains staunchly opposed to the idea of gay marriage. Many believe that the moral and social norms for Canadian society are, and should remain, the heterosexual family and repudiate claims that equality under the Charter must embrace the legal recognition of same-sex relationships. Other critics accept that same-sex partners should be permitted to legally register their relationships if they so wish, but oppose same-sex marriage, preferring instead the idea of a civil union.

Not only does the prospect of same-sex marriage represent what many critics consider to be a moral crisis of deep proportions, it also raises important questions about the respective roles of, and relationship between, Parliament and the courts. Should Parliament lead or follow judicial pronouncements when the Charter affects important matters of social policy? If the Supreme Court of Canada declares that the prohibition on same-sex marriage is unconstitutional, can Parliament establish civil unions as an alternative to marriage? How should the federal government proceed if it encounters, as it well might, a conflict between judicial judgment and the will of a majority of Parliament? Is use of the notwithstanding clause an acceptable means to resolve this disagreement?

At the time the Charter was included in the Canadian Constitution, few could have anticipated that within a period of scarcely more than 20 years, courts would outlaw social policy distinctions that deny same-sex partners benefits given to heterosexual couples and would determine whether the definition of marriage must change to embrace same-sex unions. In the lead-up to the Charter, lesbian and gay activists in Canada had little reason to look either to Parliament or to the judiciary as allies in their quest for social reforms. At the time the pattern of political behaviour was steadfast refusal to acknowledge or redress claims that discrimination occurs not only from blatant prejudicial treatment of lesbians and gay men, but also from an exclusive reliance on heterosexuality as the basis for determining the legal recognition of spouses and families, benefits and responsibilities. Legislation was not the only source of discrimination. Employers and landlords could discriminate against lesbians and gay men with relative impunity. Judicial relief was rarely forthcoming. Courts and tribunals regularly ruled that since legislation did not conceive of lesbians and gay men as constituting families or spouses, and since human rights codes did not identify sexual orientation as a prohibited ground of discrimination, they had no reason to conclude that differential treatment based on sexual orientation was discriminatory.

When the Charter was first drafted it was extremely difficult to anticipate whether and how it would offer lesbians and gay men protection from discrimination. The equality rights in the Charter do not specifically mention sexual orientation as a prohibited ground of discrimination, because the Charter's political drafters were not prepared to include it. Jean Chrétien, who was justice minister at the time, made it clear that although the federal Liberal government was not willing to include sexual orientation as a prohibited ground for discrimination, it was aware that courts might one day interpret equality as if the Charter did preclude this form of discrimination. The equality rights in section 15 (1) of the Charter stipulate:

> *Every individual is equal before and under the law and has the right to the equal protection and equal benefit of the law without discrimination and, in particular, without discrimination based on race, national or ethnic origin, colour, religion, sex, age, or mental or physical disability.*

Lesbian and gay activists did not initially see the Charter as a likely tool for their liberation from social, political and legal discrimination. It is hardly surprising that many at the time doubted the prudence of relying on a legal rights tradition that previously had not questioned the legitimacy of discriminatory treatment of lesbians and gay men. Moreover, many lesbians and gay men had, and continue to have, misgivings about reliance on the Charter's paradigm of liberal rights, particularly those who have no desire to construe their relationships in terms that are analogous to heterosexual families. Nevertheless, many lesbian and gay activists are relying on Charter equality claims as an important component in their strategies for legislative and social reforms.

Within a few years of equality rights coming into force (this was delayed three years to give governments an opportunity to review and redress existing discrimination in legislation), a steady stream of lower court and tribunal decisions revealed sympathy for the position that section 15 of the Charter should be interpreted to protect against discrimination on the basis of sexual orientation. In 1993 the Supreme Court of Canada indicated for the first time that it might also be receptive to this idea. Two years later the Supreme Court unanimously declared in *Egan and Nesbit v. Canada* that section 15 prohibits discrimination on the basis of sexual orientation, despite the absence of any explicit reference to sexual orientation in the Charter. In the Court's view, sexual orientation is analogous to the prohibited forms of discrimination that the equality rights in the Charter address. At issue in *Egan* was the legitimacy of the federal *Old Age Security Act,* which provided an allowance for the spouse of a pensioner who was already receiving a guaranteed income supplement. Both entitlements were based on need. Spouse was defined and interpreted by administrators as meaning persons of the opposite sex. Consequently when James Egan applied for the monthly spousal allowance on behalf of his same-sex partner, his application was denied because his partner did not satisfy the definition of spouse.

Although the Court ruled that in principle the Charter's equality rights prohibit discrimination on the basis of sexual orientation, not all judges believed that the denial of benefits in this case constituted discrimination. Four judges ruled that the denial did not violate equality, arguing that the policy distinction between heterosexual and same-sex partners is "firmly anchored in the biological and social realities that heterosexual couples have the unique ability to procreate." Five judges disagreed, ruling that the "opposite-sex" restriction in the definition of spouse in the *Old Age Security Act* violates equality, emphasizing the importance of protecting human dignity by according equal concern, respect and consideration to all. But one of the five concluded that this infringement should be upheld under section 1 of the Charter as a reasonable limit on equality, suggesting that parliament should be given time to determine how to extend social benefits within the context of newly recognized social relationships. This view, when combined with the four judges who did not think equality had been violated, constituted a narrow majority that upheld the constitutional validity of the legislation.

Thus the decision conveyed mixed messages about whether and when governments must extend social policy benefits to same-sex partners. On the one hand, it confirmed that discrimination on the basis of sexual orientation violates equality rights in the Charter. Yet, on the other hand, it held out the possibility that some judges were willing to accept the denial of benefits to same-sex partners, either because they did not believe this denial constituted discrimination, or because parliament should be given more time to redress the problem. The *Egan* decision was interpreted by federal and provincial departments and ministers as removing the immediacy for legislative reforms and therefore reinforcing the status quo.

The turning points for compelling governments to change legislation so as not to deny lesbians or gay men protection or benefits given to heterosexual spouses were the back-to-back decisions of *Vriend v. Alberta* in 1998 and *M v. H* in 1999. These decisions made it clear that a majority of the Supreme Court was not willing to countenance continued legislative inaction. At issue in *Vriend* was the termination of employment of a laboratory assistant in an Alberta college after the college learned that he was gay. After his termination, Mr. Vriend attempted to file a complaint with the Alberta Human Rights Commission but was advised that this was not possible because the province's human rights legislation, the *Individual's Rights Protection Act* (IRPA), did not include sexual orientation as a prohibited ground for discrimination. The Supreme Court unanimously ruled that his equality rights were violated, suggesting that the Alberta government's decision not to include sexual orientation in the IRPA was tantamount to "condoning or even encouraging discrimination against lesbians and gay men," and that it conveyed a "sinister message" that lesbians and gay men are less worthy than others. The Court interpreted the IRPA so that it would henceforth include this protection, a remedy many found controversial because it is tantamount to the judiciary acting as if it were the legislature.

The next and most significant Supreme Court ruling in terms of putting pressure on governments to introduce broad legislative reforms was *M v. H*. At issue was the failure of Ontario's *Family Law Act* to recognize same-sex relationships in its processes for resolving property and other issues arising from the dissolution of family relationships. The act utilized a heterosexual definition of spouse. The Supreme Court ruled 8–1 that this definition of spouse violated equality in a manner that could not be justified as a reasonable limit on equality.

The importance of *M v. H* for prompting significant and far-reaching legislative reforms stemmed from the Court's unambiguous statement that same-sex partners must be treated with the same degree of respect and recognition given to heterosexual spouses. The majority emphasized that the purpose of equality rights in the Charter is to "prevent the violation of essential human dignity and freedom through the imposition of disadvantage, stereotyping, or political or social prejudice" and to promote a society where all persons are recognized as "equally capable and equally deserving of concern, respect and consideration." Although the decision applied specifically to Ontario, Justice Iacobucci provided a warning, applicable to all governments, that the Court's ruling "may well affect numerous other statutes that rely upon a similar definition of the term 'spouse'." At the time of this decision, more than 360 federal and substantial numbers of provincial legislative provisions recognized relationships or conferred benefits where eligibility was based on a heterosexual definition of spouse.

Ottawa and a majority of the provinces have now passed legislation that extends most of the social policy benefits given to heterosexual couples to same-sex partners. In most jurisdictions, changes have come about only after courts have ruled that existing legislation is unconstitutional, and often have been attended by substantial controversy. Consider, for example, the federal government's response to the *M v. H* ruling, which was the *Modernization of Benefits and Obligations Act* (Bill C-23), introduced in February 2000. This omnibus legislation amended 68 statutes and covered 20 federal departments and agencies. The federal Liberal government tried to side-step a previous controversy that had emerged: should the term "spouse" be used to depict same-sex relationships? It did so by introducing a new term—"common-law partner"—that would include same-sex partners. The government also argued that it could respect the Charter by eliminating discrimination against same-sex partners and yet still preserve marriage as the privileged and exclusive domain of heterosexual spouses. Some critics argued that the legislation was deficient because it did not redefine marriage to include same-sex partners. But others, including many in Parliament, had the opposite reaction and argued that the legislation would alter the definition of marriage, a claim repeatedly denied by then justice minister Anne McLellan. The government eventually bowed to political pressure from the Canadian Alliance party and also from some Liberal members by agreeing to include a legislative preamble indicating that the legislative changes did not affect the traditional definition of marriage. This was not the first time the government has given into pressure to identify marriage as an exclusively heterosexual relationship. In 1999 the government supported a Reform Party motion that stated that marriage would remain the lawful union of one man and one woman to the exclusion of all others. That motion easily passed by a vote of 216–55. The overwhelming majority of Liberal MPs, including Jean Chrétien and Paul Martin, voted in favour.

When Parliament reconvened in September 2003, the Alliance Party tried unsuccessfully to obtain parliamentary approval for a motion that not only reaffirmed the traditional heterosexual understanding of marriage but also committed parliament to take "all necessary steps" to preserve this definition, which implied use of the unpopular notwithstanding clause. At the time of the motion, the federal government had promised to redefine marriage so as to include same-sex partners. This time the vote was extremely close, 137–132. It came moments after an earlier, failed attempt to amend the motion by removing the reference to "all necessary steps." The intent of this proposed amendment was to make it easier for more MPs to vote in favour of the reaffirmation of traditional marriage by removing the threat of having to use the notwithstanding clause to support this definition. Prime Minister Chrétien, who voted against the motion to retain a traditional, heterosexual definition of marriage, attributed his reversal on this issue to recognition that "society has evolved."

The question of whether the law on marriage must change remains the most significant issue yet to be resolved in terms of legislative treatment of lesbians and gay men. Under the constitutional division of powers, the federal parliament has authority over the legal capacity to marry while the provincial and territorial legislatures have authority over solemnization, which includes issuing licences. But the federal parliament has never enacted legislation that defines eligibility for marriage. Its only statements on this issue have come in the form of agreements to the motions discussed above. Thus, what has prevented same-sex partners from marrying has been a common law definition of marriage that is more than one century old and utilizes a heterosexual criterion for eligibility.

But as of the summer 2003, lesbians and gay men have been able to marry in two provinces—Ontario and British Columbia. This ability has arisen because the courts of appeal in these two provinces have ruled that the current prohibition on same-sex marriage is unconstitutional. A Quebec court agrees, and at the time of writing the case was before the province's Court of Appeal. The B.C. case, *Barbeau v. British Columbia (Attorney General),* did not immediately allow for same-sex marriages because the court suspended the effects of its judgment until July 2004 so that Parliament could legislate on this issue. But in June 2003 the Ontario Court of Appeal in *Halpern v. Canada (Attorney General)* declared a new definition of marriage, to take effect immediately in the province, which allows same-sex partners to marry. The B.C. court subsequently lifted its suspension, allowing same-sex partners in B.C. to also marry. In the remaining provinces, the earlier common law rule prevails, which prohibits same-sex marriage.

The Ontario ruling is controversial, both for its conclusion and its remedy. At the time of the judgment a parliamentary committee (Standing Committee on Justice and Human Rights) was about to embark on its report on whether and how the government should address the recognition of same-sex unions, after holding hearings across the country and listening to 467 witnesses. The majority of these, 59 percent (274), favoured extending equal marriage rights to same-sex couples, while 35.5 percent (166) opposed. Although the committee has garnered negative headlines that raise questions about whether some members' critical views on same-sex marriage are too entrenched to be influenced by testimony, the judicial decision to change the law before Parliament had completed its deliberations demonstrates contempt for Parliament. What further undermined Parliament was the federal government's attempt to secure a positive committee vote on NDP member Svend Robinson's motion to urge the government to accept the Ontario court ruling. As the vote was about to occur, the government suddenly altered the composition of its government members of the committee, replacing two members (one of whom was Derek Lee, who has expressed disagreement with the idea of same-sex marriage) with two new members who voted in favour of the motion. The vote resulted in a tie, which was resolved by the Liberal chair in favour of the motion.

The Chrétien government has now changed its position on same-sex marriage. It has decided not to appeal the Ontario ruling and has drafted legislation to change the definition of marriage so as to read: "Marriage, for civil purposes, is the lawful union of two persons to the exclusion of all others." The government has asked the Supreme Court to review its draft legislation. The Court is being asked to address three questions:

• Is the government's draft bill defining marriage within the exclusive legislative authority of the Parliament of Canada?

- If the answer to the above question is yes, is the capacity to marry to persons of the same sex consistent with the *Canadian Charter of Rights and Freedoms*?
- Does the freedom of religion guaranteed by the Charter protect religious officials from being compelled to perform a marriage between two persons of the same sex that is contrary to their religious beliefs?

What is most interesting about the reference questions is what the Court is not being asked to address. The Court is being asked whether the government's intention to change marriage to allow for same-sex unions is consistent with the Charter. It is hard to envisage any reason why the Court wouldn't affirm that parliament has the capacity to define marriage in these terms, since the constitutional division of powers gives the federal parliament authority over marriage. The real issue is whether a prohibition on same-sex marriage violates the Charter's equality rights. Although not asked to address this question, the Court in all likelihood will address it, since three courts have already declared that the prohibition on same-sex marriage violates the Charter and because the B.C. and Ontario courts of appeal have already changed the law in their provinces. What is also significant about the questions is that the Supreme Court is not being asked whether a civil union is an acceptable alternative to same-sex marriage. Many members of parliament and a substantial portion of the public prefer the concept of same-sex civil union to same-sex marriage.

In addition to the Charter dimension of the reference questions, there is also an important federalism aspect. By asking the Court if the federal government has exclusive authority over marriage, the government is in effect asking the Court to address whether the provinces can do anything that would interfere with the federal government's power to define who can marry. Three provincial governments (Alberta, Quebec and B.C.) have filed notices of intent to intervene in this reference case. Quebec has indicated it is not opposed to same-sex marriages but wants to preserve the concept of civil unions in Quebec. Alberta Premier Ralph Klein has stated publicly that his government would invoke the notwithstanding clause if necessary to prevent same-sex marriages in Alberta. This power gives Parliament and the provincial legislatures the ability to have legislation prevail for five-year renewable periods despite an inconsistency with a judicial interpretation of the Charter. But the notwithstanding clause would not give Klein power to prevent same-sex marriages in Alberta if the Supreme Court affirms that Ottawa has exclusive jurisdiction to define who can marry. This is because the notwithstanding clause does not apply to disagreements about the constitutional division of powers, it applies only to the Charter. What remains unclear is whether a province can exercise its authority for the solemnization of marriage so as to negate or frustrate the effect of how the federal parliament has defined marriage. Patrick Monahan, a noted constitutional scholar, states emphatically that a province's constitutional power to issue marriage licences cannot be used to frustrate federal law.

Both the government's decision not to appeal the *Halpern* ruling and its intent to pass legislation that recognizes same-sex marriages have been extremely controversial. The government faces deep and vocal divisions on this issue, unattended by the declining authority Jean Chrétien wields in the dwindling days of his leadership and the ambivalence expressed on this issue by his successor, Paul Martin. As of late August [2003], 50 of 171 Liberal MPs had indicated their intention to vote against the legislation as currently proposed. A newspaper poll conducted that month suggested that 126 of 301 MPs intended to vote against the same-sex marriage legislation. The vote on the September Alliance motion, which drew the support of more than 50 Liberal MPs, underscored just how seriously the governing party is divided on this issue. The government has indicated that it will wait for the Supreme Court's answer to its questions before introducing legislation in the House of Commons, which will be subject to a free vote. But since the Supreme Court will not hear the case until next spring [2004], and its ruling won't be known for some time after that, many within the Liberal party worry that the issue of same-sex marriage will become a serious political liability for Liberal MPs when they seek re-election, likely in spring 2004.

This opposition to same-sex marriage raises two important questions. One is, what will be the law on marriage if Parliament defeats the government's legislation and the Supreme Court indicates that a prohibition on same-sex marriage violates the Charter? If both events occur, Canada would temporarily have two different laws on marriage in play. Two provinces (Ontario and B.C.) would permit same-sex marriages, because courts have changed the common law definition. When Quebec's Court of Appeal rules on this issue, Quebec might become the third province to permit same-sex marriage. Lesbian and gay couples in other provinces will likely initiate Charter litigation, seeking a declaration from other provincial courts that the common law prohibition on marriage is unconstitutional. If the Supreme Court of Canada confirms that the prohibition on same-sex marriage is unconstitutional, provincial courts that have not yet ruled on this issue will likely take their lead from its opinion and the common law prohibition on same-sex marriage will gradually disappear throughout the country. This means that if Parliament is intent on preventing same-sex marriages from occurring, federal legislation will be required to define marriage as an exclusively heterosexual union. But this would likely require use of the notwithstanding clause, which is unpopular and considered by many to be an inappropriate way to resolve parliamentary/judicial disagreements.

The second question that arises in light of the conflict about same-sex marriage is, what, if anything, is a constitutionally valid alternative? Some who favour a traditional heterosexual definition of marriage believe that if Parliament were to establish civil unions for same-sex partners, it would not need to invoke the notwithstanding clause to retain a heterosexual definition of marriage. Their assumption is that the judiciary will accept a traditional definition of marriage under the Charter, as long as lesbians or gay men are permitted to register their relationship as a civil union. Although the reference decision may not shed light on this issue, it is important to remember that the Supreme Court has interpreted equality as requiring not only the equal benefit and effect of law, but also has stated that the law must confer equal dignity and respect. Although many have expressed profound differences on whether equality is violated by denying same-sex partners the opportunity to marry as long as they can enter into civil unions, the Supreme Court will be skeptical of any arrangement that has separate but equal implications, particularly in light of historical injustices perpetrated on minorities and sustained by this doctrinal approach. Thus, it seems unlikely that the Supreme Court will accept the constitutional validity of a two-tier structure that recognizes marriage for heterosexual spouses and civil-unions for same-sex partners (and also those heterosexual spouses who prefer this to marriage).

Another alternative that has been floated in this debate is the idea that Parliament should abandon authority for marriage altogether, and instead establish a national registry for civil unions. Under this model, marriage would only be conducted by religious organizations according to their beliefs and criteria, and would occur in addition to a civil union. But a large percentage of the Canadian population is not deeply religious. Many who are not religious might be offended by the idea that Parliament would no longer recognize secular marriage (even if existing marriages are protected or "grandparented"), particularly if they interpret this as diminishing the importance and legitimacy of their nonreligious marriages. This option received little support from those appearing before the parliamentary committee studying the issue of same-sex marriage. Moreover, the provinces may contest the idea that the federal Parliament has jurisdiction over civil unions. During the parliamentary committee hearings, a representative from the Canadian Bar Association advised the committee that the federal Parliament does not have jurisdiction to create a national registry of civil unions, If the provinces are recognized as having jurisdiction over civil unions, some provinces might oppose civil unions that apply to same-sex partners and, if challenged under the Charter, could invoke the notwithstanding clause.

Critics of same-sex marriage might take comfort from Paul Martin's indication that not only is he interested in alternatives to same-sex marriage, such as civil unions, but that once installed as leader he intends to revise the same-sex marriage legislation. Yet it is not obvious there are alternatives to same-sex marriage that will either be considered publicly acceptable or are considered constitutionally viable by Martin himself. As suggested above, the idea that marriage is delegated entirely to religious organizations will offend many who value and desire marriage but who are not deeply religious. As for the possibility of establishing civil unions for same-sex partners (while retaining a traditional definition of marriage for heterosexual spouses), this approach would likely require use of the notwithstanding clause if the Supreme Court continues to relate equality to human dignity and interprets equality as imposing an obligation that governments treat all persons as equally deserving of concern, respect and consideration. Martin has stated publicly that he is not prepared to proceed with an option that is inconsistent with the Supreme Court's interpretation of the Charter, and he therefore will not use the notwithstanding clause.

In the event that Parliament defeats the government's same-sex marriage legislation and the Supreme Court makes it clear that a prohibition on same-sex marriage is unconstitutional, it may be some time before Canadians know whether the Supreme Court considers a civil union to be a constitutionally valid alternative to marriage. That is, unless the Court is willing to be subject to accusations for being too activist by answering a question the government has not asked of it.

Many worry that the Charter provides a convenient refuge for politicians to avoid controversial issues, claiming a need to wait for courts to resolve the issue and then blaming judges for forcing them to pass controversial legislative changes. This hypothesis may explain prolonged government inaction to redress many other forms of legislative discrimination against lesbians and gay men. But it does not explain why the Chrétien government has now decided to legislate to allow for same-sex marriage. Had the Chrétien government genuinely wished to minimize or avoid unnecessary controversy, at least until after the next federal election, a more plausible strategy would have been to delay any new policy initiative involving marriage until after the 2004 election. This could have been accomplished by either appealing the *Halpern* ruling or by asking the Supreme Court the question "Does the Charter prohibit a ban on same-sex marriage and, if so, is the concept of a civil union instead of same-sex marriage a valid constitutional alternative?" Either of these options would have carried the government through until the next federal election without obliging it to publicly contemplate such controversial and divisive legislation. At a later date, if the Supreme Court ruled that a civil union was not an acceptable alternative to same-sex marriage, federal politicians could then have tried to deflect responsibility and "blame" the need to redefine marriage on the courts. In short, this author can only conclude that Jean Chrétien accepts, either on his own or because of pressure by others within his Cabinet, including his justice minister Martin Cauchon, that the prohibition of same-sex marriage constitutes such a serious and unjust form of discrimination that the government must now redefine marriage, despite the inevitable controversy and internal divisions this initiative precipitates. Whether or not one approves of the government's new commitment to same-sex marriage, an unfortunate consequence is that controversy on this issue will shroud political debate until and through the next election. This risks transforming the election into a single-issue event that overshadows or ignores important and pressing issues about which Canadians need to understand the parties' positions. These include health care reforms, redressing poverty, Canada's relations with the United States, foreign aid, the appropriate relationship between security and civil rights, parliamentary reforms, and electoral reform, to name but a few.

Virtual Political Parties and The Decline of Democracy

REG WHITAKER*

*Reg Whitaker is Distinguished Research Professor Emeritus at York University, Toronto, and Adjunct Professor of Political Science, University of Victoria.

A quick quiz on the major events of the political year 2000 might elicit the following list: the emergence out of the old Reform party of the new Canadian Alliance under Stockwell Day; the re-election of Jean Chrétien's Liberals to a third successive majority; the apparent stagnation of the Bloc Québécois; the continued marginalization of the federal Progressive Conservative and New Democratic parties.

Appearances can sometimes be misleading, however. Surface events and personalities mask deeper, structural changes taking place beneath the veneer. Distracted by the rise and fall of party labels and leaders, it has been easy to miss the subterranean transformation of political parties into different sorts of creatures than in the past. In an age of relentless change imposed by markets and technology, political parties have had to adapt to the challenges of globalization, the information revolution and the new media, or fade into irrelevance.

The flavour of these changes can be caught in the language used by party insiders to describe their business. Alister Campbell, one of the leading architects of Ontario premier Mike Harris' Common Sense Revolution, and a former federal Progressive Conservative official, early in 2000 wrote an open letter to PC supporters urging them to abandon their federal party for the Canadian Alliance. He complained about his own "wasted investment" in this "brand": "It was time to invest elsewhere." He went on: "If the federal PC party in which you have invested so much was a mutual fund you would have dumped it years ago."

Two of Campbell's words are particularly significant: investment and brand. Parties are no longer about commitment in the sense of principles, loyalty and tradition. Long ago, partisans rallied to Sir John A. Macdonald's Tories under the slogan "the Old Man, the Old Flag, the Old Policy." No more. A party is not a collective project. It is a "mutual fund." Commitment has become investment, and investment demands appropriate returns. If "wasted," it should be pulled out and put "elsewhere." The party's name and symbols are no longer marks of allegiance, but are merely a "brand." Brands are corporate marketing devices for products. Brand identification is intended to promote sales. If sales falter, re-branding may be required. In Campbell's worst-case scenario, the wise investor pulls out altogether and invests in a new product line with a more marketable brand. Hence, like a good investment analyst, Campbell is advising his clients to sell PC and buy CA.

According to political scientists, political parties are crucial linkages between civil society and the state: a noble calling. But in capitalist democracies, parties are poor cousins to their private sector counterparts, the corporations. Corporations sell goods and services and make profits. Parties sell promises of policy and patronage. At best, they offer insurance that profits in the private sector will not be impeded by policies pursued in the public sector, a kind of respectable protection racket. But in a competitive political market, few parties can bank promises contingent upon victory at the polls. Not surprisingly, it is the corporate sector where research and innovation in the technology of marketing and communications take place. Parties have to catch up with trends in the private sector, and struggle to cope with new techniques and tools of marketing as best they can, with limited resources.

One of the organizational forms pioneered in the new economy is the "virtual corporation," a form adapted to the flexibility required of a networked world. Old corporations were heavy, stand-alone entities, with high fixed investment in plant and product, centralized and hierarchical in structure, slow to react to changes in their environment, commanding market share by sheer weight and inertia. Exemplars of old corporate culture were the big three North American automakers before the challenge of Japanese and European competition hit home. New corporations are somewhat less hierarchical, more decentralized, more flexible and adaptive, with less fixed investment. New corporations are leaner, which does not mean that they necessarily employ fewer people. Rather, they employ fewer people directly, but many more indirectly, through outsourcing. Here is where the idea of the virtual corporation comes in. For specific purposes or projects, networks are formed that flow around and over the old organizational boundaries. They may involve temporary partnerships or alliances with other corporations, or at least components of other corporations. These networks are functionalist in design, strictly goal-oriented, and evanescent, forming and reforming around particular projects, and disappearing when the goals are achieved. These commando units may be considered, during their transitory lives, as "virtual" corporations.

Like "virtual" corporations in the networked information economy, virtual parties form and reform for specific purposes. With more tasks "outsourced" and less done in-house, the virtual party networks across traditional organizational boundaries, drawing in specialists who perform specific functions to meet specific, market-driven needs. Virtual parties form around politicians seeking the leadership of parties, as relatively small entourages or coteries of political strategists, marketing and communications experts, "spin doctors," PR flacks and policy "wonks." If successful, the same coterie then in effect colonizes the party and runs its subsequent election campaign. The party, as such, serves as little more than a convenient franchise with brand recognition, marketing "location," and ready sources of campaign funding. Sometimes, it is more convenient to "re-brand" the old party for better location. The real campaign dynamic derives from the virtual party within the shell of the traditional party. If the electoral campaign is successful, the virtual party then colonizes the strategic heights of government, around the office of the prime minister or premier, setting policy priorities, interfacing with the permanent bureaucracy and managing the government's image and media presentation. Many of the real high flyers in the team, however, will choose to return to the more lucrative private sector, only coming out again for a brief burst of activity during a re-election campaign. All this is dependent upon the leader, and the policy package he or she represents. These are the products being marketed.

There are some spectacular examples of the virtual party in operation. One of the most remarkable is the transformation of the British Labour party under Tony Blair. Blair's communications and publicity entourage, led by Peter Mandelson, the former Northern Ireland secretary, remade the party from the top down. They even re-branded it as New Labour, to distinguish it from the electorally unsuccessful and media-unfriendly "Old" Labour. Helped by a decaying Tory *ancien régime,* New Labour swept to office in 1997. Millbank, the permanent party headquarters where its publicity directors and spin doctors reside, has become a kind of rival power centre to Whitehall. In office, Blair and company have been assailed by both critics and supporters as lacking in any clear or distinctive policy direction, yet at the same time as control freaks obsessed with spin doctoring their image at the expense of substance. This is a trap that virtual parties can fall into, given that they are constructed in the first instance for the immediate purpose of getting elected, rather than for governing. Yet some Canadian experience suggests that virtual parties may be quite well prepared not only to get elected, but also to govern programmatically with distinctive policy agendas.

A remarkable case study of a programmatic, even ideological, "virtual" party is the "Mike Harris party," as the Progressive Conservative party of Ontario was re-branded in 1995, the year of its return to power from the wilderness. In the years following its traumatic defeat in 1985, after 42 years of uninterrupted rule, the Ontario Tory party was "hollowed out, broke, leaderless," as journalist and author John Ibbitson put it. The Ontario Tories had been known and feared for the "Big Blue Machine," the Conservative party organization that raised lavish funds from Bay Street, ran one successful electoral campaign after another, and then discreetly and efficiently managed the patronage that came with seemingly perpetual political power. It had over the years governed resolutely from the centre, mixing policy pragmatism with a kind of Red Tory sense of the importance of the public sector.

The Big Blue Machine was now defunct and the party a shell that could be taken over. This represented an opportunity for ideologically committed young right-wingers to seize the party franchise. A small group of young activists formed up in 1990 to back the leadership candidacy of the Tory MPP from North Bay, Mike Harris, an affable yet ambitious politician with few ties to the crumbling party establishment. With Harris as leader the moderate policy orientation of the past could be discarded, and replaced with a hard-right neoliberalism. Although initially unsuccessful in the 1990 provincial election, the Mike Harris virtual Tory party took brilliant advantage of the conjuncture in the early 1990s of an NDP government and a severe economic recession to lay the groundwork for a surprise victory in 1995 on a rigorously right-wing ideological party program, the Common Sense Revolution. Moreover, throughout their first term, the Harrisites were committed to enacting their program with unusual zeal and exactitude. Returning to the electorate in 1999, they could truthfully assert something few Canadian parties in office could claim: They had leveled with the voters about what they intended to do, and then carried out their promises.

The Harris party has been successful because it has tightly integrated marketing with policy. It was re-branded the "Harris" party not because Mike Harris is the product, but because it is a useful way of distinguishing its new policy orientation front the soft, centrist conservatism that characterized the old Tory party. The real product is the Common Sense Revolution, an ideological program that reflects the goals and preferences of its architects, the core of the virtual party. But right-wing ideological purity in itself is no guarantee of electoral success. Prior to the 1995 campaign, the Harris people had carefully identified their potential core supporters and what specifically they wanted from government. This is in line with the dramatic shift in recent years in the private sector from mass to niche, or "micro" marketing. New media and new information technologies have combined to provide tools that can profile and target ever more finely honed markets. The Harris Tories have never looked for the illusory grail of the "public." Instead they have concentrated on very specific "publics"—all those elements in the Ontario population angry and resentful over the results of previous NDP and Liberal governments—and turned to these refined marketing tools to identity specific policies that would sell to these potential buyers. As it turned out, a fortuitous synergy developed between the hard-right policy orientation of the Harris team and the policy preference profile of a critical mass of voters in the conjuncture of mid-1990s Ontario. The Common Sense Revolution was a product whose time, and market niche, had come. The virtual Ontario Tory party was the marketing vehicle that delivered the product. Following their re-election [in 1999], the Tories have seemed directionless. They await a further re-branding, this time as a party of government, no longer a party of angry outsiders, a marketing task that may present difficulties for a virtual party designed to appear as outsiders.

The federal Liberals under Jean Chrétien have been a highly successful political enterprise, winning three successive majority governments. The Liberal party too has become a virtual party, distinct from its roots, although it chooses not to re-brand itself, but rather to link its pitch with a long history of positive brand identification (since 1896, the Liberal Party has been in national office 70 per cent of the time). Yet the party of Chrétien is a different creature than its predecessors. It is neither the elite-run "ministerialist" party of the King-St. Laurent era, nor the "participatory" party of the Pearson-Trudeau era. It remains a formidable patronage machine, and an engine for organizing Parliament to pass the agendas set by the prime minister. But neither cabinet ministers nor the grass roots matter as much as they once did. National campaigns are poll and media-driven as never before, and the virtual party at the heart of the shell that is called the "Liberal Party" forms the real dynamic.

But there is one oddity about the virtual Liberal Party—its two-headedness—that sets it apart from other virtual parties, and has lent the Chrétien years a distinctive coloration. Virtual parties form up around particular leaders, in the first instance at the time they challenge for control of the party at a leadership contest. Winners then usually take all, and losers typically are isolated, neutralized and quite often blown right out of the party and/or the government. In the case of Ralph Klein when he gained the leadership of the Alberta Progressive Conservative Party, his chief competitor was blown all the way into the leadership of the Alberta Liberal Party, where she opposed him as the official opposition leader in the 2001 election, before resigning after another crushing Klein majority. More often, losers simply drop out to the private sector and are heard of no more, or at least until the leadership reopens.

When Jean Chrétien was himself defeated by John Turner for the Liberal leadership in 1984, he had felt humiliated by the winner. When he in turn won the leadership over Paul Martin, Jr. in 1990, he behaved differently toward his rival. The Chrétien virtual Liberal Party has in office controlled most of the patronage, and the prime minister runs a notoriously centralized and very tight ship. Yet Mr. Chrétien came to the top with no policy agenda whatever, other than becoming prime minister. The *Red Book* of policy promises, a crucial element in the 1993 campaign, was constructed by a team led by Martin as co-chair of the platform committee. And early on in the Liberals' first term, Martin was permitted to set the major agenda of the government: deficit elimination. The success of this priority became the defining mark of the Chrétien government, and Martin has consequently grown in stature, to the point of becoming a putative rival to the prime minister, certainly in the eyes of his own entourage (the nascent Martin virtual Liberal Party) and of the media, always alert to a saleable personality conflict narrative. Thus the Liberal Party has appeared as a strange, two-headed beast. The Chrétien loyalists argue that while the PM controls the patronage, the finance minister controls the policy agenda, a functional division of labour of sorts. It is an unusual form for the virtual party, but in the Liberals' case, who can argue with success?

The Liberals also lay claim, with some justification, to being the only genuinely national party in a system now characterized by opposition parties locked, either willingly in the case of the Bloc Québécois, or unwillingly in the case of the Alliance and the PCs, into regional ghettoes. Yet the Liberals are relatively weak in the West. The regional fragmentation of our present party system is a manifestation of an underlying feature of the virtual party system. As mass marketing gives way to niche or micro marketing, the "public" becomes fragmented into many publics, each targeted for votes by parties that tailor and hone their appeals to particular niches. In the most comprehensive examination yet published of the emerging party system (*Rebuilding Canadian Party Politics,* UBC Press, 2000), Professors R. Kenneth Carty, William Cross and Lisa Young argue that the national discussion of politics in an election campaign will "increasingly be replaced by a series of highly focused, private conversations. When coupled with the regional dynamics of campaigns, this trend is contributing to the end of pan-Canadian politics." They go on to suggest that "despite calls for further democratization of political parties, these new communication patterns ensure that pollsters, advertising and marketing specialists, and those skilled in the management and manipulation of data sets will retain a central role within campaign organizations. Fragmented and private political communication requires the skills and technology of these professionals, reinforcing their place within the party structure."

The most striking example of how the virtual party is superseding the real party can be found in the transformation of the Reform Party into the Canadian Alliance. Ostensibly designed to break Reform out of its Western ghetto and challenge the Liberals in Canada's biggest electoral battleground, Ontario, the "United Alternative" project was actually about transforming the structure of the party. When Preston Manning urged the Reform Party faithful to abandon their short-lived party attachment for a new and more efficacious vehicle (which soon showed its disdain for loyalty by ditching Manning himself), he exhorted them to "Think Big." The subtext of this message was that Reform had been thinking small, not only in terms of its regional base, but also in terms of its conception of itself as a party. For those who would like to see our parties strive to become more democratic vehicles, there is considerable irony in this message.

The rapid rise of the Reform Party from nowhere to Official Opposition was a remarkable example of innovation in the party system. Along with the Bloc Québécois, Reform brought to Ottawa a more programmatic, ideological and principled politics than the cynical old brokerage parties had offered. Above all, Reform brought an insistence upon concrete democratic accountability, and provided elaborate institutional mechanisms to ensure that accountability: referenda, initiatives, recall, free votes in Parliament, fixed terms for governments and so on. To a public jaded by such undemocratic exercises as Meech Lake, free trade, and the GST, Reform's democratization agenda seems a breath of fresh air, and indeed Reform was able to steal ownership of the democracy issue away from the NDP, which had monopolized the concept for decades. To be sure, populism of this kind is always open to a kind of plebiscitarian manipulation by the leadership. But the early Reform Party did demonstrate signs of genuine grassroots participation, in organizing and financing the party, and in asserting real influence over the party's policy directions. A populist network sprang up in western Canada that did something very unusual in this country by successfully launching and sustaining a new party from below. This could only go so far, however. It stalled in Ontario and failed to evict its Conservative rivals from the political map. Hence the Alliance, a re-branding of the Reform product designed to appeal more to the potential Ontario market.

Although the Alliance did hold a founding convention much like traditional party conventions, it made one major decision about process that moved the new party away from

Reform's structure. The Alliance's first leadership contest was to be a national primary, not a convention. The rationalization for this was that new members would be brought into the party structure as they were mobilized by competing candidates—most specifically, Ontarians mobilized by the candidacy of Tom Long, one of the architects of the Harris Common Sense Revolution, and a key catch for the Alliance's Ontario strategy. But voters mobilized by candidates in a primary-type contest are not socialized into the party in the way that those who join local constituencies and attend regional and national meetings are socialized into the solidarity and camaraderie of shared endeavour. They simply pay for a membership and cast a vote for their candidate in much the same isolation that characterizes voting in general elections. They miss the social matrix of the party, and miss learning its norms and practices, its sense of collective memory and shared identity. The Progressive Conservatives had adopted the same procedure for their earlier national leadership contest: It produced the bizarre result of the David Orchard candidacy, and a singular lack of a sense of organized purpose at the centre of the national party. The Joe Clark virtual Tory party was, and is, a large head with a tiny body or, to shift metaphors, a racing driver with a track record but a toy car to drive.

In the case of the Canadian Alliance, the Long candidacy failed to ignite an influx of new recruits from the Ontario Tory party. This failure was foreshadowed by the curious "poison pill" adherence of Ernie Eves, provincial treasurer and No. 2 man in the Harris government (since retired), and long the most prominent supporter of the federal Tories within the Harris cabinet. Eves declared that he would support the Alliance, but only if it adopted the Ontario candidate as its leader. When Long finished last, Eves was as good as his word, brusquely taking his leave of the Alliance. Although the Alliance under Day did do better with Ontario voters than Reform under Manning, clearly outdistancing the PCs in the popular vote, they were able to elect only two MPs. There was certainly no sense of gaining a durable new mass federal base to match that of the Harris Tories. The 905 suburban belt around Toronto, the very heartland of the Common Sense Revolution where Long had symbolically chosen to launch his leadership campaign, actually threw its support so monolithically to the Liberals as to run ahead of the 51 per cent the Chrétien party garnered province-wide.

The failure to mobilize lasting grassroots support in Ontario partially masked one very important contribution to the new party by Tom Long, although this only strengthened the party's virtual status. Long was able to open up financial support from Bay Street that was unprecedented in the previous short history of the Reform Party. Although Manning had the financial support of certain Western regional economic interests, especially oil money, and had gained a few supporters here and there on Bay Street, Reform had never been able to match the corporate fundraising prowess of the Mulroney Tories or the Chrétien Liberals, and had had to rely to a degree on grassroots donations. Manning and his Western supporters had appeared a bit too rough-edged and *outré* for Bay Street's liking. Long was one of their own, and, urged on by the *National Post*, they opened up their coffers for him. Unlike Long's vanishing voting support, Bay Street money stuck to the Day-led Alliance. In the 2000 election, the Alliance was able to rival the Liberals in corporate campaign funding. However important in establishing a financial base for the Alliance's future stability, this shift in funding from small, grassroots donations to big corporate giving completes a cycle within the Reform/Alliance from a grassroots populist movement to a political marketing tool for Bay Street. The Alliance as a virtual Ontario party had the money, and a vociferous mouthpiece of Bay Street in the form of the *National Post* to push it forward. All that was missing were the voters.

Stockwell Day's campaign in 2000 was of course ambushed by a far more sophisticated and ruthless marketing machine centred on the prime minister's office, and the Chrétien virtual party's pollsters and spin doctors. But the scale of the disaster should not obscure the effects of campaign exigencies on the Alliance as a party in its first, formative national campaign. Distinctive policies that set the Alliance apart from its competitors, including the Progressive Conservatives, were quickly dropped on the advice of Alliance advertising advisers. Delegates to the party's founding convention had enthusiastically adopted a flat tax. Moreover, as Alberta Treasurer, Day had already begun implementation of a flat (or at least flatter) provincial income tax, so the idea was clearly in the realm of the possible and practical. No matter: Focus groups showed there were perception problems with a flat tax, and it was unceremoniously dumped from the party platform.

Another distinctive feature of Day's ascent to the leadership had been the adhesion of pro-lifers and the Christian Right, who had flocked into the Alliance to elect a candidate who forthrightly defended their moral positions on sensitive public issues like abortion and homosexuality. Once the national campaign was launched, however, all mention of anti-abortion and anti-gay rights positions was dropped. When the Liberals cleverly ambushed Day by raising the spectre of an Alliance government encouraging referenda on abortion and gay rights, there was furtive backpedaling even on the Alliance's commitment to direct democracy. Finally, one might cite the Alliance's frantic efforts to deny any distinctive conservative position on health care, despite the Klein government's trail-blazing efforts to open up private clinics as a component of health care delivery. Their flight from principle was embodied in the rather forlorn spectacle of Day holding up his hand-lettered sign, "No two-tier health care," during the leaders' TV debate.

The 2000 election results produced very small gains for the Alliance outside the West, along with further deepening of support in the West. Whether the party can ever break out of Reform's Western ghetto, or even force a merger with the PCs, remains to be seen. But even if it does succeed, the Alliance, as a structure that has moved further along the continuum away from "party" toward "virtual party," will represent one more step in the decline of deliberative, negotiated democracy and its replacement by unmediated telemarketing.

Referring to the emergence of the modern social welfare state in Canada in the 1960s, former Ontario premier Bob Rae writes (in *The Three Questions: Prosperity and the Public Good*) that "these achievements were brought about because political parties, the little platoons of loyalty bound together by common affection and common conviction, advocated, persuaded, compromised, and negotiated their way to achieving tangible, real, practical progress. That's what politics is."

Rae draws the phrase "little platoons" from Burke, who meant all the institutions of civil society that mediate between the individual and the state. Parties were, for the political system, the pre-eminent mediating institutions. Whether they ever quite fulfilled the role Rae has lovingly ascribed to them is open to question. Ambition, patronage and venality were often enough in as much evidence as "loyalty . . . common affection and common conviction" as motives for partisanship. Yet Rae's emphasis on how parties "advocated, persuaded, compromised, and negotiated" surely gets the hang of what these peculiar institutions were supposed to do. States must arrive at authoritative resolutions of conflicts in the society. Parties were there to articulate demands, focus debates, negotiate workable solutions and then build broad support for the compromises thus arrived at. This was referred to as the "brokerage model" of parties, usually in recent years with disdain. Brokerage politics, it has been said repeatedly, were mundane, uninspiring, conservative, often corrupt and ineffective.

At one time or another, no doubt, they were all of these things. Like all other established institutions they have suffered over recent decades a decline in the trust and deference accorded them by the democratic citizenry, most spectacularly in the case of the state itself, but followed by corporations, unions, churches and so on. The reasons for this decline are many and complex, and still perhaps obscure to contemporary observers too close in time and place to fully decipher the clues. But take away the capacity of parties to link and mediate between society and the state, take away their capacity to fulfill the functions accorded them in theory, and we have a serious problem with our politics. Parties have been largely denuded of their old legitimacy, incapacitated in filling their traditional roles, and held up to public ridicule and scorn. But no new and better institutions have been invented to replace them. Interest groups act directly upon the legislative and administrative processes, without the mediation of parties, and with the result that the more powerful get their way, while leaving the losers bitter, angry and paranoiac about what is done behind closed doors and in the dark corridors of power. Social movements and public interest groups try to influence governments directly from the outside by raising their voices and making threatening gestures, but they are largely ignored, leaving their supporters further alienated. Everywhere the "democratic deficit" is identified and decried, yet the traditional instruments for making government accountable to the people—political parties—tend to be seen as part of the problem rather than part of the solution.

Neither corporatism nor populism, neither technocracy from above nor electronic direct democracy from below, have actually succeeded so far in replacing parties. In the 21st century, parties remain as crucial to the workings of liberal democratic politics as they have always been. A democratic political system without parties is like an automobile without a transmission: It might look good, but it won't take you anywhere. But this does not mean that under their old labels, "parties" are in continuity with their past. Here is where virtual parties step in. Like the body snatchers of the Hollywood horror-movie, they take over the old shells, but fill them with something quite different. Virtual parties in opposition are not so much participants in ongoing debate and deliberation as marketing tools for selling their product—themselves. Virtual parties in power do not preside over and organize the parliamentary process, as such; rather they are devices for establishing unmediated producer–consumer relations between the leader and the population, while bypassing or end-running Parliament and press and any other institutions that get in the way. Not much room is left for the "little platoons of loyalty bound together by common affection and common conviction."

Structural reforms of the electoral process and enhancing the role of Parliament are worthy objectives in themselves, but unlikely to get far under the present circumstances of Liberal self-satisfaction. Yet even such reforms might do little to dislodge the virtual party, which has sunk roots in economic and technological changes that lie deeper than political institutions. Perhaps more radical changes in forms of representation are required to address a growing democratic deficit.

The Global Entertainment Economy

JOHN HANNIGAN*

*John Hannigan is Professor of Sociology at the University of Toronto.

Sometime soon, downtown Toronto will reinvent itself as midtown Manhattan. Across from a reconfigured Eaton Centre, "Metropolis," five levels of retail anchored by a thirty-screen cinema and a Virgin megastore, will sprout up in a block now occupied by dollar and discount stores and street-level amusement arcades. Billed as a "Times Square concept," the $90 million redevelopment project will also include a public square and, to give it an extra dash of pizzazz, New York-style neon signage. Just around the corner, the International Olympic Committee plans to erect an entertainment centre of its own, with an Olympic sports theme. With an estimated cost of $32 million, "Olympic Spirit" will take the form of a fifty-metre-high media tower in the shape of the Olympic torch. Five hours down Highway 401, a similar development plan has already transformed the Montreal Forum, formerly the temple of hockey for generations of Quebeckers. Promoted as a "Times Square-style" entertainment complex, the redeveloped Forum, now called the Pepsi Forum Entertainment Centre, features a twenty-two-screen megaplex and "Jillian's," a restaurant complex that includes such entertainment facilities as virtual and real bowling alleys, a blues stage, and a disco.

The "Manhattanization" of downtown locations in Canada's two largest cities is the leading edge of a "global entertainment economy" organized around the merchandising of American popular culture brands and celebrities. In the United States, which has the most developed entertainment and media industry, as a percentage of household spending entertainment (5.4 percent) currently ranks ahead of clothing (5.2 percent) and health care (5.2 percent), generating US$480 billion in business each year in a US$8 trillion economy. Expected to double in a handful of years, entertainment is, according to American media consultant Michael Wolf, "fast becoming the driving wheel of the new world economy."[1] In the United Kingdom, annual expenditure on leisure activities rose by 50 percent between 1992 and 1997. By the end of the 1990s, British consumers spent more on leisure and tourism than on food, rent, and local taxes put together.[2] In Canada, the consumer market for entertainment services grew by almost 50 percent in real terms in the decade between 1986 and 1996, to reach $5.8 billion.[3] Since Statistics Canada's figures do not

---

[1] Michael Wolf, *The Entertainment Economy: How Mega-Media Forces Are Transforming Our Lives* (New York: Times Books, 1999), 4.

[2] Emma Rees, "Leisure Futures," *Design Week, The Big Picture: Leisure* (October 1998): 24–5. Cited in Guy Julier, *The Culture of Design* (London: Sage Publications, 2000), 146.

[3] Louise Earl, "Entertainment Services: A Growing Consumer Market," *Service Indicators/Indicateurs des Services —3rd Quarter* (Statistics Canada) (1998): 17.

include such activities as dining at a themed restaurant or patronizing a casino, this figure can be seen as being substantially higher in the developing fantasy cities of the future. European cities, long resistant to American-type commercial developments, are on the verge of undergoing a major transformation. Major urban entertainment projects are already under way in Brussels and Barcelona. Symbolizing Berlin's economic renaissance, the new Potsdamer Platz, along the former East–West boundary, is crowned by the Sony Centre, Europe's largest private sector development. Under a soaring V-shaped canopy composed of sail-like fabric and glass panels, an oval-shaped Forum, an IMAX theatre, the German Film Institute, several themed cafés, and a Sony store can be found. Across the road is a private neighbourhood that contains a casino, an Imax/Discovery Channel theatre, a three-storey retail mall, and numerous themed eateries. Despite the "Asian flu" that has battered most economies in the Pacific Rim, countries in the region are poised to welcome some major entertainment developments. New urban theme parks are being built by both Disney and Universal in Japan, and the former has announced plans to open an international entertainment facility in 2006 on Lantau Island, Hong Kong, the site of the former colony's new airport.

While rooted in the "global communications environment," the impact of the entertainment economy is profoundly felt at the level of the local urban community. Speaking at a 1998 real estate development conference in Toronto, Vancouver architect Clive Grout predicted that "entertainment and experience will begin even more strongly to shape the ways that architecture, design, merchandising, shopping, travel and leisure define themselves in our cities."[4] Elsewhere, I have described how a new form of urban development has emerged in which cities have come to represent themed fantasy experiences.[5] These "fantasy cities," as I have termed them, are often promoted as antidotes to the decades-long decline of those inner cities that have suffered from the steady exodus of manufacturing jobs and middle-class residents. However, there are indications that rather than reawakening downtown vitality and urban sociability, these new themed developments may well impose an iron cage of uniformity in which local initiative and identity are stifled and private space replaces public space. In the geographic city of the future, with its "generic urbanism inflected only by appliqué," ties to any specific space could be replaced by a universal particular that is favoured by globalized capital, electronic means of production, and uniform mass culture.[6]

Of course, the cultural invasion of American mass culture and the resulting "globalization and homogenization of values, culture and consciousness"[7] is by no means of recent vintage. Over a quarter of a century ago, in his book *Mass Communication and*

---

[4]   Albert Warson, "Entertaining Canada," *Building* 48, 3 (1998): 34.

[5]   See John Hannigan, *Fantasy City: Pleasure and Profit in the Postmodern Metropolis* (London and New York: Routledge, 1998).

[6]   Michael Sorkin, "Introduction: Variations on a Theme Park," in *Variation on a Theme Park: The New American City and the End of Public Space*, ed. Michael Sorkin (New York: Noonday Press, 1992), xiii.

[7]   Jerry Mander, "Technologies of Globalization," in *The Case against the Global Economy: And for a Turn toward the Local*, ed. J. M. Mander and E. Goldsmith (San Francisco: Sierra Club Books, 1996), 350.

American Empire, the media theorist Herbert Schiller denounced the juggernaut that flattens local identities and cultures while substituting a uniform and predominantly American character.[8] Today, even as America's hegemony in other industries ranging from automobiles to consumer electronics has been shattered irrevocably, global consumer culture has remained almost an American monopoly and is said by some scholars to have effectively eclipsed both high culture and the culture of traditional societies worldwide.[9] With the fall of the Soviet bloc, "literally the entire planet is being wired into music, movies, news, television programs and other cultural products that originate primarily in the film and recording studios of the United States."[10]

Nevertheless, the global entertainment economy in the early twenty-first century has some distinctive features as compared to its earlier forms. Of particular importance has been the merging of corporate globalization strategies with those that emphasize creating and building brand-driven synergies. To describe this process, political scientist Benjamin Barber has coined the term "McWorld": "McWorld is an entertainment shopping experience that brings together malls, multiplex movie theaters, theme parks, spectator sports arenas, fast-food chains (with their endless movie tie-ins), and television (with its burgeoning shopping networks) into a single vast enterprise that, on the way to maximizing its profits, transforms human beings"[11]

The expanding universe of entertainment described by "McWorld" pivots around the convergence of three types of consumer purchases: screened products (movies, television, computer games); packaged products (home videos, toys); and leisure activities (amusement parks, casinos, cruise ships).[12] These are brought together under the umbrella of "brand empires," colonies of products and services that draw their sustenance from a single strong and readily recognizable corporate brand. Wolf observes that brands do more than just carry a product's attributes; they convey a simple, powerful idea: family, taste, money, or fun: "Disney doesn't simply mean animated features or theme parks anymore: it means family. Martha Stewart doesn't mean a magazine or a TV show; Martha equals glamorous good taste. Bloomberg is not just a terminal on a trader's desk; it is instantaneous financial news and analysis. The NBA isn't about watching tall men put the ball in the hoop with a high degree of accuracy; it's about a fast, urban, street lifestyle, with all the glitz and glamour of showbiz."[13]

---

[8]   Herbert Schiller, *Mass Communication and American Empire* (Boston: Beacon Press, 1971).

[9]   Notably, David Rieff, "A Global Culture," *World Policy Journal* 10, 4 (1993–94): 73–81.

[10]   Richard Barnet and John Cavanagh, "Homogenization and Global Culture," in *The Case against the Global Economy*, ed. Mander and Goldsmith, 71–2.

[11]   Benjamin Barber, *Jihad vs. McWorld* (New York. Times Books, 1995), 97.

[12]   Jason Squire, "What's Your Major? Entertainment Studies?" *The New York Times*, 19 April 1998, section 3, 13.

[13]   Wolf, *The Entertainment Economy*, 224–5.

FACTORS PROMOTING THE GROWTH OF THE GLOBAL ENTERTAINMENT ECONOMY

Demographic and Lifestyle Factors

To understand why the global market for entertainment has become so large, it is first necessary to recognize some of the key demographic features and lifestyle choices of contemporary consumers.

About a third of the Canadian population, the largest single cohort, constitute the so-called "boomer" generation, born between 1947 and 1966. Of these, the majority are "front-end" boomers—that is, those entering or about to enter their fifties [in 2002]. During the decade of the 1980s, many of the older boomers spent considerable time at home rather than going out. Pop marketing guru Faith Popcorn labelled this stay-at-home behaviour "cocooning" and claimed that it was the future trend in cities, which were increasingly overwhelmed by crime and other urban problems. However, University of Toronto economist and demographer David Foot rejects this forecast, arguing that once the boomer generation's children became old enough not to require constant supervision, their parents once again began to go out in search of fun. Solidly established in their careers, entering their peak earning years, and having already made most of the major consumer purchases—most notably a house—the front-end boomers are now primed to shift to a leisure-spending mode.[14] Some have emulated the "forty-something" Vancouver trial lawyer, cited in a *Globe & Mail* article from the late 1990s, who opted for a high performance sport coupe "before I get too old to enjoy it."[15] But others have rejected new luxury consumer durables in favour of shopping and entertainment "experiences." Comparing figures from 1969 and 1996, Statistics Canada reports that spending on recreation services was especially increased for the highest income households, a category that encompasses many of the more affluent front-end boomers. Of this group, 60 percent reported attending "live staged performances," 40 percent said they had paid admission to museums, exhibitions, and the like, and 36 percent went to "live sports spectacles."[16]

Smaller in number than the front-end boomers, "Generation X," those now in their thirties, have also been important in spurring the growth of the new entertainment economy. Weaned on MTV and MuchMusic, high tech video games and computers, the Generation Xers are said to be media savvy, both multitaskers and multimedia users.[17] Furthermore, they display an entirely new outlook toward television, eschewing loyalty toward a particular channel or network in favour of the program itself. One of the consequences of this "postmodern" orientation has been to break up the long-standing domination of the airwaves by the major television networks, thus opening up access to a new flock of

---

[14]   David K. Foot and Daniel Stoffman, *Boom, Bust and Echo: How to Profit from the Coming Demographic Shift* (Toronto: Stoddart, 1997).

[15]   Jeremy Cato, "Muscle in on This Action," *The Globe & Mail*, I5 March 1999, D12.

[16]   Louise Earl, "Spending on Selected Recreation Items in Canada," *Focus on Culture* (Statistics Canada) 10, 2 (1998): 3.

[17]   Bob Losyk, "Generation X: What They Think and What They Plan to Do," *The Futurist* 31, 2 (1997): 4

competitors, including MTV, Fox, Nickelodeon, and CNN. Turow calls these channels "lifestyle parades" that invite their audiences to belong to an "ad-sponsored community" that resonates with their personal beliefs and helps them chart their position in the larger world.[18]

These qualities are even more pronounced in "Generation Y" (or the "Echo" generation, as Foot labels them), the children of the front-end boomers who are just beginning to enter the working world. According to figures cited by Michael Wolf, these "children of the multimedia" spend US$130 billion annually and are estimated to influence the spending of an additional US$250 billion.[19] Members of Generation Y are particularly avid moviegoers. Accustomed from childhood to watching videotaped movies at home, they are also more likely than older generations "to go to the cinema," and they therefore "form an important component of movie audiences."[20]

New Leisure Patterns

Contemporary leisure analysts are split on the issue of whether our leisure time is shrinking or expanding. One prominent researcher, John Robinson of Pennsylvania State University, has presented data for the period 1965–1995 that demonstrates a steady rise in the leisure time of Americans in the 18 to 64 age range.[21] Other social scientists have argued that people today are "overworked"[22] and are experiencing a "time bind"[23]; they are spending more time at paid jobs and less time in pursuit of leisure. What does seem to be clear is that the pace of both work and pleasure has increased significantly, leading to a perception that our free time has shrunk and has become a valuable commodity that must be rationed and be spent more carefully.[24] Drawing on data from three Canadian time-use surveys conducted between 1981 and 1992, Zuzanek and Smale detect a perception of significant time-related pressures in our lives—pressures that increased considerably in the 1990s. While they identify some gender and lifestyle differences, Zuzanek and Smale conclude that the mounting sense of time pressure "should be, at least in part, attributed to the harried lifestyles typical of modern industrial societies."[25]

Wolf contends that people today have begun to conceptualize time in a radically different way, treating it as a highly segmented grid—a series of small parcels or boxes that need to be filled. Leisure is no exception, requiring that free time be scheduled into man-

---

[18]   Joseph Turow, *Breaking up America: Advertising and the New Media World* (Chicago: University of Chicago Press, 1997).

[19]   Wolf, *The Entertainment Economy*, 35.

[20]   Earl, "Entertainment Services," 27.

[21]   John P. Robinson and Geoffrey Godbey, *Time for Life: The Surprising Ways Americans Use Their Time* (University Park: Pennsylvania State University Press, 1997).

[22]   Juliet Schor, *The Overworked American: The Unexpected Decline of Leisure* (New York: Basic Books, 1991).

[23]   Arlie Hochschild, *The Time Bind: When Work Becomes Home and Home Becomes Work* (New York: Metropolitan Books, 1997).

[24]   See Elia Kacapyr, "Are We Having Fun Yet?" *American Demographics* 19, 10 (1997): 28–30.

[25]   Jiri Zuzanek and Bryan J.A. Smale, "More Work—Less Leisure? Changing Allocations of Time in Canada, 1981 to 1992," *Loisir et société/Society and Leisure* 20 (1997): 95.

ageable blocks distributed over the course of the week. This has led to a kind of "time surfer" mentality in which we choose recreational activities that can be consumed in bite-sized chunks, ranging from ten minutes to several hours. Wolf goes on to argue that not only has leisure time become segmented and broken into variable-length blocks, but it is something that can be most efficiently utilized by spending money. Time-pressed business executives, for example, hire "personal trainers" to put them through physical fitness routines either at the gym or at the office. The reorientation of leisure toward this type of commoditized time surfing has stimulated the growth of an entertainment marketplace in which audio books, video games, Internet "zines" (i.e., virtual magazines), and urban theme parks all figure prominently.[26]

An associated trend is what has been termed the "localization of leisure."[27] Rather than the traditional three-week summer vacation, middle-class consumers today prefer more frequent but shorter getaways scattered throughout the year. These take the form of long-weekend retreats to urban centres within several hours of a person or family's home, by air. According to a 1991 "Futures Project" survey conducted by the Hyatt Hotel chain, frequent short vacations were preferred by executives, on the grounds that they helped to alleviate work-related stress and could more easily be programmed into work schedules. While warm weather locales in Florida and the Caribbean are still popular, vacationers are increasingly flocking to regional destinations that are perceived as offering several days worth of entertainment value. The growth of tourism in second tier cities such as Cleveland, Pittsburgh, and San Diego is moving the urban entertainment economy beyond established fantasy cities such as Orlando and Las Vegas, into the heartland of the United States and Canada.

Economic Factors

Until the early 1990s, entertainment conglomerates relied on the first-run theatrical exhibition of motion pictures as their chief money-spinning operation. These were buttressed by "ancillary" markets (network television, pay TV, home video, syndication, foreign distribution) and "complementary" markets (theme parks, toys, video games, licensed merchandise, retail chains). Over the last decade, however, the role of ancillary and complementary markets has grown significantly, triggering a major expansion and restructuring of the global entertainment industry. This is reflected in the increasing emphasis on multiple revenue streams, the growth of synergies and brand empires (see above), and the accelerating pace of mergers and acquisitions resulting in "megamedia" formation.

The growth of ancillary markets has significantly altered the calculus of media economics. It is not unusual now to hear of Hollywood films that only break even or even lose money domestically, but which are very profitable because of strong sales abroad or on video. In some cases, a movie may go directly to video without first being exhibited in theatres. In the past, television networks in the United States were legally prohibited from holding syndication rights, by the so-called "Fin-Syn" rules enforced by the Federal

---

[26] Wolf, *The Entertainment Economy*, 38–40.

[27] Michael S. Rubin and Robert Gorman, "Re-inventing Leisure," *Urban Land* 52, 2 (1993): 27.

Communications Commission (FCC).[28] The FCC's lifting of this prohibition in 1993 has encouraged the production of new programming and has made the networks more attractive prospects for takeovers by entertainment giants such as Disney.

Until relatively recently, the major player in complementary markets was the Disney Company. When he first opened Disneyland in Anaheim, California, in 1955, Walt Disney recognized that the venture's success depended upon the creation of synergistic linkages among the concept's television shows, motion pictures, theme park, and consumer products. The after-school Mickey Mouse Club TV show was a showcase for Disneyland as well as for related merchandise ranging from lunch pails to caps with mouse ears. Even more profitable was the Davy Crockett series, which was first shown on the Sunday night Disney prime-time television series on the ABC network (ABC held a one-third interest in Disneyland for the first decade, as well as receiving all profits from food concessions). The series about the Kentucky-bred frontiersman was enormously popular and was successfully spun off into theme park attractions (in the "Adventureland" area of Disneyland), merchandise (the coonskin cap worn by Crockett on the series became one of the biggest product fads of the era), theatrical releases, and even a chart-topping song, "The Ballad of Davy Crockett." As film scholar Douglas Gomery has noted, the "long-run Disney magic on TV consisted of fashioning a popular series that symbiotically promoted its core theme parks into world-class attractions."[29]

Despite Disney's success, other media conglomerates embraced complementary markets somewhat gingerly. A few other motion picture studios (Paramount, Universal Studios, and Warner Bros.) did enter the theme park market, as did Taft Broadcasting, a regional radio and television chain. In the late 1970s and early 1980s, several large entertainment companies invested directly in the toy and video game industries. After Disney had passed on the opportunity to buy in, Warner invested in the Atari home video game system while Universal/MCA flirted with toys and video games through its now long-defunct LJN Toys.

By most accounts, it was the enormous merchandising success of George Lucas's *Star Wars* [1977] that convinced entertainment companies that commercial licenses should be a "marketing goal" rather than a "marketing tool." The *Star Wars* trilogy generated US$2.6 billion worth of merchandise sales by the end of the 1980s and transformed the toy industry into a platform for branded products based on Hollywood characters. The huge sales of

---

[28] The Financial Interest in Syndication (Fin-Syn) Rule(s) was adopted by the Federal Communications Commission (FCC) in the United States to prevent the three television networks (ABC, CBS, NBC) from restricting the market for television programming. The rule(s) prohibited the networks from owning re-runs; they were allowed only to lease them. In 1993, after a protracted and contentious set of hearings, the FCC finally opened the syndications business to the networks on the grounds that changes in broadcasting—the development of cable television networks—had undermined the theory that the three networks could control the market for video programming. See Robert Corn-Revere, "Economics and Media Regulation," in *Media Economics: Theory and Practice*, ed. Alison Alexander, James Owers, and Rod Carveth (Hillsdale, NJ: Laurence Erlbaum Associates, 1993), 71–90.

[29] Douglas Gomery, "Disney's Business History: A Re-Interpretation," in *Disney Discourse: Producing the Magic Kingdom*, ed. F. Smoodin (New York and London: Routledge, 1994), 77.

Batman merchandise in the early 1990s further reinforced this trend. With the stakes suddenly much higher, media conglomerates began actively to pursue expansion strategies designed to enhance complementary markets.[30] In one extreme case, *Space Jam*, a feature film with a mix of animated characters and human actors was produced primarily as a vehicle to promote sports merchandise associated with the movie's star, basketball player Michael Jordan.

The Changing Nature of Retail

The expansion of the global entertainment economy is also a reflection of the changing nature of retailing at the cusp of the millennium. This "entertainmentization" of retailing is in no small measure a strategic response to the decline of suburban shopping malls and the twin challenge from off-price retailers and online shopping.

In response to the corporate downsizing of the early 1990s, an increasing number of consumers embraced the concept of "value retail"—brand-name goods at prices below those offered by department and specialty stores. The threat posed by value retailers to suburban and regional shopping centres was exacerbated by the fact that value retailers succeeded in capturing higher-income shoppers as well as the expected lower-income ones.[31] The Factory Outlet Mall, just across the American border in Niagara Falls, New York, has taken this concept to a new level by transforming into a discount outlet for high fashion brands such as Polo/Ralph Lauren, Saks Fifth Avenue, and Jones New York. The 1990s witnessed the entry into Canada of the American "big box" stores—Costco, Staples, Home Depot—housed in stand-alone, warehouse-like structures, as well as the discount department store giant Wal-Mart. By 1997, retail analysts estimated that Wal-Mart was taking slightly more than one out of every four dollars spent at Canadian department stores, after only three years in this country.[32] Finally, there is the growing lure of online retailing. The full impact of Internet retailing has yet to be felt, but in some product areas, notably books and records, travel, and computer software, it has already challenged in-person shopping. With these alternatives newly available in the 1990s, shoppers began to desert existing shopping centres in droves. From 1994 to 1997, more than forty anchor stores left Canadian malls, either declaring bankruptcy or relocating in more profitable retail environments outside the malls.[33]

One major way in which retailers in Canada and the United States have responded to this decline of the shopping mall is to embrace entertainment as a way of bringing back the crowds. Some have retrofitted and expanded, adding megaplex cinemas, themed restaurants, high technology amusement arcades, and other leisure retailers. The more ambitious option has been to build completely new "super-regional" shopping centres that combine value retailing with entertainment components. The leader in taking this approach

---

[30] See Dan Steinbock, *Triumph and Erosion in the American Media and Entertainment Industries* (Westport, CT: Quorum Books, 1995), 129.

[31] Michael Beyard *et al. Developing Urban Entertainment Centers* (Washington, DC: Urban Land Institute, 1998), 11.

[32] "Wal-Mart Romps ahead in Canada," *Building* 47, 5 (1997): 34.

[33] Albert Warson, "Born again Shopping Centres," *Building* 47, 5 (1997): 33.

has been The Mills Corporation, of Arlington, Virginia, which builds facilities of 450,000 to 600,000 square metres (it is rare in Canada to find an enclosed shopping centre over 300,000 square metres). Grapevine Mills, two miles north of Dallas/Fort Worth International Airport, contains an AMC thirty-screen cinema, Imax Theatre, Virgin Megastore, Rainforest Café, Sega Gameworks virtual reality arcade, and, among its ISO retail tenants, Saks Fifth Avenue and Rodeo Drive (Beverly Hills) stores. Arizona Mills, in a suburb of Phoenix, has a megaplex, a Rainforest Café, and an American Wilderness Experience store among its attractions. The first Mills supermall is planned for a Toronto area location on Highway 400 near the Canada's Wonderland theme park, while a slightly smaller Mills mall in Vancouver is also on the drawing board. Both will be built as joint ventures with veteran Canadian developer Cambridge Shopping Centres.

More generally, retailers have reacted by attempting to make the activity of shopping itself more entertaining. This convergence of shopping, fantasy, and fun is known as "shoppertainment." Fashion floors in department stores frequently feature television monitors on which rock videos continuously play. Some leading-edge retailers are embracing the concept of "experiential retailing," which means that shopping is transformed into a themed retail experience complete with interactive exhibits (at the Nike store on Toronto's Bloor Street, patrons are invited to spin a basketball to call up milestone moments in the history of that sport). The new generation of bookstores comes complete with comfortable couches, in-store cafés, and celebrity authors (I once got to meet musician, songwriter, and television star Steve Allen at a local Chapters store). In a recent, much publicized dip into the world of the Internet, the Victoria's Secret lingerie chain broadcast a fashion show on its computer. Web site entertainment, then, has diffused out into the retail environment on a major, unprecedented scale.

Technological Factors

Most contemporary accounts of globalization accord a central role to communications technology. Tony Spybey, for example, stresses the convergence of various aspects of electronic technology in the "information super-highway" that runs between North America, Europe, and East Asia and that embraces telecommunications and computer networks with the aid of high-capacity satellites and fibre-optic cabling. Such technological advances in communications, Spybey observes, have contributed to potentiating and accelerating such major events of social change as the collapse of the Soviet Union and the resurgence of Islam, and have facilitated the contemporary development of global social movements in peace, feminism, and environmentalism.[34] Richard Barnet and John Cavanagh write that satellites, cables, Walkmans, videocassette recorders, CDs, and other marvels of entertainment technology have "created the arteries through which modern entertainment conglomerates are homogenizing global culture." In particular, they cite the daily beaming of MTV programming to 210 million households in seventy-one countries as "the most spectacular technological development of the 1980s."[35]

---

[34] Tony Spybey, *Globalization and World Society* (Cambridge: Polity Press, 1996), 111–12.
[35] Barnet and Cavanagh, "Homogenization and Global Culture," 71–2.

What is noticed less often, however, is the extent to which technologies developed for the defence and motion picture industries have been downsized and rolled out across a wide array of urban entertainment destinations. Motion simulators, for example, were derived from military and pilot training technologies of the 1970s. Their compact size and portability make them highly adaptable to use in theme parks, museums, festivals, shopping centres, and urban entertainment centres. One of the first examples of this miniaturization was the "Tour of the Universe" ride, introduced at Toronto's CN Tower in 1985. Developed by Douglas Trumbull, designer of special effects for motion pictures such as *Blade Runner* and *2001: A Space Odyssey*, it evolved five years later into the acclaimed *Back to the Future* ride which debuted at the Universal Studios theme park in California. By 1993, Trumbull had developed a simulator theatre with fifteen seats, which could fit into an approximately nine-metre-square space less than five metres high. In similar fashion, IMAX Corporation, the pioneer of large-format movie technology, has introduced the new SR projection system, which is small enough to fit into multiplex cinemas and yet costs two-thirds less to build than a conventional venue. The SR projection system is designed to bring this technology to urban markets with a population base as low as 500,000, unlike conventional IMAX theatres, which need a population of one million or more.[36] This type of technological downsizing is important because it facilitates the growth of the type of regional entertainment destinations that are being developed in response to the "localization of leisure" trend. On the other hand, conventional movie theatre technology is moving in exactly the opposite direction: megaplexes such as The Coliseum and Silver City contain larger screens, stadium seating, and digital sound.

MAIN PLAYERS IN THE GLOBAL ENTERTAINMENT ECONOMY

Herman and McChesney have characterized the worldwide communications market today as a "global media oligopoly" consisting of two tiers. At the top of the primary tier are the six largest and most fully integrated global media giants—Time-Warner, Disney, Bertelsmann, Viacom, News Corporation, and TCI. Rounding out the top ten are four other firms: Polygram, Seagram, Sony, and General Electric.[37] In the two years since Herman and McChesney compiled their list, Time-Warner has grown even larger, merging with Turner Broadcasting, and, pending regulatory approval, with America Online (AOL). Seagram, through its Universal Studios subsidiary, purchased Polygram, only to be taken over itself by the French utilities and media conglomerate, Vivendi. Most of the thirty or forty firms in the second tier are built on newspaper empires, cable broadcasting systems, or broadcast chains that have evolved into national or regional conglomerates. Of these, three are Canadian: Thomson Corporation, the Hollinger newspaper group, and Rogers Communications.

---

[36] H. Enchin, "IMAX Scores Its Biggest Deal in 10-Theatre Sale to Regal," *The Globe & Mail*, 25 June 1997, B8.

[37] Edward S. Herman and Robert W. McChesney, *Global Media: The New Missionaries of Global Capitalism* (London and Washington, DC: Cassell, 1997), 70.

Rapidly entering the global media market are a number of new players such as computer software giant Microsoft and the telecommunications companies Bell Atlantic-NYNEX and U.S. West. In April 2000, Bell Atlantic Corporation (which had earlier taken over NYNEX), U.S. West, Pactel, and GTE merged to become Verizon, the largest wireless communications company in the United States. Such companies have taken advantage of the convergence of the telecommunications, media, and computer industries, usually entering the traditional media in joint ventures with existing media giants.

Most of the first tier media moguls have been leaders in recognizing the brand synergies attached to complementary markets (see above). Disney is one of the lead architects of this new landscape of leisure. In 1995, the Walt Disney Co. established a division to develop a wide range of new businesses, from location-based entertainment centres to sports restaurants, while its "imagineers" (designers) focused on ways to downsize theme park experiences for use in city locations.[38] Since then, the DisneyQuest entertainment arcades have been introduced, and the Disney-owned "ESPN Zones" in New York and Baltimore offer video games, batting cages, race car simulators, and big screen TVs on which a sports event is always being shown. One distinct advantage that Disney possesses is that it is able to debut and fine-tune its new entertainment initiatives at its theme park complex in Orlando, where a critical mass of patrons is already primed for entertainment experiences. Universal Studios, now a subsidiary of Vivendi, has been a leader in the themed entertainment industry. Universal's "CityWalk," a 460-metre private street that connects the Universal Studios Hollywood theme park with its megaplex theatre and amphitheatre, has come to be regarded as a template for urban entertainment projects and is being cloned by the company itself in Florida and Japan. Sony has joined forces with IMAX Corporation, a Canadian company, to build a series of advanced technology 3-D theatres. In New York, the Sony-IMAX theatre is located in a megaplex complex at Lincoln Square and has become the single highest grossing motion picture screen in the United States, while the four-storey Metreon centre, in San Francisco, is expected to draw over two million patrons per year.

While this global media oligopoly is a major player in the new entertainment economy, the two are not synonymous. The major initiative behind many of the urban entertainment destinations now being built or on the drawing board in fact comes from a handful of long-established real estate developers that have branched out from erecting shopping centres and office buildings. In the United States, the leader has been Simon DeBartolo, of Indianapolis, the largest real estate investment trust in the country, with a market capitalization of US$7.5 billion. Under the direction of veteran developer Mel Simon, the company is involved in some landmark projects including the Forum Shops, an upscale themed mall attached to Caesars Palace casino in Las Vegas, which boasts its own hand-painted, computer-controlled sky. The major Canadian player is Peter Munk's TrizecHahn Corporation. TrizecHahn is constructing a shopping and entertainment complex at the foot of the CN Tower, in Toronto, and another at the totally rebuilt Aladdin casino-hotel in Las Vegas. Its highest profile project, however, is the "Hollywood and Highland" redevelopment along Hollywood Boulevard in Los Angeles. The brainchild of TrizecHahn executive David Malmuth, a former Disney developer, it will wrap a US$388 million urban-destination

---

[38] Hannigan, *Fantasy City*, 111.

entertainment centre on Mann's Chinese Theatre and will include a new theatre that is to be the future home of the Academy Awards.

Since they lack experience in such key matters as determining the proper mix of retail tenants, global entertainment giants routinely join forces with experienced real estate developers. The latter usually welcome this collaboration because they need the branded concepts owned by the entertainment moguls.

Less visible than the big media companies or real estate developers, but worth watching, are a clutch of new competitors that are expanding rapidly in new and existing entertainment markets. One rapidly rising meteor in the entertainment industry is what was formerly called SFX Entertainment Inc. Now owned by Clear Channel Entertainment, a San Antonio, Texas, media company that controls 1,170 radio stations, eighteen television stations, and 700,000 outdoor advertising displays, it is aggressively expanding into the management and promotion of concert and theatrical productions. With exclusive booking arrangements in twenty-eight of the top fifty markets in the United States, Clear Channel's recent moves have raised some industry fears of an impending monopoly. In addition, Clear Channel recently acquired Integrated Sports Entertainment, a major sports entertainment company whose clients include National Basketball Association stars Hakeem Olajuwon, Jayson Williams, and John Starks; National Football League quarterbacks Steve Young and Vinny Testaverde; and corporate clients Burger King, Cadillac, Sports Illustrated for Kids, and General Mills-Wheaties. In another twenty-month spending spree in the 1990s, the company purchased four elite sports-agent firms, worth a total of about US$200 million, including super-agent David Falk's sports-management agency, FAME. What it is moving toward, suggests trade journalist Ray Waddell, is "hooking up" corporate America with live music tours that it both books and promotes, in the same way that the sporting industry now combines corporate sponsorships with live events.[39]

THE IMPACT OF THE NEW GLOBAL ENTERTAINMENT ECONOMY

While economic development has long dominated the agendas and politics of urban governments, the new consumption-based versions associated with an international market culture appear to be particularly problematic. Reichl attributes this to the stultifying effect of Disneyesque places on social diversity and democratic social life. Assessing the recent redevelopment of Times Square in New York, he observes: "In an effort to create a place marketable to mainstream tourists and corporate tenants, a coalition of public and private elites imposed a Disney model of controlled, themed public space on an area of remarkable, if unsettling, diversity. In doing so, they sacrificed the provocative, raw energy produced by the friction of different social groups in close interaction for the stultifying hum of a smoothly functioning machine for commercial consumption."[40]

---

[39] Ray Waddell. "SFX Pays $93.6 Mil. for Nederlander Interests," *Amusement Business*, 8 February 1999, 1,6.

[40] Alexander Reichl, *Reconstructing Times Square: Politics and Culture in Urban Development* (Lawrence, KA: University Press of Kansas, 1999), 179.

According to Andranovich, Burbank, and Keying, the well-crafted image of the city that we find in "tourist bubbles" such as Times Square contributes to the sense that downtowns are being reshaped for recreational users rather than for those who actually live in the city.[41] Julier notes that the conversion of focused pockets of the cityscape into outposts of the new cultural economy of postindustrial cities may be undertaken as "a local response to the globalization of capital and the demand to attract international investment," but it ends up as "a way of producing an illusion of the cultural capital of urban unity for the benefit and reward of upper- and middle-class commitment to urban living."[42] Each of these academic observers (Reichl, Andranovich, and Julier) similarly critiques the consumption-based development associated with the global entertainment economy on the grounds that it is undemocratic, socially exclusive, and rigidly predictable. The danger here is that the identities of our urban centres will be undermined even as global power relationships are being enforced.[43]

In further considering the implications of the trend toward theme-park-style urban development, three specific impact areas can be identified: urban governance, public space and community life, and Canadian cultural identity.

Urban Governance

In an article in a leading international urban studies journal, Australian social scientists Glen Searle and Michael Bounds describe some recent difficulties faced by the state government of New South Wales (NSW). With urban planning and development control constitutionally the responsibility of the states rather than the federal or local governments, New South Wales has found itself on the horns of a dilemma. On the one hand, changes in federal politics have favoured a shift to a market-driven economy in which government functions are downsized, privatized, and corporatized. At the same time, Australia has seen an escalating inter-city competition to attract global capital, notably that attached to the entertainment industry. The NSW state government has reacted to this by implementing policies that favour the reduction of local impediments to development and the sale or lease of its own landholdings to entertainment entrepreneurs on favourable terms. Drawing on three case studies—the Eastern Creek Raceway, the Sydney Casino, and the Year 2000 Olympic Games, Searle and Bounds demonstrate how the pressure to bid for facilities and events associated with global entertainment and consumption led the NSW government to appropriate local planning powers in order to fast-track the projects and circumvent environmental challenges.[44]

As is the case in Australia, the increasing emphasis of urban governance in Canada and the United States has been on "public-private partnerships" oriented toward an explicit eco-

---

41   Greg Andranovich, Matthew J. Burbank, and Charles H. Hewing, "Olympic Cities: Lessons Learned from Mega-event Politics," *Journal of Urban Affairs* 23 (2001), 115–16.

42   Julier, *The Culture of Design*, 28–30.

43   Steven Miles, "The Consuming Paradox: A New Research Agenda for Urban Consumption," *Urban Studies* 35 (1998): 1001–8.

44   Glen Searle and Michael Bounds, "State Powers, State Land and Competition for Global Entertainment: The Case of Sydney," *International Journal of Urban and Regional Research* 23 (1999): 165–72.

nomic development agenda rather than the social, redistributional one that characterized the postwar period.[45] in this new policy environment, governments increasingly play the role of urban entrepreneurs, devising place-marketing strategies that they then direct toward the global "image bank" for consumption by media, sport, and leisure corporations.[46] But some major liabilities are attached to this form of cultural "smokestack chasing."

As Grant and Hutchison have discussed in the case of foreign manufacturing investment in American states, an incongruity is growing rapidly between the devolution of development functions to government units with smaller and fixed boundaries and the rising global economic reach of the corporations with whom they must deal. That is, state and provincial governments "are being inserted into a global economy and called upon to play a larger role in deciding their economic destinies, while the forces that shape those destinies are often too overwhelming or distant for them to manage."[47] Using time series data for the years 1978–85, Grant and Hutchison found that states that were drawn far beyond their borders into the game of "global smokestack chasing" soon floundered in deep water. Four supply-side "policy packages" are commonly used to lure foreign factories: debt financing programs that make or guarantee loans to business; geographically targeted policies meant to stimulate development in selected areas within states; labour market deregulation policies—such as abolishing the minimum wage—that lower labour costs for corporations; and regressive tax policies, such as corporate income tax exemptions, designed to reduce the tax burden imposed on corporations. Only the latter measure was found to have any significant effect or influence on corporate location decisions.

In their attempts to attract sports teams, casinos, entertainment malls, and hallmark events (e.g. Olympic Games), Canadian municipal and provincial governments are beginning to confront the same kind of pressures of a spatialized global economy that have dogged American smokestack chasers. Consider, for example, the case of the "Technodome," the most ambitious urban entertainment project heretofore proposed for a Canadian urban setting.

The "Technodome"

In 1995, the Urban Land Institute, a research and lobby group for the American real estate industry, began its sponsorship of an annual conference on urban entertainment development. Among those powerfully impressed by what they were hearing was Abraham Reichmann, president of Heathmount A.E. Corp., a private company that "exists to put Canada on the theme park map."[48] With his uncle Albert, former chairman of Olympia and

45   Stephen Graham and Simon Marvin, *Telecommunications and the City: Electronic Spaces, Urban Places* (London and New York: Routledge, 1996), 42.

46   See David Harvey, "Urban Places in the 'Global Village': Reflections on the Urban Condition in Late Twentieth Century Capitalism," in *World Cities and the Future of the Metropoles*, ed. Luigi Mazza (Milan: Electra, 1988), 23.

47   Don Sherman Grant Ill and Richard Hutchison, "Global Smokestack Chasing: A Comparison of the State-level Determinants of Foreign and Domestic Manufacturing Investment," *Social Problems* 43 (1996): 22–3.

48   Eric Reguly "Reichmann: The Next Generation Takes a Shot," *The Globe & Mail*, 6 April 1999, A10.

York Developments, Ltd. (once the world's largest commercial real estate developer), on board as chairman and chief executive, Abraham set about making his mark. After unsuccessful efforts to put a movie studio attraction on the grounds of the Canadian National Exhibition (CNE), in Toronto, and build a $2 billion Theme park near Niagara Falls, New York, Heathmount had its proposal accepted in principle for the $1 billion "Technodome."

Initially designed to be built on a corner of the 525-hectare former military base at Downsview in northwestern Toronto, the 600,000-square-metre Technodome was to include an indoor ski hill, a white-water kayaking facility, a beach, a rainforest, a thirty-screen multiplex cinema, a Hollywood-style movie studio and a re-creation of Bourbon Street in New Orleans. On hearing that the project had been given the green light, Mel Lastman, the mayor of North York (and subsequently the mayor of Toronto), proclaimed with characteristic hyperbole that the Technodome "will be the No. 1 jewel in all of the GTA [Greater Toronto Area]; there's nothing like it in the whole world."[49]

In March 1999, however, newspapers in Toronto and Montreal reported that the Reichmanns were considering moving the Technodome to Montreal, on the grounds that Canada Lands Company, the Crown agency in charge of the Downsview redevelopment, insisted on leasing the site rather than selling the land needed for the project. While Heathmount's first choice was said to be federal land in the westernmost part of the Port of Montreal, it was considering a site farther west at the "Technoparc," an underutilized, high technology industrial park next to the Bonaventure Expressway. This option was made even more attractive by the provincially run industrial development corporation Société générale de financement (SGF), which was reported to have offered to invest as much as 40 to 45 percent of the $135 million Technodome start-up costs. A month later, Heathmount made its decision public and official, announcing that the Technoparc locale had won out. Both the *Globe & Mail* and the *National Post* declared this to be a "development victory" for Montreal.

Some industry observers have suggested that the Technodome project is a white elephant that is too expensive ever to be built in either Toronto or Montreal; nevertheless, this episode has raised some pertinent questions about urban entertainment destinations and public policy. As financial journalist Eric Reguly noted in his *Globe & Mail* column, projects such as the Technodome are far too large to be guided by a small, virtually unknown Crown corporation whose specialties have been helping to dispose of surplus federal property and finding new uses for redundant military bases.[50] At the same time, local governments in both cities, caught up in a current of cultural smokestack chasing, do not seem to be capable of critically appraising whether the Technodome project is feasible, affordable, and environmentally compatible. They appear instead to see it simply as something that would give their city a competitive edge in the urban growth game. Thus the Montreal city councillor in charge of economic development was quoted as saying, "the price (of land) won't be an object, it won't be a major, determining consideration."[51]

[49]   Alan Barnes, "Unveiled: A New Downsview," *Toronto Star*, 25 April 1997, A1.

[50]   Eric Reguly, "Downsview Debacle Needs Leadership," *The Globe & Mail*, 25 March 1999, B2.

[51]   Estanislao Osiewicz and Tu Thanh Ha, "Montreal's $1 Billion Coup Infuriates Lastman," *The Globe & Mail*, 26 March 1999, A1.

More generally, the Technodome negotiations highlight what Leaf and Pamuk have identified as "the central dilemma of globalization." This is the tension between the conflicting roles of the state as a "facilitator" linking nations and communities with the global economy and as a "guardian" seeking to protect its citizenry from the more negative impacts of global capitalism.[52] Reflecting on the rise and fall of property-led development in London and New York in the 1980s and 1990s, Rutgers University planning professor Susan Fainstein insists that economic restructuring and redevelopment, including the theme park development of the future, can be adequately directed only by understanding how the global and the local arenas interact. Furthermore, she recommends a new type of improved public-private partnership that would better balance the facilitator and guardian roles of the state. In Fainstein's view, it is inevitable that giant, multinational, service-producing corporations will come calling. Public policy makers therefore have to be prepared to "tap into their economic power" while making sure that urban populations do not "remain hostage to 'private' decisions shielded from democratic scrutiny despite their public significance."[53]

Public Space and Local Community Life

One of the chief attractions of the new entertainment economy has been its promise of reviving face-to-face interaction in urban settings. It is therefore treated by some observers as a much needed antidote to the disembodied form of communication found in Internet chat rooms and other such computer-mediated settings. Commenting on the recent boom-let in public lectures, *Globe & Mail* columnist Michael Valpy praised Toronto as a city of real, not virtual, meeting places: "If the cinema business knows what it is doing, cocoon-ing is tottering. Huge multiscreen cineplexes are mushrooming through Toronto from the downtown to the suburbs. Ten thousand people throng the nightclub zone on a summer's weekend night. Lunchtime pulsates with neat little cafés. Telecommuting just hasn't hap-pened."[54]

In Valpy's view, we are seeking out a more actively human experience than is possible by renting a video or surfing the Internet, although perhaps not as social as the bowling lionized by political scientist Robert Putnam as the key to civic economic success and democracy.[55]

Sociologist Craig Calhoun, in contrast, argues that new communications technologies such as the Internet have fostered the atomizing of the city into small-scale enclaves with weak local connections to each other. What he is thinking of in particular is the tremen-dous growth of gated communities in suburban and exurban areas. These gated enclaves are said to foster the compartmentalization of community life, something which is "anti-thetical to the social constitution of a vital public sphere."

52 Michael Leaf and Ayse Pamuk, "Habitat II and the Globalization of Ideas," *Journal of Planning Education and Research* 17 (1997): 71–8.

53 Susan S. Fainstein, *The City Builders: Property Politics, and Planning in London and New York* (Oxford, UK, and Cambridge, MA: Blackwell, 1994), 252–3.

54 Michael Valpy, "Flocking to Lectures: Live and in Person," *The Globe & Mail*, 30 March 1999, A11.

55 Robert Putnam, *Bowling Alone: The Collapse and Revival of American Community* (New York: Simon and Schuster, 2000).

Valpy and Calhoun share a conviction that urban public life based on propinquity is preferable to virtual communities, which rarely "pull beyond one's immediate personal choices of taste and culture." Calhoun's ideal seems to be the eighteenth-century European city, which was chock full of coffee houses, theatres, public festivals, and other "public spaces" in which people of different social identities were drawn into contact. By contrast, the industrial revolution, the rise of urban planning, and the new technologies of transportation and communication have collectively robbed cities of their public spaces and established an overwhelming plurality of what he terms "indirect social relations," those which involve no physical co-presence but instead exist only through the intermediation of information technology and/or bureaucratic organizations. Thus, sitting at the Lanterna, a café in Greenwich Village noted for its splendid apricot tarts, Calhoun concludes that electronically mediated groups and networks are limited in their capacity to enhance citizen power in democracies. Here he is reacting to a comment by William Mitchell in his book *City of Bits*, in which Mitchell refers to his computer keyboard as his "café." Calhoun counters that his café is in Greenwich Village, not the electronic village, contending that the Lanterna and the cybercafé down the street are both "sociable public space" where there are "dimensions of publicness and sociability [that are] reproduced poorly if at all in computer-mediated communication." Electronically mediated groups work best, he believes, as supplements to face-to-face encounters. With "cyberdemocracy" thus running far behind the "cybercapitalism" of globalized financial markets, local urban settings remain absolutely vital to preserving and enhancing public discourse.[56]

If Calhoun and Valpy are correct, then are the leisure-soaked, consumption-based cities that are created by the global entertainment economy hotbeds of civility and urbanity? Certainly, the promoters of fantasy cities like to think so. "Consumers crave the functionality of the city: dense, eclectic, spontaneous, pedestrian environments where entertainment, dining and retail options are in close proximity," suggest urban entertainment consultants Patrick Phillips and Jay Wheatley.[57] Reflecting on Berlin's future as a cultural capital, *New York Times* bureau chief Roger Cohen describes the Potsdamer Platz as a "sea of anonymous commercialism" but admits that "the development has proved hugely popular, one of the few places where 'Ossis' and 'Wessis' really mingle."[58] Other observers of the theme park city, however, detect a bleaker future. Paul Goldberger, the noted New York architectural critic, has identified the proliferation of "urbanoid environments," sealed-off private spaces which purport to be public places, but which lack all the energy, variety, visual stimulation, and cultural opportunities of the real thing. Intimately linked to the fusion of consumerism, entertainment, and popular culture, this counterfeit form of urban experience is measured,

56 Craig Calhoun, "Community without Propinquity Revisited: Communications Technology and the Transformation of the Urban Public Sphere," *Sociological Inquiry* 68 (1998): 373–97.

57 Patrick Phillips and D. Wheatley, "Urban Chic," in *Developing Urban Entertainment Centers*, by M. Beyard et al., 19.

58 Roger Cohen, "Building a Capital Where Triumph Is Taboo," *The New York Times*, 11 April 1999, section 2, 33. This is especially true for the adjacent shopping mall where, during a recent visit, I observed local families sitting down for a traditional midday meal.

controlled, and tightly organized—cleaner and safer but also flatter and duller. Its shops and cafés are filled with consumers of culture, not with the makers and shapers of it.[59]

Another important aspect of this policy debate revolves around the influence of entertainment development on social equity and exclusion. According to Fainstein, this issue has two facets: the direct impacts of projects on different social groupings, and the extent to which the public receives the benefits of socially created gain in the value of property.[60]

Affordability constitutes one major barrier to accessibility. By and large, these new entertainment destinations are designed to attract out-of-town tourists and affluent suburban "day trippers" embarked on "leisure safaris into the depths of the postmodern metropolis."[61] As such, they remain beyond the financial reach of local residents. Referring to recent changes in contemporary Los Angeles, Mike Davis argues they mark the demise of what was once a genuine "democratic space"—free beaches, luxurious parks, and "cruising strips."[62] In some cases, these projects may also end up forcing the poor and disadvantaged out of urban spaces that they formerly occupied and utilized.

Furthermore, the economic "spillover" effects from leisure and entertainment development are not overwhelming. In one of the most comprehensive empirical analyses of its type, American economist Robert Baade charted the impact of new stadiums and professional sports teams on income levels for the eight major regions in the continental United States between 1959 and 1987. His results indicate that professional sports teams in fact have little impact on a city's economy.[63] In a similar fashion, Marc Levine failed to detect much economic spillover to local shops and businesses from the festival marketplace development around Baltimore's Inner Harbor in the 1970s.[64] It is still too early to know whether the urban entertainment destinations of today will create any economic ripples in surrounding neighbourhoods and communities, but this result can by no means be assumed.

Canadian Cultural Identity

In contrast to the topic of foreign media ownership and cultural protection policies, which has been extensively documented and analyzed, little is known about the effects of locality-based entertainment on Canadian culture and identity.

A little more than three decades ago, *Financial Post* journalist Robert Perry published a series of controversial *Post* articles in the form of a book entitled *Galt, U.S.A.: The American Presence in a Canadian City* (1971). Near the beginning of the book, Perry profiled what he

---

[59] Paul Goldberger, "The Rise of the Private City," in *Breaking Away: The Future of Cities*, ed. J. Vitullo-Martin (New York: The Twentieth Century Fund Press, 1996), 146.

[60] Fainstein, *The City Builders*, 245.

[61] Hannigan, *Fantasy City*, 200.

[62] Mike Davis, *City of Quartz: Excavating the Future in Los Angeles* (New York: Verso, 1990), 227.

[63] Robert A. Baade, "Stadiums, Professional Sports and City Economies: An Analysis of the United States Experience," in *The Stadium and the City*, ed. J. Bole and O. Moen (Keele, Staffordshire: Keele University Press, 1995), 277–94.

[64] Marc V. Levine, "Downtown Development as an Urban Growth Strategy: A Critical Appraisal of the Baltimore Renaissance," *Journal of Urban Affairs* 9 (1987): 103–23.

called "Popcult Galt," a New Jersey-style motel and fast-food strip along Hespeler Road, which ran between the city limits and the downtown. With its 7.5-metre-high rocket ship outside the Satellite Motel and a giant snowman guarding the entrance to the Thunderbird golf driving range, the Hespeler Road strip was perhaps an early harbinger of the coming of the theme park cities of the 1990s. Even the now long-defunct Red Barn hamburger drive-in, owned and operated by a Canadian, used American marketing techniques, standards, specifications, systems, and methods, giving its American franchisers, Perry observed, "the ultimate control."[65]

A decade later, Taft Broadcasting of Cincinnati, Ohio, added to their theme park chain by opening "Canada's Wonderland" near Maple, Ontario, just north of Toronto. In a remarkably blunt assessment recorded five years earlier, Provincial Treasurer Darcy McKeough had posed some potentially sticky questions to his cabinet colleagues:

1. Why can't a Canadian business take on this type of project? On the assumption that there may be room for only one such park in Southern Ontario, would we be shutting out the possibility of a future Canadian operation?

2. This thing could be seen as a Canadian "Disneyland" (or I guess it would be "Yogi Bear Land") and some people will argue about the cultural implications of putting it into the hands of an American operation.[66]

Despite McKeough's qualms, the provincial cabinet, under pressure from the Ministry of Industry and Tourism, readily blessed the proposed theme park, as did the federal Foreign Investment Review Agency. Yet aside from the name itself, very little in the park was in any way representative of Canadian life. Writing on the eve of its opening, York University geographers James Cameron and Ronald Bordessa issued this warning: "In spite of all its sophistication in marketing techniques, the Taft Broadcasting Company cannot altogether obliterate cultural differences though the sobering conclusion is that they almost certainly will become one of the agents promoting its steady erosion."[67]

Now, the next wave of foreign cultural content is about to descend upon Canadian cities. It is aggressively themed and is branded around American pop celebrities, sports stars, and cartoon characters. If there is a template for this, it could well be DisneyQuest, the entertainment giant's major new initiative into the urban entertainment market. A multistorey interactive indoor theme park that uses computer-based virtual reality technology. DisneyQuest can be described as a sort of "portable Disney World," designed to "deliver a piece of the Disney magic closer to people's houses."[68] From the swirling Hurricane Mickey logo on the exterior of the building to the video games and rides inside—Buzz Lightyear's Astro Blaster (based on a character from the Disney movie *Toy Story*), Aladdin's Magic Carpet Ride—DisneyQuest is meant to consciously exploit synergies

[65] Robert Perry, *Galt, U.S.A.: The American Presence in a Canadian City* (Toronto: Maclean-Hunter, 1971), 65.

[66] McKeough's comments are cited in James M. Cameron and Ronald Bordessa, *Wonderland through the Looking Glass: Politics, Culture and Planning in International Recreation* (Maple, ON: Belston, 1981), 56.

[67] Cameron and Bordessa, *Wonderland through the Looking Glass*, 120.

[68] David Lasker, "A Virtual Disney World Close to Home," *The Globe & Mail*, 27 March 1999, C20.

with Disney's movie characters. With prototypes in Orlando and Chicago, Disney plans to franchise the project both domestically and internationally, including locations in Canadian cities.

Some scholars might respond to the planned rollout of the DisneyQuest model across the globe by citing the phenomenon of "glocalization," whereby the negative effects of a global consumer culture are progressively mitigated as they interact with local values and structures. For example, the contributors to editor James Watson's book *Golden Arches East: McDonald's in East Asia* (1997) demonstrate how East Asian consumers have eliminated the "fast" from fast food, transforming their McDonald's outlets into local institutions where the relations between staff and customers have become personalized (Beijing, Hong Kong) or politicized (Taipei). In many parts of the region, the Golden Arches have come to house leisure centres, after-school clubs, and meeting halls. One contributor to the book, David Wu, observes that in today's Taiwan two opposite forms of consumption, the "hyperlocal" (as symbolized by betel-nut chewing) and the "transnational" (eating "Big Macs") coexist, and to a surprising extent reinforce one another as expressions of national identity.[69]

At first glance, it is difficult, to envision how this glocalization process might operate in the Canadian context. While there are clear and documented differences in Canadian and American consumer tastes—we evidently prefer doughnuts, poutine, and Canadian Tire—our choices in music, clothing, and entertainment tend to be similar, suggesting that local values and structures are unlikely to mitigate the negative effects of global consumer culture. At the same time, some identifiable differences exist. Reporting on the most recent results of an annual poll that measures attitudes of Canadian versus American respondents on several social and cultural issues, Michael Adams of the Environics Research Group found that Canadians have fundamentally different views about dealing with conflict, about relating to their parents and children, and about relating to authority. For example, Canadians are more likely to favour accommodation rather than domination as a problem-solving strategy. "Globalization," Adams asserts, "may actually enhance the difference among cultures, rather than converge them."[70] While researchers have not provided comprehensive content analyses of the branded cultural products and images that are flowing into Canada as part of the expanding global entertainment economy, researchers have examined in great detail the ideological tropes contained in Disney movies and theme parks. These clearly emphasize such traditional American value themes as "America as the land of opportunity" and "the right to bear arms in defense of liberty."[71] When confronted with such lessons as part of the cultural discourse embedded in the current generation of

---

[69]   David Y.H. Wu, "McDonald's in Taipei: Hamburgers, Betel Nuts, and National Identity," in *Golden Arches East: McDonald's in East Asia*, ed. J.L. Watson (Stanford, CA: Stanford University Press, 1997), 110–35.

[70]   David Akin, "We're Becoming Less like Americans: Poll," *National Post*, 21 June 2001, A8.

[71]   Stephen Fjellman, for example, argues that Frederick Jackson Turner's "frontier thesis" of 1893 is "enshrined at Walt Disney World." Here, space is depicted as the new frontier, the conquering of which will permit Americans "to retain the entrepreneurial individualism that is our characteristic right as Americans." Stephen M. Fjellman, *Vinyl Leaves: Walt Disney World and America* (Boulder, CO: Westview Press, 1992), 60.

high technology rides, games, and themed attractions, will Canadian teenagers be capable of maintaining a critical distance or will they accept these messages at face value?

POLICY IMPLICATIONS AND OPTIONS

In the past, cultural industries policy in Canada has been guided by two main arguments.[72] According to the economic (or industrial) argument, the federal government is compelled to intervene in the marketplace in order to nurture and protect Canadian-owned business-es that otherwise could not survive in the hurly-burly of intense international competition. In particular, Canadian companies are said to be potentially threatened by foreign-owned branch plants that supply imported content to the domestic market at a small fraction of the cost of generating comparable Canadian content.[73] The second, and perhaps more fun-damental, argument used to establish cultural industries policy is a cultural one. This cul-tural argument maintains that telecommunications, broadcasting, film, publishing, and recordings are instruments for nation-building; they are the key to establishing and main-taining a distinct Canadian identity. Even in the midst of a continuous flood of American messages and images, Canadian personalities, viewpoints, and landscapes have continued to flourish, but only because they are shielded by a system of subsidies, tax breaks, and protective legislation.

In recent years, however, a crisis has been steadily looming. David Taras argues that the pace of envelopment by American popular culture has been accelerating as a consequence of structural changes in broadcasting, particularly television. He cites three changes that have been of special importance: new economies of scale enjoyed by the US television industry, which give it enormous advantages over its Canadian competitors; the changing circumstances of the CBC, which has been reeling under fiscal strain and is unable to rec-oncile its obligations to serve a series of minority audiences with its financial need to cap-ture a mass audience; and the advent of new technologies such as satellite, cable, and video, which have splintered audiences into narrow segments[74] and left Canadian television networks open to what Marc Raboy has called "the brutality of the gutted marketplace."[75]

What then of the rapidly diffusing global entertainment economy? Should the Canadian public policy response to this trend be neutral, supportive, or regulatory? If the latter, should it follow the dual direction that has been set by cultural policy in the past or carve out a new trail? To begin with, I detect two major difficulties.

As Magder has argued, the Canadian state is currently divided between agencies and departments that have business and economics as their focus and are committed to trade liberalization and neoliberal economics, and the cultural industries portfolio, which back-

---

[72]   See Rowland Lorimer and Jean McNulty, *Mass Communication in Canada* (Toronto: Oxford University Press, 1996), 194.

[73]   Paul Audley, *Canada's Cultural Industries: Broadcasting, Publishing, Records and Film* (Toronto: Lorimer, 1983), 320–1.

[74]   David Taras, "Defending the Cultural Frontier: Canadian Television and Continental Integration," in *Seeing Ourselves: Media Power and Policy in Canada*, ed. David Taras and Helen Holmes (Toronto: Harcourt Brace Jovanovich Canada, 1992), 178–82.

[75]   Marc Raboy, *Missed Opportunities: The Story of Canada's Broadcasting Policy* (Montreal: McGill-Queen's University Press, 1990), 250.

stops a welter of protectionist policy measures "that muddy the marketplace transparency much in vogue."[76] As was noted earlier, this tension between the conflicting role of the state as "facilitator" and "guardian" constitutes one of the central dilemmas of globalization. The problem is even more acute when we turn to local politics and administration, where an "urban growth machine" promotes the development of tourism and entertainment destinations as one of its major objectives. As Rosentraub has noted with regard to the head-long rush to attract professional sports teams to North American cities, "the provision of subsidies to influence the location of capital has been a constant and frustrating component of local economic policy" and one which has been dictated in no small part by the "imperatives of global competition."[77] An outstanding example of this trend is the current scheme to massively redevelop the Toronto waterfront. Rather than being determined by an extensive and open public debate, the future of the Port Lands, the CNE grounds, and the Inner Harbour appears set to follow from the Fung Report (Toronto Waterfront Revitalization Task Force Report), which was written with one eye on Toronto's bid to "win" the right to stage the 2008 Summer Olympic Games. This area will therefore be developed into a sports, entertainment, and leisure corridor. Local space is thus (potentially) transformed into a globalized "hub" where flows of finance, information, people, goods, and services are temporarily targeted and assembled.[78]

Second, the global entertainment economy crosses so many jurisdictions and purviews that it cannot easily be fitted into a single policy area. Mostly, decisions about megamalls and megaplexes, sports stadiums and gambling casinos, end up being made narrowly on the basis of compliance to land use and zoning regulations, with no serious discussion of the social and cultural impacts. Too often, decisions are made about individual projects and proposals without situating them within a wider policy framework. What is sorely lacking in Canada is a national urban policy. Since the demise of Urban Affairs Canada in the 1970s, the responsibility for deciding on the future of cities has been downloaded onto the provinces and onto local municipalities that rarely take into account the larger picture. Those issues that do show up on the larger radar screen—the questionable effects of casino gambling, the advisability of tax subsidies to sports team owners—tend to be debated in relative isolation. At the same time, a nearly complete policy vacuum envelops other government programs and activities that fall outside the traditional watershed of cultural/communications policy; the disposal of surplus federal lands by Canada Lands Co. Ltd. (see the case study, above, on the Technodome controversy) is a good example of this.

Before concluding whether Canadian public policy should respond pro-actively to urban entertainment development with support, neutrality, or regulation, it is necessary to document the magnitude of this type of development in Canada, its organizational co-ordinates, and its effects on the local community. In a collection of articles on "Business Elites and Urban Development," published in 1988, editor Scott Cummings suggests four general themes

---

[76] Ted Magder, "Franchising the Candy Store: Split-run Magazines and a New International Regime for Trade in Culture," *Canadian-American Public Policy* 3 (April 1998): 47.

[77] Mark Rosentraub, *Major League Losers: The Real Cost of Sports and Who's Paying for It* (New York: Basic Books, 1999).

[78] Maurice Roche, *Mega-events and Modernity: Olympics and Expos in the Growth of Global Culture* (London and New York: Routledge, 2000), 233.

related to the encounter between private enterprise and public policy in the urban context of the 1980s. First, it is necessary to identify: the preferred strategies for urban growth of urban business elites, who typically establish development coalitions and use public institutions to design and implement a growth agenda for their cities that is consistent with enhancing their own prosperity; and the conflicts that result between private benefits and the public good.[79] Second, we should consider the ability of real estate interests and others centrally implicated in the economic redevelopment of the city to mobilize resources from the local state and how this can be successfully countered by community and neighbourhood groups. Third, we need to look at how local development strategies are being influenced by extra-local events and investment trends, especially those that occur within an international economic context. Finally, it is important to document how changes in the organization of space, which are related to the changing economy, have produced a "dual city" marked by increasing class polarization.[80] Cummings's four themes can easily be applied to the case of the global entertainment economies and the city of the twenty-first century, and they provide a logical starting point for a systematic public policy analysis.

CONCLUSION

As the new millennium begins, corporate "brand empires" are rapidly hiving off from television, motion pictures, and professional sports, and "colonizing" urban downtowns and exurban malls, museums and schools, holidays and festivals. Much as fast-food giant McDonald's has already done, leisure developers such Nike, Disney, and Virgin "are trumpeting their brands by using comforting, familiar logos, thus attracting a large percentage of the population."[81] In doing so, they may well end up undermining communities of propinquity or place that for many Canadians remain a key source of identity and culture.

In its romanticized and overly simplified version of this process, Hollywood depicts a David and Goliath battle between the people-oriented "shop around the corner" and the profit driven megastore. In real communities, however, the tension between the global and the local is more subtle. Just before sitting down to write this, I went for a walk along Queen Street, the major shopping avenue in our east Toronto waterfront neighbourhood. Stopping for coffee at a Starbucks, I noted that the franchisee had mounted a new exhibition of paintings by local artists on the walls of the café and was advertising a series of poetry readings on Sunday afternoons. As I sipped my drink, I browsed through our community newspaper, noting a letter to the editor and a column by a local historian, both calling for a campaign to save a local boathouse, first built in the 1930s, which has fallen into a state of disrepair. On the way back, I saw a woman wearing a leather and suede jacket on which was prominently displayed the logo of "Silver City," a new megaplex cinema chain that has begun to ripple across the Canadian urban landscape. What these seemingly disparate events have in common is that each in some way indicates a differing brushstroke

---

[79] Scott Cummings, "Private Enterprise and Public Policy: Business Hegemony in the Metropolis," in *Business Elites and Urban Development: Case Studies and Critical Perspectives*, ed. S. Cummings (Albany, NY: State University of New York Press, 1988), 13.

[80] Ibid., 3–21.

[81] Olivier Courteaux, "The Inner City for Fun and Profit," *National Post*, 19 March 1999, B5.

on the evolving canvas of the local/global community. Neighbourhoods like mine are fast becoming sites for contrasting "economies of signs and spaces."[82] Some, like the Silver Birch Boathouse, are viewed by long-time residents as pieces of area history that should be cherished and kept. Others, such as the Silver City jacket, are mobile advertisements for new entertainment brands. Starbucks is one of the hot global brands of the 1990s, but, here at least, it has made a token gesture toward supporting the local artistic and literary scene. Indeed, it is in the context of everyday community life that we can best find the nexus between traditional values and the new outlooks associated with globalization.

Attention must also be paid to the role of the state in responding to the emerging global entertainment economy. . . . Marc Raboy observes that the pursuit of public policy objectives in culture and communication today requires a shift in focus from the national to the global policy arena and appropriate strategies for intervention through new global policy mechanisms. Yet are there any transnational fora that pertain to complementary markets and themed leisure retail experiences, as there are for telecommunications standards or intellectual property rights? Is there a disjunction between the spread of the global entertainment economy and the simultaneous movement of governance downward and outward to lower levels of the government, the market, and the community? How can we best rationalize the seemingly conflicting roles of the state as both cultural smokestack chaser and guardian of Canadian culture?

Muddying the waters somewhat is the recent surge of Canadian cultural exports, especially to the United States. According to a Statistics Canada report released in June 2001, exports of Canadian culture were worth $4.5 billion in the year 2000, up nearly 40 percent since 1996.[83] While this figure may be skewed by the massive sales of recorded music by a handful of Canadian-born performers—Shania Twain, Céline Dion, Alanis Morissette— it nevertheless also includes creative powerhouses such as Cirque du Soleil, which has become a fixture both in Las Vegas casinos and Disney theme parks. With culture becoming one of Canada's fastest-growing export sectors, governments need to become more pro-active in providing financial and marketing support to domestic producers and performers. One possible approach is to promote cultural exports more aggressively through the Export Development Corporation. Such a position would reinforce the situation that the editors of this collection [Cameron and Stein] have described as "the handmaiden state," in which public policy concentrates on facilitating entry into the global economy by producing a climate favourable to research and innovation and by providing higher levels of technical training. For example, the much heralded program in computer animation at Sheridan College, in Oakville, Ontario, can be seen as a template insofar as it provides Canadian-trained talent for Disney, DreamWorks, and other film studios that have re-embraced animated feature films. Despite such initiatives, however, the corporate conveyor belts from south of the border continue to bring in more cultural product than we export. Furthermore, Canadians must often necessarily work within the framework of American formulas for motion pictures, television shows, and themed attractions, which dictate a maximum branding potential and a minimum degree of moral complexity. As a result, national identities may erode over time, even as made-in-Canada cultural products achieve

---

[82]   See Scott Lash and John Urry, *Economies of Signs and Spaces* (London: Sage Publications, 1994).

[83]   Chris Cobb, "Pop Icons Bring Wealth into Canada," *National Post*, 21 June 2001, A8.

higher numbers. This is especially relevant at the level of local communities, which tend to become repositories of shared cultures and political loyalties in the face of the weakening of national identities.

Finally, as Cameron and Stein suggest in their conclusion to this volume [*Street Protests and Fantasy Parks: Globalization, Culture and the State*, Vancouver: UBC Press, 2002], the process of globalization cannot be expected to "march in an uninterrupted, smooth, linear sequence". This statement is especially relevant with regard to urban entertainment development, which depends on ever-increasing flows of investment money, hot new global brands, and foreign tourists. Already, there are humps in the road, with cinema chains facing bankruptcy because of the overcapacity created by an orgy of megaplex construction, and some of the better-known themed restaurant chains (Rainforest Café, Planet Hollywood) battling to stay alive. If city planners and politicians persist in investing significant sums of taxpayer dollars in infrastructure, subsidies, and promotions linked to the tourist economy while ignoring festering issues of poverty, homelessness, and widening social inequality, we most certainly risk ending up becoming, in Cameron and Stein's words, a "state of unrequited dreams". Governments, then, must find a better accommodation between their dual roles as "facilitators" and "guardians," both at the broad level of policy making and in the specific details that spell out the parameters of public-private partnerships.

SECTION 4 TERMINOLOGY

Accountability

Boomer Generation

Brokerage Party

Canadian Charter of Rights and Freedoms

Civil Society

Common law

Constituency/Riding

Convention

Crown Corporation

Electoral System

Executive

Generation X

Generation Y

Globalization

Glocalization

Hegemony

Initiatives

Judiciary

Legislature (Legislative Assembly)

Legitimacy

McWorld

Majority (majority government)

Mandate

Market-driven economy

Ministers of the Crown

MPs (Members of Parliament)

Notwithstanding Clause

Oligarchy

Oligopoly

Orders-in-council

Parliament

Patronage

Plurality

Populism

Primary

Privy Council Office (PCO)

Programmatic Party

Question Period

Recall

Referenda

Representative Democracy

Responsible Government

Spin Doctors

SECTION 4 DISCUSSION QUESTIONS

1. Increasing the executive branch's accountability would bring with it not only benefits but also certain negative consequences. List and discuss the likely results, both positive and negative, of requiring the executive branch to be more accountable to the legislature.

2. Survey evidence reveals that the Canadian public is likely to support the Courts over Parliament in cases where legislation challenges the Charter. Can you think of a situation in which Parliament should be able to overrule the Courts?

3. Political parties play an important role in the smooth functioning of the political system. What roles do parties play that interest groups and social movements cannot?

4. As a consumer, it can sometimes be hard to see the downside to having access to Starbucks coffee 24/7. Adopting a different perspective, can you think of reasons why communities should be wary of opening themselves up to generic globalized businesses?

5. Thinking of the political arena as a system made up of various parts, what evidence would you need to argue that it was functioning efficiently? Effectively?

 POLISCI SUPERSITE

Pearson Education Canada's PoliSci Supersite (**www.pearsoned.ca/polisci**) contains a set of text-specific pages for *Ideas, Interests, and Issues*. Visit the Supersite to access a list of relevant weblinks and interesting additional readings tailored to the content of each section.

Section 5

Democratic Governance

SECTION SUMMARY

Few students of political science will not have heard the term "democracy" prior to their first class. The term is commonly employed in the West to identify the "ideal" or "best" political system—a normative evaluation. Why then did Winston Churchill refer to it as "the worst form of government, except all those other forms that have been tried from time to time" (Hansard, 11 November 1947)—in other words, as merely the "least bad" system? This paradox is best understood by distinguishing between the theory that lies behind the concept and its practice. While democratic systems are the best designed to uphold the set of political values deemed central within Western civilizations, in practice they often fall short of the mark. Studying democracy necessitates understanding both what it ought to be as well as the reality of what it is.

The set of readings in this section provides a foundation for understanding democracy in its many guises and, importantly, addresses the current preoccupation with the "democratic deficit." Characterized by a lack of civic engagement in such acts as voting and party membership, and by low levels of political satisfaction and contentment, much attention has been directed, first, to understanding the nature of the phenomenon, and second, to explaining its underlying causes. Given that the success of democracies is often gauged by the levels of participation and satisfaction exhibited by citizens, governments in the West have been occupied with establishing policies and programs designed to stem the tide of unhappiness and withdrawal.

The first article, by Philippe Schmitter and Terry Lynn Karl, establishes the key concepts, principles, and procedures underlying the democratic ideal. As they make clear, the practice of democracy can take many different forms and entails more than simply the holding of elections. Additionally, their identification of the many unrealistic expectations made of democratic systems stands as an important reminder of the need for a clear understanding of the limited ability of single institutions to solve the many troubles within modern political systems.

The remaining articles each address some element of the "democratic deficit." The root cause of this political discontent, Andrew Johnson suggests, is the changed relationship between governments and citizens in Western democracies.

Where governments once adopted social responsibility as a purpose, the market now dominates. The opening up of markets that characterizes the modern phenomenon of globalization can be deemed an economic success, but along with it, governments have to yield a certain level of autonomy. In this new regime, citizens have been redefined as consumers. By definition, however, consumers focus on meeting their wants and desires; allegiance lasts only so long as the ability of the current supplier to meet these needs. In this new world of "self-interested" citizens, Johnston argues, governments' inability to meet the demands of all citizens necessarily leads to political disenchantment. But politics should not be about satisfying the desires of each and every citizen, contends Johnson; it is, rather, about making important collective decisions about whose desires will and will not be met in attempting to generate "the greatest good for the greatest number." Until consumers become citizens once again, conscious of the needs of the collective and fully engaged in the process of democratic decision-making, political discontent is unlikely to diminish.

The next two readings tackle the question of the causes of the "crisis." The Centre for Research and Information on Canada's paper provides a comprehensive review of the evidence suggesting that Canadians are no longer as politically engaged, at least in elections, as they were in the past. Evaluating several possible explanations for the decline, as well as a number of possible solutions, the piece illustrates the complexity of attempting to adopt institutional reform as a remedy when faced with less than perfect information about the problem being confronted. This message is reinforced in the reading by Elisabeth Gidengil, André Blais, Neil Nevitte and Richard Nadeau. Focusing on youth participation in politics, the authors seek to dispel several of the myths surrounding the dramatic decline in youth political engagement. As they point out, youth are more likely to engage in politics if their political interest rises, a shift that may be brought about by targeted efforts to engage them in the system. Education presents an additional avenue for redressing the decline, for it provides both the motivation and the skills that give rise to political engagement.

The final reading addresses longstanding concerns with Canada's single-member plurality (or first-past-the-post) electoral system, which some claim is to blame for much of Canada's democratic malaise. The British Columbia Citizens' Assembly on Electoral Reform constitutes an experiment in participatory democracy—its 160 members were drawn randomly from across the province to spend 11 months studying electoral systems in order to deliver a recommendation on whether it ought to be changed. The Assembly's recommendation to change to a Single Transferable Vote System will be the subject of a referendum at the time of the next provincial election in May 2005. The Assembly is not only an important resource on electoral reform but also an instructive example of citizens' willingness to commit to deliberative decision-making and, potentially, of the benefits of engaging the public in political decision-making.

What Democracy Is ...
And Is Not

PHILIPPE C. SCHMITTER AND TERRY LYNN KARL*

*Philippe C. Schmitter is Professor of Political and Social Sciences at the European University Institute of Florence, Italy. Terry Lynn Karl is Professor of Political Science, Stanford University, California.

For some time, the word democracy has been circulating as a debased currency in the political marketplace. Politicians with a wide range of convictions and practices strove to appropriate the label and attach it to their actions. Scholars, conversely, hesitated to use it—without adding qualifying adjectives—because of the ambiguity that surrounds it. The distinguished American political theorist Robert Dahl even tried to introduce a new term, "polyarchy," in its stead in the (vain) hope of gaining a greater measure of conceptual precision. But for better or worse, we are "stuck" with democracy as the catchword of contemporary political discourse. It is the word that resonates in people's minds and springs from their lips as they struggle for freedom and a better way of life; it is the word whose meaning we must discern if it is to be of any use in guiding political analysis and practice.

The wave of transitions away from autocratic rule that began with Portugal's "Revolution of the Carnations" in 1974 and seems to have crested with the collapse of communist regimes across Eastern Europe in 1989 has produced a welcome convergence toward [a] common definition of democracy.[1] Everywhere there has been a silent abandonment of dubious adjectives like "popular," "guided," "bourgeois," and "formal" to modify "democracy." At the same time, a remarkable consensus has emerged concerning the minimal conditions that polities must meet in order to merit the prestigious appellation of "democratic." Moreover, a number of international organizations now monitor how well these standards are met; indeed, some countries even consider them when formulating foreign policy.[2]

---

[1] For a comparative analysis of the recent regime changes in southern Europe and Latin America, see Guillermo O'Donnell, Philippe C. Schmitter, and Laurence Whitehead, eds., *Transitions from Authoritarian Rule,* 4 vols. (Baltimore: Johns Hopkins University Press, 1986). For another compilation that adopts a more structural approach see Larry Diamond, Juan Linz, and Seymour Martin Lipset, eds., *Democracy in Developing Countries,* vols. 2, 3, and 4 (Boulder, CO: Lynne Rienner, 1989).

[2] Numerous attempts have been made to codify and quantify the existence of democracy across political systems. The best known is probably Freedom House's *Freedom in the World: Political Rights and Civil Liberties,* published since 1973 by Greenwood Press and since 1988 by University Press of America. Also see Charles Humana, *World Human Rights Guide* (New York: Facts on File, 1986).

WHAT DEMOCRACY IS

Let us begin by broadly defining democracy and the generic *concepts* that distinguish it as a unique system for organizing relations between rulers and the ruled. We will then briefly review *procedures,* the rules and arrangements that are needed if democracy is to endure. Finally, we will discuss two operative *principles* that make democracy work. They are not expressly included among the generic concepts or formal procedures, but the prospect for democracy is grim if their underlying conditioning effects are not present.

One of the major themes of this essay is that democracy does not consist of a single unique set of institutions. There are many types of democracy, and their diverse practices produce a similarly varied set of effects. The specific form democracy takes is contingent upon a country's socioeconomic conditions as well as its entrenched state structures and policy practices.

Modern political democracy is a system of governance in which rulers are held accountable for their actions in the public realm by citizens, acting indirectly through the competition and cooperation of their elected representatives.[3]

A *regime or system of governance* is an ensemble of patterns that determines the methods of access to the principal public offices; the characteristics of the actors admitted to or excluded from such access; the strategies that actors may use to gain access; and the rules that are followed in the making of publicly binding decisions. To work properly, the ensemble must be institutionalized—that is to say, the various patterns must be habitually known, practiced, and accepted by most, if not all, actors. Increasingly, the preferred mechanism of institutionalization is a written body of laws undergirded by a written constitution, though many enduring political norms can have an informal, prudential, or traditional basis.[4]

For the sake of economy and comparison, these forms, characteristics, and rules are usually bundled together and given a generic label. Democratic is one; others are autocratic, authoritarian, despotic, dictatorial, tyrannical, totalitarian, absolutist, traditional, monarchic, oligarchic, plutocratic, aristocratic, and sultanistic.[5] Each of these regime forms may in turn be broken down into subtypes.

Like all regimes, democracies depend upon the presence of *rulers,* persons who occupy specialized authority roles and can give legitimate commands to others. What distinguishes

---

[3] The definition most commonly used by American social scientists is that of Joseph Schumpeter: "that institutional arrangement for arriving at political decisions in which individuals acquire the power to decide by means of a competitive struggle for the people's vote." *Capitalism, Socialism, and Democracy* (London: George Allen and Unwin, 1943), 269. We accept certain aspects of the classical procedural approach to modern democracy, but differ primarily in our emphasis on the accountability of rulers to citizens and the relevance of mechanisms of competition other than elections.

[4] Not only do some countries practice a stable form of democracy without a formal constitution (e.g. Great Britain and Israel), but even more countries have constitutions and legal codes that offer no guarantee of reliable practice. On paper, Stalin's 1936 constitution for the USSR was a virtual model of democratic rights and entitlements.

[5] For the most valiant attempt to make some sense out of this thicket of distinctions, see Juan Linz, "Totalitarian and Authoritarian Regimes" in *Handbook of Political Science,* eds. Fred I. Greenstein and Nelson W. Polsby (Reading, MA: Addison Wesley, 1975), 175–411.

democratic rulers from nondemocratic ones are the norms that condition how the former come to power and the practices that hold them accountable for their actions.

The *public realm* encompasses the making of collective norms and choices that are binding on the society and backed by state coercion. Its content can vary a great deal across democracies, depending upon preexisting distinctions between the public and the private, state and society, legitimate coercion and voluntary exchange, and collective needs and individual preferences. The liberal conception of democracy advocates circumscribing the public realm as narrowly as possible, while the socialist or social-democratic approach would extend that realm through regulation, subsidization, and, in some cases, collective ownership of property. Neither is intrinsically more democratic than the other—just *differently* democratic. This implies that measures aimed at "developing the private sector" are no more democratic than those aimed at "developing the public sector." Both, if carried to extremes, could undermine the practice of democracy, the former by destroying the basis for satisfying collective needs and exercising legitimate authority; the latter by destroying the basis for satisfying individual preferences and controlling illegitimate government actions. Differences of opinion over the optimal mix of the two provide much of the substantive content of political conflict within established democracies.

Citizens are the most distinctive element in democracies. All regimes have rulers and a public realm, but only to the extent that they are democratic do they have citizens. Historically, severe restrictions on citizenship were imposed in most emerging or partial democracies according to criteria of age, gender, class, race, literacy, property ownership, tax-paying status, and so on. Only a small part of the total population was eligible to vote or run for office. Only restricted social categories were allowed to form, join, or support political associations. After protracted struggle—in some cases involving violent domestic upheaval or international war—most of these restrictions were lifted. Today, the criteria for inclusion are fairly standard. All native-born adults are eligible, although somewhat higher age limits may still be imposed upon candidates for certain offices. Unlike the early American and European democracies of the nineteenth century, none of the recent democracies in southern Europe, Latin America, Asia, or Eastern Europe has even attempted to impose formal restrictions on the franchise or eligibility to office. When it comes to informal restrictions on the effective exercise of citizenship rights, however, the story can be quite different. This explains the central importance (discussed below) of procedures.

Competition has not always been considered an essential defining condition of democracy. "Classic" democracies presumed decision making based on direct participation leading to consensus. The assembled citizenry was expected to agree on a common course of action after listening to the alternatives and weighing their respective merits and demerits. A tradition of hostility to "faction," and "particular interests" persists in democratic thought, but at least since *The Federalist Papers* it has become widely accepted that competition among factions is a necessary evil in democracies that operate on a more-than-local scale. Since, as James Madison argued, "the latent causes of faction are sown into the nature of man," and the possible remedies for "the mischief of faction" are worse than the disease, the best course is to recognize them and to attempt to control their effects.[6] Yet

---

[6]   "Publius" (Alexander Hamilton, John Jay, and James Madison), *The Federalist Papers* (New York: Anchor Books, 1961). The quote is from Number 10.

while democrats may agree on the inevitability of factions, they tend to disagree about the best forms and rules for governing factional competition. Indeed, differences over the preferred modes and boundaries of competition contribute most to distinguishing one subtype of democracy from another.

The most popular definition of democracy equates it with regular *elections,* fairly conducted and honestly counted. Some even consider the mere fact of elections—even ones from which specific parties or candidates are excluded, or in which substantial portions of the population cannot freely participate—as a sufficient condition for the existence of democracy. This fallacy has been called "electoralism" or "the faith that merely holding elections will channel political action into peaceful contests among elites and accord public legitimacy to the winners"—no matter how they are conducted or what else constrains those who win them.[7] However central to democracy, elections occur intermittently and only allow citizens to choose between the highly aggregated alternatives offered by political parties, which can, especially in the early stages of a democratic transition, proliferate in a bewildering variety. During the intervals between elections, citizens can seek to influence public policy through a wide variety of other intermediaries: interest associations, social movements, locality groupings, clientelistic arrangements, and so forth. *Modern democracy, in other words, offers a variety of competitive processes and channels for the expression of interests and values—associational as well as partisan, functional as well as territorial, collective as well as individual. All are integral to its practice.*

Another commonly accepted image of democracy identifies it with *majority rule.* Any governing body that makes decisions by combining the votes of more than half of those eligible and present is said to be democratic, whether that majority emerges within an electorate, a parliament, a committee, a city council, or a party caucus. For exceptional purposes (e.g., amending the constitution or expelling a member), "qualified majorities" of more than 50 percent may be required, but few would deny that democracy must involve some means of aggregating the equal preferences of individuals.

A problem arises, however, when *numbers* meet *intensities.* What happens when a properly assembled majority (especially a stable, self-perpetuating one) regularly makes decisions that harm some minority (especially a threatened cultural or ethnic group)? In these circumstances, successful democracies tend to qualify the central principle of majority rule in order to protect minority rights. Such qualifications can take the form of constitutional provisions that place certain matters beyond the reach of majorities (bills of rights); requirements for concurrent majorities in several different constituencies (confederalism); guarantees securing the autonomy of local or regional governments against the demands of the central authority (federalism); grand coalition governments that incorporate all parties (consociationalism); or the negotiation of social pacts between major social groups like business and labor (neocorporatism). The most common and effective way of protecting minorities, however, lies in the everyday operation of interest associations and social movements. These reflect (some would say, amplify) the different intensities of preference that exist in the population and bring them to bear on democratically elected deci-

[7]   See Terry Karl, "Imposing Consent? Electoralism versus Democratization in El Salvador," in *Elections and Democratization in Latin America, 1980–1985*, eds. Paul Drake and Eduardo Silva (San Diego: Center for Iberian and Latin American Studies, Center for US/Mexican Studies, University of California, San Diego, 1986), 9–36.

sion makers. Another way of putting this intrinsic tension between numbers and intensities would be to say that "in modem democracies, votes may be counted, but influences alone are weighted."

Cooperation has always been a central feature of democracy. Actors must voluntarily make collective decisions binding on the polity as a whole. They must cooperate in order to compete. They must be capable of acting collectively through parties, associations, and movements in order to select candidates, articulate preferences, petition authorities, and influence policies.

But democracy's freedoms should also encourage citizens to deliberate among themselves, to discover their common needs, and to resolve their differences without relying on some supreme central authority. Classical democracy emphasized these qualities, and they are by no means extinct, despite repeated efforts by contemporary theorists to stress the analogy with behavior in the economic marketplace and to reduce all of democracy's operations to competitive interest maximization. Alexis de Tocqueville best described the importance of independent groups for democracy in his *Democracy in America,* a work which remains a major source of inspiration for all those who persist in viewing democracy as something more than a struggle for election and re-election among competing candidates.[8]

In contemporary political discourse, this phenomenon of cooperation and deliberation via autonomous group activity goes under the rubric of "civil society." The diverse units of social identity and interest, by remaining independent of the state (and perhaps even of parties), not only can restrain the arbitrary actions of rulers, but can also contribute to forming better citizens who are more aware of the preferences of others, more self-confident in their actions, and more civic-minded in their willingness to sacrifice for the common good. At its best, civil society provides an intermediate layer of governance between the individual and the state that is capable of resolving conflicts and controlling the behavior of members without public coercion. Rather than overloading decision makers with increased demands and making the system ungovernable,[9] a viable civil society can mitigate conflicts and improve the quality of citizenship—without relying exclusively on the privatism of the marketplace.

Representatives—whether directly or indirectly elected—do most of the real work in modern democracies. Most are professional politicians who orient their careers around the desire to fill key offices. It is doubtful that any democracy could survive without such people. The central question, therefore, is not whether or not there will be a political elite or even a professional political class, but how these representatives are chosen and then held accountable for their actions.

As noted above, there are many channels of representation in modern democracy. The electoral one, based on territorial constituencies, is the most visible and public. It culminates in a parliament or a presidency that is periodically accountable to the citizenry as a whole.

---

[8] Alexis de Tocqueville, *Democracy in America,* 2 vols. (New York: Vintage Books, 1945).

[9] This fear of overloaded government and the imminent collapse of democracy is well reflected in the work of Samuel P. Huntington during the 1970s. See especially Michel Crozier, Samuel P. Huntington, and Joji Watanuki, *The Crisis of Democracy* (New York: New York University Press, 1975). For Huntington's (revised) thoughts about the prospects for democracy, see his "Will More Countries Become Democratic?," *Political Science Quarterly* 99 (Summer 1984): 193–218.

Yet the sheer growth of government (in large part as a byproduct of popular demand) has increased the number, variety, and power of agencies charged with making public decisions and not subject to elections. Around these agencies there has developed a vast apparatus of specialized representation based largely on functional interests, not territorial constituencies. These interest associations, and not political parties, have become the primary expression of civil society in most stable democracies, supplemented by the more sporadic interventions of social movements.

The new and fragile democracies that have sprung up since 1974 must live in "compressed time." They will not resemble the European democracies of the nineteenth and early twentieth centuries, and they cannot expect to acquire the multiple channels of representation in gradual historical progression as did most of their predecessors. A bewildering array of parties, interests, and movements will all simultaneously seek political influence in them, creating challenges to the polity that did not exist in earlier processes of democratization.

PROCEDURES THAT MAKE DEMOCRACY POSSIBLE

The defining components of democracy are necessarily abstract, and may give rise to a considerable variety of institutions and subtypes of democracy. For democracy to thrive, however, specific procedural norms must be followed and civic rights must be respected. Any polity that fails to impose such restrictions upon itself, that fails to follow the "rule of law" with regard to its own procedures, should not be considered democratic. These procedures alone do not define democracy, but their presence is indispensable to its persistence. In essence, they are necessary but not sufficient conditions for its existence.

Robert Dahl has offered the most generally accepted listing of what he terms the "procedural minimal" conditions that must be present for modern political democracy (or as he puts it, "polyarchy") to exist:

1. Control over government decisions about policy is constitutionally vested in elected officials.
2. Elected officials are chosen in frequent and fairly conducted elections in which coercion is comparatively uncommon.
3. Practically all adults have the right to vote in the election of officials.
4. Practically all adults have the right to run for elective offices.
5. Citizens have a right to express themselves without the danger of severe punishment on political matters broadly defined. . . .
6. Citizens have a right to seek out alternative sources of information. Moreover, alternative sources of information exist and are protected by law.
7. ... Citizens also have the right to form relatively independent associations or organizations, including independent political parties and interest groups.[10]

---

[10]   Robert Dahl, *Dilemmas of Pluralist Democracy* (New Haven: Yale University Press, 1982), 11.

These seven conditions seem to capture the essence of procedural democracy for many theorists, but we propose to add two others. The first might be thought of as a further refinement of item (1), while the second might be called an implicit prior condition to all seven of the above.

1. Popularly elected officials must be able to exercise their constitutional powers without being subjected to overriding (albeit informal) opposition from unelected officials. Democracy is in jeopardy if military officers, entrenched civil servants, or state managers retain the capacity to act independently of elected civilians or even veto decisions made by the people's representatives. Without this additional caveat, the militarized polities of contemporary Central America, where civilian control over the military does not exist, might be classified by many scholars as democracies, just as they have been (with the exception of Sandinista Nicaragua) by U.S. policy makers. The caveat thus guards against what we earlier called "electoralism"—the tendency to focus on the holding of elections while ignoring other political realities.

2. The polity must be self-governing; it must be able to act independently of constraints imposed by some other overarching political system. DahI and other contemporary democratic theorists probably took this condition for granted since they referred to formally sovereign nation-states. However, with the development of blocs, alliances, spheres of influence, and a variety of "neocolonial" arrangements, the question of autonomy has been a salient one. Is a system really democratic if its elected officials are unable to make binding decisions without the approval of actors outside their territorial domain? This is significant even if the outsiders are relatively free to alter or even end the encompassing arrangement (as in Puerto Rico), but it becomes especially critical if neither condition obtains (as in the Baltic states).

PRINCIPLES THAT MAKE DEMOCRACY FEASIBLE

Lists of component processes and procedural norms help us to specify what democracy is, but they do not tell us much about how it actually functions. The simplest answer is "by the consent of the people"; the more complex one is "by the contingent consent of politicians acting under conditions of bounded uncertainty."

In a democracy, representatives must at least informally agree that those who win greater electoral support or influence over policy will not use their temporary superiority to bar the losers from taking office or exerting influence in the future, and that in exchange for this opportunity to keep competing for power and place, momentary losers will respect the winners' right to make binding decisions. Citizens are expected to obey the decisions ensuing from such a process of competition, provided its outcome remains contingent upon their collective preferences as expressed through fair and regular elections or open and repeated negotiations.

The challenge is not so much to find a set of goals that command widespread consensus as to find a set of rules that embody contingent consent. The precise shape of this "democratic bargain," to use Dahl's expression,[11] can vary a good deal from society to society. It depends on social cleavages and such subjective factors as mutual trust, the standard of fairness, and

---

[11]   Robert DahI, *After the Revolution: Authority in a Good Society* (New Haven: Yale University Press, 1970).

the willingness to compromise. It may even be compatible with a great deal of dissensus on substantive policy issues.

All democracies involve a degree of uncertainty about who will be elected and what policies they will pursue. Even in those polities where one party persists in winning elections or one policy is consistently implemented, the possibility of change through independent collective action still exists, as in Italy, Japan, and the Scandinavian social democracies. If it does not, the system is not democratic, as in Mexico, Senegal, or Indonesia.

But the uncertainty embedded in the core of all democracies is bounded. Not just any actor can get into the competition and raise any issue he or she pleases—there are previously established rules that must be respected. Not just any policy can be adopted—there are conditions that must be met. Democracy institutionalizes "normal," limited political uncertainty. These boundaries vary from country to country. Constitutional guarantees of property, privacy, expression, and other rights are a part of this, but the most effective boundaries are generated by competition among interest groups and cooperation within civil society. Whatever the rhetoric (and some polities appear to offer their citizens more dramatic alternatives than others), once the rules of contingent consent have been agreed upon, the actual variation is likely to stay within a predictable and generally accepted range.

This emphasis on operative guidelines contrasts with a highly persistent, but misleading theme in recent literature on democracy—namely, the emphasis upon "civic culture." The principles we have suggested here rest on rules of prudence, not on deeply ingrained habits of tolerance, moderation, mutual respect, fair play, readiness to compromise, or trust in public authorities. Waiting for such habits to sink deep and lasting roots implies a very slow process of regime consolidation—one that takes generations—and it would probably condemn most contemporary experiences *ex hypothesi* to failure. Our assertion is that contingent consent and bounded uncertainty can emerge from the interaction between antagonistic and mutually suspicious actors and that the far more benevolent and ingrained norms of a civic culture are better thought of as a *product* and not a producer of democracy.

HOW DEMOCRACIES DIFFER

Several concepts have been deliberately excluded from our generic definition of democracy, despite the fact that they have been frequently associated with it in both everyday practice and scholarly work. They are, nevertheless, especially important when it comes to distinguishing subtypes of democracy. Since no single set of actual institutions, practices, or values embodies democracy, polities moving away from authoritarian rule can mix different components to produce different democracies. It is important to recognize that these do not define points along a single continuum of improving performance, but a matrix of potential combinations that are *differently* democratic.

1. *Consensus:* All citizens may not agree on the substantive goals of political action or on the role of the state (although if they did, it would certainly make governing democracies much easier).

2. *Participation:* All citizens may not take an active and equal part in politics, although it must be legally possible for them to do so.

3. *Access:* Rulers may not weigh equally the preferences of all who come before them, although citizenship implies that individuals and groups should have an equal opportunity to express their preferences if they choose to do so.

4. *Responsiveness:* Rulers may not always follow the course of action preferred by the citizenry. But when they deviate from such a policy, say on grounds of "reason of state" or "overriding national interest," they must ultimately be held accountable for their actions through regular and fair processes.

5. *Majority rule:* Positions may not be allocated or rules may not be decided solely on the basis of assembling the most votes, although deviations from this principle usually must be explicitly defended and previously approved.

6. *Parliamentary sovereignty:* The legislature may not be the only body that can make rules or even the one with final authority in deciding which laws are binding, although where executive, judicial, or other public bodies make that ultimate choice, they too must be accountable for their actions.

7. *Party government:* Rulers may not be nominated, promoted, and disciplined in their activities by well-organized and programmatically coherent political parties, although where they are not, it may prove more difficult to form an effective government.

8. *Pluralism:* The political process may not be based on a multiplicity of overlapping, voluntaristic, and autonomous private groups. However, where there are monopolies of representation, hierarchies of association, and obligatory memberships, it is likely that the interests involved will be more closely linked to the state and the separation between the public and private spheres of action will be much less distinct.

9. *Federalism:* The territorial division of authority may not involve multiple levels and local autonomies, least of all ones enshrined in a constitutional document, although some dispersal of power across territorial and/or functional units is characteristic of all democracies.

10. *Presidentialism:* The chief executive officer may not be a single person and he or she may not be directly elected by the citizenry as a whole, although some concentration of authority is present in all democracies, even if it is exercised collectively and only held indirectly accountable to the electorate.

11. *Checks and Balances:* It is not necessary that the different branches of government be systematically pitted against one another, although governments by assembly, by executive concentrations, by judicial command, or even by dictatorial fiat (as in time of war) must be ultimately accountable to the citizenry as a whole.

While each of the above has been named as an essential component of democracy, they should instead be seen either as indicators of this or that type of democracy, or else as useful standards for evaluating the performance of particular regimes. To include them as part of the generic definition of democracy itself would be to mistake the American polity for the universal model of democratic governance. Indeed, the parliamentary, consociational, unitary, corporatist, and concentrated arrangements of continental Europe may have some unique virtues for guiding polities through the uncertain transition from autocratic to democratic rule.[12]

---

[12] See Juan Linz, "The Perils of Presidentialism," *Journal of Democracy* 1 (Winter 1990): 51–69, and the ensuing discussion by Donald Horowitz, Seymour Martin Lipset, and Juan Linz in *Journal of Democracy* 1 (Fall 1990): 73–91.

WHAT DEMOCRACY IS NOT

We have attempted to convey the general meaning of modern democracy without identifying it with some particular set of rules and institutions or restricting it to some specific culture or level of development. We have also argued that it cannot be reduced to the regular holding of elections or equated with a particular notion of the role of the state, but we have not said much more about what democracy is not or about what democracy may not be capable of producing.

There is an understandable temptation to load too many expectations on this concept and to imagine that by attaining democracy, a society will have resolved all of its political, social, economic, administrative, and cultural problems. Unfortunately, "all good things do not necessarily go together."

First, democracies are not necessarily more efficient economically than other forms of government. Their rates of aggregate growth, savings, and investment may be no better than those of nondemocracies. This is especially likely during the transition, when propertied groups and administrative elites may respond to real or imagined threats to the "rights" they enjoyed under authoritarian rule by initiating capital flight, disinvestment, or sabotage. In time, depending upon the type of democracy, benevolent long-term effects upon income distribution, aggregate demand, education, productivity, and creativity may eventually combine to improve economic and social performance, but it is certainly too much to expect that these improvements will occur immediately—much less that they will be defining characteristics of democratization.

Second, democracies are not necessarily more efficient administratively. Their capacity to make decisions may even be slower than that of the regimes they replace, if only because more actors must be consulted. The costs of getting things done may be higher, if only because "payoffs" have to be made to a wider and more resourceful set of clients (although one should never underestimate the degree of corruption to be found within autocracies). Popular satisfaction with the new democratic government's performance may not even seem greater, if only because necessary compromises often please no one completely, and because the losers are free to complain.

Third, democracies are not likely to appear more orderly, consensual, stable, or governable than the autocracies they replace. This is partly a byproduct of democratic freedom of expression, but it is also a reflection of the likelihood of continuing disagreement over new rules and institutions. These products of imposition or compromise are often initially quite ambiguous in nature and uncertain in effect until actors have learned how to use them. What is more, they come in the aftermath of serious struggles motivated by high ideals. Groups and individuals with recently acquired autonomy will test certain rules, protest against the actions of certain institutions, and insist on renegotiating their part of the bargain. Thus the presence of antisystem parties should be neither surprising nor seen as a failure of democratic consolidation. What counts is whether such parties are willing, however reluctantly, to play by the general rules of bounded uncertainty and contingent consent.

Governability is a challenge for all regimes, not just democratic ones. Given the political exhaustion and loss of legitimacy that have befallen autocracies from sultanistic Paraguay to totalitarian Albania, it may seem that only democracies can now be expected to govern effectively and legitimately. Experience has shown, however, that democracies too can lose the ability to govern. Mass publics can become disenchanted with their performance. Even more threatening is the temptation for leaders to fiddle with procedures and ultimately undermine the principles of contingent consent and bounded uncertainty. Perhaps the most critical moment comes once the politicians begin to settle into the more predictable roles and relations of a consolidated democracy. Many will find their expectations frustrated; some will discover that the new rules of competition put them at a disadvantage, a few may even feel that their vital interests are threatened by popular majorities.

Finally, democracies will have more open societies and polities than the autocracies they replace, but not necessarily more open economies. Many of today's most successful and well-established democracies have historically resorted to protectionism and closed borders, and have relied extensively upon public institutions to promote economic development. While the long-term compatibility between democracy and capitalism does not seem to be in doubt, despite their continuous tension, it is not clear whether the promotion of such liberal economic goals as the right of individuals to own property and retain profits, the clearing function of markets, the private settlement of disputes, the freedom to produce within government regulation, or the privatization of state-owned enterprises necessarily furthers the consolidation of democracy. After all, democracies do need to levy taxes and regulate certain transactions, especially where private monopolies and oligopolies exist. Citizens or their representatives may decide that it is desirable to protect the rights of collectivities from encroachment by individuals, especial propertied ones, and they may choose to set aside certain forms of property for public or cooperative ownership. In short, notions of economic liberty that are currently put forward in neoliberal economic models are not synonymous with political freedom—and may even impede it.

Democratization will not necessarily bring in its wake economic growth, social peace, administrative efficiency, political harmony, free markets, or "the end of ideology." Least of all will it bring about "the end of history." No doubt some of these qualities could make the consolidation of democracy easier, but they are neither prerequisites for it nor immediate products of it. Instead, what we should be hoping for is the emergence of political institutions that can peacefully compete to form governments and influence public policy, that can channel social and economic conflicts through regular procedures, and that have sufficient linkages to civil society to represent their constituencies and commit them to collective courses of action. Some types of democracies, especially in developing countries, have been unable to fulfill this promise, perhaps due to the circumstances of their transition from authoritarian rule.[13] The democratic wager is that such a regime, once established, will not only persist by reproducing itself within its initial confining conditions, but will eventually expand beyond them.[14] Unlike authoritarian regimes, democracies have the capacity to modify their rules and institutions consensually in response to changing circumstances. They may not immediately produce all the goods mentioned above, but they stand a better chance of eventually doing so than do autocracies.

---

[13]   Terry Lynn Karl, "Dilemmas of Democratization in Latin America," *Comparative Politics* 23 (October 1990): 1–23.

[14]   Otto Kirchheimer, "Confining Conditions and Revolutionary Breakthroughs," *American Political Science Review* 59 (1965): 964–74.

Democracy, Prosperity, Citizens and The State

ANDREW F. JOHNSON*

*Andrew Johnson is a Professor of Political Science at Bishop's University, Lennoxville, Québec. This paper was prepared for the Canadian Centre for Foreign Policy Development's Thinkers' Retreat: Clash of Civilizations?, Ottawa, May 2–4, 2002.

> The survival of the West depends on Americans reaffirming their Western identity and Westerners accepting their civilization as unique, not universal and uniting to renew and preserve it against the challenges from non-Western societies.
>
> (Huntington 1996: 20)

> The central issue for the West is whether, quite apart from any external challenges, it is capable of stopping and reversing the internal process of decay.
>
> (Huntington 1996: 303)

Democracy may be a universal value but the longevity of functioning democratic institutions has become the quintessence of Western identity. Its components—direct and representative decision-making, citizen participation as a means to good governance, and respect for individual freedom (Lenihan *et al.* 2000: 26)—are deeply ingrained in Western political institutions, laws and values.

Prosperity is another defining characteristic of Western civilization. There are myriad factors identified to explain the West's prosperity, not the least of which is democracy itself. Yet prosperity, as an independent variable, seems to have sown an inverse relationship with democracy. While prosperity has increased for nearly three decades, confidence in democratic institutions has decreased.

Prosperity is not directly linked to the political discontent that has steadily grown in Western democracies. Rather, it is the relationship that has evolved between governments and citizens, concomitant to prosperity, which has cumulated in overall political discontent. At least, such is the central thesis of this paper that describes, compares, and explains long-term political discontent in the United States and Canada. The responses of the American and Canadian governments to the erosion of confidence in government are also delineated and assessed comparatively. Finally, the concluding section relates the tensions between market relations and democratic relations, identified as a fundamental source of discontent in the U.S. and Canada, to the alleged clash of civilizations and to the supposed "decay" of Western civilization.

The decay of contentment in democratic political institutions may well be an integral part of the decay of Western civilization to which [Samuel] Huntington enjoins the West to redress by considering its values to be unique and not universal. However, Huntington also asserts "political principles are a fickle base on which to build a lasting community".

(Huntington 1996: 306) It is difficult to fathom how his assertion applies to the United States. It is also exceedingly difficult to determine whether Huntington's assertion applies to Canada, a state that is not exactly embedded in lofty democratic principles such as those that preceded the founding of the U.S.

Indeed, one should be wary of the curse of ideas—the principles of ideologies and nationalism—that plagued the Twentieth Century. (Conquest 1999) However, one should also be aware that "life, liberty and the pursuit of happiness"—not tribalism, ethnicity, race, religion, or doctrinaire economic formulae—are the very principles upon which America has built a lasting community. To be an American is to be a liberal. Seymour Martin Lipset puts it this way:

> ... in Europe and Canada, nationality is related to community; one cannot become un-English, or un-Swedish. Being an American, however, is an ideological commitment. It is not a matter of birth. Those who reject American [liberal] values are un-American.

> *(Lipset 1990: 19)*

Accordingly, adherence to liberal principles is a prerequisite to membership in the American community.

To illustrate, political principles hardly seemed fickle as a bond for America in the aftermath of 9/11. The entire nation displayed the Star Spangled Banner as the symbol of commitment to certain principles encapsulated by one word: "freedom". Freedom is emblematic of "lasting community". For Canadians, the principle of having no emotive attachment to principles, symbolized like American ones in simple emotive words, is, ironically, very much demonstrative of an attachment to principles—an attachment to the principles of diversity, tolerance, and pragmatism which define Canada's lasting community.

Additionally, the lasting community is not exclusive in the sense that it is normally reinvigorated—not hermetically sealed—in the face of challenges from non-Western influences. In the Anglo-democracies, political arrangements are much like the English language, which continuously renews itself through its absorptive capacities and tolerance of diversity. Accordingly, America is identified as a "melting pot" while Canada defines itself as a "multi-cultural society". That is precisely what makes America and Canada capable of facing, moderating and assimilating internal and external challenges. Moreover, each state's respective political principles, as expressed in their respective political institutions, may well have served to engender prosperity.

Why should democratic political institutions in America and Canada (as well as in all of the trilateral democracies) be objects of political discontent from their citizens, those who have flourished from the most accelerated and prolonged period—the post-war period—of economic growth and prosperity in the history of mankind? One is not required to look too hard for answers. The subject of political discontent in Western democracies has become a growth industry in terms of both unique and general explanations. However, one has to look hard for satisfying structural explanations. Accordingly, an overview of the former will be presented in Section II while a structural explanation will be proffered in Section Ill. These explanations, however, will be preceded by a description of the problem (in Section I) to which we now turn.

POLITICAL DISCONTENT: A DESCRIPTIVE OVERVIEW OF THE UNITED STATES AND CANADA

Recently, there has been a startling reversal of three decades of uninterrupted and cumulating political discontent that has plagued America. A *Los Angeles Times* poll of almost 2,000 American adults in late November 2001 indicated that 25 percent felt that 9/11 had transformed their lives for the better—they had better relations with neighbours and family and a new appreciation of their nation's values and of their own values. Moreover, now it is being reported there are strong indications that young Americans—previously harbouring very little confidence in politics—are embracing government as a highly respected career path. (*The Globe and Mail* 2002: A6) Accordingly, at university job fairs this year, the longest queues have been at government booths, including those for the CIA and FBI.

Such observations are supported by survey research. Robert Putnam and his colleagues conducted a nationwide survey of civic attitudes and behaviours in the summer and fall of 2000 and returned to "many of the same people and posed the same questions" in a survey conducted from mid-October to mid-November 2001. (Putnam 2002) Using a standard question to measure political confidence,[1] they found that 51 percent of respondents expressed greater confidence in the federal government than they had a year earlier while seven percent expressed less, for a net increase of 44 percent. Furthermore, political confidence increased more sharply among younger respondents than among older respondents, as did their interest in public affairs. Almost as a bonus, there were notable increases in trust of each other as well as in civic and political communities.

The Canadian opinion poll data is less comprehensive and considerably more parochial than America data, but to put it as diplomatically and as ineloquently as do Putnam and his colleague Susan Pharr, the Canadian data, "if less abundant and dramatic" at least "conforms to the general picture". (Putnam, Pharr and Dalton 2000: 10) The "general picture", as it were and according to an Ekos Poll, indicates that the Liberal government's support has increased from the election held in 2000 by almost 15 percent, that is, from 40.9 percent of the electorate to about 55 percent by the fall of 2001. (Ekos 2001) Additionally, 52 percent considered that the government was moving in the right direction in its fight against terrorism (29 percent indicated "neither" while 17 percent responded with "wrong"). As if to underscore and bolster renewed Canadian confidence in politics, President Bush, who, prior to 9/11 was not exactly a popular world figure among Canadians, received an excellent and dramatic approval rating of 68 percent among Canadians.

So does all of this conform to a "general picture" of renewed trust in government as suggested by the American data? Probably not. A Canadian Press/Leger Marketing Poll (January 2002) reveals that Canadians possess a great deal of trust in those in the safety professions (e.g., 98 percent for firefighters and 96 percent for nurses) but very little trust in politicians. In fact the lowest level of trust of all professions listed is accorded to politicians—18 percent, a rate that reaches as low as eight percent in British Columbia—substantially below car salespeople who earn the trust of 23 percent of Canadians.

---

[1]   The question was the following: "How much can you trust the government in Washington to do what is right—all of the time, most of the time, some of the time, or none of the time?"

Yet, pre-9/11 Canadian polling data may be instructive, however politically confident the American and Canadian publics may be in the recent performance of their governments. Short-term and immediate trust in politicians, political institutions, and public policy initiatives may mask long-term or structural trends of political discontent or distrust, as hard as it is to imagine in prosperous nations—nations that have delivered the goods, so to speak, for their citizens.

The long term structural patterns of political discontent in prosperous European nations, North American nations and, potentially, Japan were identified by Huntington and others just over a quarter of a century ago. The "crisis of democracy" faced by these nations was understood to be largely a consequence of "excessive" democracy. A surge of democracy had culminated in a superabundance of demands being placed on governments, a condition of "demand overload". (Crosier, Huntington and Wantanuki 1975) They forecasted a bleak future for democratic political institutions.

A "crisis" did not occur but subsequent evidence demonstrates that general unhappiness with government continued to accrue. According to the World Values Surveys, as interpreted by Nevitte (1996: 56), the overall decline of public confidence in political institutions was "consistent and substantial" in ten of twelve nations, including the U.S. and Canada, during the decade of the 1980s. As Nevitte notes, confidence in political institutions at the beginning of the decade was higher in America than in Canada but in their descent, confidence levels converged by 1991.

The erosion of political confidence continued unabated throughout the decade of the 1990s in the U.S. and in Canada, as it did in all of the other nations of the trilateral democracies. However, the U.S. endures the dubious distinction, according to Putnam and Pharr, of being the nation in which "the down trend is longest and clearest ... where polling has produced the most abundant and systematic evidence". (Putnam *et al* 2000: 8) Polling data related to questions posed on fundamental abstract (rather than ever changing concrete) associations with government declined precipitously by 1998. Thus they reported that only 39 percent of Americans felt that they could count on government to "do what is right" by that year. *Washington Post* data shows that the proportion slipped again in 1999 and in 2000, to less than one-third of respondents but then increased in one fell swoop to slightly over 50 percent of respondents in the immediate aftermath of 9/11.

Putnam and Pharr (2000: 9) also presented the *Harris Poll* on political alienation as proof positive that political discontent was in a free fall. The poll measures political alienation by presenting five statements to national samples of Americans:

- The people running the country don't really care what is happening to you.
- Most people in power try to take advantage of people like you.
- You're left out of things going on around you.
- The rich get richer and the poor get poorer.
- What you think doesn't count much anymore.

Putnam and Pharr reported that the index had won increasing assent since it was established in 1966. The tendency to feel alienated from politics continued to increase until 1995 but fell by about ten percent in the five year period between 1995 and 2000 and then plummeted by another ten percent in just one year (to 47 percent of respondents) after 9/11. Nevertheless, political alienation still remains at a rather high level.

However and despite the high levels registered on the "Harris Alienation Index", Americans continue to score high values on the "Harris Feel Good Index". Approximately three-fourths of Americans continue to feel good since 1998, according to a 16-question composite index on the quality of life. The lowest scores of approval on average, including the May 2001 poll, tend to be on "the state of the nation"—58 percent—and "the morals and values of Americans in general"—39 percent. Questions relating to economic well-being receive higher ratings.

To date, there is no evidence to suggest that the institutions of democracy are in imminent danger of collapse. However, the *Harris Poll* perceptions of "the state of the nation" and for "the morals and values of Americans in general" suggest that, whatever the case may be in the immediate wake of 9/11, democratic institutions should not be taken for granted. After all, the Council for Excellence in Government reports that, as recently as 1999, Americans feeling "disconnected" from government at all levels outweighed those feeling "very connected" or "fairly connected".

Canadians, for their part, are not normally asked to respond to questions on such an authentically American concept as the "state of the nation". They were, however, asked to register their feelings towards democracy in a poll carried out by York University's Institute for Social Research in 2000. (Howe and Northrup 2000: 6) A total of 71 percent of respondents were "very satisfied" and "fairly satisfied" with democracy. The researchers recognized, however, that respondents could have been responding positively to the notion of a democratic ethos. Thus, they were asked to register their satisfaction with concrete political structures—"government" and "politics". Satisfaction dropped markedly to a total of 58 percent and 53 percent, respectively, for the "very" and "fairly" satisfied respondents. The drop is not huge but sufficient to suggest that the 71 percent figure may overstate the general level of democratic contentment, as the researchers are quick to emphasize. (Howe and Northrup 2000: 7–8)

In addition to polling data, there are other signs of a decline in political contentment. Voluntary civic engagement, civic literacy and political participation are also falling. Significantly, they are dropping among younger citizens; this does not bode well for the future of democracy. The dip in voluntary activity is a case in point.

"Social capital", in which voluntary activity is central, refers "to connections among individuals—social networks and the norms of reciprocity and trustworthiness that arise from them", according to Robert D. Putnam, who coined the term. (2000: 19) By participating in voluntary organizations, people learn the skills of citizenship—and the values of a civic culture—by building bonds of mutual trust, tolerance and cooperation, ideally prerequisites for participation in democratic institutions. Accordingly, a nation that is rich in social capital is also likely to be endowed with a high level of political contentment.

In Canada, a national survey indicated that the number of volunteers dropped by almost one million or by 13 percent between 1997 and 2000. (*Independent Sector* 1999, 2001) Put otherwise, the number of Canadian volunteers dropped from 31 percent to 27 percent in the three-year period. In the U.S., however, the percentage decrease in adult volunteers in an even shorter time period, from 1998 to 2000, was more than double Canada's—from 56 percent to 44 percent.

It is encouraging that there are more volunteers in the U.S. as a proportion of population than in Canada but the drop in formal voluntary activity is equally discouraging. Of course, the everyday generosity of Americans cannot be overlooked. In fact, the percentage of household income (from contributing households) given to charitable organizations has increased from 1.9 percent in 1987 to 3.2 percent in 2000, that is, to a substantial dona-tion of US $1,620 per household. Despite the outpouring of trust and giving—from giving to charities to giving blood—in the weeks following the September tragedy, the American reservoir of social capital has not necessarily expanded. Paul C. Light of The Brookings Institution succinctly summarizes the notion that it is easier to give than to become involved even since 9/11:

> *Unfortunately, little of this civic enthusiasm has spilled over into volunteering. We spent more time last fall renting videos and ordering take-out food than volun-teering. Although Americans are venturing out more these days, the level of vol-unteering has not grown substantially. Americans have the will to volunteer but they do not have the time.*

(Light 2002)

Whatever the time constraints of Americans, Light's comment that they lack the will to volunteer is a matter of fact. This can be concluded from a survey of young adults, con-ducted in January 2002. (Centre for Democracy and Citizenship 2002) Young adults, according to the survey, show remarkable levels of trust in government in the wake of the terrorist attacks. However, just under half of young adults (47 percent) and 18 to 24 year-olds (48 percent) volunteer in their communities once a year compared to 54 percent of the 18 to 24 group in a survey conducted in 2000, despite a seemingly broad definition of vol-unteerism, which includes involvement as well as donations. More to the point, the data also indicate that whatever the value of the social capital accumulated by young Americans, "noticeably strong pluralities to majorities of young adults are certain that they will not engage in political activism". (Centre for Democracy and Citizenship 2002) Thus the data about those in whom the future of democracy resides are not comforting, but then neither are other rough indicators for the future of democracy. Consider, for example, the store of civic literacy in Canada and in the U.S., which, Henry Milner argues is more important to the sustenance of democratic institutions than social capital *per se*.

Civic literacy, "the knowledge to become effective citizens", from Henry Milner's per-spective, is the key ingredient in the stock of social capital required to bolster democracy. His argument makes good sense. (Milner 2001: 7) Informed individuals are likely to be able to assess policy options more effectively than the ill-informed, and thus be inclined to par-ticipate in politics. Milner cites a reliable study, which asserts "the political ignorance of the American voter is one of the best documented [findings] in political science". (Barrels cited in Milner 2001: 8) He also identifies data from the 1984 and 1997 Canadian Election Studies and other data to demonstrate that basic knowledge of civics is highly deficient. For instance, a majority of respondents were unable to identify ostensibly popular political par-ticipants. Sadly, the data shows that the least knowledgeable are young people.

Milner's findings conform to an "exam" survey conducted by Angus Reid on behalf of the Dominion Institute in late 1997. (Dominion Institute 1997). Forty-five percent of Canadians failed a mock citizenship exam similar to the one immigrants take to become Canadian citizens. Participants in the middle age bracket (35 to 54 years old) performed better (61 percent passed) than those in the older and younger age groups, each of which had a mere 52 percent pass rate. At least it was comforting to learn that respondents rec-ognized their shortcomings as citizens: 74 percent agreed with the statement, "not enough history and civics are being taught in schools".

However one might weigh civic literacy relative to social capital, as catalysts for political participation, it is clear that political participation has declined significantly in all Western democracies if we take the most basic measure, voting, as a rough indicator. Voter turnout in all elections throughout the OECD has decidedly declined since 1970. While voter turnout has remained below the OECD average in the U.S. and in Canada, the drop has been most precipitous in Canada. However, voter turnout in the OECD remains lowest in the U.S., where less than half of eligible American voters vote.

Additionally, throughout Europe, as well as in America, participation as measured by political party membership has withered. (*The Economist* 1999: 51) Membership figures for Canadian political parties are somewhat unreliable. However, the York University survey data suggest that membership diminished from 18 percent to 16 percent among those who "had ever been" members of political parties—a statistically insignificant drop. (Howe and Northrup 2000: 31) But previous surveys indicate that only two to three percent of samples respond affirmatively if asked if they are currently members of political parties. The point is that the proportion of Canadians participating in political party activity is low. Moreover, participation rates are not increasing and past members are neglecting to renew party memberships.

Perhaps most discomforting is that participation, even at these most basic and relatively effortless levels, is lowest among young people. The trend holds for Americans (Conway 2000: 19–24) as well as for Canadians. Accordingly, Brenda O'Neill concludes that:

> . . . *today's young Canadians are participating in the political system at lower levels than previous generations did at the same age, suggesting that recent declines in voting turnout and other measures of political participation will not be reversed in future years.*

> *(O'Neill 2001: 3)*

In explaining the declining membership in European political parties, *The Economist* (1999: 51) asserts "people's behaviour is becoming more private" and asks rhetorically "why join a political party when you can go fly fishing or surf the web?" The same may be legitimately asked of American and Canadian citizens, that is, if one assumes a private contractual relationship—a market relationship—between citizen and government. In such a relationship, it makes perfect sense to enjoy the leisurely self-indulgent benefits of prosperity while neglecting the civic obligations of democracy—to be politically knowledgeable, to contribute to civil society and to participate in the political process. But heretofore, the contractual nature of the relationship between citizen and government has not been fully explored as an explanation for the political malaise that infects the West, particularly in the U.S. and Canada. Instead, unique circumstances and general factors affecting specific nations, and Western nations in general, have been proffered to account for growing discontent. These factors are evaluated next and the new contractual relationship between citizen and government, as a fundamental explanation for ongoing and growing political discontent, will be discussed subsequently.

POLITICAL DISCONTENT: FROM UNIQUE TO GENERAL EXPLANATIONS FOR THE U.S. AND CANADA

In his comparative analysis of the causes of continuing political discontent in the U.S. and Canada, Richard Simeon (1995: 25) refers metaphorically to government as "a circus performer riding two horses". The performer exists perilously "precisely at the point where . . . two sets of forces intersect or collide". Democracy and globalization are identified as "the two sets of forces". And political discontent lies in a government's ability or lack thereof to balance and "accommodate" these forces.

To be sure, federal systems tend to reinforce regional and provincial or state claims on the polity. Such cleavages might be expected to add to the plethora of demands, stemming from democracy and resulting from the ever increasing complexity of government, however determined successive governments in the U.S. and Canada have been in reducing their respective functions. However, in Canada, political discontent is alleged to come from "democracy itself". (Clarke *et al.* 2000: 24) It is not just a matter of an operational "performance deficit" on the part of government—a widespread perception that it is unable to effectively deliver programs and services. It is a matter of a fundamental performance deficit on the part of the federal government—a prevalent and profound belief that it is unable and/or unwilling to resolve longstanding constitutional as well as socio-political issues.

Thus, Canada's political disaffection, its current existence as a "polity on the edge, is the end result of a ten-year accumulation of five inter-connected but unique events: two failed constitutional proposals—the 1992 Charlottetown Accord and the 1995 Quebec Referendum—combined with three elections, two of which (1988 and 1993) were on major economic issues and the last of which (1997) is characterized as "a collective frustration" which appeared to change nothing and resolve nothing". (Clarke *et al* 2000: 20) And to this we could add the 2001 election, which was very much a replay of the 1997 election.

There are events stemming from democracy, and unique to the U.S., which may also be identified as accounting for the decline in political contentment. One major factor is the alleged historical and unique mistrust of government in the USA. (Wills 1999) Mistrust is then customarily propped up by a considerable inventory of supplementary, but similarly unique circumstances. Thus, for example, Anthony King, (2000: 74–98) who is no stranger to the subject of political discontent, identifies two long-term factors—mistrust of government and "limited constituency" or limited bonds with citizens—and several short-term factors, from unmet expectations, to Vietnam, Watergate and flawed leaders, to the "incomprehensibility of government" to, finally, the "decline of comity".

Just as success of democracy has generated political discontent, so has the economic success of the state. The state has enlarged its scope and functions during the last five decades by managing demand within a Keynesian perspective and by promoting trade liberalization, international monetary stability, the mobility of capital and of labour and by stimulating and nurturing rapid technological change. In doing so, the state has unleashed internal and external forces that are alleged to have eroded the state's autonomy and sovereignty. (Horseman and Marshal 1994 and Barber 1995) The external forces, particularly multi-national enterprises, are thought to be most threatening to the authority of the modern state. (Leys 2001: 8–19) Indeed the ostensible threat posed by the primary agents of globalization, transnational corporations and international financial capital, have spawned a growth industry in publications which at worst predicts the death of the nation state and at best describes its current comatose condition. (Johnson and Stritch 1997: 9–14)

However, if the authority of the state is measured rather crudely by expenditures and revenues as ratios of GDP, then the proportions indicate that in both the U.S. and Canada sovereignty is not "at bay" as *The Economist* so aptly puts it. (1997: 8) And whatever the extent of the threat posed by globalization to the authority of the state, a World Economic Forum (WEF) survey, conducted among 25,000 respondents in 18 states during 2000 and 2001, clearly indicates that economic globalization is viewed positively in the U.S. and Canada in absolute and in relative terms. Moreover, people tend to have high expectations of economic globalization. Majorities anticipate improvements on eight of 15 factors surveyed, most notably greater access to world markets, cheaper goods, improved cultural life, a better quality of life, strengthened human rights, a more robust national economy, and a higher personal income. Significantly, respondents in a national survey voiced support for those who wish to express political discontent on a global scale. Almost half of the citizens overall, and majorities in half of the states surveyed, "support people who take part in peaceful demonstrations against globalization because they are supporting my interests". However, such support in the U.S. only stood at 40 percent after September 11.

Thus, citizens in the U.S. and Canada apparently support the prosperity that has accompanied globalization (and also express concern for those who have not profited from economic globalization). Nevertheless political discontent in both states has risen steadily despite the growth of prosperity There appears to be a negligible relationship (McAllister 1999) or, at most a tenuous relationship (Lawrence 1997) between economic performance and political confidence, a conclusion that can be deduced from the WEF survey above. In other words, strong evidence does not exist to support the notion that political discontent, however defined, fluctuates with the ups and downs of the business cycle.

Yet, a reasonably sound case can be made—and has been made—that the very success of the state in engendering prosperity has led to a shift in values—from modern to post-modern—because economic growth has lessened concerns about economic and physical security and has stimulated absorption in self-expression and self-realization which, in turn, challenges democratic institutions. (Inglehart 1997: 211) This thesis is consistent with the empirically substantiated signs that political discontent is especially rife among young adults who, as a group, are the repository of post-modern values. (Inglehart 1997: 213)

Curiously, by the middle of the 1990s the Western world had come to a stark realization that economic prosperity was not continuous and, more particularly, that a crisis in unemployment among the G-7 countries had interrupted the economic and physical security of the previous decade, especially among young people. Was there a concomitant shift from post-modern values back to modern values or in another direction to some other set of values? In the absence of suitable polling data, we do not know. We do know, however, that the erosion of political contentment has steadily persisted and is especially marked among young adults, whatever the impact of dramatically altered circumstances on post-modern values as they relate to politics. This suggests that there may be widespread and fundamental patterns of attitudinal change, which are not necessarily discerned by polling data. Put otherwise, the very success of the state in generating prosperity may have shifted modern values of participatory democracy into the self-indulgent realm of the post-modern. But let us take Inglehart's thesis one step further: the long-term economic success of the American and Canadian states may have basically modified the relationship between state and citizen in a manner which has inevitably bred structural political discontent.

POLITICAL DISCONTENT: PROSPERITY IN THE U.S. AND CANADA AS A STRUCTURAL EXPLANATION

In the last half of the last century, government fashioned a role for itself in the image of Keynesian economic theory as the harbinger, manager, and distributor of prosperity. In so doing, government relinquished its role as leader and repository of principles advancing civic virtue. Government became at once the master and servant of economic forces, inasmuch as its assumed role was to manage macroeconomic policy by way of fiscal and monetary policy in the service of its shareholders, the electorate. In other words, government's preoccupation with making the market work has eclipsed its role of making politics work.

Hence, a main role of North American governments in the 1960s was to create and distribute social policy largesse. In the following decade, they were primarily absorbed with manipulating their fiscal and monetary levers to offset the effects of a new economic phenomenon in which recession existed side-by-side with inflation. During the 1980s President Reagan and Prime Minister Mulroney advanced a new Trinity: expenditure cutbacks, deregulation, and privatization. Their governments held a common objective, which was to free the market from public sector entanglements so that the invisible hand would presumably become more effective than government in creating, sustaining and distributing the benefits of prosperity. At the same time, their governments worked, as had their successors, to "liberalize" the international market from the putative fetters of governments and to expedite the process of disentangling their own polities from the North American market by creating a free trade agreement.

Thus, by the end of the 1980s the U.S. and Canadian governments had surrendered much of their control of the market to the market. The market now eclipsed the polity, for better or for worse. This simply completed a process that began 40 years earlier when governments adopted a Keynesian path to prosperity while pretty much ignoring the need to sustain the polity. Governments had begun the last half of the Twentieth Century as agents for the market, and ended up by the 1990s as agents of the market.

Governments, much like business corporations, now define their primary role and responsibility as delivering services to "customers" or "clients", not "citizens". By the 1990s governments were re-designing themselves in accordance with business principles or with "managerialism", such as Japanese production principles embedded in Total Quality Management (TQM). Indeed, TQM, which essentially involves maintaining high quality to serve the needs of the "customer", lies at the core of the New Public Management (NPM) philosophy.

NPM has been fully embraced during the last decade by governments in the U.S. and in Canada. More to the point of our thesis, the full scale adoption of market culture in government indicates that government essentially sees itself as just another business engaged in a commercial or contractual relation with "customers"; it does not necessarily see itself as involved in social cum communal relationship with citizens. And that, according to Jeremy Rifkin (2000: 241), is the "Achilles heel" of the new age. Commercial obligations are no substitute for social obligations. More importantly, the commercial relationship that governments have developed with their citizens may well be the structural source of political discontent in the U.S. and Canada as well as elsewhere.

Social relations originate from kinship, ethnicity, geography, religion or adherence to a political ideal, i.e., from a communitarian ideal. They are long-term and sustained by notions of "reciprocal obligations and visions of common destinies". They are nurtured by communities "whose mission it is to reproduce and continually secure the shared meanings that make up the common culture". (Rifkin 2000: 241) Commercial relations, by contrast, typically involve short-term and individual—rather than group—commitment; they are explicit, generally delineated in legal or contractual terms, and are quantifiable. In short, social relationships are embedded in custom and obligation to community; commercial relationships stem from delivering the goods and commitment between individuals. Rifkin eloquently elucidates the distinctive nature of commercial relationships:

> *[They] are designed to maintain a distance between parties. It is understood at the outset that the relationship is based on nothing deeper than the exchange of money. Whatever shared experience occurs between the parties in the course of their relationship is meant to be superficial, expedient and short-lived.*
>
> *(2000: 242)*

That is precisely the nature of the relationship that governments in the U.S., Canada, and elsewhere in the OECD have cultivated with their citizens in the last half of the 20th Century.

Governments and citizens alike have traded individual freedom to participate in the decisions about their collective destiny for freedom to choose our values and ends for ourselves, as Sandel puts it. (1996: 275) Values and ends are located in the market, that is, in the commercial plenitude of prosperity.

However, commercial relationships are fleeting and shallow. They last as long as the customer gets a deal. In the world of business, Robert Reich contends that in this "age of the terrific deal" commercial relationships are not expected to last and everyone will switch to a better alternative if one becomes available. Accordingly, "disloyalty is 'normalized' and loyalty itself comes under suspicion". (2001: 83) Why should it be any different with government? It is not different, except for the discontent that accrues because government activities are comprehensive and its services are monopolistic. Government cannot possibly please all of the people all of the time in their commercial wants and needs. Yet, one cannot switch to a better deal. What better recipe for discontentment with politics, especially for young people who have only known government in its commercial role as architect and dispenser of goods and services?

In short, political discontent is an outcome of a clash between social and commercial relationships, or between the institutions of democracy and the market. At least in this day and age, governments seem to recognize the deficiencies inherent in maintaining a one-sided relationship with citizens—a predominantly commercial relationship. At the same time, they seem hard pressed to devise ways of restoring a social relationship or, at the very least, creating balance between the two.

REDRESS: GOVERNMENT AND CITIZEN ENGAGEMENT

Since 9/11, there has been a sea change in U.S. civic attitudes which has been reinforced by powerful television ads and images, promoting and fostering American unity and political community. Nevertheless, Thomas H. Sander and Robert D. Putnam (2002) of Harvard's Saguaro Seminar on Civic Engagement assert that "attitudes are outrunning our actions". Americans have not reported joining more community organizations or attending more organizational meetings despite the "historical window of opportunity for civic renewal" afforded by the tragic events of September which left Americans more united than in recent memory. Accordingly, Sander and Putnam recommend that institutional changes be made to spur and assimilate civic mindedness and that civic literacy be promoted to enhance political contentment. To date, the American response has been focussed relative to Canada's response. Social capital has been designated by President Bush, in his January 2002 State of the Union Address, as the means to rouse and foster civic engagement and, presumably, political contentment. To this end, $560 million in new funds alone in fiscal 2003 are to be allocated to the U.S. Freedom Corps, an umbrella program to reinvigorate old volunteer programs and to sustain new ones so that Americans are encouraged to devote two years—4000 hours—over a lifetime to community service.

Will stockpiling social capital, combined with a renewed determination to revitalize America's civic culture as advocated by Sander and Putnam, be sufficient to transform the commercial relationship with government to a social or genuinely civic relationship? The question must be considered against the backdrop of other broad government initiatives for the reform of government. The 2003 budget contains three such broad initiatives. (The White House 2002) First, the federal government is to be transformed into "citizen-centred" government from a "bureaucracy-centred" one. This is to be accomplished by flattening the federal hierarchy and, mainly, by improving e-government facilities. Second, government is to be made "results-oriented—not process oriented", largely by inaugurating more effective financial controls and performance indicators than are currently in place, and by applying private sector reforms to the public service. Finally, government is to be "market-based" which entails opening up government programs and activities to competition from the private sector.

The three initiatives will undoubtedly make government a better business, so to speak, and concomitantly strengthen the efficiency of its commercial relationship with American taxpayers. And overall, they may (or may not) make good sense, depending on the nature of operational designs. Yet against this backdrop of government reform, the Freedom Corps initiative seems almost futile. After all, the ultimate goal of strengthening social capital is to foster political participation and involvement. If there are few institutional means to absorb social capital into the political process and to convert it into a non-commercial relationship between citizens and government, then the structural cause of political discontent will largely remain.

The OECD's Public Management Service (PUMA) Working Group on Strengthening Government-Citizen Connections suitably frames the problem of redress by devising three separate analytic categories: information, consultation, and active participation. (OECD 2001: 23) Information, consultation, and active participation are identified as sequential but, also, intertwined, as a means to alleviate political discontentment.

Information, a one-way relationship, is expected to be enhanced by access to information laws and by the Internet. Both the U.S. and Canadian governments have long since succeeded in this category, especially in the realm of e-government services. A recent report of the Accenture consulting group ranks the Internet services of the Canadian and American governments as first and third, respectively, in the world. Accordingly, Accenture characterizes both governments as "innovative leaders" but cautions that they "still have a long way to go to providing fully mature online government". (Accenture web site) Both governments recognize as much, having committed substantial sums to further developing e-government. However, these expenditures are not necessarily designed to establish closer non-commercial ties between citizen and government as is expected in the realms of consultation and active participation.

Consultation, a two-way relationship in which citizens can provide feedback to government by way of public opinion polls and comments on draft legislation, has long since been elevated to a fine art, and provides input into policy-making on governance in Canada and, especially, in the U.S.. Indeed, experimentation has already begun in the U.S. (but not in Canada) with "deliberative polling" in which randomly selected respondents are provided with an opportunity to become informed and engaged. (Averill 2001: 11) Briefing materials are given to respondents and, subsequently, they are invited to discuss issues with each other, experts, and politicians. Then their opinions are polled. Deliberative polling may well appeal to Canadians, according to Averill, who cites a Canadian opinion poll, conducted in 2000 to verify her claim. (2001: 11) It is a reasonable step towards connecting with government but it, like polling in general, seems limited to random samples or very small groups and inclined to forge close relationships with pollsters more so than with government. However, sophisticated polling may serve as a prerequisite to forming institutions of active participation, a category which has been somewhat neglected by the U.S., in contrast to its neighbour to the north.

Active participation, "relations based on partnership with government, in which citizens actively engage in defining the policy process and content of policy-making" is expected to transpire by way of consensus conferences and citizen juries, according to the OECD. (2001: 23) Moreover, civil society organizations (CSOs) are expected to serve as intermediaries between citizen and governments. CSOs now function under a new aura of legitimacy in the U.S. and in Canada. However, third party democracy is no substitute for political party democracy in which the elector has input if one chooses to exercise it. Nevertheless, CSO activity may help to restore the stock of social capital in the U.S. and in Canada.

In the meantime, the process of generating participation seems to be far more advanced in Canada than in the U.S. Against the backdrop of Privy Council Office directives that promote better service, departmental co-operation and financial economies (PCO web site)—much like the directives in the U.S. budget—the federal government has begun to consider new ways in which to forge closer relationships with citizens. The PCO is setting guidelines for initiatives in consultation but individual departments and agencies have also devised new ways of bringing citizens back into politics.

Participation initiatives are characterized by recent attempts to re-define the nature of citizenship and citizen engagement in government. They range from heuristic devices such as the Reformcraft Project, which has sought to define and measure good governance by way of engaging 160 citizens "in all walks of life" in a series of 15 conferences (Hubbard 2000), to Heritage Canada's innovative CanadaPlace, a part of which would include a "digital commons". (Lenihan 2002: 12) The proposed digital commons would be designed to provide citizen and community interaction, including interaction with government by way of the Internet, audio, and video conferencing, all supported by full information and consultation.

Indeed, it maybe useful to re-think the nature of citizenship and citizenship engagement with government. However, the advent of new and breathtaking communications technologies should not seduce one into thinking that there may be a quick techno-bureaucratic fix for the problem of political discontent in prosperous nations. Technology is form, not substance. Technology cannot redress the unique causes, cited above, as sources of political discontent in the U.S. and Canada. Political will and determination can only resolve those issues.

More importantly, the technologies available to enhance the information, consultation and participation elements of citizenship engagement cannot redress the structural source of political discontent, as alluring as these devices may be to young people. Governments will never fully neutralize the commercial relationship that they have developed with their citizens. Politicians—especially politicians—and public servants must make a determined and concerted effort to explain to citizens the importance of what they do, and the importance of citizen involvement to guide them in doing what they do. Moreover, politicians and public servants must continuously inform citizens that public policies are truly social policies, policies that are an outcome of a covenant that requires trust and participation. Above all, governments must abandon the current vogue of applying the lexicon of the market to their own operations. After all, the public and private sectors have different goals, which are, at the most basic level, to foster social as distinct from commercial gain.

Governments using the quixotic institutional jargon, evocative of a romanticized bygone era of simple communitarian democracy—"fireside chats", "town hall meetings", "national forums" and "global villages"—will not restore citizen engagement and contentment. Quaint images may comfort older citizens but younger people, whose current convictions must be redressed, have a great deal more savvy about images than previous generations. More importantly, the younger generation—the least politically contented—have grown up in prosperity and have been gradually indoctrinated with the notion that the market is above politics, that is, as Harvey Cox puts it: the Market is God. (1999) Thus, Western governments, notably the governments of the U.S. and Canada, must de-theologize government of the Market if governments of Western civilization are to nurture political contentment and sustain democratic institutions, not only as a bulwark from attacks from other civilizations, but also as a sop and a positive channel for discontent originating elsewhere. In other words, governments of the West must continue to address political discontent from external sources in order to peacefully secure their own identities. This includes being open to new ideas from the outside as a precondition to maintaining their own security and prosperity.

CONCLUSION: ABSORBING THE CLASH OF CIVILIZATIONS?

The Market as God has eclipsed the perhaps idealistic principle of government as warden and progenitor of community values, and has transformed governments into disciples of the Market. Governments, especially the U.S. and Canadian governments, have accepted their subordinate role willingly by adopting and applying the logic and lexicon of the market to themselves. They have become agents of the market—mere instruments of prosperity. In doing so, governments have abandoned their somewhat idealized role as arbiter and repository of community values and have formed pedestrian contractual relationships with citizens. Governments and citizens are connected to each other only by the ephemeral quest for prosperity; a relationship that is bound to lead to discontent once prosperity is, as it has been, realized.

The ideal of citizens as participants in their own collective destiny has been replaced by the metaphysics of the market. The metaphysics of the market—its invisible hand—is, much like theology, accepted and sustained by faith. Accordingly, faith posits that the Market as God is omnipotent, omniscient, and omnipresent and that economic success or failure can be explained by its manifestation, the Invisible Hand. (Cox 1999)

However, Western governments must demystify the Invisible Hand by way of making a concerted effort to explain to citizens the importance of what they do and the significance of the impact of public policies on social and community relationships. Above all, governments must make it clear that they are not inert pawns at the mercy of the Invisible Hand, particularly in the guise of globalization. Nowadays, governments simply make policies differently—in concert with other nations through multilateral forums (Kapstein 1994)—than they did decades ago. In other words, governments must correct the imbalance between contractual and social relationships—the clash between the market and democracy—in order to restore political contentment and to stem the decay of democratic political institutions.

There is nothing new about tensions between these types of relationships. The conflicts between social and contractual types of relationships were pondered systematically over a hundred years ago by [Émile] Durkheim, who drew the distinction between mechanical solidarity—characterized by "social resemblances"—and organic solidarity, while [Ferdinand] Tönnies theorized about the distinctions between *Gemeinschaft* and *Gesellschaft* — a temporary and artificial mechanism of social cohesion. (Lukes 1975: 140) Similar tensions are even reported in the Old Testament wherein, unlike and diametrically opposed to the present, social covenant takes total precedence over contractual behaviour.[2] In a sense, civilizations have been confronting the same issue for more than two thousand years.

Islamic civilization seems to be no exception, although the imbalance in relationships is just the opposite of that in the West. Many Islamic governments identify themselves in terms of true faith by cloaking their activities in the tenets of Islam. However, governments clouded by theological legitimization will not likely cure Muslim nations of economic problems or propel them towards prosperity. Instead, de-theologized politics may attenuate the religious tendency to accept what exists; it may also create a political will to mend structural defects in domestic political economies that cultivate poverty. A new balance between social and contractual relationships, marked by progress towards the secularization of politics in Islamic civilizations and matched by a secularization of the market in the West, might help defuse the apparent clash between Islam and the West. In other words, a new balance might moderate the apparent prevalent Islamic view that the West is characterized by crass commercialism

---

[2]   See Numbers 15: 32–36 in which the Lord commands Moses to put to death, by stoning, a man caught gathering wood, a contractual act, on the Sabbath and in violation of laws which sustain the social cohesion of the Israelites.

in most of its relations; it might also vitiate the Western perception that the Islamic world is rife with blind religious intolerance in most of its internal and external relations.

In the meantime and to reiterate, Western governments must re-establish themselves as entities separate from the market and ennobled by social purpose as well as social covenant in order to prevent further deterioration in political contentment. Accordingly, governments must go beyond just providing better information to citizens. They must progress beyond mere consultation that has also become highly sophisticated by virtue of the rapid development of advanced communications technology. They must build political institutions that effectively require citizen engagement and effectively integrate citizen input—a formidable challenge in an age in which democracy has long since been commodified, and in which commercial relationships seem to have become infinitely more preferable to social relationships.

Governments in the U.S. and Canada have no choice but to do so. Prosperity—and their significant role in generating prosperity—in and of itself is not sufficient to meet internal challenges, let alone external challenges. Political contentment can only sustain the institutions of democracy which, to date, have proven resilient to attacks from others, not just by virtue of military capability, but by virtue of absorptive capacity. Stable, vigorous, and well-supported democratic institutions have a prodigious capacity to absorb challenges from within and from without and to assimilate those challenges into new directions in policy, to the benefit of citizens of Western nations as well as to the benefit of people from nations based on other civilizations.

REFERENCES

Accenture, *Governments Closing the Gap Between Political Rhetoric and eGovernment Reality.* www.accenture.ca

Averill, Nancy (2001). "Doing Democracy: How Deliberative Polling Works." *Canadian Government Executive,* 1.

Barber, Benjamin (1995). *Jihad vs. McWorld* (New York: Times Books).

Bartels, Larry (1996). "Uninformed Votes: Informational Effects in Presidential Elections." *American Journal of Political Science 40*:1. February.

Canadian Press/Leger Marketing (2002). *The Perception of Canadians with Regard to Various Professions,* January.

Centre for Democracy and Citizenship, et al. (2002). *Short Term Impacts, Long Term Opportunities: The Political and Civic Engagements of Young Adults in America,* March 2002. www.youngcitizensurvey.org/

Clarke, Harold D., Allan Kornberg and Peter Wearing (2000). *A Polity on the Edge: Canada and the Politics of Fragmentation* (Peterborough, Ontario: The Broadview Press).

Conquest, Robert (1999). *Reflections on a Ravaged Century* (NY: W.W. Norton & Co.)

Conway, M. Margaret (2000). *Political Participation in the United States,* 3rd ed. (Washington DC: Congressional Quarterly Press).

Cox, Harvey (1999). "The Market as God." *The Atlantic Monthly,* March.

Crozier, Michel, Samuel P. Huntington, and J. Wantanuki (1975). *The Crisis of Democracy: Report on the Governability of Democracies to the Trilateral Commission* (New York: New York University Press).

Dominion Institute/National Angus Reid Group Poll (1997). *The Dominion National Citizenship Exam Survey of 1997,* November 10.

Ekos Research Associates (2001). *Security, Sovereignty, and Continentalism: Canadian Perspectives on September 11,* September 27.

Horsman, Mathew and Andrew Marshal (1994). *After the Nation State: Citizens, Tribalism and the New World Order* (London: HarperCollins, 1994).

Howe, Paul and David Northrup (2000). "Strengthening Canadian Democracy: The Views of Canadians." *Policy Matters* (July) *11*:5.

Hubbard, Ruth (Senior Advisor to the PCO) (2000). *Good Governance: Reformcraft Final Report,* June 5. www.pco-bcp.gc.ca.

Huntington, Samuel P. (1996). *The Clash of Civilizations and the Remaking of the World Order* (New York: Simon and Schuster).

Independent Sector (1999). *Giving and Volunteering in the United States, (Executive Summary).* www.independentsector.org/.

Independent Sector (2001). *Giving and Volunteering in the United States (Executive Summary)* www.independentsector.org/.

Inglehart, Ronald (1997). *Modernization and Postmodernization: Cultural, Economic, and Political Change in 43 Societies* (Princeton: Princeton University Press).

Johnson, Andrew F. and Andrew Stritch eds. (1997). *Canadian Public Policy: Globalization and Political Parties* (Toronto: Copp Clark).

Kapstein, Ethan B. (1994). *Governing the Global Economy: International Finance and the State* (Cambridge: Harvard University Press).

King, Anthony (2000). "Distrust of Government: Explaining American Exceptionalism" in Susan J. Pharr and Robert D. Putnam, eds. *Disaffected Democracies: What's Troubling the Trilateral Countries?* (Princeton: Princeton University Press).

Lawrence, Robert Z. (1997). "Is It Really the Economy, Stupid?" in Joseph S. Nye, Jr. et al. eds. *Why People Don't Trust Government* (Cambridge, MA: Harvard University Press).

Lenihan, Donald G. (2002). Post-Industrial Governance: *Designing a Canadian Cultural Institution for the Global Village* (Ottawa: Centre for Collaborative Government), January.

Lenihan, Donald G. et al. (2000). *Collaborative Government in the Post-Industrial Age: Five Discussion Pieces* (Ottawa: Centre for Collaborative Government), May.

Leys, Colin (2001). *Market-Driven Politics: Neoliberal Democracy and the Public Interest* (New York: Verso).

Light, Paul C. (2001). An interview with Paul C. Light, Vice President and Director of Governmental Studies, The Brookings Institution, on National Public Radio's Morning Edition, February 7. www.brook.edu/views/op-edAight/20020207.htm.

Lipset, Seymour Martin (1990). *Continental Divide: The Values and Institutions of the United States and Canada* (New York: Routledge).

Lukes, Steven (1975). *Emile Durkheim: His Life and Work* (Markham: Penguin Books).

McAllister, Ian (1999). "The Economic Performance of Governments" in Pippa Norris ed. *Critical Citizens: Global Support for Democratic Government* (New York: Oxford University Press).

Milner, Henry (2001). "Civic Literacy in Comparative Context: Why Canadians Should Be Concerned." *Policy Matters* (July) 2:2.

Nevitte, Neil (1996). *The Decline of Deference: Canadian Value Change in Cross-National Perspective* (Peterborough, Ontario: Broadview Press).

O'Neill, Brenda (2001). "Generational Patterns in the Political Opinions and Behaviour of Canadians: Separating the Wheat From the Chaff." *Policy Matters* 2:5.

OECD (2001). *Citizens as Partners: Information, Consultation and Public Participation in Policy-Making* (Paris: OECD publications).

Privy Council Office *Executive and Deputy Minister Performance Agreements—Strategic Directions for the Public Service of Canada: Priorities for 2001–2002.* www.pco-bcp.gc.ca.

Putnam, Robert D. (2002). "Bowling Together." *The American Prospect* (February 11) 13:3.

Putnam, Robert D. (2000). *Bowling Alone: The Collapse and Revival of American Community* (NY: Simon and Schuster).

Putnam, Robert D., Susan J. Pharr, and Russell J. Dalton (2000). "Introduction: What's Troubling the Trilateral Democracies?" in Susan J. Pharr and Robert D. Putnam eds. *Disaffected Democracies: What's Troubling the Trilateral Countries?* (Princeton: Princeton University Press).

Reich, Robert B. (2001). *The Future of Success* (New York: Alfred A. Knopf).

Rifkin, Jeremy (2000). *The Age of Access* (NY: Tarcher/Putnam).

Sandel, Michael J. (1996). *Democracy's Discontent: America in Search of a Public Philosophy* (Cambridge: The Belknap Press).

Sander, Thomas H. and Robert D. Putnam (2002). "Walking the Civic Talk After Sept.11." *The Christian Science Monitor,* February 19.

Simeon, Richard (1995). "Globalization, Domestic Societies, and Governance" in C.E.S. Franks, J.E. Flodgetts, *et al.* eds. *Canada's Century: Governance in a Maturing Society* (Montreal: McGill-Queen's Press).

The Economist (1999). "Empty Vessels?" July 24:51.

The Economist (1997). "The Future of the State." September 20:8.

The Globe and Mail (2002). March 8:A6.

The White House (2002). *A Blueprint for New Beginnings—IX. Government Reform.* www.whitehouse.gov/news/usbudget/blueprint/budix.html.

Wills, Garry (1999). *A Necessary Evil: A History of American Distrust of Government* (New York: Simon and Schuster).

Voter Participation in Canada: Is Canadian Democracy in Crisis?

CENTRE FOR RESEARCH AND INFORMATION ON CANADA (CRIC)

INTRODUCTION

The November 2000 general election in Canada saw Jean Chrétien's Liberal Party win its third consecutive parliamentary majority. It also saw the third straight decline in voter participation—that is, in the number of registered voters who cast a ballot. And while some 12.86 million Canadians cast ballots, some 8.25 million registered voters (or 39 percent of the total) did not vote at all.[1] Never before have so many voters abstained.

The decline in voter participation, or turnout, is worrying. The defining characteristic of a representative democracy is that those who govern are chosen by the people. A democracy without willing voters is a sham. It is important to ask what the decline in turnout says about the health of Canadian democracy, and what can be done to reverse the trend.

There are countless reasons why people do not vote, and not every instance of non-voting should be interpreted as an indictment of the existing political system. Many do not vote because they are travelling, sick, or have difficulty getting to a polling station. Others are not sure whether they are eligible to vote, or about how to get their names on the voters list. Still others may be inclined to vote, but nonetheless decide that they can sit this one out because the result in their own constituency or across the country as a whole is a foregone conclusion. Few of these people can be described as overly cynical about Canadian democracy or genuinely disaffected with politics.

But as the number of non-voters grows, the situation becomes more worrisome. What is keeping more and more voters away from the polls? Is declining voter turnout a symptom of growing dissatisfaction with parliament, political parties and politicians? Is non-voting more pronounced among certain groups within the population, such as young people? Does it really matter if fewer people are voting than in the past? Is Canadian democracy really in crisis?

These are the questions that this paper will address.

---

[1] All figures related to turnout and voting results in Canada are from Elections Canada (see *www.elections.ca*). Figures for 1997 and 2000 are taken from the official voting results published by the Chief Electoral Officer. Figures for elections prior to 1997 are taken from: Elections Canada, *A History of the Vote in Canada* (Ottawa: Public Works and Government Services Canada), 1997.

VOTER PARTICIPATION IN CANADA

Federal Elections

Voter participation in Canada is declining. Consider these facts:

- Turnout has declined in three straight federal elections, falling from 75 percent in 1988 to 61 percent in 2000—a 14-point drop over the course of 12 years (see Figure 1).[2]
- Turnout at the last federal election was the lowest ever recorded in Canada.
- The average turnout at federal elections in the 1990s was much lower than it was in the decades that immediately preceded it (see Figure 2), and the lowest of any decade in Canadian history.

    Turnout at federal elections has fallen in each province, but the decline has been more pronounced in some than in others.

- Average turnout in the 1990s was at least 10 percentage points lower than it was in the previous decade in six provinces: Newfoundland, PEI, Ontario, Saskatchewan, Alberta and British Columbia. The largest drop in average turnout between the 1980s and the 1990s was in Saskatchewan and BC—almost 13 percentage points in each case.
- In Nova Scotia, Ontario, and Saskatchewan, turnout for the 2000 federal election was about over 20 percentage points lower than it was in the 1960s.
- The province where the drop in turnout has been the most moderate is Quebec. Average turnout in the 1990s was only 4 percentage points lower than it was in the 1980s.

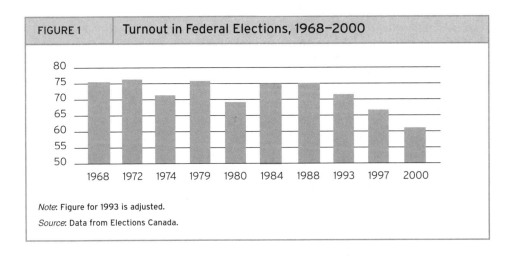

FIGURE 1 | **Turnout in Federal Elections, 1968–2000**

Note: Figure for 1993 is adjusted.

Source: Data from Elections Canada.

---

[2]   In most democracies, including Canada, turnout is calculated by dividing the number of ballots cast by the number of voters who were registered to vote. In the US, where the system of voter registration fails to reach large numbers of potential voters, turnout is calculated differently, by dividing the number of ballots cast by an estimate of the voting age population.

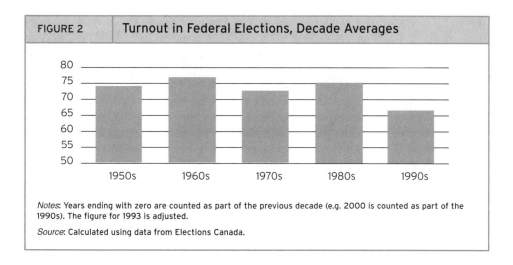

FIGURE 2 — Turnout in Federal Elections, Decade Averages

Notes: Years ending with zero are counted as part of the previous decade (e.g. 2000 is counted as part of the 1990s). The figure for 1993 is adjusted.

Source: Calculated using data from Elections Canada.

Provincial Elections

Voter participation has also been falling in provincial elections, though not as uniformly or a dramatically.

- A comparison of the average turnout within each province for elections from 1980 to 1989 with the average since 1990 gives the following results: turnout has declined in 5 provinces, risen in three provinces, and remained unchanged in two (see Appendix, Table 1). Where turnout has increased, the size of the increase has been relatively small.[3]
- Saskatchewan experiences the most dramatic change. Turnout at the last two elections (1995 and 1999) was 17 points lower than it was at the previous three elections (1982, 1986 and 1991).
- Turnout has also declined by several points in recent elections in Nova Scotia, New Brunswick, Manitoba and BC.
- Average turnout has not changed significantly in Ontario or Alberta, but the level of participation in those provinces (respectively, 58 percent and 53 percent at the most recent elections) nonetheless is very low.

An International Trend?

Canada is not unique. Researchers have noted a decline in voter participation in other democratic countries. In fact, speaking of this decline, US political scientist Martin Wattenberg

---

[3] The largest increase (+ 2.3 percentage points) was in Quebec, where the return of sovereignty to the agenda of party politics after 1990 heightened the stakes of electoral contests.

writes: "it is rare in comparative politics to find a trend that is so widely generalizable."[4] In a range of democracies, including the United Kingdom, Ireland, the Netherlands, Portugal, Italy, Finland, Austria and Japan, turnout at the most recent election was the lowest recorded in the post-war period.[5] In the case of the UK, voter turnout in the 2001 election fell by a dramatic 12 points to 59 percent, a level lower than that at the most recent election in Canada.

There are exceptions. For instance, there has been no downward trend in Australia—like Canada, a parliamentary democracy with a federal system—because voting there is compulsory. In the United States, voter turnout has not changed much over the last 30 years, but it was already very low to begin with. In many other west European countries, turnout has fallen slightly in recent years, but remains high by Canadian standards.

Despite some possible exceptions, it remains the case that voter turnout is falling in many countries, and not just in Canada. This has implications for how the causes of the problem, and the possible solutions, should be understood. At the same time, it should also be noted that few western democracies have experienced as steady and as significant a drop in turnout over the last 15 years as has Canada.[6]

EXPLAINING THE DECLINE IN VOTER PARTICIPATION

Political scientists and commentators have identified a number of factors that may be responsible for lower voter participation. But they do not agree on which is the most important. More specifically, they do not agree as to whether the decline in voter turnout in Canada is a cause for alarm. While some argue that lower turnout simply reflects the uninteresting or uncompetitive nature of recent election campaigns, others see it as a more worrying product of deteriorating public perceptions of parliament, parties and politicians.

What follows is a review of the four main explanations for low turnout in Canada, and a discussion of their strengths and weaknesses.

Liberal Hegemony

People are more likely to vote when they think their vote counts. And they are more likely to think their vote counts when the election is hotly contested, or when there are major

---

[4]   Martin P. Wattenberg, "Turnout Decline in the U.S. and other Advanced Industrial Democracies," Centre for the Study of Democracy Research Paper Series in Empirical Democracy Theory (University of California, Irvine: Center for the Study of Democracy, 1998), p. 14 (available on the website of the Center for the Study of Democracy at: *www.democ.uci.edu/democ/papers/marty.html*). See also: André Blais, *To Vote or Not to Vote: The Merits and Limits of Rational Choice Theory* (Pittsburgh: University of Pittsburgh Press, 2001): 33–36; Mark Franklin and Michael Marsh, "The Tally of Turnout: Understanding Cross-National Turnout Decline Since 1945," paper prepared for delivery at the annual meeting of the American Political Association, Washington D.C., August–September 2000, 2–3.

[5]   See the figures for turnout posted on the website of International IDEA, at *http://www.idea.int/voter_turnout/index.html*.

[6]   One exception is Japan, where turnout has fallen sharply.

issues at stake.[7] In the 1995 Quebec referendum, for instance, turnout was an unprecedented 93.5 percent. This figure is astoundingly high, yet understandable, given what was at stake and the small margin separating the two sides in the campaign.

In contrast, many observers argue that the federal election of 1997 and 2000, when turnout fell below 70 percent, were singularly uninteresting. In both cases, the Liberal Party faced a divided opposition and won by a large margin over its nearest rival. In neither case did the election appear to be fought over an issue of great importance to the future of the country, such as national unity or free trade. By and large, there was no widespread anger with the current government that could be counted on to drive Canadians to the polls to vote for change.

The decline in turnout, therefore, reflects the relatively uncompetitive period of national politics. There is no reason not expect voters to participate in greater numbers once elections become more competitive and more meaningful.

The following points support this theory:

- The number of people who said that there were no important election issues at stake was much higher in 1997 and 2000 than in previous elections (see Figure 3).[8] And research has shown that those who say there are no important election issues are much less likely to vote.[9]

- At the last election, the margin of victory for winning candidates was generally much smaller in constituencies with high voter turnout than it was in those with low voter turnout. In the 10 constituencies where turnout was highest, the average margin of victory was 17 percent. In the ten constituencies where turnout was lowest, the average margin of victory was 42 percent.[10] This suggests that there is a relation between voter

---

[7] Political scientists who have studied political participation in a large number of democratic countries have concluded one of the factors affecting turnout is the voters' own sense of whether the election is either close (in terms of the winning party's margin of victory), or important (in terms of its political consequences, or how much the outcome is deemed to matter). See Blais, *To Vote or Not to Vote*, p. 43; see 17–44; Franklin and Marsh, "The Tally of Turnout," p. 29. See also Mark N. Franklin, "The Dynamics of Electoral Participation," in *Comparing Democracies 2: Elections and Voting in Global Perspective*, edited by Lawrence LeDuc, Richard G. Niemi and Pippa Norris (Thousand Oaks: Sage Publications, 2002).

[8] Jon H. Pammett, "The People's Verdict," in *The Canadian General Election of 2000*, edited by Jon H. Pammett and Christopher Dornan (Toronto: Dundurn, 2001), p. 300; Jon H. Pammett, "The Voters Decide," in *The Canadian General Election of 1997*, edited by Alan Frizzell and Jon H. Pammett (Toronto: Dundurn, 1997), p. 235.

[9] Tony Coulson, "Voter Turnout in Canada: Findings from the 1997 Canadian Elections Survey," *Electoral Insight* Vol. 1, No. 2 (November 1999): 19. Available on the website of Elections Canada at *www.elections.ca*.

[10] The margin of victory is the difference between the number of votes won by the winning candidate and his or her nearest rival, expressed as a percent of the total votes cast for all candidates in the constituency. On this point, see the analysis of the 2000 federal election results in the province of Quebec, offered by Louis Massicotte and Édith Brochu. They note that turnout in that province declined most notably in Liberal strongholds on the island of Montreal. (Louis Massicotte et Édith Brochu, "Élections fédérales de novembre: coup de loupe sur un scrutin." *Le Devoir* 26 février 2001, page A7. Available on the website of *Le Devoir* at *www.ledevoir.com/public/client-css/news-webview.jsp?newsid=165*.)

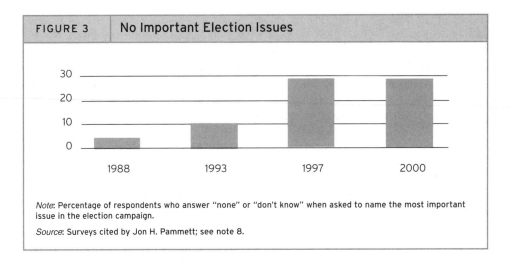

FIGURE 3 | No Important Election Issues

Note: Percentage of respondents who answer "none" or "don't know" when asked to name the most important issue in the election campaign.

Source: Surveys cited by Jon H. Pammett; see note 8.

turnout and the closeness of the election result, and implies that turnout might be higher in future elections, should they be more competitive.

However, there are several weaknesses in the argument that turnout has fallen because recent elections were not all that interesting.

First, there have been previous elections in Canada where the results were predictable, or at least not very close, but where turnout remained high. For instance, turnout was as high at the time of the 1958 Diefenbaker landslide as it was for the much more closely contested elections that ensued.

Second, citizens are called upon to vote, not only because their vote might decide a close election, or because the central issue in the campaign is also their own top priority, but because it is a civic duty to participate in selecting the government. Research conducted by André Blais has shown that most people agree that it is their duty to vote. He writes: "the feeling that voting is a moral obligation and that not voting implies a failure to fulfill one's civic duty is widespread and strongly ingrained in the population."[11] This raises a question: is the decline in turnout related not so much to the peculiarities of any one election campaign, but to more worrying changes in how people perceive and act on their sense of their obligations as citizens?

Third, the lack of an election issue or of competitiveness among parties is an explanation that begs more questions than it answers. There is simply no objective reason why this past election campaign should have been so devoid of debate about the country's priorities and the best means to achieve them. At the time of the election, the government was wrestling with a number of acute challenges—the reform of the health care system, the need to manage globalization and negotiate new trade agreements, the rapidly deteriorating environment, and the plight of Canada's disadvantaged Aboriginal communities, to name a few. Moreover, with five official parties spanning a wide range on the ideological spectrum, Canadian voters were offered a variety of choices at the ballot box. And yet the

[11] Blais, *To Vote or Not to Vote*, p. 99.

parties were collectively unable to initiate a debate about these issues, one capable of capturing the voters' imaginations and of spurring them to cast a ballot. We need to ask why this was the case.

The Permanent Voters List

The November 2000 election was the first one conducted on the basis of the new method for registering voters that Canada adopted in 1996.[12] In previous elections, a new voters list was compiled during each election campaign by enumerators, who visited every household in the country to obtain the names of those eligible to vote. Enumeration "was repeatedly hailed as a highly effective method of registration, one that produce an up-to-date and accurate list of electors" at relatively low cost.[13] Since a person needs to be correctly registered in order to vote, the accuracy of the list is very important. If the list is very complete and accurate, few people will be discouraged from voting because they are not registered, do not know how to register, or do not have the time or inclination to do what is necessary in order to register.

The decision was made to do away with door-to-door enumeration in favour of what is known as the permanent voters list. It is so named because rather than being produced from scratch at the start of each election, it is maintained from year to year and continuously updated. Unless voters otherwise object, their names remain on the list. Revisions to the list—changes of address, deletions of those deceased and addition of new citizens—are made automatically through electronic information sharing among Election Canada and different federal and provincial government departments and agencies. Those who become eligible to vote on their 18th birthday automatically receive a card from Elections Canada, asking them to agree to have their names added to the list.[14] Because it is a permanent list, the new voters list is in place at the time an election is called, although voters whose names are not on the list can register throughout the election campaign, up to and including voting day itself.[15]

---

[12] As in 2000, there was no door-to-door enumeration of voters during the June 1997 electoral campaign. But the voters' list used in 1997 was the product of a final door-to-door enumeration carried out in April of that year, in preparation of the new permanent voters' list. Therefore that election cannot be said to be the first one to have been conducted without the benefit of door-to-door enumeration.

[13] Jerome H. Black, "The National Registry of Electors: Raising Questions About the New Approach to Voter Registration in Canada," *Policy Matters* Vol. 1, No. 10 (December 2000), p. 8. Available on the website of the Institute for Research on Public Policy at *www.irpp.org*.

[14] Except in Quebec, where the names of 18 year olds are automatically added to the provincial list of electors, and then added to the federal list.

[15] In 2000, there were 959,774 net additions of names to the voters list prior to election day, and a further 872,552 voters registered on election day itself. This means that 8.6 percent of all voters who were finally registered added their names to the list during the campaign or on election day. Many more had to revise their registration, for example, by recording a change of address. See the Chief Electoral Officer's report on the 37th General Election, available on the website of Elections Canada at *www.elections.ca*.

Two points have been made about the impact of the new list on voter participation:

• The old system was better at *encouraging* people to vote, because door-to-door enumeration reminded votes that an election had been called and that they were eligible to vote.

• The new system *discourages* more people from voting. All observers agree that, because it does not rely on door-to-door enumeration, the permanent voters list is less accurate. By the time an election comes around, more voters are likely to find that they are not registered correctly or at all. At this point, the onus is on the voter to add his or her name to the list. While many find this easy, others do not.

Is there evidence to support these claims?

• On the one hand, difficulties with voter registration were not the main reasons why non-voters did not vote in the last election (see Figure 4). According to a post-election survey conducted for Elections Canada[16], only 16 percent of non-voters said that they did not vote because of a reason associated with the system of voter registration, namely: (a) they didn't have enough information about where and when to vote; (b) they weren't registered or on the voters list in their riding; or (c) they didn't receive their voter's card.[17]

• On the other hand, the number of non-voters in 2000 who did not vote because they were not on the voters list appears to have been higher than in previous elections.[18]

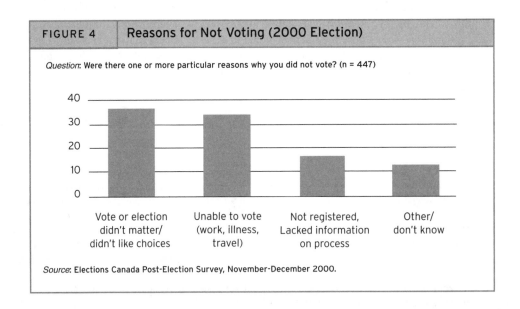

| FIGURE 4 | **Reasons for Not Voting (2000 Election)** |

Question: Were there one or more particular reasons why you did not vote? (n = 447)

Vote or election didn't matter/ didn't like choices — Unable to vote (work, illness, travel) — Not registered, Lacked information on process — Other/ don't know

Source: Elections Canada Post-Election Survey, November-December 2000.

---

[16] The survey was conducted between November 28 and December 11, 2000 by Ipsos-Reid. A total of 2,500 Canadians were surveyed, including 1,400 persons between 18 and 34 years of age.

[17] The voter's card indicates that a person is registered to vote, and states where and when votes can be cast.

[18] Pammett, "The People's Verdict," p. 310.

Thus, it could be that some people did not vote in 2000 because of the switch from enumeration to a permanent voters list. *But this was clearly not the main reason why people did not vote.* Moreover, it cannot account for the general downward trend in turnout, which began before the switch to the permanent voters list.

Yet it is important to note that the reduced accuracy of the permanent voters list, and the greater onus it placed on individual voters to ensure they are registered, likely discourages participation among *particular groups* within the population. As Jerome Black notes, "the impact of the registration system is not neutral across social categories. More demanding regimes will generally lead to under-registration and lower levels of voter turnout on the part of those who are less well-off or who are less favoured (e.g., in terms of income, occupation and education).[19] Those who already feel shut out by the political system are more likely to be put off by the need to register. And because of their mobility, students, young people and tenants are least likely to be correctly registered in the constituencies where they reside. Only about one in four 18-year-olds return the card sent to them by Elections Canada, asking them to agree to have their names added to the list. While Elections Canada tries to address these problems by various means, the fact remains that, for some people at least, the new system of voter registration places a new obstacle in the path of voting.

Changing Times, Changing Values

Canadian society has changed considerably over the past 25 years. Canadians are much better educated, and receive much more information through the media. They are less religious, more morally permissive, more likely to have grown up within a "non-traditional" family structure, and more likely to change jobs several times throughout their working life. They are more egalitarian and open to cultural and other forms of social diversity. They are less accepting of hierarchies and more interested in participating directly in decision-making at work and within society. These changes are not unique to Canada.[20] Researchers argue that many of these trends help to explain why citizens have become less likely to vote.

Religion

The declining importance of religion is especially significant. Only 34 percent of adult Canadians attended church at least once a month in 1998, down from 41 percent a decade earlier.[21] But research shows that "people who regularly attend religious services and who

---

[19] Black, "The National Registry of Electors," p. 13.

[20] See: Neil Nevitte, *The Decline of Deference: Canadian Value Change in Cross-National Perspective* (Peterborough: Broadview Press, 1996); Neil Nevitte and Mebs Kanji, "Canadian Political Culture and Value Change," in *Citizen Politics: Research and Theory in Canadian Political Behaviour*, edited by Joanna Everitt and Brenda O'Neill (Toronto: Oxford University Press, 2001), esp. p. 71.

[21] Statistics Canada, *The Daily*, 12 December 2000. See: *http://www.statcan.ca/Daily/English/001212/d001212b.htm*. For other evidence on the declining importance of religion in the lives of Canadians, see Nevitte, *Decline of Deference*, Chapter 7.

say they are very religious are more likely to vote."[22] It can be argued people who are more religious are likely to feel their obligation to vote more acutely.[23] And church groups and leaders often encourage their members to vote, especially when issues that are important to the church are at stake. But religion is also important because church attendance helps to foster people's sense of attachment to and involvement in their community.[24] In other words, participation in religious services integrates people into community life in general, and this has a positive effect on non-religious activities like voting.

Political Parties

People's changing values have also made them less likely to identify strongly with any one political party.[25] As citizens become better educated and more informed, they also become more independent in their thinking and less likely to accept the lead of any given political party over the long term. The increasing unease with rigid hierarchies also makes citizens less comfortable with traditional party organizations. Some also argue that with the rise of television as the main medium of political communication, parties have increasingly crafted their election campaigns around the party leader, focusing more on his or her image, and less on the party as a whole.[26] TV elections ads now regularly emphasize the leader's qualities (or attack the qualities of other leaders) and all but fail to mention the name of the leader's party. These trends weaken loyalty to particular parties. This, in turn, has an effect on turnout, because those who are strongly attached to a party will be more likely to vote.

Attitudes Toward Authority

Another factor underlined by political scientists is people's growing sense of personal autonomy and their changing attitudes toward authority. It is argued that citizens today tend to be more assertive and less deferential towards authority.[27] They are also more inclined

22   Blais, *To Vote or Not to Vote*, p. 52.
23   This hypothesis has been put forward tentatively by André Blais. He notes that "the process of secularization . . . has nourished a sense of moral relativism that makes it more difficult for people to be certain that voting is a good and not voting is wrong." See Blais, *To Vote or Not to Vote*, p. 114.
24   Blais, *To Vote or Not to Vote*, p. 52.
25   Again, this is a gradual but unmistakable trend that is visible throughout the industrialized world. See, for instance, Nevitte, *Decline of Deference*, p. 49; Russell J. Dalton, "Political Support in Advanced Industrial Democracies," in *Critical Citizens: Global Support for Democratic Government*, edited by Pippa Norris (Oxford: Oxford University Press, 1999) pp. 65–66. Dalton reports that "the empirical evidence now presents a clear and striking picture of the erosion of partisan attachments among contemporary publics."
26   Wattenberg, "Turnout Declines in the U.S. and other Advanced Industrial Democracies," p. 18.
27   The most well-known statement of this thesis in Canada is Nevitte, *Decline of Deference*. See also Dalton, "Political Support in Advanced Industrial Democracies," pp. 67–68 and 74. Dalton concludes that "citizens have grown more distant from political parties, more critical of political elites and political institutions, and less positive toward government. . . . The deference to authority that once was common in many Western democracies has partially been replaced by public scepticism of elites."

to look within themselves for moral guidance. Pollster Michael Adams thinks that Canadians over time have moved away from traditional values (including respect for hierarchy and authority) and have become less "socially inclined or other-directed" and more "inner-directed"—a gradual shift that represents a "significant evolution of values current in our society and culture."[28] For these reasons, contemporary citizens are somewhat less likely to vote out of a sense of civic obligation, or respect for political institutions or authorities. This does not mean necessarily that citizens have an overly negative view of politics (a point that will be covered below), but simply that they are more individualist and less willing to be guided by tradition and moral absolutes.

To sum up, researchers have confirmed that Canadian values are changing. Some will see these changes as positive, while others will not. But none of these changes is *necessarily* a sign that the Canadian political system is in crisis. Rather, they are developments that have taken shape over the longer term and across most industrialized societies. They reflect a variety of profound and likely irreversible changes such as rising education levels, innovations in information technology, the changing nature of work and shifts in family structure.

Political Disaffection

Many observers argue that the decline in voter turnout is a result of citizens losing confidence in their political leaders and becoming cynical about the political process. They see voter apathy as driven by a growing disaffection with politics that, in turn, is fueled by the perception that politicians and political parties are self-interested, dishonest and out-of-touch.

Evidence of cynicism—that is, contempt for the political system—and of a growing lack of confidence in politicians and political institutions in Canada is plentiful:

- According to a recent CRIC survey, 86 percent of Canadians agree that politicians often lie to get elected. And more than 7 out of 10 of those surveyed agree with the statement: "I don't think governments care very much about what people like me think."[29] And there is evidence that these negative views are much more pronounced than they were 20 or 30 years ago (see Figure 5).[30]

- Over the past 25 years, the percentage of Canadians who say they have a great deal of confidence in the House of Commons or in political parties has declined significantly, while the percentage saying they have very little confidence has increased (see Figures 6 and 7).

---

28 Michael Adams, *Better Happy than Rich: Canadians, Money and the Meaning of Life* (Toronto: Viking, 2000), pp. 19–23.

29 CRIC survey on Trade, Globalization and Canadian Values, 2001, February–March 2000. See: CRIC, *Opinion Canada*, Vol. 3, No. 23 (June 21, 2000); available online at *http://www.ccu-cuc.ca/en/op/archives/opv3n23.htm#file*.

30 See for instance: Lawrence LeDuc, "The Canadian Voter," in *Introductory Readings in Canadian Government and Politics*, second edition, edited by Robert M. Krause and R.H. Wagenberg (Toronto: Copp Clark, 1995), p. 371.

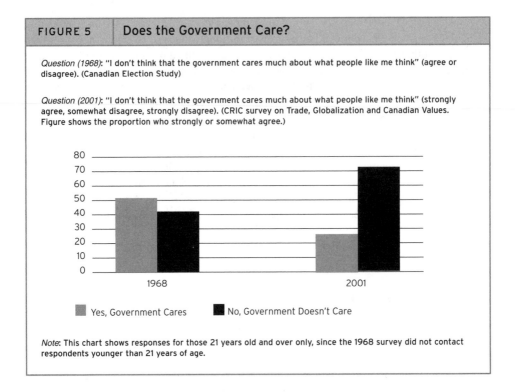

FIGURE 5 | **Does the Government Care?**

Question (1968): "I don't think that the government cares much about what people like me think" (agree or disagree). (Canadian Election Study)

Question (2001): "I don't think that the government cares much about what people like me think" (strongly agree, somewhat disagree, strongly disagree). (CRIC survey on Trade, Globalization and Canadian Values. Figure shows the proportion who strongly or somewhat agree.)

■ Yes, Government Cares   ■ No, Government Doesn't Care

Note: This chart shows responses for those 21 years old and over only, since the 1968 survey did not contact respondents younger than 21 years of age.

- Similarly, surveys conducted by Environics show that the percentage of Canadians saying they have little or no confidence in governments rose from about 40 percent in the early 1980s to over 60 percent in the early 1990s.[31]

- Over 50 percent of Canadians surveyed in the 1960s said that they could trust the government in Ottawa to do what is right "just about always" or "most of the time." By the 1990s, only about one-third took this position.[32]

- A 1997 CRIC survey of Canadians between the ages of 18 and 34 found that respondents had less confidence in political leaders than in any of the other eight groups that they were asked about. Almost two-thirds of respondents said that they had "not much confidence" or "no confidence" in political leaders (see Figure 8).

Unlike the previous explanation, which focused on changing values, this explanation clearly implies that the problem lies with the way the political system is working. The point here is not that citizens have changed, but that the political system is perceived to be less and less responsive to people's concerns.

---

[31] Data from Environics Research Group, cited in George Perlin and Andrew Parkin, "Regime Legitimacy," in George Perlin, Canadian Politics, Volume 2: Canadian Democracy in Critical Perspective (Kingston and Toronto: Queen's University and CBC Newsworld, 2000).

[32] Data from Canadian Elections Studies, cited in Perlin and Parkin, "Regime Legitimacy."

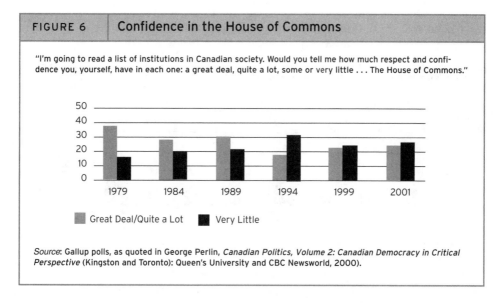

FIGURE 6   **Confidence in the House of Commons**

"I'm going to read a list of institutions in Canadian society. Would you tell me how much respect and confidence you, yourself, have in each one: a great deal, quite a lot, some or very little . . . The House of Commons."

Great Deal/Quite a Lot   Very Little

Source: Gallup polls, as quoted in George Perlin, *Canadian Politics, Volume 2: Canadian Democracy in Critical Perspective* (Kingston and Toronto): Queen's University and CBC Newsworld, 2000).

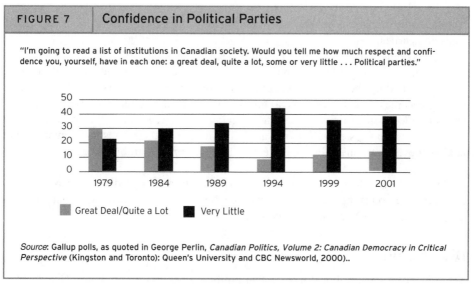

FIGURE 7   **Confidence in Political Parties**

"I'm going to read a list of institutions in Canadian society. Would you tell me how much respect and confidence you, yourself, have in each one: a great deal, quite a lot, some or very little . . . Political parties."

Great Deal/Quite a Lot   Very Little

Source: Gallup polls, as quoted in George Perlin, *Canadian Politics, Volume 2: Canadian Democracy in Critical Perspective* (Kingston and Toronto): Queen's University and CBC Newsworld, 2000)..

Political scientists in Canada have varied views on which factors are to blame for heightening voter cynicism.[33] Some point to the way in which the news media cover politics. Television news emphasizes style over substance and portrays election campaigns as strategic contests among party leaders. This reinforces the sense that there are few major issues at stake and accentuates the negative tone of the campaign—a tone that some

---

[33]   See Perlin and Parkin, "Regime Legitimacy."

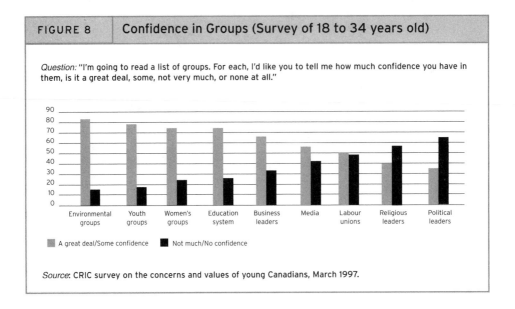

FIGURE 8   Confidence in Groups (Survey of 18 to 34 years old)

Question: "I'm going to read a list of groups. For each, I'd like you to tell me how much confidence you have in them, is it a great deal, some, not very much, or none at all."

■ A great deal/Some confidence   ■ Not much/No confidence

Source: CRIC survey on the concerns and values of young Canadians, March 1997.

American researchers have shown to "contribute to the general antipathy toward politicians and parties."[34]

    Others point to the limited role played in decision-making by the majority of members of Parliament. As power has become increasingly concentrated in the hands of the inner circle surrounding the Prime Minister and his or her key ministers,[35] parliament, as a whole, becomes less relevant as a forum for political deliberation. Backbench and opposition MPs, in particular, are seen as having no power to shape the political agenda and no input into legislation. Citizens are left to wonder if their votes really matter, since in almost every case the MPs they select will be far removed from the centre of political power.

    Furthermore, without a meaningful role to play, MPs are reduced to trying to score partisan political points through cajoling and heckling—precisely the activity that increases the public's negative view of politicians.

Discussion

There is much about political turnout that political scientists do not know. One problem that researchers face is that many non-voters simply refuse to be interviewed in telephone surveys about politics. This limits our understanding of why some people don't vote.

    Even if we cannot be sure which of the various factors in the single most important one, we can still draw the following conclusion: both the relative lack of competitiveness of the last two elections, and the problems associated with the switch to a permanent vot-

---

[34]   Stephen Ansolabehere and Shanto Iyengar, *Going Negative, How Political Advertisements Shrink and Polarize the Electorate* (New York: The Free Press 1995), p. 112.

[35]   See: Donald J. Savoie, *Governing from the Centre: The Concentration of Power in Canadian Politics* (Toronto: University of Toronto Press, 1999), e.g. pages 108, 362.

ers list, discouraged a certain number of people from voting. But even taken together, these factors cannot account in full for the longer-term trend toward lower turnout.

This means that the gradual shift in values, along with the increasing political cynicism or disaffection, have to be taken into account. The key point of disagreement is over how much weight to give to each of these two explanations. Those who argue that voter turnout is declining because Canadians, like most citizens in the Western world, are becoming more "inner-focused," more secular and less deferential to authority, are less likely to see cause for alarm. That is because these changes can be linked to developments, common to all industrialized countries, that have little to do with the performance of the political system.

But those who stress the coincidence of lower turnout and greater cynicism about politics are more apt to worry, since the implication is that declining turnout is a symptom of a deeper malaise. Given the apparent extent of political disaffection among citizens, there is little room for complacency. It should be stressed that while the above-noted changed values have been recorded in most Western democracies, the decline in voter turnout in Canada in the past decade has been especially acute. Moreover, the most common type of reason for not voting given by those surveyed in 2000 by Election Canada was that they didn't think the election or their vote mattered, or that they didn't like the choices they were offered (see Figure 4). This again prompts us to take seriously the idea that the Canadian political system may be performing particularly poorly in the eyes of its citizens.

A consideration of the case of young Canadians, which follows below, further reinforces the sense that all is not well with Canada's political system.

YOUNG CANADIANS: ACTIVIST OR APATHETIC?

Voting and Non-Voting

Younger people are less interested in politics (see Figures 9 and 10) and are less likely to vote than their elders.[36] This is not surprising. On the whole, voters who only recently have become adults will be less familiar with politics. They are at a relatively "care free" stage of life, and have had less opportunity to see how elections could affect their interests.

Many young adults are highly mobile, and so less rooted in their communities and less aware of community needs and issues. For these reasons, they are likely to be less interested in elections. But as they grow older, it is generally assumed that they will become more likely to vote.

The decline in voter turnout raises questions about this assumption. Contrary to expectations, are more and more young people continuing to abstain from voting as they grow older? And are young people today even less likely to vote than they were a generation ago?

---

[36] Blais, *To Vote or Not to Vote*, 52; Neil Nevitte, André Blais, Elisabeth Gidengil and Richard Nadeau, *Unsteady State: The 1997 Canadian Federal Election* (Don Mills: Oxford University Press, 2000), 61; Jon H. Pammett and John Myles, "Lowering the Voting Age to 16," in *Youth in Canadian Politics: Participation and Involvement*, edited by Kathy Megyery, Volume 8 of the Research Studies prepared for the Royal Commission on Electoral Reform and Party Financing (Toronto: Dundurn Press, 1991), 99–101.

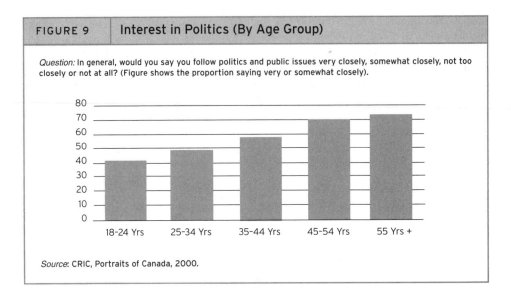

FIGURE 9 | **Interest in Politics (By Age Group)**

Question: In general, would you say you follow politics and public issues very closely, somewhat closely, not too closely or not at all? (Figure shows the proportion saying very or somewhat closely).

Source: CRIC, Portraits of Canada, 2000.

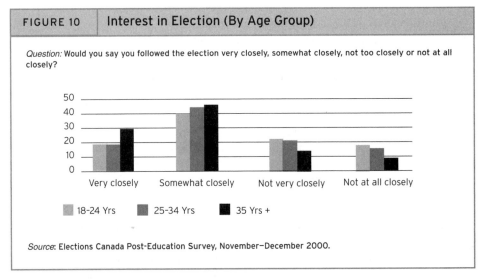

FIGURE 10 | **Interest in Election (By Age Group)**

Question: Would you say you followed the election very closely, somewhat closely, not too closely or not at all closely?

Source: Elections Canada Post-Education Survey, November–December 2000.

The answer is "yes."[37] The team or researchers leading the 2000 Canadian Election Study have found that, at the same age, turnout among those born in the 1960s is 10 points lower than it was for earlier generations, and it is a further 10 points lower among those born in the 1970s. In other words, turnout for younger Canadians (those born after 1970) is 20 points lower than it was at the same age for those born before the 1960s.[38] This

---

[37]   Nevitte, Blais, Gidengil and Nadeau, *Unsteady State*, 62.

[38]   André Blais, Elisabeth Gidengil, Neil Nevitte and Richard Nadeau, "The Evolving Nature of Non Voting: Evidence from Canada," paper prepared for delivery at the Annual Meeting of the American Political Science Association, San Francisco, August 30–September 2, 2001, p. 3.

research confirms that it is less and less the case that voters who abstain when they are young are opting to vote as they get older. And this in turn accounts for much of the decline in turnout experienced in Canada; that is, turnout is declining because, as time passes, newer generations of Canadians, who are less inclined to vote, are coming to represent a larger share of the electorate.[39]

Neither Cynicism Nor Apathy

It might be assumed that young people are voting less because they have become especially cynical about politics. But this is not the case.

Elections Canada's recent post-election survey found 18 to 24 year olds are more likely to agree that their vote doesn't really matter, and less likely to agree that it is important to vote. But the difference in the responses given by older and younger people is relatively small (see Figure 11). As expected, the same survey found a very large difference in the proportion within each age group who said they had voted in the election. Clearly, the much lower voter turnout among 18 to 24 year olds cannot be attributed to the fact that they were only slightly less likely to think that voting matters.

In addition, consider the following:

• The same survey asked those who had not voted to say why they had abstained. Nonvoters, 18 to 24, were *less* likely than older non-voters to say that they had abstained

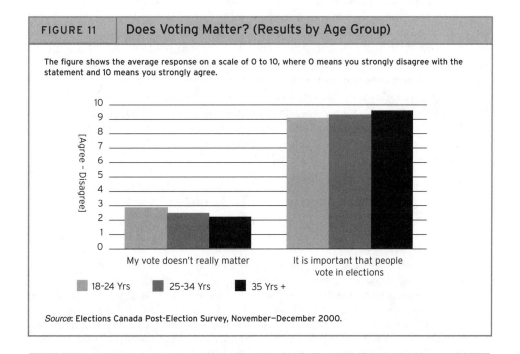

FIGURE 11 | **Does Voting Matter? (Results by Age Group)**

The figure shows the average response on a scale of 0 to 10, where 0 means you strongly disagree with the statement and 10 means you strongly agree.

[Agree – Disagree]

My vote doesn't really matter   It is important that people vote in elections

■ 18-24 Yrs   ■ 25-34 Yrs   ■ 35 Yrs +

Source: Elections Canada Post-Election Survey, November–December 2000.

---

[39] Blais, Nevitte and Nadeau, "The Evolving Nature of Non Voting," pp. 4–5. The authors note, however, that "it also remains to be explained *why* younger generations are less prone to vote than their predecessors" (p. 7). See also: Nevitte, Blais, Gidengil and Nadeau, *Unsteady State*, 63.

because they didn't think their vote made a difference, because the election didn't matter to them, or because they didn't like any of the candidates or the political parties.

- As noted above, a majority of Canadians agree that governments don't care very much about what they think, and that politicians often lie to get elected. But younger people are no more likely to agree with these statements than are older people.[40]

- Data from Environics' *Focus Canada* surveys show that the percentage of those saying they had confidence in governments fell by a dramatic 28 points between 1988 and 1992. However, the decline was less pronounced among younger Canadians: among 18 to 29 year olds it fell by 23 points, whereas it fell by 28 points among those aged 30 to 44, and by 33 points among those aged 45 to 59.

- CRIC's *Portraits of Canada 2000* survey found that young people are slightly less likely to say that the main parties running in that year's federal election are basically the same, and about as likely to say that there are real differences between some of them.[41]

These latest findings confirm previous studies' findings that "young people are less cynical about politics and have higher feelings of political efficacy than do older people."[42] Or, in the words of another group of researchers, "there is no relationship between age and cynicism. It is *not* because they are more cynical that the generation born after 1970 is less prone to vote."[43]

Some commentators also claim that the evidence that young people today are less interested in politics is misleading. While they may be less interested in federal elections, they are more attracted than ever to other political activities at the local and international levels. As is often noted, the cultural, economic and political horizons of young people have become much more global. And where conventional political institutions appear remote, hierarchical and ineffective, community politics is "hands-on," co-operative and promises to deliver concrete results in the short term. In short, many socially and politically engaged young people "do not feel that voting is an empowering form of change. They would rather put their energies into other forms of political engagement."[44]

This argument is compelling. At the same time, it is interesting to note that recent surveys have shown that the views of young adults in Canada are not all that different from those of our parents.

---

[40] CRIC survey on Trade, Globalization and Canadian Values, 2001, February–March 2001. See: CRIC, *Opinion Canada*, Vol. 3, No. 23 (June 21, 2001); available online at *http://www.ccu-cuc.ca/ en/op/archives/opv3n23.htm#file*.

[41] Similarly, the IRPP found that young people are less likely to agree with the statement that "all federal parties are basically the same; there isn't really a choice." See: Paul Howe and David Northrup, "Strengthening Canadian Democracy: The Views of Canadians," *Policy Matters* Vol. 1, No. 5 (July 2000), 88. Available from the website of the Institute of Research on Public Policy at *www.irpp.org*. There is one exception to the statement made above: in the CRIC survey, 18 to 24 year olds were less likely than every other age group, *except those over 55 years of age*, to say that all parties were the same.

[42] Pammett and Myles, "Lowering the Voting Age to 16," 101.

[43] Nevitte, Blais, Gidengil and Nadeau, *Unsteady State*, 63.

[44] D-Code Inc., *Social Vision Report: Young Adult Perspectives on Social and Civic Responsibility* (Toronto: D-Code, Inc., 2001), p. 21.

- An Institute for Research for Public Policy survey asked "what do you think is a more effective way to work for change nowadays: joining a political party or an interest group?" Only 21 percent of 18 to 29 year olds said that it is more effective to join a political party, but the proportion of 46 to 60 year olds who preferred this option was exactly the same.[45]
- Similarly, a CRIC survey found that young Canadians essentially are no more likely than their parents to approve of acts of civil disobedience. Seventy-two percent of 18 to 29 year olds said they would never engage in acts of civil disobedience, such as occupying a building or blockading a road—a figure only slightly lower than the 76 percent of 46 to 60 year olds who said the same.[46]

In each case, the real difference of opinion was between those under 60 years of age, and those over that age. In other words, it is the oldest generation of Canadians that has distinctive views about the efficacy of political parties or the legitimacy of political protest, not the youngest.

These limited findings do not invalidate the argument that, increasingly, young people are ill at ease with the country's political institutions. But they do suggest that other factors need to be considered in order to explain the growing reluctance of young Canadians to participate in elections.

Civic Education

One example is the decline in "civic education" in schools—classes that focus on the country and its political system, and encourage discussion of current affairs. Some argue that the education system is not doing as much as it once did to familiarize young people with the political system and its underlying values. This may help to explain the fact that Canadian citizens appear to be less knowledgeable about politics than they once were. As Paul Howe reports, "a sizeable and growing section of the population is woefully ill-informed about political matters. . . . Nor are things likely to improve down the road. Young Canadians are the least politically knowledgeable group in the country, and by a wider margin today than ten years ago . . . . What's more, this relative decline in levels of political knowledge also holds true of young Canadians who have received post-secondary education."[47] Howe adds that those who are less knowledgeable about politics are also less likely to vote.

Perceptions About Government

A second factor is changes in perceptions about government and its role in society. The current generation of young voters came of age during the 1990s, at a time when political debate focused on the deficit and debt problem, wasteful spending and excessive levels of

---

[45] Howe and Northrup, "Strengthening Canadian Democracy," p. 95.

[46] CRIC survey on Trade, Globalization and Canadian Values, February–March 2001. See: CRIC, *Opinion Canada*, Vol. 3, No. 23 (June 21, 2001): available online at *http://www.ccu-cuc.ca/en/ op/archives/opv3n23.htm#file*.

[47] Paul Howe, "The Sources of Campaign Intemperance," *Policy Options/Options Politiques* Vol. 22, No. 1 (January–February 2001), p. 22.

taxation. Governments were frequently portrayed as the source of Canada's problems, not the solution. Government program spending was dramatically curtailed, sending young people the message that citizens should become more self-reliant and seek more opportunities outside the public sector. Thus, it is no surprise that young Canadians question the effectiveness and relevance of government and the value of political participation.[48]

Furthermore, for young adults full of creative energy and ideals, the world of politics is arguably less inviting than it once was. Until recently, post-war governments in Canada had been preoccupied with managing economic expansion, creating the welfare state, "nation-building" through constitutional renewal, and promoting peace and justice abroad. But government's role has been curtailed, both as a result of the need to cut spending and in response to the constraints of economic globalization. Once again, it is perhaps no surprise that young Canadians with more ambitious goals are by-passing traditional political institutions.

A Fragmented Community

A third factor is the gradual fragmentation of public communication and debate. Much has been said about the Internet's impact on Canadian society. Some argue that it is a means through which young people can become socially engaged. Via the Internet, citizens with similar interests can form "virtual" communities. But virtual communities are still diffused communities. There is little that connects them to one another or to a larger, all-encompassing community. With the proliferation of virtual communities, the common community becomes less and less visible.

Similarly, developments in other forms of electronic media—including the expansion of cable, satellite and digital television—mean that there are many more channels of public communication to choose from. Fred Fletcher has argued that, among other things, the proliferation of TV channels may bring about a fragmentation of the Canadian public— turning it into numerous micro-audiences.[49] Again, common community is partially eclipsed.

Each of these three developments is important, since research has shown that voter participation is linked to the degree to which citizens are connected with the larger community. Voting is, in part, an expression of one's sense of community. As the visibility or salience of the shared community is eroded for the reasons mentioned above, then one of the most important forces that once encouraged young people to participate in the country's political life is weakened. The problem is not that more and more young people feel hostility towards the political system, but that more and more are indifferent to it.

---

[48] I am grateful to Lisa Young and Phillip Haid for bringing this point to my attention. As one indication of how the effort to contain government spending has affected the lives of young Canadians, consider that average university tuition for an undergraduate arts program doubled over the course of the 1990s. See Statistics Canada, *The Daily*, 27 August 2001, available online at: *http://www.statcan.ca/ Daily/English/010827/d019827b.htm.*

[49] Frederick J. Fletcher, "Media, Education, and Democracy," *Canadian Journal of Communication* Vol. 19, No. 1 (1994), pp. 143–44.

DOES TURNOUT MATTER?

Does it really matter if 40 percent of the electorate chooses not to vote?

No

Low turnout could be a sign of what pollster Michael Adams calls a "new consensus" about the need for smaller governments and the reduced importance of national politics in our day-to-day lives. Elections matter less than they did before, he argues, but not because there is a crisis in Canadian democracy. They matter less because governments are doing less, because globalization places more policy issues beyond Ottawa's control, and because citizens are more self-reliant and less willing to be led by traditional figures of authority. According to Adams, "there is life after electoral politics"—by which he presumably means that the health of a society must be measured by more than the tally of those willing to trudge to the polls every four years to cast a vote.[50]

It can also be noted that turnout is not necessarily the best measure of the health of a democratic society. For various reasons, Switzerland has very low turnout at national elections, yet in many ways constitutes a model democracy. Conversely, some countries whose democratic institutions rest on very shaky foundations can nonetheless boast high levels of voter participation.

Yes

There are at least three good reasons why turnout does matter.

Equality of Influence First, it matters because declining turnout sows the seeds of increasing inequality among social groups in terms of political participation and political influence.

As political scientist Jerome Black reminds us, it is important to look at who is voting, and who is not. The decline in voter participation is particularly acute among certain groups within society—young people and those who are less well-off economically. This means that, as overall turnout declines, the active electorate becomes less and less representative of society as a whole; "low voter turnout means unequal and socioeconomically biased turnout."[51] Voters no longer appear to speak with the voice of "the people"—they speak more and more with the voice of those who are relatively privileged.

This reality in turn shapes the behaviour of political parties. As noted American political scientist Arend Lijphart argues, "unequal participation spells unequal influence," a fact that he calls "a major dilemma for representative democracy."[52] Political parties craft their platforms in order to gain the votes they need to win power. There is little incentive for them to aim their appeal at those groups that are the least likely to vote. As non-voting

[50] Michael Adams, "The Revolt of the Voting Classes" (30 November, 2000). Available on the website of Environics Research Group at *http://erg.environics.net/news/default.asp?aID=424*. Published in *The Globe and Mail* under the title "Death of Politics."

[51] Arend Lijphart, "Unequal Participation: Democracy's Unresolved Dilemma," *American Political Science Review* Vol. 91, No. 1 (March 1997), p. 2.

[52] Lijphart, "Unequal Participation: Democracy's Unresolved Dilemma," p. 1.

increases among the less affluent, political parties and, ultimately, governments will tailor their messages and policies to an increasingly narrow segment of the population. The result: the political system will seem even less relevant to the less affluent than before—reinforcing their sense that there is little point in voting.

Legitimacy Second, turnout matters because the government's moral authority to govern rests on its claim that it won the support of the largest share of the electorate. Many people may oppose the current party in government, but they recognize that it has legitimacy because it won a mandate from the people.

As more voters abstain, however, the total votes won by the winning party, measured as a share of the number of eligible voters, decreases. For example, the last two Liberal majorities were elected by only 25 percent of eligible voters, whereas at least 30 percent supported the majority governments elected in 1968, 1974, 1984 and 1988. Indeed, minority governments elected in 1972 and 1979 were supported by a greater share of the electorate than were the two most recent majority governments.

What is more striking is that the proportion of the electorate who vote for the winning party is now smaller than the proportion who do not vote at all (see Figure 12). In 1988 for instance, the Conservative party attracted the support of 32 percent of the electorate, while 25 percent did not vote at all. In 2000, as mentioned, only 25 percent voted Liberal, compared to the 39 percent who abstained.

Therefore, as turnout decreases, the ability of the winning party in an election to claim that it has won the support of the public is brought into question. As the American political scientist Ruy Teixeira writes, "as fewer and fewer citizens participate in elections, the extent to which government truly rests on the consent of the governed may be called into question. As a result elites may feel they do not have sufficient legitimacy among citizens to pursue desired policy objectives, and citizens may feel the government is not legitimate enough for them to support these elites and their policy objectives."[53]

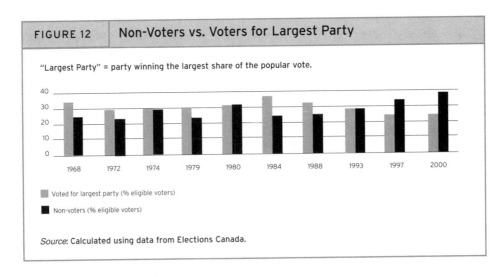

FIGURE 12   **Non-Voters vs. Voters for Largest Party**

"Largest Party" = party winning the largest share of the popular vote.

Voted for largest party (% eligible voters)

Non-voters (% eligible voters)

Source: Calculated using data from Elections Canada.

---

[53]   Ruy Teixeira, *The Disappearing American Voter* (Washington: Brookings Institute, 1992), p. 101.

Political Community Third, turnout matters because of what it tells us about the health of our political community. It is arguable that the decline in voter turnout can be seen as but one symptom of a growing disconnect between Canadians and their community, a growing distrust of public officials and institutions, and a weakening sense of civic duty or obligation. It is notable that volunteerism is also on the decline, with 1 million fewer Canadians giving their time in 2000 as compared to 1997.[54] Statistics Canada reports the proportion of Canadians who were members of a political organization also fell during that period, from 4 to 3 percent.[55] The problem, therefore, may not be simply that fewer people vote, but that fewer are engaged, as citizens, in the public life of the common community.

This does not place Canada in a very good position to meet the challenges that will likely befall it in the years to come. It is foreseeable that in the next five to ten years the country will have to respond to developments as varied as the completion of the Free Trade Area of the Americas, the need to reinvent medicare, a third referendum on sovereignty in Quebec, the coming-of-age of a young and more assertive Aboriginal population, and the moral issues raised by new medical and biological technologies. The finding of effective policy responses must be rooted in citizen participation, for at least two reasons: first, those advancing creative policy ideas must seek public support in order for these ideas to find a place on the political agenda; and second, governments that cannot connect with citizens are unlikely to be able to build the support to ensure that their policies are accepted and effectively implemented.

It is even possible to suggest that Canada's future depends at least in part on the ability of its population to cohere as a community. Many commentators have stressed how the shifting flow of trade, from an east-west axis to a north-south one, weakens the economic bonds that once tied Canada's regions together.[56] More than ever, Canadian unity must be forged through an appeal, not to economic self-interest, but to a sense of shared values and common purpose. The more citizens become non-participants in key political events, such as elections, and lose respect for political institutions, the greater the likelihood that appeals to shared values and common purpose will fall on deaf ears.

LOOKING FORWARD

If turnout does matter, can anything be done to encourage more citizens to go to the polls? A number of suggestions have been put forward. But at the outset, it should be noted that some of the principal causes of declining voter participation—notably shifting values and rising political disaffection—are not "problems" to which easy solutions readily can be found.

---

[54] Statistics Canada, *The Daily*, 17 August 2001, available online at: *http://www.statcan.ca/ Daily/English/010817/d010817c.htm*.

[55] Michael Hall, Larry McKeown and Karen Roberts, *Caring Canadians, Involved Canadians: Highlights from the 2000 National Survey of Giving, Volunteering and Participating*, Statistics Canada Cat. No. 71-542 (August 2001), p. 50; supplemented by communication with Statistics Canada.

[56] See, for instance, John Ibbitson, *Loyal No More: Ontario's Struggle for a Separate Destiny* (Toronto: HarperCollins Publishers, 2001).

Internet Voting

Some argue that new communications technology offers a possible solution. Voters might be more inclined to vote if they could do so online or by telephone. In the wake of the low turnout in the recent UK election, that country's Electoral Commission proposed a review of both these methods of voting.[57] Elections Canada has also studied the implication of information technology for the voting process.[58]

Canadians are currently divided on the question of whether such innovations are advisable. The Election Canada post-election survey found that 47 percent said they would like to vote online in future elections, if technology allowed, while 52 percent said they would not. Similarly, 38 percent agreed with the proposition that "to make it easier for people to vote, Internet voting should be allowed for a general election," but the same proportion disagreed.[59] (In the case of telephone voting, only 28 percent agreed that it should be allowed, compared to 47 percent who disagreed). Furthermore, 48 percent agreed that "there is too much potential for fraud and mistakes to ever have Internet voting for a general election," and 30 percent remained opposed to Internet voting even in the event that "systems are proven safe and secure." Those most likely to be familiar with computers and the Internet—that is, younger, better-educated and wealthier Canadians—were more supportive of voting online.

Concerns have been expressed about the potential for fraud, should voting online be allowed. For instance, hackers could disrupt the system, cause it to misallocate votes, obtain voters' passwords, or reveal whom individual voters supported.

The biggest problem with voting online, however, has nothing to do with the technology. It has to do with the potential for abuse simply because more and more voters would be voting outside of a polling station, where nothing prevents someone from looking over voters' shoulders to make sure they support the "right" candidate. If families gather to vote around the household terminal, it will be harder for spouses or children to secretly defy the political wishes of their partners or parents. More serious abuses could follow from the actions of unscrupulous political activists. In tightly fought constituencies, one can readily imagine activists armed with portable, wireless computers seeking out otherwise apathetic voters and buying their online votes.

Finally, it can be argued that the visit to a polling station has a positive influence on citizens in a democracy. It is perhaps one of the most important exercises in civic education that voters are likely to experience. The traditional voting process can be seen as a ritual that, like many other rituals in human life, heightens the sense of importance of the act in question. These intangible effects of voting would be lost in the transition to voting online.

---

[57] Kevin Ward, "Britain Looks at Internet Voting, Ballot Redesign to Overcome Voter Apathy," Canadian Press article posted on CBC News website on July 24, 2001.

[58] See "The Feasibility of Electronic Voting in Canada," in *Electoral Insight* Vol. 2, No. 1 (June 2000): 2–5. Available on the website of Election Canada at *www.elections.ca*.

[59] Respondents were asked to use a scale of 0 to 10, where 0 means strong disagreement and 10 means strong agreement. For the purpose of the results cited above, answers from 0 to 2 were coded as "disagree" and answers from 8 to 10 were coded as "agree." The remaining responses were coded as "neutral."

For all these reasons, new communications technology is not the best solution to the problem of low voter turnout.

Compulsory Voting

The simplest way for Canada to boost turnout at elections would be to adopt compulsory voting. As Arend Lijphart argues, "compulsory voting is the only institutional mechanism . . . that can assure high turnout virtually by itself."[60] Countries such as Australia, Belgium and Greece each make voting mandatory, and as a direct result, turnout in these countries is very high.

Compulsory voting does more than increase the number of ballots cast. It can have a "spillover effect," acting as a "form of civic education and political stimulation" that encourages citizens to become more interested and involved in politics.[61] And it can enhance democracy by counteracting the tendency, noted above, for certain groups within the population—notably those who are better-off—to vote in greater numbers than others.

There are two compelling arguments against compulsory voting. The first is that it likely would be opposed by a majority of the public, who would see it as an unwarranted restriction on the freedom of the individual. In a survey conduced last year by the IRPP, only 24 percent supported compulsory voting, while 73 percent opposed it.[62] Compelling citizens to vote might therefore *contribute* to their sense of anger toward the political system, even if a greater number of them turned out to vote.

Second, compulsory voting does little to address the underlying causes of low voter turnout, and might only mask the problem. It turnout were artificially high through mandatory voting, we would not have the evidence of declining turnout to alert us that something is wrong with the political system, with the level of civic education, or the sense of civic duty in Canada.

For these reasons, compulsory voting is not the best solution for Canada.

Proportional Representation

In recent years, Canada's electoral system has been increasingly criticized. Under the existing "first-past-the-post" system, the candidate who wins the most votes in an individual constituency is elected. While this seems fair, it produces results that on the aggregate are peculiar. Examples are familiar and plentiful: in 1993, the party with the fourth highest popular vote (the Bloc Québécois) won the second highest number of seats and formed the official opposition; in 1997, the Progressive Conservative Party won almost as many votes as the Reform Party, but one-third as many seats; in 2000, the Tories won more votes than the Bloc but less than one-third as many seats. And parties regularly form majority governments on the basis of the support of only 2 in 5 votes.

---

[60] Lijphart, "Unequal Participation," p. 10.

[61] Lijphart, "Unequal Participation," p. 10.

[62] Howe and Northrup, "Strengthening Canadian Democracy," p. 86. The question was: "In Australia and a number of other countries, people must vote or pay a small fine. Do you think Canada should have a law like this?"

In response, many argue that Canada should adopt a system of proportional representation (PR). Under PR, parties would be allocated a share of the seats in the House of Commons that more closely reflected their level of popular support. Advocates of PR argue that it is fairer to voters and to parties. In Canada, PR would also alleviate regionalism, as it would make it possible for each of the major parties to win seats in all regions of the country.

But it can also be argued that a switch to PR would give voters added incentives to cast their ballots, and thereby enhance turnout. There are several reasons why this might be the case:

a. PR would do away with "wasted" votes. At present, many voters know that their preferred candidate has no chance of winning in their constituency. Under PR, each vote is weighed in the calculations used to allocate seats in the House of Commons. Therefore every vote counts in a way that it does not under the existing system.

b. PR would make elections more interesting and competitive. Easy majority victories would be unlikely, and election outcomes less predictable. The electoral monopolies that certain parties exercise over specific areas of the country would be disrupted. Smaller parties would emerge as potential coalition partners, giving their supporters an added incentive to turn out to vote.

c. Since the relative standing of the parties in the House of Commons would more closely reflect their level of popular support, the political system would appear more responsive. It would no longer be the case that some parties could lose official party status despite winning a significant portion of the vote, or that others could win large majority despite being supported by less than half the electorate. The more direct relation between votes cast and seats won would contribute to the sense that voting matters.

In general, then, advocates of PR argue that it is more responsive to voters' intentions and therefore removes the disincentives to vote that characterise the electoral system as it now stands. As Mark Franklin writes, "voters are not fools, and an unresponsive system will motivate many fewer of them to vote."[63] From this standpoint, it is perhaps not surprising that researchers have found that, other things being equal, countries that use a form of PR tend to have higher turnout (although there is some disagreement as to how much of a difference PR makes).[64]

Since the lack of competitiveness in recent elections, combined with some citizens' view that voting or elections don't matter, are among factors contributing to low turnout in Canada, the need to examine PR is evident. The government could give Elections Canada a mandate to engage Canadians in a serious debate about changing the electoral system, establish a commission of enquiry to recommend alternatives, and ultimately put the question of PR to the people in a referendum on electoral reform.[65]

---

[63] Franklin, "The Dynamics of Electoral Participation."

[64] See, for instance: Franklin, "The Dynamics of Electoral Participation"; André Blais and Agnieska Dobrynska, "Turnout in Electoral Democracies," *European Journal of Political Research* Vol. 33 (March 1998), pp. 247–248; André Blais and Ken Carty, "Does Proportional Representation Foster Voter Turnout?" *European Journal of Political Research* Vol. 18 (1990), pp. 174 ff.

[65] For some thoughts on how the process of electoral reform in Canada might proceed, see Matthew Mendelsohn and Andrew Parkin, with Alex Van Kralinger, "Getting from Here to There: A Process

Institutional Reform

A change in the electoral system is only one of a number of possible reforms that could reinvigorate Canada's political system. Others include:

- Enhancing the role of individual members of parliament by relaxing party discipline and allowing more free votes in the House of Commons. (Note that, in CRIC's March 2001 survey of the four western provinces, 55 percent of respondents said that "changing the rules of the House of Commons so that members of parliament can vote more freely, rather than having to vote the same way as their party" was a high priority for making the country work better.[66])
- Further expanding the influence of MPs by strengthening parliamentary committees (Canadian parliamentary committees are much weaker than those of similar countries[67]).
- Subjecting leadership campaigns within political parties to public regulation, in order to make fund-raising and spending, as well as the voting process, more transparent and worthy of public confidence.
- Hold more referendums on key public policy issues (as was done recently in New Brunswick, on the question of video lottery terminals), or allow citizens to initiate referendums on issues of their choice.[68]

Each of these changes could be debated at length. Some may be found to be more appropriate than others. But the need to embrace at least some of these proposals is clear. The challenge is to convince citizens that elections matter, either because their own votes make a difference, or because their elected representatives do. And citizens are sufficiently cynical about politics, and sufficiently savvy, that they cannot be won over by public relations campaigns that offer nothing more than slogans. In order to rekindle their interest in politics, the political system must become more responsive. Only reforms designed to further these objectives can raise public confidence in the system. Without such changes, citizens committed to improving their communities and country will be drawn away increasingly from an ossified parliamentary system.

Thus, declining turnout can be seen as a challenge that calls for a bold, innovative and far-sighted response from Canada's political leaders. They need not look elsewhere, since they themselves have the power to reinvigorate the institutions over which they preside.

---

for Electoral Reform in Canada," *Policy Options/Options Politiques* Vol. 22, No. 6 (July–August 2001): 55–60.

[66] A report in this survey is available on the website of the Council for Canadian Unity at: *http://www.ccu-cuc.ca/en/polls/data/cric.html.*

[67] See for instance, Peter Dobell, "Reforming Parliamentary Practice: The Views of MPs," *Policy Matters* Volume 1, No. 9, p. 11. Available from the website of the Institute for Research on Public Policy at *www.irpp.org*. In this paper, Dobell outlines several ways in which the role of committees could be expanded.

[68] This idea was widely dismissed during the 2000 election campaign, but did not receive the serious consideration it deserves. See Matthew Mendelsohn and Andrew Parkin, "Introducing Direct Democracy in Canada," *Choices* Vol. 7, No. 5 (June 2001). Available from the website of the Institute for Research on Public Policy at *www.irpp.org*.

More Questions Than Answers

Electoral reform and changes to other political institutions are measures that are intended to make elections more competitive, make parliament more responsive and more relevant, and ultimately raise citizen's interest and confidence in the political process as a whole. In so doing, they clearly address some of the causes of declining voter turnout that were discussed earlier in this paper. But several notes of caution are in order.

First, there is no solid evidence from other countries that measures such as a loosening of party discipline or a revitalization of parliamentary committees will boost turnout. It could be that such measures will only impress those who are already interested and active in politics, yet fail to inspire non-voters.

Second, changes to the political institutions may not have the desired effect unless there is also a commitment among politicians, their advisors and the media to improve the tone and depth of political debate. In the US, for instance, referendums on policy issues are often manipulated by narrow interest groups with ample money to spend on negative TV advertising, and hardly serve to instill greater public confidence in government.

Third, none of these reforms directly address the issue of the long-term change in values, such as decreasing deference to authority or the declining importance of religion. Indeed, as noted above, many observers see such value change as irreversible.

For these reasons, many political scientists in Canada seem uncertain whether anything can be done to reverse the trend toward declining turnout over the long term. This uncertainty may serve to keep our expectations in check, but does not stand as a valid reason to avoid undertaking the modest reforms suggested above.

CONCLUSION: IS CANADIAN DEMOCRACY IN CRISIS?

Does the decline in voter turnout constitute a crisis for Canadian democracy? It is tempting to adopt a "wait and see" attitude—turnout might rise again at the next election, especially in the event that a stronger opposition emerges to challenge the governing party. But this is too complacent an approach. As we have seen, the problem goes well beyond the issue of the lack of excitement generated by the last two election campaigns. For this reason, the trend toward lower turnout may prove difficult to reverse. Even if turnout rises somewhat at the next election, in the coming decade we are unlikely to see, on a consistent basis, a return to the level of voter participation that we experienced in the 1960s or even the 1980s.

Whether or not this amounts to a crisis depends on the extent to which one values citizen participation in politics as a good thing in and of itself. It is true that parliament currently works equally well, whether it is elected on the basis of high voter turnout or on the basis of low voter turnout. In this sense, turnout does not really matter. But if citizen participation in politics is taken to be a fundamental characteristic of democracy, then the situation appears more grave. What is especially worrying is that the younger generations of Canadians—those who are now beginning to move into positions of leadership—are voting in lesser number than ever before. Those who must be relied upon to give the country its future direction and vision presently are much less engaged in the political process than were their parents or grandparents. It remains to be seen what implications this will have for the ability of the country's political leadership, political parties, and civil service to renew themselves and respond to Canada's needs in the years to come.

APPENDIX TABLES

TABLE 1A	Turnout at Provincial Elections

Percentages of registered voters actually voting in provincial elections since 1980 (year of election precedes turnout figure):

Province	1980–1989			1990–2001			Average: 1980–1989	Average: 1990–2001	Change
NF	1982: 70	1985: 77	1989: 81	1993: 84	1996: 74	1999: 70	76.0	76.0	0.0
PEI	1982: 78	1986: 88	1989: 81	1993: 81	1996: 85	2000: 85	82.3	83.7	1.3
NS	1981: 74	1984: 68	1988: 76	1993: 75	1998: 69	1999: 68	72.7	70.7	-2.0
NB		1982: 82	1987: 82	1991: 80	1996: 75	1999: 76	82.0	77.0	-5.0
QUE	1981: 82	1985: 76	1989: 75	1994: 82	1998: 78		77.7	80.0	2.3
ONT	1981: 58	1985: 62	1987: 63	1990: 64	1995: 63	1999: 58	61.0	61.7	0.7
MA	1981: 72	1986: 68	1988: 74	1990: 69	1995: 69	1999: 68	71.3	68.7	-2.7
SA		1982: 84	1986: 82	1991: 83	1995: 65	1999: 66	83.0	71.3	-11.7
AB	1982: 66	1986: 47	1989: 54	1993: 60	1997: 54	2001: 53	55.7	55.7	0.0
BC		1983: 78	1986: 77	1991: 75	1996: 72	2001: 71	77.5	72.7	-4.8

Sources: websites of the provincial elections agencies supplemented by communications with these agencies.

TABLE 2A	Margin of Victory for the Ten Constituencies With the Highest Turnout (2000 Election)

Constituency	Province	Winning Party	Turnout	Margin of Victory[69]
Saanich–Gulf Islands	BC	Alliance	70.6	10.9
Louis-Hébert	Quebec	Liberal	70.8	4.3
Beauséjour–Petitcodiac	NB	Liberal	71.3	15
Miramichi	NB	Liberal	71.4	26.3
Lac-Saint-Louis	Quebec	Liberal	71.7	66.6
Saint-Maurice	Quebec	Liberal	72.5	15.1
Egmont	PEI	Liberal	72.8	11.5
Malpeque	PEI	Liberal	73.2	9.7
Acadie–Bathurst	NB	N.D.P.	75.4	6.3
Cardigan	PEI	Liberal	79.2	1.6
Average			**72.9**	**16.7**

---

[69] See note 10.

Turned Off or Tuned Out?
Youth Participation in Politics

ELISABETH GIDENGIL, ANDRÉ BLAIS, NEIL NEVITTE,
AND RICHARD NADEAU*

*Elisabeth Gidengil *is Professor of Political Science, McGill University, Montréal.* André Blais *is Professor of Political Science at Université de Montréal.* Neil Nevitte *is Professor of Political Science, University of Toronto.* Richard Nadeau *is Professor of Political Science at Université de Montréal.*

Young Canadians are turning their backs on electoral politics in unprecedented numbers. The optimistic assumption is that they are turning to other forms of political engagement instead. This assumption is encouraged by the fact that today's young Canadians are much more likely than their parents' or grandparents' generation to have had a university education. The assumption gains credence from media images of young people protesting against globalization or the war against Iraq. What we are seeing, the argument goes, is a new generation of highly educated young Canadians who are frustrated with traditional electoral politics and who are turning to more autonomous forms of political action. However, as this article demonstrates, there is evidence this represents an unduly sanguine reading of the situation.

THE DEEPENING DIVIDE

There is nothing new about lower turnout rates among young people. Detailed study of voter turnout in federal elections since 1968 suggests that the propensity to vote typically increases by 7 or 8 points between ages 20 and 30 and by about 15 points between ages 20 and 50.[1] Young people are less likely to vote precisely because they *are* young. Most young people are not going to be particularly concerned about taxes, mortgage rates and access to services, and the political debate that swirls around these issues may seem remote and abstract.

What *is* new is the widening generational divide. There is something about this generation of young Canadians that makes them less likely to vote than their parents or their grandparents were when they were in their twenties. Turnout was 10 points higher among those born in the 1960s when they were young and 20 points higher among baby boomers when they were the same age. When trends are tracked for the different generations, the

---

[1]   André Blais, Elisabeth Gidengil, Richard Nadeau and Neil Nevitte, "Where Does Turnout Decline Come From?" *European Journal of Political Research* 43 (2004): 221–236. For more detailed information on issues covered in this article, see André Blais, Elisabeth Gidengil, Richard Nadeau and Neil Nevitte, *Anatomy of a Liberal Victory: Making Sense of the 2000 Canadian Election* (Peterborough, Ontario: Broadview Press, 2002), Chapter 3, and Elisabeth Gidengil, André Blais, Neil Nevitte and Richard Nadeau, *Citizens* (Vancouver: University of British Columbia Press, 2004).

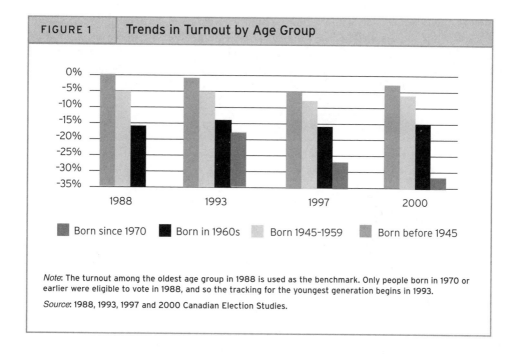

FIGURE 1 | Trends in Turnout by Age Group

Legend: Born since 1970 | Born in 1960s | Born 1945-1959 | Born before 1945

Note: The turnout among the oldest age group in 1988 is used as the benchmark. Only people born in 1970 or earlier were eligible to vote in 1988, and so the tracking for the youngest generation begins in 1993.

Source: 1988, 1993, 1997 and 2000 Canadian Election Studies.

pattern is truly striking (see Figure 1). Turnout has held more or less steady for the three older generations; it is only among the young that voting has decreased. What this means is that much of the decline in turnout since 1988 can be attributed to generational replacement. If the four generations had made up the same proportion of the electorate in 2000 as they did in 1988, turnout in the 2000 federal election would have been as much as 10 points higher.

THE EDUCATION MYTH

The declining turnout in this generation is puzzling because it has come at a time when unprecedented numbers of young Canadians continue their education beyond high school. If they are so much more likely to go on to university, why are they so much less likely to vote than their parents or their grandparents? A ready answer has been found in the very fact that they *are* highly educated. The assumption has been made that these young Canadians are turning away from electoral politics in search of more active forms of political engagement. Because they are highly educated, they aspire to something more meaningful than casting a ballot once in a while.

However, it is a serious misconception to suppose that it is the highly educated young who are failing to turn up at the polls. On the contrary, the more education young people have, the more likely they are to vote. Education remains one of the best predictors of turnout because it provides the cognitive skills needed to cope with the complexities of politics and because it seems to foster norms of civic engagement. Education makes a massive difference to whether young Canadians vote or not. The 2000 Canadian Election Study reveals that turnout in the youngest generation was almost 50 points higher among university graduates than it was among those who left school without a high school diploma.[2] Furthermore, the decline is confined to those with less than a university education. Since the 1993 general election, turnout has fallen over 30 points among those with less than a high school education and 15 points or more among those who have completed high school and/or some college (see Figure 2). Meanwhile, turnout has held steady among young university graduates.

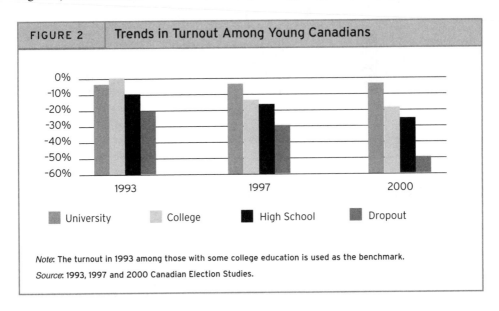

FIGURE 2 **Trends in Turnout Among Young Canadians**

Note: The turnout in 1993 among those with some college education is used as the benchmark.

Source: 1993, 1997 and 2000 Canadian Election Studies.

KNOWING LITTLE AND CARING LESS

A second misconception is that young Canadians are being "turned off" by traditional electoral politics. They are certainly dissatisfied with politics and politicians. Three in five believe that the government does not care what people like them think and two in five believe that political parties hardly ever keep their election promises. However, they are no more dissatisfied than older Canadians. In fact, they are, if anything, a little less disillusioned with politics than their parents and their grandparents are. In any case, political discontent is not a particularly good predictor when it comes to staying away from the polls. Many people who are disaffected with politics choose to vent that frustration by voting against the incumbent.[3]

[2] The 2000 Canadian Election Study involved a rolling cross-section campaign survey with a representative sample of 3,651 Canadians, a post-election survey with 2,862 of the campaign survey respondents, and a mail-back questionnaire filled out by 1,535 of the post-election respondents. The campaign survey response rate was 62 percent. The field work was conducted by the Institute for Social Research at York University and by Jolicoeur et Associés. It was funded by the Social Sciences and Humanities Research Council of Canada, with additional funding from Elections Canada and the Institute for Research on Public Policy.

[3] Elisabeth Gidengil, André Blais, Neil Nevitte and Richard Nadeau, "The Correlates and Consequences of Anti-Partyism in the 1997 Canadian Election," *Party Politics* Vol. 7 (2001), pp. 491–513.

Young Canadians are not so much "turned off" as "tuned out". They tend to be much less interested in politics than older Canadians and to know much less about what is going on politically. Interest in politics and political knowledge are two of the best predictors of who will vote and who will not. If young Canadians had been as interested in politics and as informed as older Canadians, their turnout in the 2000 federal election would have been 14 points higher.

When they were interviewed right after the 2000 federal election, almost one young Canadian in five was unable to name Jean Chrétien as leader of the Liberal party, and one in two failed to come up with Joe Clark's name when asked to identify the Progressive Conservative leader (see Figure 3). The skeptical might charge that this knowledge test is biased against the young: given how long both men have been active in federal politics, older Canadians have simply had more time to become acquainted with them. However, younger respondents were also much less likely to know the names of the newer party leaders: one in three could not name Stockwell Day as Canadian Alliance leader, and more than half failed to identify Alexa McDonough as leader of the New Democratic Party.

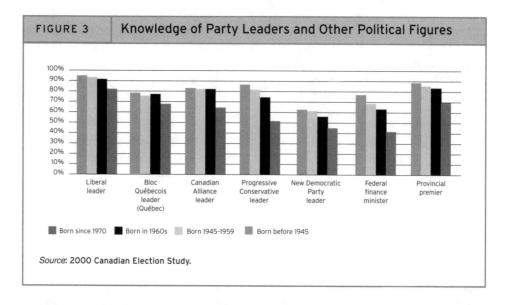

FIGURE 3 | **Knowledge of Party Leaders and Other Political Figures**

Legend: Born since 1970 | Born in 1960s | Born 1945–1959 | Born before 1945

Source: 2000 Canadian Election Study.

Knowing the names of the federal party leaders is not mere political trivia. After all, the leader of the winning party will be Canada's prime minister. At the same time, only two in five could come up with the name of the federal finance minister, and only two in three managed to name their provincial premier. Young Canadians knew even less about the parties' positions than older Canadians. Only one in four could identify the Alliance as being on the right and even fewer could locate the N.D.P. as being on the left. The one factual question on which young Canadians did as well as the older age groups was naming the capital of the United States.

According to the optimistic scenario, however, this low level of knowledge could be just what we would expect if young Canadians are turning their backs on traditional electoral politics. If many of them are finding electoral politics to be irrelevant to their real concerns, perhaps it is hardly surprising that they seem to know so little about it. If this line of argument were correct, we would expect to find much higher levels of knowledge when young Canadians are asked about the issues that *are* supposed to concern them. This is not so. The sight of young Canadians protesting at economic summits suggests that globalization is exactly the sort of issue that is of special interest to them. In truth, however, their lack of awareness seems to extend to this topic as well. According to a survey conducted in March 2001 for the Centre for Research and Information on Canada, only 57 percent of Canadians born since 1970 had heard anything about globalization, only 53 percent had heard anything about the demonstrations against the World Trade Organization the previous year in Seattle, and a mere 40 percent had heard anything about the upcoming Summit of the Americas in the city of Québec.[4] On all three questions, awareness was lowest among the young.

WHO ARE THE ACTIVISTS?

The third misconception is that young Canadians who are giving up on electoral politics are involving themselves in other ways. In fact, according to the 2000 Canadian Election Study, young Canadians were the least likely to have been active in a voluntary association or community group during the previous five years, and when they had been active, it was typically in a sports association (40 percent). If young Canadians were turning to more meaningful forms of engagement, this should show up in membership of environmental groups. The environment is an issue that matters to young people, and it has hardly been a priority on the country's political agenda. Active involvement in an environmental group might seem to offer a more effective way of working for change. However, young Canadians are no more likely (9 percent) than Canadians in general to have been active in an environmental group. This calls into question the optimistic assumption that declining participation in traditional electoral politics is being offset by greater involvement in grassroots-level activities.

Involvement in protest activities tells a similar story. The activists are actually most likely to be found among the middle-aged, a pattern that holds across national boundaries.[5] The young are the least likely among Canadians to have been active; more than one in five have engaged in no form of protest whatsoever—even signing a petition or joining in a boycott. To be sure, there is a core of young people who are seeking to effect change by engaging in protest activities. Indeed, this generation ranks second only to their baby-boomer parents when it comes to involvement in three or more different protest activities. But far from turning their backs on more conventional means of making their voices heard, these young activists are *more* likely than other members of their generation to belong to a political party or to an interest group, and to vote.

It is not really surprising that many of the same young people who fail to vote also fail to get involved in grassroots organizing or protest activities. Involvement presumes a

---

[4]   For details, see the Canadian Opinion Research Archive at Queen's University under CROP Political Survey (March 2001), CROP, Inc., Montréal, Quebec (CRIC0103). Neither the original collector of the data, CORA, nor the relevant funding agency bear any responsibility for the use of the data made here. The results of the survey are analyzed in "Trade, Globalization and Canadian Values," *The CRIC Papers* Vol. 1 (April 2001), available at http://www.cric.ca/pdf/cahiers/cricpapers_april2001.pdf.

[5]   Pippa Norris, *The Democratic Phoenix: Reinventing Political Activism* (New York: Cambridge University Press, 2002).

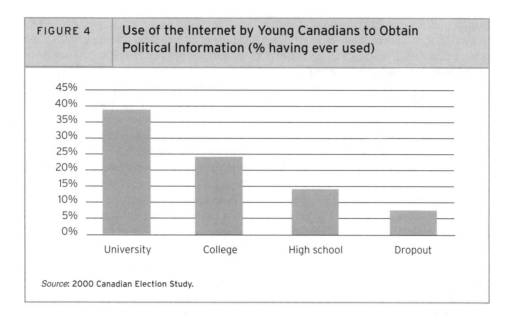

FIGURE 4 | Use of the Internet by Young Canadians to Obtain Political Information (% having ever used)

Source: 2000 Canadian Election Study.

degree of awareness of what is going on in the world. If people do not pay a modicum of attention to the news, issues such as globalization or the environment may simply be "off the radar screen".

THE ON-LINE MYTH

This brings us to the final misconception, namely that the Internet is helping to counteract young Canadians' tendency to tune out of politics. It is certainly true that young Canadians are the most likely to go on-line in search of information about politics. However, the numbers are not very impressive. At the time of the 2000 federal election, less than a quarter of young Canadians reported that they had *ever* used the Internet to track down political information. Moreover, there was a clear education gradient: the more education they had, the more likely they were to have used the Internet for this purpose (see Figure 4). Almost two in five university graduates had gone on-line to find some information or other about politics, compared with fewer than one in ten of young Canadians without a high school diploma. More to the point, those young people who had used the Internet to obtain political information were also the most likely to be following politics in the traditional media. These Internet users scored fully two points higher on average than the non-users (on a scale from zero to ten) when it came to the amount of attention they paid to television news and/or news in the newspaper.

HOW CAN YOUNG CANADIANS BE ENCOURAGED TO VOTE?

The key to encouraging young Canadians to participate in politics is to get them to "tune in". Political engagement presupposes political interest. If young Canadians are not interested in politics, they are not going to spend much time or energy keeping up with public affairs, and still less participating actively in the country's democratic life. We need to recognize, though, that interest runs both ways. One very tangible form of interest is to have a campaign worker or even a candidate turn up at the door: people who reported being contacted by *any* of the parties during the 2000 campaign were more likely to vote. This was true of young Canadians, too, but they were the least likely to report being contacted. This suggests that a concerted get-out-the-vote effort on the part of political parties could help to stem the downward trend in voting among the young. A recent study in the U.S.A. points to the importance of getting young citizens to vote for the first time: once they have paid the "start-up costs of voting", young voters tend to keep on voting.[6]

For the longer term, the single most important step would be to find ways to keep more young people in school. The more education young people have, the more interested they are in politics and the more likely they are to vote, to join groups working for change and to be active in their communities. Canada's dropout rates may not be out of line with other OECD countries, but Canadian dropouts tend to have very low levels of literacy compared to these countries because they typically quit high school at an earlier age.[7]

Education not only equips citizens with the cognitive skills that active engagement requires, it also seems to instill norms of civic obligation. Sense of duty is one of the most powerful incentives for turning out to vote.[8] However, this sense seems to be diminishing: fewer than one young Canadian in five expressed a strong sense of duty to vote in 2000, compared with one in three of those born before 1945.

Just what has impaired the development of a sense of duty to vote on the part of this generation of young Canadians is unclear, but it may well have something to do with the fact that they were reaching adulthood at a time when disaffection with politics was growing. This disaffection had a number of sources: the rise of a neo-conservative outlook that advocated a smaller role for the state, a perception that governments were relatively powerless in the face of global economic forces, and a series of constitutional crises and failed accords. All of these factors could have combined to produce a disengaged generation that often tunes out politics altogether. But these circumstances are changing. Political disaffection peaked in the mid-1990s and seems to be waning. Meanwhile, security concerns at home and abroad have highlighted the role of the state. One result may be a renewed sense that politics does indeed matter.

---

[6]   Eric Plutzer, "Becoming a Habitual Voter: Inertia, Resources, and Growth in Young Adulthood," *American Political Science Review* Vol. 96 (2002), pp. 41–56.

[7]   Canada, Human Resources Development Canada, Applied Research Branch, *Dropping Out of High School: Definitions and Costs* R-01-1E (Ottawa: Human Resources Development Canada, 2000).

[8]   André Blais, *To Vote or Not to Vote: The Merits and Limits of Rational Choice Theory* (Pittsburgh: University of Pittsburgh Press, 2000).

A Preliminary Statement to the People of British Columbia

ISSUED BY THE CITIZENS' ASSEMBLY ON ELECTORAL REFORM AT
MORRIS J. WOSK CENTRE FOR DIALOGUE, MARCH 21, 2004.

The Citizens' Assembly on Electoral Reform has completed the first phase of its work and eagerly looks forward to hearing the views of all British Columbians. We have organized public hearings to be held in communities all over the province during May and June. In this report, we indicate what we have accomplished to date and provide a preliminary assessment of the strengths and weaknesses of our current electoral system. We invite comments on this as well as on the features of electoral systems which we feel merit further discussion and debate.

At this stage, the Assembly has not come to any conclusion about whether the present system needs to be reformed. In fact, we have deliberately refrained from doing so. We are still busy learning about democratic electoral systems and want to hear from our fellow citizens about what they think. This is a time for discussion and debate and we invite all British Columbians to join us in this process.

THE BC CITIZENS' ASSEMBLY ON ELECTORAL REFORM

The British Columbia Citizens' Assembly on Electoral Reform was established by the government and Legislature in the spring of 2003 with a clear mandate. It is to *"assess models for electing Members of the Legislative Assembly"* and specifically the *"manner by which voters' ballots are translated into seats in the Legislative Assembly"*. If the Assembly concludes that an alternative model to the one now used ought to be adopted, then its recommendation is to be put to a referendum of the province's voters on May 17, 2005, the time of the next scheduled provincial election. In making any recommendation, the Assembly is to ensure that any change would *"be consistent with both the Constitution of Canada and the Westminster parliamentary system"*.

The Citizens' Assembly was established by an order-in-council which provided that its membership was open to all British Columbians on the provincial voters list with the exception of working politicians. Jack Blaney was designated, by a unanimous vote of the Legislative Assembly, to chair the Assembly and direct the work of its staff. A two-stage random selection process—carefully balanced by gender and age and structured to include individuals from all electoral districts in the province—led to a further 160 citizens being randomly chosen from the provincial voters list to constitute the Assembly's membership.

The Assembly constitutes a representative group of non-elected British Columbia citizens. Its members range in age from 19 to 78. They come from a diverse set of backgrounds, ethnic communities and occupations, but all are concerned with the health of the province's democracy and its common political life. The members have committed to working together over most of 2004 in a serious and sustained effort to evaluate the electoral system and determine if there is another system that might serve the province better.

The Assembly's work is divided into three phases:

1   The first, now completed, involved detailed study of the range of electoral systems used in modern democracies. Given that no two countries use exactly the same system, this proved to be a major undertaking, but it has given the Assembly an appreciation of the fact that there is no such thing as a perfect system. All electoral systems involve trade-offs among desirable elements, and any system must reflect the values and aspirations of the community that will use it. In a subsequent section of this statement, we report on our understanding of the strengths and weaknesses of the system now used in British Columbia.

2   The second phase of the Assembly's work will involve listening carefully to the views of all British Columbians. What kind of politics would they like to see? What sorts of electoral systems do they believe are appropriate or desirable? Assembly members will participate in public hearings around the province and study formal submissions made to them (available on our website: www.citizensassembly.bc.ca).

3   In the third phase, scheduled for the fall of 2004, the Assembly will meet to hear formal presentations on the merits of alternative systems and then to discuss and debate the issues around its mandate so members can then draft a set of final recommendations for their fellow British Columbians. The mandate requires that the Assembly either endorse the current system or propose a specific alternative.

This statement signals the end of the first phase and invites British Columbians to consider and respond to the preliminary assessment that Assembly members have made of the electoral system now in use and their suggestions for further consideration.

THE ASSEMBLY'S WORK TO DATE

The learning phase of the Assembly stretched over six busy weekends from January through March. Assembly members came together and worked hard to learn about the way our political system works, and then to study five different families of electoral systems. With presentations from staff members and visiting experts from across Canada and around the world, the Assembly learned how variations in constituency size, ballot paper formats and counting formula combine to produce a wide variety of different systems.

The families studied include:

• Majority systems (as in France or Australia)
• Plurality systems (as in Canada or India)
• Proportional representation by list systems (as in Finland or the Netherlands)
• Proportional representation by transferable vote systems (as in Ireland or Australia)
• Mixed systems (as in Germany or Japan)

The Assembly has taken the measure of these different kinds of systems and discovered that each has its advantages and disadvantages. (For details, please consult our website or contact the Assembly or its members for 'fact sheets' outlining these systems.) In accordance with its mandate, the Assembly has paid particular attention to the effects of these different electoral models *"on the government, the Legislative Assembly and the political parties"*. This intensive study has involved the mastery of complex concepts and the appreciation of relevant comparative experience through absorbing formal presentations, engaging in small group discussions, and undertaking considerable private study of advanced political science literature. All Assembly members have been active participants—attendance at Assembly meetings has been virtually 100%—and all members have participated fully and equally in the discussions that have led to this preliminary statement.

Assessing the comparative merits of differing systems is neither easy nor straightforward but Assembly members identified several criteria to use as benchmarks:

- The extent to which electoral outcomes reflected votes cast (the issue of vote–seat relationships)
- The nature of the linkage between voters and their representatives (the character of local representation)
- The range and nature of choice offered to voters (issues ranging from the number and nature of competing parties to the form of the ballots)
- The impact of the system on governance (the issues of effective government and the working of the legislature)

The Assembly quickly realized that there is no perfect system. The problem for it has been one of weighing the relative merits of the different systems and the trade-offs in desirable features that they require. At this stage in the work of the Assembly, members have reached a general consensus on the basic strengths and weaknesses of the present electoral system and believe that, before any decisions are taken, further reflection and debate is needed.

THE CITIZENS' ASSEMBLY ASSESSMENT OF THE CURRENT BC ELECTORAL SYSTEM

Assembly members are cognizant that our current single-member plurality electoral system—sometimes known as First-Past-the-Post—has much to recommend it. The system has been in widespread use in British Columbia and most other parts of Canada for most of our history and has served us well. We have a flourishing democracy in which voters hold politicians and governments accountable and we would not want to abandon such a system unless it was clear that: 1) the system had deficiencies that detracted from the evolution and maintenance of healthy democratic politics in the province, and 2) we were convinced that there was an alternative system that could be adopted that would speak to the identified deficiencies.

In an attempt to advance discussion about our electoral system, the Assembly has identified the following basic advantages and disadvantages of the system as it operates in British Columbia. This points to features that Assembly members believe need to be central to an assessment of the system.

Strengths of the Current System

Local Representation and Accountability The current system provides for individuals to be elected representing specific and identifiable areas of the province. This fosters a direct link between voters and their representatives and ensures that all areas of the province have a spokesperson in the legislature. This system allows politicians to speak authoritatively for their area, enables issues of local concern to be placed on the public agenda, and provides a mechanism for voters to hold representatives directly accountable for their actions. All Members of the Legislative Assembly (MLAs) have equal standing in the legislature and share common obligations and relationships to the electorate.

Style of Government and Representation The current system promotes the creation of majority governments that can claim an electoral mandate. These governments have a security of tenure that allows them to plan confidently for the life of the Legislative Assembly and to implement their program as they see fit. By stimulating winner-takes-all competition, the electoral system fosters two-party competition and works to limit the place and influence of minor parties and marginal interests. Elections generally revolve on the issue of the choice of governments.

Simplicity, Familiarity and Transparent Counting The single-member plurality system is familiar and straightforward. Voters are simply required to indicate their preferred candidate from the list of names presented. Winners are determined by a simple count of the ballots and are known almost immediately.

Weaknesses of the Current System

Lack of Proportionality Our single-member plurality system is one in which there is no direct connection between the number of votes a party receives and the number of seats it wins in the Legislative Assembly. The system favours large parties over small ones, creating governments with 'artificial' majorities and depriving minority views from finding expression in the legislature. This tends to limit effective voter choice, leads to many votes not contributing to electing any MLA, and sometimes leads to parties with the most votes not winning an election.

Government-Dominated Parliaments The system fosters an adversarial style of two-party politics in which government domination of the legislature becomes standard practice. With strong party discipline this ensures centralized decision-making with no effective opportunity for the legislature to hold the government accountable between elections. The system cannot ensure a strong opposition and, with MLAs required to put party interests above those of their constituencies, local and minority interests are often excluded.

Impacts on Governance and Voters Adversarial politics often result in sharp swings in public policy as newly elected governments often undo or reverse the programs of their predecessors. This style of politics contributes to a growing alienation of voters from the political process, which has been reflected in falling voter turnout rates, especially among young voters.

APPROACHES TO ALTERNATIVE ELECTORAL SYSTEMS

The Assembly has considered a wide range of alternative electoral systems and studied their impact in other democracies. It has given particular attention to the values that underlie the basic features of these other systems and their potential consequences for the style and character of British Columbia's democracy. While it is difficult to predict in detail how any other specific system would work in British Columbia, the Assembly is convinced that any alternative system it considers must reflect the values it believes are central to the political health of the province's democracy. At this point it draws attention to important defining features of electoral systems:

Local Representation

Our tradition has long valued a system of representation that provides for local representation—for its politicians to speak for and answer to the distinctive communities that make up the whole province. Citizens believe it is important that the interests of their particular communities be represented in public debate and policy-making. This is accomplished when MLAs have an intimate knowledge of the communities they represent and the concerns of the people in them.

With elected politicians rooted in specific geographic areas, it is possible for voters to hold them directly accountable for their performance in defending the values and interests of their local constituents.

Having a local representative gives individual citizens a direct personal channel into the government, a local contact they can use to obtain help or advance their concerns. The Assembly is aware that British Columbians in rural areas, and in locations far removed from the heavily populated Lower Mainland region, feel especially strongly that they must struggle to have their concerns heard. It is sensitive to the reality that for them, a vigorous system of local representation remains a highly valued dimension of their political life. It anticipates that any reformed electoral system would need to maintain an element of effective local representation.

Creating an electoral system that ensures effective local representation is an important challenge. The practice of party discipline obliges MLAs to vote as their party decides, not always as their voters prefer. The Assembly is interested in considering electoral systems whose features help ensure that elected representatives are more responsive to the concerns and views of their constituents.

Proportionality

The Assembly believes it is important that the outcome of an election, in terms of the distribution of seats in the legislature, should reflect the expressed intentions of citizens as expressed in their votes. This is the principle of proportionality—seats won should be proportional to votes won.

Beyond an acceptance of this basic principle, the Assembly has learned that there are a number of important reasons why British Columbians might want to consider moving to an electoral system based on proportional representation. Such systems typically ensure that more parties are able to compete successfully and so provide voters with more choice. A direct consequence is that more interests and groups are able to have their voices heard in a legislature that is more reflective of the social composition of the electorate. Given the province's increasing diversity, this offers the possibility of more genuinely representative politics at a time when voter turnout is falling and apathy is rising among young British Columbians.

The Assembly is aware that proportional electoral systems are likely to end the dominance of one-party majority governments and lead to a more consensual, or at least coalitional, style of politics in which opposition and small-party MLAs have the opportunity to play a greater role in the government of the province. It believes that a move away from the highly charged adversarial politics that have characterized the province in recent decades might foster politics more in keeping with the values of contemporary British Columbians.

Most modern democracies incorporate some proportional element in their electoral systems. The Assembly is aware that, by increasing the number of political parties, such systems can alter the balance of forces in the legislature. To avoid excessive political fragmentation some consideration might have to be given to establishing a modest threshold that parties would be expected to meet before being guaranteed representation.

There are a number of possible proportional systems—some that exist in pure party-list form, others which combine with features of constituency-based systems in different ways. In terms of its basic value position, the Assembly believes that many of these offer rich possibilities for British Columbia and deserve careful consideration. On the other hand, systems that are not responsive to the goal of increasing the proportionality of the system would seem to offer little in the way of advantage over the single-member plurality system we now use. In the same way, the choices offered voters are an important and integral part of any electoral system and the Assembly would not want to see it constrained.

WHAT KIND OF VOTING SYSTEM DO *YOU* WANT IN BRITISH COLUMBIA?

The Assembly wants to hear from British Columbians. It wants to hear if they share its conviction that local representation needs to be an important element in the province's electoral system. It wants to hear if they agree with it that a more proportional system would better reflect the basic values of our province's population. It wants to hear what kind of choices they would like to see at the polls. And it is anxious to hear what kind of electoral system our fellow citizens believe can best express our common values.

We welcome feedback on these and any other aspect of the electoral system that British Columbians feel would contribute to our province's democratic process. We look forward to hearing a full expression of public views at our public hearings to be held across the province during May and June, and encourage formal submissions through our website or to the Assembly office.

SECTION 5 TERMINOLOGY

Autocratic

Checks and Balances

Charlottetown Accord
(1992)

Citizen

Civic Literacy

Civil Society

Civil Society Organizations
(CSOs)

Concurrent Majority
(Double majority)

Constituency

Democracy

Elections

Electoralism

Enumeration

Factions

Federalism

Interest Group

Invisible Hand

Keynesianism

Majority Rule

Majority Systems

Mandate

Melting Pot

Mixed Systems

Multicultural Society

New Public Management

Order-in-council

Parliamentary Sovereignty

Party Discipline

Pluralism

Plurality System

Political Cynicism

Political Efficacy

Post-modern Values

Permanent Voters List

Presidentialism

Proportional
Representation (PR)

Proportionality

Public Realm

Qualified Majority

Quebec Referendum
(1995)

Referendum

Regime

Representatives

Rule of Law

Security of Tenure

Single-member Plurality
System (First Past the
Post)

Social Capital

Social Movement

Threshold

Trilateral Democracies

Turnout Rate

Western Civilization

SECTION 5 DISCUSSION QUESTIONS

1. The principles of proportionality and local representation were identified by the Citizens' Assembly as crucial to the selection of an electoral system for British Columbia. Which of these two do you see as most important, and why?

2. Does Schmitter and Karl's definition of democracy differ from what you have normally understood it to mean? If so, in what way? Why do you think it is so important to come up with a clear definition of concepts such as "democracy" in the study of politics?

3. How would you characterize the relationship that exists between the government and yourself? Do you think that government does more than "simply meet your demands"? Are you a customer or citizen?

4. Given the data assembled by the Centre for Research and Information on Canada, do you think that Canadian democracy is in crisis?

5. If you are eligible, do you vote? Why—or why not? If you are not eligible, would you vote if you could? Why—or why not? Does it matter whether people vote?

POLISCI SUPERSITE

Pearson Education Canada's PoliSci Supersite (**www.pearsoned.ca/polisci**) contains a set of text-specific pages for *Ideas, Interests, and Issues*. Visit the Supersite to access a list of relevant weblinks and interesting additional readings tailored to the content of each section.

Section 6

Going Global

SECTION SUMMARY

In this section of the reader, we introduce global politics, a field also referred to as International Relations (IR). IR is one of the most prominent sub-fields of Political Studies, and is similar to domestic politics in that there are a number of actors competing for limited resources. But unlike domestic politics, IR is about the distribution of resources at the global level. That means that the "actors" in IR include the nation state, non-governmental organizations (NGOs), international institutions, and corporations. In a domestic environment, the various participants provide checks on each other's powers. For instance, legislatures offset the powers of the courts or the executive. But in IR, there is no set order to the hierarchy of powers. This leads to the eventual question: who has ultimate authority?

Global politics differs drastically from domestic politics when we consider the matter of authority. All nations have levels of authority, and governments theoretically have the ultimate say concerning policies for their citizens. But IR has no "world government," meaning that states themselves are their own highest authority. This creates all manner of disagreements about who, or what, has the right to decide proper conduct on the world stage. Since we are more connected than we ever have been in the past, some have taken to referring to the global environment today as a "global village." This may be true in part, but it is perhaps also true that we are still as divided as we were in the past. Sometimes, learning more about each other shows us things we don't like about each other.

Many, but not all, of the readings in this section link up with those in the final section, which concerns issues in politics. That shows how international events have more and more consequences for domestic affairs. Global politics covers many different aspects of affairs at the international level. The mixed set of readings contained in this section of the book illustrates this.

Kim Nossal's critique of Canadian foreign relations, and Daniel Schwanen's assessment of Canada's free-trade relations, offer a perspective of Canada's place in the world. Nossal's line of reasoning, that Canada has lost much of its former influence in international affairs, is widely acknowledged by observers of Canada's foreign policy. Schwanen notes that Canada's past success in free trade could pose future problems, if not cautiously managed. Looking more widely, Ramesh Thakur considers how international security has changed since the end of the Cold War. Hardly less important than it was then, he suggests that security now is more complicated and multi-faceted than ever before, but he cautions that our old definitions may not be up to the task. Louise Arbour and Elizabeth May take on issues that at one time may not have received much attention at all. Humanitarian intervention and the international environment are more than "trends"; rather, their growing importance shows the implications of greater connection in the international system. If globalization is occurring (and most agree it is, even if they can't agree what it looks like), then the issues presented by Arbour and May will require more attention in the future. And Denis Stairs examines a subject that is not new, but has more meaning than ever: terrorism. Anyone with a passing interest in modern global politics is conscious of the threat that terrorism poses to nation states. Moving beyond the threat and reaction surrounding terrorism, Stairs asks deeper questions about understanding the phenomenon. He concludes that better knowledge about the causes of terrorism will not necessarily lead us to solving the problem.

Global politics is a many-sided field. The readings in this section may leave you with more questions that you had before you started, but perhaps with some different answers as well.

Canada: Fading Power or Future Power?

KIM RICHARD NOSSAL*

Kim Richard Nossal *is Professor and Head of Political Studies at Queen's University, Kingston.*

While by some measures Canada might be described as a principal power—its member-ship in the G-8 and the Quad, for example—by many other measures it is simply no longer as prominent in world politics as it used to be. Canadian spending on international affairs, on security and defence, on development assistance, has declined over the past decade. The government is no longer as active in international affairs as it used to be. Its capacity to be involved has shrunk. And when it seeks to be active, Canadian influence on key interna-tional events and issues appears limited.

Needless to say, debates about the kind of power Canada is in world politics are by no means new. How to measure Canadian power and influence in world politics has been the subject of a running academic—and political—debate for at least two generations. Nor is the idea that Canadian diplomacy is in decline new. In 1993, Arthur Andrew, a seasoned Canadian diplomat, argued in *The Rise and Fall of a Middle Power: Canadian Diplomacy from King to Mulroney* that the foreign policy of the Progressive Conservative government of Brian Mulroney finished the process of decline.

However, the 'fading power' theme became more pronounced after 11 September 2001, when the international system changed so dramatically. There was perhaps nothing more emblematic of the supposed growing 'invisibility' of the government of Jean Chrétien on the international stage than the treatment accorded Canada in the speech delivered by President George W. Bush to the United States after 11 September. Bush's speech was framed by the Manichean assertion that all countries had a stark choice: 'If you are not with us, you are with the terrorists.' The president made a point of mentioning a number of friends and allies by name, but did not mention Canada, despite the various Canadian con-tributions on 11 September, notably the emergency care of some 30,000 stranded air trav-ellers barred from US air space. The absence of any mention of Canada might not have been intentional, but it caused a great deal of angst in Canada because it was so highly symbol-ic and reflected the growing distance between Ottawa and Washington.

The fading power thesis was given a particular boost by the sub-title chosen for the 2002 volume of *Canada Among Nations*. The editors of the collection, Maureen Appel Molot and Norman Hillmer, used the 'fading power' motif to explore the degree to which Canadian foreign policy in 2002 was a mere shadow of the robust presence in global politics that Ottawa had enjoyed in the 1950s.[1]

---

[1] Maureen Appel Molot and Norman Hillmer, eds., *Canada Among Nations 2002: A Fading Power* (Toronto: Oxford University Press 2002).

The motif was picked up by numerous commentators in the months before the American-led attack on Iraq loomed and the distance between Canada and the US widened. For example, Richard Gwyn noted in the *Toronto Star* that Chrétien's major foreign policy address to the Chicago Council on Foreign Relations in February 2003 was not mentioned in any of the major papers in the United States and got only passing reference in the Chicago media.

Andrew Coyne of the *National Post* went further: in a column under the headline 'Canada on the sidelines,' Coyne asserted that the prime minister's Chicago speech demonstrated how irrelevant Canada had become. No one listens to us any more, he wrote, not least because nothing we say is worth listening to. 'If a Canadian speaks in Chicago and no one gives a damn,' Coyne concluded, 'does he make a sound?'

And indeed it would appear: the so-called Canadian proposal at the Security Council, which sought a middling way between the two polar positions on the Security Council, was dismissed by all sides. Christopher Sands, of the Center for Strategic and International Studies in Washington—one of the few American Canada-watchers—put it succinctly: Canada is simply not thought about in Washington. 'That is where Canada is. Not at the margins. Not whispering in the ear of the global power. But outside the game.' And in the spring of 2003, Andrew Cohen published *While Canada Slept: How We Lost Our Place in the World*, an argument that detailed the nature and extent of Canada's decline in world politics.

To what extent is Canada the fading power that the pundits suggest? Looking at the evolution of Canadian foreign policy in the spring of 2003, one might go further than the pundits and suggest that in the months before the attack on Iraq in March 2003, the Chrétien government transformed Canada from a fading power to an utterly irrelevant power in Washington. The deterioration was the result of a combination of both substantive policy decisions and symbolic rhetorical attacks on the United States.

For many months, the Chrétien government refused to rule anything in—or anything out—as a conscious policy. Canada might go to war if the United Nations Security Council gave its approval; but Canada might go to war if the UN didn't approve. Perhaps the best measure of the success of the government's efforts to make its policy as ambiguous as possible were the entirely contradictory headlines in the English-language press on 24 January 2003 reporting Chrétien's comments on Canada's approach to a possible war in Iraq: in the *Globe and Mail*, the headline was 'PM to Bush: Hold off on war—Canada will break with U.S. if it hits Hussein without mandate from UN.' By contrast, the *National Post* headline claimed that 'Chrétien opens door to possibility of Canada joining U.S.-led attack on Iraq.' (Given Ottawa's purposeful ambiguity, it is perhaps not surprising that the British ambassador to the United Nations would publicly admonish the Canadian government to make up its mind.) Eventually, of course, the Chrétien government did make up its mind: refusing to lend either concrete or even symbolic legitimacy to the attack on Iraq.

In the process, the government in Ottawa made a couple of decisions that ensured its marginality as war grew closer. First, it arranged things so that Canada could not contribute forces even if it had wanted to. In February the prime minister dispatched fully 3000 troops for stabilization force work in Kabul, Afghanistan. Since the Canadian Forces found it impossible to sustain 750 troops in Kandahar for more than six months, the 3000 troops committed to Kabul are sure to stretch capabilities to the breaking point. But there was method in this: with such a large force in Kabul, there simply were no Canadian troops left for any coalition of the willing, even if the Chrétien government had been willing.

Second, even though it was not ruling anything in or anything out, the longer it played its hide-and-seek game, the more it distanced itself from Washington and London. With each passing week, the Canadian government sharpened its opposition to the unilateral option the closer the war got. Eventually the prime minister openly criticized the regime change agenda of the Bush administration, noting that if we embraced regime change for the regime in Iraq, who might be next? By that time, while it was still possible for Canada to join the coalition at the last minute, Chrétien no longer had any entrée in Washington.

Third, Ottawa also made little effort to engage in traditional Canadian diplomatic behaviour—by working alongside the United States but behind the scenes trying to use quiet persuasion to constrain American behaviour. It is useful to contrast the Chrétien government's diplomacy on Iraq with the diplomacy of the government of Louis St. Laurent over the Korean conflict. In Korea, the Canadian government worked hard to constrain the impulses of the Democratic administration of Harry S Truman and its expanding war aims. There was a real concern in Ottawa about the implications of widening the war to include the on-going civil war between the Chinese Nationalists on Taiwan and the newly established communist Peoples Republic of China. And Canadians tried on a number of occasions to change the course of American policy. For Lester Pearson, the foreign minister, the key assumption was 'that the possibilities for containing the behaviour of great power decision-makers are increased if they can be induced to operate within a multilateral arena. In such a context they are subject to the demands and pressures of smaller states, whose representatives can sometimes be mobilized in concert. At the same time, however, it is vital to recall that the essence of great power status . . . is the capacity in the final analysis to treat lesser powers as incidental. This being the case, the leverage of small power statesmen is always limited by the degree to which their views are regarded as important . . . Hence, in the Korean case, Washington could be constrained, but only to a point.'[2]

Pearson's assumptions remain as relevant today as they were in Korea in the early 1950s. However, there was an essential necessary condition: for the Canadian government to be able to exercise influence in Washington on matters of global policy, the government in Washington had to be willing to listen to what Canadians had to say on such matters.

But over the last six months prior to the start of the war against Iraq, the Chrétien government made itself progressively more irrelevant in Washington. Thus when Ottawa did float an eleventh-hour compromise proposal, it came far too late—by then the Canadian government was completely irrelevant in the eyes of the major players, including the United States. By that time, no one cared. And indeed, when the Canadian government finally abandoned its ambiguity and announced that it was not participating, no one was really surprised.

It can be argued that the concrete decision not to join the 'coalition of the willing' was made worse by the parade of insulting, rude, insensitive, short-sighted behaviour on the part of the Chrétien government. The list is long: Chrétien wondering on the first anniversary of 11 September whether the inattentiveness of Americans to global poverty might have brought the terrorist attacks on themselves: Chrétien's communication director, Françoise Ducros, calling the president a moron, not being disciplined by Chrétien, and

---

[2] Denis Stairs, *The Diplomacy of Constraint: Canada, the Korean War, and the United States* (Toronto: University of Toronto Press 1974), 311.

only falling on her sword when American commentators refused to let the comment go; Liberal members of parliament such as Carolyn Parrish claiming that she 'hated' Americans, terming them 'bastards,' or Karen Kraft Sloan sniggering at Bush's religious beliefs; cabinet ministers such as Herb Dhaliwal slagging Bush for his lack of statesmanship, or Bill Graham, the minister of foreign affairs, not bothering to call the US ambassador prior to the prime minister's announcement to inform him of Canada's decision, and then saying that Paul Cellucci was quite capable of watching Canadian TV; or the video clip of the entire Liberal caucus jumping up in joyful applause when Chrétien finally announced to the House of Commons that Canada was not going to support the US.

What are the likely consequences of Canada's stand on Iraq? First, it is likely that until there is 'regime change' in either Ottawa or Washington, the Canadian government will cease to have any meaningful voice in Washington on matters of global policy. This means that at the very time that the United States government is embarking on what is a radically different kind of foreign policy, Canadians will have no means of even trying to influence the direction and nature of that revised course. Canadians will be reduced to kvetching from the sidelines, and we can be fairly sure that whatever advice comes from Ottawa will be ignored with great pleasure by anyone who matters in Washington.

Second, the decision on Iraq is likely to have an adverse effect on the well-being of Canadians. This is not the tired old argument that Canadians will face overt retaliation from the US government for having diverged from American policy on this issue. That is not how politics in North America works. Rather, it is the argument, most commonly associated with John W. Holmes, that Canadians have an enduring interest in maintaining a certain kind of relationship with the United States. Holmes used to make this point on many occasions. For example, in *Life With Uncle*, a book written in 1981 when the administration of Ronald Reagan had just arrived in Washington, and Canadian-American relations were heading into one of their cyclical downturns, he put it this way: 'It is of very great importance to Canada to maintain amicable relations with whatever administration the Americans elect. That does not mean supine agreement, but it suggests caution in picking a quarrel. The danger [of not picking one's quarrels carefully] is that we forfeit not only our vested interests but also the disposition in Washington to listen to our arguments on world affairs.'[3]

Twelve years later, in an era when even more of Canada's wealth depends on cross-border trade, Denis Stairs would restate the Holmesian prescription when he wrote that there is 'only one imperative in Canadian foreign policy. That imperative is the maintenance of a politically amicable, and hence economically effective working relationship with the United States.'[4]

In other words, it is not that the United States government—or ordinary Americans—will lash out at Canada in retaliation. Rather, the consequences of cocking a snook at the US on such an important issue as the war against Iraq will be far more subtle, and thus far more damaging to Canadian interests. The real danger is to the smooth management of the

---

[3] John W. Holmes *Life with Uncle: Canadian–American Relationship* (Toronto: University of Toronto Press 1981), 91.

[4] Denis Stairs, 'Canada in the New International Environment,' Inaugural Meeting, Canadian Consortium on Asia Pacific Security, York University, Toronto 3–4 December 1993.

vast complexity that is the Canadian–American relationship. To be sure, this will probably only be manifest in a number of small ways, but the very size of the Canadian–American relationship tends to take small things and magnify them. For example, if a mere fifteen seconds of processing time were added for every border visitor, the impact would be profound if that were multiplied by 550,000—the number of people who cross the border each day. Likewise, if Canada is unable to secure extensive exceptions to the Draconian provision of the US Patriot Act of 2002, just-in-time production arrangements in North America will be seriously affected. In the long term, it is likely that investment decisions in the next five years will be affected by the degree to which the border starts to become a real impediment to the flow of goods and people, since rational investors are unlikely to invest in Canada when getting goods to market is impeded by a border that slows flows down to a crawl.

The argument here is not that the Canadian government should have joined the Bush coalition of the willing simply in an effort to keep the border open. Rather, the argument is that there are clever ways to deal with the US and not-so-clever ways. And while it may be very satisfying to stick one's finger in the American eye and give it a little wiggle, such satisfaction is not only juvenile but could be highly damaging to the interests of those who do not have fat parliamentary pensions to cushion them from the effects of recession or unemployment that may be one of the consequences of puerile approaches to global politics.

This leads to a second argument, which has a more positive aspect: we have been here before, and there is an interesting historical dynamic that appears to play out in Canadian politics. Canadians, it would appear from their voting behaviour, tend to understand, however inchoately, the wisdom of the argument advanced by policy-makers like Holmes and academics like Stairs. They appear to understand, again however inchoately, that Canada's aggregate wealth—and the wealth of those in the Quebec-Windsor corridor in particular—is heavily dependent on amicable political relations between Canada and the United States. Canadians get uncomfortable when the relationship sours. By the same token, however, Canadians appear not to like it when relations between Ottawa and Washington get too close or chummy.

When the relationship between the two governments veers into the outer zones of overly friendly or overly antagonistic, an interesting phenomenon appears to occur in Canadian politics: a strong counter-reaction emerges that provides fertile soil for a political force to bubble up to argue the importance of changing the relationship.

In the 1950s, for example, when the Liberals under Prime Minister Louis St Laurent were seen to be climbing far too deeply into bed with the United States, the Progressive Conservatives under the leadership of John Diefenbaker were encouraged to make the Canadian–American relationship an election issue and to formulate an alternative vision. But when Diefenbaker's relationship with the US deteriorated, the Liberals under Lester Pearson were able to make the improvement of the relationship an important element of their 1963 election campaign.

Likewise, in the early 1980s, when relations between the government of Pierre Elliott Trudeau and the Reagan administration deteriorated, Brian Mulroney was able to make refurbishing the relationship with the US a priority. Mulroney enjoyed an exceptional relationship with both Reagan and his successor, George H. Bush. And it was the very exceptional nature of that relationship that provided considerable fodder for Jean Chrétien to attack Mulroney's record on Canada–US relations during the 1993 election campaign.

We can see this dynamic unfold at present. No sooner had the Canadian–American relationship sunk to the low point in March 2003 than the pendulum began to swing yet again. The forces of reaction gathered steam with considerable alacrity, forcing the prime minister to muzzle the more anti-American voices in his government and prompting Paul Martin, the leading contender for the Liberal leadership, to speak out about the need to repair the relationship.

However, while the new Liberal leader may be able to repair the relationship sufficiently to forestall some of the more damaging economic effects, it is likely to be more difficult to recover Canada from its faded diplomatic status and to ensure that Canadian views are considered by the American administration. The United States has embarked on a new course in global politics; Canadians have a deep interest in being able to influence that course as much as possible. Unfortunately, to recover our voice in Washington will likely require more political capital than any contender for the Liberal leadership possesses.

Security in the New Millennium

RAMESH THAKUR*

Ramesh Thakur is Senior Vice-Rector, Peace and Governance Programme, United Nations University, Tokyo, Japan.

The business of the world has changed almost beyond recognition over the course of the last 100 years. There are many more actors today, and their patterns of interaction are far more complex. The locus of power and influence is shifting. The demands and expectations made on governments and international organizations by the people of the world can no longer be satisfied through isolated and self-contained efforts. The international policy-making stage is increasingly congested as private and public non-state actors jostle alongside national governments in setting and implementing the agenda of the new century. The multitude of new actors adds depth and texture to the increasingly rich tapestry of international civil society.

In today's seamless world, political frontiers have become less salient both for national governments whose responsibilities within borders can be held up to international scrutiny, and for international organizations whose rights and duties can extend beyond borders. The gradual erosion of the once sacrosanct principle of national sovereignty is rooted today in the reality of global interdependence: no country is an island unto itself any more. Ours is a world of major cities and agglomerations, with nodes of financial and economic power and their globally wired transport and communications networks. Cumulatively, they span an increasingly interconnected and interactive world characterized more by technology-driven exchange and communication than by territorial borders and political separation.

The meaning and scope of security have become much broader. The number and types of security providers have grown enormously, and the relationship between them has become more dense and complex. As welt as armed terrorism, for example, states have to contend with eco-terrorism and cyber-terrorism, e.g., the "I love you" bug. All three are cross-border phenomena of global scope and ramifications requiring active collaboration among the defence and constabulary forces, law enforcement authorities and non-government groups and organizations.

In this period of transition, the UN is the focus of the hopes and aspirations for a future where men and women live at peace with themselves and in harmony with nature. Over a billion people living in abject poverty have had neither the spirit nor the means to cheer the arrival of the new millennium. The reality of human insecurity cannot simply be wished away. Yet the idea of a universal organization dedicated to protecting peace and promoting welfare—of achieving a better life in a safer world for all—survived the death, destruction, and disillusionment of armed conflicts, genocide, persistent poverty, environmental degradation, and the many assaults on human dignity of the Twentieth Century.

The UN has the responsibility to protect international peace and promote human development. The UN Charter codifies best practice in state behaviour. Universities are the market place of ideas. Scientists have a duty to make their knowledge available for the betterment of humanity. The United Nations University has the mandate to link the two normally isolated worlds of scholarship and policy-making. It lies at the interface of ideas, international organizations, and international public policy. In an information society and world, the comparative advantage of the UNU lies in its identity as the custodian and manager of knowledge-based networks and coalitions that give it a global mandate and reach.

One recurring refrain in our projects in recent times has been the tension between the twin processes of globalization and localization; a second is the need for partnerships between different actors, including individuals, at all levels of social organization; and a third is the comprehensive and interconnected nature of many of today's major problems that require urgent policy measures. Solutions must be individual-centred, within a framework of human security that puts people first; they must be integrated and coordinated; and they must be holistic, tackling the roots of the problems even while ameliorating the symptoms of stress and distress.

Globalization refers both to process and outcome. National frontiers are becoming less relevant in determining the flow of ideas, information, goods, services, capital, labour, and technology. The speed of modern communications makes borders increasingly permeable, while the volume of cross-border flows threatens to overwhelm the capacity of states to manage them. Globalization releases many productive forces that, if properly harnessed, can help to uplift millions from poverty, deprivation, and degradation. But it can also unleash destructive forces—uncivil society—such as flows of arms, terrorism, disease, prostitution, drug and people smuggling, etc., that are neither controllable nor solvable by individual governments. At the same time, and indeed partly in reaction to globalization, communities are beginning to re-identify with local levels of group identity.

Recommended solutions to the dilemma include decentralization and subsidiarity, on the principle that the locus of action and solution should be where the problems are. There must be active participation of the local government, non-government organizations, and private actors in all phases of planning and implementation. Thus, international democracy promotion should be directed at building local capacity—supporting, financially and technically, the various pillars of democratization processes, the rule of law and the judicial system, and the legislatures, in addition to assisting the conducting of elections.

The combined effect of globalization—both the process and the outcome—and localization is to erode the legitimacy and effectiveness of national governments and intergovernmental organizations. There has been a corresponding decline in levels of resources and support for international organizations, including the UN. In the meantime, a host of new actors from civil society—NGOs, labour unions, churches—have become progressively more assertive in demanding a voice at all top decision-making tables. Sometimes developing countries attach their concerns to NGOs, while at other times NGOs attack the state of affairs in developing countries (slave labour, child labour, environmental laxness).

The solution to many of these challenges lies in global governance. The goal of global governance is not the creation of world government, but of an additional layer of international decision-making between governments and international organizations which is comprehensive—not merely piecemeal social engineering—multisectoral, democratically accountable, and inclusive of civil society actors in the shared management of the troubled and fragile world order.

Partnerships are called for between governments, international organizations, NGOs, other civil society organizations, and individuals. Some countries are beginning to involve citizens more substantially in the political decision-making process through well-designed public choice mechanisms like referenda. We are likely to witness increasing issue-specific networks and coalitions. The UN has the moral legitimacy, political credibility, and administrative impartiality to mediate, moderate, and reconcile the competing pulls and tensions associated with both the process and outcomes of globalization. Human security can provide the conceptual umbrella that brings together the main themes of the Millennium Summit—security, development, environment, and governance—within one coherent framework. This would help to give practical content to the opening words of the UN Charter, We the peoples. . . .

TRADITIONAL SECURITY PARADIGM: TOWARDS A WORLD FREE OF WARS

War lies at the heart of traditional security paradigms, and military force is the sharp edge of the realist school of international relations. The incidence of war is as pervasive as the wish for peace is universal. At any given time, most countries are at peace and long to keep it so. Yet most are also ready to go to war if necessary. Some of the most charismatic and influential personalities in human history—from Gautama Buddha and Jesus Christ to Mahatma Gandhi—have dwelt on the renunciation of force and the possibility of eliminating it from human relationships.

The Twentieth Century captured the paradox only too well. On the one hand, we tried to emplace increasing normative, legislative, and operational fetters on the right of states to go to war. Yet the century turned out to be the most murderous in human history, with over 250 wars, including two world wars and the Cold War, twice as many dead than in all previous wars of the past 2,000 years. Another six million more have died since the Cold War ended.

Confronted with a world that cannot be changed, reasonable people adapt and accommodate. The turning points of history and progress in human civilization have come from those who set out to change the world. This section is a story about a group of unreasonable people who met recently for the first steering committee of "GlobalAction to Prevent War: An International Coalition to Abolish Armed Conflict and Genocide".

The causes of war are many and complex. Our call to end it is single-minded and simple. Cynics insist that war is an inherent part of human society. To end war would indeed be to end history. Maybe. But, so too have crime and poverty always been part of human history. Any political leader who admitted to giving up on the fight to end crime or poverty would quickly be returned to private life by voters. Paradoxically, in the case of war it is those who seek to abolish it who are considered to be soft in the head.

The deadly situation does not have to continue into the new century. We already have resources and knowledge that can drastically cut the level of armed violence in the world and make war increasingly rare. What has been missing is a programme for the worldwide, systematic, and continuing application of these resources and knowledge. GlobalAction offers such a programme, and it is building a worldwide coalition of interested individuals, civil society organizations, and governments to carry it out (www.glocalactionpw.org).

For internal conflicts, GlobalAction proposes a broad array of conflict prevention measures to be applied by the UN, regional security organizations, and international courts. For conflicts between neighbouring states, it recommends force reductions, defensively oriented changes in force structure, confidence-building measures, and constraints on force activities tailored to each situation. The possibility of conflict among the major powers can be reduced by fostering their cooperation in preventing smaller wars and through step-by-step cuts in their conventional and nuclear forces, eliminating their capacity to attack each other with any chance of success.

GlobalAction's conflict prevention and conventional disarmament measures will promote nuclear disarmament. Nuclear cuts, in turn, will facilitate conflict prevention and conventional disarmament. Achievement of nuclear disarmament will very probably require both reduced levels of conflict worldwide and some effective and acceptable way to cut back the conventional forces of the major powers, especially their force projection capability with naval and air forces. Countries like China, Russia, and India are not likely to relinquish their nuclear weapons if the main effect of doing so is to enhance the already large conventional superiority of the U.S. Other governments are unlikely to be prepared to reduce their conventional armed forces drastically unless there is evidence that nuclear weapons are on the one-way road to elimination.

GlobalAction's deliberate focus is on violent armed conflict. The world also faces fundamental crises of poverty, human rights violations, environmental degradation, and discrimination based on race, gender, ethnicity, and religion. All of these challenges must be met before human security and a just peace can be fully achieved. To meet these challenges, many efforts must be pursued; no single campaign can deal with all of them. But efforts to address these global problems can and should complement and support one another. The abolition of war will make it possible to focus all remaining energy and efforts on resolving the fundamental structural problems.

One analogy is with domestic violence. Faced with incidents of violence within the family, the first and most urgent order of business is to stop the violence. Only then can we look at probable causes and possible solutions, including if necessary separation and divorce.

FROM NATIONAL SECURITY TO HUMAN SECURITY

The shift from the national security to the human security paradigm is of historic importance. The object of security changes from the state to the individual; the focus changes from security through armaments to security through human development; from territorial security to food, employment, and environmental security. The fundamental components of human security—the security of people against threats to life, health, livelihood, personal safety, and human dignity—can be put at risk by external aggression, but also by factors within a country, including security forces. Over the course of the Twentieth Century, 30 million people were killed in international wars, seven million in civil wars, and an additional 170 million by their own governments. *(The Economist* 1999)

In his Millennium Report, (Annan 2000) Secretary-General Kofi Annan writes of the quest for freedom from fear, freedom from want, and securing a sustainable future. A recurring theme in his report is the importance of making the transition from the culture of reaction to the culture of prevention. This is even more fundamental for the attainment of human security than for national security, as even a cursory glance at threats to human security will show.

Mankind—including the rich countries—will not be able to live free of fear, will not be able to secure a sustainable future, so long as over a billion people live in servitude to want. That is, freedom from want is a precondition of the other two elements in the trinity. The safest and most peaceful communities are composed of individuals who have their basic needs and aspirations met.

The multidimensional approach to security sacrifices precision for inclusiveness. In order to rescue it from being diluted into nothingness, we need to focus on security policy in relation to crisis. Short of that it is more accurate to assess welfare gains and losses rather than increased security and insecurity. Security policy can then be posited as crisis prevention and crisis management, with regard to both institutional capacity and material capability.

Even if we limit security to anything which threatens the core integrity of our units of analysis (namely, human lives), many non-traditional concerns merit the gravity of the security label and require exceptional policy measures in response: environmental threats of total inundation or desertification; political threats of the complete collapse of state structures; population flows so large as to destroy the basic identity of host societies and cultures; structural coercion so severe as to turn human beings into de facto chattels; and suchlike. The annual mortality correlates of Afro-Asiatic poverty—low levels of life expectancy, high levels of maternal and infant mortality—run into several million. Annual deaths—preventable killings—even on this scale cannot be accommodated within the analytical framework of national security, but they can in human security.

The traditional, narrow concept of security leaves out the most elementary and legitimate concerns of ordinary people regarding security in their daily lives. It also diverts enormous amounts of national wealth and human resources into armaments and armed forces, while countries fail to protect their citizens from chronic insecurities of hunger, disease, inadequate shelter, crime, unemployment, social conflict, and environmental hazards: *Na roti, na kapara, na makan—par Bharat mera mahan.*[1]

When rape is used as an instrument of war and ethnic 'impurification', when thousands are killed by floods resulting from a ravaged countryside, and when citizens are killed by their own security forces, then the concept of national security is immaterial and of zero utility. By contrast, human security can embrace such diverse phenomena. To insist on national security at the expense of human security is to trivialize the concept of security in many real-world circumstances to the point of sterility, bereft of any practical meaning.[2]

A recent report on health as a global security challenge concluded that health and security converge at three intersections. (CSIS 2000) First, faced with domestic economic crises and shrinking foreign assistance, many developing countries have had to make difficult budgetary choices to reduce the level of public services. But the failure of governments to provide the

---

[1]   The first part is a popular saying in India; the second is a patriotic boast. The two have been combined for ironic effect: *Neither food, nor clothing, nor shelter—but my India is great.*

[2]   For an attempt to apply the human security concept to the Asia Pacific region, see Tow, Thakur, and Hyun 2000).

basic public health services, including garbage removal, water treatment, and sewage disposal, has two further consequences. It erodes governmental legitimacy, and encourages the spirit of self-help and 'beggar thy neighbour' among citizens at the expense of the public interest. Often the competition degenerates into violence. Thus, the withdrawal of the state from the public health domain can be both a symptom and a cause of failing states. Second, there has been an increasing trend in recent internal armed conflicts to manipulate the supplies of food and medicine. Indeed, the struggle to control food and medicine can define the war strategies of some of the conflict parties. And third, the use of biological weapons represents the deliberate spread of disease against an adversary.

The narrow definition of security also presents a falsified image of the policy process. The military is only one of several competing interest groups vying for a larger share of the collective goods being allocated authoritatively by the government. Environmental and social groups also compete for the allocation of scarce resources. There is, therefore, competition, tension, and conflict among major value clusters. The concept of military security as a subset of the national interest serves to disguise the reality of inter-value competition. By contrast, the multidimensional concept of security highlights the need for integrative strategies that resolve or transcend value conflicts. If they are rational, policy-makers will allocate resources to security only so long as the marginal return is greater for security than for other uses of the resources.

Once security is defined as human security, security policy embraces the totality of state responsibilities for the welfare of citizens from the cradle to the grave. The mark of a civilization is not the deference and respect paid to the glamorous and the powerful, but the care and attention devoted to the least privileged and the most vulnerable. Children, in particular, need and should have the most protection in any society. Regrettably, the many hazards to children's survival, healthy growth, and normal development, in rich as well as poor countries, constitute a pervasive threat to human security at present and in the foreseeable future.

UN calculations[3] show that in the last decade alone, two million children have been killed, one million orphaned, six million disabled or otherwise seriously injured, 12 million made homeless, and ten million left with serious psychological scars. Large numbers of them, especially young women, are the targets of rape and other forms of sexual violence as deliberate instruments of war. The steps taken in defence of the rights of children remain small, hesitant, and limited. The biggest danger is compassion fatigue: we will get so used to the statistics that they will cease to shock us, and we will learn to live with the unacceptable.

Being wedded still to national security may be one reason why half the world's governments spend more to protect their citizens against undefined external military attack than to guard them against the omnipresent enemies of good health. Human dignity is at stake here. How can one experience the joys and the meaning attached to human life, how can one experience a life of human dignity, when survival from day to day is under threat?

---

[3] For details, see Annan 2001. For the latest annual publication of the most authoritative compilation on the state of the world's children, see UN 2002.

FROM ARMS CONTROL TO INTERNATIONAL HUMANITARIAN LAW

Human security gives us a template for international action. Canada and Japan are two countries that have taken the lead in attempting to incorporate human security into their foreign policies. A practical expression of this was the Ottawa Treaty proscribing the production, stockpiling, use, and export of anti-personnel land mines. The first to impose a ban on an entire class of weapons already in widespread use, the convention was a triumph for an unusual coalition of governments, international organizations, and NGOs. Such 'new diplomacy'[4] has been impelled by a growing intensity of public impatience with the slow pace of traditional diplomacy. Many people have grown tired of years of negotiations leading to a final product that may be accepted or rejected by countries. They look instead for a sense of urgency and timely action that will prevent human insecurity, not just react to outbreaks of conflict.

It would be as big a mistake to interpret the Ottawa Treaty from the analytic lens of national security, instead of human security; as to judge it by criteria devised for the evaluation of arms control regimes. Instead, it falls into the stream of measures that make up international humanitarian law.[5] Such measures derive from motives different from those which prompt the negotiation of arms control regimes, are concerned with different subject matters, involve radically different compliance mechanisms, and ultimately have different political functions. The basic purpose of international humanitarian law is not the exacting one of securing the absolute disappearance of particular forms of conduct, but rather the more realistic one of producing some amelioration of the circumstances which combatants and non-combatants will confront should war break out. While its rules are cast in the language of prohibition, it operates through the process of anathematization.

Sceptical observers of the Ottawa process have focused on such important non-signatories as the U.S., Russia, China, and India; the allegedly perilous simplicity of the treaty, which creates scope for disagreement as to its exact meaning; and the relative ease with which a perfidious state party could move to violate its provisions. These criticisms are, for the most part, misconceived, and arise from a misunderstanding of the functions that the Ottawa Treaty can appropriately be expected to perform. In principle, every country whose participation is vital to the credibility and integrity of an arms control regime must be party to the Treaty. A humanitarian treaty seeks to make progress through stigmatization and the construction of normative barriers to use and deployment. While major power endorsements of the convention would have added significantly to its political weight, amending the Treaty provisions to accommodate their preferences would have greatly diluted the humanitarian content of the regime. The integrity of the convention, as a humanitarian treaty, was held to be more important than the inclusion even of the U.S. The humanitarian impulse proved stronger than the arms control caution. Even those key states that have not signed the Treaty have voiced sympathy for its objectives. To that extent, it has changed the parameters of discussion of anti-personnel mines from a strictly military framework to one that is strongly shaped by humanitarian concerns.

---

[4] Matthews 1989: 176. Matthews was writing in the context of environmental negotiations.
[5] This section summarizes Thakur and Maley 1999: 273–302.

NON-GOVERNMENTAL ORGANIZATIONS

In recent major diplomatic landmarks, like the Ottawa Treaty banning of anti-personnel land mines, the Rome Treaty establishing the International Criminal Court, and humanitarian interventions in Kosovo and East Timor, the impact of NGOs on international public policy has been very evident. The consequence of the rise of NGOs as significant policy-influencing actors is to tilt the balance away from hard to soft security.

There are four broad reasons for the rise of NGO influence. Political space for them opened up with the end of the Cold War. New issues like human rights, environmental degradation, and gender equality came to the forefront of public consciousness. These are issues on which NGOs enjoy many comparative advantages over governments in terms of experience, expertise, and often, let it be noted, public credibility. These are also issues on which it is more difficult to marginalize and exclude NGOs than was the case with the hard security issues during the Cold War.

Second, the global scope and multi-layered complexity of the new issues increased the need for partnerships between the established state actors and proliferating NGOs. They are partners in policy formation, information dissemination, standard-setting advocacy, monitoring, and implementation.

Third, the opportunities provided to NGOs have expanded enormously as a result of modern communications technology that enables people to forge real-time cyberspace communities on shared interests, values, and goals. The Internet and the fax machine have expanded the range, volume, and quality of networking activity. Globally networked NGOs can serve as focal points for mobilizing interests shared by people living in different countries.

Fourth, and finally, people with special skills and expertise have increasingly been drawn to work for and with NGOs, thereby muting some of their earlier amateurishness. The more effective and credible NGOs are increasingly professional in personnel and operations, including research, lobbying, fundraising, advocacy, and networking.

The expanding worldwide networks of NGOs embrace virtually every level of organization, from the village community to global summits, and almost every sector of public life, from the provision of microcredit and the delivery of paramedical assistance to environmental and human rights activism. Much of the UN's work in the field involves intimate partnerships with dedicated NGOs. They can complement UN efforts in several ways.

1. The presence of NGOs in the field can be a vital link in providing early warning for dealing with humanitarian crises.

2. Their specialized knowledge and contacts can be important components of the post-crisis peace-building process.

3. They can mediate between the peace and security functions of intergovernmental organizations and the needs and wants of local civilian populations.

4. They can exert a positive influence on the restoration of a climate of confidence for rehabilitation and reconstruction to take place.

This is not to imply that states are being replaced by NGOs and international organizations—far from it. Nor does it mean that all NGOs are 'good' ones, always on the side of angels. Instead we must confront, address, and redress the problem of unelected, unaccountable, unrepresentative, and self-aggrandizing NGOs. They can be just as undemocratic as the governments and organizations they criticize, and represent single-issue vested interests such as the gun lobby. By contrast, most industrialized country governments are multipurpose organizations trying to represent the public interest by the choice of the voters. In many developing countries, societies are busy building sound national governments as the prerequisite to effective governance: good governance is not possible without effective government. However, it does imply that national governments and international organizations will have to learn to live with the rise of NGOs. Indeed, those who learn to exploit the new opportunities for partnership between the different actors will be among the more effective new-age diplomats.

HUMAN RIGHTS

NGOs have been especially active, often intrusive, and sometimes even obtrusive on human rights. Fifty years ago, conscious of the atrocities committed by the Nazis while the world looked silently away, the UN adopted the Universal Declaration of Human Rights. It is the embodiment and the proclamation of the human rights norm. Covenants in 1966 add force and specificity, affirming both civil-political and social-economic-cultural rights, without privileging either. Together with the Declaration, they map out the international human rights agenda, establish the benchmark for state conduct, inspire provisions in many national laws and international conventions, and provide a beacon of hope to many whose rights are snuffed out by brutal regimes.

A right is a claim, an entitlement that may be neither conferred nor denied. A human right, owed to every person simply as a human being, is inherently universal. Held only by human beings, but equally by all, it does not flow from any office, rank, or relationship.

The idea of universal rights is denied by some who insist that moral standards are always culture-specific. If value relativism were to be accepted literally, then no tyrant—Hitler, Stalin, Idi Amin, Pol Pot—could be criticized by outsiders for any action. Relativism is often the first refuge of repressive governments. The false dichotomy between development and human rights is often a smoke-screen for corruption and cronyism. Relativism requires an acknowledgement that each culture has its own moral system. Government behaviour is still open to evaluation by the moral code of its own society. Internal moral standards can comply with international conventions; the two do not always have to diverge. The fact that moral precepts vary from culture to culture does not mean that different peoples do not hold some values in common.

Few, if any, moral systems proscribe the act of killing absolutely under all circumstances. At different times, in different societies, war, capital punishment, or abortion may or may not be morally permissible. Yet, for every society, murder is always wrong. All societies require retribution to be proportionate to the wrong done. All prize children, the link between succeeding generations of human civilization; every culture abhors their abuse.

The doctrine of national security has been especially corrosive of human rights. It is used frequently by governments, charged with the responsibility to protect citizens, to assault them instead. Under military rule, the instrument of protection from without becomes the means of attack from within.

The UN—an organization of, by, and for member states—has been impartial and successful in a standard-setting role, selectively successful in monitoring abuses, and almost feeble in enforcement. Governments usually subordinate considerations of UN effectiveness to the principle of non-interference.

The modesty of UN achievement should not blind us to its reality. The Universal Declaration embodies the moral code, political consensus, and legal synthesis of human rights. The world has grown vastly more complex in the 50 years since. But the simplicity of the declaration's language belies the passion of conviction underpinning it. Its elegance has been the font of inspiration down the decades; its provisions comprise the vocabulary of complaint.

Activists and NGOs use the declaration as the concrete point of reference against which to judge state conduct. The covenants require the submission of periodic reports by signatory countries, and so entail the creation of long-term national infrastructures for the protection and promotion of human rights. UN efforts are greatly helped by NGOs and other elements of civil society. NGOs work to protect victims, and contribute to the development and promotion of social commitment and the enactment of laws reflecting the more enlightened human rights culture.

Between them, the UN and NGOs have achieved many successes. National laws and international instruments have been improved, many political prisoners have been freed, and some victims of abuse have been compensated. The most recent advances on international human rights are the progressive incorporation of wartime behaviour and policy within the prohibitionary provisions of humanitarian law, e.g., the Ottawa Treaty, which subordinated military calculations to humanitarian concerns about a weapon that cannot distinguish a soldier from a child. In 1998 the world community established the first International Criminal Court. The U.S. absence from both shows the extent to which human rights have moved ahead of their strongest advocate in the past.

HUMANITARIAN INTERVENTION

The refusal to accept the discipline of universal norms of international humanitarian law is especially difficult to fathom in the case of a country that insists on the right to humanitarian intervention. We cannot accept the doctrine that any one state or coalition can decide when to intervene with force in the internal affairs of other countries, for down that path lies total chaos. Nevertheless, the doctrine of national sovereignty in its absolute and unqualified form, which gave the most brutal tyrant protection against attack from without while engaged in oppression within, has gone with the wind. On the other hand, war is itself a major humanitarian tragedy that can be justified under only the most compelling circumstances regarding the provocation, the likelihood of success—bearing in mind that goals are metamorphosed in the crucible of war once started—and the consequences that may reasonably be predicted. And the burden of proof rests on the proponents of force, not on dissenters.

If the Gulf War marked the birth of the new world order after the Cold War, Somalia was the slide into the new world disorder and Rwanda marked the loss of innocence after the end of the Cold War. Worse was to follow in the 'safe area' of Srebrenica in July 1995 in a tragedy that, in the words of the official UN report, 'will haunt our history forever'. (UN 1998: 503)

While Rwanda stands as the symbol of inaction in the face of genocide, Kosovo raised many questions about the consequences of action when the international community is divided in the face of a humanitarian tragedy. (Schnabel and Thakur 2000) It confronts us with an abiding series of challenges regarding humanitarian intervention: is it morally just, legally permissible, militarily feasible, and politically possible? What happens when the different lessons of the Twentieth Century, encapsulated in such slogans as 'no more wars' and 'no more Auschwitzes', come into collision? Who decides, following what rules of procedure and evidence, that mass atrocities have been committed, by which party, and what the appropriate response should be?

To supporters, NATO cured Europe of the Milosevic-borne disease of ethnic cleansing. The spectre of racial genocide had come back to haunt Europe from the dark days of the Second World War. Military action outside the UN framework was not NATO's preferred option of choice, Rather, its resort to force was a critical comment on the institutional hurdles to effective and timely action by the UN. To critics, however, the NATO cure greatly worsened the Milosevic disease. The trickle of refugees before the war turned into a flood during it, and afterwards the Serbs were ethnically cleansed by vengeful Albanians.

The sense of moral outrage provoked by humanitarian atrocities must be tempered by an appreciation of the limits of power, a concern for international institution-building, and a sensitivity to the law of unintended consequences. In today's unstable world full of complex conflicts, we face the painful dilemma of being 'damned if we do and damned if we don't'.

- To respect sovereignty all the time is to be complicit in human rights violations sometimes.
- To argue that the UN Security Council must give its consent to humanitarian war is to risk policy paralysis by handing over the agenda to the most egregious and obstreperous.
- To use force unilaterally is to violate international law and undermine world order.

The bottom-line question is this: faced with another Holocaust or Rwanda-type genocide on the one hand and a Security Council veto on the other, what should we do? Because there is no clear answer to this poignant question within the existing consensus as embodied in the UN Charter, a new consensus on humanitarian intervention is urgently needed.

The UN Charter contains an inherent tension between the principles of state sovereignty with the corollary of non-intervention, and the principles of human rights. In the first four decades of the Charter's existence, state sovereignty was privileged almost absolutely over human rights, with the one significant exception of apartheid in South Africa. The balance tilted a little in the 1990s, and is more delicately poised between the two competing principles at the start of the new millennium. The indictment of President Slobodan Milosevic as a war criminal, as well as the arresting saga of former Chilean President Augusto Pinochet, shows the inexorable shift from the culture of impunity of yesteryears to a culture of accountability at the dawn of the Twenty-first Century.

The UN Security Council lies at the heart of the international law enforcement system. The justification for bypassing it to launch an offensive war remains problematic, and the precedent that was set remains deeply troubling. By fighting and defeating Serbia, NATO became the tool for the KLA policy of inciting Serb reprisals through terrorist attacks in order to provoke NATO intervention. Communities, bitterly divided for centuries, cannot be forced by outsiders to live together peacefully. Another lesson that has been reinforced is that it is easier to bomb than to build. The willingness of the strong to fund a campaign of destruction stands in marked contrast to the reluctance of the rich—who happen to be almost the same group of countries—to find far less money for reconstruction. In turn, this seriously, if retrospectively, undermines the humanitarian claims for having gone to war.

Many of today's wars are nasty, brutish, anything but short, and mainly internal. The world community cannot help all victims, but must step in where it can make a difference. However, unless the member states of the UN agree on some broad principles to guide interventions in similar circumstances, the Kosovo precedent will have dangerously undermined world order. Not being able to act everywhere can never be a reason for not acting where effective intervention is both possible and urgently needed. Selective indignation is inevitable, for we simply cannot intervene everywhere, every time. However, community support for selective intervention will quickly dissipate if the only criterion of selection is friends (where the norm of non-intervention has primacy) versus adversaries (when the right to intervene is privileged).

In addition, we must still pursue policies of effective indignation. Humanitarian intervention must be collective, not unilateral. And it must be legitimate, not in violation of the agreed upon rules that comprise the foundations of world order. Being the indispensable power can temper one into being indisposed to accept the constraints of multilateral diplomacy. However, being indispensable does not confer the authority to dispense with the legitimacy of the UN as the only entity that can speak in the name of the international community. The reason for much disquiet around the world with the precedent of NATO action in Kosovo was not because their abhorrence of ethnic cleansing was any less. Rather, it was because of their dissent from a world order that permits or tolerates unilateral behaviour by the strong, and their preference for an order in which principles and values are embedded in universally applicable norms with the rough edges of power softened by institutionalized multilateralism.

THE UNITED NATIONS

It used to be said during the Cold War that the purpose of NATO was to keep the Americans in, the Germans down, and the Russians out. Does Kosovo mark a turning point, changing NATO into a tool for keeping the Americans in, the Russians down, and the UN out?

International organizations are an essential means of conducting world affairs more satisfactorily than would be possible under conditions of international anarchy or total self-help. The UN lies at their legislative and normative centre. If it did not exist, we would surely have to invent it. Yet its founding vision of a world community equal in rights and united in action is still to be realized.

For the cynics, the UN can do nothing right and is the source of many ills. For the romantics, the UN can do no wrong and is the solution to all the world's problems. Its failures reflect the weakness of member states, prevented only by a lack of political will from fulfilling its destiny as the global commons, the custodian of the international interest, and the conscience of all humanity.

The UN Charter was a triumph of hope and idealism over the experience of two world wars. The flame flickered in the chill winds of the Cold War, but has not yet died out. In the midst of the swirling tides of change, the UN must strive for a balance between the desirable and the possible. The global public goods of peace, prosperity, sustainable development, and good governance cannot be achieved by any country acting on its own. The UN is still the symbol of our dreams for a better world, where weakness can be compensated by justice and fairness, and the law of the jungle replaced by the rule of law.

The innovation of peacekeeping notwithstanding, the UN has not fully lived up to expectations in securing a disarmed and peaceful world. As with sustainable development, which seeks to strike a balance between growth and conservation, the UN must be at the centre of efforts to achieve sustainable disarmament, i.e., the reduction of armaments to the lowest level where the security needs of any one country at a given time, or any one generation over time, are met without compromising the security and welfare needs of other countries or future generations.

The UN system can take justified pride in mapping the demographic details of the human family, and also in the stupendous improvements to human welfare that have been achieved. The advances in health, life expectancy, and satisfaction of basic needs and other desires were truly phenomenal over the course of the Twentieth Century. The symbolic six billionth child was born just recently.

At the same time, as the sun rises on the new century and illumines some of the darker legacies of the last one, we should engage in sober reflection and sombre introspection. It is simply not acceptable that:

- at a time of unprecedented economic prosperity and stock market booms in some parts of the world, millions of people should continue to be condemned to a life of poverty, illiteracy, and ill-health;
- the combined GDP of the 48 least developed countries should be less than the assets of the world's three richest people;
- the annual income of 2.5 billion—47 per cent—of the world's poorest people should be less than that of the richest 225.

The need for international assistance in many continents is an unhappy reminder of man's inhumanity against fellow man and his rapaciousness against nature. Secretary-General Kofi Annan has noted that there were three times as many major natural disasters in the 1990s as in the 1960s. (Annan 2000: 58, fig. 11) Moreover, most disaster victims live in developing countries. Poverty and the pressures of population force growing numbers of people to live in harm's way at the same rime that unsound development and environmental practices place more of nature at risk. The rich reap the benefits, the poor pay the price.

Success that is sustained requires us all to make a greater commitment to the vision and values of the UN, and to make systematic use of the UN forum and modalities for managing and ending conflicts. People continue to look to the UN to guide them and protect them when the tasks are too big and complex for nations and regions to handle by themselves. The comparative advantages of the UN are its universal membership, political legitimacy, administrative impartiality, technical expertise, convening and mobilizing power, and the dedication of its staff. Its comparative disadvantages are excessive politicization, ponderous pace of decision-making, impossible mandate, high cost structure, insufficient resources, rigid bureaucracy, and institutional timidity. Many of the disadvantages are the products of demands and intrusions by the 188 member states that own and control the organization, but some key members disown responsibility for giving it the requisite support and resources. For the UN to succeed, the world community must match the demands made on the organization with the means given to it.

The UN represents the idea that unbridled nationalism and the raw interplay of power must be mediated and moderated in an international framework. It is the centre for harmonizing national interests and forging the international interest. Only the UN can legitimately authorize military action on behalf of the entire international community, instead of a select few. However, the UN does not have its own military and police forces, and a multinational coalition of allies can offer a more credible and efficient military force when robust action is needed and warranted. What will be increasingly needed in the future are partnerships of the able, the willing, and the high-minded, with the duly authorized. What we should most fear are partnerships of the able, the willing, and the low-minded, in violation of due process. What if the UN Security Council itself acts in violation of the Charter of the UN? Unlike domestic systems, there is no independent judicial check on the constitutionality of Security Council decisions. No liberal democracy would tolerate such a situation domestically; why should liberal democrats, who generally lead the charge for humanitarian intervention, find it acceptable internationally?

The UN has to strike a balance between realism and idealism. Its decisions must reflect current realities of military and economic power. It will be incapacitated if it alienates its most important members, but it will also lose credibility if it compromises core values. The UN is the repository of international idealism, and utopia is fundamental to its identity. Even the sense of disenchantment and disillusionment on the part of some cannot be understood other than against this background.

The learning curve of human history shows that the UN ideal can be neither fully attained nor abandoned. Like most organizations, the UN is condemned to an eternal credibility gap between aspiration and performance. The real challenge is to ensure that the gap does not widen, but stays within a narrow band. Sustained, coordinated efforts can turn killing fields into playing fields and rice fields. Success comes from having the courage to fail. If you have never failed, then you have not tried enough: you have not pushed yourself hard enough, not tested the limits of your potential.

REFERENCES

Annan, Kofi A. (2000). *We the Peoples: The Role of the United Nations in the 21st Century* (New York: UN Department of Public Information).

Annan, Kofi A. (2001). *We the Children: End-decade review of the follow-up to the World Summit for Children,* Report of the Secretary-General: A/S-27/3 (New York: United Nations) May 4.

CSIS (2000). "Contagion and Conflict: Health as a Global Security Challenge. A report of the Chemical and Biological Arms Control Institute and the CSIS International Security Programme," (Washington DC: Centre for Strategic and International Studies) January.

GlobalAction website address: www.globalactionpw.org.

Mathews, Jessica Tuchman (1989). "Redefining Security," *Foreign Affairs* (Spring):68.

Schnabel, Albrecht and Ramesh Thakur (2000) eds. *Kosovo and the Challenge of Humanitarian Intervention: International Citizenship, Selective Indignation, and Collective Action* (Tokyo: United Nations University Press).

Thakur, Ramesh and William Maley (1999). "The Ottawa Convention on Landmines: A Landmark Humanitarian Treaty in Arms Control?" *Global Governance 5.3* (July–September):273–302.

The Economist (1999). "Freedom's Journey," survey. September 11.

Tow, William T., Ramesh Thakur, and ln-taek Hyun, eds, (2000). *Asia's Emerging Regional Order: Reconciling Traditional and Human Security* (Tokyo: United Nations University Press).

UN (1999). "Report of the Secretary-General Pursuant to General Assembly," Resolution 53/35 1998 (New York: UN Secretariat) November.

UN (2002). *The State of the World's Children 2002* (New York: United Nations Children Fund).

9/11 "Terrorism," "Root Causes" and All That: Policy Implications of the Socio-Cultural Argument

DENIS STAIRS*

*__Denis Stairs__ is McCulloch Professor in Political Science at Dalhousie University, Halifax.

The attacks on New York and Washington a year ago were ghastly phenomena. They killed (most Westerners would argue) the innocent. They also killed by surprise. They killed, too, in large numbers. And they killed to extraordinarily symbolic effect. Of the two primary targets, one—the Pentagon—was the official home of the most powerful and sophisticated military machine ever devised by humankind, and the other—the World Trade Center—manifested the capitalist enterprise not only of the United States, but of the entire OECD world. If the Great Republic presides over a hegemonic empire, this was a frontal assault on the two core components of its imperial being.

It was an unfamiliar experience, and stunningly exotic. Continental Americans had not been so directly attacked by forces emanating from an overseas politics since the War of 1812. That the explosive projectiles used against them should be contrived of their own civilian airliners compounded the horror, deepened the disbelief. Hasty conclusions were drawn. Things would never be the same. A new kind of vigilance was required, and a new kind of "war" had to be fought. For the instrument of the enemy was "terrorism," and terrorism is "special."

As understandable as this last conclusion may be, it warrants a closer look. _Why_ do we think of terrorism as "special"? Why, indeed, do we think of it as "terrorism" at all? For the term itself is politically loaded. One observer's "terrorism" may be another's legitimate act of resistance to oppression. Such arguments over terminology, the contrarious often assert, reflect nothing more than a difference of perspective—a difference very reminiscent of a similar phenomenon in the disarmament trade. As the old saw has it, whether you think a weapon is "defensive" or "offensive" depends on whether you're standing behind the trigger or in front of it.

But there may be a difference. We think of terrorism as both "special" and objectively identifiable not just because our security personnel have trouble dealing with it, but also because it seems _aberrational_. In effect, we regard it as a pathology—a pathology that is particularly awful (a) because it's violent, (b) because the violence is often (although not always) directed to the random slaughter of the innocent, and (c) because it sometimes (again, not always) requires for its successful execution the certain death of the terrorist—a characteristic that seems to connote the presence of an alarming dose of wantonly fanatical "irrationality." And since it _is_ "special" in these ways, the phenomenon appears also to require a special kind of explanation, and possibly a special kind of policy response.

From the political scientist's point of view, on the other hand, terrorism is not a manifestation of pathological behaviour at all. Quite the contrary. It is simply an *instrument of politics,* a technique for getting one's way, a means of changing the prevailing pattern of who gets what, when and how.

Moreover, it is not in the least bit unusual in being violent. All sorts of instruments of politics involve death and destruction, and most political authorities are quite good at mounting "just cause" reasons for their deployment.

Nor is terrorism unique in its targeting of the innocent. We could ask the ghost of Hermann Goering. Or the bombers of Dresden. Or the architects of the cataclysms of Hiroshima and Nagasaki. Or the inventors of the doctrine of Mutual Assured Destruction. Or any of a multitude of others, great and small.

Nor, finally, is it singular in demanding the death of its perpetrators. In this respect (although perhaps not in other respects), *everyone* compares it with the performance of *kamikaze* pilots in World War II. But it could be compared in modern times also with the behaviour of self-immolating Buddhist priests in Vietnam. It could even be compared with the extraordinary courage exhibited by many of those who have received, posthumously, the Victoria Cross (Canadians among them).

"Terrorist" behaviour, in short, is not "psychotic" behaviour, even if we were to find on close examination that some individual terrorists (like many of the clandestine members of the Communist Party in the United States in the 1950s and 1960s) give evidence of having social or psychological problems of one sort or another.

It may therefore be more instructive to think of terrorism as a political activity akin to guerrilla warfare—a phenomenon upon which there is a massive literature, much of it linked in the 20th century to the politics of decolonization, and informed by the writings and practices of Mao Tse-tung, Che Guevara, General (Vo Nguyen) Giap and others of that ilk. Among other things, this has the advantage of reminding us that terrorism, like other forms of guerrilla warfare, is a very *unpleasant* activity, entailing enormous—and often the ultimate—sacrifice. As an instrument of politics, therefore, it is not the instrument of first choice but the instrument of last resort. It is used only where other instruments are unavailable, or, if available, are unequal to the political task—that is, in situations where the tactics of conventional politics are denied to the political actors involved, or have no prospect of being effective, and where the advantage in terms of the more conventional instruments of force (armies and police) is very clearly held by the other side.

Cognoscenti will regard these as commonplace observations, but they help to open up the question of "root causes" and thereby lead us directly to a consideration of the socio-cultural factor as a source of terrorist behaviour. This is because playing politics with the intensity of motivation that recourse to terrorism entails requires a deep attachment to a *cause*—a cause for which the terrorist is actually prepared to die, and to die, moreover, not by accident but wilfully, by his or her own hand.

Usually, attachment to the cause has to be shared (although perhaps not so intensely) by others as well, since such sharing of purposes is essential to the creation of a wider base of support. Hence Mao Tse-tung's famous dictum that guerrilla fighters have to be like "fish in the sea"—a view which has been echoed by almost all modern authorities on the subject, irrespective of which side of the battle they have been on.

In the 9/11 context, of course, the guerrillas, or the terrorists (like the corporate and other agents of the secular world of modern liberalism and Western capitalism that they appear to so profoundly hate), have gone "transnational," so that the areas in which they are operating are geographically distant from the sea that ultimately provides their sustenance. Their local target communities don't even know they're there—until it's too late. But that is simply a new wrinkle on an ancient political phenomenon, a wrinkle introduced (like so much else in the modern world) with the help of technology.

For the purpose of the present discussion, however, the focus needs to be on the "cause" itself, because this, presumably, is where the socio-cultural factor (like other potential candidates for "root cause" status) comes into play. Culturally bound assumptions, after all, help human beings everywhere to define themselves, and what they want. They also help them to define their enemies, and what they think their enemies want. Above all, they help them to determine how much they *care*—how much they think the contested issues really matter.

The prevailing societal culture, along with the processes by which it is either spontaneously learned or systematically inculcated, helps, in short, to give definition to the politics. (it does this, incidentally, as much for the forces of the establishment—and in the present situation that means for *us*—as it does for the forces of those who see themselves as gravely dishonoured, or gravely dispossessed.)

But this analysis leads to a problem. Certainly it leads to a problem when we focus on terrorism as organized political behaviour, as opposed to concentrating on the motivations of particular individuals who may happen to engage in terrorist acts. Simply put, this is because the cultural variables—the cultural drivers—affect a much larger proportion of the population than the one we associate with the relatively small community of terrorists and their immediate supporters. That being so, it appears that other things have to be going on—that the cleavages of identity and culture have to be reinforced by cleavages of another kind—before the terrorist behaviour is triggered.

While the socio-cultural environment may be a permissive, or even facilitating, factor in the emergence of certain kinds of terrorist activity, therefore, it cannot be sufficient in itself as a cause of the behaviour (although conceivably it could be sufficient as a foundation upon which to build the indoctrination of individual terrorist "warriors"). The cultural element, in other words, does not appear to have enough causal power to account for the phenomenon as a whole, even if it can account for why certain individuals are prepared to commit extraordinarily self-sacrificial political acts.

The problem of weighting the cultural factor relative to other variables is compounded by the fact that the leaders of any terrorist campaign are unlikely to be as simply motivated as those who follow them. Their political thinking is likely to be far more calculating, far more complex, and probably far more pragmatic and "instrumentalist" in orientation. For them, the cultural factor may be more pertinent as a vehicle for the mobilization and indoctrination of others than as a recipe from which they seek guidance for their own behaviour. On the other hand, it may well affect the "lens," or the "intellectual prism," through which they interpret the world around them—influencing, as it were, their "intelligence assessment."

This relatively modest interpretation of the importance and role of the cultural variable as a stimulus for terrorist activity (relative to the role played by variables of other kinds) could easily be wrong-headed. Reaching conclusions on such issues is ultimately, after all, a matter of judgment. But whether the judgment offered here is wrong-headed or not, there can be no doubt that the weights we assign respectively to the various causal factors that may be driving the behaviour involved have profoundly significant implications for our views of the appropriate policy response.

To illustrate this point, it may be useful to consider three commonly suggested propositions about what may have been going on in the minds of Osama bin Laden and his senior colleagues over the past decade or so.

One account has it that he was profoundly offended—and ultimately radicalized—by the presence of the American military on the soil of Saudi Arabia.

Now, if that were truly the driver of al-Qaeda behaviour, the long-term solution might seem relatively simple—although certainly not strategically or politically "cost-free" from the Washington vantage point. On such an interpretation, to de-escalate the problem it is necessary only to remove the American armed forces contingent from Saudi Arabian territory (obviously not the stratagem that the Americans have adopted thus far, and probably not one they are likely to pursue in the immediately foreseeable future).

A second account of the problem holds that the core source of the radicalism of the terrorists is the presence of Israel in a land that Palestinians and their supporters elsewhere in the Islamic world regard as properly Palestinian, and not Israeli.

Here again, the solution is technically straightforward, but from the political point of view it may be even more difficult to achieve. Israel has to give up some of its land (or the land it currently controls). On some accounts, it has to give up *all* of its land. The former might conceivably happen in the context of a negotiated settlement. The latter won't.

But a third account has it that the current round of terrorist radicalism has roots that are deeply imbedded in the Islamic culture, or at least in one or more versions of it. They are imbedded specifically in that part of the culture that leads to the perception that the "West" represents a way of living that is so fundamentally a violation of the will of God that it creates for true believers an obligation to try to bring it down.

This is not very difficult to understand. For a start, the West has insisted (after a centuries-long struggle in Europe) on separating Church from State, or the world of God from the world of Caesar. This, clearly, is a position that makes for a more civilized politics in largely secular societies, but it also has the effect of demoting the salience of "God" to the conduct of an important and pervasive part of our lives. The West has concluded, in effect, that our relations with our respective gods are private matters entirely, and that theological considerations have no place in the way we do our community politics—which is a quite extraordinary idea when one thinks of it from the vantage point of those of deeply committed faith.

Moreover, if one's view of the will of God incorporates an attachment both to family and to what Westerners describe as "puritan" values, the offensiveness of the West assumes truly monumental proportions. It requires only a moment's reflection on how an evening of North American television would look to someone holding such beliefs to grasp the implication. The experience would seem like an odyssey in corruption and decadence—an almost unbroken display of violence and greed, along with illicit (and alarmingly public) sexual activity, an overwhelming fascination with the pampering trivia of personal hygiene, a voyeuristic portrayal of the responses of the police to the degraded vulgarities of the gutter, and so on. What, after all, would John Milton have made of Jerry Springer? What must a committed Muslim make of him in our own time?

On this account of the problem, however, there is no policy "cure" at all—not, at least, a policy cure short of the conversion of a dedicated and militant Islam to what we may have to acknowledge is a world-view akin to the libertarian.

This list of potential "root causes" could easily be expanded. Some would be inclined to argue that the disaffection of the terrorists is ultimately the product of economic deprivation, or perhaps more accurately, in the present context, of gross disparities in the distribution of wealth. Their leaders may be wealthy and be guided by other considerations—considerations typical of authoritarian elites everywhere, in every time—but their capacity to recruit their foot-soldiers is nurtured by the poverty of the many, and it would go away if the pertinent populations were appropriately enriched. Alternatively, it can be held that the true source of the alienation lies with political regimes that are transparently corrupt, oppressive and undemocratic, so that the solution must ultimately rest on the advance of democratization. It can also be suggested that the difficulty really lies with the structural integration of *both* these conditions—the underlying poverty and the disparities in the distribution of wealth being themselves the inevitable consequence of an oligarchical politics.

Here, too, the implications of the argument—even if the analysis itself is well-founded—are such as to leave little hope of effective remedy in the short term, since the necessary reforms are unlikely to occur in the absence of invasive interventions of the imperial sort—interventions that would be no more acceptable to the indigenous populations than they would be to the constituencies of the intervening powers.

In practice, these various interpretations (and others like them) of bin Laden's behaviour, and perhaps even more of the behaviour of those who follow him, may *all* be right—in the sense that they are all "in the picture" and actually serve to reinforce one another. Israel, in such an account of the bin Laden view, is not just the stealer of Palestinian land; it is also the purveyor in the Middle East of Western corruption—a corruption that among other things has turned the leadership of Saudi Arabia into a comprador elite, willing to lend part of its territory to the armed might of the United States in a way that helps the Saudi leadership to sustain its own position of political, economic and social privilege.

If there is any merit in this assessment of the "root causes" analysis of the current terrorist problem, the practical implication from the Western point of view is both clear and depressing, since it effectively denies the viability of remedies based on root-cause engineering. Attempting, for example, to change the substance of a given socio-political culture, much less the institutions and processes by which the socialization of the culture occurs, is not an easy or reliable undertaking. Certainly it is not a *short-term* undertaking. That being so, the security problem that terrorist "guerrilla warfare" represents has to be regarded as just that—a *security* problem. The liberal world that Canadians and others in the West inhabit has enemies—and some of them are understandably determined. We can fiddle at the margins in attempting to dissuade them of their views, and here and there we can even make policy changes in the hope that this will make us appear less offensive to them. But in the final analysis, we will need to defend ourselves against their belligerence.

The defensive strategy required is obviously multi-faceted, and there can be no surprise in the fact that almost every major agency and department of the federal government (and many at other levels of government, too) have been involved in both the Canadian and the American responses.

But one particular requirement may warrant special emphasis. For to do the job as effectively as possible we need to understand not only the "terrorists" and their "culture," along with the ways in which they are "socialized," but also the reality of the circumstances they face, and the various cleavages of wealth, power and status that help to sustain their alienation. In effect, we need first-class "intelligence." Even more, we need first-class intelligence *analysts*.

For the reasons already indicated, this is not a matter of finding a "cure." It is a matter of knowing one's adversaries, and of being able to think like them. This, in turn, is not just a question of being able to understand their culture, but of being able to understand their world in *all* of its dimensions, so as to be better equipped to predict their behaviour and make the most of their vulnerabilities.

For such a purpose, research is required. So is higher education. And the two go together. We cannot properly staff CSIS, or the DND, or the RCMP, or DFAIT, or the PCO, or the folks in Customs, or in Immigration, without both. Canada is a trifle short of educational and research personnel with these sorts of capacities in most of the fields in which we now seem to need them. We need them, moreover, with "critical mass." And to get them, we need to fund their training and make it financially possible for them to do their research— not only here, but in the field.

To fill the gap in the short term, of course, we can rely in some measure on our capacity to borrow enlightenment and instruction from our friends—not just our friends in the United States, but those elsewhere, too. This cannot be a substitute, however, for having effective analytical capacities of our own. For there is a strong case for maintaining a certain distance from the assumptions and perspectives that guide the assessments, in particular, of our neighbours. Information liberates. Informational dependency imprisons.

That said, it should be noted that the cultivating of our own analytical capacities can be as useful to our neighbours as to ourselves. This is partly because there are things that researchers from a small power can do that researchers from a hegemonic superpower cannot. Canadian social scientists asking questions in the Middle East may be tolerated. American social scientists trying to do the same may not. More importantly, however, there are perspectives on "reality" that flourish in smaller powers but are quick to die in the more muscular world of the great powers.

In this arena, as in others, there is value in diversity. It inhibits myopia, and inhibiting myopia is helpful to the making of sound policy.

The Responsibility to Protect and the Duty to Punish: Politics and Justice in a Safer World

LOUISE ARBOUR*

***Louise Arbour**, former Supreme Court of Canada Justice (1999–2004) is the United Nations High Commissioner for Human Rights.

Prior to her appointment to the Supreme Court of Canada, Arbour was Chief Prosecutor, International War Crimes Tribunals for the Former Yugoslavia and for Rwanda. This is a slightly amended version of the first H.R. MacMillan Lecture, held by the CIIA in Vancouver in February 2002.

On 17 April 2002, Canadians celebrated the 20th anniversary of the coming into force of the Canadian Charter of Rights and Freedoms. Much was said on that happy occasion about the immeasurable impact of that constitutional document on our lives and on our aspirations, not only for ourselves, but also for others because this is indeed the genius of the charter. Inasmuch as it is truly a document asserting individual freedoms, liberties, and rights, its implementation invariably brings to the forefront of public awareness the existence of the rights and aspirations of others, usually those who claim to be ill-served by a democratic process reduced to a self-serving majority rule. One does not think of the charter as having any particular international significance. It has, of course, had implications for immigration and refugee law, and in that sense its impact is felt outside our immediate boundaries. It has also brought us closer to those, like the European Union, who are engaged in similar human rights litigation. And there is no question that Canadian charter jurisprudence is having an important influence on the thinking of constitutional courts in many jurisdictions confronting the difficult issues we have so recently tackled.

Beyond this, I believe that the contribution that Canada has made on the international scene, particularly in the last decade, reflects our new identity, born of charter awareness, about the universality of rights and the imperative of enforcing those rights. Michael Ignatieff addressed this issue in *The Rights Revolution*.[1] But in a sense he spoke even more forcefully about the idea of rights in *Virtual War,* his book about the war in Kosovo,[2] in which he documents the dilemma, very overtly expressed in particular in the United Kingdom, about the morality, the legitimacy, and the legality of waging war in defence of someone else's rights. His book precipitated a vigorous public debate about state sovereignty and military intervention. That debate led the secretary-general of the United Nations to question whether

---

[1]   Michael Ignatieff, *The Rights Revolution* (Toronto: Anansi 2000).
[2]   Michael Ignatieff, *Virtual War: Kosovo and Beyond* (Toronto: Penguin 2001).

we had entered a new era of internationalism, one essentially dominated by concerns over the protection of fundamental individual rights.

The probing of these issues could not have been mote timely for Canadians, who had themselves examined the outer limits of the state's obligations to support human rights and fundamental freedoms in two decades of charter litigation. We heard and understood the implications of the question raised by the secretary-general, and in particular I suggest that we understood that there had to be a legal framework, not just a political one, within which to search for answers. This led to the Canadian initiative of convening the International Commission of Intervention and State Sovereignty, which published its report in December 2001. The report, *The Responsibility to Protect,* is concerned primarily with establishing guidelines for triggering military intervention in the face of human catastrophes fed by either the collusion or the impotence of national states.[3]

To be fair, the report is not narrowly preoccupied with militarism. it argues that the international community has a responsibility to prevent, to react, and to rebuild: not surprisingly, it stresses prevention as the most important aspect of the responsibility to protect. But the most striking aspect of the conclusions reached by this international body of experts is the recognition that the concept of state sovereignty is not just a question of state prerogative, representing the always superior interest of the state, but that it is a voucher for human security. The rationale for the international order deferring to the will of individual states in the management of their own affairs is that the vindication of state sovereignty will best serve peace and, therefore, safety and security. In other words, sovereign states have a responsibility to protect their citizens, and if they forfeit that responsibility they surrender part of their sovereignty accordingly. In that sense, international intervention for human protection purposes is justified if and when a state no longer lives up to the obligations imposed upon it by its sovereign status.

There is little doubt that these ideas are rooted in part in the growth of international legalism. Since the Second World War, we have witnessed a proliferation of legal instruments, particularly in the human rights field, which have led to a similar growth of domestic legislation and, although at a much slower pace, a growth in enforcement of these international norms that are now universally accepted, if not universally implemented. We have witnessed, particularly since the end of the cold war, a gradual consensus that the rule of law can and should override the pragmatism of the rule of necessity, the rule of convenience, and the rule of force.

The events of 11 September 2001, which now dominate so many concerns in international relations, in a sense have temporarily obscured the common trends on security issues that had prevailed since at least the end of the cold war, in particular the proliferation of deadly armed conflicts within states or, as in the former Yugoslavia, between states emerging from the disintegration of previously sovereign states. What 11 September has not obscured, in fact what it has highlighted in the most tragic fashion, is the pernicious vulnerability of civilians, who are indeed often deliberately targeted by those who claim, explicitly or otherwise, to be waging war.

---

[3] International Development Research Centre, *The Responsibility to Protect: Report of the International Committee on Intervention and State Sovereignty* (Ottawa: IDRC 2001).

The report of the Commission on intervention and State Sovereignty stresses the need for a framework for anticipating and then responding to acute crises in human security. it is not surprising that its existence was essentially a by-product of the multinational military intervention in Kosovo, the culmination of more than a decade of attempts at conflict management in that region. Indeed, the level, the diversity, and the intensity of international attention devoted to the Balkans will probably provide one of the most complex case studies in international diplomacy, NGO monitoring and pressure, and sustained media attention, all within the oversight of sophisticated organizations such as the United Nations (UN), the North Atlantic Treaty Organization (NATO), the European Union, and the Organization for Security and Co-operation in Europe (OSCE).

It is interesting, from my point of view, that the insertion, for the first time ever, of an operational international judicial institution both complicated matters and provided a fresh and promising outlook for the management of that unmanageable conflict. The original perception that international criminal justice was very much a misfit within this array of political interveners became acute with the Dayton Peace Agreement. There was to be an inevitable operational interaction between the theoretical and the practical international law enforcers in Bosnia and Herzegovina. Leading the former was the International Criminal Tribunal for the former Yugoslavia (ICTY), created two years earlier by the Security Council under its chapter VII powers. The tribunal, as a judicial organ of the Security Council, was mandated to investigate and prosecute serious violations of international humanitarian law on the territory of the former Yugoslavia from 1991 onwards. It was specifically directed to apply the law of command responsibility, and no immunities from prosecutions were given to anyone, including heads of state. The tribunal's jurisdiction encompasses genocide, war crimes, and crimes against humanity—crimes that continued to be perpetrated during the existence of the tribunal—and it had jurisdiction, some of it very theoretical indeed, to conduct on-site investigations. Under article 29 of the tribunal's constituting stature, all states were required to co-operate with it, and all states were compelled to obey its orders.

The more practical law enforcers in the field were, of course IFOR, subsequently SFOR, and then, in Kosovo, KFOR. IFOR, the Dayton implementation force, was a NATO-led, Security Council mandated military force in which more than two-dozen countries were represented, including Russia and other eastern European countries. At its peak, it deployed over 50,000 troops. It took over from UNPROFOR, the long-serving UN peacekeeping mission, first in Croatia then in Bosnia-Herzegovina. UNPROFOR had struggled with its ever-expanding mandate of providing humanitarian assistance as well as managing safe areas. Both the political and the military command of IFOR were firmly in NATO (the North Atlantic Council and the Supreme Allied Commander Europe). Its rules of engagement provided for the robust use of force both for force protection and to ensure the discharge of its mandate.

In annex 1-A of the peace agreement, the parties agreed to authorize and assist IFOR in the discharge of its mandate, including the use of necessary force. The Dayton agreement also dealt with the ICTY. Under article IX of annex 4 on the Constitution of Bosnia and Herzegovina the agreement said: 'No person who is serving a sentence imposed by the International Tribunal for the Former Yugoslavia, and no person who is under indictment by the Tribunal and who has failed to comply with an order to appear before the Tribunal, may stand as a candidate or hold any appointive, elective or other public office in the territory of Bosnia and Herzegovina.'

Referring to the role of IFOR vis-à-vis ICTY, the Dutch commentator, Dick A. Leurdijk, had this to say: 'The role of the IFOR troops when it comes to apprehending war criminals has been an extremely sensitive issue both for the military and diplomats. The position of the international community was, as so often before, ambiguous.' He added, with reference to the paragraph in the Dayton agreement quoted above: 'This paragraph would become one of the most contentious provisions of the Dayton implementation process. It was also directly related to another Dayton provision, which obliged all parties "to cooperate in the investigation and prosecution of war crimes and other violations of international humanitarian law." Similarly, Security Council Resolution 1031, which authorised the deployment of IFOR, recognised that the "parties shall cooperate fully with all entities involved in implementation of the peace settlement, as described in the Peace Agreement, or which are otherwise authorised by the Security Council, including the international Tribunal for the Former Yugoslavia."' At NATO'S headquarters, the consensus was that this paragraph did not provide a 'clear mandate for IFOR to arrest indicted war criminals, suggesting that it was up to the UN Security Council to take a decision.'

I will spare you the detailed account of the efforts deployed by tribunal officials at persuading IFOR and then SFOR to take a more robust stance on the issue of arresting persons indicted by The Hague tribunal. Much of it was widely reported in the international press at the time. NATO's position was clearly expressed in a press release of 14 February 1996, which stated that the North Atlantic Council strongly supported the tribunal and that IFOR would provide logistical assistance, within its means, to ICTY and concentrate on providing a safe environment in which organizations like ICTY could best operate. As for apprehension of indictees, ICTY would provide detailed information about them to IFOR, and IFOR would apprehend them if and when 'they come into contact with such persons in carrying out their duties.' This was the 'no manhunt' policy that captured so well NATO's lack of enthusiasm for another chapter VII institution, one that it preferred to view as another NGO, intent on doing good, but frankly just standing in the way of getting things done. That lack of enthusiasm, I must add, was not exclusive to NATO but was endemic even among some members of the Security Council, such as Russia, who just three years earlier had launched this unprecedented initiative.

This was the first of many interactions between international criminal justice and what it thought were its partners in the peace implementation process. Nowhere more than on this thorny issue of arrest was the latent conflict between peace and justice brought to the surface—a conflict, in my view, that has no rational foundation but that served to express the profound ambivalence of those who, unlike Canadians under their Charter of Rights and Freedoms, had difficulty embracing an international rights revolution.

Although the Report on Intervention and State Sovereignty does not address explicitly international criminal law enforcement, it is clear that the framework that it proposes will be relevant to the decision-making process of the Office of the Prosecutor of the imminent International Criminal Court (ICC). The report envisages a responsibility to punish as integral to the responsibility to protect. As I indicated earlier, the responsibility to protect is broken down into three elements: the responsibility to prevent, to react, and to rebuild. The duty to react encompasses the use of coercive measures such as sanctions and international prosecutions, with military intervention reserved for the most extreme cases. In the duty to rebuild, the report expresses the need not only for reconstruction but also for reconciliation— a task often linked to justice, particularly criminal justice. This endorsement of the continuing role that international accountability through criminal justice is likely to play in serious conflict management comes at a critical moment in the rapidly moving history of the enforcement of the laws of war.

Under the Rome Statute that created the ICC, signed in the summer of 1998, 60 ratifications are necessary to bring the court into existence. This number was reached in April 2002. The consensus is that the court will be in existence before the end of the year [2002]. Despite the considerable assistance that he or she will derive from the work of the existing ad hoc tribunals, the work of the ICC prosecutor will be truly unprecedented.

The prosecutor will be dependent on the co-operation of many states, and that co-operation will not always be nudged along by the threat of Security Council intervention, if only in the form of an expressed concern or disapproval. The prosecutor will also have to exercise discretion over whether or not to launch an investigation, in an environment that is likely to be much more political than that which surrounded most of the decisions of the prosecutor for the Yugoslav and Rwanda tribunals. The work of the ICC prosecutor will be prospective only. It will therefore inevitably deal with ongoing conflicts, where the prosecutor's initiative will be intermingled with other forms of international attention and intervention. In short, it will have all the features that were so conducive to the SFOR-ICC clashes that marked the early years of the tribunal's attempt to impose itself as a genuine law enforcement institution in the Balkans.

On the eve of the launch of the ICC, it is more important then ever to recall the basic imperatives of any functioning and trustworthy criminal justice system. I can do no better here than to refer to a short speech that I delivered in The Hague on 13 May 1999. The occasion was the launch of a global ratification campaign for the ICC, organized by the Coalition for International Justice, during the height of the NATO bombing campaign in Kosovo. In my remarks, 'Despair and Hope: Kosovo and the ICC,' I added my voice to the call for an immediate, universal, and effective repression of the most serious violations of the most fundamental international human rights, perpetrated against civilian populations rendered particularly vulnerable by the collusion, the impotence, or the indifference of governments. We did nor then have a language within which to cast that obligation. It can now be referred to as the responsibility to protect, in the terminology of the Commission on Intervention and State Sovereignty. The three arguments I advanced in support of the speedy ratification of the ICC stature—authority, universality, and urgency—are as cogent today as they were then.

My first point is that any international criminal jurisdiction has to be authoritative, both in theory and in reality. The existing ad hoc tribunals are powerful judicial institutions. The prosecutor of the tribunals is explicitly empowered by the Security Council of the United Nations, through resolutions that all member states have agreed will bind them, to conduct investigations and prosecutions, acting independently and on her own initiative, and, in the exercise of that power, to question witnesses and to conduct on-site investigations. Furthermore, all states are required, by the same binding Security Council resolutions to comply with requests for assistance and court orders issued by the tribunal.

It was in that empowering environment that I affirmed publicly in March 1998 the jurisdiction of the tribunal over alleged war crimes and crimes against humanity being committed in Kosovo. It was in that same empowering environment that the Security Council in three separate resolutions throughout 1998 supported that position and reaffirmed the obligations of all states to assist our efforts to investigate. And it was also in that empowering environment that the tribunal's investigators and I were systematically denied visas for Kosovo and that I was turned back at the border of the Federal Republic of Yugoslavia, two days after the Racak massacre, on my way to conduct an on-site investigation, as I was mandated to do by the Security Council.

That experience has persuaded me that when it comes to the exercise of lawful authoritative powers, empty threats are a grave folly. The political spirit of accommodation and compromise, which is so crucial for the peaceful resolution of many types of conflicts, is entirely inappropriate when it comes to compliance with the law. It is an affront to those who obey the law and a betrayal of those who rely on it for protection.

What was activated in Rome in the summer of 1998 was the promise that something greater than force will govern, something that does not get traded away, something worthy of trust.

My second point deals with the need to expand the reach of accountability. Irrationally selective prosecutions undermine the perception of justice as fair and even-handed and therefore serve as the basis for defiance and contempt. The ad hoc nature of the existing tribunals is indeed a severe fault line in the aspirations towards a universally applicable system of criminal accountability. There is no answer to the complaint of those who have been called to account for their actions that others, even more culpable, were never subjected to scrutiny. Why Yugoslavia? Why Rwanda? Not that the impunity of some makes others less culpable, but it makes it less just to single them out. It therefore runs the risk of giving credence to their claim of victimization, and, even if it does not cast doubt on the legitimacy of their punishment, it taints the process that turns a blind eye to the culpability of others.

The broader the reach of the International Criminal Court, the better it will overcome the shortcomings of ad hoc justice. That is why the ratification of the Rome Treaty by 60 states should be only the beginning. A broad-based and ongoing ratification drive should deploy all efforts to ensure that its reach is truly universal.

My last point is to stress the continued urgency of establishing this indispensable institution. The willingness to submit to impartial, unbiased scrutiny is not only the hallmark of law-abiding persons and institutions; it is, in my view, a prerequisite of their moral entitlement to calling others to account. The 120 countries that signed the text of the Rome treaty recognized that we live in a world where warfare inflicts unspeakable harm to many, often in the most unexpected ways, ranging from hand combat with agricultural implements and cheap landmines to high-tech precision instruments that still sometimes fail in catastrophic ways.

Justice Robert Jackson, the United States Supreme Court judge who was one of the four prosecutors at Nuremberg before the International Military Tribunal set up by the victorious allies to try the leaders of the Nazi regime for war crimes and crimes against humanity, made a powerful and often quoted opening statement at that extraordinary trial. Referring to the unprecedented nature of the international tribunal, he said: 'That four great nations, flushed with victory and stung with injury, stay the hand of vengeance and voluntarily submit their captive enemies to the judgement of the law is one of the most significant tributes that Power has ever paid to Reason.'

This statement lays the foundation of the morally superior choice of justice over brutal revenge. it also lays very explicitly the foundation for victor's justice. The choice that faces the international community today is of the same nature but of a different order.

Justice Jackson might well have put it this way, referring to the countries who have and will ratify the Rome treaty creating the ICC: That these great nations willingly submit themselves to the judgment of the law is not only another vindication of Reason over Power, but is a most significant step towards equality, justice, and peace.

The legitimacy of the ICC cannot simply be asserted. It will have to be established, day by day, as is the case for all institutions in a democracy, under the scrutiny of the press and the public. Much has been said in Canada on the theme of the legalization, and indeed the judiciarization, of politics. There is no doubt that since the advent of the Canadian Charter of Rights and Freedoms, the courts have indeed become for many Canadians the forum of choice for the vindication of claims based essentially on an idea, or an ideal, of justice. That was certainly the situation with the early cases dealing with procedural fairness in the criminal context, and it has become even more acute in the litigation dealing with fundamental freedoms and with equality. I am not so naive as to suggest that we are on the eve of experiencing a primacy of the juridical over the political on the international scene. But I do think that legalism is the by-product of globalization of rights.

It is fair to say that in liberal democracies, not everyone views the legalization of politics as a positive development, just as the emergence of a juridical international regime of accountability for gross human rights violations is encountering everything from scepticism to outright hostility. Yet international criminal justice has become an inseparable component of the international efforts to make and to keep peace and security. Our ruling generation holds in trust the enforcement of the rules of governance. If we are to embark on wars of values, I think it is worth fighting for international justice. Authoritative, universal justice.

From Montreal to Kyoto, How We Got From Here to There—Or Not

ELIZABETH MAY*

*Elizabeth May, an environmentalist, writer and lawyer, is Executive Director of the Sierra Club of Canada, and a former vice chair of the National Round Table for the Environment and Economy.

The macro-environmental issue of climate change was first seriously addressed by the 1987 Montreal Protocol to reduce ozone depletion. The 1992 Rio Earth Summit agreed to the first global treaty on climate change. The 1997 Kyoto Protocol agreed to reducing greenhouse gas (GHG) emissions to 6 percent below 1990 levels by 2008–2012, but needs support by 55 countries responsible for 55 percent of 1990 global emissions to come into effect. When George W. Bush walked away from Kyoto in 2001, he took 25 percent of the world's 1990 GHG emissions with him. Canada's support became all the more important both as one of 55 signatories and as the producer of 2 percent of global GHG emissions. Prime Minister Chrétien told the world at the Johannesburg Summit that Canada would ratify the accord. Elizabeth May recounts Canada's journey on the road from Montreal to Kyoto, a road she has personally travelled with passion and conviction.

Since the Prime Minister's confirmation in Johannesburg of Canada's intent to ratify before year's end, the intensity of the Kyoto debate has certainly increased. It has not, unfortunately, uniformly led to a deeper public understanding. In fact, as huge amounts of money are thrown into last minute scare tactics from the anti-Kyoto forces it is harder to sort out rhetoric from reality. The most frustrating part of the propaganda campaign has been the claim that the Government of Canada is "rushing to ratify." The notion that there has been any haste in confronting the threat of climate change in Canada would be laughable if it were not so dangerous. In walking through the key milestones leading to Kyoto ratification, the pace has been leisurely.

I clearly come to this debate as no unbiased observer. I became convinced that climate change was the largest looming threat to humanity, civilization, and potentially all life on Earth, sometime during my tenure working within the Mulroney government. From 1986–88, I worked as senior policy advisor in the office of the environment minister Tom McMillan. My background in environmental issues had taken me from grassroots campaigns against pesticide spraying and nuclear energy into a policy position within the minister's staff. An issue of importance to the department's scientists, but for which there was not as yet any environmental group campaign focus, was the threat of climate change.

In dry, technical briefings the scientists from Environment Canada would review what was known, what was likely and what uncertainties remained about the impact of ever-increasing emissions of greenhouse gases, primarily from burning fossil fuels. Canada was taking a lead in the quiet discussions among scientists globally. The Government of Canada offered to host a major scientific conference, in collaboration with the United

Nations and the World Meteorological Programme. The conference, "The Changing Atmosphere: Implications for Global Security," took place in a Toronto heat wave in June 1988. The public and media impact likely made many Canadians aware of the issue for the first time. The debate at the conference was largely whether the climate changes which were already being observed in the late 1980s were attributable to human-caused (anthropogenic) forces. One of Canada's most distinguished and conservative scientists, the late Dr. Ken Hare, was the first expert to stake his reputation on the fact that climate change was already upon us.

By conference end, scientists from all over the world agreed on a consensus statement and a target for emission reductions. The statement opened, "Humanity is conducting an unintended, uncontrolled, globally pervasive experiment, whose ultimate consequences could be second only to global nuclear war." The target: global reductions of carbon dioxide emissions to 20 percent below 1988 levels to be achieved by 2005.

Within the year, the United Nations established an international scientific peer review group. The Intergovernmental Panel on Climate Change (IPCC) was created to review the emerging science and provide advice to policy makers. The IPCC was composed of scientists appointed by their governments. Their conclusions require an enormous effort at consultation, negotiation, and testing of evidence in order to report a consensus assessment of the science. One thing the IPCC is *not* is an advocacy group. It does not present the worst case scenario. The potential for nasty surprises is recognized, but the reported warnings are based on a consensus which is, by definition, conservative.

By 1990, the United Nations General Assembly set in motion the negotiations leading to the Rio Earth Summit and the first global treaty on climate change. The Toronto target became a starting point for negotiations. Canada, with then environment minister Lucien Bouchard taking the lead, set a less ambitious target: freezing emissions. Canada committed that our emissions in 2000 would be no higher than they were in 1990.

Two years later, the largest gathering of heads of government in the planet's history gathered in Rio and agreed upon the Framework Convention on Climate Change (FCCC). Due to last minute pressure tactics from then-president George Bush, the treaty was completed without any targets or deadlines. Bush threatened that if deadlines and targets were included, he would boycott the Earth Summit: "The American lifestyle is not on trial," he famously proclaimed. The FCCC was signed and ratified by virtually every nation on Earth, including Canada and the United States.

In the FCCC, the nations of the world accepted that climate change was a serious threat and that efforts should be undertaken to avoid a buildup of greenhouse gases to "dangerous" levels. It also set in motion the negotiating process to get the world to mandated targets and deadlines. This process takes place within the Conference of the Parties (COP), in which every nation which has signed and ratified participates. Mulroney was responsible for the signing and ratification of the FCCC, but it has been the Chrétien government that has negotiated through the various COPs.

There was every reason to expect faster action to reduce greenhouse gases with the election of the Chrétien Liberals. The 1993 Red Book promised to meet the Toronto target: obtaining 20 percent reductions against 1988 levels by 2005. Compared to the stabilization goal of the Mulroney government, the Chrétien Liberals, with environment critic Paul Martin playing a key role, seemed destined to overtake the Tory environmental lead.

Sadly, the last ten years have been characterized by one step forward, two steps back. While Canada continued to move internationally toward mandated reductions through a binding agreement, attempting actual emission reductions took a back burner. Largely to appease Alberta interests, the prime minister undercut his first environment minister, Sheila Copps, to buttress his Alberta-based minister of natural resources, Anne McLellan. The impact was to leave business and industry convinced that it was business as usual. Greenhouse gas emissions continued to rise. In fact, on a per capita basis, through the 1990s, Canadians became more energy wasteful, not less.

Nevertheless, Sheila Copps negotiated a mandate leading to Kyoto that established the importance of following the successful model of the Montreal Protocol to reduce ozone depleting substances. To protect the ozone layer, the international community had agreed that the most important first step was for the industrialized countries, which had caused the problem in the first place and which had the resources to innovate and develop alternatives, to take on reduction targets, while leaving developing countries to allow emissions of ozone depleting substances to rise in the short term. It had succeeded with the subsequent ozone protocols accelerating reductions in industrialized countries while bringing in the developing countries to cut back as well. The same approach was to be taken for the reduction of global greenhouse gases. What seemed non-controversial at the time has clearly had an unforeseen public relations impact.

By COP3 in Kyoto, Canada had spent five years in multi-stakeholder consultations on how we would reduce emissions. The provinces had been consulted and a target of 3 percent below 1990 levels was set for our negotiating team in Kyoto. Chrétien was in Russia when he got a call from US President Bill Clinton. Clinton reportedly asked Chrétien to help break a predicted impasse in Kyoto. The European nations wanted the protocol to mandate reductions on the order of 15 percent. Canada, the US and Japan were only prepared to move much more slowly. Clinton asked Chrétien to offer deeper cuts in order to be able to achieve success in Kyoto. Chrétien agreed, but allegedly obtained Clinton's support for some Canadian loopholes—credits for our forests (for the benefits of holding carbon out of the atmosphere) and for the export of greener technology. Chrétien's much reported "Beat the Americans" negotiating mandate to Canada's delegation was strategic collaboration with the US, not competition.

In any event, by the conclusion of Kyoto, the US had taken on a 7 percent target. Canada was committed to 6 percent reductions, but as then-environment minister Christine Stewart explained to angry provinces, the 6 percent target was really the same as the provincially agreed negotiation mandate of 3 percent. Once you counted in all the loopholes Canada had achieved with US support, the amount of reduction required would be about 3 percent below 1990 levels.

Environmental groups bemoaned the weak target. Counting credits from various loopholes, Canada was committed to a very small advance over the Mulroney stabilization target, to be delivered over ten years late. Meanwhile, the US Senate proclaimed that it opposed ratifying any agreement which left out developing countries. In a move that had all the earmarks of messages developed through focus groups, the forces of Big Carbon had found their wedge issue. They did not have to be against action on climate change—just appeal to a North American sense of fairness and selfishness. It has been virtually impossible to communicate through the media the precedent of the Montreal Protocol and all the reasons why leaving emission reduction targets to poorer countries until later had not been accidental, but a deliberate negotiating mandate since 1993.

Since Kyoto, we have experienced more of the same. Carbon dioxide emissions continue to climb. Canada has sought and obtained even more loopholes, which the government prefers to call "flexibility mechanisms." A new multi-stakeholder, federal provincial consultation process was created. To date, over $20 million has been spent on such processes, while the positions of the key antagonists remain unchanged. In an effort to mollify Ralph Klein, the federal government placed the Government of Alberta as the co-chair of the process to write our implementation plan. Issue tables met sector by sector hoping the oil industry would come to consensus with wind energy, car makers with environmentalists. The magical consensus did not emerge. In May of this year, the Alberta government quit the process and blamed the federal government for not having delivered the implementation plan. The plan had been due for over a year and a half. Alberta's role as co-chair is certainly suspect in the failure of the process to deliver.

But the money spent over the last five years was not entirely wasted. Canada now has a vast amount of information about how a wide range of emission reduction measures will impact the economy, impact on jobs, and provide cleaner air. The Assessment and Modeling Group has run economic model after economic model. Even with pessimistic assumptions built in, every region and every province of Canada experiences continued economic growth under Kyoto. The distorted threats of job losses from the anti-Kyoto crowd come from estimates of the difference in employment between economic growth of 30 percent without Kyoto and about a percentage point less with Kyoto. Even then, those future hypothetic job losses are more than offset by the 1.8 million hypothetical future job gains under Kyoto.

Of course, discussions of the last five years are entirely incomplete without including the Bush factor. In late 2000, the sixth COP in The Hague was in trouble. Canada was holding out for more loopholes. The Europeans were intransigent, and disgusted with the efforts to undermine the Protocol. The Hague COP ended in an adjournment in hopes things would go better once the session reconvened. They might have if not for the butterfly ballots and hanging chads and judges placed on the US Supreme Court by the next president, George Bush.

By mid-December 2000, it was clear the White House was going to the Republicans. Still, it was not automatically clear that Kyoto was in trouble. George W's election platform actually set more ambitious greenhouse reduction targets than Al Gore. Newly appointed head of the US Environmental Protection Agency, former New Jersey governor Christine Todd Whitman explained to international gatherings that the US would continue to work toward Kyoto. When George Bush announced to the contrary in March of 2001, it was evident he had not bothered to alert Whitman. White House press secretary Ari Fleisher is reputed to have predicted that withdrawal from Kyoto would be a one-headline, one-day media event. He also explained the White House view. The American lifestyle is based, he explained, on access to cheap and abundant energy. It involves the freedom of driving where you want when you want. "The American way of life is blessed."

Interestingly, following the Bush rejection Chrétien wasted no time in reconfirming Canada's commitment to Kyoto. In fact, when Environment Minister David Anderson was unable to attend the COP6 meeting's continuation in July 2001 in Bonn, Chrétien dispatched his deputy prime minister, Herb Gray.

Kyoto's survival hung by a thread. In order for the protocol to enter into force, it needed ratifications from 55 countries. In addition those 55 countries had to have collectively emitted 55 percent of the world's greenhouse gases in 1990. When George W. walked away, he took 25 percent of the world's 1990 greenhouse gas emissions with him. Saving Kyoto meant obtaining ratification support from at least the European Union, Japan and Russia.

With Chrétien in Genoa for the G8 Summit, Gray was in Bonn. Reportedly, the two spoke every day. Canada helped keep Japan in the protocol. And Canada won even more concessions from the European Union—as much as 40 mega-tonnes of carbon credit for forests.

By the end of the Bonn COP6 continuation, the Kyoto Protocol was saved. At least in principle, enough nations were committed to ratification to bring the treaty into force as binding international law—even without the United States.

Despite Bush's rejection of Kyoto, however, the US is doing a great deal to reduce greenhouse gases. Much of it is at the state level. California has passed a referendum mandating significant fuel economy improvements in its automobiles by 2007. The New England governors have banded together with Canada's Maritime premiers in agreeing to air quality targets that fall in line with Kyoto. Many states in the US have adopted Renewable Portfolio Standards which set a requirement for "green and renewable" energy within the state's energy supply mix. As well, technological innovation is moving faster in the US than in Canada. Due to a mix of these factors, the Pembina Institute study on Competitiveness and Kyoto found that if Canada failed to ratify Kyoto, we would become less competitive.

Eventually, the US is likely to rejoin the emissions reduction effort. The US remains an active player in global negotiations. Interestingly, at the COP8 meetings in New Delhi in October–November 2002, the US urged developing countries not to take on targets. The transparency of its hypocritical claims that it would not ratify Kyoto as long as developing countries were not mandated to cut emissions is exposed as the US argues against emissions reductions by any country. Clearly, anything is possible in US politics. Strategically, one hopes that the next big negotiation to reduce emissions takes place in Houston.

The one player in all this to not give a damn about negotiations is the atmosphere. Piling on carbon dioxide, methane and other greenhouse gases means only one thing to the atmosphere—climatic destabilization. The global average temperature continues to rise. It has seen a one degree celsius increase in the last century, with the rate of warming three times faster in Canada's Arctic. The melting of permafrost in the MacKenzie Valley basin was one of the first pieces of empirical evidence that climate change was upon us. The melting permafrost releases methane. Methane is a powerful greenhouse gas, providing a positive feedback loop, producing yet more warming. Polar bears are starving; Peary Caribou are at risk of extinction—both because of climate change. The loss of sea ice is striking. In fact, with a doubling of atmospheric concentrations of carbon dioxide, the Arctic ice cap would become a seasonal event, with open ocean at the top of the world.

Sea level rise has begun with noticeable storm surge damage on Canada's coasts. Extreme drought conditions plague Canada's prairies. Losses to severe weather events continue to mount. Floods, ice storms, forest fires and drought are all on the rise. The climate models have proven to be remarkably accurate, with observations of climate change tracking tightly with what were mere projections in the briefings I received in 1986. On current emissions trends, we could see an absolute doubling of global concentrations of carbon dioxide as soon as 2030. Meeting Kyoto targets only delays the doubling point by six years. Kyoto detractors use this as a point to criticize Kyoto and argue for inaction. In fact, this unsettling reality points only to the need to act aggressively and soon. Back to the IPCC warnings: to avoid a doubling of carbon dioxide we need 70 percent reductions.

To meet those levels of reductions we need to start now. Over the next five decades we will likely see steeper cuts with the entire global community of nations on board. A healthy transition away from our addiction to fossil fuels will likely take place. Economies will benefit from access to inexhaustible energy supplies of wind and solar, as well as from more efficient end use of the energy we generate by any means.

Perhaps, as people like Bjorn Lomborg, the self-proclaimed "Skeptical Environmentalist," suggest all this will happen by the natural action of the market. Perhaps fossil fuel exploitation will go the way of the dinosaur for purely economic reasons. There is not much evidence for that. We did not wait for the economy to solve acid rain or ozone depletion. The economy and rational economic choices kick in once the rules are clear. The Kyoto Protocol begins a long road to reduction. It starts with a fairly modest effort to monetize carbon. It is just the first step, and we should take it now.

Canada and Free Trade: 15 Years On

DANIEL SCHWANEN*

***Daniel Schwanen** is Senior Economist at the Institute for Research on Public Policy, Montreal.

January 1, 2004, marked the 15th anniversary of the implementation of the Canada–US Free Trade Agreement (FTA), which largely formed the basis of the North American Free Trade Agreement (NAFTA), including Mexico as a partner, that came into effect exactly five years later at the beginning of 1994.

Both agreements were seen as epochal and were the subject of intense scrutiny and debates in Canada (at least with respect to the FTA) and the United States and Mexico (at least with respect to NAFTA). In retrospect, they also must be put in context of the broader trend toward the increased liberalization of global merchandise trade, investment, and flows of services and peoples after the Second World War, as well as technological changes affecting transportation and communications. These trends toward more deeply interconnected world economies called for new rules, beyond simply those affecting trade in goods at the border that had been the mainstay of the rounds of negotiations on the multilateral General Agreement on Tariffs and Trade [GATT] until the 1970s. In some ways the FTA and NAFTA served as role models for the subsequent agreement on the Uruguay Round of multilateral trade negotiations.

Given that various proposals have recently surfaced to facilitate even further the exchanges between the US and Canadian economies, it may be useful to look back on what we know about how the FTA and NAFTA did or did not work and about economic integration in North America more generally, and to ask what questions remain or what lessons can be drawn as we look to the future. To that end, this article reviews some of the recent analysis and data relevant to the evaluation of how the FTA and NAFTA have affected Canada, and attempts to draw some conclusions relevant to the future of Canada's economic position in North America.

Economic integration is typically analyzed by looking at four broad types of cross-border flows: trade in goods, trade in services, investments and people. These distinctions are useful in terms of examining the breadth of North American integration across a range of activities. I summarize the evolution of these four variables between Canada and the other two NAFTA countries in Table 1. The table compares data for the years 1988 (the year before the FTA came into effect), 1993 (the year before NAFTA came into effect), and 2002. For investment, I show the accumulated stock of foreign direct investment (FDI, as distinct from portfolio investments) in Canada by NAFTA nationals, and by Canadians in other NAFTA countries. A sub-category of services transactions called "commercial" services, which excludes travel, transportation (which often reflects trends in goods trade) and government-provided services, is also shown. Commercial services include, for example, cross-border flows of royalties and licence fees, financial services, management services, and architectural, engineering and other professional services.

TABLE 1	Some Basic Statistics		
Yearly average	**1988**	**1993**	**2002**
As % GDP			
Goods exports to NAFTA	17.3	20.6	30.6
Goods imports from NAFTA	15.3	18.4	23.5
Services exports to NAFTA	1.9	2.3	3.1
(excl. travel, transport., govt.)	0.9	1.2	1.7
Services imports from NAFTA	2.6	3.6	3.7
(excl. travel, transport., govt.)	1.3	1.7	2.1
Direct investment stock to NAFTA	8.4	9.4	18.0
Direct investment stock from NAFTA	12.4	12.5	19.7
As % of transactions with all countries			
Goods exports to NAFTA	73.7	78.8	84.3
Goods imports from NAFTA	70.7	75.6	75.1
Services exports to NAFTA	60.8	58.1	61.0
(excl. travel, transport., govt.)	69.3	64.0	64.8
Services imports from NAFTA	62.7	63.2	62.6
(excl. travel, transport., govt.)	75.2	71.8	73.1
Direct investment stock to NAFTA	64.2	55.7	47.5
Direct investment stock from NAFTA	66.6	64.1	64.2
As % employment			
Temp. migrants to NAFTA		0.4	1.1
Temp. migrants from NAFTA		0.2	0.2
% US imports from Canada	18.5	19.2	18.0
(excl. imports from China, Mex.)	19.9	21.8	23.2
Labour statistics			
Unemployment rate	7.8	11.4	7.5
Employed: manufacturing as % total	16.6	13.9	15.1
Mfg. weekly earnings (all Ind. = 100)	116.0	118.1	121.9
Average for period	**1984–88**	**1989–93**	**1994–2002**
Unemployment rate	9.6	9.7	8.4
Bus. fixed capital spending as % GDP	12.0	11.2	12.0
Labour income as % nat'l income	53.0	54.5	51.7
Corp. profits as % nat'l income	10.1	6.1	10.6
% return on Canadian FDI in US	6.2	2.93	3.4
% return on US FDI in Canada	9.6	5.7	8.7

Notes: Most data are from Statistics Canada CANSIM data base, and author's calculations. Data on temporary migrants are from Papademetriou (2003); his data on entry into the US reflect admissions, and the same individual may thus be counted several times. In calculating NAFTA trade in commercial services for 1988 and 2002, the author used Mexican data from 1989 and 2001, the only ones publicly available currently. Both these figures are from Canada Department of Foreign Affairs and International Trade (2003).

These data are, in a first block of rows in the table, expressed as a share of Canada's GDP, except the data on temporary worker movement (only shown for 1993 and 2002), expressed as a share of Canada's total employment. The picture that emerges from these lines is unambiguous: all the key trade and investment cross-border flows with NAFTA countries, as well as the temporary presence of Canadians working in other NAFTA countries, have assumed a much bigger importance relative to Canada's economy since 1988.

These flows overwhelmingly represent transactions with the United States. Canada's merchandise imports from Mexico, Canadian direct investment to Mexico, and two-way flow of temporary workers between Canada and Mexico have grown markedly faster than the corresponding transactions between Canada and the United States since 1988, but they did so from a very small base, and hence they have slightly reduced but not challenged the dominance of US flows for Canada as far as intra-NAFTA relations are concerned.

These intra-NAFTA data can also be expressed relative to similar transactions between Canada and all countries, and I have done this for trade and FDI flows in a second set of rows in the table. Of note here is how much more subdued, when not in fact submerged, the just-noted increased importance of intra-NAFTA transactions becomes, when compared to the increasing flows that Canada has also experienced with the rest of the world. Note however, that 2001 and 2002 were years of exceedingly slow growth for the United States economy, and also ushered in noticeable increases in the costs of transacting business across the US border due to the fallout from the September 11, 2001 terrorist attacks. (Total Canadian goods and services trade as a share of GDP are shown in Figure 1.)

In other words, while our interdependence with NAFTA increased across all key indicators, Canada's relationships with the rest of the world in some cases grew even faster, notably with respect to flows of Canadian direct investment abroad. Furthermore, even though Canada's goods trade with its NAFTA partners rose much faster than that with the rest of the world, Canada has not actually increased its share of the total US import market during the period.

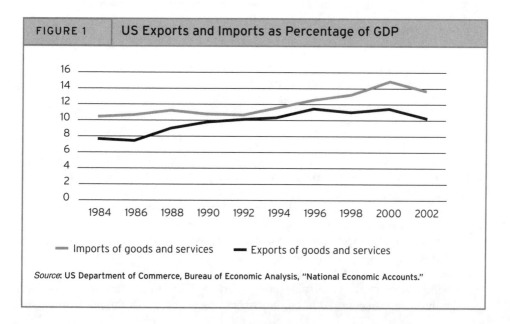

| FIGURE 1 | US Exports and Imports as Percentage of GDP |

■ Imports of goods and services   ■ Exports of goods and services

Source: US Department of Commerce, Bureau of Economic Analysis, "National Economic Accounts."

It could be tempting to conclude on that basis that North American free trade has had little overall impact, and that most of the explosion in trade is due entirely to the booming American economy for much of the period and attendant rise in US imports (Figure 2). But this would not likely be the correct conclusion. We cannot expect North American integration to proceed in isolation from other rapidly evolving global trends and events, and the broad numbers may hide significant shifts on the ground. For example, while Canada has not gained share in total United States imports, it has in fact done quite well, relative to many traditional competitors, since the FTA. If one excludes the emergence of Mexico on the US market since NAFTA (and the 1994 peso devaluation), and the huge progress that a rapidly modernizing China is making in the world's major markets (including Canada, where China has displaced Japan as the number two importer), Canadian producers have done well relative to the rest of the field (see Table 1). Indeed, early signs clearly had shown that by 1995 Canada–US trade was booming specifically in those sectors that were liberalized by the FTA, and relative to trade with other countries, suggesting a positive impact on trade flows from the trade agreement.

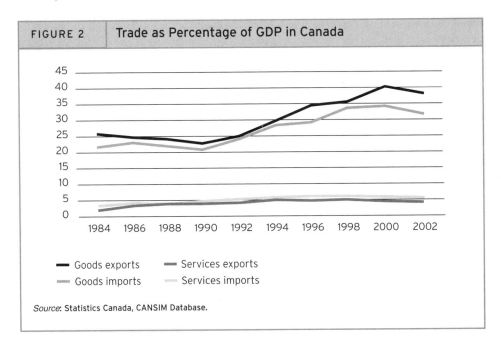

| FIGURE 2 | Trade as Percentage of GDP in Canada |

- Goods exports
- Services exports
- Goods imports
- Services imports

Source: Statistics Canada, CANSIM Database.

This is not to say that subsequent competition from Mexico or China is to be taken lightly. On the contrary, it is important both to understand who the competition is and to adjust our strategies accordingly, a point to which I will return below.

A similar observation applies with respect to FDI. China and other large and promising markets have opened themselves up to foreign investors since the FTA came into effect. It is not surprising that these new and fast growing markets exert a profound attraction on global firms, including Canadian ones, leading to a neglect (but only a relative one) of markets that in any event are already well "mined" by foreign investors, such as Canada's.

Another factor might be at play in the Canada–NAFTA investment relationship. Foreign direct investment used to be, in part, the means by which foreign firms could "jump" over a country's tariffs and access its market. With tariffs between Canada and the United States falling to zero for the vast majority of products, some of the increased cross-border trade could have substituted for products that might have otherwise had to be made locally by a subsidiary. In other words, trade reduced the need for FDI as a means of accessing markets, which would be consistent with the increasingly standard finding that investment is now in large part a complement to trade, not a substitute for it.

Having said this, there appears to have been a structural shift in Canadian investments in the United States toward services industries rather than goods production. During the first year of the FTA, in 1989, 33 percent of Canadian FDI in the United States was in services. Today, that ratio is close to 65 percent. This shift, which seems to be continuing with recent announcements of substantial Canadian acquisitions of US firms in the insurance and retail sectors, including Manulife's purchase of John Hancock, may be a sign that many Canadian services companies are pursuing, through investments, the vertical integration achieved through trade by their colleagues in manufacturing. Indeed, Statistics Canada has shown that, relative to manufacturers, Canadian service providers tend to serve their foreign clients more through majority-owned affiliates in foreign countries (Marth 2003). In part, this is because the nature of certain services makes it difficult to provide them without having a significant physical presence in the market. Having said this, the US services market remains more open to Canadian services exports than most others around the world.

Clearly, vertical integration (countries specializing in various stages of production in a wide range of products, as opposed to each country specializing in different industries) has been more intensively pursued than specialization by industry between the NAFTA partners. Indeed, a key trend there has been the increased use of imports from each other as inputs into our exports to each other. Thus, the typical Canadian export was made up of 33 percent imported goods and services in 1999, up from 26 percent in 1988, according to Statscan in 2002. This increased ratio—evident across resources, manufactured goods and commercial services exports underlines the greater sensitivity of North American production to potential border disruptions, as well as the increasingly self-defeating nature of protectionist measures between countries. A similar phenomenon has sprung up from more open trade between Mexico and the United States.

The temporary movement of people for economic reasons has also experienced a significant leap during the period. Here again, one may speculate that these temporary exchanges of talent may well be the sign of more vertically integrated economies and are often supportive of Canadian exports or Canadian investments.

Greater integration has had a positive effect on Canada's productivity performance. The importance of productivity (producing more or better goods and services with a given amount of resources) is hard to overstate as a key underpinning of wellbeing, regardless of whether one thinks that standards of living are sufficiently approximated by GDP (economic output) or not.

A number of micro-economic studies show that greater trade integration with the United States has been positive for Canada's productivity performance. They suggest, simply, that free trade fulfilled its mission by raising the productivity of Canada's manufacturing industry beyond what it would have been otherwise. A by-now classic reference is Dan Trefler's 2001 paper "The Long and Short of the Canada–US Free Trade Agreement." In the same vein, a more recent 2003 Statistics Canada study by John Baldwin and Wulong Gu concludes Canadian manufacturing plants that have increased their exposure to export markets accounted for three-quarters of manufacturing productivity growth in the 1990's, even though they accounted for less than 50 percent of manufacturing employment.

While Canada's manufacturing employment continued on its secular downward trend relative to total employment, its decline since the FTA was nothing like the decline in manufacturing employment that characterized the US economy during the same period. The establishment survey conducted by the US Bureau of Labor Statistics shows that US manufacturing employment now stands at less than 12 percent of total US employment, compared to 17 percent in 1988. Canada appears, relatively, like a manufacturing powerhouse, with average weekly earnings in manufacturing (including overtime) rising by five percent in Canada since the free trade agreement, relative to earnings in other sectors of the economy. Furthermore, the structure of Canada's goods exports under the FTA has shifted markedly away from the traditional resource base, and toward non-resource exports, now accounting for some 55 percent of all exports, and no longer absolutely dominated by automobiles (see Figure 3).

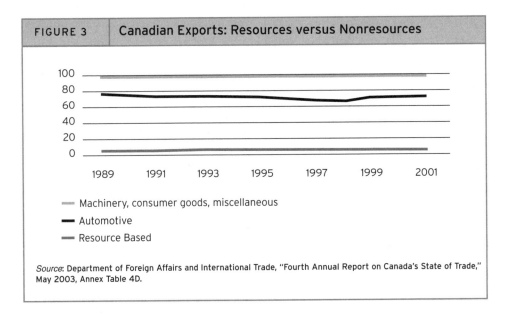

| FIGURE 3 | Canadian Exports: Resources versus Nonresources |

— Machinery, consumer goods, miscellaneous
— Automotive
— Resource Based

Source: Department of Foreign Affairs and International Trade, "Fourth Annual Report on Canada's State of Trade," May 2003, Annex Table 4D.

To be sure, there are serious clouds on the horizon. As useful as free trade has been in helping Canada shed its image of hewer of wood and drawer of water, there are dangers in the position that Canada finds itself in. It is clear that the low Canadian dollar during much of the period has also been a very significant factor in sustaining the Canadian manufacturing success. The recent rise in the Canadian dollar is now testing the basis of this success. And in a way this will be a good thing, for as Mexico is finding out, low costs are not a sustainable basis for competitiveness in the face of emerging economies. If Canada is to sustain its penetration of the US market, it will have to be on the basis of innovative products and superior quality.

Having said this, as is widely known, and in spite of the boost provided by free trade, Canada's overall productivity performance did not keep pace with that of the United States. OECD statistics show that labour productivity in the business sector increased by

26.5 percent in the United States since 1988, or 1.7 percent per year, compared with 20.3 percent or 1.3 percent per year in Canada. This result runs explicitly against the hope that, thanks to free trade, Canada's productivity could catch up to that of the United States.

What went amiss on that score, then? Recent studies point to two possible explanations: a rise in self-employment, and a lack of innovation. Rather than reaping huge economies of scale from free trade as some had predicted, Canada's productivity initially increased through the shedding of workers in non-competitive firms, according to a 2003 Statscan analysis. To be sure, workers remaining in industries that modernized in the face of foreign competition, and the myriad consumers benefiting from lower prices and greater choice, were "winners" from free trade. But, as the table shows, this was also a period of high unemployment due not only to those initial losses to liberalized imports, but to other factors that made it hard for employment to gain traction at the time, such as the punishingly high level of the Canadian dollar at the beginning of the 1990s, undermining export efforts in the short run, and the beginning of serious fiscal retrenchment in the public sector.

This period coincided with an extraordinary mushrooming of self-employment, with the self-employed not having the level of productivity as those remaining in the incorporated business sector. This factor alone can account for most of the productivity differential between Canada and the United States, according to a Statscan analysis.

Another, possibly complementary explanation focuses on innovation. Kais Dachraoui and Terek Harchaoui in another 2003 Statscan analysis found that while there was a revival of Canadian productivity after 1992 relative to US levels, this revival was due to the progressive adoption of best-practice existing technology in Canada, presumably in the face of greater international competition. However, while Canada was copying best practices, the United States was able to keep its lead by pushing the innovative frontiers in new industries.

While many of the studies of the impact of free trade just mentioned have focused on manufacturing wages and employment, there is no doubt that services were also profoundly affected. This was not necessarily due to any liberalization that was contained in the FTA or NAFTA, since many trade and investment restrictions remained in the service industries under these two agreements. Rather, the need to serve customers who were themselves coming under greater competitive pressure provided the backdrop for changes in the Canadian services sectors. CN is the prime example of this, having reoriented its entire rail and service infrastructure from being geared to east-west trade to being able to serve north-south trade. While CN did shed workers in the process, there is evidence that free trade favoured employment and earnings of workers in trade-related services industries—those services most linked to both export and import activities.

This exploration of the impacts of the FTA on the nature of North American integration and on Canada's economy, while short and inherently incomplete, raises a number of questions moving forward.

Thanks to more open trade, Canada has improved and in many cases realized its potential to become a more productive economy overall than would otherwise have been the case. Thanks in part to the low Canadian dollar relative to its US counterpart, it has certainly been competitive in NAFTA. But, as I have sketched out, the world is moving rapidly and simply holding the line on competitiveness is not sufficient.

Mexico provides a sobering object lesson in this respect. Quite apart from the difficulties that had been predicted and that have sadly come true with respect to Mexico's newly liberalized agricultural sector, with attendant social and migration and environmental problems, the Mexican economy faces formidable emerging competitors. Yet Mexico has not fully taken advantage of the opportunities afforded by NAFTA to transform itself into a dynamic economy that could, among other things, provide better employment for displaced agricultural workers. The main lesson there is the role that domestic policies do or do not play in ensuring that economies can properly compete under conditions of more open transactions with the rest of the world. In the Mexican case, an energy sector struggling for capital under state ownership, and a poor tax structure and tax collection that in turn starve the public sector of much needed funds for infrastructure and education, seem to be key culprits.

The point made above concerning the productivity travails of the Canadian economy under free trade also suggest some lack of flexibility and innovation domestically, preventing the capture of potential benefits from the larger market. It is remarkable that innovation has been such a buzzword of public policy for so long, and that governments at all levels have produced countless studies and strategies aimed at improving Canada's innovation performance, and that we still find ourselves with a major shortcoming on that score. Yet there are strong reasons to think that the larger and richer the markets in which we operate, the greater the returns to innovation and, conversely, the lower the relative incomes of those who do not have the skill or talent to innovate. In that light, every policy area and major public investment, from health care to cultural policies to the subsidies being sought by the automobile industry, should be reviewed to ensure that it does not stifle or discourage innovation. Similarly the case is strong that some elements of Canada's tax mix are out of synch with building a more innovative and productive economy in the context of open trade, notably our relatively strong reliance on income-based rather than consumption-based taxes (note that this is not necessarily a question of the overall tax levels needed to fund public services).

The emphasis I have just put on bringing domestic policies more in synch with the more open economy does not mean that we should not address the many flaws and unfinished business of existing trade agreements. But it is important to take the time to do this right, because the experience of the FTA and NAFTA also shows that partial liberalization has a cost, and indeed can corner participants into clearly sub-optimal situations. For example, the incomplete liberalization of transportation services is a major element preventing the full realization of the benefits of trade in goods, as noted by Mary Brooks in her 2003 paper, "Mapping the New North America." This is just one illustration of the fact that it makes less and less sense to discuss strictly goods trade liberalization (for example, under a customs union), without also considering how we can improve the cross-border relationship more generally (for example, concerning dispute avoidance and settlement) or address complementary flows of services, investments and peoples.

Thus, while NAFTA remains a major asset in Canada's economic arsenal, the lessons from our own experience and elsewhere is that the world keeps moving, and that continued adaptability, as well as taking greater account of the complementarity of policies in various areas, is the name of the game.

SECTION 6 TERMINOLOGY

Arms Control

Civil Society

COP (Conference of the Parties)

Dayton Peace Accord

Democracy

Development Assistance

Disarmament

EU (European Union)

FCCC (Framework Convention on Climate Change)

FDI (Foreign Direct Investment)

FTA (Free Trade Agreement)

G8

GATT (General Agreement on Tariffs and Trade)

GDP (Gross Domestic Product)

GHG (Greenhouse Gas)

Globalization

Guerrilla Warfare

Human Security

Humanitarian Intervention

ICC (International Criminal Court)

ICTY (International Criminal Tribunal for the former Yugoslavia)

IFOR (Implementation Force)

Interdependence

International Law

International Organizations

Internationalism

IPCC (Intergovernmental Panel on Climate Change)

Kyoto Protocol

Middle Power

Mutual Assured Destruction

NAFTA (North American Free Trade Agreement)

National Security

NATO (North Atlantic Treaty Organization)

NGO (Non-Governmental Organization)

OECD (Organization for Economic Cooperation and Development)

OSCE (Organization for Security and Cooperation in Europe)

Ottawa Process

Ottawa Treaty

Paradigm

Quad

Security Council

SFOR (Stabilization Force in Bosnia and Herzegovina)

Sovereignty

Terrorism

UN (United Nations)

UNPROFOR (United Nations Protection Force)

SECTION 6 DISCUSSION QUESTIONS

1. Is it fair to speak of our world as a global village? Is the world more separated or more united than it used to be?

2. How is globalization causing both "connection" and "division"? What are the implications for growing nationalism?

3. Environmentalism is a relatively new ideology. Is it a fad, or does it have long-lasting potential?

4. Is Canada's effectiveness as an international actor weakened by its close relationship with the United States?

5. Can we reconcile humanitarian intervention with the principle of national sovereignty?

POLISCI SUPERSITE

Pearson Education Canada's PoliSci Supersite (**www.pearsoned.ca/polisci**) contains
a set of text-specific pages for *Ideas, Interests, and Issues*. Visit the Supersite to access
a list of relevant weblinks and interesting additional readings tailored to the content of
each section.

Section 7

Issues in Politics

SECTION SUMMARY

Creating categories for our studies is a useful way to organize our thoughts and our ideas. But sometimes our categories can't be cleanly divided, or there may be topics that don't fit neatly into our groupings. This final section of the book contains six readings that could be placed in several different sections, but none of them wholly belong in any of them. These are selected issues in politics that deserve our attention, and cause us to think about other themes that other readings in the book have brought up.

Politics is an inevitable part of our lives, and therefore the innumerable activities that take place in society have political characteristics. In this section of the book we have assembled some readings that apply some of the concepts, issues, and approaches that we have dealt with earlier.

The Right Honourable Beverley McLachlin is Chief Justice of the Supreme Court of Canada. In "The Civilization of Difference," McLachlin addresses identity and conflict in the world. She suggests that despite the seemingly insurmountable obstacles placed before us, there is more that binds humans together than separates them. Canada, she feels, offers a good example of how nations might better achieve peace among communities through what she terms "accommodation."

Gerard Boychuk takes on the myth of unsustainable health care in Canada in "The Illusion of Financial Unsustainability of Canadian Health Care." Contrary to the common and popular view that Canada's health care is in crisis, Boychuk shows that health care expenditure is more at risk from flawed federal–provincial relations than from a lack of money or services. In "Report to the Shareholders," Maurice Strong tackles a different scenario: the potential effects of continued environmental degradation. In his futuristic essay, Strong imagines the domino effect of related problems that could be connected back to the way we treat our environment today. While his picture of impending events may be implausible, Strong challenges us to consider the inter-relationship of politics, economics, resources, environmental damage, and spirituality. He suggests that the world as we know it is already experiencing a shifting balance, and that inaction could bring about the kind of doomsday setting he describes.

Quebec identity, Claude Couture and Nathalie Kermoal feel, has been too often portrayed in simplistic terms. They argue in "The Multiple Affiliations of Quebec" that there are many affiliations in Quebec society, creating a unique balance between "Quebec" and "Canada" in that province. They use competing approaches to show the complexity of affiliations felt by Quebecers. In the next reading in this section, Kent Roach describe the outcome of the terrorist attacks on 11 September 2001 in the Canadian context. Roach contextualizes 9/11, moving from the immediate effects of the attacks, to the feelings expressed by Canadians, to the consequences for Canada's relations with the United States and the world. Finally, Darren O'Byrne discusses one of the most challenging concerns in modern politics: human rights. There are no universal ideas of human rights, he points out, but that shouldn't stop us from trying to understand why different societies see fit to interpret so differently a topic that for many of us seems so simple. O'Byrne shows us that, like so many issues in politics, there is no simple answer.

The Civilization of Difference

THE RIGHT HONOURABLE BEVERLEY MCLACHLIN, P.C.*

*__Beverley McLachlin__ is Chief Justice of the Supreme Court of Canada.

One problem, more than any other, dominates human history—the problem of how we deal with those who are different than us. Human beings share a vast catalogue of commonalities. Our genetic differences are negligible; women and men are equally creative and capable; those we label as ill or old or disabled are no less virtuous, deserving, or capable of contribution than others; and people from all cultures and societies share similar aspirations to be safe, to be loved, and to feel fulfilled. In sum, the similarities that unite human beings by far overshadow their differences.

Why is it then that our differences dominate discourse on every level—political, legal, social and domestic? Our headlines tell the story. East against west in the cold war. Serb against Croat in the Balkans. Hutus against Tutsis in Rwanda–Burundi. Barely do these crises subside than a new schism seizes the front pages—fundamentalist Islam versus the western world. On the legal, social and domestic front we debate our differences with passion—the right of women to equal pay, the legitimacy of same-sex families, the place of religion in public life.

Tonight I propose to explore with you this issue. Why does difference dominate? How can we better manage difference? Canada, like other countries, has struggled with these questions. Sometimes we have answered them with exclusion and violence. Yet even in our beginnings we find another response—the response of respect, inclusion, and accommodation. Accommodation, in this context, means more than grudging concessions. Accommodation, in the strong sense in which I wish to use it, means ending exclusion, encouraging and nourishing the identity of the other, and celebrating the gifts of difference. It is this response that has come to characterize the modern Canada, shaping our thinking and our policy on women, First Nations people and the profusion of races and cultures that constitute Canada in the 21st century.

I will return to the Canadian experience. But first, let me take a few moments to explore the underlying dynamic of difference.

THE DYNAMIC OF DIFFERENCE

Why, despite our manifest commonality, do our differences, real and perceived, tend to define our world and dominate our discourse and our conduct? Philosophers have long debated the phenomenon. Jean-Paul Sartre wrote of the "other" as the concept by which we define ourselves. In his book on identity and language, *Oneself as Another*, Paul Ricoeur wrote of the "work of otherness at the heart of selfhood".[1] Michael Ignatieff has written movingly of "The Stranger in our Midst" in his book *The Needs of Strangers*, tracing the

---

[1] P. Ricoeur, *Oneself as Another*, trans. K. Blamey (Chicago: University of Chicago Press, 1992) at 318.

dialectic of difference and need in history and literature. Despite their varying contexts and perspectives, all agree on the essential role of difference in human experience.

An answer to the question of why we place so much emphasis on our differences lies in the inescapable human need to construct one's identity within a social context. For all the celebrated individualism of recent decades, human beings are social beings. "A person only becomes a person through other people," proclaims the African aphorism. To be human is to communicate, speak, and relate to other human beings. As Charles Taylor reminds us, group living is a prerequisite to full human agency. Yet in this intercourse with others, we are confronted by difference; and in the face of this difference we are impelled to a sense of what distinguishes us as physically, historically, and culturally unique. Indeed, we need this sense of identity to make sense of our worlds. Yet identity does not remain purely personal; identity itself becomes social. As we discover our distinguishing attributes—those elements in ourselves, our history, and our culture that we value—we bind ourselves to others who share these attributes and values. In the process, each person becomes a constellation of group identities—race, ethnicity, language, gender, religion and a host of other affiliations.

Group identity is a good thing. It binds us to a horizon formed by a common history and shared memory in which we can orient ourselves and give meaning to our lives. It tells us who we are and reassures us that we are worthy. And it grounds our cultures—the aggregations of norms, achievements, and institutions that are peculiar to a people. So long as group identity focuses on shared values, it is enriching and constructive.

But group identity can also be a bad thing. The obverse of commonality is difference. To say I am part of a group is also to say that I am *not* part of a *different* group. From here it is but a short step to seeing the different group as less worthy than the group to which we belong. What we see in the other but not in ourselves may seem strange and abject. The celebration of the attributes of one group quickly slips into the denial of the attributes of others; the affirmation of one group's identity into the undermining of another group's identity. The positive "We are good", becomes the superlative "We are best", with its implication that those different from us are less worthy and less entitled to the full measure of human dignity and respect. Differences are magnified, even imagined, to serve the end of vaunting the merits of the dominant group. In its ultimate manifestation, this distortion of the group ethic results in the dehumanization of those perceived as different. They are no longer perceived as human beings, but as some lesser species whose rights may be denied with impunity.

The negative aspects of group identity tend to be self-reinforcing. Treating others as less worthy or able makes us feel stronger, more righteous, more powerful. We are doubly affirmed, first by our kinship with other members of our "superior" group, second by the presumed deficiencies of those outside the group. Treating those whom we perceive as different or whom we do not understand with dignity and respect is much more difficult.

The force of this dynamic of difference should not be denied, but faced full on in its historical reality. As John Ralston Saul stated in his 2000 Lafontaine-Baldwin Lecture, "the past is not the past. It is the context. The past—memory—is one of the most powerful, practical tools available to a civilized democracy".[2] The history of human beings is the

---

[2]   J.R. Saul, A. Dubuc, G. Erasmus, *The Lafontaine-Baldwin Lectures: A Dialogue on Democracy in Canada*, vol. 1, ed. by R. Griffiths (Toronto: Penguin, 2002) at 3.

history of oppression based on real and imagined difference. The Athenians invented democracy, but women and slaves were not recognized as part of the polis. The Romans treated the peoples they conquered as slaves. Medieval Christians crusaded against the Infidel. Societies from Russia to India relegated ordinary folk to the sub-human rank of serf or "untouchable", denying them the most basic rights and opportunities. And in an atrocious distortion of group identity, the twentieth century witnessed the calculated dehumanization and destruction of Jews, gypsies and the mentally and physically disabled. We ignore this history at our peril.

This past is not our past; it is ever-present. Modern society condemns slavery, yet still women and children suffer its ravages. The world community decries discrimination, yet people are still treated as less worthy because of their race, ethnicity, gender, religion or disability. In Canada, we vaunt our multi-cultural society, yet still racism, anti-Semitism and religious intolerance lurk in our dark corners. The modern world holds out the promise of inclusion, but delivers the reality of exclusion; the exclusion of refugees driven from their homes; the exclusion of women and minorities from mainstream institutions; even the more mundane exclusion of the schoolyard bully. We proclaim the right of every human being to life, yet so long as the memory of the events of September 11, 2001 remains we cannot deny that the stark goal of eliminating those seen as different dominates the agendas of many.

The imperative seems clear. President Wilson's observation that "nothing . . . is more likely to disturb the peace of the world than the treatment which might . . . be meted out to minorities" is as true today as it was in 1920.[3] If we are not to perpetuate the tragedies of the past we must tame the dark side of difference. But how? Two solutions emerge.

The first solution looks at world history, deduces that human beings cannot be relied upon to treat those different from them with decency and dignity, and concludes that the only solution is to separate groups within autonomous nation states. Michael Ignatieff, in *The Needs of Strangers*, argues that ethnic groups "cannot depend on the uncertain and fitful protection of a world conscience defending them as examples of the universal abstraction Man",[4] and therefore must be secured "their own place to be". The reorganization of Europe along ethnic lines and the creation of Israel reflect this thinking. And it is not without its virtues. As Georges Erasmus explained in his 2002 Lafontaine-Baldwin Lecture, self-rule confers a measure of respect and cultivates self-reliance and dignity. The sense of security gained from community self-determination is particularly important in cases where the countries of the world have been historically unable or unwilling to tend to the needs of given minority groups.

Yet for all of its attractions, the solution of finding an ethnic home for each of the peoples of the world does not offer the complete answer. First, in a world where most nation-states contain ethnic minorities and global movement of peoples is the norm, the ethnically defined nation state is difficult to maintain. Second, even if one could achieve and maintain the ethnically defined nation-state, this would not prevent the confrontations between groups of states and ethnic blocks that dominate recent history. Third, the ethnic nation

---

[3]   Plenary Session, 31 May 1920: HWV Temperley, *A History of the Peace Conference of Paris*, vol 5 (London/New York: Oxford University Press, 1969).

[4]   M. Ignatieff, *The Needs of Strangers* (London: Penguin, 1984) at 53.

state solution only addresses part of the problem—the political part. It leaves untouched and even threatens to conceal other forms of discrimination and exclusion within the nation-state because it says nothing about respect or the essential value of human beings. Finally, as Alain Dubuc warned in his 2001 Lafontaine-Baldwin Lecture, nationalism, "if it is exalted, can easily become a tool of exclusion rather than a window on the world".[5] We should not abandon the idea of the nation-state as one means of attending to the struggles of a pluralistic democracy; to quote John Ralston Saul in his 2000 Lecture, "[d]emocracy was and is entirely constructed inside the structure of the Western nation state".[6] Yet if the goal is to address the negative potential of group identity, the nation-state solution simply cannot go the whole distance.

This brings us to the second way of addressing the negative aspects of difference—promoting mutual respect and accommodation within the nation state. This approach rests on a single proposition—the intrinsic worth of every human being. In historical perspective, the idea is revolutionary. Throughout human history, the powerful and privileged have always treated those they view as different as less worthy. When historians look back on the last half of the 20th century and the beginning of the 21st, they will describe the idea that all people are equally worthy as one of the seminal ideas of our time.

Yet the ethic of respect and accommodation possesses venerable roots. One hears its echo in the declarations of western religion that all humans are created "in the image and likeness of God". The European Enlightenment contributed to the secular conception of fundamental human worth by celebrating the universality of reason, and Immanuel Kant urged that we treat humans as ends and never only as means. The Romantic movement furnished a robust notion of authenticity, premised on the idea that each person held a unique and intrinsically valuable potential that would be unlocked through genuine expression in life. These and other streams of thought converged and were filtered through the horrors of the first half of the 20th century.

The result was a coalesced notion of the intrinsic worth of all humans and a palpable sense that social and political recognition of this idea was critical. John P. Humphrey, one of Canada's great contributors to the project of recognizing human rights, reflected this historical truth when he stated that, although human rights did not figure on the international stage prior in time, "[b]y 1945 . . . the historical context had changed, and references to human rights run through the United Nations Charter like a golden thread".[7] We can now look back to the ultimate product of the work of Humphrey and others, the *Universal Declaration of Human Rights*, and find the clarion assertion that "recognition of the inherent dignity and of the equal and inalienable rights of all members of the human family is the foundation of freedom, justice and peace in the world."

The new idea of the equal worth of every person finds expression in the legal language of rights—human rights. If all people are equal, it follows that all people are equally entitled to freedom, fair treatment, and respect. The rights are easily stated. The more difficult problem is to move them off the sterile page and into the reality of people's lives.

---

[5]   *Lafontaine-Baldwin Lectures*, *supra*, at 59.

[6]   *Ibid.*, at 24.

[7]   J.T.P. Humphrey, *Human Rights & The United Nations: A Great Adventure* (Dobbs Ferry, NY: Transnational Publishers, 1984) at 12.

Formal declarations of equality are not enough to remove discrimination and exclusion. Indeed, they may perpetuate them. Formal equality is the equality of "separate but equal". The group is hived off, labeled "different", and told that they are equal with one important qualification—equal within their designated sphere. Cloaked by the façade of formal equality, group difference perpetuates denial. Examples are not hard to find. Formal equality allowed African Americans to live in forced segregation for decades. In the eyes of many, it still justifies treating women as different. You are equally worthy, these groups are told. It is just that you are different. Understanding and accommodating difference is essential to true equality. But when differences are manufactured, exaggerated or irrelevant, the result is to perpetuate inequality. True equality requires an honest appraisal of actual similarities and differences—an understanding of the context in which human devaluation occurs. To make equal worth a reality we need more than what Michael Ignatieff calls "rights talk". We need to look beyond the words to the reality, or context of the individual and group, to understand the other in his or her full humanity. This requires an open and honest mind, a willingness to bridge the gap between groups with empathy. Only when we look at the member of a different group in this way are we able to give effect to the promise of equal worth and dignity.

Understood in this way, rights, like the nation-state, create a protected space for difference within society; a space within which communities of cultural belonging can form and flourish under the broad canopy of civil society. This applies to the traditional "individual" rights which enable individuals to form and maintain the groups that constitute civil society, to adapt these groups to changing circumstances, and to promote their views and interests to the wider population. Will Kymlicka states: "It is impossible to overstate the importance of freedom of association, religion, speech, mobility, and political organization for protecting group difference."[8] But a second kind of rights—group rights—are also important. These are rights that inhere in an individual not qua individual, but by reason of the groups to which he belongs, like protections for minority language and religion. "[W]ere it not for these group-differentiated rights, the members of minority cultures would not have the same ability to live and work in their own language and culture that the members of majority cultures take for granted".[9] Together, individual and group rights contribute to an ethic of respect for difference and meaningful inclusion of multiple "others" in a diverse society.

Rights that acknowledge people as members of groups do not lead to a fragmented state. True, they are important to the communities they protect. But they also help us reach across the borders between groups and to establish a civic community embracing sometimes profoundly different groups. The language of rights can serve as a common language of understanding. As Harvard Law Professor Martha Minow puts it, "[r]ights provide a language that depends upon and expresses human interconnection at the very moment when individuals ask others to recognize their separate interests".[10]

We must confront the dark side of human difference. We must recognize the price the marginalization of the other in our midst exacts—a price we pay in the coin of war, suffering

---

[8]   W. Kymlicka, *Multicultural Citizenship* (Oxford: Oxford University Press, 1995) at 26.

[9]   *Ibid.*, at 126.

[10]   M. Minow, *Making All the Difference* (Ithaca: Cornell University Press, 1990) at 296.

and unrealized human potential. We must provide refuges for our minorities—the physical refuge of the protective nation state and the conceptual refuge of respect and accommodation embodied in the principle that all people, regardless of the group to which they are born or assigned, are equally worthy and equally deserving of respect. Only thus can we combat the discrimination and exclusion that have marred so much of human history.

THE CANADIAN EXPERIENCE

With this backdrop in mind, I now wish to turn to Canada's experience with the dynamic of difference and what it means for us as Canadians as we enter the 21st century. Formed as it was from powerful groups with different linguistic, religious and cultural attributes, Canada, from its earliest days, recognized the need to practice the habits of respect and tolerance and to enshrine them in the law through the language of rights. In order to form a nation, Canadians had to come to terms with difference by learning to respect other cultural and linguistic groups and by expressing a commitment to this respect through the provision of rights. Yet Canada was born in an era of ethno-nationalism, religious and linguistic intolerance, racism and gender inequality. These aspects of our past manifested as exclusionary, assimilationist, and discriminatory practices at various periods of our country's life. We must also look at these dark points in our past and be humbled by their existence. So a close examination of Canada's past can disclose both a strong foundation in the ethic of tolerance and inclusion, as well as the dark side of group belonging in the form of intolerant treatment. I want to explore both of these aspects of our heritage, in the hopes of ultimately demonstrating that, as Canada has matured and grown as a nation, we have embraced and cultivated the first of these traditions in order to do a better job of confronting the second—we have learned to value and institutionalize the ethic of respect for difference as a means of combating exclusionary thinking.

Canada is one of the few countries in the world which has from its beginning dealt with the issue of minorities and sub-groups by the two-pronged mechanism of the nation-state and respect and tolerance of minorities within the nation-state. Most of the world's countries grew up around and continue to adhere to the model of the ethnic nation-state, often in the face of diverse ethnic groups within their borders. European nations like Germany and France still cling—with increasing difficulty to be sure—to the ideal of ethnic nationalism.

Canada's history is quite different. Other countries are only now awaking to the critical issue of dealing with the other in their midst. Canada, by contrast, was forced to come to terms with this reality from its very inception. The peace accords that ended the century-long wars between England and France in the late 18th century, left England in possession of France's former colonies in America. Two of the most important—Quebec and the Maritimes—lay within the territory of the future Canada. People in these lands spoke a different language and adhered to a different religion than their new rulers. England dealt with these two distinctive colonies in different ways.

The first epitomized the ethnic-exclusionary approach to dealing with minorities. England required the Maritime Francophones, the Acadians, to conform, at least to the extent of swearing oaths of allegiance to the British Crown. The failure to conform, perceived or real, led to the deportation of the Acadians to what is now the United States and to far-flung points of Europe. Many eventually found their way back, but only after the separations and sufferings that inevitably follow such dispersion. The treatment of the Acadians remains a paradigmatic illustration of an exclusionary nation-state policy.

The Lower Canadian French population, on the other hand, was too large and too firmly implanted to be uprooted and disposed of in this way. England had little appetite for a conflict with its colonists in Quebec. And so, in the end, to truncate a long and complex story full of historical intricacies, it acceded to the demands of Governor Carleton (who camped three years in London insisting on his position) that the French-speaking people of Quebec be allowed to retain their language, religion and civil law tradition. Although motivated largely by pragmatic considerations, the product was a commitment to accommodation, embodied in the Quebec Act of 1774—respect and tolerance, implemented through the mechanism of rights. Half a century later, discontent with colonial strictures led to democratic movements and rebellion in both Upper and Lower Canada. Lord Durham was sent out from England to find solutions. Lord Durham's Report of 1840 turned its back on Canada's history of accommodation and tolerance and recommended return to an assimilationist policy that gave prime place to England and English traditions. But, under the leadership of Lafontaine and Baldwin, the colonials rejected Lord Durham's vision of the assimilated unitary nation-state. The former colonies of Upper and Lower Canada, Nova Scotia and New Brunswick that met in 1866 and 1867 to create the country of Canada had learned a critical lesson: the only way the new country could succeed was on the basis of a constitution that guaranteed mutual respect and tolerance. And so Canada was born, not of nationalism, but of the pragmatic necessity to accept difference.

This beginning created the space in which the colonies, soon to be joined by the colonies of British Columbia and Vancouver Island, Prince Edward Island, the prairie territories, and later Newfoundland and Labrador, could come together and grow. Confederation and the constitutional guarantee of rights provided a mechanism through which the dialogue of accommodation could be pursued—a dialogue that is still being pursued today on all manner of subjects, from government provision of medical care and federal-provincial views on the environment to the rights of sexual minorities and Aboriginal land claims.

One of the most discussed issues regarding group difference in Canada has been the provision of guarantees for minority language rights. Language, as much as any other feature, marks the minority as different than the majority since language forms the basis of communication. Human beings seem instinctively to view those who do not speak their own language as outside their cultural group. It is thus no surprise that despite the reality that many countries are multi-lingual, a single common language continues to be seen by many as the essential glue without which a nation will fall apart. Thus the distinguished American historian Arthur Schlesinger Jr. in *The Disuniting of America* argues that it would be folly for the United States to permit Spanish to achieve any sort of official status. Schlesinger argues that "[i]nstitutionalized bilingualism shuts doors. It nourishes self-ghettoization, and ghettoization nourishes racial antagonism . . . Using some language other than English dooms people to second-class citizenship in American society".[11]

In fact, however, the Canadian experience with bilingualism can be argued to support the opposite conclusion—that in states facing the reality of widely entrenched linguistic difference, recognition of the right to use minority languages furthers national unity.

---

[11]   A. Schlesinger, *The Disuniting of America: Reflections on a Multicultural Society* (New York and London: W.W. Norton & Co., 1998) at 113.

Canada's minority language and religion guarantees continue to serve their intended purpose—the purpose of providing security to minority citizens that the majority will respect their identities. Minority linguistic rights serve as a bulwark against fear of marginalization, allowing them to participate as equal citizens secure in the knowledge that they will not be excluded because of their linguistic identity. The economic cost of bilingual services is far outweighed by the benefits of inclusion. As Chief Justice Dickson stated for the Supreme Court of Canada in 1990, "any broad guarantee of language rights . . . cannot be separated from a concern for the culture associated with the language. Language is more than a mere means of communication, it is part and parcel of the identity and culture of the people speaking it. It is the means by which individuals understand themselves and the world around them".[12] To draw linguistic interests into the protective embrace of the state is, therefore, a means of expressing society's commitment to the integrity of cultures and respect for the dignity of individuals.

Canada's foundation in the ethic of respect and tolerance provided space for citizens of two diverse cultures to work out their political, linguistic and religious differences in a climate of mutual accommodation. It did not, however, mean that the old exclusionary way of thinking did not persist. Sadly, against the backdrop of our remarkable history of accommodation and respect, Canada's first century was marred by the ethic of the assimilation and exclusion of peoples it slotted into special groups—its first inhabitants, the Aboriginal Peoples; immigrants of so-called "different" races—that is, neither French nor English; and the 52% or so of the population who were women.

Our country's policy toward the ancestral inhabitants of Canada's lands, the Aboriginal Peoples, has throughout its history veered between exclusion and assimilation on the one hand and respectful acceptance on the other. Prior to Confederation, Aboriginal groups were more often than not treated as autonomous nations. Indeed, the Huron and Mohawk nations played important opposing roles in the Franco–British wars on what was to become Canadian Territory. But in the 19th Century, as settlement progressed, exclusion, confinement and assimilation came to dominate Canadian policy. The results, most now agree, were at best a failure, at worst tragic. Only in recent decades have First Nations people begun to reclaim their group identity and their rightful place in our country.

The 1996 report of the Royal Commission on Aboriginal Peoples laid bare for Canadians a history which can without exaggeration be characterized as institutionalized discrimination. The Royal Proclamation of 1763 recognized the entitlement of Aboriginal Peoples to their lands and stipulated that these must not be taken from them unless they consented by agreement with the Crown. Translated into the Realpolitik of the 19th Century, this meant the Treaty system, whereby the Indians, as they were called, gave up right to their larger territories in return for a small parcel of reserved land—the reservation—and minor gifts. In British Columbia, treaties were not entered into; First Nations people were simply allotted parcels upon which to live.

The second-class status of Aboriginal Peoples was clear. In 1857 Upper Canada passed the *Act to Encourage the Gradual Civilization of the Indian Tribes in this Province*, which provided for the enfranchisement of Indians of "good character" who would, thereafter, be declared to be "non-Indian." The theory was clear. Aboriginal Peoples were regarded as

---

[12]   *Mahe v. Alberta*, [1990] 1 S.C.R. 342, at para. 32.

"uncivilized savages". The only solution was to change them to "non-Indians", or in words of Prime Minister John A. Macdonald to "do away with the tribal system, and assimilate the Indian people in all respects with the inhabitants of the Dominion." Following passage of the first *Indian Act* in 1876, native cultural institutions and spiritual practices came under attack. On the west coast, the potlatch ceremony was prohibited. On the plains, the police were called in to break up the sun dance, a ceremony thick with cultural significance for the Aboriginal Peoples of the prairies.

In illogical locked step, assimilationist policies were paired with exclusionary practices in the pervasive reserve system. The very peoples the leaders were proclaiming should be assimilated found themselves virtual prisoners on their reservations with the Department of Indian Affairs' adoption of the pass system in 1885. The residential school system, established first in 1849 in Alderville, Ontario, and subsequently expanded, likewise combined exclusionary and assimilationist impulses, with the often tragic consequences that are only now coming fully to light. Policies were no better in the early part of the 20th century. The assimilation-exclusion model persisted. On the exclusionary side, Canadian Aboriginals were not permitted to vote until the 1950s and 60s, unless they renounced their aboriginal status. On the assimilation side, Duncan Campbell Scott, Deputy Superintendent of Indian Affairs, stated in 1920 that government policy was "to continue until there is not a single Indian in Canada that has not been absorbed into the body politic and there is no Indian question and no Indian department."

The simultaneous pursuit of exclusion and assimilation produced cultural displacement, marginalization, and tragic loss of identity and self-esteem. The policy of exclusion cut Aboriginal Peoples off from opportunities available to the rest of the country. At the same time, the policy of assimilation undermined their identity as members of a group—their shared history, language and culture. The good aspects of the group dynamic—a solid identity rooted in one's history and culture—were weakened; the negative aspects—isolation, alienation and lack of opportunity—enhanced. Despite the often good intentions of well-meaning men, it is difficult to conceive in retrospect of a more problematic approach to the other.

Aboriginal Peoples responded to the policy of assimilation-exclusion with "consistent resistance", as Georges Erasmus explained in his 2002 Lecture.[13] Recent years have witnessed community renaissance. Aboriginal Peoples have begun a process of rediscovering their traditions and values, rebuilding communities, and exploring and sharing their cultures. Constitutional protections have been extended to the Aboriginal community, providing a legal safe-haven in which Aboriginal group interests can flourish. On the non-Aboriginal side, paternalism and exclusion are increasingly being replaced by respect and accommodation. To quote Georges Erasmus once more: "[g]aining recognition of Aboriginal rights in the courts and entrenchment in the Constitution have been critical to restoring Aboriginal peoples as active agents in directing our collective lives".[14]

Canada's history of minority exclusion and marginalization of those belonging to groups labeled "different" is not confined to the Aboriginal community. Chinese-Canadians came to Canada to help build our railroads. Their task completed, they found

---

[13] *Lafontaine-Baldwin Lectures*, *supra*, at 118.
[14] *Ibid.*, at 104–105.

themselves burdened with oppressive and discriminatory laws. Head taxes were imposed on entry. Impediments to the immigration of women were adopted. The lack of Chinese women in turn gave rise to irrational fears that Chinese men would prey on white women, and led to prohibitions on the employment of white women by Chinese men.

Black Canadians too felt the cold touch of exclusion and racism. Between 1782 and 1785 about 3,500 blacks, most former slaves who had fought for Britain in return for freedom, fled to what is now Nova Scotia and New Brunswick at the close of the American Revolution. Once in the Maritimes, they were cheated of land, forced to work on public projects like road building and denied equal status with whites. Disappointed, 1,190 men, women and children left Halifax on 15 ships for Sierra Leone. Sixty-five died on route. In 1796 six hundred Maroons—people with a long tradition of resistance to European rule—arrived in the Maritimes to face the same miserable conditions as the freed Black Loyalists. They too left for Sierra Leone. In 1814–15, 3,000 or so American black refugees from the war of 1812 settled in the Maritimes, and in the 1920s hundreds of Caribbean immigrants, called "later arrivals", came to Cape Breton to work in the mines and steel mills. Quebec and Ontario saw similar migrations, and black colonies were established in the west of Canada. Black people came to Canada expecting respect and accommodation. They found little of either. Despite the abolition of slavery in 1833, black Canadians found themselves excluded from schools, churches, restaurants, hospitals and public transportation, and denied equal housing and employment opportunities.

The list of racial groups that have suffered exclusion and discrimination goes on and on. Ukrainian Canadians were interned in World War I. Japanese Canadians, as well as men of German and Italian origin, were sent to camps during World War II. Well into the 20th century anti–Semitism forbade Jewish Canadians from holding property in designated areas. And in a dramatic expression of intolerance and lack of respect for the "other" who is labeled as different, legislation in the mid-twentieth century permitted the eugenic policy of sterilizing people deemed mentally deficient.

Perhaps the most far-reaching example of exclusionary-thinking is the history of our treatment of women. Women make up 52% of the Canadian population. Yet for much of Canadian history, women have been relegated to an inferior status in society. Why? Again the familiar premise—women are different. The obvious biological difference between men and women was extrapolated to apply to all forms of feminine functioning. Women had smaller and less clever brains. Women were congenitally weaker. Women functioned emotionally; only men could think. From here it was but a short logical leap to conclude that women should not be permitted to vote or practice medicine or law and should be barred from public office. The effect of these illogical leaps into stereotype was to deny women first-class status. Their identity as thinking, responsible human beings was challenged, their humanity denied. People perhaps, full persons, certainly not.

Women in Canada, as elsewhere in the western world, began to challenge these assumptions at the end of the 19th century. They fought for legal rights and they won them. It took a long time. Canadian women did not win the right to vote in federal elections until 1920. And it was only in 1929, with the now-famous "Persons Case", that the law recognized that women were "persons" entitled to hold public office.

However, as with the struggle of Aboriginal Peoples, legal equality for women did not translate into actual equality. Old ideas die hard. In the minds of many, women remained a fundamentally different kind of human being, with corresponding fundamental limitations. Women were fit for domestic roles, fit to serve as secretaries and nurses and other kinds of assistants. They clearly were not, however, up to the big jobs. This exclusionist thinking was buttressed by ingrained attitudes that the primary place of women was in the home with the children. Women who wanted to serve in law, medicine or politics could attempt to do so, but they faced an up-hill struggle against the prevailing attitudes of the day and seldom got to the top. The difficulties they faced led to statements like that of French journalist Françoise Giroud, "Women's problems will be solved when a mediocre woman holds a major job".[15]

It is now widely accepted that there is no justification for sweeping negative generalizations about the ability and temperament of women. It is accepted that women can and do play with equal effectiveness in all walks of life. And it is accepted—by many if not all—that cooking and childcare is not an exclusively feminine gift; men too can enjoy and excel in these activities. Why then did we persist so long in our belief that women were fundamentally unsuited for anything but working in the home and assisting men in grander pursuits? The answer brings us back to the dynamic of difference. Instead of evaluating the differences between men and women honestly and with an open mind, people magnified those differences and extrapolated them into conclusions which bore no relation to the actual abilities of women and paid no respect to their right to choose their path in life. In a word, stereotype transmuted into popular, hence unassailable, wisdom. Myth supplanting reality shut women out.

Why did the myth of female inadequacy persist so long? Why indeed does it still exert a tenacious power over our deepest attitudes and actions? Why can we not simply acknowledge, as we increasingly do with ethnic minorities, that the biological differences between men and women should not limit their place in society? Why, in short, can we not, where women are concerned, move from an exclusionary mentality to and inclusionary mentality? The answers are complex. Social and religious institutions may buttress an exclusionary mentality, as may the very structures of our institutions.

For example, many Canadian offices and workplaces continue to be organized on the Edwardian model of a century past. The family breadwinner (presumptively Papa) is expected to be available for work and travel at any time. This is made possible because the family homemaker (presumptively Mama) devotes her exclusive efforts to the home and family. This model no longer fits the reality of Canadian families, where increasingly both parents must work outside the home to earn the necessary income and both parents are involved with domestic and child-rearing tasks. We are beginning to explore ways to bring our workplace organization into synch with the reality of our lives—day care centres on the jobsite, childcare programs, flex time and working from home are among the options being explored. So long as we organize our workplaces on Edwardian lines, women will find themselves at best stressed and at worst falling back into the default role of sole domestic care-giver, reinforcing the old attitudes.

If Canada has not won the war against the exclusion of women, we have fought the first important battles. We have rejected the exclusionary politics that once denied women access to the levers of influence, power and full societal participation. We lead other nations in the opportunities we open to women. We have more senior female judges, more female university professors, more practicing physicians than many western countries. Personally, I

---

[15] From Lysiane Gagnon column in *The Globe & Mail*, weekend of Jan 27–28.

believe that in my own profession, the law, it is easier for a woman to succeed in Canada than almost anywhere else. Yet despite these achievements—and they are not inconsiderable—we still have terrain to take. Women's equality issues remain very much alive. Few women occupy the highest seats of political office and commerce. Statistics Canada tells us we have not achieved pay equity.[16] And violence against women is a persistent problem.

Canada's record on the treatment of Aboriginal Peoples, racial minorities and women—not to mention gays and lesbians—teaches us that notwithstanding our nation's foundation in the ethic of tolerance and accommodation, we are not immune from the evils of exclusionary thinking. The natural inclination of the majority and the powerful to see the minority and less powerful as less worthy and less entitled to share in all aspects of the country's life, has repeatedly surfaced on Canadian territory. We devalued Aboriginal Peoples, ethnic minorities, disabled people, and women, much as others elsewhere devalued the same groups. This must not be minimized. Yet from this complex and troubling history, we are slowly progressing towards a society where all people are fully valued, whatever their race, religion or gender. Since the Second World War and the international acknowledgment of the equal worth of all and the concomitant right to equal treatment, Canada has moved more quickly than many other countries to a more inclusionary, respectful model of society.

The law, while not the entire answer, has played a pivotal role in this progression. Canadian legislators reacted swiftly in the wake of World War II and the horrors of the Holocaust to protect minority rights. In 1944 Ontario passed the *Racial Discrimination Act* which prohibited the publication or dissemination of materials that expressed racial or religious discrimination. In 1947, the *Saskatchewan Bill of Rights Act* began a revolution in legislation that sought to be broadly protective of rights and civil liberties. These legislative innovations dove-tailed with the momentum building at the international level around the adoption of the Universal Declaration of Human Rights. In 1962, the first *Ontario Human Rights Code* proclaimed "the inherent dignity and the equal and inalienable rights of all members of the human family . . . in accord with the Universal Declaration of Human Rights as proclaimed by the United Nations." Nova Scotia's *Human Rights Act* came in the next year, followed by Alberta, New Brunswick, and P.E.I. By 1973, all provinces had enacted human rights laws and in 1976, the federal government followed suit.

The adoption of the *Charter of Rights and Freedoms* in 1982 elevated the basic human rights, aboriginal rights and equality to the status of supreme law, against which all government actions and legislation must be assessed. The *Charter* stands as Canada's ultimate expression of our commitment to freedom and human dignity.

The *Charter* has had a monumental impact on Canadian law and, indeed, in what Kent Roach has called a "heavy export trade in the *Charter*",[17] the law of other countries. Yet the *Charter* is more than a litigation tool or a lawyer's text. A glance at our newspapers shows the extent to which the *Charter*, and the values and principles it embodies, have been internalized by Canadians. Alain Dubuc has argued that the speed and readiness with which the rights enshrined in the *Charter of Rights and Freedoms* were taken up by Canadians was the product of an abiding national insecurity about our identity.[18] I prefer to think that the

---

[16] Statistics Canada, *Average Earnings by Sex and Work Pattern*, based on CANSIM II, Table 202–0102.

[17] K. Roach, *The Supreme Court on Trial: Judicial Activism or Democratic Dialogue* (Toronto: Irwin Law, 2001) at 60.

[18] *Lafontaine-Baldwin Lectures, supra,* at 72.

Charter manifests an ethic of respect and inclusion that has been part of Canada's fabric from its beginnings, and the way in which Canadians have embraced the *Charter* demonstrates its tremendous resonance with our country's identity. As I have tried to show, in Canada a unique political and cultural history is intertwined with a universalized ethic of respect and accommodation. The former constitutes our roots and shows us the path we have traveled as a nation. The second expands our sense of ourselves by including a commitment to respect for all kinds of difference in an unknowable future. Both are now immutable aspects of our country's identity, and both are reflected in the *Charter*.

In this way, the *Charter*, more than any other document, expresses the Canadian ethic, the country's sense of itself. The *Charter* also provides all of us, regardless of race, religion, or gender, with a secure space in which to realize our aspirations. Finally, the language of the *Charter* provides a common vocabulary in which we can cast our various perspectives, giving all Canadians access to the public space in which some of our country's most difficult and contentious issues are debated. The *Charter* has not created consensus. But by expressing our most fundamental values—above all the respect we hold for others, regardless of their differences—it has strengthened us and given each of us a place to stand. And by giving us the common vocabulary of rights it has provided a forum for understanding one another's circumstances and working out the accommodations so essential in a diverse, multi-cultural society.

The *Charter* protects difference. But, independent of any particularized rights, respect for minorities has become an inseverable component of our constitutional fabric. On August 20, 1998, the Supreme Court of Canada rendered its judgment in the *Reference re: the Secession of Quebec*.[19] Noting our long tradition of protecting minority rights, the Court recognized the protection of minorities, along with federalism, democracy, constitutionalism and the rule of law, as one of the foundational principles subtending our constitutional architecture.

Canada, as a nation grounded in difference and respect, has erected an impressive legal structure to protect difference. But this structure is not merely law. This is no alien, imposed legal order. It is a structure that expresses our history of respecting minorities and our ever-strengthening commitment to the policies of inclusion and accommodation and to the belief in the fundamental dignity and worth of each human being. Inclusion and equality cannot be achieved by mere rights. But when the rights reflect a nation's values and are accepted as a means of brokering our differences and finding accommodation, they take on profound importance. And when we add to the mix attitudes of tolerance, respect and generosity—attitudes which Canadians possess in good measure—the prospects become bright for the inclusive society of which we dream. Michael Ignatieff writes in *The Needs of Strangers* that "Love ... is perhaps the most desperate and insistent of all human needs. Yet we cannot force someone to love us. We cannot claim love as a human right."[20]

My hope is this. If we cannot claim love, we must strive for respect and accommodation. And as national ambitions go, that's not bad.

---

[19]   [1998] 2 S.C.R. 217.

[20]   *The Needs of Strangers*, *supra*, at 18-19.

The Civilization of Difference was presented by the Right Honourable Chief Justice of Canada, Beverley McLachlin, PC, as part of the Dominion Institute's March 2003 LaFontaine-Baldwin Symposium (www.lafontaine-baldwin.com).

The Illusion of Financial Unsustainability of Canadian Heath Care

GERARD W. BOYCHUK*

Gerard W. Boychuk is Associate Professor of Political Science at the University of Waterloo. This article is based on the author's paper, "The Changing Political and Economic Environment of Health Care in Canada," prepared for the Royal Commission on the Future of Health Care, 2002.

Public health care in Canada is portrayed with increasing frequency and urgency as being financially unsustainable. However, current patterns of public health expenditures in Canada provide little evidence for this claim. The real crisis of the Canadian health-care system lies in the paradoxical situation by which its institutional underpinnings—especially the nature and dynamics of federal–provincial relations—undermine rather than bolster public support for the system.

The political weakness of the health-care system is the result of powerful dynamics generated out of nearly a decade of federal–provincial wrangling over funding in a context of fiscal restraint. The incentives built into federal–provincial arrangements and the resulting patterns of federal–provincial interaction have led to increasingly widespread perceptions that the public health-care system in Canada is of rapidly declining quality, is wracked by a funding crisis, is unable to control costs, and is ultimately unsustainable. Because these perceptions are rooted in its institutional framework, pressures on the health-care system have not eased—and should not be expected to ease—as fiscal pressures abate or as mechanisms to control future cost pressures are implemented. Reorienting the health-care system to a more politically sustainable basis requires a serious rethinking of the relative roles and responsibilities of the federal and provincial governments in the funding and delivery of public health care.

The Canadian Institute for Health Information (CIHI) data on provincial health expenditures are unequivocal. Total provincial public health expenditures comprised *exactly* the same proportion of gross domestic product in 2001 (6.2 percent) as they did in 1990 and were actually down slightly from their peak level of 6.9 percent in 1992 (see Figure 1). Where, then, do the claims that health care is now financially unsustainable come from?

Two approaches generally underpin arguments regarding the financial unsustainability of health care. The first is to extrapolate future health-care costs from current spending patterns (primarily since 1996); the second is to focus on expenditures expressed as a proportion of total provincial program expenditure. But there are serious problems with both approaches.

Extrapolations of health-care costs based on the late 1990s tend to ignore the fact that expenditure restraint in the middle of the decade created pent-up demand that was reflected in higher annual spending levels later in the decade. Annual provincial health expenditures did increase significantly after 1996. However, from 1993 to 1996, actual expenditures were

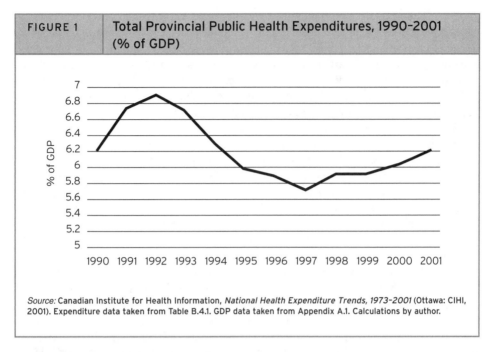

FIGURE 1	Total Provincial Public Health Expenditures, 1990–2001 (% of GDP)

Source: Canadian Institute for Health Information, *National Health Expenditure Trends, 1973–2001* (Ottawa: CIHI, 2001). Expenditure data taken from Table B.4.1. GDP data taken from Appendix A.1. Calculations by author.

lower than if they had simply been maintained at 1992 per capita levels. While provinces began to reinvest in health care after 1996, actual cumulative expenditures by 2001 did not—but almost—reached the amount that provinces would have spent in the 1992–2001 period if 1992 levels of per capita expenditure had simply been maintained. As the provincial and territorial ministers report on health care costs notes, the "severe restraint directed toward health care in the early-to-mid 1990s produced a very low annual average growth rate" and [s]ince 1996, provinces and territories have been reinvesting, partly to make up for the restraint applied in the early years of the decade."

Cost expansion driven by pent-up demand resulting from earlier (and sometimes ill-considered) programs of expenditure restraint is not evidence of the inevitability of future cost increases. One only has to think of the costs incurred by Ontario in first laying off and then recruiting and rehiring thousands of nurses. Extrapolating from current expenditure patterns without clearly demarcating the various underlying drivers of cost escalation and identifying their different implications for future expenditure patterns is not an appropriate methodology for forecasting future expenditure patterns.

The second explanation for the perceptions of financial unsustainability is that numerous reports and public debates have increasingly focused on health-care expenditures expressed as a proportion of total provincial program expenditures. While provincial public health expenditures are no higher relative to GDP than they were a decade ago, they have increased relative to total provincial program expenditure. There are two dynamics and each provides a partial explanation for this apparent discrepancy.

First, *total* provincial program expenditures remained static from 1991 to 2000 in real dollar terms and have dropped to 78 percent of their 1991 levels relative to GDP. Thus, provincial health expenditures rose as a proportion of total provincial program expenditures even while remaining static relative to GDP.

Second, the overall contribution the federal government makes to provincial total revenues has declined. (All major federal transfers to the provinces including those under the Canada Health and Social Transfer (CHST) for health go directly into the consolidated revenue fund, so to identify particular transfers for health, as is often attempted, is simply not relevant to the question of the overall fiscal sustainability of provincial health-care expenditures. At the same time, the issue of federal contributions to health is an extremely important issue in discussing the legitimacy of the conditional nature of specific transfers.)

Restraint in federal transfers has meant that an increasing proportion of the growth in provincial revenues is going to health care rather than other provincial programs or provincial deficit reduction or debt retirement. To this extent, health care is crowding out the provision of other public goods and, clearly, this is a serious problem from the provincial perspective. The financial sustainability of health-care expenditures is a very real problem *from the provincial perspective*. It is not, however, indicative of the unsustainability of the overall financial burden of health care relative to the overall ability of Canadian governments to bear this burden.

In the longer term, the financial sustainability of public health care in Canada becomes a serious issue under two scenarios; provincial governments become increasingly unable (or unwilling) to maintain current taxation levels (for which there is currently no evidence); alternatively, there is a future escalation of health-care costs. However, according to the provincial and territorial ministers of health report, *Understanding Canada's Health Care Costs*, which presents a detailed forecast of health-care costs to 2026–2027, cost drivers such as aging and population growth are *not* expected to increase the burden of public health expenditures relative to GDP in the foreseeable future. Including the effects of population growth, aging, inflation and a 1 percent per year increase to reflect "other" health-care service needs, the report concludes that *health expenditures will remain fairly constant as a share of GDP over the next 25 years.*

Questions of fiscal sustainability emerge only under a scenario of *accelerating* costs and, indeed, there are compelling reasons to expect considerable future cost pressures. The fact that current patterns of expenditure are not demonstrably unsustainable does not mean that questions of affordability pose no future threat or that there is no need for fiscal restraint in health management. The main question is whether the acceleration of costs to unsustainable levels is inevitable. The claim that inevitable cost acceleration will make public health expenditures unsustainable in the future is a much different claim than the one that current levels of health expenditure are unsustainable.

Despite the fact that provincial health expenditures relative to GDP are the same as they were at the beginning of the 1990s, there is now an increasingly widespread perception of a financial crisis in public health care. The roots of this perception lie, to some significant degree, in the institutional underpinnings of health care—especially federal–provincial fiscal arrangements.

The preponderance of jurisdictional responsibility for the provision of health services lies with provincial governments, while the federal role lies primarily in sharing the costs of provincially provided health services under terms governed by the federal Canada Health Act (CHA). Given this division of responsibility, the dynamics of federal–provincial relations regarding health are relatively straightforward. The federal government strives to minimize its fiscal commitment to the degree possible while ensuring both its visibility in health and its ability to claim credit for enforcing the CHA. Provincial governments, for their part, strive to maximize federal fiscal commitment while also preserving their room to manoeuvre vis-à-vis constraints imposed directly or indirectly through public pressure as a result of the CHA. Pressures on these arrangements began to build as the federal government restrained transfers first under the Established Programs Financing (EPF) arrangements and then, more drastically, under the CHST. Three crucial effects were thus generated.

The first is the illusion of health care as a rapidly growing fiscal burden relative to the ability of governments as a whole to bear this burden. Public health-care expenditures do not constitute a higher proportion of GDP than they did a decade ago. Yet, as a result of federal transfer restraint, provincial governments now make a compelling case that public health care as it currently exists is no longer affordable. From the provincial perspective, this concern is real.

Second, partly as a result of federal transfer retrenchment, the federal government's fiscal position is disproportionately brighter relative to the provinces. The situation in which surpluses are held at the federal level (which has limited direct involvement in the delivery of health-care services) and deficits or near deficits are held at the provincial level of government (whose most important single program responsibility is health care) contributes to the political construction of a strong linkage between health care and the issue debts and deficits. The goals of providing public health care and debt/deficit reduction are cast into sharp political competition as a result of the fiscal imbalance between levels of government that has been exacerbated by the capricious federal manipulation of health-care transfers.

Finally, these fiscal arrangements have generated perverse incentives for provincial governments. Provinces face limited incentives to forcefully combat public perceptions regarding the declining quality of health care and the sensationalist media coverage that strongly reinforces such perceptions. There are incentives for provincial governments to leverage their demands for greater federal funding by allowing such perceptions to flourish (if not actually encouraging them) so long as some measure of the blame can be successfully shifted to the federal government.

Provinces have a similar incentive to focus disproportionately on the funding aspect of the health-care issue, emphasizing the perception that a central explanation for problems with the health-care system is a lack of financial resources. Also as part of the blame-shifting strategy, provinces have an incentive to claim that the CHA is a straitjacket that does not allow for serious innovation in the health-care system and limits their ability to respond to the problems of health care themselves. Not surprisingly, the *National Post* recently called for the CHA " . . . to be scrapped, given the intolerable constraints it imposes on provinces' freedom to innovate", as noted by Andrew Coyne on January 11, 2002.

This provincial approach has culminated, somewhat predictably, in claims that the current public health-care system is unsustainable. In concluding a recent meeting of premiers in Victoria, Premier Gordon Campbell of British Columbia noted, "We all agree as premiers that health care under the current situation is not sustainable", as reported in the *Globe and Mail* on January 25, 2002. The *National Post* reported the following comments by Don Mazankowski: "Public health care in Canada will soon collapse unless bold reforms are introduced" (January 5, 2002). A final illustration is the Ontario government advertisements which, in a banner headline, claim: "Unless Ottawa pays its fair share for health care, the prognosis isn't good." These responses simply represent the provincial calculation of a rational response to the incentives structured into existing federal–provincial arrangements.

Public perceptions regarding health care, which otherwise might seem puzzling, are more clearly explicable in light of these political dynamics which help explain three relatively stable and well-documented trends in public opinion.

1) *A belief that the system is in crisis and that the quality of health care is declining despite personal experiences to the contrary.*

The growing perception among Canadians that health care is the highest priority facing the country is nothing short of astounding. Over the course of the 1990s, health care has shifted from being a non-issue to being far and away the highest priority among Canadians. While concern for other more perennial issues such as the economy has waxed and waned, health care emerged out of nowhere to become the top issue of concern in less than five years. In part, health care has become such an important issue because of growing perceptions that the system is in crisis—a belief now held by nearly four out of five survey respondents.

This increase in the salience of health care as an issue is related to the staggering decline in public perceptions of the quality of the Canadian health-care system. This shift did not take place gradually; rather, it first emerged only in the early 1990s, accelerated rapidly in the mid-1990s, and has remained relatively stable since 1997 despite the fact that provinces have begun to reinvest in health care.

The most obvious explanation for such a pattern would be that the system is in crisis. However, to the degree that Canadians' perceptions of their own personal interaction with the health-care system have been overwhelmingly positive, the image of crisis must lie elsewhere.

There is evidence of a decline in the positive nature of personal experiences with the health-care system but it is limited and has emerged only relatively recently. For the most part, individual perceptions regarding the quality of care in Canada have been strikingly high and any decline in perceptions of personal experiences have followed—rather than led—declining perceptions of the quality of the overall system. Similarly, Canadians have been much more sanguine about the system's ability to meet their own personal health needs and those of their families than to meet the needs of the population as a whole. This discrepancy is most plausibly explained by media reports of many stories depicting the stresses and strains in the health-care system. While these problems are certainly not imaginary, neither are they are representative of the norm in health-care provision. Key in this process is the apparent willingness of provincial governments to allow and sometimes even encourage such perceptions.

2) *A belief that we are now in a major funding crisis and that the system needs more resources.*

There is a widespread belief that the system is either currently facing a funding crisis or that a funding crisis is imminent. These public perceptions are not surprising given ongoing provincial government efforts to publicly demonstrate the existence of a health-care funding crisis. In this context, it is also not surprising that four out of five Canadians believe that too little is being spent on health care. Certainly, while most citizens do not believe that increased funding alone is the answer, most Canadians are skeptical that the system can be improved without increased funding.

3) *A striking decline in public approval ratings for how both the federal and provincial governments are handling the issue of health care and a belief that governments are losing ground in solving the issues facing health care.*

Public satisfaction with both the federal and provincial governments' handling of health care reached a peak in the early 1990s. After 1992, public approval ratings for both governments' performance on this issue began a precipitous yet enduring decline and have not recovered much beyond their lowest points in the late 1990s. This trend has certainly been exacerbated by intergovernmental strategies in which each level of government, in an effort to avoid accepting public blame for problems with the health-care system, attempts to shift responsibility to the other.

Despite the fact that the sustainability of the health-care system has been overwhelmingly portrayed in current debates as a financial issue, political sustainability must also be considered. Political sustainability requires ensuring the ongoing ability of the health-care system to maintain widespread popular support sufficient to guarantee that there are incentives for governments to adequately fund and effectively provide public health-care services. The trends in public opinion outlined above are suggestive of how seriously this ability is coming to be challenged. Fiscal sustainability is a moot issue if the health-care system is politically unsustainable and *vice versa*. Reforms that address only one of these components of sustainability—without consideration for the other—are likely to founder.

The most simplistic solution to the problems of political sustainability, yet one we are likely to repeatedly hear echoed from various quarters this autumn [2002], is to suggest that the federal and provincial governments simply "get their act together and fix health care." Certainly, the public is unlikely to disagree with this motherhood prescription. The failure of both orders of government to collaborate effectively has significantly contributed to fuelling public cynicism regarding governments' ability to deal with health-care issues.

Naively suggesting that the two orders simply work together, without fundamentally rethinking the incentives faced by each order of government under the current set of institutional arrangements, will merely raise public expectations for such cooperation without significantly increasing the likelihood that governments will deliver. It is a facile prescription that avoids the toughest issues and entails greater risk than promise. In the absence of institutional change that addresses the incentives generated by existing federal–provincial arrangements, a continuing and not easily reversible decline in public perceptions of both the quality and the sustainability of the public health-care system in Canada seems likely. It is here that the real potential for crisis lies.

Report to the Shareholders

MAURICE STRONG*

*Maurice Strong is Senior Advisor to United Nations' Secretary General Kofi Annan and former Secretary-General of the United Nations Conference on the Human Environment and Executive Director of the United Nations Environment Programme.

This is how it might go, unless we're very, very lucky, or very, very wise:

1 JANUARY 2031
REPORT TO THE SHAREHOLDERS, EARTH INC.

The best that can be said of the past year—and the past tumultuous decade, the most devastating in human experience—is that it's behind us. If this were a business, the board of directors would have recommended shutting the doors and padlocking the gates, turning the workforce loose to pick up scraps where they might. But of course this is not a business; it is the Prison of Life, and there is nothing beyond the gates of Planet Earth but the formless void. Since we cannot escape, we must endure, and since we cannot give up, we must continue the struggle. We must also grasp at what straws there are. Perhaps the past decade has been so awful that it must get better. Perhaps in the chaos and degradation we have experienced, the seeds of a new order have finally been planted, and deep in the muck strong new wood is growing.

Perhaps not. But life without hope is a living death.

The year began with another grotesque failure, that of world leaders at the Global Summit held in The Hague to agree on how to reverse the accelerating breakdown in relations between states, to agree even on co-operating to discuss the lack of international co-operation. The summit was supposed to bring nations together on key issues affecting the security and future of the world community. It was also supposed to revive the United Nations as the only available forum for doing this, to attempt to bring that once august body back to a semblance of the prestige and authority it had briefly enjoyed at the end of the Cold War between the former Communist empires and the former American one—a prestige dealt a fatal blow by its contemptuous dismissal by an America confident still of its own manifest destiny.

On both these issues the summit failed dismally, with the predictable consequences we have all seen: the chaos that has engulfed the world in the past decade shows no sign of abating. Central authority has now broken down in thirty-two more nations, from which sixty-nine (or is it seventy? seventy-one?) new nations emerged, declaring themselves sovereign and independent. The greatest of these was of course China, whose central government finally had to succumb to the centrifugal forces that had already resulted in the breakup of Indonesia and smaller states like Sri Lanka. A severely weakened government in Beijing has had to acquiesce in conceding virtually full autonomy to Guangdong, Tibet, Manchuria, Hunan and the former commercial enclaves of Shanghai and Hong Kong, which insisted on fully independent status and resisted inclusion in what Beijing is forlornly describing as a "new Chinese Federal Union."

India has long since disintegrated. It's hard to remember what really set the process off—the Sikh separatists in the northwest, or the squabble between Tamil Nadu and Karnataka over the water of the Cauvery River. In a way it no longer matters: frontier posts have gone up all over the formerly united subcontinent, and minor conflicts flare every few months.

The other formerly great power in Asia, Japan, has thus far been able to contain these tendencies. But it has, nevertheless, had to concede a much greater degree of autonomy to its principal regions, while at the same time resorting to an increasingly authoritarian style of government.

Korea split apart again at the beginning of the decade and this year continued to fragment.

Attempts to revive the moribund European Union collapsed—again. The European Parliament, which hadn't met for five years, was called into special session, but it failed even to achieve a quorum—no one could agree on how to assess the credentials of many of the delegates who bothered to show up. Was Scotland an independent country, as its delegates declared? Was Alsace? Brittany? The new Basque state carved from parts of Spain and France at least seemed viable. The big news from Eastern Europe was the further breakdown of what had been called Russia. The small "states," governed mostly by warlords, that had sprung up along the banks of the Volga met briefly in the Tatar city of Kazan, but failed to agree not only on a constitution but even on a style of government, and after the convenor was assassinated, the delegates fled. A whole series of new "countries" sprang up around the Black and Caspian seas, and some of the Siberian tribes declared that their allegiance to Moscow had ended, following the lead of the Asian republics, some of whom had joined with Iran earlier in the decade, only to split again in a disastrous civil war as the mullahs came into conflict with the oil oligarchy.

Almost everywhere in the region law and order have disintegrated, and local governments are run by strong autocratic leaders who ignore or are no longer bound by normal principles of accountability. Some are closely allied with and strongly influenced by criminal elements, which wield much of the economic power. In other cases there is no distinction at all between the local "mafias" and government, and governance has become a protection racket. Gang warfare, too, is common: the region is rife with local conflicts that claimed the lives and property of many thousands of citizens while terrorizing and exploiting the remainder.

In other places there is precarious order. The tiny nation of Chechnya has exploited the breakdown of government and order in its neighbours and has assumed de facto control of the region. Although it has imposed its rule and the constitutional measures purported to legitimize it, it has nevertheless received the passive support of the people concerned for the discipline, order and stability that the regime has restored. Much of the economy of the region has been paralyzed by shortages and disruption of energy supplies.

Of the seventy-three nuclear power plants in Russia, only three are now functioning, and attempts to refurbish others have foundered for lack of capital and components. As we have learned to our cost, there is a flourishing criminal trade in the deadly components of nuclear weapons, many looted from power stations or the former Russian arsenals. The sabotage of transmission lines and relay stations has deprived large segments of the population and industry of power supplies. Gas pipelines also have been sabotaged, which has severely disrupted supplies to domestic markets and to Ukraine and Western Europe, where it has exacerbated already serious energy shortages. Massive forest fires in Siberia have effectively destroyed a number of key towns, cities and industries there, while the continuing drought in the Trans-Ural regions and torrential rains in the Ukrainian lands mockingly called the "breadbasket" area have devastated crops and produced severe short-age of food.

Nine more countries in Latin America reverted to military dictatorships, but the rever-sion to authoritarianism has been even more extensive, as the democratic process in many countries that retain a formal commitment to democracy has been effectively subverted by or come under the control of the military, often in collaboration with criminal elements.

In the United States, where the office of the president has been severely weakened since the assassination of President Brady in 2023, President Reynolds has become even more politically impotent with effective power increasingly concentrated among the extremists who now control Congress in concert with the military and the FBI. Their action in push-ing through Congress a motion calling for a new constitutional conference constituting a powerful Preparatory Committee under the chairmanship of Senator Torrence McKelvie ostensibly to deal with the decisions taken by the state governments of Texas and Florida to secede from the union, has effectively consolidated the shift of power to this group and left the president with the formal trappings of power but devoid of its substance. Speculation about why they did not use their majority in power to impeach the president centres on their need to resolve rivalries within their own group before acting to claim presidency.

At the same time there is effectively a state of guerrilla warfare in several mountain states, as "citizen militias" become increasingly assertive.

Canada has been luckier. Two decades ago, prodded by Quebec and British Columbia separatist movements, the Canadians opted for an innovative system that divided the coun-try into four separate sovereign states united in the Canadian Union, which helped to keep a functioning democracy. The members of the Canadian Union have suffered the same eco-nomic devastation experienced world-wide, and many parts of the union have reverted to locally managed subsistence-level economies. Overall, Canadians have thus far done a bet-ter job of managing their crisis than most. They have been able, with the help of volunteer brigades, to maintain security, so violent conflicts have been avoided or contained. A notable exception was the outbreak of violent clashes in Vancouver's Chinatown in July, when it was invaded by a large mob bent on seizing the hoards of food and medicine they believed had been stockpiled there. The rioting was eventually brought under control, but not before much of the area had been looted and destroyed.

THE STATE OF THE ENVIRONMENT

The short period of benign weather experienced in many parts of the world as the year began inspired hopes that there would be a return to more stable and reliable weather. Unfortunately, it was not to be: 2030 gave us hitherto unprecedented extremes of weather. Hurricanes, tornadoes, and record rainfall took more lives and caused more damage than both world wars of the twentieth century. Much of Florida is now under water, and the low-lands of the Carolinas are lagoons. The devastation of much of the California coast has accelerated the exodus of people from what was once one of the most attractive places in the world to live. Its economy has been shattered by the almost complete devastation of its infrastructure, particularly the road system, much of which was earlier destroyed or weak-ened by the Great Earthquake of 2026. Many other coastal areas around the world were similarly devastated. An estimated 6 million people died as a result of the flooding of the low-lying plains of Bangladesh, and many more are now dying of starvation and disease. Widespread flooding has also occurred in the Netherlands, despite reinforcements of its unique system of dikes, and much of its productive farmland has been lost. The rise of several centimetres in the sea level has exacerbated the effects of storms and required the evacuation of many coastal areas and several South Pacific Islands as well as the Maldives in the Indian Ocean.

Another consequence of the turbulence and destructiveness of the weather in the past year has been the disruption of water supplies. Shortages and the progressive contamination of existing supplies have deprived many cities and towns of potable and even non-potable water. In Central Asia, cities like Bukhara and Tashkent have faced the forced evacuation of most of their residents and the closing-down of industries. Twenty years ago more than a billion people were without safe water. The number has more than doubled and is still increasing.

Oil supplies are increasingly erratic. Seizure by remnants of the military of some of the principal oil and gas fields and related facilities have been tolerated because they have restored production, despite the fact that they control the output in order to sell it to the highest bidders in a world market starved for energy.

The heavy blanket of grey smoke that hung over Siberia during the summer affected the people of this once pristine region with air pollution, while, paradoxically, their compatriots in most of the cities of the region who had long suffered from air pollution experienced some relief because of the closing of the industrial plants that had caused it. Unemployment became so bad that people were actually clamouring for pollution—at least that would have meant the reopening of the factories and plants that provided their jobs. Later in the year the pollution indeed resumed. But it was useless, unproductive pollution, the result of the coal and wood fires that warmed houses when gas and oil supplies dried up.

In the Middle East the precarious peace persisted. Iran and Iraq consolidated their control of the oil-producing states of the region, which now produce some 70 percent of the world's oil. Their reconciliation in 2021, for the purpose of freeing the region of foreign control, led to a joint guardianship of Gulf States that has proven remarkably effective, particularly now that both Kuwait and Saudi Arabia are ruled by regimes installed with the support and agreement of both Iran and Iraq.

During the year there were renewed but increasingly futile calls in the United States in particular for military action to assert Western control of the region on which its economic lifeblood depends. Cooler heads knew it was too late. It might have been feasible immediately following the rapprochement of Iran and Iraq, but was then judged unnecessary. No one expected the alliance to survive, and there were fears even then that an invasion would seriously disrupt oil supplies. A year or two afterwards was already too late. By then Iran and Iraq (the United Islamic Republic) had demonstrated their power and their joint control of OPEC by raising oil prices again to $50 a barrel. All the West could do was bluster futilely: the UIR had by then made elaborate and sophisticated arrangements for the demolition of all oil fields and facilities in the region in the case of an attack. America made noises but took no action. The price would have been too high—much higher than just paying up.

In point of fact most sober observers now admit that the new Middle Eastern power has conducted itself responsibly vis-à-vis the rest of the world and has ensured security and a certain stability of supply in an otherwise uncertain international political climate.

Although the stability of the oil situation in the region was reinforced during the year, there has been no end to the conflicts over water—which is now, barrel for barrel, more expensive than oil in many arid regions of the world. Concerted attacks by Arab guerrillas supported by Iraq have failed to dislodge Israel's control of the Jordan River, but they have demonstrated Israeli vulnerability to future attacks, particularly as the weakened economy makes it extremely difficult for the Israelis to maintain, let alone strengthen, their occupation of the basin. After an incursion of Iraqi troops deep into Turkey the two countries have reached a truce of sorts in their conflict over the Tigris, but the fundamental problems of sharing the depleted water flows of the river have not been resolved. Even more complicated is the struggle over the Euphrates. Iraq's control of Syria has strengthened its hand in the conflict with Turkey, but its preemption of a major portion of Syria's historical share of Euphrates water is creating immense human and economic problems for Syria and strong resentment against its new overlord.

Elsewhere, the Great Plains area of the midwest United States and Canada suffered the seventh consecutive year of drought, and the dried-out soil of what was once the world's most productive farming region has been swirling away on great clouds of dust, which have darkened the Prairie skies and buried whole farms and towns. Grain and animal production now barely meet local needs, and no one foresees the time when surpluses will again be available for export to those who had long relied on this source of supply. Elsewhere, too, the granaries of the world have been ravaged by either continuing drought or debilitating floods—Ukraine, Australia, the grain belt of Argentina, all have suffered. And even where grain has been produced in export quantities, the deteriorating infrastructure has meant it can't get to markets. As a consequence the price of wheat rose above $50 a bushel, but with the disruption of commodity markets, much of what was traded was sold in the black market at even higher prices.

The Ogallala aquifer, which had been the main source of groundwater for eight of the states of the Great Plains, has been sucked dry and is not being replenished. Which means the whole area—comprising farms and cities—is entirely dependent on rainfall. Consequently, the plains are among the areas hardest his by the drought.

The Colorado River was long since stolen from the Mexicans by California, but now only a trickle is reaching California itself, and farmers in the Imperial Valley have either reverted to subsistence farming or have fled. For the first time water vendors with armed guards roam the streets of Los Angeles, providing the only source of water for the few people left in those parts of the city where the water system is no longer functioning.

Last summer's record heat wave added to the toll of deaths and suffering in many parts of the world. Washington, D.C., came to a standstill as the failure of electric power left the city without air conditioning. The deaths from heat-related causes exceeded a hundred thousand, many of whom could undoubtedly have been saved if the district's remaining hospitals and medical services had not been overwhelmed.

The year has been catastrophic for humans, but insects and rodents have thrived, and the explosion in their populations has contributed immensely to the death and suffering. The outbreak of plague, which took so many lives in Russia and Central Asia, is attributed to the proliferation of the rat population; a new strain of killer bee played havoc in the southern and western United States; great swarms of locusts devoured what little there was of crops in North Africa; and mosquitoes and flies have multiplied to the point that they have made many places in the tropics as well as in northern regions virtually uninhabitable for humans. For example, a new and virulent strain of mosquito-borne malaria has emptied the bayous of Louisiana and turned New Orleans into a shrinking fortress held only with poisonous amounts of increasingly lethal pesticides.

The fires that continue to rage in the Amazon region and the forests of West Africa have reduced these to some 20 percent of their original size, and unusually dry weather, in some cases bordering on drought, combined with the relentless cutting of trees, seems to ensure that these regions will be stripped of their original growth within the next five years.

Reliable figures are not available at this point, but one of the world's leading experts at the Smithsonian in Washington has estimated that in this year alone some 25 percent of the world's prime concentrations of biological diversity have been lost, and something like the same proportion of species of animals and bird life have become extinct. There is no sign that this process is being arrested. Not only is it robbing many people who are immediately dependent on these resources for their livelihoods, but it is depriving all people of the resources that will be required to create a sustainable future for those who survive the current tumult.

The human tragedy is on a scale hitherto unimagined. In earlier periods there would have been an outpouring of sympathy and convoys of relief to the stricken areas, but no longer. People preoccupied with their own survival have little alternative but to turn their back on the more distant tragedies of others.

It's not possible to more than hazard a guess at the total number of those who have died as a result of these calamities. But for the decade it certainly must be on the order of 200 million if the victims of disease are included, a large proportion people weakened by hunger and malnutrition. The outbreak of cholera in Brazil in June has claimed at least 1.5 million victims and has still not been brought under control. A combination of famine and pervasive outbreaks of malaria, cholera and other water-borne diseases, as well as a particularly virulent virus for which there is no known cure, has further devastated the populations of much of sub-Saharan Africa, deepening the region's slide into economic chaos and anarchy. The populations of China, India, Pakistan, Bangladesh, Indonesia and other Asian countries have suffered deaths that surely exceed 1000 million. Europe, America, Australia, New Zealand and Japan have not escaped, as some 2 million people in these countries have fallen victim to the virulent nerve-destroying "virus X," originating in Africa, and to resurgent communicable diseases.

One consequence of these multiple disasters is that the troubled peoples of the world are on the move, in numbers previously beyond imagining. In great urban centres such as Cairo, Bangkok, Lagos and São Paulo, the lack of potable water and food and the breakdown of services have forced the exodus of the majority of the population. In the countryside they are almost always met with hostility by the rural population. There is frequent violent conflict. Some people resort to every possible means of entering America, Europe and other countries thought to offer refuge, waves of desperate refugees crashing against every border. Even the brutal measures that these countries have adopted to keep them out have not been sufficient, and the number of illegal immigrants to the United States, Canada and Western Europe has increased by at least 50 percent in the past year. Armoured vehicles patrolling the full length of the border between the United States and Mexico with "shoot on sight" instructions have failed to stem the flow. It has proven impossible to monitor the thousands of kilometres of coastline, and tens of thousands more come by boat. Refugees are even entering North America from the north, stumbling over the polar ice-caps, perishing in their hundreds.

The Europeans have set up huge "confinement camps" to contain the flow, but they have proven unmanageable. Even basic services are lacking, and in the past few months alone, rioting inmates have broken out of at least a third of the camps in Europe and are to be seen everywhere along the roads and in the streets and cities and towns. Feelings against immigrants run high, and they are often shot on sight. The authorities are helpless to intervene.

Some take comfort from the fact that no new official war was declared last year, but it is scant comfort indeed. By year's end there was scarcely a region in the world free of conflict and few places where life and property were secure. If there are no new wars in the formal sense, it is because the limited capacity of most governments to mobilize and deploy conventional military forces is needed to try to keep order at home. Most conflicts involved armed gangs, criminal syndicates or local warlords. In many places police and former military forces have become the main predators, and those who do still provide security do so at a steep price. The wealthy retreated into gated and armed enclaves long ago, but even their guards are now turning on them, and the number of incidents of the wealthy becoming the hostages of their hired security are increasing.

Some of the most dramatic conflicts of the past year have taken place at sea. The shrinking of land-based food supplies drove many more to turn to the sea for sustenance. A number of the main species have been depleted to the point of extinction, and the lesser species are following as the oceans are sucked clean of life. There has been a resurgence of piracy on the seas. Much of the conflict is between individual boats and groups of boats, or between those who resort to piracy when their fishing is unsuccessful. A hysterical mob recently hacked to pieces a whale that had been beached on the coast of Maine, and when they had finished with the whale they turned on each other. One of the most dramatic fights at sea occurred in August, when private gunboats sank a fleet of twenty-seven Spanish fishing boats in international waters on the Grand Banks.

What about the good news, if any?

There is, of course, good news—much of it from people who had faced up to their difficulties—but even some of the good news is in fact bad. For example, the best estimates of emissions of carbon dioxide and other greenhouse gases from human sources indicate that they have now stabilized and should be in the process of receding somewhat. But this is not because we have become more prudent or disciplined. Our use of fossil fuels has been drastically reduced because of the breakdown of the world economy. Scientists can only speculate about the degree to which this may be offset by the large-scale desecration of the forests and grasslands, which provide sinks for the absorption of carbon dioxide.

And there is still one island of relative calm. The strongest and most resourceful political leader of the years is undoubtedly Germany's new chancellor, Rolf Schmidt. Elected in a landslide on a platform of restoring stability and discipline in Germany, he has set out to make it an island of strength, security and survival in a troubled world. He's no Adolf Hitler, but he nevertheless borrowed from Hitler the tactic of winning his office democratically and then granting himself emergency powers, giving him virtually total authority. Unlike Hitler, however, he has in his few months in office demonstrated a remarkable combination of benevolence, fairness and toughness. In instituting reform and marshalling the resources of German society he has sought to ensure that all Germans work together for the common good and share equitably in both the sacrifices and the benefits achieved through a total mobilization of citizens to deal with their problems. Schmidt's initiatives have ignited a new spirit of determination and optimism among his people, and at this point he enjoys their virtually unanimous support. Already the tough new regimen of national mobilization he has imposed is producing results in establishing personal security throughout the country, increasing food production and ensuring that food and other essential supplies are made available to all on an equal basis.

But benevolent dictators are increasingly rare. The majority of other authoritarian regimes that have emerged around the world are neither so benevolent nor so effective.

Still, other scattered islands of sanity and order are to be found in many regions, beacons of civility and hope, playing the same role in our modern chaos as the medieval monasteries did in the European Dark Ages, keeping alive the flickering embers of learning and wisdom. In Crestone, Colorado, for example, a community created as a spiritual retreat in recent materialistic times has proven to be a haven for the virtues of sustainability, harmony and "ethical husbandry."

Similar havens have appeared in the Altai in Russia and in the remote fastnesses of Tibet, a traditional refuge for asceticism and spirituality. A farmer in Manitoba has synthesized the best attributes of the Hutterite self-help communities and the Amish farmers and has set up a refuge around a large groundwater reservoir. Its ready success has prompted him to expand it to include others, as the capacity to absorb them permits, giving priority to displaced children and young families. Everywhere, indigenous peoples are rediscovering their traditional way of life. The Inuit in the Chesterfield Inlet of northern Canada have once again established a community like that of their ancestors; tribes in the Brazilian Amazon have abandoned their new-found reliance on chainsaws and tobacco and are once again dwelling in harmony with the forest—albeit with an "educational facility" set up for foreigners who wish to learn how it is done. In the war-ravaged cities of Mozambique, a demobilized soldier named João has helped to restore order and basic amenities through an innovative system of volunteer cadres supported and paid for by the grateful community. A similar system was set up in Texas by an enterprising former colonel of the U.S. Army, Mike Ryan, who put together a volunteer security service for schools, hospitals and other institutions serving the needs of people, particularly young people. This "volunteer security corps" has spread rapidly to other parts of America and Canada, and counterparts are now springing up throughout the world.

THE STATE OF THE SOUL

In the face of these multiple disasters, massive numbers of people turned away from science, which was blamed for the chaos, and toward religion. There was a resurgence of religions and spiritual movements of all sorts. Some have been promulgating messages of hope and calling to their followers to help relieve the distress and suffering of others, while an increasing number have been pointing to the current travails as a sign that the end of the world is near. The prudent habits and communal practices of the Mormons have enabled them to maintain a reasonable degree of security, order and subsistence in communities they dominate. But their commitment has been challenged by the growing migration of others to these communities, and their hostility toward these newcomers has in some cases turned violent.

Old ethnic and religious conflicts, such as the continuing open warfare between Catholics and Protestants in Ireland, have flared up again. The return of "the church militant" has also given rise to new conflicts as religious groups band together to stake competing claims to living space and livelihoods.

One of the more dramatic events of the past year was the emergence of a new movement for spiritual unity under the charismatic leadership of the man who calls himself Tadi.

As almost everyone by now knows, his message is deceptively simple, little more than an exhortation to people to return to the roots of their own religions, while tolerating and respecting all others as differing expressions of a universal spirituality that unites all people. Simple, perhaps, but exceptionally sophisticated. Tadi has persuasively isolated the basic spiritual, ethical and moral values underpinning all the world's religions, from the imperial legions of Christianity and Islam to Judaism, the many variants of the Tao, Buddhism and even the smaller, more isolated philosophies like those of Nummo, the great god of the Dogon in North Africa. Ecumenism or unitarianism is not, of course, a new notion. What is new and remarkable is that people of all faiths have embraced Tadi's formulations. This is due as much to the timeliness of the message as it is to the exceptional qualities of the messenger.

Tadi is of mixed Welsh, Armenian and Moroccan origin. After being educated in the United States and spending some ten years as a Christian missionary in Guyana, he came to reject his own narrow fundamentalist vision of the world, concluding that in this Time of Troubles God must call all to a new and transcendent unity. By now he has come under intense media and security service scrutiny, but nothing has been found that would cast doubt on his integrity. His modest style of living sets an example for all to whom it has become a necessity as well as a virtue, and he works tirelessly not only to promulgate his message but to give effect to it in practical ways. Tadi disclaims formal leadership of the movement, yet he is clearly the inspiration for the proliferation of Spiritual Unity groups and communities throughout the world.

The movement has also evoked vigorous and often hostile responses from fundamentalists of various religions. Tadi has been condemned by the Christian Alliance in the United States as the voice of the devil who seeks to undermine the commitment to Christ as the only saviour and the exclusive route to heaven. In the Sudan fundamentalist Muslims have rallied to the call of a new Mahdi, personally leading attacks on Christian churches and communities and threatening death to anyone who joins the Spiritual Unity movement. A few of the more militant Orthodox rabbis in Jerusalem have labelled Tadi a blasphemer.

PROGNOSIS

Most people can't afford the luxury of looking to the long-term. But at year-end we must have faith that there will be a future for the human family. Those who survive and the generations that will follow them will eventually benefit from the traumatic chastisement that nature has visited on our generation. Soothsaying is always risky, but surely it is revealing (as well as ironic) that some of the concerns commonly expressed at the beginning of this century have proven unfounded, and that certain worrying trends have even reversed—as a result not of good sense but of cataclysm.

Population growth, for instance. At the end of the twentieth century the exponentially expanding human population was perceived as the greatest problem facing humankind, the "ur-problem" underpinning all others. Yet now population growth has ceased; population levels are declining precipitously almost everywhere, and some areas of our planet have been almost entirely depopulated. More people are dying, and dying younger—birth rates have dropped sharply while infant mortality increases. At the end of the decade, the best guesstimates of total world population is some 4.5 billion, fewer than at the beginning of this century. And experts have predicted that the reduction of the human population may well continue to the point that those who survive may not number more than the 1.61 billion people who inhabited the Earth at the beginning of the twentieth century.

A consequence, yes, of death and destruction—but in the end a glimmer of hope for the future of our species and its potential for regeneration.

Tadi teaches us what we should already know: that we must inculcate in those of our children who survive the bitterest lesson of all, which is that the human suffering and cataclysms we are now experiencing need never have happened, that they occurred not through chance or the will of malevolent gods, and that the revenge of nature and the devastation of our civilization are direct results of the uncaring arrogance of our forebears and of our own self-indulgence, greed and neglect. What we have suffered is our own fault, and only through our own efforts can it be reversed and a hopeful and sustainable future secured.

The Multiple Affiliations of Quebec

CLAUDE COUTURE AND NATHALIE KERMOAL*

***Claude Couture** is Professor of History at the Centre d'Études Canadiennes de la Faculté Saint-Jean, University of Alberta. **Nathalie Kermoal** is Instructor at the School of Native Studies, Faculté Saint-Jean, University of Alberta.

INTRODUCTION

This chapter explores the place of Quebec in contemporary Canada by explaining several important narratives in Québécois social science, which purport to reveal both the origins of Quebec nationalism and the likely path of its future evolution. The chapter begins by contesting the ethnic-based narrative about Quebec, which is all too frequently encountered in political science textbooks and other analyses of Quebec written primarily in English for a francophone audience. Such a textbook narrative represents Quebec nationalism as ethnically based and a throwback to earlier times. However, as the chapter explains, independantist writers reject this narrative by providing three very different interpretations of Quebec's past and future. This chapter examines three models in detail—the Dumont Model, the Bouchard Model, and the "Revisionist Model." This discussion demonstrates that the Quebec narrative continues to hold a complex and contradictory place in any narrative about the contemporary Canadian community.

In most of the textbooks on Canadian politics, Quebec nationalism (that is, the nationalism of French Canadians living in Quebec) is described as "ethnic" (Dickerson, 1994; Jackson, 1994; Landes, 1995) or essentially racially based, comparable, for example, to the Afrikaner nationalism in South Africa, as described in the *Concise Oxford Dictionary of Politics* (McLean, 1996). This conclusion is generally based on a particular narrative comprising the following components. It begins with a depiction of Quebec as a seventeenth-century white settler colony, one grounded in an *ancien régime* of rural and religious values. The Conquest of 1760, it is argued, stigmatized those values in what became a very religious and rural French Canada in the nineteenth century, while the British—secular and urban—embraced the project of modernity. Finally, it is asserted that Quebec is still haunted by the ghosts of its past, and thus remained a pre-modern society until the Quiet Revolution of the 1960s. Consequently, its nationalism remains, in the twenty-first century, essentially "ethnic" and "racial."

This view of Quebec, apart from a few nuances, is basically reproduced everywhere in the literature, whether the authors claim to write from the "neutral" perspective of liberalism (Beiner and Norman, 2001), a comparative perspective (Modood and Werbner, 1997), "gender" and "race" perspectives (Yuval-Davis and Stasiulis, 1995), or "ex cathedra" (Habermas in Taylor, 1994; Habermas, 1998). The same narrative about Quebec, particularly before 1960, is also present in Taylor (1992, 1994). Kymlicka too has his "cut and paste" paragraph on traditional Quebec before the 1960s (1989, 1995). Michael Ignatieff reaped a fortune from his simplistic representation of "petty" nationalisms, including Quebec's, while francophone "experts" have also made a lucrative career out of these "miserabilist" visions (Gagnon, 1990; Maclure and Gagnon, 2001; Thériault, 1995; Sarra-Bournct, 2000). The list is endless.

But to what extent does this almost universally accepted narrative of Quebec's past reflect the complexity of the debates among francophone political writers and the historiography of the last 30 years? Since the 1960s, numerous schools of thought have emerged in Quebec about the definition of nation and the content of nationalism. Francophone Québécois have been divided in three different political camps: the Trudeauistes, the "soft federalists," and the independantists (McRoberts, 1997). Among the latter group, the independantists, there are at least three schools of thought. The first is represented by the work of sociologist Fernand Dumont. The second and third, the Gérard Bouchard paradigm and the "revisionist" view, are essentially reactions to the Dumont paradigm. Feminism, the First Nations issue, and multiculturalism have challenged each of the three models.

In order to avoid a simplistic reading of Quebec, "à la Ignatieff" for example, one should at least try to go beyond the usual narrative and consider the complexity of the discourses involved even among the strict advocates of an independent Quebec. The political ramifications are important because common understandings of nation guide both political opinion and action. Gérard Bouchard's argument, for example, advances the notion that Quebec will reach its full potential as a society of the New World only when it cuts its ties with the old colonialists, the British monarchy. Bouchard's project of an independent Quebec is thus shifting, using the "ethnic" nationalism stigmata as a tool to portray Canada as a society of the Old World, colonial and racist. Quebec thus could only reach its full progressive potential notably through a wider inclusion of diversity, which would only be possible by cutting its ties with a monarchist Canada. Even if today the support for sovereignty is shrinking, it does not necessarily mean that the sovereigntist project is dead. One has only to recall that in 1976, a few weeks before the election of the Parti Québécois, Prime Minister Trudeau declared the death of the separatist movement in Quebec. But the paradigm had shifted in 1976, from a nostalgic right-wing agenda to a social democratic one. Now, at the beginning of this new millennium, the paradigm is shifting again, from a vague, social-democratic project to a multicultural one, with French defined as the public language of a diverse society.

THE FERNAND DUMONT MODEL

The late Fernand Dumont was, in Quebec, the most important sociologist of his generation. Dumont thought that Quebec was not a nation, as indicated by the title of his *magnum opus—Genèse de la Société Québécoise*. He thought, to the contrary, that there was a "French" North American nation, mostly concentrated in the province of Quebec, but present in other regions of Canada as well as in the United States. In his *Genèse de La Société Québécoise* (1993), he advanced a narrative based on the idea of the "French" as a francophone nation or "people."

Dumont reminded his readers that the French North American empire before 1763 was a vast territory including the St Lawrence River valley, the Great Lakes region, and territories around the Missouri and Mississippi rivers from the Ohio River valley to the Gulf of Mexico. The James Bay region and the northern part of Quebec were officially British territories after the Treaty of Utrecht in 1713, half a century before the Conquest of 1760.

It is important to note that the word Canada (meaning "village" in Iroquois), not Québec, was used by the French to refer to the territory of New France that lay along the St Lawrence River (Morin, 1997). There was a strong sense among the French population of belonging to North America (Couture and Cardin, 1996). The inclusion of the vast interior of the continent, reinforced by the fur trade and French exploration, has never completely disappeared from the complex sense of identity of francophone Québécois, or "Canadiens" as they have referred to themselves since the eighteenth century (Choquette, 1997). For example, in 1995, at the peak of the referendum in Quebec on sovereignty, still an important number of francophone Québécois kept some element of a Canadian identity. Asked about their identity, 20 percent of the people interviewed said they were Québécois only, another 20 percent said they were Québécois and Canadians, a third 20 percent answered that they were Canadians and Québécois, and only 6 percent said they were Canadians only. The Canadian identity of the old New France never vanished, thus confirming Dumont's emphasis on the French-Canadian identity (McRoberts, 1997).

Dumont, who was a religious man, also insisted on the religious factor as a founding element of New France (1993). At the end of the seventeenth century, religious minorities in Europe sought to emigrate in order to build societies according to their religious beliefs. France's minorities, such as the Huguenots, mainly moved to Central Europe, while religious minorities in Britain emigrated to North America. The refusal of the Church to allow religious minorities to move to New France, and the fertile soil and temperate climate of the Atlantic seaboard, led to a great disparity in the populations of New France and New England. Between 1608 and 1713, despite the success of its expansion on the continent, New France's population had grown from several hundred to only 15,000 inhabitants (1993). In comparison, New England had a population of 400,000 in 1715 and more than 2 million in 1763. Between 1715 and 1763 the population of New France grew from 15,000 to almost 70,000 inhabitants. But it was too late. Oddly, it was under the English regime after 1763 that the remaining French-speaking population grew substantially. From less than 70,000 the French population increased to some 100,000 in 1784, over 400,000 in 1825, and almost a million in 1860. By 1911, the French-speaking population in Quebec was about 2 million people, 4 million in 1951, and almost 6 million in 1960. Between 1840 and 1930, 1 million French-Canadians, most of them seeking jobs in the manufacturing sector in New England, left Quebec for the United States. Today, according to some authors (Balthazar and Hero, 1999), the Franco-American population could approximate 10 million people.

In 1791, with the *Constitutional Act*, the frontiers of the colony were reduced to what is essentially southern Quebec today (Couture and Cardin, 1996). The colony was also granted an elected assembly. But the territory, like any other British colony, was directly and undemocratically governed from the metropolis through a governor named by London and a body of councils also composed of non-elected members. The assembly, moreover, had limited powers.

The Canadiens developed a distinct identity by the end of the eighteenth century, and the initial struggle for democracy became, according to Dumont, synonymous with nationalism (1993). It is worth noting, according to Dumont, that the Patriots were defined as *Canadiens*, and included all of those who were against the British monarchy and in favour of democracy. Consequently the idea of the "multi" was a key element of the political project of the *Canadiens*. After failed rebellions and amalgamation with Upper Canada

(Ontario) in 1841, Quebec became part of a legislative union as a result of Lord Durham's recommendations. Quebec became a province of the Canadian federation in 1867.

According to Dumont (1993), the failure of the 1837–38 Rebellion, which meant the failure of the "civic humanist" ideal, or the Republican project, provoked a realignment in the "French" nation and the emergence of a new project and a new national content called "survivance." Instead of creating a multinational republic, the elite of French-Canadian society, among them a new powerful Church after 1840, shifted their focus from politics to culture. They accepted the *BNA Act* of 1867 but for them Confederation was based on the principle of a federation of nations, namely the British and the French (both the French and the British of the era excluded the First Nations in their equation). But that interpretation of Confederation was never shared by the majority of English-speaking Canadians. British Canada tended to see Canada as a homogeneous nation composed of different regions represented by the provinces (Dumont, 1993; Bouchard, 2000; Létourneau, 2000). This unresolved debate about the nature of the federation has been at the core of every political and constitutional crisis in Canada and the province of Quebec since 1867. For Dumont, the Métis Rebellions of 1870 and 1885, the hanging of Louis Riel, the illegal and unconstitutional abolition of the use of the French language in Manitoba in 1890, the conscription crises in 1917 and 1942, the constant marginalization of the French language at the federal level until the Official Languages legislation of 1969—all these events contributed to a negative perception of the Canadian federation, and saw the rise of a siege mentality that focused on Quebec.

Also, for Dumont, the project of sovereignty for Quebec was crucial to reinstating the Republican project of the Patriots. A sovereign Quebec, he argued, should create institutions based on the recognition of the numerous nations comprising Quebec, among them, as a majority, the "French" Canadian nation. Thus, Quebec, comprising, was not a nation, according to Dumont, but an eventual multinational state where the French as a majority were better positioned to help or even attract the other French Canadians of the continent. Dumont's detractors pointed out that his project of transforming a cultural nation into a political majority was ethically suspect in terms of avoiding the traps of ethnic nationalism, even if Dumont insisted on forming a federation of nations inside Quebec.

This federation would have included the First Nations as "founding people" (Morn, 1997; Dupuis, 1997, 2001), a major difference compared to the situation prevailing in the nineteenth century. For several leaders of the First Nations in Quebec, the concept of "founding people" was not necessarily perceived as colonialist (Bernard Cleary in Seymour, 1999). The recognition of the First Nations as "founding people" would mean their political acceptance in Canada and, consequently, would lead to "nation to nation" pacts. In fact, in February 2002, the Cree Nation in the James Bay area signed a treaty called "Ia paix des Braves" with the province of Quebec based on the principle of a "nation to nation" negotiation. Dumont would have recognized his project in this "paix des Braves" (*Le Soleil*, March 25, 2002),

However, if Dumont's notion of a federation of nations was inclusive when it came to the First Nations, his paradigm was not as clear about the inclusion of groups commonly associated with contemporary multiculturalism. Dumont's work did not provide a clear solution for the recognition of other cultural/ethnic groups—nor of [women]. In fact, his paradigm was particularly hostile to feminism (Lamoureux, 1995; Lamoureux, Maillé, and de Seve, 1999), a fact that is consistent with Dumont's strong Catholicism. Some of

Dumont's current followers (Cantin, 1997) also seem to be indifferent, if not hostile, to feminism (Létourneau, 2000). Overall, although Dumont paradigm is still stigmatised as "cultural" nationalism, the content of its vision is more complex than the simple reproduction of an "ethnic" form of nationalism. Dumont, like many Catholics, was morally tormented by questions of ethics and did not seem to find a satisfying solution, in moral terms, to the problem of Quebec nationalism. More recent writers believe they have.

THE GÉRARD BOUCHARD MODEL

A student of Fernand Dumont in the 1960s, Gérard Bouchard completed his doctoral thesis in social history in Paris in 1971, and like Dumont, he has had a very prolific career (Mathieu, 2001). Gérard Bouchard's intellectual project can be divided into two periods. The first period, from 1971 to 1996, was devoted to a thorough study of the Saguenay population. This study concluded that there was a discrepancy between the representation, by the elite, of the popular classes in Quebec and what seemed to be the more complex reality of the popular classes. Following from that, Bouchard embarked on a comparative history project that led to his book *Genèse des Nations et Cultures du Nouveau Monde*, in which he compares the evolution of national identities in Quebec, Canada, the United States, Latin America, New Zealand, and Australia. He, too, seemed to be fascinated by the origins of identity formation.

Despite the first incursions of the French in 1534, the real beginning of French colonization in the St Lawrence Valley was in 1608, when Samuel de Champlain established a fort at Cap Diamant, today the site of Quebec City. The French North American empire expanded considerably during the seventeenth century (Choquette, 1997). In 1672 and 1673, Jolliet and Marquette explored the Mississippi River and, in 1682, Robert Cavelier de LaSalle reached the Gulf of Mexico by following the Mississippi River. Many institutions were established—hospitals such as the Hôtel-Dieu de Québec in 1639 and the Hotel-Dieu de Montréal in 1657. In 1664, the Coutume de Paris became the law in the colony; in 1663, Bishop Laval opened the first seminary, the Grand Séminaire de Québec, while the Séminaire de Saint-Sulpice opened in Montreal in 1677 (Greer, 1997; Choquette, 1997). In 1713, the Treaty of Utrecht, following France's defeat by a coalition of European countries in the War of the Spanish Succession, demanded that France surrender Acadia (in Nova Scotia, excluding that area which is today Cape Breton Island), Newfoundland, and the lands around Hudson's Bay. Several thousand Acadians thus became part of the British Empire in North America. Following the Seven Years' War, Quebec City and Montreal were claimed by the British. It was the end of the French Empire in North America (Couture and Cardin, 1996).

According to Bouchard's narrative (2000), a few years after the Conquest, the remaining French population of the new British colony benefited from tension between the Thirteen Colonies and Britain with the Quebec Act of 1774. The Quebec Act enlarged the frontiers of the Province of Quebec, recognized freedom of religion for Catholics, and established the legality of the seigneurial system and the French civil code. After the American War of Independence, the *Constitutional Act of 1791* reduced the frontiers of the province for the purpose of establishing a new colony, Upper Canada (eventually Ontario), and guaranteed a legislative assembly, although with limited powers, in each colony (Upper and Lower Canada).

French Canadians were, during the years between 1791 and 1867, extremely active both politically and in every aspect of economic life. Local markets were extraordinarily complex and diversified. Some French Canadians, like Augustin Cuvillier and Joseph Masson, were also involved in international commerce and banking. Both men were administrators of the Bank of Montreal while other French Canadians opened French-Canadian banks such as the Banque du peuple in 1835 (Couture, 1998).

As for Dumont, for Bouchard the key period of the nineteenth century was 1837–38. The rebellions in Upper and Lower Canada over the principle of self-government resulted in military repression and the Durham Report of 1839. Lord Durham recommended the application of the principle of self-government but suggested that the only solution to the French Canadian problem was the union of the two colonies. The aim was to assimilate the French Canadians. That plan was implemented in 1841 through the Union Act, passed in London in 1840. Section 41 of the Union Act stipulated that English was the only language of the new colony (McRoberts, 1997). But, when Britain abolished the mercantilist system between 1846 and 1848, the principle of self-government was granted to the colonies as compensation for the loss of protected access to the British market. Following that decision, a coalition of reformists lead by Robert Baldwin and Louis Hippolyte Lafontaine formed the first democratic government of United Canada (the colony formed by the union of Lower and Upper Canada) in 1848 (McRoberts, 1997). The right of the French language was recognized by the reformists. By 1864, during negotiations for a new federation of British North American colonies, it was clear that there was a growing recognition of the French reality in the proposed federation. However, Bouchard argues that from the 1840s until the 1950s, Quebec elites were obsessed by a cultural approach defined as "la survivance." It was in "la survivance," the struggle to ensure the survival of French language and culture in an English continent, that one could find the root of the discrepancy between the "learned culture" and the "popular culture" (2000).

For Bouchard, French-Canadian cultural roots can be traced to the beginning of the nineteenth century in literature, painting, and sculpture. Debate about the significance of the arts in the francophone community has been passionate since the nineteenth century. In literature, Father Henri-Raymond Casgrain in the nineteenth century and Bishop Camille Roy in the twentieth century both sought to create a literature that would reflect what they defined as the essence of French-Canadian society. After the Quiet Revolution, many writers were, like Casgrain and Roy, exploring the identity of the French-speaking society now referred to as Quebec society. There was a constant search for identity and self-confidence (Lamonde, 2000).

A century later, the cultural infrastructure in Quebec is impressive by any standard (Andrew, 1999). There are 150 theatre companies; a dynamic music scene with over 100 musical organizations, including two that started their activities in the nineteenth century.

The Orchestre Symphonique de Montréal is ranked among the top orchestras in the world, while a large number of music schools, in universities and conservatories, provide musical training. In dance, Quebec enjoys an international reputation with companies like les Grands ballets canadiens and La La La Human Steps. Montreal has around 230 commercial cinemas and is the host of the prestigious Montreal Film Festival (Andrew, 1998). No wonder that even Mordecai Richler, the prominent English-language novelist well known for his mockery of Quebec nationalism, once described francophone Québécois as the most cultivated people in Canada (Bouchard, 2000). Also, there are 29 television stations in Quebec and a high proportion of the television watched by francophone Québécois is French-language programming produced in Quebec. Quebec has 58 AM and 77 FM radio stations and more than 150 rebroadcasting radio stations. The province has 10 French-language and 2 English-language daily newspapers, more than 200 weeklies, more than 300 periodicals, and over 30 publications in languages other than French and English (Andrew, 1998).

Thus, according to Bouchard and contrary to his mentor Dumont, this massive cultural infrastructure indicates that Quebec is a nation capable of including everyone who lives within its territory and is willing to use a public language, in this case French, the same way that English is the public language in the United States (2000). But like all the colonies of the New World that became independent and progressive new nations, at least in Bouchard's mind, Quebec has to cut its ties with the British monarchy or the symbolism of the old colonialism (the British colonialism) (2000). Consequently, according to Bouchard, since Canada has not fundamentally cut its ties with the old colonialism, despite its claim of embracing "civic" nationalism, Quebec must achieve independence in order to fully embrace the project of a nation of the "new world" (2000). This point of view has been shared recently by several commentators, one of them being Michel Seymour.

A philosophy professor at the Université de Montréal, Michel Seymour has authored or co-authored nearly a dozen books on nationalism since 1995. The starting point of Seymour's analysis is his refutation of the Dumont paradigm and the notion of "survivance," or cultural nationalism. According to this philosopher, Quebec was indeed a priest-ridden and ethnic society before the Quiet Revolution. Since the 1960s, however, modern Quebec has rejected the "survivance" model and embraced a more social-democratic and inclusive project. Thus Quebec is a nation composed of all the people living within its territory. But, as Canada has a socio-political majority with British roots, Quebec also has a socio-political majority, which is French. While more than 80 percent of Canadians outside Quebec speak English at home, more than 80 percent of Québécois speak French at home (Seymour, 1999). Thus, the public language in Canada is clearly English while the public language in Quebec is French.

Quebec constitutes a nation with a clear capacity to integrate its minorities with all due respect to their origins. Both Bouchard and Seymour dedicate a great deal of their writing to the question of the integration of the non-French Canadians in a "civic" form of nationalism, while they seem to assume that the question of feminism has been dealt with successfully since the 1960s by the inclusion of the most powerful feminist lobby in Canada in Quebec's institutions. This view is not shared, however, by many prominent feminists in Quebec (Lamoureux, Maillé and de Seve, 1999). Although these feminists were extremely critical of the condescension towards Québécois displayed by Canadian feminists during both the Meech Lake and Charlottetown crises, they do not engage easily in the new discourse about the justification of independence and remain conscious of the struggle of women in Quebec despite the gains of the last decades (Lamoureux, Maillé and de Seve 1999; Strong-Boag et al., 1998).

THE "REVISIONIST" MODEL

The word "revisionist" is used by the Quebec historian Ronald Rudin to refer to the work of certain historians who mainly wrote from the end of the 1970s to today (Rudin, 1997). This work is said to be revisionist because it challenges the notion of a traditional and monolithic society before the Quiet Revolution. These historians argue that there was no discrepancy between the popular classes and the elites in Quebec before 1960. On the contrary, support for liberalism was widespread and a French-Canadian bourgeoisie was influential in Canada. Thus, in the eyes of some of the revisionists, the idea of a separate Quebec would be a predictable conclusion for a normal evolution. The revisionists claim that many of the changes that occurred in Quebec were typical of political and social forces operating in all modern societies at the time.

For example, the revisionists point to the ample evidence of urbanization and migration in Quebec in the 1800s. During the nineteenth century, large numbers of French-Canadians moved to urban centres throughout North America. Despite the official but sometimes ambiguous opposition of the Church on the subject of migration, Québécois left their rural homes as early as 1840 and moved to urban centres in New England or to cities in the province of Quebec. From 1850 to 1930, the province's urban population grew steadily. In 1871, only 15 percent of Québécois lived in cities. Two decades later, the number had doubled, and by 1921, 52 percent of the people were urban. This figure was above the Canadian average and comparable to that of Ontario. By 2001, Quebec's urban population was 80 percent, the second highest proportion in Canada, just behind Ontario with 83 percent (Linteau *et al.*, 1979; Roy, 1988; Couture and Cardin, 1996).

According to the revisionists, Quebec also housed considerable diversity. At the end of the eighteenth century, people of British origin made up 12.5 percent of the total population. Several thousand of these people were Loyalists who had come to Canada after the American Revolution. During the nineteenth century, the primary source of immigration was Britain, particularly Scotland and Ireland. In this period, 17 million people left Britain, 9 percent of whom came to Canada. These included over 200,000 Irish between 1825 and 1834, and approximately 200,000 more during the Great Famine of 1845–49. About 20 percent of the Irish immigrants settled in Quebec. By the end of the nineteenth century, the predominantly Irish immigration was replaced by East European Jews and Italians. The Jewish population in Quebec grew from 1.5 percent of the total population in 1901 to 5.7 percent in 1941. The Italian population was only 0.5 percent in 1901 and 2.3 percent in 1941. In 1996, the number of people claiming Italian origins totalled 4.2 percent of the Quebec population, while 2.6 percent claimed Jewish origins. According to the 1996 census, the other important groups, each of them making up between 0.5 and 1 percent of the population, were Greek, Portuguese, Chinese, Haitian, Lebanese, and Southeast Asian. Since the Irish immigration of the 1830s and 1840s, Quebec society has been demographically and culturally diverse (Linteau *et al.*, 1979; Bouchard, 2000).

At another level, the history of political parties in Quebec reflects both the evolution of the identity of Québécois and, as in all societies, contradictions within that identity. From 1867 to 1897 the Conservative Party dominated provincial politics, ruling for all but five of those years. The power of the Conservative Party symbolized the alliance between the Church and business, and a commitment to a socially conservative society led by private enterprise. Wilfrid Laurier's victory at the federal level in 1896 propelled the provincial Liberals to power in 1897. They remained in power for half a century, except between 1936 and 1939, until 1944. The Liberals maintained the alliance between the Church and private enterprise. The Church was given a free hand in social affairs and education while the political and economical spheres were left to politicians and business people (Couture and Cardin, 1996).

The domination by the Liberals was interrupted in 1936 when Maurice Duplessis and the Union Nationale party took power. That party resulted from the 1935 merger of the provincial Conservative Party and a group of young Liberal dissidents active during the Depression. The name of the group was l'Action Libérale Nationale and among its aims was nationalization of the private hydroelectricity companies. Once in power, however, Maurice Duplessis, leader of the Union Nationale coalition, did not implement any of the reforms proposed by l'Action Libérale Nationale, and instead ruled the same way the Liberals had.

It was the new leader of the provincial Liberal Party, Adélard Godbout, re-elected in 1939, who enacted the Union Nationale's promised reforms. The Godbout government was perhaps the most socially progressive provincial government of the twentieth century in Quebec. Among its reforms were the right to vote for women at the provincial level, the formation of Hydro-Québéc, and reforms in education. But World War II overshadowed its accomplishments when the federal government used its special wartime powers to intervene in provincial affairs. In 1944, the domination of the Liberal Party since 1897 came to an end when, with only 35 percent of the popular vote, Maurice Duplessis was elected and governed until 1959 (Couture and Cardin, 1996),

The Duplessis government was characteristic of the Cold War, being both right-wing and vehemently anti-communist. Opposition to Duplessis' extremely conservative style of government in the 1950s prepared the field for the reforms of the 1960s. When a group of young liberals led by Jean Lesage took power in 1960 it was the beginning of a new era and the period of reforms known as the Quiet Revolution. The Church was replaced by the provincial state in social affairs and the state intervened in the economy to promote French business interests. The emphasis on the provincial state corresponded with a change in the self-identification of many French Canadians in Quebec. Historians still debate the nature and effects of the Quiet Revolution. For some experts, the Quiet Revolution was a period of immense change that at last brought Quebec into the modern world (Bouchard, 2000). For others, the alliance of the Church and business, beginning from at least the second half of the nineteenth century, was a typical contradiction of modernity (Couture, 1998). To these observers, the changes of the 1960s, despite their magnitude, were simply a realignment of political and social forces in an already modern society, which is essentially what the "revisionists" argued.

POST-REVISIONISM

Most of the "revisionist" historiography was written when the Parti Québécois was a dominant force in Quebec polities. Formed in 1968, the Parti Québécois was elected less than a decade later on a clear social-democratic platform. Indeed, between 1976 and 1980, the government of the Parti Québécois initiated many controversial reforms, among them the reform of the automobile insurance system and the enactment of the famous Bill 101 on the regulation of the French language in the province. In 1980, as promised by René Lévesque, the Parti Québécois organized a referendum on the mandate to negotiate a new partnership with Canada referred to as "sovereignty-association" (Taucar, 2000). Many commentators have argued that this new partnership was in fact a proposal for a new confederation, a system where the central state could have very limited powers (Seymour, 1999). Others believe it would have represented a form of secession (Taucar, 2000).

Despite the fact that the question asked at the referendum seemed moderate, the federalist No side won convincingly—60 percent "no" to 40 percent "yes." However, in 1981, the Parti Québécois was re-elected, mainly because the Quebec voters were satisfied with its performance as a responsible government.

In 1983, the Parti Québécois appeared to turn to the right ideologically, coming into conflict with public sector unions and abandoning some of its social-democratic practices. This shift in policy posture played a crucial role in the Parti Québécois defeat in 1985. Robert Bourassa, who had patiently rebuilt his control over the provincial Liberal Party after his astonishing defeat in 1976, became once again the premier of Quebec in 1985. Caught in the debate and eventual failure of the Meech Lake Accord between 1987 and 1990, and in the controversy of Bill 178 on language regulation in Quebec allowing French and other languages on signs inside stores or public buildings but French only on signs outside buildings, Bourassa managed his way to victory again in 1989 (Couture and Cardin, 1996). Rut this second mandate was also very controversial, marked by the Oka crisis in the summer of 1990, just after the failure of the Meech Lake Accord, and the no less catastrophic failure of the Charlottetown Accord in 1992. Bourassa was replaced by Daniel Johnson, and in 1994 the Liberal Party was defeated by the Parti Québécois, led by Jacques Parizeau. One year after this victory, the Parti Québécois, in a second referendum on sovereignty, lost narrowly when the Yes side finished with a surprising 49 percent of votes (Taucar, 2000).

CONCLUSION

Since 1995, Quebec has continued its juggling act between its Quebec identity and its Canadian one. On the question of identity, the American author David Hollinger (1995), referring to the three major political identities of America, proposed the term affiliation instead of identify. It seems that Quebec also could be referred to as a society with several affiliations. These affiliations are complex, and this chapter only dealt with three affiliations used by several intellectuals to justify the project of an independent Quebec. However, it is clear that such a simplistic representation of Quebec does not do justice to all the contradictions of a society derived from European colonialism and still dealing with the consequences of that colonialism. It would be extremely naive to think that larger nations or societies, like Canada or the United States, do not have to deal with the same fundamental problems (Satzewich, 1992; Yuval-Davis and Stasiulis, 1995). It seems however that, in Quebec, the debates about the content of nationalism are broader and more public. Somehow, the international and national literature in English on Quebec should better reflect these debates.

REFERENCES

Andrew, Caroline (dir.). 1999. *Dislocation et permanence: l'intervention du Canada au Quotidien.* Ottawa: Les Presses de l'Université d'Ottawa.

Balthazar, Louis and Alfred O. Hero Jr. 1999. *Le Québec dans l'espace américain*, Montréal: Québec-Amérique.

Beiner, Ronald and Wayne Norman. 2001. *Canadian Political Philosophy*. Don Mills: Oxford University Press.

Blais, François, Guy Laforest et Diane Lamoureux (dir.). 1995. *Libéralismes et nationalismes: philosophie et politique*. Ste-Foy: Les Presses de l'Université Laval.

Bouchard, Gérard, 2000. *Genése des nations et cultures du Nouveau Monde. Essai d'histoire comparée*. Montréal: Boréal.

Cantin, Serge. 1997. *Ce pays comme un enfant*. Montréal: L'Hexagone.

Choquette, Leslie. 1997. *De Français à paysans. Modernité et tradition dans le peuplement du Canada français*. Sillery: Septentrion.

Couture, Claude. 1998. *Paddling with the Current*. Edmonton: University of Alberta Press.

Couture, Claude and Jean-François Cardin. 1996. *Espace et différences*. Ste-Foy: Presses de l'Université Laval.

Dickerson, M.O. 1994. *Introduction to Government and Politics*. Scarborough: Nelson Canada.

Dumont, Fernand. 1993. *Génèse de la société québécoise*. Montréal: Boréal.

Dupuis, Renée. 1997. *Tribus, Peuples et Nations: les nouveaux enjeux des revendications autochtones an Canada*, Montréal: Boréal.

Dupuis, Renée. 2001. *Quel Canada pour les autochtones: la fin de l'exclusion*, Montréal: Boreal.

Gagnon, Alain. 1990. *Quebec: Beyond the Quiet Revolution*. Scarborough: Nelson Canada.

Greer, Allan, 1997. *The People of New France*. Toronto: University of Toronto Press.

Habermas, Jurgen. 1998. *Après l'État-nation: une nouvelle constellation politique*. Paris: Fayerd.

Hollinger, David A. 1995. *Postethnic America*. New York: Basic Books.

Ignatieff, Michael. 1993. *Blood and Belonging: Journeys into the New Nationalism*. Toronto: Penguin Books.

Jackson, Robert J. 1994. *Politics in Canada*. Scarborough: Prentice-Hall Canada Inc.

Kymlicka, Will. 1989. *Liberalism, Community and Culture*. Don Mills: Oxford University Press.

Kymlicka, Will. 1995. *Multicultural Citizenship*. Toronto: Oxford University Press.

Laforest, Guy. 1992. *Trudeau et la fin du rêve canadien*. Québec: Septentrion.

Lamonde, Yvan. 2000. *Histoire sociale des idées au Québec (1760–1896)*. Montréal: Fides.

Lamoureux, Diane. 1995. "Le patriotisme constitutionnel et les Etats multinationaux." In Blais, François, Guy Laforest, and Diane Lamoureux (dir.). *Libéralismes et nationalismes: philosophie et politique*. Ste-Foy: Les Presses de l'Université Laval.

Lamoureux, Diane, Chantal Maillé, and Micheline de Sève (dir.). 1999. *Malaises identitaires: échanges féministes autour d'un Québec incertain*. Montréal: Les éditions du remue-ménage.

Landes, Ronald. 1995. *The Canadian Polity*. Scarborough: Prentice-Hall.

Le Soleil. "Les Cris à l'heure de la Paix des braves" (Special dossier on La Paix des braves). (2002, March 25).

Létourneau, Jocelyn. 2000. *Passer à l'avenir, histoire, mémoire, identité dans le Québec d'aujour-d'hui*. Montréal: Boréal.

Linteau, Paul-André, *et al.* 1979. *Histoire du Québec contemporain*. Montréal: Boréal.

Maclure, Jocelyn and Alain Gagnon. 2001. *Repères en mutation. Identité et citoyenneté dans le Québec contemporain*. Montréal: Québec Amérique.

Mathieu, Genevieve. 2001. *Qui est Québécois? Synthèse du débat sur la redéfinition de la nation*. Montréal: VLB Editeur.

McLean, Iain (ed). 1996, *The Concise Oxford Dictionary of Politics*. Oxford/New York: Oxford University Press.

McRoberts, Kenneth. 1997, *Misconceiving Canada: The Struggle for National Unity*. Don Mills: Oxford University Press.

Modood, Taria and Pnina Werbner, 1997. *The Politics of Multiculturalism in the New Europe*. London/New York: Zed Books.

Morin, Michel. 1997. *L'usurpation de la souveraineté autochtone*. Montréal: Boréal.

Roy, Fernande. 1988. *Progrès, Harmonie, Liberté: Le libéralisme des milieux d'affaires francophones à Montréal au tournant du siécle*. Montréal: Boréal.

Rudin, Ronald. 1997. *Making History in 20th Century Québec*. Montreal/Kingston: McGill-Queen's University Press.

Sarra-Bournet, Michel (dir.) avec la collaboration de Jocelyn Saint-Pierre 2000. *Les nationalismes au Québec du XIXe au XXe siècle*. Ste-Foy: Les Presses de l'Université Laval.

Satzewich, Vic (ed). 1992. *Deconstructing a Nation: Immigration, Multiculturalism and Racism in '90s Canada*. Halifax/Saskatoon: Fernwood Publishing/University of Saskatchewan.

Seymour, Michel (dir.). 1999. *Nationalité, citoyenneté et solidarité*. Montréal: Liber.

Seymour, Michel. 1999. *La nation en question*. Montréal: Editions de l'Hexagone.

Strong-Boag, Veronica, Sherrill Grace, Avigail Eisenberg and Joan Anderson (Eds.). 1998. *Painting the Maple: Essays on Race, Gender, and the Construction of Canada*. Vancouver: UBC Press.

Taucar, Christopher Edward. 2000. *Canadian Federalism and Quebec Sovereignty*. New York: Peter Lang Publishing.

Taylor, Charles. 1992. *Rapprocher les solitudes*. Québec: Presses de l'Université Laval.

Taylor, Charles. 1994. *Multiculturalism*. Princeton: Princeton University Press.

Taylor, Charles. 1994. *Multiculturalisme*. Paris: Aubier.

Thériault, J. Yvon. 1995. *L'identité à l'épreuve de la modernité: écrits politiques sur l'Acadie et les francophonies canadiennes minoritaires*. Moncton: Les Éditions d'Acadie.

Yuval-Davis, Nira and Daiva Stasiulis, 1995. *Unsettling Settler Societies: Articulations of Gender, Race, Ethnicity and Class*. London: Sage.

September 11, 2001

KENT ROACH*

*__Kent Roach__ is Professor of Law and Criminology at the University of Toronto.

The September 11 terrorist attacks on the United States had immediate consequences for Canada. Alexander Filipov, a Regina-born engineer, had switched his reservation at the last minute to be on American Airlines Flight 11. This flight was the first 767 aircraft driven into the massive twin towers of the World Trade Center. Another Canadian, former NHL hockey player Garnet "Ace" Bailey, was on United Airlines Flight 175 as it smashed into the south tower. Twenty-two other Canadians were among the 2,813 people killed in the subsequent collapse of both towers. The Canadians were in the World Trade Center for a variety of reasons. Some had business appointments; others were working at the New York offices of their firms. Some had moved to New York for employment opportunities, and a few were visitors to the city. David Barkway, a managing director of BMO Nesbitt Burns in Toronto, had a business appointment at the 105th-floor office of the bond-trading firm Cantor Fitzgerald. He paged his Toronto office asking for help but was never heard from again. He left a two-year-old son and a wife pregnant with their second child. Christine Egan, a nurse, had accompanied her younger brother Michael Egan to his office to view the city. She was to meet an old schoolmate in the lobby at 9.30 am, but both brother and sister perished. No Canadians were involved in the crashes of a third hijacked aircraft into the Pentagon in Washington or of a fourth in Pennsylvania, after passengers attempted to seize the aircraft from the hijackers.

Canada had experienced terrorism before. To much public approval, the War Measures Act had been proclaimed in force at 4.00 am on October 16, 1970, in response to the kidnapping of British diplomat James Cross by one cell of the Front de Libération du Québec (FLQ) and the kidnapping of Quebec Cabinet minister Pierre Laporte by another cell. The Cabinet declared the FLQ to be an unlawful association, and the police arrested close to 500 people on suspicion they were guilty of the new offences of being a member or supporter of the FLQ. These repressive measures did not prevent Laporte's subsequent murder. Those involved with his kidnapping and death were eventually apprehended and convicted of murder, kidnapping, and other crimes that existed before the October Crisis. Cross was recovered in late December and his kidnappers allowed to take a plane to Cuba. In an eerie coincidence, Canadian newspapers on the morning of September 11, 2001, featured a story about the arrest in New York City of a man who had hijacked an Air Canada flight in 1971. When the plane landed safely in Havana, two other hijacked aircraft were already on the ground. Terrorism took a more deadly turn with the 1985 bombing of an Air India flight from Vancouver, killing all 329 passengers on board. Still, Canadians, like the rest of the world, had never experienced suicide hijackings of the scale of the September 11 attacks.

Within forty five minutes of the attacks on the World Trade Center and the Pentagon, Canadian officials decided that airports from Vancouver to St John's would accept 224 planes destined for the United States. A Canadian official later told the *Los Angeles Times*: "This government took a big risk that day. Nobody knew if there would be more attacks."

Once American officials had decided to close their airspace, there was little else that Canada could do as it accepted only those aircraft that did not have enough fuel to return to their point of departure. Some of the planes were deliberately diverted to remote, less-populous parts of Canada. A Korean 747 airliner was allowed to land in Whitehorse, Yukon, even though it was thought to be highjacked. Gander, Newfoundland, with a population of 10,000, accommodated over 6,000 people in thirty-eight aircraft in the three days before full air service was resumed. Stranded passengers in Halifax were housed in a Canadian military base.

Many stories emerged of warm Canadian hospitality and new friendships. Passengers who stayed at Gander later established scholarships for local residents, and some made return trips to see new friends. Stephen Jay Gould, the famed Harvard scientist who was soon to die of cancer, wrote that while stranded with 9,000 others in Halifax, "I heard not a single harsh word, saw not the slightest gesture of frustration, and felt nothing but pure and honest welcome … And so Canada, although you are not my home or native land, we will always share this bond of your unstinting hospitality to people who descended upon you as frightened strangers and received nothing but solace and solidarity in your embrace of goodness." Another American passenger on the last of forty-two planes diverted to Halifax commented that she was "humbled by the empathy and support of the Halifax community … I would thank the military personnel and support staff and airport staff for their many kindnesses and frequently the response would be 'Glad to do it. We're neighbours.'"

Along with much of the world, Canada declared a national day of mourning after September 11. More than 100,000 people attended a memorial service on Parliament Hill. Prime Minister Chrétien told the audience: "We reel before the blunt and terrible reality of the evil we have just witnessed." Addressing the American ambassador to Canada, Chrétien added: "Our friendship has no limit. Generation after generation, we have travelled many difficult miles together. Side by side, we have lived through many dark times, always firm in our shared resolve to vanquish any threat to freedom and justice. And together, with our Allies, we will defy and defeat the threat that terrorism poses to all civilized nations. Mr. Ambassador, we will be with the U.S. every step of the way. As friends, as neighbours, as family." Ambassador Paul Cellucci replied that he had "been touched, at times overwhelmed, by the outpouring of support." The tragedy "has brought us together as never before. It has, once again, shown us that the differences that divide us are far, far less important than the ties that bind us." As one American analyst stated: "For millions of Canadians, Americans are friends, family and business partners. The choice between international terrorists and helping a neighbour was simple, and most Canadians made it without equivocation or calculation of national interest." Canadians, as individuals, were deeply affected by the September 11 terrorist attacks and responded generously and compassionately to the suffering of their neighbours.

But the relationship between the governments of Canada and the United States has never been easy. Soon after the attacks, reports surfaced that as many as five of the terrorists entered the United States from Canada, as had Ahmed Ressam, an al-Qaeda terrorist caught at the border in 1999 with a Canadian passport and explosives to bomb the Los Angeles International Airport. These reports were quickly found to be erroneous, but the impression that Canada was a terrorist haven lingered. Late in September 2001 the *Christian Science Monitor* commented that Canada, "the giant, genial nation—known for its crimson-clad Mounties and great comedians—has also become an entry point and staging ground for Osama bin Laden's terrorist 'sleeper cells.'" Although the *New York Times* stated that Canada had altered many of its security policies in an "attempt to reassure the United States that Canada is not a sanctuary for terrorists," it still reported in 2001 "that Canada's liberal refugee and immigration policies are of particular concern."

A Toronto memorial service for the thousands of victims of September 11 was marred when one of its coordinators, an American minister who was also the president of Republicans Abroad, "spoke at length about Christianity being the only salvation." To applause from the audience, a Toronto lawyer criticized these remarks as insensitive to the non-Christians in the audience. This would not be the last time that differing Canadian and American sensitivities to multiculturalism would clash. Canada would subsequently protest American border policies that targeted Canadian citizens born in the Middle East and other Muslim countries for particular attention. Stories mounted of Canadians, mainly from these groups, being poorly treated by American officials. There were also some hurtful but apparently deliberate slights. In his dramatic address to a joint session of Congress on September 11, 2001, President Bush failed to mention the Canadians who died in the attacks or Canada's warm reception for the hundreds of American-bound flights, even though he mentioned fifteen other countries. He subsequently thanked Canada, but suspicions lingered that Canada's response to September 11 was not appreciated enough by the American government.

There were also concerns that Canada was trying too hard to please the American government in its new war against terrorism and that the long-term consequence of September 11 would be an erosion of Canadian independence and difference from the United States. Shortly after September 11, Canadian leaders pledged their support for American-led military operations against the Taliban and al-Qaeda in Afghanistan, even if it meant that some innocent people would be hurt. This early support was backed up by Canada's largest military contribution since the Korean War, involving nearly 3,000 troops and including a 750 Light Infantry Battle Group that operated as part of a U.S. Army Task Force. It remained in Afghanistan for only six months because of resource constraints. Canadian military participation in Afghanistan was controversial. Some argued that placing Canadian troops under de facto American control harmed not only Canada's sovereignty but also its reputation for peace-keeping and respect for international law. They also supported Canada's autonomy from a new American Northern Command with a mandate to defend all of North America by land, air, and sea. Others, however, argued that Canadian participation in American military operations in the defence of North America, missile defence, and in a possible invasion of Iraq was necessary. For them, the experience in Afghanistan demonstrated the urgent need for Canada to spend much more money on the military. The degree of Canadian participation in the war against Afghanistan did not overly impress the United States, as the American ambassador repeatedly called on Canada to spend more on its military, but it was not lost on Osama bin Laden. The al-Qaeda leader, who is believed to have planned the September 11 attacks and apparently survived the massive bombings of al-Qaeda strongholds in Afghanistan, noted that Canada, along with Great Britain, France, Italy, Germany, and Australia, had joined the United States in its attack on Afghanistan. With reference to terrorist bombings on October 12, 2002, that killed over 180 people in Bali, Indonesia, including many Australians and two Canadians, bin Laden chillingly threatened revenge on all of America's allies.

Four Canadian soldiers did not return home from Afghanistan. They were killed by "friendly fire" from an American "top gun" pilot. The pilot, who had taken "go pills," or amphetamines, during his long flight mission, had observed ground fire from the Canadians' routine live-fire exercises outside Kandahar, an Allied stronghold. He was flying at high speed and altitude and was told to hold fire. Still, the pilot, who had been nicknamed "psycho" because of his aggressiveness, declared self-defence, descended, and released his 250 kilogram laser-guided bomb on the Canadians, only to be told 32 seconds later that the ground fire came from "friendlies." The pilot and his wingman were subsequently charged with involuntary manslaughter, but also received substantial support from their home state of Illinois. The *New York Times* reported: "The case has been a national obsession in Canada, and a source of continuing friction between the Bush administration and the Canadian government."

There was less controversy in Canada when it was discovered that elite Canadian special forces had given captives to the Americans for detention and interrogation at Guantanamo Bay, Cuba, in probable violation of the Geneva Conventions. There was almost no controversy when the Canadian Navy subsequently handed over captured al-Qaeda suspects to the Americans. The Americans continued to detain and interrogate 600 captives from Afghanistan at Guantanamo Bay. The captives included Omar Khadr, a Canadian teenager who had apparently thrown a grenade that killed an American soldier during hostilities near the Afghanistan-Pakistan border. The Canadian government expressed concerns about Khadr's youth and lack of access to Canadian consular officials. Nevertheless, he remained in American custody at Guantanamo Bay without being accorded the rights of a prisoner of war not to be interrogated or the rights of an accused charged with a crime. If Khadr is eventually charged, he may face the death penalty, since the United States is one of the few countries in the world that still executes juvenile offenders.

The Canadian government made efforts on the home front to respond to the threat of terrorism and to satisfy both American and United Nations expectations. A little more than a month after September 11, it introduced a massive and hastily drafted *Anti-terrorism Act* (Bill C-36). The bill included new legal concepts such as investigative hearings, preventive arrests, broad motive-based crimes for participation in or support for terrorist groups at home or abroad, as well as new powers to list terrorist groups, deprive them of charitable status, and take their property. There were fears that the bill, as introduced, would define some anti-globalization protests and illegal strikes as terrorist activities. A broad coalition of civil libertarians, lawyers, unions, Aboriginal people, the refugee community, anti-globalization protesters, and groups representing Muslim and Arab Canadians all expressed fears about the breadth of the bill. Before it became law in December 2001, Bill C-36 was amended to respond to some of the criticisms, but concerns remain about the necessity and breadth of the new anti-terrorism law.

September 11 also revived criticism that the Supreme Court of Canada had engaged in judicial activism by ruling that fugitives generally could not be returned for trial to the United States without assurances that the death penalty would not be applied. Would this decision mean that Canada could not return an al-Qaeda operative to the United States without such assurance? Criticisms of the Supreme Court were renewed when, in January 2002, it ruled that the same reasoning applied to prevent the deportation of suspected terrorists to face a substantial risk of torture. Would this decision mean that Canada could not return a terrorist to a country such as Jordan or Saudi Arabia which might use torture in interrogations? Arguments were made that it was the elected government of Canada, not the independent courts, that should make decisions affecting Canadian security and foreign relations. At the same time, the Court would not commit itself to an absolute rule that extradition or deportation of a terrorist to face the death penalty or torture would never be constitutional. Would the Court condone the torture of terrorists in some cases, as Harvard law professor Alan Dershowitz argued it should, if necessary to prevent another September 11? Many judges, including Chief Justice Beverley McLachlin, recognized that September 11 would place pressures on the courts to readjust the balance between liberty and security, but also that the courts might have to take unpopular stands in terrorism cases.

After passing the *Anti-terrorism Act*, the government introduced another massive bill, the *Public Safety Act*, but it was withdrawn after criticisms that it would give ministers dangerous new powers to declare military security zones around places of protest such as the 2002 G8 meeting in Kananaskis, Alberta. The bill also provided for greater controls over airport security and dangerous biological and explosive materials, and it increased efforts to make nuclear plants and pipelines more secure from possible terrorist attacks. Biological terrorism became an issue after post-September 11 mailings of anthrax in the United States resulted in five deaths. In January 2002 Canadians were reminded of the insecurity of their water supplies as a judicial inquiry concluded that budget cuts leading to less monitoring of water quality had contributed to the death of seven people in Walkerton, Ontario, in 2000 because of accidental *E. coli* contamination. If water could be accidentally poisoned without the government responding, what would ensure that the government could prevent or respond to the deliberate poisoning of water, air, or food? The *Public Safety Act* was reintroduced with new restrictions on some ministerial powers, but it has yet to be enacted. Canada's legislative and administrative response to the terrifying prospect of biological and nuclear terrorism and its preparation for emergencies such as September 11 lags behind the American response, which includes a new agency for "homeland security," the vaccination of a million military and health-care personnel, and plans to provide free smallpox vaccinations for all Americans who want them.

Although the *Public Safety Act* was not pushed forward, a separate bill dealing with exchange of information about airline passenger lists was quietly passed to ensure compliance with new American security requirements. In December 2001 the Supreme Court unanimously ruled that Canadian travellers did not have a reasonable expectation of privacy in their customs declaration forms to outweigh the government's interests in determining whether they were on vacation while receiving unemployment insurance. Elinor Caplan, the minister responsible for customs, has defended "advance passenger information" as a "major investigative tool" that "puts investigators hard on the trail of suspected killers and terrorists" and "significantly increases our ability to track pedophiles, find criminals trying to enter our country, identify potential drug smugglers, and protect the health of Canadians." The federal privacy commissioner, George Radwanski, however, questioned the use of advance airline passenger lists for general law enforcement purposes. He strenuously opposed plans to keep a "big brother" database on the foreign travels of Canadians over the past six years. Supported by a legal opinion from retired Supreme Court of Canada Justice Gérard La Forest that allowing government agencies access to detailed, travel-related information of millions of innocent Canadians would violate the Charter, Radwanski raised concerns about the "unprecedented creation of government dossiers of personal information about all citizens." He also took exception to the idea that those who oppose the database are "indifferent to terrorism, murder and armed crime, drug smuggling, pedophilia, the plight of children, even plagues." As in other countries, there were concerns that new powers in the war against terrorism were spreading to wars against other serious crimes and that privacy was being sacrificed in the new quest for security.

In December 2001 the federal government allocated almost $8 billion in spending on security in its self-proclaimed "security budget." The new spending was devoted to policing, the military, increased airport security, and border and immigration controls, but not to matters such as health care that many Canadians saw as a more immediate threat to their personal security. The budget focused on more police officers, security officials, immigration officials, and border guards. Much less money was devoted to responses that might prevent or respond to nuclear and biological terrorism or deliberate or accidental contamination of food and water supplies. The 2001 security budget made it seem as though terrorism was the only threat to the security of Canadians. Even with respect to a possible repeat of September 11, it is not clear that Canadians were getting their money's worth for a new security tax of $24 per round airline trip. A year after September 11, the chair of a Canadian Senate committee worried that box cutters similar to those used by terrorists could still be placed on aircraft at Canada's busiest airport. Armed marshals were placed on some flights, especially those into Washington, but not all baggage was screened for bombs. Air Canada pilots demanded that better security doors be installed on their cockpits or that they be given taser guns.

The immediate concern for many Canadians after September 11 was not distant events in Afghanistan, new legislation, or even aviation security, but ensuring that the almost $2 billion in trade that crosses the American-Canadian border every day continued to flow. The American *Patriot Act*, enacted with overwhelming support in Congress in October 2001, did not allay concerns about increased border delays and bottlenecks. It provided for the tripling of border guards and customs and immigration officials on the "northern border," one many Americans believed was a threat to their security. Such a mobilization at the American border would have inconvenienced the people who make a total of almost 200 million crossings every year. It might have harmed the American economy, but it would certainly have devastated the Canadian economy, which relies on exports to the United Stares. In December 2001 broad framework agreements were signed between Canada and the United States calling for increased collaboration in identifying security risks and facilitating the flow of low-risk goods and people over the border. The "smart border" agreements went beyond safer and more efficient flows of goods and people, however, and led to the initialing of a "safe third country" agreement between Canada and the United States. This agreement prohibited most refugees from applying to Canada if they reached the United Stares first. It may have responded to American concerns about Canada's "liberal" refugee policies, but it did not ensure free trade—as witnessed by bitter trade disputes that raged over American softwood lumber tariffs and farm subsidies.

The border agreements did not ease frictions between the two governments. Canada protested that Canadian citizens born in the Middle East and Muslim countries were being singled out for photographing, fingerprinting, and registration in the United Stares. The Canadian government temporarily issued a travel advisory to Canadian citizens born in these countries about the American practices. The Americans responded that such practices were not automatically tied to place of birth and did not constitute racial profiling. Speaking at Niagara Falls, New York, United States Attorney General John Ashcroft warned that "no country is exempt from the war against terrorism" and that the National Security Entry and Exit Registration System, which had already fingerprinted and photographed 14,000 people, including 1,400 Canadians, would continue to operate. Some Canadians protested the system as racial and religious profiling. Rohinton Mistry, a prominent Canadian author who was born in India, cancelled his American book tour because of the way he had been treated in American airports.

September 11 had consequences for the tenor of Canadian democracy. There was a widespread outcry after a University of British Columbia professor, Sunera Thobani, criticized American foreign policy shortly after September 11 as "bloodthirsty" and "vengeful." She also raised concerns about Canadian complicity with the American-led war in Afghanistan and a possible war against Iraq. The negative reaction to Thobani's speech at an academic conference included police investigations into whether she should be charged criminally with wilfully promoting hatred against Americans; denunciations of her speech by both the prime minister of Canada and the premier of British Columbia; and arguments in the media that it was somehow inappropriate for her, as an immigrant to Canada, to make such harsh criticisms of either Canada or the United States. Nevertheless, many Canadians agreed with Thobani that American foreign policy was one of the causes of September 11. Even Prime Minister Chrétien was later prepared to relate September 11 to global disparities of power and wealth, but his comments on the first anniversary of September 11 that the "Western world is getting too rich in relation to the poor world" were greeted with criticisms that he was being "anti-American" and blaming the victim for the crimes of September 11.

The Thobani and Chrétien comments relating September 11 to broader issues of American foreign policy and global justice prompted debates about Canadian nationalism and Canada's place in the world. Veteran journalist Robert Fulford argued that the Thobani speech was a symptom of a more general anti-Americanism that was an unacceptable part of Canadian nationalism and a denial of the many values Canada shares with the United States. Historian Michael Bliss went further: he predicted that September 11 was "the end of Canadian nationalism" and was "driving us faster along the road we had already chosen, the road of continental integration." In the immediate aftermath of September 11, many Canadians seemed prepared to sacrifice sovereignty for continued security and prosperity. Former foreign affairs minister Lloyd Axworthy expressed concerns that September 11 may have started a "slippery slope" that will erode "Canada's ability to speak with an independent and considered voice" on a range of matters. The notorious picture of Canadian troops roughly handing over detainees at Kandahar Airport to the Americans for possible detention in the open-air cages of Camp X-Ray in Guantanamo Bay, Cuba, may symbolize a shift towards greater integration with the United States at the expense of civil liberties, respect for international law, and sovereign foreign, immigration, and military policies. At the very least, the aftermath of September 11 has prompted fundamental debates about the nature of Canadian law, democracy, sovereignty, and security.

LAMENT FOR A NATION?

In my more pessimistic moments, I find myself thinking of George Grant's *Lament for a Nation*, in which he declares Canadian sovereignty and a distinctive Canadian democracy to be dead. That book was written in response to Canada's decision to accept nuclear arms in the wake of the Cuban Missile Crisis of October 1962. Although September 11 was traumatic, the Cuban crisis was even more so. Canadians feared they would be caught in the middle of an impending nuclear war between the United Stares and the Soviet Union. Nevertheless, Prime Minister Diefenbaker refused to cooperate with the Americans or accept nuclear weapons. He persisted even after his minister of defence resigned and he was strongly criticized by the American government. Diefenbaker lost the 1963 election to Lester Pearson, who had decided that Canada must accept nuclear arms. Grant argued that Diefenbaker's error was his failure to recognize "that a branch-plant society could not possibly show independence over an issue on which the American government was seriously determined." Diefenbaker's defeat, he said, was "the defeat of Canadian nationalism" and, indeed, the death of the Canada. In his view, Canada could remain distinct from the United States only by resisting involvement in the new American empire, including the war in Vietnam. Canada had to develop those aspects of its political culture that were both more conservative and more socialist than the liberalism and faith in limited government and modern progress shared by Democrats and Republicans south of the border.

There was some support for Grant's arguments that the Cuban Missile Crisis revealed Canada as no longer a fully sovereign nation. When Diefenbaker hesitated to place Canadian forces on full alert during the crisis, the military, acting in coordination with the Americans, did so in any event. Michael Bliss has suggested that the fact that Canadian officials, without consulting the prime minister, decided to accept stranded aircraft when American airspace was closed on September 11, 2001, similarly underlines that, "in a real North American crisis," Canadian "sovereignty is an illusion." He questioned whether Canada can afford to have "more liberal immigration and security procedures than the United States . . . If Americans implement ethnic 'profiling' as a sensible security procedure, can we refuse to do the same?" Certainly on some issues, Canada has followed the American lead in the war against terrorism. In February 2002 the *New York Times* concluded that "Canada has thoroughly overhauled its security policy since the Sept. 11 attacks on the United States, tightening coordination with Washington in military, intelligence and law enforcement matters while easing its traditional concerns over privacy and other civil liberties." It quoted a senior Bush administration official that the Canadians "have done a lot, yes, but at the same time, they have a lot to do, and they know it." There are legitimate fears that September 11 is driving Canada towards Americanized criminal justice, immigration, and military and foreign policies that depart from such Canadian values as multiculturalism, peacekeeping, and respect for international laws and institutions.

In my more optimistic moments, however, I believe that it is unwise to lament a Canada that was lost on that surreal morning of September 11. Grant was premature in declaring Canadian sovereignty to be dead once Diefenbaker was defeated and the government accepted nuclear weapons. Indeed, Grant's death notice for Canada was the start of a new Canadian nationalism. Prime Ministers Pearson and Trudeau subsequently took stands on a variety of issues, including Vietnam and nuclear disarmament, which were very unpopular with both Democratic and Republican administrations to the south. The history of Canadian relations with the United States has been one of continual pushes towards continental integration and pulls towards sovereign nationalism. The shock of September 11 tilted the balance towards integration, but it also provided Canada with opportunities to reaffirm its differences from the United States. Realizing this potential, however, will take more imagination and will than we have generally seen since September 11.

SEPTEMBER 11 AND OTHER CHALLENGES TO LAW, DEMOCRACY, SOVEREIGNTY, AND SECURITY

Within the short span of less than two years, how do we assess Canada's response to September 11 and situate the new challenges faced by Canada into a larger context of recent challenges for Canadian law, democracy, sovereignty, and security? Although the challenges of September 11 are particularly dramatic and intense, one of the arguments of this book is that they are not fundamentally different from those we have faced in the past. In other words, September 11 did not change everything. Rather, it accelerated a number of preexisting challenges already faced by Canada. This is an important message, given the many apocalyptic statements that have been made about September 11.

Before September 11, we were already in the habit of expanding our criminal law in a symbolic attempt to respond to well-publicized crimes that threatened Canadians' sense of security. The 1990s had seen an expansion and toughening of the criminal law in more or less direct response to a number of well-publicized murders, including the massacre of fourteen women at École Polytechnique in Montreal and murders in biker gang wars. As in the United States, there has been a tendency to "govern through crime." Complex issues such as crimes against women and minorities, and now terrorism, have been dealt with in a symbolic and punitive manner through the enactment of tougher criminal laws, including new offences that denounce conduct that was already criminal. Both before and after September 11, Canadian governments have prided themselves on advancing equality and victims' rights by enacting more criminal laws, despite the absence of evidence that criminal laws make real such laudable rights. Canadians have relied on the criminal law in a desperate and frequently vain quest for an increased sense of security and an understandable desire to express concern for those victimized by crime. September 11 only continued this trend.

The difficulty for Canadian courts as they make decisions with regard to terrorism mirrors the larger phenomenon of Canadian courts being put on trial and held up to increased public and political scrutiny of their decisions. The pressure placed on our courts by governments and the public, most of whom, it seems, would prefer that their Supreme Court be elected, makes it vitally important that courts exercise their role independently and fearlessly. At the same time, however, some recent deferential developments in jurisprudence under the *Canadian Charter of Rights and Freedoms*, as well as the historical records of courts in times of wars and other crises, should make us uneasy with the arguments of the former minister of justice Anne McLellan that the *Anti-terrorism Act* was acceptable because it was consistent with the Charter. The fact that most of the legislation may be Charter proof, in the sense that it will not be struck down by the courts, does not mean that it was necessary, wise, or even just. September 11 continued a trend of Canadian courts being put on trial and of governments Charter-proofing questionable laws.

Before September 11, not all was well with Canadian democracy. Since the protests against the World Trade Organization in Seattle, similar Canadian protests against globalization, poverty, and the treatment of Aboriginal people have often been greeted with intimidating police presences and other security measures that are not conducive to a robust democracy that invites dissent. Many expressed legitimate fears that the *Anti-terrorism Act* as first introduced could be used against illegal protests that disrupted essential public or private services. The subsequently introduced *Public Safety Act* was dubbed the "Kananaskis Act" because of the ability it would have given the minister of defence to declare the already isolated site of the G8 summit an off-limits military security zone. Since September 11 there has been an increased temptation to brand the most strident of Canada's dissenters as terrorists. Nevertheless, such dissenters were already seen as dangerous before September 11. Efforts to curb democratic debate, including debate about the causes and consequences of terrorism, are unfortunate. As a nation that regularly debates secession in a democratic manner, Canada should be a shining example of a free and democratic society. Robust democracy at home and abroad will not always prevent terrorism, but it will reaffirm the illegitimacy of violence in the pursuit of political ends.

Since September 11, terrorism has been linked with Canada's immigration and refugee policies, even though none of the September 11 terrorists entered the United States through Canada. Concerns about systemic discrimination in the criminal justice system and linkages between criminal justice and immigration are not, however, new. There was evidence of the profiling and over-incarceration of Aboriginal people and African Canadians long before September 11. Similarly, the immigration system was already being used to achieve punitive objectives such as the deportation of permanent residents convicted of crimes. Both before and after September 11, Canada faced the danger of Americanized criminal justice policies in which underclasses and groups stereotypically associated with crime were exposed to heightened state surveillance and incarceration. Although the federal government was eager to defend the *Anti-terrorism Act* as legislation that promoted human rights and protected racial and religious minorities from hate crimes, it resisted calls to commit itself in the act to nondiscrimination in the administration of the many new powers given to police and prosecutors. This refusal has led to fears that new and existing security powers could be used, as they have been in the United States, to target or profile people simply because they are perceived to be of the same race, religion, or country of birth as the September 11 terrorists. The government's claims that the act advances human rights ring hollow, and the proposed legislation was opposed by many groups which feared that their human rights would be harmed by the new anti-terrorism law. The fallout from September 11 has presented new threats to equality, but even before September 11 there was a need for Canadians to renew their commitment to non-discrimination in the administration of all our laws.

Well before September 11 the forces of globalization and continental integration were buffeting Canadians. Nationalists had long expressed fears for the preservation of Canadian sovereignty, but these concerns increased in the wake of the 1988 Free Trade Agreement and the hollowing out of Canadian governments and corporations during much of the 1990s. Canadian nationalism was not particularly healthy before September 11. Some influential Canadians had lost confidence in Canada's future as a humane and peaceful alternative to the United States. There was much envy of American prosperity, importance, and low taxation rates and increasing interest in American practices of privatized public goods, including health and education. The greater integration of the Canadian economy into the American economy and the need for a free flow of goods across the border make Canada vulnerable to American demands about security and attempts to link security concerns with broader issues of Canadian foreign, military, immigration, refugee, and criminal justice policy. These demands in turn reduce Canadian confidence in the wisdom of maintaining distinctive policies on these fronts. There are real concerns that Canada has not done enough since September 11 to preserve a sovereign foreign policy, with its traditional post-Second World War commitments to peacekeeping, respect for international law, and a generous refugee policy. Still, Canadian sovereignty was under siege long before September 11.

The horrible events of September 11 and their non-stop media coverage made Canadians feel more insecure. But Canadians had plenty of reasons to feel insecure before that fateful day. Governmental cuts in the 1990s affected a range of government services that contributed to the security of Canadians. The seven deaths in the summer of 2000 from the *E. coli* in Walkerton's water supply made many Canadians worry about the safety of their food and water. Other fears relate to nuclear and aviation safety, our reliance on computer systems and power grids, and the declining quality of Canada's health care system and its air and water. The prospect after September 11 that terrorists could poison our water and air, crash our planes, hack our computers, and blow up our nuclear reactors only added to the existing risk of accidents with respect to such materials. Although the world certainly seemed more dangerous to Canadians after September 11, it also seemed quite risky before that time. The challenge is to respond rationally to the many risks we face and to integrate the threat of terrorism with other risks in modern society.

CONCLUSION

This book [*September 11: Consequences for Canada*, 2003] has two main goals. The first is to provide a critical assessment of the consequences of September 11 for Canada. To this end, I will examine post-September 11 developments in Canadian law and democracy and in its immigration, military, foreign, and security policies. Much of the focus will be on Bill C-36, the *Anti-terrorism Act*, because it remains Canada's prime legislative response to September 11 and the one that has been subjected to the most public debate. The government's claims that this new law is needed to prevent terrorism and that it will advance human rights will be critically assessed in light of evidence that many of it most controversial provisions were not used during the first year of the law's existence and the fears of many groups that the law will infringe their human rights. The government's claims that the new law is consistent with the Charter will also be examined. Although the act violates a wide range of Charter rights, the courts may well find that these limitations are reasonable. The successful Charter-proofing of the new law reflects the ambiguous nature of the Charter in both guaranteeing rights and legitimating limitations on rights. This ambiguity is underlined by the fact that courts have refused to commit themselves to never send a suspected terrorist from Canada to face torture or the death penalty.

Looking beyond the *Anti-terrorism Act*, I will suggest that the Canadian government has been too quick to allow the imperative of keeping the border open and secure to be linked with more contentious issues of foreign, military, and immigration policy. Such linkages can undermine sovereignty and adversely affect Canada's international reputation. They may not even succeed in keeping the border open for trade. Canada can, as it is doing with respect to American softwood lumber tariffs, use existing trade mechanisms to keep the border open. Ceding sovereignty in the hope of free trade and security is not, however, the answer. Canada should not resist sensible cooperation with the United States on common border and security issues, but it should not rush towards measures that will adversely affect Canada's ability to devise its own independent policies. Since September 11, Canada has placed its enviable reputation for peacekeeping, a generous refugee policy, and respect for international law and institutions in jeopardy.

The second goal of this book is to provide a sense of how Canada's anti-terrorism policies should evolve in the future. Although September 11 has, in the short-term, hastened Canada's integration with the United States, it need not do so. It could result in renewed Canadian nationalism and a more measured and moderate Canadian response to terrorism. The Canadian approach to terrorism could place less emphasis on the criminal sanction and military force than the American approach and more emphasis on respect for international law, robust democracy, non-discrimination, and a welcoming multiculturalism. The Canadian approach could also integrate terrorism into the broader context of other threats to human security. Terrorism should be integrated into a broader human security agenda that includes better protection of food and water safety, nuclear and biological safety, public health, and emergency response. Attempts to increase the security of places and materials vulnerable to terrorism may protect Canadians not only from catastrophic terrorism but also from the greater risk of accidents and natural disasters. A broader security agenda that targets places and systems may avoid some of the threats to equality, liberty, and privacy that occur when people are targeted as potential terrorists. It may also avoid some of the conflicts with courts that should vigorously protect civil liberties and equality, even at the risk of public opposition.

Abroad, concerns about terrorism should be integrated into broader concerns about achieving human security, arms control, keeping the peace, and building democracies. Canadian policy should resist efforts to link the need for an open and secure border with broader issues of Canada's sovereign foreign, military, and immigration policy. Canada's interests are not necessarily America's interests. Canada is in a good position to help separate legitimate concerns about terrorism and security from more controversial aspects of American foreign policy. A broader security agenda will not be achieved by enacting more criminal laws and giving the police greater powers, as was done with the *Anti-terrorism Act*. It will not be achieved by spending the massive amounts required to ensure that the Canadian Forces can fight in combat with the high-tech American military. It will not be achieved by heavy-handed policies at home and abroad that may only increase grievances and produce more terrorists. Without more imagination and will, however, Canada may continue to fall into the slipstream of America's war against terrorism.

Thinking About Human Rights

DARREN J. O'BYRNE*

*Darren J. O'Byrne is Senior Lecturer and Programme Convener (Human Rights), University of Surrey, Roehampton.

At some point in their higher education careers, many students undertaking degree courses in the humanities or social sciences will probably encounter some aspect of what we might call human rights research. For example, in history they will almost certainly discuss the transatlantic slave trade and, of course, the Nazi Holocaust. In criminology they might learn about the death penalty. In media studies they will be introduced to aspects of censorship. In psychology they may be asked to consider the making of a torturer. In anthropology a lecturer may offer a session on female genital mutilation. In philosophy students will be expected to dedicate time to understanding ethics and moral behaviour. If they take electives in law, international relations, or politics, they will probably be introduced to various human rights legislations and conventions.

So, it would not be fair to say that the academic world has ignored human rights—far from it. However, from the perspective of human rights, disciplinarity brings its own problems. Where censorship is discussed in media courses, the focus is likely to be on censorship as media regulation, rather than as human rights violation. The making of a torturer is likely to be included under the banner of abnormal psychology and thus detached from questions concerning torture as a human rights abuse. Historians will undoubtedly treat slavery and the Holocaust as obscene assaults on human dignity, but slavery and genocide are more than historical issues—they are also contemporary problems. Sociologists have contributed to these debates in various forms, but … the discipline of sociology has shied away from embracing 'human rights' as a general term. It seems particularly odd that sociologists have done exceptional work on aspects of human rights—one thinks of Patterson on slavery, Sellin and Radelet on the death penalty, Bauman and Fein on genocide, numerous media sociologists on censorship—but their discipline has resisted the need to bring these disparate aspects together.

The purpose of this volume [*Human Rights: An Introduction*, 2003] is to right this academic wrong, to bring together for the first time the rich studies which have illuminated our thinking about these different aspects of human rights. In some respects, it requires us to leave our preconceptions about disciplinarity at the door. Research carried out in the field of social psychology is as valid as that in political economy—each contributes to our understanding of a given substantive area. If we want to understand a contemporary concern, such as torture or slavery, then we do ourselves no favours by closing ourselves off in secure disciplinary boxes, ignoring material that would enhance our understanding. This is particularly true if we wish to understand such a problem not just as an academic but as a concerned citizen, an activist. And this is where some aspect of disciplinarity returns, albeit in modified form. I want, if you like, to treat human rights *as a discipline in its own right*. It has its own subfields—slavery, genocide, and the various other topics discussed in this book. It has its own rich theoretical tradition, comprised of such luminaries as Kant,

Arendt, and Bobbio. It draws on the research carried out within its sibling disciplines, but it utilises this research for its own purpose, in keeping with its own logic. Its logic, of course, is the promotion of human rights awareness and its ultimate goal the eradication of all forms of human rights abuse. Thus, the discipline of human rights is more than a mere *pot pourri* of interests drawn from other, more traditional, fields. It occupies its own space, located broadly within the social sciences but as far removed from the fallacies of value freedom and scientific objectivity as any discipline could possibly be.

Even more exciting, though, are the *possibilities* that arise from this integrated approach. . . . There is considerable discussion of the theoretical approaches provided by such unlikely bedfellows as Popper, Foucault and Habermas, as well as Althusser, Arendt, Adorno and Marcuse. While these major writers may not have concerned themselves with censorship *per se*, the theoretical traditions that have arisen from their ideas are all in some way applicable to it. For example, the Habermasian paradigm presupposes the possibility of unhindered communication as a foundation for true democracy. Working within such a paradigm, we can thus reach a theoretically informed understanding of censorship in the context of its relationship to democracy. Similar applications can be made following Popper's work on the 'open society', Foucault's on surveillance, Althusser's on ideological state apparatuses, Adorno's on authoritarianism, Arendt's on totalitarianism, Marcuse's on the 'closing down of alternatives', and more besides. This is not, it seems to me, a case of poaching from the canon; rather, it would be a serious omission on our part if we were to try to understand censorship *without* considering the possibilities offered by these paradigms. Additionally, how can we even begin to understand political imprisonment within a theoretically informed framework without reference to Althusser and the idea of repressive state apparatuses? These writers and their ideas are not the private property of any one discipline, and it is clear that they have much to contribute to the integrated approach to human rights advocated here.

It is therefore not inconceivable to envisage the emergence of degree programmes dedicated to this logic, and it is certainly true that individual modules have already been established, under the broad banner of one or another 'traditional' discipline, which seek to adopt such an integrated approach to human rights research. Students sitting these modules may, with good reason, feel rather annoyed when they encounter an unfortunate consequence of the dispersed nature of human rights studies—the lack of an integrated textbook which covers most of the ground they will expect to cover in their course. Having devised a module of this kind myself, I am more than aware of the confusion that can arise when students are sent in different directions, to different corners of the library or bookshop, in order to learn more about a specific important study on, say, censorship or torture. While this is understandable, in so far as disciplines have never really needed to make any links between censorship and torture, and publishers, guided by traditional disciplinarity, have never needed to commission volumes which make reference to both, this volume is intended to fill this gap for an emerging academic audience.

But if there is to be a disciplinary logic to the integrated study of human rights, it must reside primarily in its resistance to any separation between academic research and the 'real world' of human rights abuses. The purpose of human rights studies is to utilise this research for the advancement of an overt political and ethical goal, that is, the betterment of human existence. As Herbert Marcuse famously said, the task of a critical theory is to realise that human life is, or should be, worth living, and to identify the conditions that exist to make it less than it should be.[1] Human rights studies are born out of Marcuse's unapologetic call to arms. . . . The academic discourse should not be treated as abstract because it reflects a harsh social reality. Human rights should be understood both in theory, and in practice. . . .

Human rights violations do not only take place in the civil and political realms, and are not only committed by state actors. Poverty is a violation of human rights, as are cultural practices such as female genital mutilation. Of course, to include research on everything which might be included under the human rights banner would be virtually impossible. Constraints imposed upon me by space have forced me to concentrate the bulk of the book on this traditional approach to human rights—favoured by many activist organizations because it allows them to target states as perpetrators of the violations. . . .There is, however, another reason why I concentrate on these rights, and that pertains to the relationship between human rights, social theory and the idea of the state. . . .

HUMAN RIGHTS ABUSES IN THE WORLD TODAY

When the United Nations introduced the Universal Declaration of Human Rights in 1948, it was seen by many as a sign of optimism, of the possibilities of a better world. Yet, over 50 years later, observers recognise that we live in an age when human rights abuses are as prevalent as they ever have been—in some instances more prevalent. The world is littered with examples of violations of basic rights: censorship, discrimination, political imprisonment, torture, slavery, the death penalty, disappearances, genocide, poverty, refugees. The rights of women, children, and other groups in society continue to be ignored in atrocious ways. The environmental crisis takes the discourse on rights to a different level.

In 1998, as the Declaration celebrated its fiftieth birthday, the *Observer* newspaper in Britain published a poll called the 'Human Rights index', which it described as 'the World Cup that no country wants to win'. The Index ranked 194 nation-states according to their record on human rights abuses. The results made for interesting reading. Algeria took first prize, ahead of North Korea. The United States featured in 92nd place, the United Kingdom in 141st. Russia was 32nd, while China was 10th. The poll was based on a points system allocated to countries according to their use of torture or capital punishment, their political prisoners and disappearances, and their denials of basic rights. The totals were then adjusted according to the Human Development Index (HDI) which measures countries in terms of their level of economic and social development. Table 1.1 identifies the different indicators used and how the ten highest-placed countries scored on each.

Another attempt to rank countries [was] featured on the website of the *Guardian* newspaper (Table 1.2). This list featured a slightly different set of indicators, and a slightly simpler ranking system. On this occasion, the Democratic Republic of Congo shared first place with its neighbour Rwanda, Russia and the United States shared 62nd position, the United Kingdom came in joint 126th, while China was 12th.

Both indexes provide only a guide to the state of human rights in the world today—no country can afford to be complacent about its performance on such a scale. Campaigning

---

[1] Herbert Marcuse (1991, original 1964). *One-Dimensional Man: Studies in the Ideology of Advanced Industrial Society*, London: Routledge, pp. xlii–xliii.

TABLE 1.1   The *Observer* Human Rights Index[2]

	Algeria	North Korea	Burma	Indonesia	Libya	Colombia	Syria	Iraq	Yugoslavia	China
Extra-judicial killings	30	19	19	19	17	20	8	24	14	10
Use of torture	24	16	20	16	16	15	20	26	16	23
Disappearances	24	19	16	19	14	20	14	24	2	1
Use of the death penalty	0	8	10	10	7	0	10	10	5	9
Denial of free speech	10	10	10	10	8	5	9	10	7	9
Denial of political rights	10	10	10	10	8	4	9	10	75	6
Political prisoners	10	10	10	10	9	6	9	10	7.5	6
Denial of free movement	5	10	10	10	8	6	4	10	5.5	4
Denial of child rights	10	4	10	7	4	8	3	8	3	3
Denial of religious freedom	8	10	10	10	5	0	4	1	4	9
Denial of fair trial	7	5	10	5	7	4	6	10	7.5	9
Denial of minority rights	10	10	10	10	7	6	5	10	8	4
Denial of women's rights	2	4	7	8	8	5	9	2	8	5
Total	150	135	152	144	118	99	110	155	95	101
HDI	0.737	0.765	0.655	0.668	0.801	0.848	0.755	0.531	0.86	0.774
Total x HDI	**110.55**	**103.275**	**99.56**	**96.192**	**94.518**	**83.952**	**83.05**	**82.305**	**81.7**	**78.174**

© *The Guardian/Observer*

[2]   The Index appeared in the *Observer*, 28 June 1998, p. 10. The top three categories were scored out of 30, the remainder out of 10. The totals were then cross-matched against the United Nations Human Development Index, which ranks countries by their level of development.

TABLE 1.2	The Guardian Human Rights Index[3]									
	DR Congo	Rwanda	Burundi	Algeria	Sierra Leone	Egypt	North Korea	Sudan	Indonesia	Yugoslavia
Extra-judicial executions	3	3	3	3	3	–	1	3	3	3
Disappearances	–	3	2	2	–	1	2	3	3	3
Torture	3	3	3	3	3	3	3	3	3	2.5
Deaths in custody	–	2	3	–	2	2	1	1	–	1
Prisoners of conscience	3	–	–	2	1	2	2	2	3	1
Unfair trials	3	3	3	3	3	3	3	2	2	3
Detention without charge or trial	3	3	3	3	3	3	3	2	2.5	3
Executions	3	2	–	–	2	2	3	1	–	–
Death sentences	3	3	3	3	3	3	3	1	2	1
Abuses by armed opposition groups	3	3	3	3	3	2	–	3	2	3
Total	**24**	**24**	**23**	**22**	**22**	**21**	**21**	**21**	**20.5**	**20.5**

© The Guardian/Observer

organisations such as Amnesty International are usually reluctant to rank countries in this way because it detracts from the central issue: it is not how you perform compared to other countries that matters, but the fact that you have violated human rights at all! Nevertheless, the indexes allow us to ponder the enormity of our task as students and activists concerned with human rights. These lists are also informative as much because of what is not ranked as for what is. . . . What is apparent, though, is that some *types* of human rights abuse are more common in some countries than in others, The United States of America, for example, may consider itself something of a moral guardian of basic civil and political rights, such as freedom of speech, but is regularly criticised for its use of the death penalty. The United Kingdom is frequently targeted for its mistreatment, including arbitrary detention, of refugees and asylum seekers. Disappearances and extra-judicial executions are usually associated with Latin America, apartheid with South Africa, while censorship is of course a major problem in many authoritarian states and most 'liberal' ones as well. . . .

THE SCOPE OF HUMAN RIGHTS RESEARCH

. . .

For the most part, as I stated above, I have focused primarily on *civil and political rights*, sometimes called 'first-generation rights'. These tend to be easier to locate in so far as they usually have a direct relationship with the *state*. Complications arise when we introduce 'second-generation rights'—*economic, social and cultural rights*—and 'third-generation rights'—*collective rights and land rights*. . . .

The inclusion of torture is unlikely to stimulate debate, because it is (in principle) universally condemned and illegal. Yet most official definitions of torture actually include corporal punishment (indeed, torture itself has often been used as a form of judicial punishment), and this often does result in disagreements between parties. Nevertheless, human rights abuses can and do occur within the legal system as well as the political system (which is where most of the formal human rights discourse is often directed). . . . Human rights abuses can actually form part of a legal and judicial system, for the purpose of punishing criminals. If the currency of politics is power, then the currency of law is order. 'Enemies' of the law are referred to as criminals, and they need not be political agents. Thus, this constitutes an analysis of human rights abuses as *punishment*, where the law infringes upon our civil rights (to life and respectful treatment)—even though, in its application, the death penalty clearly has *political* undertones.

Progressively this discourse has extended further beyond the limits of the political realm to incorporate social and economic issues. . . .

Few people in the human rights field would deny that apartheid, slavery, genocide, and the plight of refugees constitute human rights violations, Actually, the logic behind this is not always clear. It is true that they are forms of *social* exclusion—that is to say, they exist within the social sphere in so far as the *victims* of these atrocities are targeted not because they are enemies of the state or because they are criminals, but because of their characteristics as *groups of people*. However, they are condoned, or carried out in the name of, the state and its agents, and they (usually) constitute violations of civil and political rights. Discrimination—the root of many of these evils—is effectively a social problem, although it becomes a legal one when it is formalised as apartheid or segregation. Slavery is another example of how social exclusion becomes formalised in the legal sense, that is, where the *law* pervades *society*. The primary difference between apartheid and slavery is that the former is the legal violation of the right to equality, while the latter is the legal violation of the rights to equality *and* freedom, although boundaries are never really this clear. Quite clearly, the absence of political equality under apartheid necessarily results in a denial of freedom as well. Genocide is often (but not always) explained in terms of similar reasons to apartheid and slavery, although while these violations constitute legal strategies for social exclusion, genocide is quite clearly a political one, which threatens not the right to life, but the right to existence. The problems faced by refugees are also social problems, problems of belonging, although once again they tend to be fought out in the legal sphere. That is to say, questions of existential belonging evolve into questions of legal belonging. That we end on the problem of refugees seems apt, since these problems challenge the very assumptions—to sovereignty, legitimacy, and exclusivity—upon which the theory of the modern state rests.

So, clearly, while we have strayed to some extent from our starting point in the political sphere, we have maintained an attachment to some kind of state involvement. Table 1.3 lists the various substantive areas covered in this book, locating them within the relevant sphere (that is, the appropriate *rationale* for the violation in question), and, where it is different, the relevant medium (that is, the *arena* through which the violation is articulated), and identifying the particular *right* which is violated in each case. This should be read as a very rough table. . . . No single human rights issue is so simplistic as to fit so neatly into any one category, especially if, as intellectuals, we are able to look beyond the obvious and uncover the hidden agendas which may be at work in each case, Nevertheless, it is a useful analytic tool.

. . . It is true, as I have already indicated, that most of the formal discussion on human rights has been concerned primarily with the political, and to some extent the legal, spheres; that is, *the state*. However, should we always limit our thinking about human rights to these areas? Surely, economic, social and cultural rights also need to be addressed. We need to be aware, at least, of the multitude of human rights violations which occur outside the state sector.

One, very broad, area deals with violations of rights which take place within the cultural sphere, and which have so far been marginalised by the mainstream debates. Two such practices are aimed directly at women and justified wholly according to cultural tradition: the practices of female genital mutilation and *sati*. A third violation aimed at women, that of forced sterilisation, . . . is an example of how the state seeks to regulate the social dimension through intrusion upon the body. Other topics . . . are . . . children's rights, and the debates concerning the relationship between human rights and business. Poverty is also included as a human rights concern, a violation of the right to economic welfare and security, even though it is not always reducible to the state. Mention is also made of the emerging discourse on environmental rights as well as to questions of indigenous land rights. . . . Thus, we can include in Table 1.3 the additions shown in Table 1.4.

Needless to say, I introduce this useful table at this point only to problematise it! It is true that I have stretched the definition of human rights beyond the standard, state-centred model, by including poverty and female genital mutilation. Does this mean that we can, or should, refer now to human rights issues without necessarily relying upon some degree of state involvement? Let us see how such a shift would impact upon four of our other categories, which are recognised as human rights issues. Let us start with slavery. . . . While the popular definition was applicable to earlier forms of this abuse, it is less relevant with

TABLE 1.3	Traditional Forms of Human Rights Abuse	
Substantive area	**Sphere (medium)**	**Rights violated (type)**
Censorship	Political (Cultural/Legal)	Information/Expression(Civil/Political)
Political imprisonment	Political (Legal)	Justice (Civil)
Torture	Political/Legal(Biophysical)	Respectful treatment(Civil)
The death penalty	Legal (Legal/Biophysical)	Life (Civil)
Apartheid	Social (Legal)	Equality (Civil)
Slavery	Social (Legal)	Equality/Freedom (Civil)
Genocide	Social/Cultural (Political)	Existence (Civil/Cultural)
Refugees	Social (Legal)	Citizenship (Political/Civil)

TABLE 1.4	Emerging Forms of Human Rights Abuse	
Substantive area	**Sphere (medium)**	**Rights violated (type)**
Poverty	Economic	Welfare/Security (Social/ Economic)
Female genital mutilation	Cultural (Biophysical)	Personal autonomy (Civil)
Sati	Cultural (Biophysical)	Life (Civil)
Forced sterilisation	Social (Biophysical)	Reproduction (Biological)

regard to modern slavery, much of which is arranged through illegal, private exchanges, not sanctioned by the state or its agents.[4] Furthermore, in so far as modern slavery does not constitute the deliberate targeting of a particular social group, it is no longer even a form of social exclusion—instead, its rationale (sphere) and its arena of contestation (medium) are both *economic*. Does this make modern slavery any less of a human rights abuse, simply because it occurs within the economic sphere? Clearly not.

If, then, it is acceptable to include modern slavery in our discussion of human rights, what else is it possible to include? Murders are committed every day, and they are undoubtedly violations of someone's right to life. Yet these are never treated as human rights issues, because they take place between social actors, in the social sphere. Similarly, while torture is clearly a human rights concern, when a man attacks his partner with intense violence, this is considered a crime, and a despicable one at that, but not an issue of human rights, because once again it occurs within the social (indeed, the domestic) arena. If we include modern slavery, how do we exclude domestic violence from our discussion on torture? If not, how, within what arena, is it best articulated?

---

[4]   Kevin Bales (1999) *Disposable People: New Slavery in the Global Economy*, Berkeley: University of California Press.

Similar complications arise when we turn to the cultural sphere. Female genital muti-lation has been a recent addition to the discourse on human rights. However, there are many such practices which have not, as yet, been elevated to that status. There is certainly considerable discussion over the extent to which legal or political violations might some-how be related to cultural traditions. An interesting such discussion concerns the extent to which apartheid can be equated to the caste system. Should we include caste within our discussion of human rights? It is useful for us to be aware, as concerned social scientists, of the debates which seek to understand both caste and apartheid as forms of social strat-ification. . . . Readers are at liberty to critique what they may feel is an arbitrary decision on my part to include these but not to discuss murder or domestic violence (or any other form of social violence) in the chapters on the death penalty and torture. These omissions highlight the difficulties inherent in any discussion of human rights.

Table 1.5, then, re-evaluates these four human rights violations in respect of their exe-cutions in both the state and the non-state sectors.

TABLE 1.5	Taking a Closer Look at State and Non-State Human Rights Issues		
State	**Sphere (medium)**	**Non-state**	**Sphere (medium)**
Apartheid	Social (Legal)	Caste	Social (Cultural)
Slavery	Social (Legal)	'New' slavery	Economic
Torture	Political–Legal (Biophysical)	Domestic violence	Social (Social/Biophysical)
Death penalty	Legal (Legal/Biophysical)	Murder	Social (Social/Biophysical)

These debates—what to include, what not to include—are taking place not only in academic circles, but in activist ones as well. Amnesty International, which is probably the best known campaigning organisation dedicated to human rights issues, has long debated the possibility of expanding its mandate to take into consideration human rights abuses which take place in the non-state sector. There are, though, additional complica-tions which such social movements have to take into account. The question is not, then, whether 'new' slavery is a human rights issue because it clearly is, regardless of whether or not it is practised by the state. Instead, the question is whether 'new' slavery is an appro-priate concern for this organisation. This is a pragmatic, not a philosophical question, which relates to resources, and to organisational structure and profile. At least when human rights abuses occur within the state sector we can identify the target of our cam-paigns, and utilise our resources accordingly. It is for this reason, more than all others, that human rights have tended to be synonymous with civil and political rights, but this should not exclude economic, social and cultural rights (or environmental ones for that matter) from the philosophical discourse on human rights.

I think it is fair to say, in conclusion, that although human rights violations can and do take place in any sphere, through any medium, the *discourse* on human rights is articulat-ed primarily through the state. The very idea that we have rights *at all* presupposes that we need them, and that the machinery exists to *protect* them. The liberal traditions which stem from the philosophies of Hobbes and Locke presume that the state exists in some kind of contract with its citizens. *Both* traditions require us to view this contract as a kind of balancing act of rights and duties. As Hannah Arendt acutely observed, rights are only meaningful in the context of a state that recognises them.[5] This is true whether we advocate a strong state in the Hobbesian sense or a weaker one as conceived by Locke. One of the great scholars of human rights and duties, Immanuel Kant, argued that the only incontrovertible right is freedom. . . . How, though, can freedom be an incontrovertible right, when it is legally denied every day, whenever we legally—and more often than not justifiably—imprison criminals? If we allow this right to be violated in such frequent and unexceptional circumstances, surely it cannot be an incontrovertible right. But does this mean that slavery, which seems necessarily to be a violation of the right to freedom, is not, in fact, a human rights abuse? Clearly it is, but why? The only response is that it violates social justice, and social justice is necessarily tied to concepts of *society* (how we live with one another), and *the state* (how we regulate the way we live together). Equally, the death penalty is not in fact treated as a human rights concern *because it denies the right to life*, but *because it requires the state to exceed its powers vis-à-vis the citizen*. Norberto Bobbio is quite right to say that the problem we face when dealing with human rights today is not how to justify them, but how to protect them.[6] In that respect, the state—in its political, judicial, or military manifestations—is still central to the debate.

HUMAN RIGHTS AND THEORETICAL TRADITIONS

If we are to make inroads into an integrated social science study of human rights, we need somehow to make sense of the varying theoretical perspectives that dominate the different disciplines, as a number of such traditions will feature throughout this volume and may cause confusion. Because so many of the substantive areas included in this book have been subjected to detailed examination by various social science practitioners, then in many cases the debates within each field take the form of debates between major theoretical traditions in the social sciences, There is, of course, in existence a *general* theory of human rights. . . . Other traditions, approaches, or schools of thought may be more familiar to students from one background than to those from another. For the most part, however, these traditions are applicable and comparable across the disciplines—it is their subject matter which distinguishes them, and often they go by different names in different disciplines. It stands to reason that many of the major writers and traditions whose work has illuminated or might illuminate our thinking about a given human rights issue have not written about human rights *per se*. To help us make sense of these approaches and how they relate to one another, and to see how they might be applicable to human rights, we can identify five key propositions which we need to address:

1 That human rights violations *are carried out by individuals*. So, what is it that leads a person to commit such an act? Here, we need to consider *theories of human nature*.

---

[5]   Hannah Arendt (1949) 'The "Rights of Man": What Are They?' in *Modern Review* 3, 1, Summer; reproduced in Arendt (1951) *The Origins of Totalitarianism*, New York: Harcourt Brace, pp. 290–302.

[6]   Norberto Bobbio (1996) *The Age of Rights*, Cambridge: Polity Press, p. 10.

2 That human rights violations *have to be understood in their social context*. What are the social conditions within which the acts occur? Here, we turn to *theories of society*.

3 That human rights violations *are by their very nature condemned by members of global civil society*. This is logical, because otherwise these rights and their violations would not have been debated in the first place. But what *makes* them so wrong? Can they ever he justified? In this case, we should consider *theories of ethics*.

4 That human rights violations *usually involve the state, either directly or indirectly*. What, then, is the role of the state in this respect? We are guided here by *theories of politics*.

5 That human rights violations *occur in spite of human 'civilisation' and 'rationalisation'*. So, is 'progress' a myth, or are we still able to imagine a better world? Here, we contrast competing views of the *'logic' of modernity*.

THEORIES OF HUMAN NATURE

Is the human animal innately bad, good, or indifferent? In fact, the question is unfair, because it seeks to apply a social category to a presocial condition. Nevertheless, this question lies at the heart of so many debates within the social sciences—even if contemporary social science practitioners seek to distance themselves from it.

The primary distinction we can make here is between essentialists and constructivists. *Essentialists* will argue that there is some innate human condition. *Constructivists* will argue that the human being begins *tabula rasa*, and that her or his characteristics are learned, shaped by conditions, or constructed in some other way. This crude distinction is not altogether helpful, for it hides many other important areas of debate.

Social science has generally followed a more constructivist line. The idea that there is some pre-social human nature is largely antithetical to its disciplinary purpose, and is often dismissed as crude biologism or psychologism. It would be unwise, though, to underestimate the influence of essentialist thinking upon social science disciplines.[7] Indeed, in respect of human rights, essentialist arguments are still frequently used. The most common form of essentialism derives from the writings of Thomas Hobbes, for whom the pre-social human is inherently savage. Various forms of Hobbesian social science begin with the assumption that humans, as animals, possess an inherent biological impulse towards self-preservation and violence. Society and culture serve to restrain this urge, but certain traits of human existence can nonetheless be explained according to it. The Hobbesian approach to human nature has evolved into the discipline of *sociobiology*. Essentialist views of human nature presupposing its tendency towards violence have influenced debates on apartheid (Van der Berghe), genocide (Lorenz), and torture (Zimbardo).

An important counterbalance to biological or psychological essentialism can be found in the psychological school of *behaviourism*. Behaviourism assumes that individuals act in

---

[7] Consider, for example, the impact of Hobbesian essentialist thought upon the social sciences. Realism in international relations, control theory and 'right' realism in criminology, sociobiology in anthropology, public choice theory in political science, and classical elite theory in political sociology, are all varieties of neo-Hobbesian social science.

certain ways not according to some inherent nature but in response to external stimuli. When we learn about such things as punishment and reward we modify our behaviour, thus making rational decisions which maximise our happiness. Behavioural psychology may, for example, help us understand what drives a torturer to commit cruel acts (Milgram).

Behaviourism may stand in marked contrast to essentialist reductionism, but it has been subjected to as much criticism. The behaviourist believes, ultimately, that all forms of behaviour, of emotion, of consciousness, are learned. Human nature is thus wholly dependent upon the environment. An alternative viewpoint, phenomenology, sees humans as creative agents engaged in the active construction of their social worlds. This approach focuses on the strategies employed by social actors to make sense of their worlds, and construct (or maintain) their sense of self. We might adopt it if we want to look at how someone becomes a torturer (Festinger), or how an individual copes while facing execution (Johnson).

THEORIES OF SOCIETY

Sociology is rife with theoretical traditions, and many of them will contribute to the debates contained within this volume.[8] Theories of society ask what 'society' might be, and how it is driven. They thus (usually) explain things in terms of external influences, rather than according to 'human nature', although, typically, they do begin with certain ontological assumptions. A very general distinction can be made between two competing approaches—one which suggests that society is driven by consensus, and one which argues that it is driven by *conflict*.

There are two main types of consensus approach:

1 *Functionalism.* According to functionalists, society operates as a system of interlinked component parts. Each part fulfils a distinct function in the management and maintenance of the system as a whole. Like any other system, societies can become unstable—that is, social order can break down—when something goes wrong with their internal dynamics. Thus, a functionalist analysis of genocide (Dadrian) looks at instabilities within the social system.

2 *Structuralism.* This method is concerned with locating the hidden meanings which give rise to cultural practices. Structuralists might observe a particular ritual of social life, but rather than take it for granted, or indeed presume that the ritual is important only in so far as it is meaningful to the participants themselves, they would seek to explain it in terms of meanings embedded in the culture. A study of the caste system in relation to apartheid (Dumont) might be subjected to a structuralist analysis.

These theories begin with the assumption that societies are stable. They spend little time addressing, or critiquing, inequalities and power relations in the social structure. By contrast, *conflict* theories begin with the assumption that societies are arenas of contestation. We can distinguish between three broad conflict perspectives:

---

[8]   It would not, of course, be fair to expect the reader of this volume to be familiar with these traditions, and in this introduction space allows only for a 'beginner's guide'. Students wishing to explore the complexities of social theory in more depth are advised to consult George Ritzer (1992) *Sociological Theory*, New York: McGraw Hill.

1 *Marxism*. The writings of Karl Marx have resulted in various interpretations, so in fact there are many different Marxisms. However, generally speaking, Marxists agree that the fundamental distinction in societies, historically and geographically, is between those who have, and those who do not have, access to the means of production. This is because, for Marxists, the driving force behind history is the economic system, and all other spheres of life, such as politics, law, religion, and so on, are dependent upon this base. Capitalist societies, driven by a market economy, are characterised by distinctions of social class. The *bourgeoisie*, or ruling class, profits under capitalism by exploiting the labour of the marginalized *proletariat*, or working class. While various Marxists disagree on the extent to which they see the economy as all-powerful, Marxism as a broad category has illuminated debates on apartheid and slavery (Cromwell-Cox, Ste. Croix, Genovese), genocide (Sartre), and other human rights concerns.

2 *Weberian conflict theory*. Max Weber was a diverse theorist who contributed to many fields. With regard to the structure of modern society, Weber provided a critique of Marx. He believed that Marx's account was too simple because it reduced conflict in modern societies to one root cause—social class. Weber argued instead that stratification operates according to three distinct hierarchies: class, status, and party, and that there is no singular driving force of history. These hierarchies—which roughly correspond to economic, social, and political action—occasionally overlap, but they are distinct. Weberian conflict theories are therefore interested as much in non-economic (e.g. ethnic) conflict as they are in economic conflict, so it should not be surprising to see them used to help us understand genocide (Kuper), caste/apartheid (Warner), and slavery (Patterson).

3 *Feminism*. While Marxists argue that the driving force which steers society and creates inequalities is capitalism, feminists argue that it is in fact male domination—patriarchy—which is at fault. There are, though, just as many feminisms as there are Marxisms. . . .

THEORIES OF ETHICS

Although there are many theories of ethics, we can group most of them into two camps which provide alternative answers to the question: What makes an act 'good'? The first camp is associated with *moralism*. Moralism (sometimes called deontological ethics) draws on such thinkers as Kant, and it stresses that the value of an act resides in the act itself. Thus, one should not censor, or torture, or execute, because to do so would violate an inherent and universal right. Alternatively, a moralist might argue that one *should* censor certain material, because the material itself is inherently vile, or execute a criminal, because his or her crime was deserving of such punishment.

By contrast, *causalism* (or consequentialism) focuses not on the act but on its consequences. An act is good if it brings about a desired end, or bad if it has undesirable consequences. Causalist approaches often draw on utilitarianism, in so far as the desired end tends to be the 'greatest good' for the 'greatest number'. For the causalist, nothing is inherently evil, it can only be the right or wrong thing to do in certain circumstances. However, few causalists would want to condone such vile acts as torture, so they seek to avoid being subject to relativism by appealing to more abstract notions of the greater good.

THEORIES OF POLITICS

Theories of politics operate at two levels: the level of the state, and the level of international relations, Our concern here is primarily with theories of power—that is, theories of where power is located and what role the locus of political administration, the state, has in managing that power. There are three dominant traditions that we need to address: *realism*, *liberalism*, and *Marxism*.

Realism takes as its point of departure the ontological assumptions of Thomas Hobbes, that is, that humankind is an innately violent species, in need of protection from itself. Hobbesians thus call for a strong state which acts to guarantee the security of its people, in return for which the people surrender a degree of their natural freedom and rights. It is not too difficult to imagine, then, a realist defence of the death penalty (Van den Haag). When applied to the international political arena, the central premise of realism is that the world is made up of competing, self-interested nation-states, and it is with these that power rests. The world of international politics is thus portrayed as an anarchic war of all against all, from which the strongest emerge as dominant.

Liberalism begins by inverting the Hobbesian presumptions about human nature, drawing on the ontology of John Locke. Locke believed that in the 'state of nature' humans are in fact innately peaceful, but competitive. The liberal position, following Locke as well as classical economists such as John Stuart Mill, Adam Smith and David Ricardo, calls for a minimal state that serves only as arbiter on economic transactions, and should not interfere unduly in the lives of private citizens. Liberals such as Karl Popper have written fiercely about the need to defend individual freedom against the tyranny of the state. Unsurprisingly, the liberal school has been the most outspoken on matters of censorship. In the international realm, liberalism adopts a more pluralistic position than realism, maintaining that power rests not only with nation-states but also with individuals (citizens), groups, organisations, and markets.

Finally, the *Marxist* position, which we have already introduced, tends to see the state as a mere functionary, serving the interests of the market. Power in national and international terms tends to reside in the economic system. However, this position has probably caused more debate and disagreement within Marxism than any other aspect of the wider theory.

THEORIES OF MODERNITY

Theories of modernity did not begin with Max Weber, but he is a good point of departure for our purposes here, because he provides a sociological critique of both liberalism and Marxism, and because he grounds his critique in a theory of rationalisation which has influenced subsequent traditions. *Liberal* ideas, which have influenced pluralist and functionalist thinking, tended to adopt an optimistic and wholly *evolutionist* view of progress, that societies were evolving into more 'civilised' states. Some accounts, inspired by Lockean ontology, behavioural psychology, and utilitarianism, presume that human actors are constantly engaged in rational decision making. One such approach, *rational choice theory*, has been applied to the study of slavery as a social relationship (Fogel and Engerman). Most liberal accounts, then, have equated modernity with progress. *Marxist* accounts, by contrast, have tended to equate modernity with capitalism, and have concentrated primarily on the evolution of the economic system—Marx called his method historical materialism. However, it was Weber, in his critique of Marx, who presented the definitive pessimistic view of societal rationalisation. Rather than understanding modernity in terms of the emergence of the capitalist system (as Marx did), Weber understood capitalism in terms of the rise of a particular kind of rationality, associated with Protestantism. Indeed, following Weber, one can equate modernisation with rationalisation, in so far as the latter relates to a particular type of bureaucratic, means–end mentality. The manifestation of this bureaucratic rationality is the modern nation-state, which holds administration over a particular territorial space, devises laws which regulate action within that space, and serves as the centralised means of violence. So, Weber not only replaces the Marxist model with a state-centred alternative, he also provides an informed critique of naïve liberal theories of progress. Furthermore, his cultural sensitivity—his commitment to what some might call *historicism*—is a useful alternative to the alleged reductionism of the liberal and Marxist models.

By linking questions of 'rationality' with the role of the state, Weber laid the foundations for a debate which has moved on significantly since his time. Two significant developments—both of which engage with Weber's equation of modernity with instrumental, bureaucratic 'rationality', with the emergence of the state as the centralised locus of violence, one of which is broadly optimistic and the other of which is wholly pessimistic— are *critical theory* and *post-structuralism*.

Critical theory is a blend of Marxist concerns about capitalism and domination with Weberian ones about rationality, together with insights from Freudian psychoanalysis. Devised by members of the Frankfurt School prior to the Second World War, the perspective is primarily concerned with how domination comes about. The task of critical theory is to bring about emancipation, and this can be achieved by stepping outside the system in order to realise one's position within it, and to identify the inherent contradictions in a system which purports to be rational. Critical theory juxtaposes false rationality—associated with the instrumentalist logic of political and economic action which dominates the modern world—with true rationality—associated with human freedom. Thus, critical theorists recognise the bleak picture painted by Weber, but stress that this is only one kind of rationality, and there is always an alternative. The language of human rights is clearly part of this alternative rationalisation. While much of the original Frankfurt School library is either abstract and philosophical or polemical in nature, a second generation of scholars, led by Jürgen Habermas, has sought to develop more sociologically grounded foundations for critical theory.

Post-structuralism is a vague (and unhelpful) term applied to scholars who broke away from structuralism during the 1970s, embracing instead a variety of radical, challenging perspectives concerned with how language, interaction and everyday life are imbued with power relations. These disparate perspectives share a reluctance to accept that grand ideas such as progress, justice, truth, or rationality, are anything but stories. Where critical theorists search for hidden rationalities which might free us from repression, post-structuralists find only subtle techniques through which systems of power operate. The most celebrated writer of this kind is Michel Foucault, whose comments on torture and the death penalty are essential reading. Foucault's writings appear at first glance to be the antithesis of Habermas's. Habermas holds on to a commitment to the (liberal) Enlightenment ideals of progress and freedom. Foucault understands the various practices which many consider to be synonymous with progress (more 'humane' prisons, more 'advanced' forms of medical care) not in respect of some imaginary evolutionary line, but as reflections of social conditions. Superficially, they appeal to some concept of rationality, but really, however well they are disguised, they are just new ways of telling a familiar story, a story of violence and power.

Habermas and Foucault have set the standard when it comes to trying to make sense of rationality, and both have influenced my thinking on these issues. In many of the chapters that follow, I will attempt to contrast, and if possible synthesise, appropriate ideas drawn from these two different but comparable writers. Readers may decide that my attempts at synthesis are unsuccessful, perhaps undesirable. In true Kantian style, it is not, I would say in response, the success which matters as much here as the attempt—the attempt to make the best use of modern and classical social theory in order to make the most sense of the atrocities and acts of violence which occur daily in the allegedly rational and civilised world in which we live.

SECTION 7 TERMINOLOGY

Al-Qaeda	Cold War	Refugees
ancien régime	EPF (Established Programs	Rights
Anti-Semitism	Financing)	Self-Determination
CHA (Canada Health Act)	GDP (Gross Domestic	Sovereignty
CHST (Canada Health and	Product)	Sovereignty-Association
Social Transfer)	Lower Canada	Taliban
Civic Nationalism	Quiet Revolution	Terrorism
Civil Liberties	Racism	Upper Canada

SECTION 7 DISCUSSION QUESTIONS

1. Is there any hope of extending the Canadian tradition of "accommodation" to the rest of the world?

2. Health care is commonly ranked as the number one public policy issue in Canada. Is this justifiable? Are there other issues that demand more attention?

3. Is Quebec separation inevitable? What are the alternatives?

4. In what ways has the fear of terrorist attacks changed the world? Are Canadians at risk?

5. Some say that environmental threats bind all humans together. Is this an overstatement?

 POLISCI SUPERSITE

Pearson Education Canada's PoliSci Supersite (**www.pearsoned.ca/polisci**) contains a set of text-specific pages for *Ideas, Interests, and Issues*. Visit the Supersite to access a list of relevant weblinks and interesting additional readings tailored to the content of each section.

GLOSSARY OF TERMINOLOGY

Accountability: requirement that a person or group accept responsibility for an action or outcome.

Activist: a person who takes direct and sometimes militant action to bring about political or social change.

Agora: In ancient Greek cities, the open marketplace, where public meetings were also held.

Alienation: feeling of disconnection or separation from ourselves and other people, systems or things; frequently employed to explain political phenomena.

Al-Qaeda: (also Al-Qaida, from the Arabic "the foundation") terrorist Islamist organization most noted for the attacks against the United States on 11 September 2001; reportedly active in more than 60 countries.

Analytical approach: perspective that views politics as an empirical discipline, rather than a science. The basis of this approach is that politics cannot be broken down into parts, and must be viewed as a whole.

Anarchy: In political philosophy, a theoretical society without formal law or system of government. In more general use, a state of disorder and lawlessness caused by absence of government (from the Greek, "without rule").

ancien régime: old regime or old order.

Anti-Semitism: racial prejudice in theory, action, or practice that is directed against Semites (Arabs and Jews). In practice, it is used almost exclusively against Jews.

APEC: Asia-Pacific Economic Cooperation group, which promotes open trade and economic cooperation among Asia-Pacific economies.

Arms Control: Cooperative agreements among two or more states/blocs to regulate arms levels by restricting their growth or use.

ASEAN: Association of South-East Asian Nations, a group devoted to peace, security, progress and prosperity in the South-East Asian region.

Autarky: condition of complete self-sufficiency and isolation from the rest of the system; used to describe states that seek to be economically self-sufficient.

Autocracy: uncontrolled and absolute rule by one person.

Authoritarianism: political system requiring absolute obedience to a constituted authority.

Behaviouralism: perspective that concentrates on the "tangible," measurable aspects of political life, rather than values; original objective was to establish a scientific and objective discipline.

Bicameral: term describing a legislative or parliamentary body made up of two assemblies (Latin, *camera* = chamber), as opposed to a unicameral legislature with just one assembly. Canada has a bicameral legislature (the House of Commons and the Senate).

Bretton Woods agreements: post-World War II system of fixed exchange rates and heavy controls on private banks and other financial institutions so that their role

in international finance could be controlled. Named after the conference that took place at Bretton Woods, New Hampshire in 1944.

Boomer Generation: generation of individuals born between 1946 and the early 1960s (i.e. those born in the post-war baby "boom").

Brokerage Party: in any given political situation, a party whose actions are dictated by the desire to maintain harmony between various social divisions in society.

Budget: sum of money available or needed for a given period of time for a specified purpose.

Bureaucracy: branch of government responsible for carrying out public policy, and staffed by public employees (public or civil servants).

Campaign: organized movement to raise awareness of a political platform leading up to elections.

Canadian Charter of Rights and Freedoms: Constitutional amendment adopted in 1982, setting out Canadian individual and collective rights and freedoms.

Capitalism: economic system in which production and distribution of goods relies on private capital and investment.

Centralization: concentration of power in a single body, usually a national government.

CHA: Canada Health Act.

Charlottetown Accord (1992): agreement on major constitutional changes between the Canadian federal and provincial governments and Native groups, which was defeated in a nationwide referendum.

Checks and balances: system of mutual oversight and countervailing powers between different levels and branches of government, with the aim of preventing centralization of power in any one branch or level.

CHST: Canada Health and Social Transfer.

Citizen: status of an individual, whether claimed by right (of birthplace or parentage) or granted by law, that confers certain rights and freedoms and establishes certain duties vis-à-vis the state.

Civic Literacy: level of political knowledge and ability that allows citizens to effectively engage in the political system.

Civic Nationalism: form of nationalism where the state gains political legitimacy from active participation of its citizenry, or the "will of the people."

Civil Liberties: individual freedoms that are protected by law from government interference.

Civil Servants: employees of government departments.

Civil Society: body or community of citizens.

Civil Society Organizations (CSOs): associations that are neither of the state nor of the family, often characterized by voluntary organizations.

Cold War: a period of rhetorical hostility not marked by violence; most often referenced to the period of 1945–91 that existed between the alliance systems centred around the United States and the Union of Soviet Socialist Republics (USSR).

Colonization: process of establishing colonies abroad, whereby people of one country are subjected to the rule of another, dominant country.

Command Economy: a planned economy where economic decisions are made on behalf of the public by government.

Common Law: legal system characterized by unwritten law generally developed through decisions of the court rather than by statute.

Communism: political theory based on the writings of Karl Marx (1818–83) and Friedrich Engels (1820–95) that espouses class conflict as a means to form a system where all property is publicly owned, and each citizen works to his or her own best ability with equitable compensation.

Comparative approach: method of political analysis that compares different systems of political authority, based on system type, time period, or form of leadership.

Comparative politics: a subfield of political studies that examines politics using the comparative approach.

Comparative advantage: in classical economic theory, the idea that every individual, business, and nation ought to focus on an activity at which they have the greatest natural advantage in skill or resources relative to other actors.

Concepts: abstractions employed to describe phenomena according to their characteristics, e.g. political alienation, social class.

Concurrent Majority (Double Majority): procedure requiring majority support of at least two sub-units within a unit for approval.

Confederalism: political system of divided powers where added power is given to the non-central governments, and limited authority

and power is conferred on the central government.

Congress: legislative chamber of government in the United States, made up of the House of Representatives and the Senate.

Conservative: person who adheres to conservatism, or a perspective related to it.

Conservatism: political perspective that seeks to conserve the best of what has come before for future generations and is concerned with maintaining political and social traditions and customs.

Constituency: territorial or geographical locality (riding) represented by a politician chosen through the electoral process. Or, a group whose interests are represented by a politician or party, whether or not they live in a certain locality.

Constitution: the fundamental laws and principles upon which a political system is governed.

Constitutionalism: form of rule based on the belief that government power should be limited by the rules and principles enshrined in the constitution.

Convention: meeting of party members to discuss and determine policy and/or to select a party leader.

COP: Conference of the Parties (Kyoto).

Crown Corporation: term adopted in Canada to describe an organization wholly or partly owned by the state that provides a good or service.

Culture: way of life, language, art, customs, and institutions of a community, whether that community is defined ethnically, historically, or politically.

Dayton Peace Accord: agreement that ended the war in the former Yugoslavia, negotiated at Dayton, Ohio, in November 1995.

Decentralization: process whereby power and authority is taken from central government and conferred to a lower tier of government (e.g. state, regional or provincial).

Decision-making: mechanism or pattern of relations involving different levels of government where determinations and judgments regarding the governance of political system are made.

Democracy: political system based on the principle that governance requires the assent of all citizens through participation in the electoral process, articulation of views, and direct or indirect representation in governing institutions.

Democratization: the process of transition to a democracy.

Despotism: government rule of absolute and arbitrary authority.

Dependency Theory: related to structural theory, which argues that the structure of the international economic system has been such that close integration into that system would not benefit the economies of the developing world.

Depression: extended period of economic, industrial, and financial stagnation or decline.

Détente: a warming of relations, especially the period of enhanced relations between the United States and the Soviet Union in the 1970s.

Developed World (First World): industrialized nations, including Western Europe, North America, Japan, Australia and New Zealand, that are part of a structurally integrated system of global capitalism. (The term "Second World"

used to refer to the former communist countries of the Soviet Union and China, and their satellites.)

Developing World (Third World): largely non-industrialized or industrializing countries that are economically and technologically deprived; they are primarily located in Africa, South America, and Asia.

Devolution: political system where some authority is given to regional governments, but the power to oversee, dismiss, or entrench these authorities is still held by the central government.

Direct Democracy: political system where citizens are directly involved in the decision-making process.

Disarmament: reduction of military forces and destruction of equipment by negotiated agreement between countries or groups of countries.

Econometrics: application of mathematics to economic data or theories.

Elections: procedure normally employing a vote to select the winner of a political office or position.

Elected Assembly: (*see* Legislature).

Electoral System: the complete set of legal rules governing the selection of political representatives.

Electorate: body of those who have the right to vote in an election to a given representative chamber.

Electoralism: belief that the holding of elections is a sufficient condition for the existence of democracy.

Empirical Research: analysis that bases knowledge claims on

things that can be observed or subjected to experiment.

Enumeration: the process of determining the number of individuals eligible to vote in a constituency; in Canada, this consists of door-to-door contact by enumerators.

Environmentalism: political ideology based on the notion that modern economic systems are the main source of damage for the natural world; it also views modern industrialism as a hierarchical system that restricts human freedom.

Epistemology: the investigation of the conditions and nature of knowledge.

EPF: Established Programs Financing.

EU: European Union.

Executive: branch of government that initiates and enacts policy, according to the preoccupations of the dominant political party. The head of the executive branch is usually considered a country's head of government (such as the prime minister, in Canada), and may also be that country's head of state (such as the president, in the United States).

Factions: groups of people holding similar beliefs and opinions within a larger group.

Fascism: ideology that holds that the nation should be organized by the state, under the unquestioned authority of a national leader; in practical terms this means a combination of ethnic nationalism and extreme authoritarianism, and the will to use force to ensure order and compliance.

FCCC: Framework Convention on Climate Change (Kyoto).

FDI: foreign direct investment (also DFI, or direct foreign investment).

Federalism: form of governance that divides powers between the central government and regional governments, with particular roles and capacities being given to the different levels of government.

Feminism: an ideology based on the demand for the complete legal, political, economic, and social equality of women with men.

First Past The Post: electoral system (also known as a simple plurality) where the winner is the person or party receiving the greatest number (but not necessarily a majority) of votes.

First World: *see* Developed World.

Free Market: economic system governed by supply and demand and not restrained by government intervention, regulation, or subsidy.

Free Trade: international trade among political systems unimpeded by restrictions or tariffs on imports or exports.

FTA: Free Trade Agreement (Canada–United States).

G8: Group of Eight (formerly G7—Group of Seven, without Russia) major industrialized nations: United States; United Kingdom; France; Germany; Canada; Italy; Japan; and Russia.

Game Theory: research method that analyzes interactions and predicts actual behaviour by using formalized "games"—situations where "players" try to maximize their effectiveness by anticipating responses to their actions.

GATT: General Agreement on Tariffs and Trade.

GDP: Gross domestic product—total value of goods and services produced in a country in one year.

GHG: greenhouse gases.

Generation X: generation of individuals born during the late 1960s and the 1970s (i.e. the children of baby boomers).

Generation Y: generation of individuals born during the 1980s and the 1990s in Western countries (children of the later baby boomers; sometimes called the echo generation).

Glass Ceiling: an unofficial obstacle to occupational advancement, especially for women or ethnic minorities.

Globalization: the intensification of economic, political, social, and cultural relations across borders.

Glocalization: creation of products and services designed for the global market but customized to suit the local culture (combination of the words "globalization" and "localization").

GNP: Gross national product—total value of goods and services produced in a country in one year plus total of net income earned abroad.

Gold Standard: monetary system where currencies are linked to a standard unit of gold, which has a value of a fixed weight.

Government: the institutions and people responsible for carrying out the affairs and administration of a political system.

Guerrilla Warfare: irregular—usually politically motivated—armed forces fighting regular forces; from the Spanish for "little war."

Hegemony: dominance of one group of beliefs, practices, and groups over all others.

Hierarchy: A classification of successive ranks (e.g. grades,

classes) or of authority, one above another.

Human Nature: human behaviour that is believed to be instinctive rather than learned; important in the study of political philosophy.

Humanists: group that stresses the individual dignity, worth, and capacity of human beings for self-realization through reason and logic.

Humanitarian Intervention: intrusion in another state, often without the agreement of that state's government, to deal with a humanitarian disaster, usually the contravention of human rights.

Human Security: security that places primary emphasis on the individual rather than the nation state.

Hypothesis: a proposed and falsifiable (i.e. testable) explanation for observed phenomena.

ICC: International Criminal Court.

ICJ: International Court of Justice. Body of the United Nations responsible for settling international legal disputes, and for giving advisory opinions on legal questions referred to it by duly authorized international organs and agencies.

ICTY: International Criminal Tribunal for the former Yugoslavia.

Ideology: set or system of ideas that form the basis of a political or economic system and provide guidance and direction for political leadership.

IGO: Inter-Governmental Organization.

IFOR: Implementation Force (in the former Yugoslavia).

INGO: International Non-Governmental Organization.

Indirect Democracy: political system of representation where citizens elect a representative to act on their behalf (also see representative democracy).

Industrialization: process whereby countries improve and strengthen their industrial capability and production.

Initiatives: mechanisms that allow citizens to petition the government to introduce or adopt specific pieces of legislation or force a referendum on an issue.

Institutionalism: an approach within political science that focuses on the rules, powers, and processes of institutions and the role they play in shaping individual and group behaviour.

Interdependence: mutual dependence; a method of measuring dependent relationships among countries, based on the level of sensitivity and vulnerability one country has to the actions of another.

Interest Group: organization in a political system that seeks to either alter or maintain the policy of government without taking a formal role in elections or an official capacity in government (also called pressure groups).

International Anarchy: condition where there is no "world government;" the sovereign nation state is the highest authority in the international system.

International Law: law based on treaties between states.

Internationalism: political movement urging greater interaction between states in a spirit of peaceful cooperation.

International Organizations: international alliance involving many different countries; may be governmental or non-governmental.

International Political Economy (IPE): political and economic activity on an international stage that demonstrates the intimate connection between national and international processes.

International Politics: relations of a political nature that exist at the international level.

Invisible Hand: Adam Smith's notion that economic forces, if left to themselves, would automatically maximize efficiency and economic growth over time as the actors in an economy engage in competition with each other; benefits to society as a whole would arise from this competition without political interference.

IPCC: Intergovernmental Panel on Climate Change.

Judicial Review: power of the courts to interpret the constitution, varying from the ability to resolve disputes between levels of government in federal systems, to the ability to annul legislative and executive actions outright.

Judiciary: The branch of government responsible for the interpretation and application of the law and for the administration of the court system.

Keynesian System (Keynesianism): economic system based on the writings of John Maynard Keynes, who proposed that governments should stimulate business and employment through monetary and fiscal programs.

Kyoto Protocol: proposed amendment to the FCCC that would commit signatories to reduce emissions of carbon dioxide and other greenhouse gases, which are linked to global warming.

Laissez-faire: "to let be"—economic theory that suggests that a reduction in political control will benefit the economic system.

Legislature (Legislative Assembly; Elected Assembly): legislative branch of a political system, with the responsibility to make laws. In Canada, the legislative assembly is Parliament, made up of the House of Commons (or simply, the House) and the Senate.

Legitimacy: government's or individual politician's legal and moral quality of having the right to exercise power, based on a mandate (usually an election) from the people; by extension, also a quality possessed by their actions.

Liberal: person who adheres to liberalism, or a perspective related to it.

Liberal Democracy: political system based on freedom and individual liberty, and on the principle that governance requires the assent of all citizens through participation in the electoral process, articulation of views, and direct or indirect representation in governing institutions.

Liberalism: view of politics that favours liberty, free trade, and moderate social and political change.

Liberty: freedom from despotic control.

Lower Canada: historical name for the province of Quebec between 1791 and 1841 (when it occupied only the southern portion of the area covered by today's province). It merged with Upper Canada (Ontario) in 1841 to form the Province of Canada. The name derived from its geographical position downstream from Ontario along the St. Lawrence River.

McWorld: term popularized by Benjamin Barber to describe the universalizing forces of economic and cultural globalization, such as the global expansion of the McDonald's chain of fast-food restaurants.

Macro-Economic Policy: monetary and fiscal policies that affect the economy as a whole.

Majority Government: government by the party that received a majority of seats in an election to a legislative assembly.

Majority Rule: principle that the numerical majority (50 percent + 1) of an organized group can make decisions binding on the whole group.

Majority Systems: electoral systems that require candidates to earn more than 50 percent of votes to be elected.

Mandate: command or authorization given by a political electorate to its representatives.

Market: economic and legal environment—domestic or international—within which the exchange of goods and services takes place.

Market (-driven) Economy: economy that is subject to and determined by free competition.

Melting Pot: term employed in U.S. cultural history to describe the assimilation of immigrant groups with disparate ethnic origins into the dominant culture.

Middle Power: state that is not considered a superpower or great power, but still has influence in the international system, often due to relational power and reputation.

Ministers of the Crown (or Cabinet Ministers): members of cabinet in a parliamentary system, who collectively form the government of the day.

Minority Government: government by party that won the most, but not a majority of, seats in an election to a legislative assembly.

Mixed System: an electoral system that combines elements of two or more electoral systems to govern elections, e.g. the Mixed Member Proportional System used in Germany.

MNC: Multinational Corporation; business organizations that operate in more than one country.

Morality: good conduct and behaviour, in conformity with customary conduct and duty.

MPs (Members of Parliament): representatives of constituencies elected to the House of Commons.

Multicultural Society: society that emphasizes and encourages the retention of unique cultures, particularly immigrant-receiving nations such as Canada.

Multi-party System: competitive party system with more than two parties.

Multilateralism: integration or coordination of policies or decision-making by three or more nation states.

Multinational Corporation: *see* MNC.

Mutual Assured Destruction: doctrine prevalent in the Cold War period (1945–1991) among countries possessing nuclear weapons, recognizing that the use of those weapons would result in the destruction of both the attacker and the defender.

NAFTA: North American Free Trade Agreement, involving Canada, the United States, and Mexico.

Nation: groups of persons who share an identity that is based on, but not limited to, shared ethnic, religious, cultural, or linguistic qualities.

Nation State: state formed on the basis of national identity.

Nationalism: political movement, based on national identity, to create a political state; may also be interpreted as a strong feeling of patriotism.

National Security: the safety of a nation and its people from threats.

NATO: North Atlantic Treaty Organization.

New Public Management: an approach in public administration that adopts principles acquired in the private sector in the hope of improving the efficiency, effectiveness, and general performance of public services in modern bureaucracies.

NIC: Newly industrialized country.

NGO: Non-governmental organization—term popularized with the creation of the United Nations (1945) to describe international private groups (other than corporations). Often development, social, or cultural bodies, they are independent from government control, and are non-profit, and non-criminal.

Normative (research): analysis that focuses on establishing standards or prescriptions for action.

Norms: pattern of standard or expected behaviour in a political community.

OECD: Organization for Economic Cooperation and Development.

Notwithstanding Clause: section 33 of the Canadian Charter of Rights and Freedoms that allows legislatures to pass legislation that violates or limits the rights and freedoms outlined in sections 2, and 7 through 15 of the Charter, under certain conditions.

Oligarchy: government by the few.

Oligopoly: a market in which there are few sellers (e.g. because of high capital start-up costs), a condition that distorts the proper operation of market forces by allowing sellers to collude in maintaining higher prices than they would be able to in a more competitive market.

Order-in-council: an order issued by the cabinet, either on the basis of authority delegated by legislation or by virtue of the prerogative powers of the Crown.

OSCE: Organization for Security and Cooperation in Europe.

Ottawa Process: partnership of civil society and governmental groups, with leadership from middle powers such as Canada that led to the Ottawa Treaty (1997), which banned the production, sale, or use of anti-personnel landmines.

Overseas Development Assistance: Foreign aid given to developing countries either bilaterally, or through multilateral institutions such as the Development Assistance Committee of the Organization for Economic Cooperation and Development (OECD).

Paradigm: general theory, model, or "worldview" influential in determining a discipline or sub-discipline.

Parliament: legislature in Westminster form of government.

Parliamentary Sovereignty: the principle in parliamentary systems that there is no higher authority than Parliament and no external limits on what a Parliament can do.

Party: group of individuals engaged in the attempt to control government through the election of their members.

Party Discipline: the practice of elected party members voting in

the legislative assembly as a collective, according to the policy of their leadership.

Patronage: the appointment of individuals to positions or the granting of government business on the basis of rewards for past service rather than merit.

Permanent Voters List: permanent list of eligible voters employed in Canada derived from, among other things, income tax returns and provincial driver's licence data.

Pluralism: society where several disparate groups (minority and majority) maintain their interests, and a number of concerns and traditions persist.

Plurality: requirement that the winning candidate or option receives more votes than any other, but not necessarily a majority of votes cast.

Plurality System: a type of electoral system in which candidates are required to earn a plurality rather than a majority of votes in order to win seats

Policy: aims, based on political principles, that a governing party attempts to put into practice through legislation or executive order.

Polis: Greek city-state.

Political Action Committees (PACs): conglomerations of several interest groups in the U.S. that band together to more effectively influence the decision-making process.

Political Alienation: dissatisfaction with politics and governments characterized by low levels of trust and feelings of ineffectiveness.

Political Culture: set of political attitudes, beliefs, and values that underpin any political system.

Political Cynicism: belief that politicians, political institutions and/or the political system are inherently corrupt.

Political Efficacy: degree to which people feel they have an impact or can exert some influence on public affairs.

Political Philosophy: branch of political science that tries to understand both what we do and what we ought to do, normally flowing from assumptions about human nature.

Political Theory: body of work within political science devoted to the critical and systematic development of models, concepts and prescriptions related to power in both its public and private forms.

Political System: conglomerate of numerous political structures that work together to drive the political aspects of a country's social interaction.

Politics: the governance of social units, allocation of power and responsibility, and relationship among political actors in society.

Polity: the form or process of organized government; can mean a state, or it can refer more generally to a collection of individuals in a community that have a political relationship with one another.

Populism: support for the preferences of ordinary people, as opposed to those of political or business élites.

Positivism: rejection of value judgments in the social sciences; concentration on "facts" rather than "values."

Post-Cold War: period following the end of the Cold War, generally accepted to have begun in 1992, following the formal dissolution of the Soviet Union on December 31, 1991.

Postmodern Values: emerging set of post-war values identified by

Ronald Inglehart, giving priority to self-expression and quality of life rather than to economic and physical security.

Post-War Order: political arrangements that emerged from the balance of power existing after World War II.

Power: ability to achieve goals in a political system and to have others do as you wish them to.

Prescription: rule or direction to be followed based on sustained customs.

Presidentialism: Political regime in which executive power is independent and separate from the legislative power; normally contrasted with the parliamentary system.

Pressure group: organizations that seek to either alter or maintain the approach of government without themselves taking a formal role in elections or seeking an official capacity in government (also called interest groups).

Primary: an election held within a party to select candidates for election to public office.

Privy Council Office (PCO): central agency that works for the Canadian Prime Minister, and which is responsible for coordinating the work of cabinet, and cabinet committees.

Programmatic Party: political party that prioritizes adherence to an ideologically consistent set of policies over pragmatic strategies for winning elections.

Proportional Representation (PR): electoral system where seats in the legislature are won more or less in proportion to the the parties' popular vote. The main alternative systems are plurality and mixed systems.

Proportionality: the principle that the share of seats in a legislature won by a party should reflect the share of electoral votes obtained in an election.

Protectionism: tendency of countries to safeguard their own economic sectors or industries by using tariffs, quotas, or other forms of trade and investment legislation as a means to limit competition from abroad.

Prudence: discretion regarding the most appropriate course of action.

Public Administration: management of public affairs and government by politicians and public servants.

Public Interest: common comfort and security; well-being.

Public Opinion: the aggregate views of citizens about political issues and actors.

Public Policy: laws or principle of performance adopted by a government that affect a political system.

Public Realm: arena in which government activity legitimately occurs.

Quad: USA, the EU, Japan, and Canada, the world's largest market economies.

Qualified Majority: requirement that a proposal (or bill) achieve greater than simple majority support (50 percent + 1) in order to pass.

Quebec Referendum (1995): second referendum in Quebec (the first took place in 1980) on the question of whether Quebec should pursue a path towards independent statehood ("sovereignty"); in both cases, the majority voted against the proposal.

Question Period: specific time period in a sitting of the legislative assembly in parliamentary systems where the Prime Minister and cabinet must respond to written and oral questions posed by the Members of Parliament.

Quiet Revolution: phase of rapid change in Quebec in the 1960s characterized by secularization, formation of the welfare state, and development of the *Québécois* national identity.

Racism: discrimination against people based on their perceived or ascribed race; theory that human characteristics and abilities are determined by race.

Recall: mechanism that allows citizens to petition to remove their political representative before the next election period.

Referenda (Referendum): mechanism that allows citizens to vote directly on pieces of legislation or constitutional amendments.

Refugees: those who avoid political persecution by seeking refuge in a foreign country.

Regime: the set of rules, individual personalities, institutions and process comprising a system of government.

Regionalism: economic or political integration in a defined territorial area.

Regionalization: process of forming regional associations.

Regulation: laws governing the conduct of business or public activities in order to prevent fraud and ensure conformity to given standards of health, pollution control and fiscal probity.

Representation: standing for the views of others; election of a representative to symbolize the collective view of all constituents.

Representative Democracy: political system in which voters elect political representatives to govern in their interests (*also see* Indirect Democracy).

Representatives: individuals elected or appointed to act in the political interests of a constituency.

Republic: political system where supreme power is held by the people or elected representatives of the people.

Responsible Government: convention of the Canadian parliamentary system that the executive must retain the confidence of the elected assembly in order to remain in power.

Riding: *see* Constituency.

Right: privilege, immunity, or authority to act, to which members of a political community are entitled. They range in importance from the most fundamental, which are claimed by humans simply by virtue of being human (human rights), and citizens of a state (civil rights), to the less crucial, which can be characterized as privileges granted by legislation.

Rule of Law: principle that law rather than arbitrary authority should govern actions by all actors in a society, and that the law should be known by and applied equally to all in society.

Security Council: body of the United Nations primarily responsible for the maintenance of international peace and security.

Security of Tenure: principle that individuals have the right not to be fired without just cause, normally justified on the basis that in jobs where an exercise of political judgment is involved, protection allows for greater impartiality.

Self-Determination: people's act of deciding their own form of government free from outside influence.

SFOR: Stabilization Force (UN troops deployed in the former Yugoslavia).

Simple Plurality: electoral system (also known as first past the post) in which the winner is the person or party receiving the greatest number (but not necessarily a majority) of votes.

Single Member Plurality System: electoral system that requires the winning candidate to receive more votes than any other in order to win the seat—that is, to receive a plurality of votes—and which selects a single candidate within each electoral district (e.g. Canadian federal electoral system).

Social Capital: the collective value of the norms of trust, reciprocity, and relationships developed within societies that can be argued to be crucial to building and maintaining democracy.

Social Contract: hypothetical agreement between people before the rise of political authority, specifying the terms by which they agree to submit to political authority.

Social Movement: broad and fluid political associations attentive to a particular political issue; e.g. feminist and environmental movements.

Socialism: economic and political theory of society that holds that citizens as a whole should own the means of production, exchange, and allocation.

Socialist: person who adheres to socialism, or a perspective related to it.

Society: persons living collectively in a ordered community.

Sophists: group of thinkers in the 5th century BC who employed debate and rhetoric to teach and disseminate their ideas, and taught these skills to others, usually for high fees.

South: term referring to the less-developed nations of the world, that are not part of a structurally integrated system of global capitalism. The term derives from the fact that most such countries lie to the south of the developed countries ("the North").

Sovereignty: political community's independence and self-determination.

Sovereignty-Association: concept originating with the Parti Québécois in 1967, involving a sovereign Quebec maintaining a political and economic association with the rest of Canada.

Spin Doctors: skilled practitioners of "spin"—the art of portraying an event or group in the best possible light often in a heavily biased, even deceptive, manner.

State: a recognized political unit with a defined territory and citizens, and a central government responsible for administration and considered to be sovereign.

Suffrage: the right to vote.

Sustainable Development: model of economic growth that seeks to use renewable resources so as not to destroy the environment in which human beings, as well as all other organisms, have to live.

Systems Theory: approach that views politics as a system of interaction, binding political structures such as government to individual action. It argues that politics is a dynamic process of information flows and responses that encompasses political institutions, groups, and individuals.

Taliban: fundamentalist Islamist movement that ruled Afghanistan from 1996 until 2001; permitted Al-Qaeda to use Afghanistan as a base for its activities.

Terrorism: use of violence and fear by individuals and organized groups to achieve political goals.

Third World: *see* Developing World.

Threshold: a minimum proportion of the vote required to obtain a seat in electoral systems based on the principle of proportionality.

Totalitarian: person who adheres to totalitarianism, or perspectives related to it.

Totalitarianism: authoritarian political system that controls not only the economy and most social interaction, but is also marked by the government's desire to force its citizens to accept its objectives and values in an unlimited manner.

Trilateral Democracies: Democractic industrialized nations of the Trilateral Commission (Japan, European Union, and North America), which was created in 1973 to increase co-operation among its members and share global leadership responsibilities.

Turnout Rate: proportion of the registered electorate (or population) that turns out to vote in an election.

Typology: study and interpretation of political classifications.

Tyranny: corrupt form of political power in which rulers rule only in their own interest.

UN: United Nations.

Undeveloped World: *see* Developing World.

Unicameral: term describing a legislative or parliamentary body made up of one assembly (Latin, *camera* = chamber). Canada has a bicameral legislature (two chambers—the House of Commons and the Senate).

Unitary System: political system that concentrates political authority and powers within one central government, which alone is responsible for the activities of the political unit, both domestic and foreign.

UNPROFOR: United Nations Protection Force (deployed in the former Yugoslavia).

Upper Canada: historical name for the province of Ontario between 1791 and 1841 (when it occupied only the southern portion of the area covered by today's province). It merged with Lower Canada (Quebec) in 1841 to form the Province of Canada. The name derived from its geographical position upstream from Quebec along the St. Lawrence River.

Utopia: ideal social, legal, and political system, as imagined by philosophers and writers.

Values: principles, standards; what an individual or community esteems as meaningful.

Welfare State: political system that creates the means for individual protection and quality of life, such as health care, employment insurance, pensions, social programs for the elderly, children, and the unemployed.

Western Civilization: the culture and societies of Europe and their genealogical, colonial, and philosophical descendants (such as North America, Australia and New Zealand), characterized by political systems enshrining personal liberties, the rule of law, and free-market economies.

Westminster System: British model of parliamentary representative government.

World Bank: development bank (formally known as the International Bank for Reconstruction and Development, or IBRD), which provides assistance to low and middle-income countries.

WTO: World Trade Organization, created in 1995 as a forum for promoting and regulating free trade between nations in goods and services, and for resolving trade disputes between member countries.